AFRICAN SERIES STUDIES
General Editor: DR J. R. GOODY

THE PRICE OF LIBERTY

1 Adelabu in London (note the robe made of 'Ade' cloth)

THE PRICE
OF LIBERTY

PERSONALITY AND POLITICS
IN COLONIAL NIGERIA

by KENNETH W. J. POST

Institute of Social Studies, The Hague

and GEORGE D. JENKINS

The Urban Arts Foundation, Stanford, California

CAMBRIDGE
AT THE UNIVERSITY PRESS, 1973

OTHER BOOKS IN THIS SERIES

1 *City Politics: A Study of Léopoldville, 1962–63* – J. S. LA FONTAINE
2 *Studies in Rural Capitalism in West Africa* – POLLY HILL
3 *Land Policy in Buganda* – HENRY W. WEST
4 *The Nigerian Military: A Sociological Analysis of Authority and Revolt, 1960–67* – ROBIN LUCKHAM
5 *The Ghanaian Factory Worker: Industrial Man in Africa* – MARGARET PEEL
6 *Labour in the South African Gold Mines* – FRANCIS WILSON

Published by the Syndics of the Cambridge University Press
Bentley House, 200 Euston Road, London NW1 2DB
American Branch: 32 East 57th Street, New York, N.Y. 10022

© Cambridge University Press 1973

Library of Congress Catalog Card Number: 70–186251

ISBN: 0 521 08503 9

Printed in Great Britain by
Western Printing Services Ltd, Bristol

CONTENTS

PLATES

MAPS

ACKNOWLEDGEMENTS

The people who had come out to learn about us needed our utmost help...and we must encourage them by giving them our full support.
> A Nigerian research assistant commenting on this project, July 1967

This is not Political Science...
> An American political scientist, commenting on an early draft of this book

We first agreed to go ahead with this biography in January 1964, so it has been a long time in the making. Our chief regret about this is the disappointment which the delay must have caused to the members of Adegoke Adelabu's family. To them, and especially to B. A. Adeyemi, we owe our greatest debt, for giving us unrestricted use of the late Alhaji's personal papers. Their generous disregard for family privacy and their contribution to Nigerian history are worthy of the greatest praise. Further sources used in this study are described in the Bibliographical Note, where more detail about the Adelabu Papers will also be found. Special mention must be made here of three other collections of documents without which this study could not have been written. First, the Ministry of Local Government of the Western Region gave access to its records for the period during which Adelabu was Chairman of the Ibadan District Council. Second, officials of the Ibadan City Council gave access to the archives at Mapo Hall. Third, the late Chief Akinpelu Obisesan, whose papers one of the authors restored and preserved with the aid of the University of Ibadan Library, gave virtually unrestricted permission for their use. The importance of his collection to Ibadan, and indeed to Nigerian history, will be seen by the reader of this book. Interview materials we owe to more people than can be mentioned here, and we hope that each will accept our general thanks. An exception should be made in individual acknowledgement of the many kindnesses received from Olubadan Isaac Akinyele and Chief J. L. Ogunsola, both now deceased.

Several people helped this book attain its final form. Emmanuel Oluyemi Latunji collected information for us after we left Ibadan, Robert Cameron Mitchell allowed us to adapt some of his maps, Koos van Wieringen drew all of ours, and Christopher Fyfe and Michael Vickers brought material to our

Acknowledgements

attention. The Western Nigeria Information Service and Captain W. J. W. Cheesman gave us permission to use photographs. A. G. Hopkins and Peggy and Charles R. Nixon (not the political scientist mentioned above!) read early drafts of the manuscript with great care, as did Michael Lofchie (likewise a positive critic) and Bernth Lindfors, persuading us to make more changes than we like to remember. Akin Mabogunje also read some of the early chapters.

Financial support for our research came from the Committee of the Centre of West African Studies of the University of Birmingham, the Program of Comparative Politics at Northwestern University (financed by a grant from the Rockefeller Foundation), the Nigerian Institute of Social and Economic Research, and the Graduate School of the University of Wisconsin.

Help of various kinds came from the staff of the University of Ibadan Library. Our mothers, Florence Jenkins and Doris Post, typed great quantities of material. In the final stages our editor, T. F. Wheatley, by pointing out our prolixities at least gave us the chance of self-improvement.

1972   K.W.J.P.
                                                                                              G.D.J.

MAPS

Map 1 Nigeria, 1958: provincial and regional boundaries

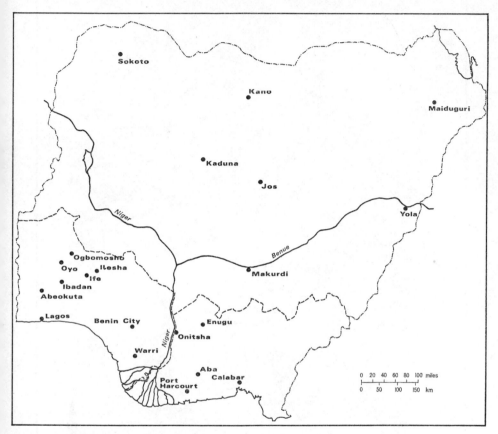

Map 2   Nigeria, 1958: some important towns

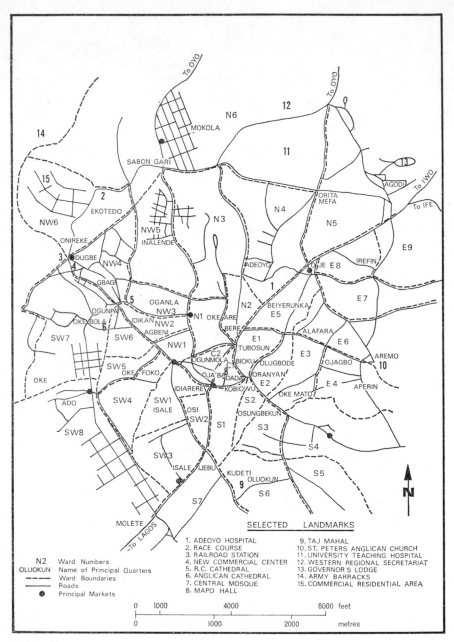

SELECTED LANDMARKS

1. ADEOYO HOSPITAL
2. RACE COURSE
3. RAILROAD STATION
4. NEW COMMERCIAL CENTER
5. R.C. CATHEDRAL
6. ANGLICAN CATHEDRAL
7. CENTRAL MOSQUE
8. MAPO HALL
9. TAJ MAHAL
10. ST. PETERS ANGLICAN CHURCH
11. UNIVERSITY TEACHING HOSPITAL
12. WESTERN REGIONAL SECRETARIAT
13. GOVERNOR'S LODGE
14. ARMY BARRACKS
15. COMMERCIAL RESIDENTIAL AREA

N2　　Ward Numbers
OLUOKUN　Name of Principal Quarters
– – –　　Ward Boundaries
———　　Roads
●　　Principal Markets

| 0 | 1000 | 4000 | 8000 feet |
| 0 | 1000 | 2000 | metres |

Map 3　Ibadan in 1958

CHAPTER 1

SETTING FOR A CAREER

As a son of Ibadan I welcome you to the Yoruba Sparta, the Giant City set on the Hill. I hope the Spirit of the Founders...of all the valiant Generals and illustrious statesmen who founded this republic as a Bastion of Freedom against Fulani invasion and steered her through her stormy history will guide and counsel us in our deliberations so that the seeds sown here may blossom into...freedom and Nigerian independence.

Adelabu, *The Turning Point*, 1952

This is the biography of Adegoke Adelabu, whose political career spanned all levels of Nigerian politics during the crucial last years of colonial rule. Above all, Adelabu saw himself as a son of Ibadan. Our story begins in this city.

Ibadan is the capital of the Western State of Nigeria, known before June 1967 as Western Nigeria. Its 900,000 residents are packed into some 24,000 living units, whose houses are mostly one-story buildings constructed from the red clay soil of the hills over which the city spreads.* Traditional thatched roofs have been replaced with corrugated iron, mottled by rust in the older, denser, central part of the city, still shiny and new in the more recently and sparsely developed outskirts. From the roof of the City Council's offices in Mapo Hall, a Parthenon-like structure on a hill in the center of the city, one sees the surrounding ring of modern hospitals, schools, universities, military establishments, industrial undertakings and residential areas, which have surrounded the old city in more recent times and virtually cut it off from the rain forest in which many of the city-dwellers have their farming plots. Mapo Hall is the focal point of Ibadan's political life and a good place from which to get a view of the city.[1]

From the front of the courtyard surrounding Mapo Hall one looks downhill along a divided roadway named King George V Avenue. It divides a number of important compounds before becoming Agbeni Street, which proceeds still further westward down the slope toward Ogunpa, a swampy

---

* A population of 900,000 can be estimated from school enrollments and what is known of age pyramids more accurately than from the census of 1963 which gives a figure of 670,000.

area. Leading westward from the Motor Park in the Ogunpa basin are Lebanon Street and New Court Road, the main thoroughfares of the major commercial area. The open-fronted and windowless buildings of West African trading company architecture are here interspersed with the house-over-shop structures of the Lebanese and Syrian merchants (who dominate the imported cloth market), transporters, grocers and a restaurant operator who form a relatively self-contained – and unpopular – community. At the top of these two thoroughfares, farthest away from Ogunpa Stream and its estuary, are the large, concrete and glass buildings of the European-owned enterprises, joined in recent years by the Obisesan Centre and Ibadan's only sky-scraper, headquarters of the State's Produce Marketing Board. This commercial area, offering a startling array of imported goods, is in fact an intrusion into the city of a segment of the encompassing ring of the modern portion of the city, a segment which includes the railway station and Dugbe Market, and beyond these a warehousing and processing district, a new residential suburb and the New Army Barracks.

One may also turn to the right on leaving Mapo Hall and proceed north on Ogunmola Road, named after a former head chief of the city. This double carriageway was built to link the Council offices to the headquarters of the Colonial District Officers at Agodi. Between the New Army Barracks and Agodi, proceeding clockwise around the ring, one finds Ekotedo, Sabon Gari and Mokola, the respective residential areas of Yoruba, Hausa and Nigerian immigrants generally, and the University Teaching Hospital operated by the Federal Government through the University of Ibadan, which lies farther to the north. Between these two educational establishments is the Secretariat of the Western State.

Still a third road circles around Mapo Hill and heads eastward through Oranyan, a low swampy area crossed by a stream, and on to the edge of the city where a number of schools are located. Between Agodi and this point are to be found cemeteries, a Roman Catholic hospital, the Adeoye Hospital and the Methodist Wesley College.

If one proceeds southward, to the left, from Mapo Hall, he passes through Oja'ba Market, where the installation of the head chief occurs, and behind which was the Central Mosque. Down the slope from Oja'ba is the less crowded and newer residential area known as Isale Ijebu, where many Ijebu Yoruba residents have built or rented houses and where most of the city's doctors, lawyers, surveyors and businessmen live. At the end of this road one again finds warehouses, the Ibadan Grammar School, the Sports Stadium, and another government housing reservation. Set some distance from the city are King's Barracks, Moor Plantation, which is operated by the Department of Agriculture, the Government College, and industrial developments. A commercial and residential area and rail yards lie between this and the railway station.

What holds the central city together is thus the barrier created by the encircling modern sector owned principally by the State and national governments and large institutions, a barrier which is less than two miles from Mapo Hall at most points. It effectively prevents the city from expanding, which means the center becomes even more congested as the population grows. Around Mapo Hall, the Central Mosque and the traditional market which adjoin the Mapo Hall grounds to the south, population densities of 250 per acre are common, although this figure may in fact double on weekends when the call to Friday prayers, Christian and Yoruba religious observances and holidays, and opportunities for leisure and amusement attract to the city those who spend the rest of the week in the rural areas. It is thus at the center of the city where most people live, work and know each other, where the noise from the radio-diffusion speakers is loudest, the small shops the most numerous, the scavenger animals the thickest and the traffic the most alarming and entertaining.

If this is where Ibadan is most exciting, it is also the place where its problems from a modern point of view are most pressing. The amenities of water, electric light and sewage are rare, and central Ibadan today is thus close to its nineteenth-century form. Much of this book deals with the continuity of nineteenth-century Ibadan into the twentieth century as it was surrounded by, but only partially integrated into, the wider activities of Nigerian national life.

Founded in 1829, Ibadan became one of a dozen or so city-states of the Yoruba people whose principal cities today have populations exceeding 50,000. Although Ibadan is one of the youngest of these city-states it quickly became the largest, its capital growing to a population of perhaps a quarter of a million during the first sixty years of its history prior to being incorporated into the British Empire in 1893.

Historically Ibadan is a relatively new city-state, but it is directly linked to traditions which centered on two more ancient states to the north – old Ife, founded sometime between A.D. 700 and A.D. 1000 and old Oyo, which with Ife exercised some central political and religious authority over other Yoruba polities.[2] To these traditions the northern Yoruba people in particular looked for their cultural identity, and it was in this area that Adegoke Adelabu hoped to re-create a Central Yoruba State in the 1950s. South of Ibadan, deeper into the rain forest, lay Abeokuta, also founded in the nineteenth century when the Egba branch of the Yoruba was pushed from its original place around Ibadan, which was one of its villages. At Abeokuta the Church Missionary Society of the Anglican Church opened a school which educated

3

many of the African C.M.S. agents who later went to Ibadan. In the coastal lagoons was the town of Lagos, now the national capital of Nigeria and the headquarters of such foreign firms as the United Africa Company, for which Adelabu worked at various times. Strategically located between Ibadan and Lagos was Ijebu Ode, whose traders controlled the Ejinrin route along which slaves moved south to Lagos and the sea, and munitions north for the internal Yoruba wars. (Adelabu was later to claim that his father was 'one of the shrewdest pioneers' of this trade route.) Friction occasionally arose between Ibadan and Ijebu Ode, but this did not prevent Ijebus from living at peace in Ibadan.

In the late eighteenth century, protest grew among the subjects of the Alafin (or King) of Oyo against his waning and arbitrary exercise of power, and in the first decade of the nineteenth century Ilorin, one of his subordinate cities, revolted and allowed the northern Muslim Fulani people to move southward into Yorubaland, whereupon they took over Ilorin, engulfed Ife and Oyo (then situated to the north of their present locations) and destroyed whatever functional unity still existed among the Yoruba people.[3] The Fulanis, however, proved unable to press farther into Yoruba territory, in part because their horses could not survive in the tsetse fly-infested forest and in part because of resistance offered by the Ife and Oyo refugees and military bands who had made the secluded Egba village of Ibadan into a 'Bastion of Freedom against Fulani invasion'. Situated, as its name suggests, 'at the edge of the field' between open farm land and the dense forest, it occupied a particularly advantageous strategic position. Their cities set against each other, the Yoruba people spent the rest of the century in turmoil; one debilitating by-product of which was the growing use of slaves for labor and export for the overseas slave trade. Even today, the various branches of the Yoruba people, harboring their nineteenth-century histories of diplomatic, military and economic conflict, often command a political allegiance which challenges that paid to the Yoruba nation as a whole.[4]

Ibadan from its inception was thus at the very center of critical Yoruba problems, not the least of which was the problem of violence, which destroyed old cities, created new ones and altered the relations among the Yoruba city-states.[5]

The principal constituent element of Ibadan society was the extended family or kinship group called a patrilineage. The patrilineage included all the male descendants of a given male forbearer and their immediate families. This kinship group, in the usage of the anthropologist, was also patri-local, which means that the married sons continued to live in their father's compound. The founders of the Ibadan lineages were the first architects and town planners of the city. Their original walled-in settlement on Mapo Hill, where the City Council offices now stand, was filled with the lineage compounds, or great connected groups of apartments, verandahs, and courtyards of traditional Yoruba architecture. As Mapo Hill filled up, the original settlement spread across low-lying swamps and streams to new high ground. Public passageways and roads were simply the spaces remaining between one compound wall and the next, or wet areas unsuitable for building. Even today, most houses in Ibadan do not face on a public road.

About 1840, the quarter within whose traditional architecture and social patterns Adelabu lived and maintained his home throughout his lifetime was established by the Oluokun lineage. There is an account of the coming of the Oluokun lineage to Ibadan which is interesting because it also describes the relationship between the Oluokuns and the Adelabus.[6] According to this, the founder of the Oluokun lineage and Adegoke Adelabu's grandfather were cousins, sons of brothers from Oyo-Ekiti, who settled in old Oyo. When that city collapsed, the brothers fled to Igbetti where they learned the art of weaving, a speciality of that town, and where Adegoke's great-grandfather married a daughter of the Alafin of Oyo. A result of this union was grandfather Adelabu; his cousin, Oluokun, was also born at Igbetti. The cousins became weavers and migrated to Ibadan where they settled in an area containing the compounds of a number of earlier settlers. It was after the fortune and fame of Oluokun had waxed, and he had become the most influential of its residents and holder of a chiefly title, that the quarter was given his name. Although his cousin, Adelabu, continued to live in the same compound, his fortune did not prosper equally and no chiefly prerogatives were extended to his branch of the family.

From its earliest days, Ibadan's chiefs were drawn largely from the heads (known as mogajis) of its important lineages. Since the army consisted of the followers of the individual chiefs (known in this context as babaoguns or war leaders) rather than of conscripts or volunteers loyal to a central authority, the lineage was the basic military organizational unit. Slaves captured in war often became farm laborers or part of a chief's fighting contingent, thus adding to his power. A critical restraint on the arbitrary exercise of this power was the fact that freemen could pledge their loyalty to leaders of their own choosing. Considerable social, economic and military opportunity existed in this loose and flexible system, even for slaves. One source refers to 'the thousands of slaves brought in annually' to the city.[7] By the middle of the nineteenth century, however, they had become so important a part of the population and the military economy that their general condition was hardly a repressive one by existing standards, and they could look forward to improving their lot and indeed to freedom.

In addition to organizing urban spatial arrangements and military and social

5

life, the lineage also controlled the agricultural hinterland. Agriculture was and remains Ibadan's main economic activity. Land was corporately held by and distributed through the city-based lineage, which meant that to have primary land holding rights one had to be a city-dweller. Thus there was no functional distinction between urban and rural in Ibadan agriculture. Virtually everyone was a part-time farmer, but since most crops of Yorubaland do not require intensive labor throughout the year, Ibadan farmers have much time for urban life. Typically those with lands close to the city walked daily to their farms; those whose land was farther away stayed there for longer periods during clearing, planting and harvesting time. Agricultural commuting was thus an aspect of urban life. Particularly at festival time or for the celebration of marriages, deaths and births the members of a lineage would be at their urban compound. Politically this meant that the organization of the rural hinterland proceeded through the major urban lineages, which as we shall see later was of some significance as modern institutions developed for organizing agricultural unions, winning the rural vote at election time, and in deciding whether Ibadan as a governmental unit should include the city with its rural areas or whether separate and specialized governmental agencies should be provided to meet urban and rural needs. Use of farm land, as opposed to its ownership, was open to followers and slaves of a lineage and their children after them for an annual payment of *ishakole*, a gift in kind, later in cash, which symbolically identified the owner and the user. The user was obligated to provide such services as helping clear lineage lands at planting time, harvesting, and contributing to extraordinary lineage expenses at the time of a chieftaincy promotion or a death. In return, however, he became a quasi-member of the lineage, entitled to physical protection, justice in the lineage court and a permanent place in the corporate life of the lineage. He was a significant link in the social network, which was based on urban residence, urban definition of rights and an agricultural economy.

Other organizational aspects of the economy included the craftsmen and retailers and the market places. Blacksmiths, cloth weavers, dyers, chicken sellers and yam flour manufacturers were all organized into guilds which regulated the quality and price of goods as well as the number of persons engaged in a particular economic activity. The heads of these guilds were recognized in their offices by the Bale (i.e. Baba Ile, or father of the town, head civil chief) as were the heads of the markets, which were usually controlled by the chief on whose property they were located. It was a pre-industrial economy, but nevertheless well organized, the various guild hierarchies not only providing order within the economy but also serving as structures through which communication with the political institutions and the masses could be achieved. However, there were virtually none of the public and indivisible goods such as roads, water wells, civic buildings and public places which were the common property of pre-industrial cities as viewed by Sjoberg.[8] Furthermore, since control of the agricultural hinterland was divided among lineages, no single urban group could exploit the rural areas for the creation of urban monuments and amenities.

It was the major chieftaincy lineage, then, and the compound which it controlled, which was the most important structure in pre-British society. In fact, in each compound there lived a microcosm of the city's wealthy and its poor, its politically powerful and its slaves, so that the various types of persons and classes were scattered evenly across the cityscape. Kinship and allegiance united those of different economic, ethnic and political characteristics into subcommunities whose authority extended even to the rural areas; the differential use of space that characterizes the modern industrial city was not to be found in Ibadan. Unfortunately, not even the crudest estimate exists of the proportions of Ibadan's modern population which stem from slaves, freemen, chieftaincy lineages or from mixtures of these backgrounds. Such a determination might be useful in explaining the twentieth-century decline of chieftaincy and the rise of elected political leaders, particularly if one guess that the chieftaincy lineage population of Ibadan was never more than twenty per cent is correct.

The lineage organized within the compound a large and diverse population subject to the disputes of a small town. The lineage council served as a court of first instance in the hierarchy of Ibadan courts, settling matters of limited geographical import and lesser political consequence. More serious cases could be initiated in or appealed to the courts of the senior chiefs or to the Ibadan Council sitting in its judicial capacity. Even in the late 1960s, with an elaborate system of local regional and national courts all prescribed by law, the lineage courts still met regularly, usually on Saturday mornings, to settle compound matters.

Thus, for the lineage member and to a considerable extent for all residents of the compound, the first identification was his lineage affiliation. Each lineage had its own facial scarifications by which its members could always be identified. To leave the compound to walk the streets was to represent the lineage, not to escape it. Yet the lineage could be authoritatively represented only by its head, its mogaji, and it was the mogajis who were citizens in the fullest sense of the word.

Sometimes strengthening, sometimes cutting across the lineage organization of society, was the principle of 'followership'. Insofar as they could, warriors, land-holding clients and freemen attempted to attach themselves to successful military leaders, to the rich and generous. Since this allegiance could be transferred at will, wealthy and ambitious leaders could thus bid for the allegiance of the followings of other lineage heads. The lineage, although it pervaded nearly every other relationship, was thus itself not impervious to the cleavages introduced by popular choice and patronage. This form of patronage is known today as the popularity of the 'big man'. In its rawest forms, it simply allows the indigent to live off the wealthy, who fear the danger of mass violence. In its more subtle use, through 'begging', a supplicant could place his political errors, his financial debts or his economic welfare at the feet of a public figure, who by 'forgiving' him assumed the prestige and the responsibility of a patron. Throughout Ibadan history, the practice has served to make the economy a distributive one and keep the well-to-do mindful of the problems and needs of the masses.

The lineages were also the recruiting ground for new chiefs. As older chiefs died and younger ones were promoted up the hierarchical ladder to fill their places, the mogajis, or heads of the important lineages, were appointed to the vacant positions. In this way, civic office rotated from person to person and thereby from lineage to lineage, and the lineages and their economic and military power were linked to a common central system. Thus, after the death of Oluokun his successor as head of the family was recognized by the Council as a mogaji, or person eligible to become a chief, which he and his successors indeed became. By 1893 there were about a hundred lineages whose heads were recognized as mogajis. Since mogajis tended to be senior men in their lineages, the deference paid to age in the kinship structure also accrued to the political system.

During the nineteenth century, there were five types of chiefs arranged in parallel hierarchies or 'lines'. The earliest line was that of the Balogun, or Warlord, and at its inception it provided both civic rule and military command. Later the line of Bale was established as the structure of civil authority, although it was in fact subject to the approval of the more influential chiefs of the Balogun's line. Parallel in organization but also formally subjected to the Balogun (War Chief) were the lines of the Seriki (Head of the Young Men) and the Sarumi (Head of the Cavalry). The fifth line was that of the Iyalode, or Mother of the Town, who had authority in women's affairs, the markets, trading guilds, and civil affairs generally.

The Council of Ibadan consisted, roughly, of the senior chiefs in each line, but there was no fixed rule concerning membership, nor traditionally was there any formal logic which determined where the line between senior and junior chiefs was drawn. Usually 'senior' meant the head of each line plus the next six chiefs of the lines of the Balogun and the Bale.* Of course

* The chieftaincy titles in the lines of the Olubadan and Balogun were eventually more or less standardized as follows (approximate translations are given): (1) Otun (right hand); (2) Osi (left hand); (3) Ashipa (leader of the vanguard); (4) Ekerin (fourth

warfare and death brought constant rotation in office. Although the chiefs became more wealthy through the accumulation of the spoils of war, on their death their wealth was divided within their lineages and their successors as mogajis did not inherit their offices as chiefs. Thus political power, although constantly striven for, was constantly re-allocated.

The Ibadan Council could in theory deal with any question, although in practice it left minor problems to the lineage councils for which it served as an appellate body while it concentrated on broader military, diplomatic and economic matters. However, it was without tax powers, relying on the wealth of the chiefs to finance common ventures such as military expeditions. It provided no services and supervised no public works that required revenue. The army, as we have seen, was organized by the chiefs and the lineages, not by a bureaucracy. Nor did the Council have a police force at its disposal, relying on the lineages to surrender criminals voluntarily to its power, which was in fact that of its head, the Bale. In extreme cases, particularly those involving public outrage against murder, treason or carelessness with fire (a capital crime in a city of thatched roofs), when a lineage refused to surrender a miscreant his compound might be declared by the authorities to be an object of public wrath, whereupon its devastation would promptly follow. Property would be stolen or burned, animals slaughtered and the inhabitants sold into slavery. We shall consider in Chapter 15 of this book a suggestion that this practice was not entirely forgotten in later times.

In marked contrast to the divine kingships found in other Yoruba cities, Ibadan politics were highly secular. No Ibadan Bale would be permitted to claim descent from Oduduwa, the Yorubas' legendary ancestor, and establish a dynasty, thus blocking access to the benefits of office to other important lineages. Ibadan could choose the elements of Yoruba custom which it would observe, and divine rulers and inheritance of political office were clearly rejected. The installation of new chiefs was conducted by the Oluwo, the descendant of the chief who had first installed the other chiefs; the cult of the worshippers of thunder and lightning was important in war; and the advice of the diviners of the Ifa oracle was important in the selection of chiefs and of dates for significant undertakings. Yet none of these held any place in the Council.

chief); (5) Ekarun (fifth chief); (6) Abese (leader of the footmen); (7) Maye ('does not move an inch'); (8) Ekefa (sixth chief); (9) Agbakin (leader of the old men); (10) Arealasa (head shield bearer); (11) Ikolaba (wearer of the apron of Shango); (12) Asaju (shield bearer to the great chief); (13) Ayingun (warrior); (14) Areago (head of a family); (15) Lagunna (one who fights on the highway); (16) Ota (*not known*); (17) Aregbeomo (head of the youths); (18) Gbonka (keeper of the chamber); (19) Areonibon (head of the rifles); (20) Bada (head of the swordsmen); (21) Ajia (messenger); (22) Jagun (ordinary warrior).

9

In sum, the emphasis placed on merit, secularism and kinship kept Ibadan politics pragmatic, flexible and close to the people.

Six decades of Ibadan history and intra-Yoruba warfare preceded British colonial rule in Ibadan. During this time, it came to differ from other Yoruba cities in that its population was drawn from all sub-groups of the Yoruba people – the Oyo, the Egba, the Ekiti, the Ijebu, the Ife and the Ijesha – rather than from a homogeneous area. These people and those of such discrepant ethnic origins as the European missionaries and Hausa northerners, were allocated land by the earlier settlers and ethnic variety, like wealth and social status, was scattered across the face of the city. During this same period, Ibadan accumulated an empire which extended beyond the Oshun River thirty miles away, consisting of some one hundred towns and villages taken in war or allied with it for purposes of defense against the Fulani. The city was thus always heterogeneous in its make up and imperial in its external ambitions and responsibilities.

Yorubaland during these sixty years was undergoing modifications of its religious institutions which were also to have long-lasting and deeply political consequences in Ibadan. Islam came to Ibadan in the 1830s and its agents quickly found an audience among the chiefs and the general population. In the twentieth century the major focal point for Ibadan Muslims has been the Central Mosque, with its Chief Imam, but allegiances to individual Alfas, or religious teachers, and to the numerous Muslim mutual-aid societies have sometimes counted for more than any sense of a community of believers. Christianity came to Ibadan with the Anglican Church Missionary Society (C.M.S.) in 1851. Land for a chapel and school in Kudeti quarter, on the outskirts of the city and a few hundred yards from the Oluokun compound, were provided by Chief Olunloyo, whose son became the first student in the mission and later an ordained priest. It is also worth noting, however, that Christian proselytization was more effective among slaves and members of the less important families than with the major chieftaincy houses. Nevertheless, because of their education, the English-speaking C.M.S. agents frequently advised the chiefs on diplomatic affairs involving the British Governor of Lagos, and enjoyed their support in educational, medical and religious activities.

In 1860, rapidly rising Ibadan clashed with the city-state of Ijaye for hegemony over what was still formally the domain of the Alafin of Oyo.[9] During the Ijaye war, in August 1861, the British annexed the city-state of Lagos on the coast less than a hundred miles from Ibadan. In alliance with Ibadan, the new Governor of Lagos helped defeat the Egba, who had allied themselves with Ijaye as that state collapsed, an intervention marking the shape of things to come. As the tiny British enclave became economically more dependent on the interior, the reluctance of the far-distant Colonial Office to establish a larger domain was overcome by arguments justifying intervention to halt warfare and slave trading and to encourage commerce in palm products, cotton, European spirits and cloth.[10] As British interest grew, the C.M.S. agents were increasingly used as intermediaries between the Governor of Lagos and interior authorities and in August 1893, fearing British military power, and on the advice of the C.M.S. agents, the Ibadan chiefs signed an Agreement which brought the Ibadan empire into the British empire.

Late in 1893, then, an officer responsible to the British Governor of Lagos, known as the Resident, was stationed at Ibadan with a troop of constabulary recruited from the Hausa people of the North and, in the words of the Governor, Ibadan became an occupied town.[11] The Ibadan army never again took the field.

Prior to this time, the Balogun, having proven himself in battle, was entitled to retire and assume the civil title of Bale upon a vacancy in that office. In this way, new and vigorous leadership could continually be brought to the senior post in the military line, since an aging Balogun could always relinquish military control gracefully by becoming Bale, a procedure which also ensured that the civil affairs of the city were in the hands of a chief who was conscious of the needs of the army. With the arrival of the British, however, the Balogun could no longer prove himself in battle and shortly a new Balogun who had not yet led the army refused to resign his position upon the death of the Bale. For the first time the second ranking chief in the Bale's line was promoted to the Baleship. Adapting their argument to this exigency, subsequent Baloguns insisted that success in war need no longer be a prerequisite for the Baleship and the chiefs in the Bale's line insisted that the title be given to a member of their line in alternation with the Balogun. A premium was thus put on displacing the heads of the two lines as rapidly as possible so as to give more junior chiefs, who could no longer rely on death in battle to create vacancies at the top of the lines, an opportunity to become Bale. Plotting and intrigue came to outweigh leadership and military skill as criteria for title holding; the resulting disarray frequently invited British intervention. We shall have to deal later with this aspect of 'chieftaincy politics'.

While this was occurring, the British were undertaking reforms of the judicial system. Concerned particularly with cases involving slaves and bonded servants and instances where charges of 'juju' were made, and appalled by sentences of death or mutilation for crimes of theft and adultery, the Resident or one of his subordinates began to sit regularly with the Council when it acted as a court. Soon the British began to feel that the lineage courts, over which they had little control, were dens of bribery and corruption and, labelling them 'secret' courts, they attempted to abolish them. To discourage cases being tried in the 'secret' courts, chiefs sitting in the 'recognized' courts were paid a salary and a percentage of fines assessed in cases which the Resident could review. The chiefs who were allowed to sit in the 'recognized' courts as judges, however, were the senior chiefs and the incomes they now derived from their judicial activities became added incentives to the younger chiefs in their attempts to oust the senior chiefs. In these struggles, one faction or the other always enlisted the support of the Resident, whose approval was required to receive a salary as a judge. Within fifteen years, no chief could advance to a senior title without the prior approval of the Governor of Lagos. The line of cavalry chiefs disappeared and that of the Seriki was greatly attenuated.

The custom of slavery waned, as did the autonomy of the chiefs and the courts, but it was not initially outlawed by the British. Although the taking of new slaves was banned there was no general emancipation, in part because the British recognized the practice to be less brutal than they had previously imagined, in part because they did not wish to upset the labor supply upon which they hoped to establish a more peaceful agricultural economy, and in part because an emancipation could not have been enforced with existing resources. As a result slavery disappeared only as slaves redeemed themselves, ran away or died, and their children were considered freemen, a growing part of what Adelabu was to call 'the teeming masses of Ibadan'.

The British administration also encouraged production of rubber, palm oil and kernels, cotton and eventually cocoa for the world market. In 1897 the construction of a railroad was begun which was to run from Lagos to Ibadan through Yorubaland and on into Northern Nigeria to evacuate the products of the hinterland. With the railway, which was opened through to Ibadan in 1901, came European trading companies whose local managers supervised the purchase and shipping of local products and the sale of European cloth, hardware and alcohol in return. The trading companies operated through middlemen who bought and sold on a commission basis and thus became involved not only in the cash economy but in widespread credit relationships. Trading generally, although not always, was quite profitable, and since the middlemen also became the repositories of a great deal of information about Europeans and about the producers from whom they purchased and to whom they sold, they became increasingly important political figures. The story of one of the most successful of them, Salami Agbaje, figures prominently throughout the first half of this history.

The railroad, and the new opportunities for trade, also brought to Ibadan Africans who wished to settle there. The earliest of these were usually

Lagosians and Egbas. As motor transport became increasingly important in the 1920s and 1930s, Ijebus came to figure more and more in the ranks of the 'native strangers', as the immigrants were collectively called by the British administrators. In these later years, non-Yoruba people, particularly Ibos, also became a more prominent part of the 'stranger' element.[12]

The increase in trade after 1901, particularly the liquor trade, was fostered as a source of revenue for the Ibadan Council. In 1903 a customs collection was established to supply the newly established Treasury with revenue, most of it derived from customs dues imposed on imported gin, brandy and whisky. Since the operation of the system required collectors who could read and keep records, a new form of employment was created for the slowly growing group of men literate in the English language. Because the only schools that Ibadan had at this time were operated by the C.M.S., the customs inspectors were Christians or had at least been exposed to a Christian training. Among these was a young man, Isaac Akinyele, a contemporary of Salami Agbaje, whose own success as a trader was in no small part due to the fact that he had taught himself to read, write and speak English. These two young men as boys had seen the arrival of colonialism, they began their adult careers just as the colonial system was becoming firmly entrenched, and by the time Adelabu began his political life they represented part of an established order against which Adelabu fought at least as vigorously as he opposed the colonial power of Britain.

Commerce and the Christian church thus became important sources from which the new men of Ibadan politics were recruited, yet the chiefs did not see in an English education an opportunity to be seized for themselves and their children. The C.M.S. was more interested in saving souls than in educating minds, and with literacy large dosages of the virtue of monogamy and of the peaceful and industrious life were administered. The chiefs, whose power and prestige depended on warfare and large families, could never be persuaded that a son who might one day be head of the house should be educated, forced to help with the many chores of a mission school, or limited to a single wife. Education was not a neutral force but a threat to the basic military and kinship values of the society. In 1893 not one chief was literate.

In 1904 the Resident of Ibadan therefore attempted to create a school specifically for the sons of chiefs which would be free from religious implications and restrictions, and a bye-law was passed compelling each chieftaincy house to enroll at least two boys in the school. Unfortunately, the school was inadequately staffed, the chiefs refused to send their sons in spite of the law and the attending schoolboys were the sons of slaves and Christians not so closely tied to the chieftaincy kinship structure or the military traditions of

13

the city. By 1950 only two of the Ibadan senior chiefs were literate: Isaac Akinyele and Salami Agbaje, neither from a traditional chieftaincy house.

This, then, was Ibadan before it was greatly modified by European influences. Although pre-industrial, it was hardly 'traditional', emphasizing as it did success over appeals to precedent, opening its gates to all comers regardless of ethnic origins, stressing individual opportunity rather than some concept of communalism, even when this included opportunity for slaves and even when it came at the expense of kinship units. Its population grew as rapidly as did those of European or American cities of its time and its population was 'mobilized' for political, economic, religious and social action through a wide variety of institutions. As we shall see, its inclusion in the British empire often impeded the development of these 'modern' characteristics.

Nevertheless, while the overwhelming percentage of the population remaintained illiterate the written word for political purposes was used and appreciated by people who could not read it. Indeed, the society had had literacy at its disposal long before the colonial rulers arrived, using it then in its correspondence with the British power and the C.M.S. headquarters at Lagos, later in court records, land documents and tax receipts. While the link between Christianity and literacy is frequently and correctly stressed, the further development of a relationship between literacy and politics, and to a lesser extent the economy, is frequently ignored. In 1952, only 45,400 of the District's 745,448 people were able to write in Roman script. Of these, 39,855 were in the urban area whose total population was 459,196.

The years since the signing of the Ibadan Agreement had witnessed the extension of British rule over an enormous area of West Africa, known by the all-embracing name of 'Nigeria'. The fact of British rule, however, and the use of a common label (which had no real meaning even for the white administrators) implied neither homogeneity, cohesion nor even uniformity of the imposed administrative practices. Areas which were later to become the Eastern, Western, Mid-Western and Northern Regions of Nigeria were brought under colonial rule by at least four separate processes, involving different groups of British agents. In particular, the North, the dominant part of which was made up of Muslim states of considerable complexity and antiquity, had not been brought under full control until the suppression of the Satiru rising in 1906 and it remained a law unto itself for long after. Frederick Dealtry Lugard, as commander of the forces of the Royal Niger Company (until it was taken over by the British government in 1900) and from 1900 to 1907 High Commissioner of the Protectorate of Northern Nigeria, had been the major figure in establishing this control and he retained throughout his life the belief that the North was the 'real' Nigeria (as did generations of British administrators after him).

Lugard became Governor of the Colony of Lagos and the Protectorate of Southern Nigeria in 1912 before being made Governor-General in 1914 to begin the 'amalgamation' of the British Protectorates of Northern and Southern Nigeria and the Colony of Lagos into the new Colony and Protectorate of Nigeria. This change was mainly inspired by the need to have the economically more active Lagos and Southern Provinces subsidize the as yet almost untapped and huge North. Certainly, except for general purposes of budgeting, the North remained aloof, administered by the British as a separate entity according to policies which they felt accorded best with its own special nature.

One such policy, initiated by Northern Protectorate officials before the amalgamation of 1914 and later given full theoretical expression by Lugard, was that of Indirect Rule, the use of existing authorities as the local agents of the new British administration. In 1914 this policy was adopted in the South as well, and immediately ran into trouble. It was one thing to use the highly centralized structure of emirs (kings), bureaucracies, and legal systems of the Hausa–Fulani people of the Muslim North, but quite another in the non-Muslim North and among the peoples of the South where there were either no 'chiefs' at all, in the sense of men with well-defined political leadership roles, or where the chiefs were so confined by a network of other institutions and relationships that they could not easily act in the authoritarian manner which close co-operation with British officials required.[13]

In Ibadan, radical changes in the relationships among the chiefs, the British, the Christians and the traders began to emerge when in 1913 Lugard replaced the former liberal Resident with Captain W. A. Ross, who was instructed to prepare for Lugard's impending scheme of Indirect Rule. Under Ross this proved to be not some sort of partnership, but an unprecedented assault on the chiefs' authority. Non-compliant chiefs were summarily deposed, and those who remained in office were required to supply free labor and, after 1918, to collect tax in their capacities as babaoguns (war leaders) from their followers. In return for their work of collection, the chiefs were given a ten per cent rebate on the total, an incentive to efficiency and a perquisite which was much prized but not, of course, a traditional right attached to office. Ross further humiliated the Ibadan chiefs in the eyes of all Yorubaland by insisting that every Yoruba must have his king. Since Ibadan's highest title, the Baleship, was no more important than that of the Bale of any bush village, Ibadan was subjected to the authority of the Alafin of Oyo, to whose city Ross moved his provincial headquarters.*

* For the deposition of another West African chief and the dismemberment and reorganization of his empire, see William A. Tordoff's *Ashanti Under the Prempehs* (London: Oxford University Press, 1966). A number of British officers who served in

Initially in response to the general decline of traditional institutions apparent even before Indirect Rule, and as an opportunity to exercise their new literary skills, six young Christians formed in 1914 the first long-lived Ibadan voluntary association for which any record exists.* The Egba Agba O'Tan, a cultural preservation society, was formed by Alexander Akinyele, an ordained Anglican clergyman and founder in 1913 of the Ibadan Grammar School, his younger brother Isaac, a local printer and three others. At first they sought only to record and preserve Ibadan's history, poetry and medicinal formulae, but almost immediately they became involved in politics in reaction to the excesses of the Alafin and Captain Ross and their disgust with the Ibadan chiefs. The Egbe was a secret society, however, dominated by the C.M.S. clergymen, and it proved to be politically ineffective. In the political fervor that followed the First World War a number of other groups emerged under the leadership of various Egbe members who were the most successful members of the new commercial classes.

These latter groups are important, even though they were all short-lived, because they mark the first interplay of political ideas between Ibadan and Lagos. Their leaders came not only from Ibadan but from Ijesha, Egba and Lagos Yorubas who had recently come to Ibadan and they shared the new consciousness of an African identity which was represented on the international level by the Pan-African Conference of 1918–19 and at the level of British West Africa by the National Congress of British West Africa, founded in March 1920 at a meeting in the Gold Coast of delegates from all four of the British territories. A branch of the Congress existed in Ibadan for about two years, as did a branch of the Negro Literary Society which had at least eight members.[14] By March 1920 there was an active branch of Blyden's Temple, named after the West Indian writer on African matters, and from 1920 to 1922 the Jamaican Marcus Garvey's newspaper, the *Negro World*, also attracted much attention among the Ibadan educated elite, prompting Akinpelu Obisesan (who plays an important part in this story) to note in his Diary on 3 March 1922 that 'My conviction is that Africans will [be] free from European bondage, but when and at what hour no mortal African can say.'[15]

The determination of the British administrators to prevent 'trouble-

Ibadan and its empire were veterans of the Ashanti campaign of 1896, the military expedition which subjugated the central portions of what is now Ghana and brought them under British rule.

* We are grateful to the late Chief Akinpelu Obisesan for the use of the Minute Book and Correspondence of the Egbe Agba O'Tan, which were in his keeping. These sources allow the correction of Richard L. Sklar, *Nigerian Political Parties* (Princeton: Princeton University Press, 1963), where he says the Egbe emerged in 1920, and that it 'functioned mainly to advise the chiefs on matters of town welfare' (p. 289).

makers' from Lagos from penetrating the interior and the Lagos leaders'
lack of interest in the hinterland led to a cooling of Ibadan's interest in Lagos
by 1923, in spite of the importance of the years 1922 and 1923 in Nigerian
constitutional history. In 1922 a new constitution established a Legislative
Council, a minority of whose members were to be 'unofficial' (that is, not
British administrators), while four of this group were actually to be elected,
on a very narrow franchise, three from Lagos and one from Calabar. In June
1923 Herbert Macaulay, one of the best known Lagos 'trouble-makers', and
some of his associates founded the Nigerian National Democratic Party,
which swept the board in the election in September, but neither of these
events seems to have attracted much attention in Ibadan.*

The history of Ibadan itself in the period from 1913 to 1931, when Captain Ross finally relinquished his control, is well illustrated in the lives of
three of its most important figures, Isaac Akinyele, Salami Agbaje and
Akinpelu Obisesan, three men who were in later years the main figures in
several of the most important events of Adelabu's career.

Isaac Akinyele was the son of Josiah Akinyele, a commoner convert to
Christianity who raised his four sons in the Christian faith and the C.M.S.
mission schools. Born in 1880, as a boy Isaac followed the Rev. Oyebode of
the C.M.S. on his calls, including one that morning in August 1893 at
5.00 a.m. when Oyebode persuaded the Ibadan chiefs to acquiesce in the
Agreement of 1893 which brought Ibadan under British rule. Isaac's schooling was terminated when the C.M.S. offered a scholarship to study at Fourah
Bay College in Sierra Leone either to him or his brother Alexander, and
Isaac deferred. In 1903 he became customs inspector for the Ibadan Council,
a post he held until 1913 and after a brief interlude as a farmer he again
entered government service as Treasury Clerk and then clerk to the Bale
until 1921. During this time he assiduously collected from the chiefs such
old documents as he could find, dating back to 1888, which were the basis
from which he began to prepare the first edition of his book, *Iwe Itan Ibadan*,
a chronicle of Ibadan history. In the early 1920s Akinyele became deeply
involved in an attempt to establish a newspaper and printing shop in Ibadan,
an effort in which Salami Agbaje was the major financier and Akinpelu
Obisesan a candidate for the position of editor.

Salami Agbaje was born in 1880 in Lagos. His father came from Iseyin
and his mother, as far as can be determined, from Ibadan. Although he never

---

* The founding of the party passed unnoticed in Obisesan's Diary; the election and its
result are noted without comment. For the N.N.D.P. see Tekena N. Tamuno,
Nigeria and Elective Representation, 1923–1947 (London: Heinemann, 1966),
pp. 45–9; James S. Coleman, *Nigeria; Background to Nationalism* (Berkeley and
Los Angeles: University of California Press, 1958), pp. 197–200; and Sklar, *Nigerian
Political Parties*, p. 317.

attended school, he was the favorite of a Roman Catholic priest in Lagos who persuaded him of the value of education sufficiently to inspire him to learn to read and write by himself and to provide English university education for all his children. Agbaje was a Muslim, but was so concerned with modern business, education and politics that he was considered 'one of us' by the Ibadan Christians. He came to Ibadan in 1904 and worked for a European sawmill operator, whose business he shortly took over, and for which he hired a European bookkeeper. As a produce middleman, he hired a number of other Africans to work for him and was one of the few who could hold his own against the European companies. Although not an early member of the Egbe Agba O'Tan, Agbaje was the wealthiest of the new commercial class in Ibadan and it was to him that the Egbe turned in 1920 for financial support in their publishing venture. His outlay of £625 for equipment prompted Obisesan to record in his diary:

No doubt Agbaje will one day be called 'King of intelligent Natives'. He has proved himself able to lead without motive to cheat.[16]

Yet Agbaje was never completely trusted in spite of the outbursts of appreciation his great wealth and generosity frequently inspired. Although he was willing to have the entire publishing operation controlled by a group of leading Christians and Muslims, it collapsed amid bitter arguments among Obisesan, Agbaje and the Akinyele brothers over who should be manager and editor.

Akinpelu Obisesan was born in 1888, the son of an Ibadan chief and a slave woman, and it is said that this was the reason his father allowed him to attend school. After a few years of school, he became a clerk on the railway then being constructed through Yorubaland. In 1916 he returned to Ibadan, renewed his boyhood ties with the Akinyele brothers, joined the Egbe Agba O'Tan and became its secretary, and attempted to make a living as a cocoa farmer. Perhaps because he felt his education had been too abruptly terminated, Obisesan threw himself into all of the activities of the Christian, educated group with great passion, but his tenuous economic position always left him in great awe of Salami Agbaje, 'the Prince Merchant'. His continuing sense of economic uncertainty – what good, he asked, were books and intelligence without money? – led him into Agbaje's employ as a middleman, Agbaje 'the man God has sent to give me manna...', but also Agbaje 'a man notorious for his business unscrupulousness...'.[17]

Merchant Agbaje was also beginning a political career as the driving force behind the Ilupeju Society ('The Community Together'). The Ilupeju was initiated as a public political organization, particularly of traders, which could unite Christians and Muslims, and Agbaje vigorously attempted to use his wealth to fill the gap between these two groups as the basis for his political activities. He found it easier to profess than to convince however – he was accused of converting the Ilupeju's funds to his own purposes, he was never allowed into the inner circle of the Egbe Agba O'Tan, and he did not become a member of the Agricultural Society (founded in 1905) until 1925, by which time he had disbanded the Ilupeju, reportedly at the request of Captain Ross. Worse, it was thought that a petition signed by the Egbe members protesting Ross's deposition of Bale Shittu in 1925 had been given to Ross by Agbaje with details of its origins.[18] The effect of these allegations was in no way diminished by the fact that they were unproven, and by 1925 it was clear that Agbaje could not be an undisputed leader of men. Obisesan had left his employ in spite of the fact that he owed Agbaje money, and he had dropped out of the Ilupeju Society, which the Akinyele brothers had never joined.

The divergent paths taken by these three men contributed to and were typical of the malaise in Ibadan's political leadership from 1925 to 1931.* In the latter year the situation began to change. Ross was replaced as Resident by H. L. Ward Price, and this, coupled with the death in 1930 of Ross's personally selected Bale and the installation of the much more capable Aleshinloye, meant that the Captain's influence remained only in the person of Salami Agbaje, whom Ross had selected in 1930 to represent Oyo Province as a nominated Unofficial Member of the Legislative Council. Ward Price was much more receptive to the views of men like Obisesan and the Akinyeles than his predecessor, and this was made even more significant by the fact that by the time he arrived in Ibadan the educated elite there had grouped themselves in a new organization, the Ibadan Progressive Union.

The I.P.U. was formed in July 1930. Victor Owolabi Esan, a young clerk in the Public Works Department, had originally proposed the formation of a new social club, but S. A. Oloko, a clerk in the Agriculture Department, wanted something more serious. One Sunday morning Oloko and his friend D. T. Akinbiyi, a young merchant, got on Oloko's motorcycle and rode to

---

* Isaac Akinyele had also undergone a personal religious crisis and left the C.M.S. for the Nigerian-controlled Faith Tabernacle (later called the Christ Apostolic Church). His own disappointment with the National Congress of British West Africa and other 'foreign' bodies seems to have been reflected in a letter which he wrote in January 1930 to the Faith Tabernacle leader, in which he said 'my advice is that we should be slow indeed to adopt any foreign method, there are hundreds of them'. See Robert Cameron Mitchell, 'Religious Protest and Social Change: the Origins of the Aladura Movement in Western Nigeria, in Robert I. Rotberg and Ali A. Mazrui (ed.), *Protest and Power in Black Africa* (New York: Oxford University Press, 1970), pp. 472–3.

St Peter's Church, where they found J. L. Ogunsola, the schoolteacher. The three of them then met Esan and the I.P.U. was born.* The impetus behind the I.P.U. thus came from men who were about fifteen years younger than those who made up the Egbe Agba O'Tan, and this generational gap was certainly significant in the origins of the new society. The members of the I.P.U. were Christians, almost without exception, and they were willing to include Egbe members like Obisesan and Isaac Akinyele in their activities even to the point of giving them important offices in the new Union, which thus began with much good will and little self-seeking.

It was not only in Ibadan that change was becoming apparent in 1931. In that year Sir Donald Cameron became Governor of Nigeria, and he brought to a head a growing realization on the part of the British that throughout the Southern Provinces of Nigeria the ideas of Indirect Rule were failing to meet the challenge of the emerging educated elite. Cameron encouraged involving educated men in the work of the local Native Authority Councils at a time when Lagos's political ideas were no longer of interest to men like Obisesan and the Akinyeles. Macaulay was virtually a spent force in the early 1930s and Garveyism was dead.

The policies of Cameron and his local subordinates like Ward Price contributed greatly to a regrouping of indigenous economic and political forces in the hinterland. In Ibadan the crash of 1929–30 had ruined a cocoa exporting company run by Isaac Akinyele, his friend and co-author from the earlier years of the Egbe Agba O'Tan, J. C. Aboderin, and Akandi Akinloye, a cocoa planter and trader who had frequently disputed several pieces of land with the Obisesan family. Charges of fraudulent use of the company's funds were brought against Akinloye, who served a prison sentence, and to prevent a similar occurrence of inadequate organization and responsibility the colonial government began a co-operative marketing organization which would return a larger profit to the producers than they were able to receive through middlemen and foreign trading companies. Akinpelu Obisesan, because of his family's many cocoa farms, was keenly interested in this development and in 1932 became the President of the Ibadan Cocoa Producers' Marketing Union, then of the Co-operative Union which was the Western Provincial producers' apex organization, and, later, in the 1950s, of the Co-operative Bank. United with him in this effort were his old friend Isaac Akinyele and other Egbe Agba O'Tan and Ibadan Progressive Union

* The authors are grateful to S. A. Oloko for this account, in which Chiefs Akinbiyi and Ogunsola concurred. Sklar, *Nigerian Political Parties*, p. 289, errs in saying the I.P U. resulted from the addition of literate elected Councillors to the Ibadan Council. The I.P.U. preceded this event by three years, its members requested the change, and in any case the Councillors were not elected.

members, in what by the late 1930s was becoming an establishment group of the Christian, educated elite of Ibadan.

Politically, the I.P.U. knew it had a friend in Resident Ward Price, who had moved his Oyo Province headquarters to the Govérnor's Lodge at Ibadan in 1931, and in the I.P.U. Ward Price knew he had a body of conscientious and articulate citizens who would support his policies when they out-ran those of the Government in Lagos. In 1933, when the I.P.U. requested Ward Price to place literate men on the Council to advise the chiefs, two of its Elders, Isaac Akinyele and J. C. Aboderin, were appointed after their nomination by the I.P.U. These two men, with the backing of the Resident, the chiefs and the I.P.U., led the campaign which in 1934 saw Ibadan re-established as a Native Authority independent of Oyo and the Alafin.

Ibadan thus reasserted itself against Oyo, but the major towns of its own empire were also changing and they now turned their attention to their own 'independence' from Ibadan. As late as 1935, their increasing autonomy was being discussed as an elaboration of 'the fuller understanding of the principles of indirect administration' and official policy persisted that nothing was to be done 'that is likely to weaken the unity of the Ibadan Native Administration. . .'[19] Undermining these assertions, however, was a feeling reflecting Cameron's reforms, that 'the method of government of Ibadan was hardly best calculated to ensure the progress of the Town under present day conditions'.[20] This feeling was shared in the districts, where ambitious young administrators sought to demonstrate their own competence and improve their individual towns through reforms in taxation and the courts and the improvement of local services, rather than contributing to that vague entity, the Ibadan Empire. This development, and the way it had come about, ran counter to the philosophy and practice of the Lugardian system introduced in 1914, and proved to be the first phase in the tortuous rethinking of the nature of the Ibadan Empire.

The silent abandonment of Indirect Rule did not mean that traditional chieftancy no longer had a place. In 1936, when it was decided that more men should have the experience of being Councillor, Akinyele and Aboderin were made chiefs by the grateful Council, in the Balogun's and Bale's lines respectively, in spite of the fact that neither of them came from 'a ruling chieftaincy house'. This honor was in part in recognition of their deference to traditional authority and diligence in the solving of modern problems which the aging and illiterate chiefs found it difficult to comprehend, and in part because they had struggled so hard and successfully to have Ibadan's 'sovereignty' wrested from the Alafin of Oyo. Thus, as we shall see on later occasions, the interests of the I.P.U. and the chiefs could converge on particular issues.

Nor was the I.P.U. strictly a political organization. One of its first programs was the establishment of a 'Reading Room' which developed into a small club and a library. Another early project was the Higher Education Fund, a scholarship program. One of the earliest I.P.U. scholars was Adegoke Adelabu, who had as a schoolmaster J. L. Ogunsola, an I.P.U. officer and founder. In Adelabu, whom they supported for six years at Government College, Ibadan, and Yaba Higher College in Lagos (he received his pocket money at D. T. Akinbiyi's shop in Lagos while at Yaba), the I.P.U. hoped they had found a representative of the next generation who would eventually take his place in their ranks and carry on their work.

Indeed, this sense of continuity which the I.P.U. demonstrated in their concerns with history and with modern education, with the elders and the schoolboys, was one of their principal strengths. It derived in part from the fact that their efforts were appreciated by the chiefs and the colonial administrators and were therefore effective and satisfying, and in part from the fact that the principal movers of the I.P.U. also enjoyed a considerable sense of individual security. As we have seen, they were all well employed for the time; for none of them was politics the only area in which they could advance or be effective. This is not to say that they were without keen political ambitions or that the I.P.U. was not frequently riven by strife.

The I.P.U. was not the only center of political initiative and power in spite of its close contacts with the co-operative movement, education, the civil service and the Ibadan Council. Salami Agbaje was never closely identified with the group, and after being made a chief and the President of a customary court in 1936 he was able to advance his own political career without I.P.U. help. The strongest organizational rivalry came from the Ibadan Patriotic Association (I.P.A.) founded in 1936 when Bale Aleshinloye was given the more prestigious title of Olubadan, meaning 'Owner of Ibadan', a title whose royalist implications the Yoruba kings and some citizens of Ibadan strongly resented. They feared Aleshinloye might be attempting to establish a dynasty by passing on his new title to his son Bello Abasi, who founded the I.P.A. to gain popular support for his father.* The I.P.A., according to its constitution and early membership list, was a federation of thirty-two other groups, including trade and craft guilds, dance societies and Muslim religious organizations, and all of the records show that the I.P.A.

---

* Sklar, *Nigerian Political Parties*, p. 289, states that the I.P.A. was founded by Muslim members of the I.P.U. who were disturbed by its overtly Christian tone. In fact, some of the early I.P.A. members and associates were I.P.U. officers and members in good standing, none of the Muslim I.P.A. members had been in the I.P.U., and the religious aspect of their differences, while real, was always a secondary one. Our thanks are due to Chief Bello Abasi for the use of the I.P.A. records (now deposited in the Library of the University of Ibadan) on which this account is based.

2 Adelabu as a Co-operative official (seated, extreme right)
3 Adelabu and Awolowo share a car

4 Politicians at play: Ade and Awo at the London dance
5 Alhaji Adelabu and Alhaji Adegbenro pose together

continued to consider itself the apex of other organizations. This meant that its most important members were already the heads of other existing groups, and nearly all were illiterate.

However, the I.P.A. was heavily involved in 'chieftaincy politics'. Educated supporters were thus of critical importance to it, for the control of the Council still rested in the hands of the colonial officers who preferred to work with literate men and who disdained, as did the I.P.U., intervention in chieftaincy politics. Under its first group of literate officers, and later under T. L. Oyesina, a teacher at the Ibadan Grammar School who became its Secretary in 1937, the I.P.A. managed its business effectively.

Under Oyesina, an attempt was made to link the I.P.U. and the I.P.A. J. L. Ogunsola, Akinpelu Obisesan and D. T. Akinbiyi of the I.P.U. attended I.P.A. meetings regularly. The split between the two groups came over the selection of Councillors in 1939. The I.P.A. now asserted its own right to nominate Councillors, and although I.P.U. members continued to meet with the I.P.A., no mutual agreement on candidates could be reached. The Association, which translated its title in Yoruba as Egbe Omo Ibile, or Society of the Sons of the Town, by about 1939 claimed fifty-eight constituent societies, of which only a few may have had literate heads. When Oyesina resigned as its Secretary in 1940 due to the pressure of his other enterprises, the I.P.A. became moribund for a number of years.

With each successive selection, the democratic basis of choosing Councillors was expanded; their number was increased, an Advisory Board made up of Representatives elected from the various quarters of the town was created in 1942 to act as an electoral college, and for several years it was possible for junior chiefs to be elected to the Council by the Advisory Board. The I.P.U. could now get more of its members on the Council than ever before, since it was the only body organizationally capable of taking advantage of this reform from above, and it continued to be influential in many important issues before the Council, particularly when literacy was a required skill. It was hoped by the administrative officers that the increase in the number of popularly elected Quarter Representatives acting as advisers to the chiefs would make it possible to articulate the demands of the people for more modern governmental services. As the number of Quarter Representatives expanded and the number of contestants for these positions grew, some I.P.U. members occasionally failed to be elected to the Advisory Board.

Olubadan Aleshinloye, who had been in office since 1930, was by 1944 an old and feeble man. The power of his office was actually wielded by his son Bello Abasi, whom Obisesan flatly called 'the whole authority for Ibadan'.[21] In the last two years before his death in 1946, Aleshinloye had ceased to attend Council meetings or to deal with the matters which required at least his formal approval. Nor did his death improve matters. His long tenure of office meant that the chieftaincy ranks were filled with aged men awaiting promotion. Worse, the constitutional question of access to the Olubadanship by the civil, as opposed to the war, chiefs had not been resolved, because it had not had to be considered since the time of Captain Ross who decided such matters largely for himself. The answer, in a totally uncustomary declaration of native custom, was phrased by the I.P.U. leaders.[22] It stated that each line should alternatively have the right to nominate candidates for the Olubadanship for consideration by the senior chiefs of both lines, whose vote should be decisive. It was anticipated that each line would nominate from among its own members, but that the final selection might fall upon, say, the third chief in the line rather than the first or second, who might be too old. It proved in fact easier to pick the most senior man in strict alternation between the lines, and to tolerate his rule because his senility ensured its brevity. Aleshinloye's successor lasted less than five months, his successor thirty-four days, the third man a year, bringing into office in February 1948 Fijabi II, the grandson of Bale Fijabi who had signed the Agreement of 1893.

By that time the situation of the Ibadan administration was approaching a crisis point. The governmental machine was described as 'clogged with arrears of work, [while] there is no appreciation of what subjects are urgent and important and what is not'.[23] The continuing failure of the Olubadan and Councillors to work together in executing policy had been reinforced by the effects of the reforms of 1944, which had widened the deliberative process to include not merely the chiefs but the Advisory Board and Quarter Representatives as well and so made it almost impossible to make decisions on policy. Profoundly dissatisfied with the way things were going in Ibadan, the British administrators came to feel that the only answer was the complete reform of the local government system there, based on the creation of the post of Administrative Secretary, who would act as the chief executive of the Council.

Thus by 1948 the I.P.U. was running into difficulties in administering the city, while at the same time it was in the plenitude of its social and political power. Its members controlled the major Christian churches, including St Peter's Cathedral, the Agbeni Methodist Church, and through Chief Isaac Akinyele the Christ Apostolic Churches of which he was President. Through the churches and the relationship of Christianity to education, they controlled two major schools, including the Ibadan Grammar School, which Bishop Akinyele had founded and which his son-in-law the Rev. E. A. Alayande, an I.P.U. member, now headed. From that school had come the teachers and headmasters of many other schools, including T. L. Oyesina, who now owned no less than six, among them the Ibadan Boys High School. The I.P.U. controlled some of Ibadan's most important economic institutions also, a control which was greatly strengthened by the fact that they tended to marry other Christians, so that virtually every Christian I.P.U. member was well-related to a variety of organizations. Their control was thus a long-standing one in terms of political generations, it was self-perpetuating and interlocking, and it effectively controlled policies affecting the lives of non-members. At a time when the illiterate chiefs were still nominally in control of the Council, its work was effectively done by special committees for court reform, town planning, civil service regulations and revenue and expenditure planning, which regularly included Isaac Akinyele, J. L. Ogunsola, H. V. A. Olunloyo and D. T. Akinbiyi.

All this power did not endear the I.P.U. to others in Ibadan. It cannot be said that the leaders had sought power for the sake of personal aggrandizement alone. They had entered the public life of Ibadan during the 1930s in the knowledge that their city was in need of reform and that they were the only people equipped with the education necessary to work with the administrative officers in carrying this out. Nevertheless, their prominence was bound to attract resentment, not only from individuals like Abasi with whom they actually clashed, but from wider sections of the population, Muslims who disliked their insistence on Christian morality, for example, or the unsuccessful entrepreneurs who envied their wealth. In broader terms, what was happening in Ibadan in the late 1940s was an elemental and often painful debate. The question was simply, who should govern and to what ends? The venerable chiefs, with their greatly diminished traditional authority and low level of competence in modern administration? Corporate groups such as the colonial administrators and the I.P.U. leaders, who were often motivated by the highest standards but were not responsible to the population at large? The I.P.U. had demonstrated to Africans and Europeans alike that the concepts of racial inferiority inherent in the thought of Indirect Rule were invalid, and for almost two decades they had worked with the chiefs and administrative officers to implement some of the most important local reforms. The colonial system was now in question, just as chieftancy was in decline, and in the context of Ibadan the I.P.U. had done much to hasten both these processes.

The constitutional debate in Ibadan was made the more complex by the fact that it became part of a greater debate which was in progress throughout Nigeria as a whole. In order to understand this, and to see how Ibadan became involved in larger-scale developments, it will be necessary to go back in time to the late 1930s when the I.P.U. was beginning to play a major part in the affairs of the city.

27

Earlier in this chapter it was noted that by 1930 the educated elite of Ibadan had lost interest in political events in Lagos. Toward the end of that decade, however, Lagosian organizations were again impinging on the hinterland. Late in 1935 the Nigerian Youth Movement came into existence in the coastal city; during the next two years it took the political initiative there away from the N.N.D.P. and Herbert Macaulay and spread inland, establishing branches in Ijebu Ode, Abeokuta and in Ibadan where it recruited some I.P.U. members. In 1938 its local President was Dr A. Agbaje (Chief Agbaje's eldest son and the first Ibadan to become a medical doctor) and its Secretary was T. L. Oyesina.

The most active N.Y.M. leader in Ibadan, however, was Obafemi Awolowo, a native stranger from Ijebu Province. Awolowo will figure largely in our story, since Adelabu came to regard him as a personal rival politically. Born in Ikenne in 1909, Awolowo had received some of his education in Ibadan and worked there as a clerk in Wesley College from 1932 to 1934. After joining the staff of the Lagos *Nigerian Daily Times*, he returned to Ibadan at the end of 1934 as its correspondent. He soon gave this up, however, became a money-lender and public letter writer, and then entered trade. Late in 1935 he had his first brush with Ibadan interests when he incurred the wrath of Ward Price and the chiefs for criticizing the administration of the Reading Room which the I.P.U. had sponsored.[24] It was probably as one of the founders of the Native Settlers Union of Ijebu immigrants that he became best known in Ibadan, however, and we will have to return to this body later.

Notice should also be taken of another man who figured largely in the life of Adelabu, Nnamdi Azikiwe, an Ibo from Onitsha who returned to Nigeria from the U.S.A. in 1934 as one of the first of his people to gain a university degree. Unable to find suitable employment in Nigeria, Azikiwe left again and took a post as newspaper editor in the Gold Coast, where he was noted for the new spirit of criticism of the colonial system which he helped to foster. In July 1937 he returned to Nigeria, this time to stay, and in November launched his new nationalist newspaper, the *West African Pilot*. Through this, and his membership of the Nigerian Youth Movement, Azikiwe was thus involved in, and largely responsible for, the more radical criticism of the British administration and economic interests which now began to be expressed by the younger men. In 1941 he broke with the N.Y.M., and spent the next few years in a kind of political wilderness, making his future plans.

In August 1944 Awolowo left for the United Kingdom, where he intended to study law, and on the 26th of that same month Nnamdi Azikiwe again swept into prominence with the launching of the Nigeria National

Council, soon to be renamed the National Council of Nigeria and the Cameroons, a grouping of trade unions, literary societies, social clubs and local improvement unions, which also incorporated Herbert Macaulay's N.N.D.P. Macaulay, by now the grand old man of Nigerian politics, became President of the new N.C.N.C. and Azikiwe its General Secretary.

The launching of the N.C.N.C. gave much greater strength to the demand which had been growing since the foundation of the N.Y.M. for changes in the constitution of Nigeria, which was still that sponsored by Governor Clifford in 1922. In 1945 and 1946 political interest and excitement in Lagos were high. This period saw the general strike of June 1945, the resultant banning of the *West African Pilot* and the *Daily Comet* (another of Dr Azikiwe's newspapers), the N.C.N.C. leader's assertion that 'unknown persons' were plotting to kill him, and the inauguration of the Zikist Movement as a radical wing of the N.C.N.C. in February 1946. It also brought to Ibadan its first newspaper since the decline of *Ijoba Ibile Marun*, edited by D. T. Akinbiyi. On 13 November 1945 Azikiwe's chain of newspapers transferred the *Southern Nigeria Defender* from Warri to Ibadan, where it continued to support the nationalist cause while appealing primarily to the stranger element in Ibadan, which was more literate and more attuned to national events than most of the population.

Another development began to have its effect on the whole of Nigeria from 1945 onwards: the decision by the British Government, now controlled by the Labour Party, to begin a process of constitutional change in the West African territories. The new Richards Constitution, as it was popularly called after the Governor of Nigeria, Sir Arthur Richards, did nothing to satisfy the nationalists; indeed, its publication in March 1945 contributed significantly to the growth in support for the N.C.N.C., since, for example, the fact that there was now to be a majority of 'unofficial' members in the Legislative Council was felt to be scanty recompense for the constitution's complete failure to extend the principle of direct election.

Three other features of the Richards Constitution, which came into effect finally in 1946, must be noted. First of all, it introduced into Nigeria a further measure of 'regionalization'. In 1939 Southern Nigeria had been regrouped into two units, the Eastern and Western Provinces, divided roughly by the River Niger. Now this administrative convenience was to be reinforced by the creation in the Eastern, Western and Northern Provinces of a House of Assembly for each; these Houses were to have budgetary powers, but no general ability to legislate. A second important feature of the Richards Constitution was that for the first time it gave the northern Provinces some effective voice in the affairs of Nigeria as a whole by granting them representation on the Legislative Council in Lagos. The Northerners were not long in making themselves felt. Akinpelu Obisesan (an Unofficial Member of the new Legislative Council, as of the old) recorded in his Diary how, in the budget debate in March 1947,

The member for Northern Provinces who hails from Bauchi electrified the House; indeed his delivery and intonation and pronunciation were the admiration of everyone. In his note of warning to those agitating against [the] British, he said that if [the] British withdrew from Nigeria, the Hausas would carry their conquest to the sea.[25]

The Member in question was Abubakar Tafawa Balewa, a militant spokesman for northern interests, later to be a ministerial colleague of Adegoke Adelabu, then the first Prime Minister of Nigeria, and, in January 1966, a victim of the military coup which overthrew the first Nigerian Republic.

A third aspect of the Constitution of 1946 was that for the first time it linked the Native Authorities throughout Nigeria to the central institutions of government by leaving to these local bodies the selection of the majority of the Unofficial Members of the three Houses of Assembly. These in turn selected the Unofficial Members of the Legislative Council. This was in accord with the new colonial policy enunciated by Arthur Creech Jones, the Secretary of State for the Colonies, in February 1947, which stated that sound local government was to provide the basis upon which an independent Nigeria could eventually be built.[26]

This doctrine had profound implications for the Ibadan Native Authority, but by 1948 the Richards Constitution was clearly outmoded (if it had not been so from the very beginning) and a new Governor, Sir John Macpherson, had in August 1948 initiated a process of constitutional revision which involved close, if manipulated, consultation with the Native Authorities, political parties and other groups. Politically, the direct result of this and certain other reforming measures was to take much of the impetus out of the campaign of the N.C.N.C. against the British.[27] At the level of local administration, the process of change was accelerated under Macpherson. In the Eastern and Western Provinces, the whole Native Authority structure was called into question. Far from witnessing an even maturation of a tutelary local colonial system into a national democratic structure at independence, Nigerian administration and politics at the local as well as the national level were in fact to undergo disruption, or as Adelabu was to term it, 'revolution'. Ibadan from 1949 to 1954 witnessed the virtual elimination from the political scene of the chiefs and the I.P.U., the products of the tutelary and evolutionary approach upon whom the British had once hoped to build the modern nation of Nigeria.

The immediate issues which provoked the launching of the 'revolution' in Ibadan were three in number, though at first one dominated popular attention. An issue which did not seem immediate was that of the Native Settlers Union. In 1948 the Council was considering a proposal to levy taxes on buildings, deliberately aimed at native strangers in Ibadan. The Ijebus, who were particularly affected, led by Obafemi Awolowo, who had returned from Britain in 1946 and become a successful lawyer, complained bitterly about the proposed building rate and about the fact that the Ibadan Native Authority would not allow them land on purchase or long lease. By 1948 the Ijebus, as particularly keen traders, had begun to grow generally unpopular in Ibadan. Abuse, and even physical mistreatment, were being meted out to them at popular festivals in the city.*

A second issue which did not seem to be pressing, to Ibadan people at least, was that of the Northern Districts. We have already noted the pressure towards a greater autonomy of these with regard to the Olubadan and chiefs of Ibadan. In opposing this independence movement, the I.P.U. found itself firmly aligned with the most conservative elements in Ibadan and in conflict with the British administrators, anxious to create more effective administrative units and pursue development plans without the hindering hand of the Ibadan Council.

The issue which actually provoked the crisis which gradually deepened to include the other two and led to radical change in Ibadan was in fact centered in the chieftaincy system. The death of three Olubadans in less than two years had meant a rapid series of promotions, and suddenly, early in 1949, the chiefs realized that Salami Agbaje, now the Otun or second ranking chief in the Balogun's line, was eligible for the Olubadanship. Agbaje was a 'foreigner', having been born in Lagos. He was a capitalist, who owned more property in fee simple than any other man in Ibadan. Although a Muslim and a financial supporter of the Central Mosque, he had spent his wealth on the English university education of six of his children. Probably more damaging was the fact that virtually all of the chiefs were heavily in debt to him, having borrowed hundreds of pounds from him to finance their own sudden rise in the chieftaincy ranks, which required very considerable outlays in initiation fees and entertaining expenses, not to mention bribes. The realization that such a man could quite possibly become their traditional

---

* In March 1948 Awolowo wrote to the city authorities complaining about the words sung in the streets during the Oke Badan festival, when Ibadan's origins and separate identity were celebrated:

> The penis of an Ijebu man is like a jousting pole.
> The vagina of the woman is like a grinding bowl.

(Awolowo to Olubadan and Council, 8 March 1948, Secretary of Western Provinces File 12674, vol. iv.)

leader, in spite of the fact that he respected so few of the traditional controls, was unbearable. A plot was begun to deprive him of his post, but it soon got out of hand. Before its repercussions were over, the old Ibadan empire had been divided, the chiefs had been deprived of their remaining control over tax collection, the courts and the Council, the position of the native strangers had become an intense issue, and the Ibadan Progressive Union's control over the city's affairs was slipping.

CHAPTER 2

EARLY LIFE

I am a living laboratory of my age. My continuous bathing in the social strains and stresses of my environmental community has made of me not a dexterous swimmer but a part of the stream. I am at once the cocoa farmer, the mercantile clerk, the civil servant, the petty trader, the transporter, the capitalist and the intellectual – all materials for the study of the social scientist. I have no prejudices, religious, tribal, racial, social, personal, economic or temperamental.

> Adelabu to the Secretary, Institute of Social Sciences, University College, Ibadan
> November 1949

Gbadamosi Adegoke Oduola Adelabu Akande was born in 1914 or 1915. In a list of birthdates of his family members 3 September 1914 is given, but Adelabu himself used the year 1915 most often and we accept it for the sake of convenience.* His father, Sanusi Ashiyanbi Adeyege Adelabu, was born in 1854 according to his son's reckoning, and appears to have prospered rather more than Grandfather Adelabu. A trader along the route to Lagos and a weaver like his father and grandfather before him, he seems to have been a somewhat cantankerous individual. He eventually settled in the compound of the Adeliyi family, from which came his second wife, the mother of Adegoke Adelabu. Here he built a two-story house in 1920, a mark of prosperity, but by 1930 his economic fortunes seem to have declined, perhaps as an indirect result of the collapse of the world market, leaving him unable to pay his son's school fees.

Adelabu's earliest description of his mother, Awujola Ajoke, is not an unusual one for the junior wife in a Muslim Yoruba family.

My mother was a typical Yoruba woman. She was a hard worker. She also had a

* On the flyleaf of his book, *Africa in Ebullition*, Adelabu gives his birth year as 1915, and in June 1943 he gave his age as twenty-eight, but in January 1944 he called himself 'about' thirty. This uncertainty is not at all unusual in Ibadan, since to this day there is no compulsory birth registration. Unless the date was recorded by a clergyman in the case of a Christian family, or the mother had gone to a maternity center, it usually went entirely unmarked.

large dose of the spirit of independence and during the short span of her married life she lived on terms of perpetual rivalry with my father.[1]

She was a trader in *adire*, a dyed cloth, and apparently enjoyed some success, for Adelabu claimed that she kept 'over half-a-dozen' *iwofa*, or bonded servants, an indication that she had surplus capital for lending purposes. In 1952 he wrote that she died 'during the Influenza in 1919–20', though the epidemic seems, in fact, to have hit Ibadan earlier.*

We can presume that his mother and father had rejoiced with their friends and relatives on the eighth day of his life, the traditional day for naming a child and celebrating the fact that he had survived the dangerous early period that claims so many African children.† He was given the traditional five names of a Yoruba child, including the praise name of Adegoke – the Crown Rises High – and he was visited by a specialist in the art of cutting into the cheeks of newborn infants the marks which would distinguish him for life as a member of his lineage, in this case, the eight *abaja* marks of a house of Oyo. Thereafter his mother probably nursed him until he was at least two, a Yoruba child's best assurance of protein content in his diet.

Adelabu was still only a small child when his mother died. After her death Adelabu was taken by his mother's sister to Ita Alade compound in Isalejebu Quarter, but shortly thereafter he was returned to Sinotu Adeitan, Adelabu's father's sister. Adeitan lived at her husband's compound of Ile Olola in Isalebode, but after a quarrel with her husband she moved with Adelabu and her own son back to Oke Oluokun. Adeitan was a woman of character. She was illiterate, but saw the value of education and, although not a Christian, she realized the importance of being one in ensuring entrance to Church Missionary Schools. She had both boys baptized, and in January 1925 Joseph Adelabu and his cousin were admitted to St David's school in Kudeti. Although his cousin's school career was temporarily interrupted in December 1925 when his father withdrew him to work on his farms during the harvest season, the young Adelabu was allowed to continue. In 1926 he returned to Ita Alade, and apparently lived there until he became a boarder at Government College in 1931. Thus he spent little of his boyhood in his father's compound, and became separated from him not merely physically, but also by his education: family tradition has it that he refused to help his father with his weaving from the time he began his schooling.

Our knowledge of Adelabu the child is thus fragmentary but it seems fair to say that he had an uncertain childhood which perhaps gave him

* Akinpelu Obisesan noted in his Diary on 20 October 1918, 'The serious diseases are raging [and] women are dying like flies.'
† Mortality rates may have been as high as 500 in a thousand for children under the age of five at this time.

34

some personal independence. Certainly his father's will, written in 1943, testifies that the estrangement of his boyhood years continued throughout his father's lifetime. While Adelabu, his father's only son, and Adeitan, his aunt who had raised him, were to share in the inheritance, the will orders

That after my death, before they bury me, the people in my compound must call Adeitan and my son Gbadamosi Adegoke and ask why they calumniate of me during my life.*

Adelabu commented frequently in later life about his parents, his estimation of them varying according to his own fortunes. In 1936, immensely elated about leaving Yaba Higher College for a position with the United Africa Company, he wrote, 'I come from a long line of ancestors, Yoruba sages, men who were famed for their dynamicism [*sic*] and independence.'[2] Having lost that position two years later, he begged his former employer to aid him in his plight since he possessed 'no atom of experience and no family influence or tradition of any kind. . .'.[3] Nevertheless, in 1950, when he had suffered his first bruises in the political arena, he called himself 'the scion of a noble house. . .sacrificed like a soulless beast on the altar of political expediency. . .'.[4] In 1952, in the book he hoped would further his political career, he refers first to his 'muslim middle class parents' and yet only a few paragraphs later, borne along on the tide of his own eloquence, he states that

Both father and mother belonged to the social caste called Igbonnas. They are citizens of the Old Oyo Metropolis and looked down on other Yorubas of the outlandish areas and rural districts as Epos and Ibolos, or 'boorish rustics'.[5]

They were not ordinary citizens, however, for according to his account, his father 'belonged' to the Oluokun ruling chieftaincy house, from which had come two of Ibadan's most important chiefs, and was a quite distinguished person. For his mother, he claimed an equally impressive background. This 'typical Yoruba woman', he now declared, was the daughter of an Ifa Priest 'famed far and wide for his righteousness and uprightness', and related to Olubadan Aleshinloye. A maternal aunt, he claimed, was 'the greatest Hostess of her days', was married variously to senior chiefs and

---

* The will, dated 15 March 1935 and preserved in the Adelabu Papers, is itself an unusual document. The old man was entirely illiterate, and the will must therefore have been prepared by a letter-writer. It left the father's estate to his two daughters, Wolemotu Adeyeola and Rafatu Adejoke, to Adelabu, and to one Asuiru, who cared for the old man when he was sick. The will is also further evidence that he was not a member of the Oluokun lineage, which would have presided over the distribution of his inheritance if he were.

merchants and had attained the title of Otun Iyalode, the third most important woman's title, before her death in 1938.[6]

The son of commoner parents, Adelabu was fascinated with questions of status, often at the expense of self-contradiction. Even had his most exaggerated claims been true, the changes brought about by over four decades of foreign rule had made it clear by the time Adelabu reached manhood that chieftaincy (much less being merely related to long-dead leaders, however prestigious) was no certain guarantee of political or economic success. As his cousin commented on Adelabu's alleged family ties, 'We are all cousins'. Today none of Grandfather Adelabu's line lives at Oke Oluokun and his grandson's family is scattered throughout the city. Only one of his seventeen wives continued to live at the 'Taj Mahal', where Adelabu's earthly remains were buried.

The death of his mother began the chain of events which snatched Adelabu from the oblivion of most Ibadan children to give him a place among Nigeria's elite. For when the aunt who cared for him after his mother's death had him baptized Joseph, probably in 1924, his baptismal certificate became his license for an education, a most important Christian characteristic denied to the overwhelming majority of Ibadan children including the sons of most chiefs, but already a second generation trait in the Christian community.*

As a schoolboy, Joseph soon established his cleverness and delighted in doing his classmates' work, leaving his own undone until the last minute, as much to mock his fellows and his teachers as to be genuinely helpful. In 1929, he was promoted from Standard II to Standard IV, the highest class offered at St David's at the time, thus gaining the first of three double promotions of his academic career. In January 1930 he entered the Central School at Mapo, also run by the C.M.S., where Standards V and VI were taught. His teacher was Headmaster J. L. Ogunsola, who was soon to become a founding member of the Ibadan Progressive Union. One of his classmates was the son of D. T. Akinbiyi, a co-founder of the I.P.U. and Ogunsola's next door neighbor, and it was he who first brought the brilliant new boy to his father's attention. At the urging of these two men, the I.P.U. encouraged Adelabu to apply for a government scholarship to attend the Government College, one of the few secondary schools in Ibadan. His successful

---

* Universal education did not begin until 1955. In 1925 there were only a half dozen Anglican, Methodist and Catholic mission schools and the Bale's School, and the best of these, the Ibadan Grammar School, was hardly a model of modern education. Only the Rev. Akinyele in the entire city possessed a Bachelor of Arts degree, from the University of Durham, England, through Fourah Bay College in Sierra Leone. Thus an educated minority, among them the Akinyele, Ojo, Ayorinde and Olunloyo families, formed the 'Christian aristocracy' which gave Adelabu his education and which he later bitterly opposed.

application nearly went for nothing when his impoverished father was unable to pay the 'six, six and six', the £6. 6. 6d. additional sum demanded for utensils, bedding and school supplies, but Ogunsola paid these fees at the last minute, whereupon the grateful old man exclaimed that 'God meant you to be his father' and in January 1931 Adelabu entered Government College. By 1936 he was head of the school and, in spite of his diminutive size, he participated successfully in such sports as swimming, diving (second place in the diving-for-plates contest!) and track and field events. At the end of the year he left, having attained Middle Six Standard.

In a job testimonial two years later, Government College Principal V. B. V. Powell remembered Adelabu as a boy with 'outstanding' mental ability, who could have passed through the college in even less than five years had he been allowed to, and who turned his 'surplus mental energy' to extracurricular subjects such as shorthand and typing, wherein he gained 'a very fair degree of proficiency' through self-teaching.

His mind, for an African, is unusual. He possesses a fine critical ability and prefers to draw his own conclusions from fundamentals. These conclusions are at times unsound, but this does not detract from the value of his ability to reason deductively. I have disagreed with him on many subjects and, while I do not claim I have always been right, I feel that there is a certain obstinacy in his tenacity to his own opinion that amounts almost to a weakness.[7]

In private, his European tutors warned the I.P.U. patrons that the boy was headed for trouble. The Rev. Field called him a 'demagogue' and Powell stated flatly that he would come to no good end.[8] The I.P.U. leaders were unwilling to accept what appeared to be Powell's typical European prejudices against a bright Nigerian – 'We thought he was a Negrophobe.' They were accordingly pleased when Adelabu passed first in the entrance examination for the three year commercial course at Yaba Higher College in Lagos, then the highest educational institution in Nigeria, and became the first winner of a scholarship of £50 per annum given by the United Africa Company. He began in January of 1936 and studied economics, shorthand, typewriting, book-keeping, elementary statistics and English economic history 'besides other subjects'. Although in 1938 he referred to this curriculum as '6 months of Specialized Education in the Rudiments of Business Economics. . .' which had given him an 'appetite. . .for Research Work. . .', this preparation for clerkdom could not hold him.[9]

At the end of June 1936 Adelabu suddenly left Yaba Higher College, his scholarship unused, to return to Ibadan to take 'a special job' as personal secretary to the District Manager of the United Africa Company. A few weeks in July and August of 1935 as a 'learner' at the Ibadan branch of the

U.A.C.-controlled company of MacIver's, when he was paid twenty shillings a month from the Cotton Manager's own pocket, had presumably been helpful in obtaining the U.A.C. Yaba scholarship. In 1936, a 'practical course in general goods' in the U.A.C. Martins Street office in Lagos led to the sudden end of his academic career.* While working there, he was discovered by E. H. L. Richardson from the U.A.C. Ibadan branch. 'He chatted with me and on hearing my story it became a matter of love at sight. He got the General Manager's permission to transfer me to his Ibadan office.'[10]

The reaction of his patrons was mixed. His 'god' at the time, according to his old teacher at Government College, whose advice against leaving Yaba he ignored, 'was certainly Mammon'.[11] Generally pleased with Adelabu's return to Ibadan was D. T. Akinbiyi who had been instrumental in getting the Yaba scholarship and to whom Adelabu's new position augured a breakthrough in U.A.C.'s anti-African hiring policy: 'Hire a Syrian and you get a Syrian. Hire an African and you get a family.' (While helping his protégé in his first task with U.A.C., Akinbiyi was unwittingly to come to grief himself.)

Adelabu told U.A.C. officials that he had left Yaba because his family wanted him employed, saying that he 'had to return home to come and support my aged father and my three motherless sisters'.[12] It is probable, however, that he was simply tired of school.† The education available in colonial Nigeria was basically directed toward a rather simple purpose – the production of African elementary school teachers, clergymen to fill the lower levels of the missions, and clerks to staff the ranks of the administration and the trading companies. With such an education, the exceptional young man had few possibilities left open to him. He could, of course, read voraciously beyond the limits of his school curricula, as Adelabu read George Bernard Shaw (for whom, as a master egotist, he had a particular respect), H. G. Wells, Harold Laski, James Jeans, Tom Paine, Havelock Ellis, R. G. Ingersoll, Adolf Hitler and many more. As we shall see in later chapters, all these were lumped together and interpreted against a totally different cultural background. Such catholicity of influence was a common feature of many of those who were later to become Nigeria's political leaders.[13]

A second possibility was that the intelligent young Nigerian might travel abroad, usually to the United Kingdom seeking a university degree in order

---

* Adelabu had written to D. T. Akinbiyi on 6 June 1936, but did not mention the 'practical course' or his impending return to Ibadan, which must have materialized later in the month.

† It was about this time, also, that he began once more to refer to himself as Adegoke, rather than Joseph, his schoolname, although he continued to sign letters for the most part as J[oseph] A[degoke] S[anusi] Adelabu.

to join the charmed ranks of the 'Been to's', those who had been to overseas institutions and 'returned with the Golden Fleece'. Both Azikiwe and Awolowo succeeded in this venture, having amassed the necessary funds. Adelabu attempted the same course, but, as we shall see later in this chapter, he was unable to pass the necessary examinations and to secure the funds to travel to Britain.

Another possibility remaining for those bored with their colonial education was to leave the institution whose limitations they had discovered, plunge into some other career, and see what happened. Adelabu, lured by the thought of a business career, left Yaba Higher College in 1936 and joined the United Africa Company as we have seen.

Politics, less than three decades before independence, was no alternative. The Lagos in which Adelabu spent the first six months of 1936 had not specially caught his imagination; there seems to have been no particular issue that gripped his attention, nothing about the cosmopolitan nature of the city that drew him toward it and away from his own. This was not a period of great intensity in Lagos politics. The new Nigerian Youth Movement (N.Y.M.), formed the previous November by the Yoruba journalist H. O. Davies and other representatives of a new political generation, was beginning to challenge the hegemony of the Nigerian National Democratic Party and the seventy-two-year-old Herbert Macaulay. The agitation from which the N.Y.M. in part originated, over the charge that Yaba Higher College was founded purposely to offer only an inferior education to Africans, had now died away, and the N.Y.M. was just beginning to build up the support which was to give it victory over the N.N.D.P. in the 1938 election to the Legislative Council. Indeed, we have no evidence that Adelabu took any interest in political matters at all.

On the other hand, Ibadan was the locus of considerable successful political development. His patrons in the I.P.U. had established themselves as Councillors in 1933 and had successfully fought against continued Oyo domination in 1934. Now the first I.P.U. Councillors were to be made chiefs, the Bale was to be made Olubadan and Oba of his city, D. T. Akinbiyi had become an editor of the small journal *Ijoba Ibile Marun* and was Councillor nominee of the Ibadan Progressive Union. Although in a sense a migrant to Lagos, through the pocket money he received at Akinbiyi's Lagos store Adelabu was constantly reminded of home. A letter to Akinbiyi just before he left Yaba shows that he had considerable interest in Ibadan affairs. Congratulating him on his nomination as Councillor, Adelabu praised Ibadan's democratic institutions and said that the city needed electric lights, water, tarred roads, clean food (an item which appeared several times in Adelabu's political program) and improvement of the Ibadan Grammar School, for

'The next generation will not tolerate illiterate Chiefs.'* He ended by noting that Akinbiyi's business successes would help him in politics, which, however, was 'a dirty game'.[14]

Thus, while the language he used not many months after the event to describe his decision to leave Yaba makes it clear that he had been affected by some of the ideas of African nationalism which were becoming more and more current, it also is clear that he saw his own fulfillment of them to be in Ibadan, not Lagos. In November 1936 he wrote:

My sudden withdrawal from the Higher College marks the beginning of a new era in my wonderful life. It is a high example of Radical Self-Determination and African initiative and I am proud of the achievement.
  This is a wonderful life.[15]

This is our first real taste of Adelabu's ebullience, and the first indication of concern on his part with wider issues. Writing nearly sixteen years later he was to speak of his educational experience in much more strongly 'racial' terms:

In January, 1931 I entered the Ibadan Government College. I met the white man. His too easy asumption that England was the hub of the Universe, that the European perspective was the only correct vantage point to survey life, that we less fortunate species of homo sapiens were created mainly to exhort, applaud and pay homage to the mighty empire on which the sun never sets exasperated and infuriated me. It ignited the glowing ember of freedom into a burning flame.[16]

There is no indication, however, that Adelabu was as 'nationalistic' in his outlook as this in 1936 at the age of twenty-one. Clearly he was deeply affected by the nature of his colonial education, but (like Obafemi Awolowo at this time) he was also quite conventional in his desire to use his new employment to finance further higher studies at some later date.

He now set out to establish himself in the adult world. Curiously, he did not appear to be a part of it, for he was only five feet high; his musculature, which was lithe and trim, compensated to some extent for his diminutive stature. He wore his hair closely trimmed as did most Yoruba men, and usually at this time he dressed in Western clothing. Despite his unimpressive height he gave a first impression of tense and unlimited energy, of striking alertness and of such overall activity that he was necessarily the center of every group of which he was a part. Europeans remember him as being 'like a cat'.

Perhaps his intense gregariousness, which we shall see throughout his life,

* His judgement of the Grammar School was one shared by others. Obisesan noted that 'It is understood that the school is failing badly in its duties as a first class institution.' (Obisesan Diary, 4 January 1938.)

is best demonstrated by the involvements he now created around himself as head of a family, such demanding involvements that they were to impinge continually on his ability to pursue wider purposes. On 28 November 1936, soon after joining the staff of U.A.C., he married his first wife, Mopelola, and within the year, to the sorrow of his Christian patrons, had taken the full Islamic complement of four. Each was important to him, and for each he was able to determine a natural place in a greater cosmic scheme of medieval physics. Calling himself the 'Sun', he described them in a rumination about his marital state in 1937 entitled 'The Character of my Wives' as typifying the elements of Earth, Air, Fire and Water. 'The four elements,' he concluded, 'are correct and I am the Soul infusing life into the parts and regulating their movements as organs in a comprehensive whole.'

Such marital bliss was not untouched by sorrow. Mopelola suffered two miscarriages before bearing a son who died shortly after birth. By the end of 1943, only one of the first four wives remained with him, and three others had simply 'come and gone'. Adelabu had only four children alive in 1944, more having died than survived.* At the time of his death in 1958, only nine of his seventeen current wives had born him children (a total of sixteen still alive). Such a number of wives was, of course, in vast excess of the limitations of Islam and a roundly number even by Yoruba standards. All with the exception of one were Ibadans, and apparently none of the Ibadan wives came from important chieftaincy houses.† Certainly, then, he did not attempt to solidify political ties with convenient or useful marriages.

His older children remember him as a strict but not an unpredictable father. None of them played a significant role in their father's public life, and we shall hear little of them until they became the subjects of a legal dispute after his death.

Although Adelabu's family responsibilities rapidly increased, in the five years after November 1936 he made sporadic attempts to continue his education and so increase his income. In 1939 he wrote to the University

---

* A daughter who survived, Afusatu Adepate, was born on 11 May 1938. By this time Mopelola had had two stillbirths. By the end of 1938 both Mopelola and another wife had given birth to sons who died almost immediately. (Incomplete details of births, marriages and deaths are to be found in a document entitled 'Memorandum' and in notes on the back of an envelope in the Adelabu Papers.) Adelabu sent his wives to hospitals and birth clinics for maternity care and used the services of Dr Okechukwu Ikejiani and Dr Samuel Manuwa. His family and his records indicate that he never relied on Yoruba traditional medical practitioners. Nevertheless, the infant mortality rate in his family was extremely high.

† One wife, Omoriyeba, was the daughter of Adeyemi, the Alafin of Oyo. She apparently married him in August or September 1954, about a year after he became involved in Oyo politics, and divorced him, after the birth of a daughter, Fatimatu.

Correspondence College in Cambridge and to Wolsey Hall in Oxford for information regarding admission, but he did not continue negotiations with them.[17] He also requested entrance regulations from the University of London in November 1939, but it was not until January 1941 that arrangements could be made to take the Matriculation Examinations, the prerequisite for admission to the university. During the next seven months he waited while the university processed his answers. Finally, on 25 August 1941, Candidate 6672 was sent a notice that he had received an F for Failure in Elementary Mathematics, Mechanics and Biology. Thus ended two years of application to the University of London for one of the brightest products of Nigeria's pre-war educational system.

Decisive as his failure was, he did not relinquish his hope. In the second septennial comment in his 'Diary', written eighteen months later, he set himself a program to attain it.*

...in the next seven years I must consolidate my position. Economically I must reach the £2000 standard. I must rear up my four sons. I MUST KEEP TO THE GOVERNMENT. On 22nd June 1950 I hope to be writing the next story upstairs with Raufu, Rashidi, Mosudi and Mojidi [his sons] standing around my table... my £1000 Bank Book in front, a pensioner, a matriculant, about to proceed to England to study LAW.

One God, One Aim, One DESTINY 22/6/43

sgnd Adelabu

As we shall see later, his attempts to enter the legal profession eventually led him into the thick of Ibadan politics without ever having studied law. There is no reason to believe he saw the law as a basis for a political career, nor is there any evidence that he saw it as a stimulating intellectual activity or even just as a chance to see England and something of the world outside Nigeria. Adelabu was not anti-colonial enough at this point to study his enemy, nor was he apparently influenced by other 'been to's'. Probably prestige and the promise of a substantial income were his principal motivations; this utilitarian approach did not foresee using British law, with its fixed procedures and 'sense of justice and fair play' which he was later to try to exploit, to institute reforms within or to overthrow colonialism.

In the middle of 1936, however, in the first flush of his new job, Adelabu as yet felt no immediate pressure to study further. His first assignment, for U.A.C., he recalled, was 'to tour the Cocoa Belt of the Western Provinces with a view to formulating a scheme of re-organization. I set to work in

---

* The 'Diary' in fact consists only of two comments upon the progress of his career, written in 1936 and 1943. It is interesting that at the time of the above comment Obafemi Awolowo also set himself a 'five-year plan' to get to Britain to study law.

earnest and in a few weeks submitted a Report...'[18] His 'Survey of the Ibadan Cocoa Trade' dealt principally with the middlemen who purchased cocoa and palm kernels from the producers in rural areas and brought them to the depots of the expatriate-owned (mainly British) trading companies in the city.* For linguistic and economic reasons, the middlemen were Africans, under very little company supervision. The most successful of them was Salami Agbaje, but in contrast to him most middlemen had inadequate purchasing capital and transport vehicles. As cocoa prices rose between 1933 and 1936 it therefore became a widespread practice for companies to grant a cash advance to the middlemen prior to the buying season, against some collateral such as a car. Using the cash advance and the same car again, some middlemen then went from company to company, adding further vehicles and acquiring further capital, sometimes with the result that more capital had been advanced by all the companies than could be covered or indeed utilized in the purchase of an annual crop. The middlemen passed the advance payments to the producers. When the advance was lower than the market price turned out to be, the middleman pocketed the difference as his profit. When it was higher, the middleman made no profit, but the companies were left holding the credit liabilities. Prosecution in court was rarely successful. Prior to the Adelabu report, the companies had sought to protect themselves and increase profits by keeping their purchasing price as low as possible, which required concerted action with other companies if individual companies were not to price themselves out of the market entirely. This, of course, opened them up – not unfairly – to charges of price-rigging. The whole credit and middleman system, however, introduced an element of inflexibility unwelcome to the companies in a fluctuating world market and made it very difficult for them to control the local market.

Adelabu's report, documented partly from the personal records of D. T. Akinbiyi, revealed how the middlemen inflated their capital by playing one European company off against another. It proposed that salaried buyers located in established market depots under European supervision replace the middlemen operating on advances. The report was sent to the London head office of the United Africa Company and in October 1936, just as the buying season was beginning, Adelabu was hired as Assistant Produce Manager at £180 per annum to oversee the implementation of his own recommendations. During the next five months, he claimed to have travelled 20,000 miles and supervised the purchase of £70,000 of produce. In so doing he held the highest position any African had ever held in U.A.C. up to that time.†

* We have not seen this document. This account of it is based on Adelabu's references to it and interviews.
† Traders up to this time were making immense profits. Money lenders received 100

Adelabu later accused Richardson of having ulterior motives in having him investigate the middlemen, for if Richardson could suggest how 'to oust the middlemen from the invulnerable position' which they had acquired, he would be given a voice in the formulation of the Company's Produce Department policies, which he much desired. The result of the report for Adelabu was the enmity of both Produce Department officials and the middlemen, many of whom, including D. T. Akinbiyi, were now sued in court by U.A.C.

In February 1937, as cocoa prices plummeted downward, Adelabu was suddenly released from his post. His I.P.U. patrons, two of whom were in the Agricultural Department at the time, claim that he cheated the producers outrageously, the farther from town and Company supervision the more nefarious his dealings. Richardson, however, was later willing to recommend him to the Co-operative Society as having 'successfully' completed a job which included 'taking to bush very considerable sums of money'.[19] He also explained that the post was but a temporary one, since it had always been held by a European, and that U.A.C. was 'forced' to terminate Adelabu's employment when the London Office sent a replacement. Adelabu, as did Richardson, attributed it to racial discrimination.

To the junior European Coastal staff my appointment was anathema, a dangerous precedent and an unwarranted encroach on the White Man's preserve. An undercurrent of resentment gradually gathered momentum and representations by personal letters and contact were made to the home Authorities.[20]

Certainly the relationship between Manager Richardson and Assistant Produce Manager Adelabu appears to have been one between patron and client, as Adelabu revealed in a plea for help to Richardson. Heart-broken, unemployed, out of school and in disfavor with his I.P.U. patrons who had suffered the first of several disappointments they were to receive at his hands, Adelabu threw himself at Richardson's feet.

What am I today? A rejected lover, an unemployed bookworm, a courtier fallen from the favour of his king, an object of ridicule in society, a useful target for the supposed vengeance of the supposed sins of the company that I tried my best to serve, a fallen man with no ray of hope for the future. Yet I am still the unsophisticated schoolboy that I was. I STILL TRUST YOU. I cannot yet believe that you will forget me as one forgets a discarded tool. I still believe in your humanity.[21]

Thus ended the career of 'the first African manager'. His colonial educa-

per cent return on loans in three to six months, and presumably Adelabu could have made more than £180 per annum as a trader, rather than as a company official. On the other hand, he may not have felt he had the necessary contacts with producers, and he was understandably unpopular with the traders following his report. A smaller salary was at least a secure income.

tion had of course given him neither the technical qualifications nor the organizational experience necessary for success in such a post and his pathetic letters to his patron demonstrate how sparse a philosophy, either concerning himself or his society, it had given him to fall back on in such times. It had, however, aroused great personal expectations, which required both a formal position with some recognized status, and a substantial and regular income, and he was therefore willing to change his course and accept his third chance with U.A.C. when he was made a credit customer dealing in produce and merchandise. On 1 October 1937 he was given £1200 credit, with one-third of one per cent interest a month on the unpaid balance to be debited to his account, 'with a view to affording him a training in merchandise markets'.[22] As Adelabu put it, he 'burst into Trade' with a lorry, a Chevrolet and a Ford taxi cab, a general goods shop, a foodstore and a cocoa buying station at the village of Awo-Oju, but this too failed. Although he 'grappled pluckily' in the 'uncharted sea of individual enterprise' he was also

...at the height of my unpopularity with the big produce buyers, with no atom of experience and no family influence or tradition of any kind, and in a highly organized market and at the onset of a most terribly rapid decline in trade...I failed along with hundreds more favourably circumstanced than myself.[23]

In 1933 cocoa had been worth £16 a ton. By 1936 it had more than tripled in price, to £52 a ton.[24] By February 1937, however, the price at Ibadan for main crop cocoa had dropped to £17. 17. 6d. a ton, and it continued to fall; by November it was £12. 12. 6d.[25] By the middle of November 1937 Adelabu calculated that he had lost 'anything from three to five hundred pounds,' and he later figured his losses at 'roughly' £1000. He was now in the same position of indebtedness other middlemen had occupied when his report had exposed them.*

Adelabu therefore requested to be taken out of the selling business and re-instated in his former job as Assistant Produce Manager at £220 per annum, with £100 per annum of this being paid toward his debt.[26] Instead of a salaried position, however, U.A.C. granted Adelabu further credit, which he accepted in spite of sharp words and the fact that it was the off season during which vehicles had to be maintained and funds had to be

---

* Obisesan well expressed the uncertainty of the times. 'Everybody depends upon the European and the Cocoa grower is the greatest among this class of dependents; has the African any other source to look up to for his economic salvation and ability besides this? I say none at present! The African it seems has taken a drug which renders him unconscious of what to do and how to do it save what the whiteman says. Must one therefore conclude that the whiteman is his God or one in whose hand his maker places him for protection etc? We have got to write and think about this big problem in times to come.' (Obisesan Diary, 22 June 1938.)

advanced to the farmer for the coming season's crop, the price for which was steadily declining. As the season advanced, so did Adelabu's financial difficulties. By mid-February 1938, he was charging U.A.C. with failure to honor an oral agreement to pay his petrol bills, of which there were now thirteen outstanding. As the season ended, with prices in mid-May down to £8. 9. od. a ton, he urged them to buy his lorry for £150; eventually they also bought his two taxi cabs with which he had 'burst into trade' only a few months earlier.[27] By July 1938 he confessed his credit venture to be 'a definite failure', and while he accepted part of the blame, he attributed his dilemma mostly to the rapid decline in trade and his own inexperience, over which, he said, he had no control. In desperation in July he begged the Lagos General Manager 'in the humble spirit of an old Servant who is most willing to serve again' for a job in the Lagos area.[28] But U.A.C. could no longer be persuaded. As Richardson put it, the 'grave credit risks' involved tended to 'resolve the average African trader into a common speculator'.[29] U.A.C. was apparently more willing to be rid of Adelabu and accept his credit losses than to continue his employment.

Adelabu was destitute and in debt. The largest employer in the private sector no longer had a place for him. He had no apparent interest in becoming a schoolteacher in spite of his intellectual pretensions and his virtuoso command of the English language, and perhaps because his break with Bishop Akinyele and his increasing number of wives prohibited his finding a place in the Christian-dominated educational system. A career in journalism, which Richardson suggested for him, would have meant going to Lagos, since Ibadan had no press worthy of his talents. Some kind of government employment might have been an alternative, but the Ibadan Council was increasingly under the influence of members of the Ibadan Progressive Union. Foremost among these, as we have seen, was Bishop Akinyele's brother Isaac, who had been awarded a chieftaincy title for his good services, and their half brother, Emmanuel Akinyele, Ibadan Council Treasurer and in charge of most of the senior staff positions. Still on the Council was Adelabu's life-long enemy-friend D. T. Akinbiyi, whose business was soon to be sold in public auction to repay his debts to U.A.C. and who was threatening 'legal steps' if Adelabu failed to settle his accounts with him, which amounted to less than £8. o. od. Furthermore, the I.P.U. had split into several factions on 11 August in its attempt to select new Councillors and it is doubtful that Adelabu could have found adequate support for his cause while they were thus distracted. Such factors meant that he stood little chance of finding a job at Mapo Hall.

Virtually the only other alternative, which he quickly accepted, was also suggested by Richardson and supported by the Acting Principal of Government College.* Less than three weeks after his plea to U.A.C. to be retained as a willing old servant, he offered his services to the Union of Co-operative Societies, 'a Movement in which I am intensely interested'.[30] His application was approved at the monthly meeting of the Union on 30 August.[31] While waiting for his duties to begin, he read what literature he could find on the co-operative movement, including articles in the *Encyclopaedia Britannica*, and in February 1939 he served on a committee with Co-operative President Akinpelu Obisesan, his former schoolmaster J. L. Ogunsola, and J. A. Ayorinde, a cocoa officer in the Agricultural Department, to prepare recommendations for a memorandum on the report of the Nowell Commission which had been inquiring into the cocoa industry and its pricing structure.[32]

On 1 April 1939, when he signed an 'African Staff' Agreement for employment as an Inspector, he was finally 'rescued into the government service' from what had become an eighteen month 'ordeal' of unemployment. His main duties included checking the records of the individual growers' co-operatives, advising them on business procedures and compiling annual financial and statistical reports. In 1942, with the Second World War depleting the numbers of expatriate officers, he served as Acting Registrar for four months in place of a British officer in charge of the co-operative societies in Kumba Province in the Southern Cameroons.[33] In 1943 he was consulted by Obisesan concerning a desire of member unions to federate for purposes of being designated by the Government as a cocoa shipper, a status which would give them a competitive position with the European trading companies, which under war-time measures shipped the entire crop on a quota basis.[34] By 1944 he was supervisor of nineteen societies in Oyo, Ijebu and Abeokuta Provinces, with a gross seasonal turnover of some £24,000.

---

* Thus Richardson to E. F. G. Haig, 19 August 1938, A. P.: 'Adelabu possesses a remarkable brain, and can give forceful expression to his views by word and on paper. But, because of his youth, his brain requires harnessing. Forceful individualism in one so young cannot and will not be accepted in competitive business either by Europeans or by Africans.

'If his intelligence can be utilized unselfishly, and harnessed over a protracted period to interests allied with the welfare of Africans or with the right school of Journalism, then he has every qualification for a highly successful career.

'He is a glutton for knowledge and not afraid of study. It would be a real tragedy if at any time his abilities became harnessed in the wrong school, as they are well worth the right kind of development.'

Powell wrote to Haig, 22 August 1938, A. P.: 'I feel that Mr Adelabu has it in him to be of the greatest value to his people and the Government. Nothing would please those of us who have watched him grow up more than to see him working under such a man as yourself and associated with a movement such as you control. Under such conditions I think the best in him would be developed and the best use made of that development.'

His success was not without discord. In 1939 Obisesan complained of his 'insolence' before the Co-operative Committee, which so aggravated the Registrar of Co-operatives, Captain Cheesman, that he left the meeting in anger even after Adelabu had prostrated in apology and several members had begged for him.[35] In his own 'Diary' entry 'On the 7th Anniversary of Manhood' written on 22 June 1943 during his last year as co-operative inspector, Adelabu noted that 'I have been persecuted by all because of my faith and my age.' Nevertheless, he felt he had 'carved a place for myself' in the Service. 'Many old enemies have become friends and allies; I am tolerated, respected and even admired.'[36] He also claimed to have found the 'special truth' his life was destined to demonstrate. 'Spiritually I have found the key to the Universe in the cosmic Series of Seven'; 'To amplify it, to preach it, to publish it, to live it. . .' was his mission. As he wrote, this required during the next seven years that he '. . . KEEP TO THE GOVERN-MENT.' He also remained on cordial terms with Obisesan, visiting him occasionally, presenting him with a gift of cloth on one visit.[37] His European superiors thought he was strongly motivated by 'the co-operative ideal', and when in January 1944 he unsuccessfully applied to the Ibadan Council for the position of Treasurer upon the resignation of Emmanuel Akinyele, Captain Cheesman wrote in a strong letter of recommendation that he would be 'sorry to lose him from my staff. . .'.

At this juncture, Adelabu possessed a 'clean record of Service'. By November this was no longer true. Sometime during his five years of service he had turned the co-operative ideal to his own advantage. As one of his superiors said in retrospect, 'If honesty was necessary to get on he followed that course.' By 1944 honesty was no longer necessary. One of his duties was to make unannounced inspections of member societies' financial records in order to discover irregularities.* This involved travelling to remote and uncomfortable villages to appear as the long arm of the bureaucracy, an unwelcome role for a young man of Adelabu's gregarious nature. He therefore began to station himself in a central and more comfortable resthouse and to call in the society Treasurers to his 'headquarters'. This procedure, of course, allowed time for records and cash boxes to be put in order, a practice which

---

* Treasures of societies were under great pressure to lend funds to friends, relatives and society members as trading capital. Although profits could reach fifty and one hundred per cent in six months and interest rates of twenty-five per cent were common in the private loan business, loans from societies' funds to such closely related persons were made without interest. Such conversion of funds was therefore not considered to be corrupt since the money would otherwise be lying idle. Chief Issac Akinyele and Akinpelu Obisesan frequently rescued treasurers from dismissal or prosecution by granting time to replace the money or even by making private loans to cover the converted funds.

negated the value of the inspection and endeared him to local co-operative officials. All this was revealed when Adelabu continued to submit expense accounts for 'bush allowance' and mileage re-imbursements to the villages when in fact he was comfortably ensconced at a resthouse. Confronted with these charges by the Registrar, who had visited the villages at the time Adelabu claimed in his expense reports to have been there himself, Adelabu first shouted charges of racial discrimination and threats of retaliation, then broke into a smile and admitted his guilt. His behavior was, of course, criminal and punishable in the courts, but the co-operative movement had not yet gained enough public support, more critically the support of the administrative officers, to admit all its internal difficulties in public. Thus Adelabu agreed to resign in exchange for a promise on the part of the co-operative officials not to prosecute. He submitted with his resignation the sum of £8. 13. 4d., the portion of his salary required in lieu of notice, and was again unemployed.*

Adelabu had always dabbled in a number of economic ventures. In 1937 he had acquired 200 acres of land at Badeku, but lost it when the owner's brothers protested his loss of the patrimony to their father, who was also the village chief. By 1940, further negotiations and a total expenditure of £37. 2. 6d. had recovered the land, whereon he invested in cocoa trees and built a house he referred to as 'my country residence'. He had opened a cocoa-buying center at Awo-Oju and bought other land at Apomu while working for U.A.C., but lost it all and abandoned his farms. Nevertheless, in January of 1944 he wrote that he had had 'a very versatile career as Private Secretary, Trader, Farmer, Produce Magnate and Civil Servant...', that he had 'earned a good name as a modest, successful young man' and that he derived 'a considerable unearned income from several properties in the city...', which included a 'modern Yaba-style building' at Kudeti, presumably his father's house which he attempted to rent in 1944 to Igbobi College, and another ten-room mud house which he sold in 1945 for £300.[38] It was a significant accomplishment indeed for an Inspector with an annual salary of only £180 and a family to support to claim, as he did, to be 'worth' £900 and to be able to 'garner in' £300 to £400 a year.

It was not the case in 1944, therefore, that he was without money as he had been in 1938. Rather, his income was vastly uncertain and still inadequate for his hopes of going to England to study law or to continue his

---

* Members of Adelabu's family first told us that his departure from the Co-operative Society had been a clouded one, an opinion held by others as well. The details of this story were given by Captain Cheesman, who promised Adelabu he would not prosecute. Adelabu's letter of resignation dated 31 October 1944 was accepted by Haig in a letter of 9 November as of 1 November.

careless spending habits in Ibadan. He accordingly sought and continued to seek official positions with regular salaries, including his second application in January 1944 for the post of Council Treasurer, which foundered on the opposition of the Ibadan Progressive Union. Certainly there was no sign of any political interests in his application:

As is the tradition with Civil Servants in England, I have no politics. My motto is 'SERVICE FIRST'. I am convinced that if Yorubaland is to reap the full benefit from the admirable system of Government by Native Authorities, then level-headed young men combining the enthusiasm and drive of youth with the better judgment and staying power of maturer years must be willing to assume posts of responsibility in the Administration and ultimately of leadership in the evolving new communities.[39]

The reasons for Adelabu's change of employment, as he explained them later, were not those given here. His father had died in September 1943, 'and as an only son domestic responsibilities necessitated my resignation from the government service'.[40] Why it necessitated his resignation six months after his father's death, and how it allowed taking a job only a short time later in Lagos, a half day's journey from Ibadan, is not clear. He had upon his dismissal from the Co-operative Society immediately drawn up what he called a 'Produce Buying Scheme', and when he saw Richardson of the U.A.C. 'on a casual visit to Lagos', Richardson immediately asked him to submit a copy of it, which he did in April 1945. The scheme was in fact a report on the internal organization and future prospects of the Co-operatives as purchasing and shipping agents able to compete with the European firms, a report which was quickly sent off to London and for which Adelabu was rewarded with another job in U.A.C. On 22 April 1945, he became Factory Production Assistant at the U.A.C. Martins Street singlet factory in Lagos. He was also in charge of a tailoring shop in Elegbeta and supervised the delivery of finished goods to the interior. He claimed to have had 300 production personnel plus clerical staff under his control and to have raised revenues from the sale of waste pieces of cloth by 300 per cent.

This period of re-employment with U.A.C. lasted just over a year. According to a family member, his managerial skills contributed significantly to his resignation. By raising the number of shirts cut from each bolt of cloth and the number of shirts sewn per hour, he was able to siphon off for sale through his own channels enough U.A.C. goods – twenty-five per cent according to his cousin – to more than double his income. He began to appear for work in the morning late and inebriated, and his arrogant statements about cleverly arrived at wealth began to irritate both superiors and subordinates who, he taunted, would 'die copying numbers'. It seems that he was thereupon unofficially transferred to the Haberdashery Department. In December of 1945 his patron Richardson suddenly resigned, as a result of what Adelabu called 'reasons of higher policy', warning Adelabu that he, too, would not last 'more than one month'. As Adelabu learned six weeks later, one of his immediate superiors had indeed urged that he be fired. Adelabu's suspicions that he was involved in high company politics, over which he had no control, were confirmed when he was called to the Manager's office 'for reasons [he] failed to disclose to me to assure me that so long [as] I was loyal to the Company and kept all the secrets which came into my possession through my friendship and close association with Mr Richardson I could keep my job'.[41] In Adelabu's mind it appeared that he was 'too closely associated with him to be spared in the purge' which followed the quarrels leading to Richardson's displacement.

He had also been accused, however, by a co-worker in the anti-Richardson group of taking money from a customer above the value of goods received. According to Adelabu, this accusation derived solely from his co-worker's unfounded claim to the right to make all sales and his conspiracy with the customer to make charges of corruption against him.

In any case, Adelabu was suspended from working in the Haberdashery Department on 20 March and placed in the Staff and Welfare Department as Assistant Chief Clerk. He refused to accept this as a permanent post. On 30 March, in a bitter letter laying out the above events, he notified the Manager that he would 'not wait and starve and languish in Lagos' while management decided what to do with him. He could be reached in Ibadan. He apparently did not go to Ibadan as he had threatened. He discussed his case with the head of the Welfare and Staff office on 3 April and again on 9 May, at which time he was told that his case would not be referred to the General Manager, but that he was willing to offer Adelabu another appointment in a new department, which Adelabu refused.[42] His Certificate of Employment, issued to him on his release, stated he had been employed from 22 April 1945 to 9 May 1946 as Assistant Chief Clerk in the General Manager's Office, denying him an official record of his previous managerial status.

Adelabu's second period of residence in Lagos had thus ended ignominiously, with his rejection by the biggest of the expatriate trading companies. His stay had coincided with the most hectic period of nationalist activity that Lagos had yet witnessed, but there is no evidence that this had any effect on him. He had been far too busy trying to make another career with U.A.C. to become 'zikified', as he was later to put it, that is, a follower of 'Zik' – Nnamdi Azikiwe.

Once back in Ibadan, where he allowed his astonished cousin to count a bundle of notes worth £2000, he quickly established himself in the cotton piece goods trade, of which he had now had some experience. (Although he now had the finances for legal studies in London, he had made no attempt to pass the matriculation examinations.) His wholesale suppliers were 'Syrian' merchants according to his own account. (The term as used in West Africa includes Lebanese, who in fact predominate.) Among them may have been Anthony Younan, a Lebanese who had established his business in Ibadan in 1923, and his son, Albert, who had struck up a close friendship with Adelabu upon returning from his education in the Lebanon. The Younans may not have been dealing with him at this time, however, since his attitude toward his Lebanese suppliers was scarcely a friendly one; he blamed them, in fact, because his profit toward the end of March 1948 was 'only' between 4 and 5 per cent on an average monthly turnover of £1000, or between £480 and £600 a year.[43] Furthermore, the Younans claim that it was Anthony Younan who advanced Adelabu's business by putting him in touch with C. M. Booth of G. B. Ollivant's, who secured him a further supply of textiles for sale. This was extremely important, since under the 'quota' system, which persisted after the war, only the big expatriate companies were able to get assured supplies of such goods, making the middlemen traders more than ever dependent upon their favors. March 1947, indeed, found Adelabu trying to exploit further contacts along these lines, seeking to renew an acquaintance with the manager of MacIver's, for whom he had worked as a schoolboy in 1935.

The years 1946–9 must have been successful ones for Adelabu, for on 4 November 1947, when wartime scarcities still made building materials difficult and expensive to obtain, he began the construction of his own house, the Taj Mahal, in part replacing and in part incorporating his father's house. Into this, according to his own estimate, he eventually sank £4000. It was a concrete block structure, two stories high, adorned on two sides with Brazilian style balconies and many glass windows.* In 1948–9 he had a profit of £700, whereupon he rented a three-door shop from Anthony Younan and Sons for £230 for the year April 1949 to April 1950.

Again, he was financially able to begin his legal studies, but he still had not passed the matriculation examinations and the opportunity to make money and to speculate in the housing market then booming in Ibadan kept him at home. The years 1949–50, however, proved to be economically disastrous. In November 1949 he wrote to the Secretary of the Institute of Social Science at the newly-founded University College of Ibadan, more in

* The 'Brazilian' style had first been introduced into Lagos by Yoruba former slaves who had returned from Brazil during the latter part of the nineteenth century and had gradually spread back into the hinterland. Its ornate use of balconies and decoration marked both private houses and mosques in Yorubaland.

discouragement and anticipation than in truth, that he had 'just wound up' his produce, transport and textile enterprise with a view, once again, to going to the London School of Economics to study economics, law and public administration. He sought a position for an interim year in which he might have a salary of £500 and an intellectual atmosphere to prepare him for his further studies.

Yet it was as if he offered himself as an object rather than as an agent of inquiry, an unwitting but poignant commentary on the preparation his education, and his reaction to it, had given him.

I am a living laboratory of my age. My continuous bathing in the social strains and stresses of my environmental community has made of me not a dexterous swimmer but a part of the stream. I am at once the cocoa farmer, the mercantile clerk, the civil servant, the petty trader, the transporter, the capitalist and the intellectual – all materials for the study of the social scientist. I have no prejudices, religious, tribal, racial, social, personal, economic or temperamental.[44]

In short, he was an indistinguishable product of his times, apparently without any special skills to contribute or demands to make, and there was no particular place for such a man at the University College. Since his trading losses for 1949–50 were £100, he closed his shop in April, delaying renewal of his lease until May, then subletting each door separately in August of that year. His efforts to find a new economic footing in 1949 and 1950 can only be described as frantic. A new note, however, had been introduced, and although it was initially but one note in the clamor of his life, it became the dominant theme. On 20 December 1949, as he recorded in his Diary, 'I entered the politics of Ibadan.' It was a furtive entry, full of scheming and conniving and bitterness, which was to leave him in September of 1950 'at the very margin of starvation' and desperately searching for either trading capital or an academic scholarship. This, in fact, was to be the pattern of the remainder of his life, a search for personal security through political office and the accommodation of himself to the resultant disappointments.

CHAPTER 3

A POLITICAL APPRENTICESHIP

Great men in all spheres of life belong to a class apart and in weighing their virtues and their vices we must avoid the too easy mistake of adopting conventional standards. The moment they fit into our common mould they cease to become great and become ordinary and commonplace. Peculiarity is the price of greatness.

Adegoke Adelabu to the Senior Officer,
Ibadan
November 1950

Adelabu's first step into what he viewed as the political arena was so precise that in retrospect he could note in his Diary, 'I entered the politics of Ibadan on Tuesday the 20th December 1949.' From his point of view, this was simply an event in his own life, an unexpected opportunity to fulfill his private hopes of studying law in England by exploiting the desire of the chiefs to deprive Chief Agbaje of his title. He did not really intend to enter politics, and at first he paid little attention to the place of the Agbaje agitation in the congeries of issues facing Ibadan and Nigeria at the time. As we shall see, however, Adelabu entered on his political apprenticeship while the chiefs of Ibadan were attempting to defend what they viewed as their traditions and while the new system of Nigerian national politics was intruding itself ever more insistently into Ibadan life. It is this coming together of the three entities of our story which provides the substance of this chapter.

The way to his legal education, Adelabu believed, lay through the post of the Administrative Secretary to the Ibadan Council, which he was led to believe the chiefs would give him in return for his help against Agbaje and which would involve sending him to England to acquire the necessary legal qualifications for the job. As we saw in Chapter 1, by 1948 the British administrators had come to the view that reform of the local government system in Ibadan Division was essential, and that part of this was to be the creation of an Administrative Secretaryship as the chief executive office of the Olubadan-in-Council, combining tasks which had hitherto been divided among several Councillors. The administration did not wish to appoint a European to this post. As was pointed out as early as May 1947, 'Some suitably qualified and locally acceptable African would be the solution, although

54

such a person would admittedly be fairly hard to find.'[1] This prospect was most alarming to Olubadan Fijabi, who found himself faced with this problem soon after his accession in February 1948, and to the chiefs, who shared the fear that such an office, filled by an African, could only lead to their own loss of power and prestige.

It was not surprising, therefore, that when the Ibadan Progressive Union proposed S. Ade Ojo, an Ibadan man then making a very successful civil service career in Lagos, for the job in April 1948, there was little enthusiasm among the traditional members of the Council. The proposal of Akinpelu Obisesan in May met with a cool reception by the Resident. The idea was nevertheless kept alive over many months by Acting Resident A. F. Abell, who agreed that the Administrative Secretary 'should be a man of proved character' and Obisesan, who honestly continued his efforts to see the post created.[2] Obisesan's advice was pragmatic. Warning in September 1949 that the Northern Districts might accept the idea of an Administrative Secretary, thus aligning themselves with the colonial administrators against Ibadan, he advised the Olubadan to accept the idea also and then register a complaint against it, for total refusal would only brand him as 'an improgressive chief'.[3]* On the other hand, Obisesan then went to Oyo where he 'forcibly' presented the point of view of the Ibadan chiefs to the Resident.

For their part, the chiefs relied on a variety of subterfuges to prevent the establishment of the Administrative Secretaryship. In August of 1949 they protested that they had not been aware of the wide variety of powers to be given him and 'were not yet highly civilised to check a bad secretary'; in September they suggested that an increase in the number of Councillors might make it unnecessary to have an Administrative Secretary and his appointment should therefore be postponed; they finally urged that, while they did not reject the idea entirely, false rumors and propaganda were being spread about the post and it should not be filled until public protest against it had died.[4] Early in November Obisesan was charged by the Council 'with responsibility to put Council's affairs in better position & to set up committees to deal with its affairs'; it was an obvious move to put off the Secretaryship. By the end of 1948 the British officials had begun to lose patience. In his report for the year, the District Officer described the Olubadan's office as 'a monument to inefficiency', and spoke of the year as one

---

* On 6 September he noted in his Diary that 'Ibadan needs one who will be able to direct her well, i.e., one with enough courage and good intentions and who would not bend to the wheel of customs to drive him away from saying what is right...' This, of course, is precisely what the chiefs feared, since it meant a strengthening of the administrative structures in ways beyond their control, just as the legislative activities of the Council were increasingly falling into the hands of Council members other than the chiefs.

during which the Olubadan had distinguished himself for failure to take the advice of his Administrative advisers, for a disregard of public opinion and interest, and for exhibiting a propensity to intrigue which is almost beyond comprehension.[5]

In the last month of this unsatisfactory year, another issue arose to try the patience of the District Officer and his colleagues. This was the agitation against Chief Salami Agbaje, occasioned by the fear of the Olubadan and his chiefs that this man, to whom so many were indebted, had risen to a position where he might soon become Olubadan. We have already noted that, from Adelabu's position at least, this issue was from the first linked with that of the Administrative Secretaryship. It became quickly associated in fact with the whole range of problems confronting Ibadan. The colonial administrators wanted reform, but not at the cost of upsetting the entire Ibadan system at a time when Nigeria as a whole was changing, nor at the cost of losing the confidence of the I.P.U. leadership. The I.P.U. wanted reform, but not the loss of the Northern Districts nor a diminution of the chiefs' prestige if that could be avoided. The longer these two elements delayed in taking a firm position, however, the more complex the situation became, the more bitter grew the various antagonisms, and the more elements of the Ibadan polity were brought into play.

The original elements grouped against Agbaje shared opportunism as their strongest common feature. As Lawani Latorera, the President of the Maiyegun League, put it,

Everything that the town supports, all the societies in the town support it too. Whether [Agbaje] is good or bad I do not know but I know that the whole people of Ibadan are fighting with him.[6]

Thus in the name of 'the town' and of a rather dubious and eroded tradition the forces gathered to pull down a strong man.

One ally of the Olubadan and chiefs at the end of 1949 was the Maiyegun League. Its attitude toward Agbaje was probably mainly determined by the fact that its rival, the Maiyegun Society and its Balogun and Treasurer, Mustafa Alli, supported Salami Agbaje, with whom Alli had been in business and for whom he had preserved respect.* The League had broken away from the Society in July 1949 partly because of personal rivalries and partly

---

* Alli has shown us a letter of 20 January 1951 he wrote to H. L. M. Butcher saying that 'I learnt the rudiments of produce trade in his large enterprise...He used to advance money during the seasons and at off seasons he used to give us [i.e. his regular customers] £25 free of any interest to buy pretty goods until the cocoa season comes on again. Over 50 of us were treated this way. Many of us through his kindness became rich and were able to feed our family.'

over the issue of the latter's support for the Government Agricultural Department's 'cutting-out' of diseased cocoa trees in an attempt to cope with an epidemic which was becoming a serious threat to Ibadan's economy. The date when the Society was founded is very difficult to establish. It variously claimed 1928 and 1930 itself, but Latorera, after leaving it, claimed to have founded it in 1938.* Certainly it was in 1938 that he asked to bring it into the Ibadan Patriotic Association, and the list of twenty-eight members it gave then did not include Mustafa Alli.[7] At that time the Society seems to have been a dancing group; Latorera was a popular performer and therefore welcome to the I.P.A. as a source of support. Possibly Alli had some older organization of his own concerned with farmers' interests, which merged with the Society and took its name, perhaps in 1947, for about that time it emerged as a farmers' organization.

In January 1945 the Olubadan had signed the Ibadan Native Authority (Control of Swollen Shoot) Order, creating penalties for obstructing the cutting-out of cocoa trees affected by that disease. It was intended that his representatives should travel with the Agricultural Department's Cocoa Survey teams to explain what was happening to the farmers, who were to get sixpence compensation for each tree cut. In 1948, when cutting-out really got under way, compensation was increased to 1s. 6d. a tree, but there was great unrest among the farmers, and the Maiyegun Society became active on their behalf. In March of that year it engaged a solicitor, C. Harrison Obafemi (who, exactly ten years later, was to act as Coroner at the inquest on Adegoke Adelabu), and began to plan obstructive action in the courts. It also began to campaign among the farmers, raising money from them for the fight against the Government. Already by July, however, it was representing itself to the Government in a rather different light. In that month its Secretary wrote to the Secretary of the Western Provinces that

The Government should realise that but for Maiyegun Society who have impressed the farmers that 'The King does no wrong' [and] that our remedy lies in the Court of Law, riot and unrest would have spread from the villages to the town. The Government should be grateful to us in this.[8]

By December, in fact, the Society had changed its policy and was willing to co-operate with the Cocoa Survey officers by sending round its own representatives with the official parties to smooth the way with the farmers. In return the Maiyegun leaders were to get fees and allowances from the

* The Yoruba version of its Rules and Regulations gives 1928, the English version 1930; both are undated, but were probably printed in January 1949. In a statement in the *Defender* on 1 October 1949 Alli mentioned 1928 and listed its original officers, with himself as Treasurer, claiming to have brought Latorera into the Society in 1947.

Government, and they also handled the payment of compensation, an opportunity for financial betterment which the Society clearly understood.

Cutting-out progressed much more smoothly after this, but in July 1949 the Society split; at a meeting at the Central Mosque on the 9th, Lawani Latorera was dismissed from the post of President and replaced by Bello Saberedowo, a partisan of Mustafa Alli. The causes of this quarrel are obscure; possibly the sharing of funds may have been involved, since one of Latorera's demands was for a proper rendering of accounts.[9] It also seems likely that this represented a cleavage between the more wealthy leaders, often cocoa middlemen, who found co-operation with the Government lucrative, and those who identified themselves more closely with the farmers. In any event, Latorera's new Maiyegun League began to campaign against cutting-out, and early in November 1949 recruited Fred Anyiam from Lagos to act as their political adviser.[10] Anyiam, by origin an Ibo from the East, owned a small textile store in Lagos, had been a founding member of the N.C.N.C., in 1946 its National Financial Secretary, and a militant member of the Zikist Movement, the radical wing of the nationalists. When contacted by the Maiyegun League he had only just finished a year in prison for his nationalist activities. This gave a more militantly anti-Government air to the League, reinforced by the fact that in late 1949 and early 1950 it was involved in series of disturbances in and around Ibadan. The most serious of these was on 28 November, when a Cocoa Survey team which intended to mark diseased trees at Olojuoro Village was turned back by an armed mob, led by some of the Maiyegun League and singing 'If Cocoa Survey officers and staff refuse to quit the farms, let them be beheaded.'[11] In the trial which resulted, four League leaders were sentenced on 14 December to pay a fine of £55 each or go to prison for six months; among them were Salami Tolorunioshe, Yesufu Mogbonjubola and an Alfa (Muslim leader), Akano Eleshinmeta, who were later to become some of Adelabu's most devoted and militant followers. Demonstrations by the League continued, directed against the Society and, on 1 March 1950, against Salami Agbaje. On this last occasion Latorera and Obadara Atanda, later another follower of Adelabu, were arrested for unlawful assembly and some two hundred farmers invaded Agodi Prison demanding their release.

Other, more personal and individual antagonisms worked against Agbaje. The catalogue of the real and imaginary complaints against him is long and we need not dwell on them. Together they point up the fact that it was marvelously unclear in Ibadan in 1949 what the long-term political interests were; the most personal, ancient and opportunistic elements entered into the dispute in the absence of any clear rules as to the boundaries of the conflict. The conflict, as we have already suggested, was increasingly involved in the encroaching national situation, a situation which from the point of view of the Ibadan politicians was not only changing but erratic and unpredictable. Adelabu entered this situation keenly aware that his own future was uncertain, fearful of the chance blows that fell upon him, not quite honest about himself and naïvely hopeful that his aid to the Olubadan (but not his entry into politics, which at the time he did not envisage) would bring him in reach of the personal goals which he had set himself.

To achieve these limited goals he willingly and vigorously engaged in a plot. As he later recounted, his part in it had begun at 8 p.m. on the night of 20 December, when Akinpelu Obisesan called him to his home 'for a very important discussion'.[12] Adelabu, accompanied by his cousin, found Obisesan sitting under the great tree in front of his two-story house at the edge of the city. Obisesan, who had returned only two days before from a week of meetings of the West African Cocoa Research Institute in the Gold Coast, told him, he alleged, that the Ibadan chiefs wished to have Chief Agbaje, now the Otun Balogun, deprived of his chieftaincy to preclude his chances of becoming Olubadan.* Opposition to Agbaje as a chief had supposedly begun to grow as early as 1936 when he had sought to become Otun Balogun without working up through the chiefly hierarchy, an attempt which Obisesan had opposed by leading an I.P.U. delegation to protest to the administrative officers. Agbaje had later secured a title, Adelabu reported Obisesan as saying, by giving Olubadan Aleshinloye a piece of land at Dugbe Market. Finally, Obisesan was supposed to have in his possession documents to show that Agbaje was signing papers 'as late as 1905', as a member of the native strangers' community. Nevertheless, Adelabu claimed, Obisesan said he would not help in depriving Agbaje of his title unless an 'ill-got-up' petition already prepared by the chiefs listing charges against Agbaje was revamped: to this end the chiefs would first have to secure 'by any means the services and co-operation of a first-class brain like myself'.[13] Obisesan was now seeking to secure Adelabu's services for the chiefs.

Obisesan's Diaries throw considerable doubt on the veracity of Adelabu's report. Adelabu's alleged visit is not mentioned. Nor is Adelabu's account of Obisesan's discussion with him on that evening a credible one. Agbaje had originally requested the Otun Balogun title in 1933, and Obisesan recorded at that time that the I.P.U. sympathized with his seeking a title but not such a high one.[14] Agbaje was installed as Ikolaba Balogun in 1936 and, after this accelerated beginning, had a normal rise through the ranks. To suggest that

* Sklar, *Nigerian Political Parties*, p. 289, suggests Agbaje was 'next in line' for the Olubadanship at this time. Although he was eligible, it would have required an extraordinary alignment of the 'king-makers' to elect him, since the Balogun and the Otun Olubadan would be normally elected in that order prior to the Otun Balogun.

Obisesan thought Agbaje was a member of an organized native strangers' group 'as late as' 1905 is, at best, a typographical error, since the term 'native strangers' was not then in use.*

Even more difficult to accept is the implication that Obisesan was requesting Adelabu to help him write a petition that Obisesan could not write. As officer of the Egbe Agba O'Tan and the Ibadan Progressive Union, as Councillor and Member of the Legislative Council, Obisesan had prepared innumerable petitions, letters and statements, and while he wisely took them for correction to his schoolmaster cousin, J. L. Ogunsola, he never shrank from such literary tasks. On the contrary, he sought them out as opportunities to use and to perfect his own English.

Nevertheless, according to Adelabu, he agreed to undertake the task as an injunction from a father (Obisesan) to a son (Adelabu), but not as a request from the chiefs, who 'were notorious for treachery and lack of good faith'. There was another motive also, as we have seen. Although Adelabu claimed that he sought the Administrative Secretaryship for 'no monetary reward', he calculated that if he insisted on this appointment as his reward, he would be able to spend £1000 of his savings to finish his house, the Taj Mahal, on the assumption that after hiring him the Council would pay for his legal studies in England.

Whatever Adelabu's doubts concerning the good faith of the chiefs, in December 1949 it was they who were instrumental in recruiting him against Chief Agbaje. As we have seen, there is reason to doubt that Obisesan played the major role here; indeed, he specifically warned the young man of the Olubadan's sensitivity concerning the new post, and urged him to seek the help of Adelabu's distant relative, Chief Omiyale, the Agbakin Balogun.

While Obisesan seems to have given little further thought to this decision (it is at least not mentioned again in his diary until 28 December), Adelabu was now heavily involved. As his account continues, Chief Omiyale called on him on 21 December, while Adelabu was taking his evening bath, stating he was sent by the Olubadan.† Omiyale, Adelabu alleged, stated that the Olubadan wished to be rid of Agbaje before the end of the year and that Obisesan for himself 'insisted that he would not countenance any petition not written by me'.[15] In return for his services, the chiefs would reward

---

* All of Obisesan's private papers were examined for this study without finding such documents, nor is there a document to our knowledge in the Ibadan Council records with Agbaje as a signatory in this capacity. If it exists in Obisesan's papers, it is after 1930 and in his official correspondence, which we have not read.

† If Adelabu indeed had been at Obisesan's at 8.00 p.m. the previous evening (although Obisesan does not mention it and it is difficult to see how the conversation could have been over by 9.00 p.m. when Chief Omiyale arrived), it is possible that Obisesan told Omiyale at that time that he had found a petition writer in Adelabu.

Adelabu 'in any manner' he chose. Adelabu then was given the chiefs' draft petition to read and found it 'loose, lacking in substance and badly worded'. He could put up a better one but 'was averse on principle to mercenary political journalism because it was degrading and the Ibadan chiefs' words were not to be relied upon'. Then he stated his terms: 'In plain language I said that I had ambition to become the first Administrative Secretary of the Ibadan Local Government.'[16] On the following day, Adelabu claimed, Omiyale returned with a messenger of the Olubadan and both assured him that the Olubadan had accepted his terms. Adelabu had thereupon agreed to attempt the petition, having decided that he 'had enough wits and experience' to protect his interest and if there were 'any breach of faith', the Olubadan, Obisesan and Chief Omiyale would 'have the worst of the encounter'. The document was completed on the 25th and supposedly shown to Obisesan that night. Obisesan was also given a summary of the negotiation up to that time, with which he declared he was pleased. He was claimed to have said that he had discussed Adelabu's request with the Olubadan 'who was in entire agreement'. Here again one searches in vain for corroboration in Obisesan's Diary. On the contrary, after attending on 22 December the first meeting of the new Ibadan Town Planning Authority (of which Chief Agbaje was also a member), he went early on the morning of the 24th to his farm at Amurire, a distance of thirty miles from town along a difficult road, where he stayed until 28 December. Upon returning to his Ibadan house, he learned that the Olubadan wished to see him and proceeded directly to Mapo Hall, where he found the other Councillors waiting for him with the news that a petition had been filed requesting Agbaje's removal from the ranks of the chiefs.

According to Adelabu, after showing his petition to Obisesan on the 25th, he then read it to Chief Omiyale and the Olubadan's messenger at 5 p.m. on 26 December, no mean trick of translation (into Yoruba) in itself, although he indicated no dissatisfaction with their comprehension of it. 'They were jubilant.' Adelabu then demanded a security deposit of £1000, to be returned upon his appointment as Administrative Secretary. This demand was carried to the Olubadan. At a second meeting that night, on the new pews waiting outside to be installed in the new Kudeti church, the Olubadan's son begged that the security requirement be dropped, a request which Adelabu refused. On the 27th Chief Omiyale again returned, and begged for a reduction of the amount, which Adelabu then lowered to £500. A few hours later they came back with only £50, which Adelabu accepted as 'a token deposit' without a receipt or an agreement being drawn up. Chief Omiyale was given the original draft petition and told to get a registered letter-writer to prepare copies and translations and affix the signatures and

61

thumbprints of the junior chiefs and mogajis in whose name the petition was filed.

The petition of 27 December listing charges against Agbaje was not one of Adelabu's best literary or analytical efforts.[17] Writing for a group of men, nearly all of whom were illiterate, he described Agbaje as a tyrant 'besides whom Nero and Caligula pale into insignificance'. He spoke of Henry Ford, John 'Pierpont' Morgan, 'Delano Roosevelt', 'Mr Philip I of Macedon' and Charles XII of Sweden without making much point. The historical facts which he adduced as justifications were crudely construed to suit his purposes. For example, he spoke of the Agreement of 1893, which the chiefs at that time bitterly opposed, as 'a treaty of amity, friendship and abolition of slave trade'. In flat contradiction to his own later statements about Ibadan's early history being a period of 'the rule of the privileged few', he referred to Ibadan's 120 years of existence as '200 years old republican freedom'. The charges themselves were in his weakest laundry-list style, accusing Agbaje of a multitude of sins including injustice, exploitation, deceit, vindictiveness and ruthlessness. In spite of these stylistic shortcomings, an accusation such as injustice carried considerable weight in the Ibadan system of values and sanctions controlling the activities of a president of a court which had been 'turned into a counting house' where 'Perquisites were manufactured on such a scale and with such a cool efficiency as astounded everybody and lowered the morale of the other courts in general.'

Adelabu charged Agbaje with exploitation of his business associates and employees; as Obisesan's Diaries from the 1920s show, this reputation had cast a long shadow over Agbaje's career. While it is difficult to believe that Agbaje was in fact more corrupt or necessarily even more clever than his contemporaries, his success came largely in the modern sectors of the economy, in companies, associations, factories and share-holding operations, and he conducted his business on contractual lines or at least with contractual implications. When business partners failed their obligations, Agbaje frequently took them to court, although he also frequently carried debtors for years. If Agbaje was no worse than others his reputation was much worse, and that was itself a reality. It was the failure to attempt to erase this public view of himself within the framework of the traditional system that made Agbaje-the-modern-capitalist so disliked.

Agbaje's real sin was thus that he was disliked and that he did so little about it, that he used his power derived from the modern economic sector to acquire the symbols and influence of the traditional political sector, without subjecting himself to the claims of tradition to which others deferred with the largesse of the 'big man'. While his sources of power were always beyond the limits of popular understanding or control, he was now constitutionally eligible to represent the masses as Olubadan. The objective problem was that in the political system of Ibadan there was no way to get rid of a man who was unpopular, since he arrived at his position by virtually automatic promotion and could be removed only after criminal charges (by the colonial administration) or by death. In the interests of colonial stability the traditional constitution of Ibadan had been stripped of methods for keeping the chiefs responsible to the public. Those who remained in office did so not because they had done anything well, but because they had done nothing terribly wrong. The Adelabu petition could bring no charges against Agbaje that would stand up in a court of law, or that would have been the most efficient way to ruin him. It had therefore to appeal to the discretion of the colonial administration. Agbaje, it said, was a 'poisonous morsel' in Ibadan's stomach. Adelabu did not know whether the stomach would 'vomit him out' – that is, a mass protest in the streets – or whether 'a surgical operation' would be necessary – a formal inquiry and deposition by the administration – but Agbaje must go.

With the petition formally presented to the Olubadan and Council, the issue was out in the open. The British officials, however reluctantly, were forced to take some cognizance of this new development, as were the I.P.U. leaders, though they became involved as individuals rather than as a group. Thus Dr A. S. Agbaje was naturally active on behalf of his father, defending him in the columns of his newspaper, the *Western Echo*, and seeking to enlist the support of Akinpelu Obisesan early in February 1950.[18] Interviews with a number of the people involved in 1963 confirmed that they all believed that Obisesan was at the center of the whole interrelated complex of disputes over the Administrative Secretaryship and Chief Agbaje. Although Adelabu's picture of him as the organizer of the agitation is almost certainly untrue, and painted after the fact for reasons we will see later, it is not to be doubted that the I.P.U. leader was at the heart of things, valued not the least for his contacts with a whole range of the interested parties. He was also in close contact with non-Ibadan elements such as his lifelong friend, the Oni of Ife, one of the most senior Yoruba Obas, who was anxious to mediate, and the British administrators.

The British officials in Ibadan were all the more sensitive about the dangers implicit in the Agbaje agitation because early in January 1950 Ibadan acted as host to the Constitutional Review Conference which brought together delegates from all over the country to discuss the final form of the new Macpherson Constitution. With this reminder on their doorsteps of the fact that while Ibadan was facing change the whole system was changing round it, they became more and more incensed with the Olubadan for embarrassing them. On 19 January, Obisesan discussed affairs with the District

Officer, W. M. Milliken, who assured him with such certainty what Government would do if the crisis increased that Obisesan thought 'his mind had been poisoned against Olubadan...'.[19] On 1 March the Resident came to Obisesan's house, and 'appeared strongly inclined to do away with Olubadan who in his judgment is unsuitable to rule'.[20] The following day Obisesan returned the visit and met Sir Chandos Hoskyns Abrahall, Chief Commissioner of the Western Provinces, who confirmed that it was in fact Government's intention to depose the Olubadan 'if necessary'.[21]

Under this pressure the Olubadan and chiefs seem to have yielded somewhat. Although the details are obscure, it would appear that some time in February they did indicate that they would be prepared to accept the office of Administrative Secretary. It would seem also that at this juncture Adelabu therefore applied for the post, only to have his application rejected by the I.P.U. members of the Council's Appointments Committee (Obisesan was in Enugu at the time). Adelabu's grief and disappointment at this rebuff was by his own account tremendous. Ruin seemed near.

As we saw in the last chapter, although he made a profit of £700 in the 1948–9 cocoa-buying season, he concluded the following season with a net loss of £100. According to his own estimate, he had sunk about £4000 in the building of the Taj Mahal, but his hope of covering that investment through Council employment was lost in the soft sands of the financial agreements he had made concerning the writing of the Agbaje petition. In December 1949 when he agreed to write the Agbaje petition, he collected £50 from the chiefs for his services. Between 15 February and 4 November 1950, according to his own various reckonings, he spent between £250 and £600 on bribes to officials and the chiefs in his attempts to be given the post of Administrative Secretary. One specific accounting, for £250, suggests the busy nature of his life at this time; he claimed to have given £50 worth of cloth to the Olubadan (who had originally paid him £50 to write the petition), £37 to Omiyale, and £25 to Chief Aminu through Obisesan who received, according to Adelabu, £50 for himself. Others received £88. In the same letter in which he claimed to have made these bribes, Adelabu described how upon learning that the post would not be given to him, 'I was panic-stricken and ran helter-skelter...crying in tones of great anguish that I had been betrayed. I went frantically about with a bundle of £500 notes [*sic*] giving liberally to all and sundry like Father Christmas...'[22]

His appointment was compounded by the connivings he believed to be behind the chiefs' reversal of their decision to accept the Administrative Secretaryship. It was 'through material inducements', he charged, that the Council Clerk got the Chiefs to reverse themselves while Obisesan was in Enugu and unable to keep track of what was going on, and Adelabu's response was to run 'helter-skelter' handing out money to all who might help reverse the decision. Apart from agreeing in general with Adelabu that such handouts are not unknown in Ibadan politics, it is only clear in one specific case that money changed hands in this instance.[23]

Adelabu also stated that Obisesan was amazed upon his return from Enugu at the change in Adelabu's fortunes. According to Adelabu, Obisesan now promised him that he would get the post of Chief Clerk for him, shifting the present Chief Clerk to the post of Lands Registrar, which was about to be vacated through a resignation under considerable but unprovable suspicions of corruption against the incumbent. Again, Obisesan's Diaries offer no corroborative evidence, but Adelabu continues that Obisesan then discovered that the Chief Clerk could not be shifted while the Lands Office was being reformed. Whether Adelabu's recounting of the details was correct is uncertain and perhaps unimportant; as the position of Administrative Secretary proved to be an ever-distant mirage, his comprehension of his limited ability to shape his future must have become ever clearer. He was in fact slowly learning his first important political lessons. Realizing his own powerlessness, he could gradually see that he had been drawn into a situation in which he had no source of support but the promises of the chiefs, no organization behind him, no large supply of money, and not even a useful reputation. He was not at this time an important figure in Ibadan. He was still a young man, of a generous nature, known to be fluent in English with tongue and pen, in short, the kind of person whom the Olubadan and chiefs would feel they could use and cast aside again. Although his claim in November 1950 was to be that 'Today as one of the Civilized Minority and a member of the Aristocracy of Intellect, I don the toga of an Independent National Statesman', he must have known this to be very far from the truth.

While Adelabu was having his own troubles, the Agbaje crisis was deepening. As soon as Obisesan understood the Government's position, he attempted to influence the chiefs toward moderation but his influence over them was not a decisive one. Having decided to dismiss Agbaje summarily, the chiefs invited him to 'a sort of private meeting' on 25 February at the Olubadan's house, but Agbaje refused to appear.[24] On 4 March the junior chiefs and mogajis offered to settle the dispute by allowing Agbaje to keep his existing rank as long as he was not further promoted. This Agbaje promptly refused. According to the subsequent inquiry, the Olubadan-in-Council thereupon 'rejected' Agbaje and asked that he no longer participate in the Native Authority's affairs. On 24 April the Council voted seven to nothing to remove Agbaje from its ranks, the I.P.U. leaders, including Chief Isaac Akinyele, announcing their neutrality and not voting. Nothing was done, however, until 5 June, when Chief Agbaje was formally suspended from the Council, a power which it is doubtful that the Olubadan-in-Council actually possessed. Nevertheless, their hand was considerably strengthened when the new District Officer, who replaced Milliken on 7 March, requested Agbaje to absent himself from his court until the dispute was settled.[25] This he had done on the order of the Resident and at the request of two of the Chiefs and Obisesan 'in the interest of peace pending settlement of his trouble'.[26] At this point the British administrators were hesitating, hoping the dispute would not erupt, thereby endangering their own plans for reform.

With the Agbaje agitation six months old, it also became clear that attempts to mediate were bound to founder on the obstinacy of both sides. In spite of a protest from the senior Ibadan chiefs, the Obas of Yorubaland met late in June 1950 at the Western House of Assembly to examine the Agbaje dispute.[27] Although the Olubadan was not a crowned Yoruba king, they had accepted the idea that the Olubadan, as the head of the largest Yoruba city, was recognized as an Oba in the eyes of colonial administrators, who were now anxious to revise the constitutional arrangements in the Western Provinces. The Agbaje dispute, by threatening the position of one of the most powerful of the Obas, threatened them all. However, because they could not command the compliance of the Ibadan senior chiefs, their efforts also came to naught. Early in July, the Chief Commissioner of the Western Provinces called in Obisesan and asked him to attempt once more to reconcile the parties. At a meeting with the Olubadan and Chief Omiyale later that same day, Obisesan accepted a gift of £15 from the Olubadan. Two days later he met with the Chief Imam in an attempt to quiet the protests of Muslim leaders who felt they had been snubbed by Agbaje when they tried to help him. Obisesan's report to the Chief Secretary of the Government later that week must have been an empty one.

It seems possible that at this point Adelabu and some of the other active organizers of the agitation were also trying to bring it to an end and turn it to their economic advantage. In his testimony at the subsequent inquiry (which was substantiated in interviews in 1963), one witness stated that 'about June' he had taken two of Chief Agbaje's sons, Mojid the lawyer and Anthony the doctor to a meeting with Adelabu, L. Ade Bello, D. T. Akinbiyi and R. Ola Oke, Secretary of the Ahmadiyya Mission in Ibadan. Adelabu, the witness testified, had declared them to be the ring leaders and stated their willingness to halt the conspiracy, since the Olubadan had not made him Administrative Secretary nor D. T. Akinbiyi a court president, if Agbaje would give them £1500 and withdraw the court action he had recently won against L. Ade Bello, as well as one against the *Southern Nigeria Defender*, the N.C.N.C. newspaper in Ibadan.[28] This offer was rejected. Whether this story is true or false, it was clear that in July 1950 Adelabu had little choice but to continue to play his part in the agitation and hope for the best.

In fact new pressure began to be applied to Agbaje. The Olubadan, in Adelabu's words, 'got nervous', and again through his blind son, Ladimeji, enrolled a 'panel of writers' to prepare petitions and write newspaper articles for his cause. According to Adelabu, these included D. T. Akinbiyi, K. O. S. Are, Bello Abasi and four others in addition to himself. They met regularly at Ladimeji's house, read each other's 'contributions' and were 'freely entertained' with food and drink. In some cases one of the team composed and another signed articles, and Ladimeji paid £10 and £50 to 'facilitate' the publication of articles in the press.* During this period, Adelabu himself published several articles.[29] He also authored petitions for the Iyalode and Women Titled Chiefs.[30] Also deeply involved was a new political society, the Ibadan Welfare Committee. According to Adelabu, this was the organizational weapon of Bello Abasi, the son of Olubadan Aleshinloye. Adelabu called him 'the mainstay' of the whole movement, whose 'money and sound counsel' and 'toughness' often prevented the whole agitation from collapsing.[31] Abasi was Chairman of the Welfare Committee, which 'sponsored' the Junior Chiefs and Mogajis at a meeting in August 1950. The Committee's President, Lasupo Layanju, was a cloth trader, as was L. Ade Bello its Secretary. Presumably the availability of the services of political entrepreneurs of such caliber suggested to Abasi that it was unnecessary to prevail upon the Egbe Omo Ibile to undertake the agitation against Agbaje, a public venture its members might have chosen to avoid. According to Adelabu, Bello Abasi supported the Welfare Committee's activities because he held against Agbaje 'a personal grudge connected with the disappearance of certain property deeds and conveyances' at the time of the death of his father, Olubadan Aleshinloye. Adelabu also maintained that Agbaje had interfered with the selection of a new mogaji of the Aleshinloye House at that time, and that Olubadan Fijabi had promised Abasi to put this matter right upon the deposition of Agbaje. To this end, then, Abasi used Lasupo Layanju and L. Ade Bello, 'two practiced rabble-rousers' who employed the membership as 'mere tools' in Adelabu's later words:

They whip up public hatred against Chief Agbaje with preposterous rumours and collect innocent signatures with lying propaganda. The Committee are the extreme left of the anti-Agbaje front consisting mainly of credulous yokels, loquacious braggarts and neurotic sadists. Their aim is destruction for its own sake.[32]

* It was common to have to pay to have articles printed in newspapers.

Under these proddings from the articles in the *Southern Nigeria Defender* and the less public activities of Bello Abasi and the Welfare Committee, the traditional members of the Council took action against Agbaje once more. When the Welfare Committee pointed out that the Otun Balogun was attending neither Council meetings nor his court sessions, the Olubadan in Council stopped his salary in September. At the meeting of the Divisional Council the following month, it was pointed out that Agbaje's salary was paid from Divisional funds, not just from the Ibadan Council, and that the Ibadan Council therefore had no power to withhold his salary. The Ibadan Council at its November meeting thereupon declared that it was useless to continue attempts to settle the dispute, a declaration which was quite promptly interpreted in the Northern Districts as a further presumption by the Ibadan chiefs over matters which concerned them as well.

A further result of the new campaign against Agbaje was to force Adelabu to think much more about the contemporary situation in Ibadan and his role in it. He now began to write regular newspaper articles which, despite his high-flown language, showed that he was acquiring a knowledge of the nature of the changes in Ibadan which was essential if he was to continue his political activity here. The conflict, he declared in 'Ibadan Nobility – Old and New', published late in September, was between two factions of the 'nobility', the 'heirs of the great houses whose original owners were co-founders of this city in the age of banditry', and the more recent 'first products of local capitalism'.[33] Briefly he analyzed the characteristics of the two groups. The 'old nobility'

born into very large families and taught from childhood to consider their acts, not in a narrow way, but in their affects on a very large number of people...are tolerant, broad-minded, compromising and conservative. Born into positions not readily purchasable with gold and silver they look down on go-getting and get rich quick plebeians. Instead of narrow personal success they live for the welfare and prosperity of their extended family and quarter.[34]

In complete contrast, the 'new nobility'

...are mostly people who have risen by personal merits. They are ambitious, self-assertive, confident, progressive, efficient, shrewd and individualistic. ...They look on tribal affiliations and family fetters as weaknesses to be exploited or at best evils to be tolerated for a time and ultimately swept aside.

It was education, he felt, which had given the second group the advantage over the first. The former had 'looked askance' on it, while the latter had used it to gain 'a monopoly of lucrative positions to the exclusion of the haughty unlettered sons of the old nobility'. As an analysis of the origins of the educated elite, and the difference between them and the chiefs, this was exaggerated but perceptive.

Similarly, in another two-part article a month earlier, Adelabu had painted a picture of the relationship between the educated elite and the chiefs which was unequivocally hostile to the former, but nevertheless showed an understanding of the position in 1949–50. Of the new men he said,

For seventeen years these ungrateful self-seekers have formed an effective cordon around our traditional Chiefs disguised as loyal subjects. They bored their way into their confidence with suave smiles and gentle obeisance, coaxing them to sell their ancient birth-right for a mess of counterfeit progress, stifling the aspiration of our best talents by slamming against their faces the doors of the public service.[35]

Although there can be no doubt that it was primarily of himself that he was thinking in his reference to these 'best talents', it was in perceiving the emergence of this third group in Ibadan that he showed that he was learning from experience. Now, he pointed out in his September article, 'a new-generation has grown up drawn from the grandchildren of the old nobility'.

They are highly educated, steeped in the mellowest Yoruba culture, proud of their lineage and their past and glorifying in the wisdom and the democratic character of our Native representative institutions. They see their fathers handicapped from playing their proper role in the scheme of things by lack of education, humiliated and imposed upon by a semi-educated boorish 'New Rich'. They are exasperated and resentful. Their first instinctive reaction is to fight.[36]

Exaggerated though some of this might be (his family was not part of the 'old nobility', and he was not on the educational level of the 'new generation'), Adelabu had perceived an important fact about contemporary Ibadan. There were now young men who because of their education were ambitious, some of whom held junior posts with the civil service or the Ibadan Council, but who were not being absorbed into the ranks of the I.P.U., even through its Youth Group. Adelabu himself came into this category, and, like many of the others, he had the relative disadvantage of being a Muslim. This applied also in the case of a range of traders and contractors, like L. Ade Bello or K. O. S. Are, who could not be described as well-educated young men, but who felt excluded by the wealthier elite. The I.P.U. was beginning to provoke a reaction against itself as a Christian, wealthy clique which monopolized much of the economic and political power in Ibadan. Men like Adelabu, who aligned themselves against Agbaje in support of the chiefs in the name of tradition, were now using the same battle cry against the I.P.U. leaders, who had no wish to quarrel with the chiefs.

While Adelabu was acquiring new political knowledge and acumen, he was also in trouble and he knew it. As he wrote in a letter on 30 September,

For the last nine months I have been lobbying to get myself appointed as the Administrative Secretary to the Ibadan Native Administration. I have spent over £600 for the Chiefs and Councillors but to my great grief they keep putting me off.[37]

Not that he had yet given up hope of employment by the Native Authority; on the same day he applied to the Council's Discipline and Appointments Committee, seeking a job 'in any capacity'. At first it looked as if this time he might be successful; a month after his application was submitted he was recommended by the Olubadan and the other Senior Chiefs on the Committee for appointment, not as Administrative Secretary admittedly, but to the new post of Lands Registrar. Once again, however, as in March, his hopes were dashed. Chief Obisesan was away in Britain this time, and so could not put his weight behind Adelabu, and the three other Councillors refused to sign the recommendation. Adelabu had still not learned that the I.P.U. leaders regarded him as an untrustworthy young man, with insufficient qualifications for an important job.

During September, Adelabu was forced to borrow £10 from the Olubadan's son for 'maintenance'. On 30 September, in the letter already referred to, he had appealed to one of his old European benefactors, C. M. Booth of G. B. Ollivant's, who had secured him the textile supply in 1946 which had enabled him to go into business on his own. Heading his letter 'S.O.S. from Mr. Adegoke Adelabu', he asserted dramatically that 'I am now, with a family of 10, at the very margin of starvation', and went on to list three ways in which Booth might help him, carefully stating them in order of preference.* His first choice was to go to the United Kingdom to read for a law degree, his old ambition, this time financed by Booth. Alternatively, he hoped Booth might get him an appointment as one of the new Government Development Officers. As a third and least desirable choice he was prepared to turn his back on his beloved native city, asking Booth to 'Fix me up outside Ibadan as an African Manager under your Company.' His letter concluded in characteristic style:

People, in their unknowing wisdom, call me 'Oyinbo Dudu' meaning 'Black White Man'. Is it any wonder if my lucky star is always with the White Man? You are the last link in the pre-destined chain of white patrons – Field – Powell – Williams – Richardson – Haig – Cheesman – Booth. As an artist and idealist I am always working my life into a series of crises. YOU MUST HELP ME if you do not want it flashed on front pages that the brilliant career of a genius was cut short in his home the Taj Mahal by grief [and] starvation.

While he waited for a reply, however, he had other irons in the fire.[38]

* As we shall see, he was head of a family of '18' only one month later.

Seeking to realize something on his capital assets, on 10 October he wrote to both the Deputy Director of Medical Services and Dr Okechukwu Ikejiani, an Ibo private practitioner who had his own hospital in the city offering to lease them the Taj Mahal. A perhaps more ingenious idea was the draft prospectus he drew up for 'The Western All-Service Bureau', with himself and R. Ola Oke as joint managers, and the motto, 'Malice is a poor match for Destiny.' Membership in the Bureau was to cost five shillings a year and the brochure which the subscriber was to receive was planned to contain an impressive list of more than twenty-five proffered services, beginning with Accounting and Auditing, Journalism and Secretaryship, Native Law Consultancy and Estate Agency, and proceeding by way of Laundry and Dry-Cleaning, Career Consultation and Psychological Treatment to Hire of Chairs, Tumblers and Gas Lamps and Taxi-Call Agency. He also thought of putting his own 'appointment wanted' advertisement in the newspaper, offering the chance to employ a 'Young man aged 35 with sound post-secondary education and 15 years experience executive work in Civil Service and Mercantile Houses', who, 'Versed in Accounts and Correspondence & used to arduous touring duties' required a minimum salary of £300 a year, but was willing to put up a £5000 surety (though it is difficult to see where this was to be obtained). Needless to say, none of these projects came to anything.

In November he resolved on desperate measures. He drafted two documents, the first a letter to Chief Obisesan, in which he threatened to reveal the full inside story of the Agbaje agitation, including his own authorship of the petition against Chief Agbaje and the responsibility of Obisesan, the Olubadan and Omiyale for the whole affair if the post of Administrative Secretary was not forthcoming. The second document was the letter to the Senior District Officer carrying out this threat. Obviously he now blamed Obisesan for his continuing disappointment. In his letter to him he held him 'responsible for baiting' him from what he now called his 'prosperous textile business', and charged that Obisesan had 'condoned' by his silence the 'treachery' of the Olubadan in not allowing Adelabu to get the job of Chief Clerk and submitting to pressure from his Ibadan Progressive Union colleagues in making the Lands Office post impossible for him to accept.[39] He warned Obisesan that unless the Olubadan and chiefs fulfilled their share of the original contract (in which Adelabu was to get the post of Administrative Secretary in exchange for writing the Agbaje petition) by signing the draft of a letter he had composed for them recommending that he be given the post, he would make the letter revealing the roles of the Olubadan, Chief Omiyale and Obisesan available to the colonial government on 5 December.*

* Adelabu's draft letter, found in his papers, composed with even the file number upon it, read in part: 'We attach herewith an application received from one of the most

The letter which Adelabu threatened to circulate gave the history of the plot and its financing, as already outlined. Adelabu went to great length to establish that he was the author of the Agbaje petition, in part, one suspects, to defend his own skill as a thinker and writer. As he pointed out, the text showed that

...the writer has read widely in history, classics, economics, biology, philosophy, psychology, physics, chemistry, astronomy, sociology, anthropology, metaphysics, modern political theories and contemporary literature and point unerringly to a background of the Ibadan Government College and the Yaba Higher College.

In his analysis, Adelabu revealed something of what he had learned from the entire agitation about men and politics in a changing Ibadan.

From the narrow view of private conduct [Agbaje] may be detestable but from the broad outlook of prevalent political standard he will stand comparison with his compeers. His moral delinquencies are so significantly prominent because he is so materially successful. Would he have survived the turbulent vicissitudes of Ibadan political life if he had been less hardy, tough and ruthless? I think not. He may not be a paragon for our children to copy but there he is, a creature of his parentage, upbringing, environment and age. Where we may withhold our love we are at liberty to bestow our admiration if we are truthful and realistic. Too complex for summary judgment today he will become a simplified understandable personality with the passage of time. Great men in all spheres of life belong to a class apart and in weighing their virtues and their vices we must avoid the too easy mistake of adopting conventional standards. The moment they fit into our common mould they cease to be great and become ordinary and commonplace. Peculiarity is the price of greatness.

For unknown reasons, the documents were never sent to Obisesan.* Obisesan's surprise seems genuine when he records in his Diary of 29 December, 'Mr Adelabu whom I have been trying to assist to secure a job under N. A. sent a damning petition to all the officers of Government accusing me...' In an interview, Chief Obisesan explained that he was suddenly sum-

intelligent sons of Ibadan, Mr Adegoke Adelabu, putting his services in any capacity commensurate with his ability at the disposal of the Ibadan Native Authority. His application led to the re-opening and reconsideration of this question. We strongly recommend him for this post because his high educational qualifications and wide managerial experience should make him an efficient co-ordinator and a valuable asset to the Ibadan Native Administration. His precise functions and powers will be the subject of discussion and agreement after Government's approval of his appointment.' A delegation, made up of two Chiefs (Omiyale and Adebisi) and two Councillors (Adelabu's old patron, D. T. Akinbiyi, and his prospective business partner, R. Ola Oke) was to wait on the S.D.O. to present the recommendation.

* A careful search of Obisesan's papers failed to locate the Adelabu letter there, nor was any mention of it to be found in Council or Government records.

moned to the office of the Chief Commissioner who showed him the Adelabu letter. According to Obisesan, the following conversation ensued.

Chief Commissioner: 'Is it true?'

Obisesan: 'It is not!'

Thereupon the Chief Commissioner tore up the document and threw it in the waste-basket. What happened at this point must remain obscure. In interviews in England in 1965, the administrative officers who were in Ibadan at this time stated they had never previously heard even a rumor of Adelabu's authorship of the Agbaje petition, much less seen his admission of it in writing. We do not even know if Chief Omiyale or Olubadan Fijabi knew of Adelabu's 'damning petition'; both were dead by the time we were in Ibadan. We only know for sure that by the end of 1950 the principals privy to the planning of the Agbaje agitation and Obisesan were once again reconciled to each other, and that Adelabu was no nearer fulfilling any of his ambitions.

His best hope, then, still seemed to be a successful application for a post with a commercial firm, or else to devise some workable scheme of his own. On 14 December he wrote to the General Manager of the British–American Tobacco Company, applying for the advertised post of Station Manager of a new scheme for extending the cultivation of tobacco at Oyo.[40] As with the Taj Mahal, he also endeavored at this time to capitalize on his other fixed asset, the land which he owned at Apomu. He was informed by a friend in the Cocoa Survey Department that the Government, through the Western Region Production Development Board, was interested in extending its plantation projects, in which it sought to improve production and methods by providing selected groups of farmers with capital and technical help. On 19 December he went to see the Assistant District Officer about this, and followed up the interview with a letter on 1 January 1951 in which he set out an elaborate table of respective advantages and disadvantages to the Western Region Production Development Board if he were either employed to manage the Project on behalf of the W.R.P.D.B. or else given a £5000 loan to develop the farm himself.[41] Insistently he urged the need to set up men of experience and substance in such farming schemes, comparing himself favorably with those already engaged in such a project at Alara:

Illiterate farmers cannot co-operate effectively in this scheme. Taking no money risk they lack incentive to keep costs low. Consequently critics will justly attribute success to artificial government subsidy.[42]

Finally, the use of relatively poor and illiterate farmers would give the impression that they were merely employees of the Government, and 'The Board must avoid laying itself open to the charge of attempting a White Plantation System.'

In the midst of his calculations regarding his future as a capitalist farmer, Adelabu had also finally sunk all his pride and asked the United Africa Company to take him back. On 27 December, exactly one year from the day he had provided the chiefs with the Agbaje petition, he wrote a long letter to the General Manager, headed 'Petition for re-employment by the first African Manager'. 'Nothing will give me greater joy', he claimed, 'than to get back into harness and have the opportunity to put my accumulated experience at the Company's service.'[43] It was true, Adelabu said, that he had suffered 'a raw deal' in the past at U.A.C., but it now appeared to have been without 'any deliberate wickedness on anybody's part'; in any case he cherished his past association with the Company's 'bigwigs' and its 'lesser fries'. The United Africa Company, however, was not disposed to take advantage of Adelabu's offer of assistance. On 13 January the Labour/Staff Manager answered somewhat tersely:

Dear Sir,
In reply to your letter dated the 27th December, addressed to the General Manager, we regret to inform you that we have no vacancy on our Establishment in which you could be re-employed.[44]

Just before this Adelabu had also heard officially that his offer to the Government of his farm at Apomu was not to be taken up, and less than a week later he was informed that the British American Tobacco Company did not consider him suitable for training as a tobacco farm manager, since they wanted younger men they could train themselves, though they promised to keep him in mind in case of further vacancies. This last was of no comfort. For more than three months Adelabu had been writing letters and lobbying administrative officers, chiefs and councillors, and nothing had come of it. The sphere in which all his hopes had been centered ever since he left Yaba Higher College in 1936, that of economic activity, seemed now to be closed to him. Despite the expansion of the Government's economic interests since the war – as in the Alara plantation scheme or the appointment of Development Officers – and despite the attempts by expatriate firms like U.A.C. and B.A.T.C. to expand their African managerial staff, there was no place for 'the first African Manager'.

It was at this time, at the lowest ebb of Adelabu's fortunes, that, on the advice of his subordinates, the Governor of Nigeria finally concluded that he must intervene in the affairs of Ibadan. On the Governor's instructions, the Senior Resident on Wednesday, 10 January 1951, informed the Council that 'Strong Reasons' were necessary for the removal of a chief or the withholding of his salary, and that these were not present in the Agbaje case. Government had therefore decided to call a Commission of Inquiry into the

Agbaje agitation and into the allegations of misconduct and inefficiency on the part of the Council; the Inquiry was, in his words, 'a slur on Ibadan'.[45] In an impassioned speech, Obisesan noted that many had spoken ill of him and asked the chiefs to 'knock their heads together' to find a solution. Ibadan had never been subjected to a Commission of Inquiry before and he begged the Resident for more time. Although the Resident assured the Council that the Commission would abide by any settlement the chiefs might arrive at if it were a permanent one, on the following day, Hugh Louis Montaguc Butcher, Administrative Officer, Class I, was appointed to begin the investigation.

CHAPTER 4

THE BLOODLESS REVOLUTION

> The sincere and informed patriot has no alternative but to rely on his own initiative, trust that the coming generation will be different and hope that, before it is too late, the Protecting Power will discover, understand, appreciate and co-operate with him to substitute order and purpose for chaos and ineptitude.
>
> Adelabu, the 'Master Plan', March 1951

> We knew precisely what we wanted to do. The only question was how much we could do at any one time.
>
> ex-District Officer Hayley, interview, 1965

H. L. M. Butcher took his oath as Commissioner in the Ibadan Magistrate's Court on 16 January 1951, the day his Commission was received there, and was immediately hard at work. On 17 January, in an announcement heard throughout Ibadan's market places and compounds by means of the radio diffusion service, he announced 23 January as the opening day of the hearings. A press release of the same day explained the terms of reference and announced 22 January as the deadline for persons or organizations to indicate intention to give oral evidence. On 19 January Butcher faced and mastered the possibility that there would be little to investigate. A telegram was received by the Chief Secretary from the chiefs and Councillors protesting the Commissioner's appointment on the grounds that as an administrative officer he would necessarily be biased towards Government's position. Since no intention to give evidence had yet been indicatd by Agbaje's antagonists, and since it was rumored the chiefs would either boycott the Inquiry or stage a shouting demonstration at the opening session, the Resident and Senior District Officer, N. E. Whiting, met the Advisory Board on 20 January and the Council on 21 January, a Sunday, to ensure that the complainants would co-operate. The chiefs were given the 'strongest possible advice to co-operate', in the face of which they adopted 'a more reasonable attitude'.[1]

The hearings began on 23 January and continued until 8 February. Testimony was given by some forty persons and twenty-nine memoranda were submitted. Adelabu's petition on behalf of the junior chiefs and mogajis was accepted as the basic list of allegations made against Agbaje and was reprinted in full in the Commission's report, although without any indication of its authorship. Adelabu testified not as the author of the petition but in a new role as General Secretary of the Egbe Omo Ibile. After identifying himself as a Muslim and then swearing on a Bible, Adelabu asserted that the Egbe was 'a federal organization consisting of social clubs, unitary political parties, pagan peoples and women's societies, representing the overwhelming majority of the taxable adults of this town'.*

The Egbe, claimed Adelabu, resented Agbaje as 'a white man's creation' who had been a partner in a white man's business, had himself employed white men, and been made a member of the Legislative Council and finally a chief by white men. Bombast marked all of Adelabu's testimony and did little to convince the Commissioner of the validity of the charges against Agbaje or of the public support for them. This failure is not totally surprising. Adelabu had as yet had no experience in translating and transmitting the views of the chiefs or the masses to other public authorities. Moreover, he had entered the agitation long before he entered the Egbe Omo Ibile, and indeed it seems that he was appointed its general Secretary by Bello Abasi purposely in order to act as a spokesman before Butcher. Early in 1951 Adelabu still had no important place in Ibadan politics. He was merely regarded as a 'pushfull Ibadan youth', the caption which the *Defender* had used for his photograph in September 1950.

Much more commanding, and indeed pathetic was the testimony of the Olubadan and the three chiefs – Memedu, Igbintade and Isaac Akinyele – who were to succeed him in office. In spite of their differences over other matters they repeatedly stressed that the basic question was one of public opinion and popularity.[2] Their admitted powerlessness must have made a great impression on Adelabu.

We need not examine in detail the working of the Butcher Commission in regard to Chief Agbaje. Butcher concluded somewhat simplisticly that the charges against Agbaje were petty, often misconceived or simply untrue, that the agitation had been engineered by the junior chiefs and mogajis, and that Chief Agbaje's admitted unpopularity was a momentary product of the plot against him. The second part of the Inquiry's work requires a little closer examination.

It will be remembered that Butcher had also been ordered 'to inquire into and report' on the efficiency and administration of the Ibadan Council, a

---

* Bello Abasi had seen the officers and the organization of the I.P.A.-Egbe altered several times in the past and Adelabu's prestigious title and great energies posed no threat to the power and experience of Bello Abasi. Indeed Abasi had often exercised his power through others anxious to appear as public leaders, a use he apparently now chose to make of Adelabu.

charge that had been given to him at the request of the administrative officers and which met with the approval of such 'progressive elements' as the Ibadan Progressive Union. As a result, all the issues noted in the latter part of Chapter I were drawn into the discussion. As Butcher summarized the allegations against the Council, there was concern that its staff was inadequately supervised, inefficient and corrupt, that its financial policy was confused, that co-ordination between the Council and its operative departments was lacking, that the affairs of the Districts were unnecessarily centralized into the Ibadan Council's hands, that the junior chiefs and mogajis exercised undue influence over the Council's affairs and that the Council was out of touch with the general population. Much evidence of malfeasance was compiled, previously unheeded recommendations for reform were reviewed, and the history of the failure to appoint an Administrative Secretary was examined. In addition to these points, some considerable time was devoted to the study of the tax system. In this regard, Butcher discovered to his great shock that taxes in Ibadan were still paid to the chiefs and mogajis, who were free to 'recruit' taxpayers according to their own popularity and regardless of the geographical location of the taxpayer. In return for this service, the tax collectors were paid a five per cent rebate. While attending a Council meeting at which the Council's financial problems were discussed, Butcher observed three chiefs 'fast asleep, and they were evidently unable to grasp the issues involved'.[3] Butcher found the tax system to be 'highly inefficient' and marked by 'large scale evasion', a condition which he felt was a consequence of the fact that each of the collectors was continually hoping for a promotion to a higher chieftaincy title and was therefore anxious to avoid such unpopular tasks as rigorous collecting of taxes. 'Territorial collection', he pronounced, 'is the only efficient system' and the insistence the Council made on maintaining the old system condemned them absolutely. The financial problems of the Council were thus directly related to the role of the chiefs in the city's politics.

From this, and from complaints and representations made by the Native Settlers' Union, Butcher concluded that the traditional authorities of Ibadan were 'out of touch with the people' of the city and the Districts. As we saw in Chapter I, the Native Settlers Union was an association of immigrants to Ibadan, for the most part Ijebus, many of whom lived in a planned sector of the city on either side of the road to Ijebu Ode known as the Ijebu Bye-Pass. The area had been laid out by a Town Planning Committee of the Council, which included Chief Agbaje and Chief Akinyele, to encourage the residents of the increasingly overcrowded center of the city to re-settle in a less densely populated area. Unfortunately, the area had become the object of much land speculation by Ijebus, but also by members of Ibadan's entrepreneurial class, including I.P.U. members, whose business ventures were often in competition with those of Ijebu businessmen. In accord with definitions of 'native' and 'native stranger' adopted during the period of 'indirect rule', the Ijebus were excluded from voting, although not from paying tax. That this 'large and progressive section of the tax-paying community, consisting of lawyers, doctors, merchants, teachers and other such persons...' should have no representation in the Council, Butcher, and the leaders of the Settlers' Union including Obafemi Awolowo, found to be an anomaly 'contrary to modern democratic practice'.

While these findings of the Butcher Commission were not announced until later, the line of inquiry that Butcher pursued made it quite clear in the above instances that he disapproved of existing arrangements. Even before his report, including recommendations for reform, was sent to Government on 21 February, countermeasures were being undertaken throughout the city.

It was the activities of the 'native strangers' which first attracted attention. Throughout February they held a series of meetings in order to state their case, which were met by countermeetings of the I.P.U. (Youth Group), the Egbe Omo Ibile and others. The Native Settlers' Union was anxious to unite with other 'native strangers' in Ibadan on the basis of their common local interests, despite the fact that on a national level many of their leaders held quite opposite allegiances. Thus, at a meeting on 8 February the speakers included Obafemi Awolowo, legal adviser to the Native Settlers' Union and enemy of Nnamdi Azikiwe and the N.C.N.C., Abiodun Akerele, his law partner, and such other associates of his as M. S. Sowole and J. O. Adigun. Among the speakers, however, were also Dr Ikejiani, a close personal friend of Azikiwe, and other N.C.N.C. stalwarts, including Oshilaja Oduyoye, a prominent local Ijebu baker, Abderahman Bida, a pharmacist from the northerners' quarter known as the Sabo, and Alfred des Dokubo, the editor of the *Southern Nigeria Defender*. The *Defender* indeed remarked of the list of speakers that it had been 'judiciously selected in order to ensure consensus of opinion'.[4] In answer to this, the Youth Group of the I.P.U. on 10 February called on Government to re-affirm the Settlers' status as strangers ineligible to purchase land although they had been 'allowed to mix indiscriminately' with native Ibadans.[5]

In response to the meeting of the Settlers on 8 February, a mass meeting was called for 21 February by a new 'United Front Committee' to discuss 'The new threat of the native settlers in Ibadan over the questions of alienation of land to non-Ibadans and representation of non-Ibadans on N.A. Council.'[6] The list of sixteen speakers reveals how a threat could temporarily unite Ibadan leaders in spite of former cleavages. On the rostrum were to be

Chief Omiyale, Adegoke Adelabu, Bello Abasi, R. Ola Oke and A. M. A. Akinloye (a young lawyer newly prominent as representing the chiefs at the Butcher Inquiry), as well as J. A. Ayorinde, E. A. Sanda and Dr Agbaje.

Ibadan's two major newspapers also joined the strangers' cause in a manner not likely to increase their indigenous readership. We have mentioned the arrival of the *Defender* in 1945. On 16 November 1949 the *Nigerian Tribune* began publication. It was owned by the African Press, whose five directors included Obafemi Awolowo and his wife. Thus both papers were owned and directed by non-Ibadans unfamiliar with local events and in March 1950 the *Defender* editorialized in favor of the separation of the Northern Districts, while the *Tribune* looked upon the Olubadan as 'an aged person who combines ignorance with stubborn resistance to all forms of progress...'. Adelabu found himself the object of abuse by both journals, Alfred des Dokubo, editor of the *Defender*, denouncing him and his associates as 'propaganda rascals' after Awolowo had recognized him as a trouble-maker in regard to the activities of the United Front Committee.

Thus the indigenous Ibadans found themselves without any external support when in early March they received further confirmation of their worst fears concerning Butcher's recommendations, when Senior Resident P. V. Main told Akinpelu Obisesan in confidence what the 'probable' main points would be.[7] The existing Ibadan Division, Butcher felt, should be carved into three separate divisions, dividing the city of Ibadan and its immediate rural areas from the Northern Districts and from the Central Districts of Binukonu and Igboora; the tax collection powers should be taken from the chiefs and mogajis and placed on a territorial basis; the chiefs should no longer be eligible to act as judges as long as they acted as chiefs on the Council (the time-honored separation of the executive and the judiciary); the appointment of an Administrative Secretary should be made as quickly as possible; and finally, the power of the senior chiefs in regard to 'subjects requiring close attention to facts and figures' should be diminished as quickly as possible.[8] Although Butcher's suggestions were put forward 'very tentatively', he urged that they could serve as a 'basis of discussion' by local leaders in the search for 'a more efficient and progressive local government'. It was this 'discussion' which Government would shortly set in train to continue the reform process which the now rejected attempt to get rid of Agbaje had given it the opportunity to hasten.

Adegoke Adelabu was at this point attempting to resolve the uncertainties that beclouded his personal and political life. He was still suffering financial embarrassments (the Electricity Corporation was threatening him with discontinuation of his supply because of an unpaid bill of £5. 4. 6d.), and he was without regular employment. Perhaps in search of a job, he spent the first two weeks of March in Lagos. In a mood rarely expressed to others he spoke in a letter written at this time of feeling exhausted by his exertions of the last months. The Agbaje agitation had been both a personal financial failure and a humiliating first venture into politics, and his appearance on behalf of the United Front Committee had created for him such important enemies as Awolowo and the *Defender* without earning the appreciation of any important friends. In this totally unpromising situation, he mustered the resolve to set out on his own course, unclear as he now knew it to be in his new realization of the complexity and uncertainty of the political forces and personalities of the hour. As he wrote from his retreat in Lagos, he must now return to Ibadan 'to face the battle of life'.[9]

It is almost certainly during this visit to Lagos that he wrote his contribution to the forthcoming discussion of Ibadan's future, the 'Master Plan', which we will discuss shortly. He also attempted to state his views on the current situation in Ibadan in a draft entitled 'Ibadan Has Turned Over a New Leaf' which was apparently intended to be the first in a series of newspaper articles justifying the fact that he was now in effect abandoning the anti-Agbaje camp. Claiming to have been 'inundated with a barrage of requests by letters, telegrams, oral messages and calls in Person' from people seeking his views on the Butcher recommendations, he declared that:

Whether we like it or not and without any deliberate intention in that direction we have casually stumbled upon a bloodless revolution. It is sheer futility for anybody at this stage to shed crocodile tears over the rights and wrongs of the recent momentous upheaval.

One of the objects of this draft article was to represent the results of the Agbaje agitation as a victory for the anti-Agbaje forces, since Ibadan had been saved from 'the danger of falling a prey to the unprincipled rule of an unscrupulous tyrant'.* At the same time, the events which this struggle had set in train now posed a new problem for Ibadan, and a second purpose of Adelabu was to warn its sons of the need to face up to this:

I am here concerned to drive home with all the emphasis at my command...that if you insist against all prudence on exacting your pound of flesh by forcibly removing Chief Salami Agbaje from Ibadan Chieftaincy it will divert your attention from your more important and more urgent duties. It boils down to a choice between the lesser of two evils. As a sincere patriot and an honest man I cast my vote unhesitatingly for allowing sleeping dogs to lie.

* Although we do not know the exact date of its composition, this essay (a typescript in A.P.) makes no reference to the suspension of the Olubadan which occurred on 15 March. It was probably thus written within two weeks of the submission of the *Butcher Report*. No trace of any 'barrage' exists in the remaining papers.

Having stood back from the problems of his native city and given his advice – which his fellows were never to receive, since the article remained unpublished – Adelabu returned home to a newly-heightened crisis. On 15 March Olubadan Fijabi was suspended by Government from the Ibadan Council with the applause of the local papers, and on the following day from his Presidency of the Judicial Court of Appeal, the highest court in the local judicial system. The District Officer now became 'Sole Native Authority' for Ibadan Division and District, 'assisted' by the Council in an 'advisory' capacity. At the same time, the Northern Districts increased their agitation for independence from Ibadan. The Ogbomosho Parapo (League), a political organization of that northern town, supported the Butcher recommendations and viewed 'with grave concern the undue publicity given to an alleged treaty of 1893', which in their opinion was null and void from the beginning since it lacked the signature of the Bale of Ogbomosho.[10] Moreover, through the skillful guidance of Obafemi Awolowo, the barrister leader of the Ibadan Native Settlers' Union, and S. L. A. Akintola from Ogbomosho, the interests of the Native Settlers and the Northern Districts were rapidly moving together. Furthermore, as everyone knew it must, Butcher's suggestion that further 'discussion' should ensue to consider his recommendations was realized in a Government decision that a committee of Ibadan representatives should be established, under the guidance of a 'District Officer – Special Duty', to encourage local participation in the reforms.

Although the United Front Committee still existed, its interests were too disparate for prompt response. Nor did a new committee proposed by Akinyele, Obisesan and Akinloye see the light of day. Before anything could materialize, the Colonial Government fixed the format in which the future debate would take place when it informed the Council in the last days of March that an official body, known from its chairman as the Hayley Reform Committee, would begin its considerations immediately. Reactions to this varied. Chief Aminu, Chief Akinyele and others agreed that this committee should be made up of two representatives from each political group in Ibadan. A sophisticated constitutional argument was made by the Iyalode and her subordinate women chiefs that since the Butcher recommendations were 'utterly unsatisfactory', it would be a violation of the Agreement of 1893 if the dispute were not first inquired into by a committee composed half of persons appointed by the Governor and half by the Ibadan Council.[11] Fred Anyiam, on behalf of the Egbe Omo Ibile, the Ibadan Welfare Committee and the Maiyegun League, protested to Governor Macpherson that '...the people view [the Olubadan's] removal as nothing short of victimisation and a deliberate attempt on the part of your Government to encourage rancour and unrest'.[12] The senior chiefs, including Memedu, Igbintade, Kobiowu and Aminu, all of whom would one day be Olubadan, protested that John Hayley's 'past record' was remembered in Ibadan 'with misgivings'.*

In an even more revealing statement of position, Chiefs Aminu and Kobiowu joined with Chief Akinyele, Obisesan, E. A. Sanda, T. L. Oyesina, A. M. A. Akinloye and others, to

condemn the British Government in Nigeria, for this arbitrary act and unilateral abrogation of the Treaty in 1893 in order to perpetuate their doctrine of Divide and Rule and to create employment for their army of Administrative Officers and weaken the People's resistance to imperial bondage.[13]

They went on to declare that 'a state of grave crisis' had arisen in Ibadan, that they would employ 'non-violence and non-co-operation as a first step' in the 'bitter strife and struggle' to restore the unity of Ibadan and the supremacy of the Olubadan over all of Ibadan Division, that they would seek redress from His Majesty's Government in London and 'expose to the whole world the breach of faith and injustice of the British Government in Nigeria in this matter'. Adelabu was no partner to this most anti-colonial statement in decades of Ibadan history, or to any other protests. His own statement was in curious contrast.

The Hayley Reform Committee, consisting of representatives of a dozen political and economic organizations, began its sessions in the second week of April.† As with the Butcher Inquiry, statements from other groups and individuals were solicited to aid the Committee in its considerations of Butcher's recommendations. Adelabu was not a member, but on 14 April, before the second meeting was held, he had already submitted a seventy-page single-spaced typescript memorandum. As he informed Hayley,

The question of Constitutional Reform, though a proper subject for discussion by the tax-paying public at large, contains several aspects which really belong to the sphere of the expert...

In this light I hope, as an ex-student of the Yaba Higher College Commercial Course, a keen student of the theory and practice of Native Administrations in Tropical Africa and a Business Executive with fifteen years experience in various

---

* John Frederick Hayley, born in 1916, the son of an Indian Civil Service officer, joined the Colonial Service in 1939 and served as Assistant District Officer in Ondo and Oshogbo, where he replaced Thomas Shankland in 1941. After the war, he served two tours in London in the Colonial Office and the Nigeria Office before returning to Ibadan.

† Those who took part were representatives of the Senior Chiefs and Council, the junior chiefs and mogajis, Quarter Representatives, the Citizens Committee, the I.P.U., the Muslim Aid Movement, the Ibadan Farmers Association, the Maiyegun Society, the Islamic Missionary Society, the Ibadan Produce Traders and Scales Union, the Oke'Badan Trading Company and the Ibadan Motor Transport Union.

government and commercial undertakings, you will find my advanced views and balanced treatise a useful guide and a convenient basis of discussion by all interested parties.[14]

The memorandum entitled 'A Master Plan for the Reorganisation of the Ibadan District and Divisional Native Authorities' was his first lengthy political analysis, the product of his political experience so far. It spoke therefore to the specific problem of constitutional reform in Ibadan, and the audience to which it was addressed was a local one; indeed, Adelabu knew the names and political careers of everyone he could reasonably expect might read it. Furthermore, the Reform Committee was sorely pressed by the administrative officers throughout its existence to make a number of concrete decisions, based in part on the alternative proposals before it, and the Master Plan was intended to persuade the Committee to accept Adelabu's views as its own.[15] One of these was essentially if incredibly that Adelabu's appointment as Administrative Secretary of the Ibadan Council followed logically from an analysis of Ibadan's political situation at the time.

Since the setting was a local one, Adelabu felt that other city-states such as Athens and Sparta, not modern European or even Yoruba cities, were the most helpful models for reform. Much as Polybius views the Greek city-states, Adelabu saw Ibadan going through a cycle of political development, in which political participation and welfare were expanding. The first or medieval period of 'unbridled tyranny and "might is right"' had been abruptly and beneficially terminated in 1893 with the advent of colonialism. The colonial period, which he determined had ended in 1949, was one of 'benevolent paternalism' and 'the rule of the traditional few'. Colonialism he viewed as an accidental intervention in the history of Ibadan, not as a consequence of imperialist expansion. In 1949, the year of the Agbaje agitation, Ibadan had entered upon an area of 'social democracy dedicated to the welfare of the common people'. This era had not been brought on by a revolution against the forces of industrial collectivism or the domination of an imperial power as much as by the growing envy harbored by the common people against the success and selfishness of indigenous commercial classes, whose position was increasingly strengthened by the education the Christian members in particular had received.

The new era, which Adelabu hoped the Reform Committee's deliberations would usher in, would thus be local in scope, constitutional and structural in implementation, industrial in content and intellectual in its planning, guidance and evolution. It was particularly this intellectual quality which he felt eminently qualified to provide, as the length and detail of the Master Plan demonstrate beyond doubt; Adelabu explicitly promised he would be 'detached, impersonal, objective, rational, impartial, scientific, disinterested, factual, dispassionate and just. . .' This approach was not temperamentally an easy one for him, nor easily come by in the circumstances of Ibadan – 'In my intellectual mood, I fell among my own people like a sojourner among foreigners in a strange country.'

Keeping in mind the 'veritable pandemonium' of political tensions in Ibadan, seven in number, and guided by the 'necessity for compromise', he had therefore prepared as the solution 'A Work of Art', whose 'Organic Unity' and 'Intrinsic Beauty' would be marred should any 'amateur dabblers' attempt to combine parts of it with other plans 'conceived in another spirit with another purpose in view'. In fact, as Adelabu made quite clear, its implementation would require the firm support of the colonial government. 'This is one of the few instances', he argued, 'where one informed head is better than many superficial ones.'

A striking characteristic of this document is that Adelabu promised, in the teeth of precisely the forces with which he would have to contend should his plan be implemented or even revealed, that virtually no one would be satisfied with what they would receive at his hands. His stigmatization of all the political leadership groups except the colonial officers alone would have been enough to defeat his purposes, or undermine his method of compromise. In quick succession he dismissed the general population, the chiefs, and the modern elite. The masses of the common people were less the source of democratic strength and virtue than the barrier against which reforms undertaken in their behalf would eventually come to a halt:

. . .the masses of the common people just tolerate these innovations, decry any new imported ventures, resist any ultra-modern untested moves and put a great premium on their indigenous mode of living.

Between the masses and their chiefs were the mogajis who were shrewd enough to see in the extension of the vote the decline of their own power. Yet they were supported by the masses.

Illiteracy and Chieftaincy via Mogajiship are legally married couples. To put them asunder without due process of law which is no other than the education of the masses is to sin against His Law which says 'Let no man put asunder what I have joined together.'

The goal of the mogajis, of course, was to become chiefs, whom he typified as 'a bewildered and decadent but harmless set of natural rulers' who found in a monopolistic control of political power 'a useful investment for the manufacture of perquisites and unearned incomes. . .'. Hence the discouraging traditional scene.

The modern components of the political spectrum were no less hopeless and were made the worse by their shameless effort to exploit traditional weaknesses with new tools. 'Financial barons' had made the chiefs into 'poor middle-class second-raters' economically, and 'the native capitalists and intelligentsia are making a desperate bid for the capture of political power' from the chiefs. Within the staff of the Council 'Tammany-Hall Practices' existed. The clerks had been taught in schools where texts were recited as though by parrots at a time when radios did not exist to combat narrow-mindedness. Their recruitment to government service was based on family, church affiliation, party loyalty and the size of their purses for bribes. Once in office they were 'nurtured under a leisurely regime where scribblers were kings'. Worst of all was the behavior of the Christians:

Amidst this alarming shortage of competent manpower the selfish Christian Minority (10% of the population) who for 18 years have dominated the commoners' participation in Ibadan Local Government have enforced scandalous & rigorous restrictive practices, much to their everlasting shame! It is to be seen and suffered to be believed.

Despite the clarity of his understanding of the problems facing Ibadan, one cannot escape the impression that Adelabu was essentially engaged in his first major clarification to himself of Ibadan's political problems. The Master Plan is rushed, incomplete and imbalanced, and from the point of view of public administration so impracticable and full of fantasy as to be considered the work of someone without political experience or access to the people, documents and ideas which the I.P.U. establishment took for granted. An initial example in support of this interpretation can be found in his views on the problems of the rural areas. He correctly observed that the Ibadan District tax structure levied rates against farmers for urban improvements in a way which ran counter to the traditional unity of urban and rural areas, and admonished the city dwellers to 'give the farmers their due before their sons return from schools to teach them their rights'. To improve the rural economy, he urged a scheme of 'Local Government Socialism' to bring capitalists into co-operation with government in developing land resources.* The implementation of this program, however, was to be through an intricate system of councils whose total effect would in fact be to reduce the 'farmers' mouthpiece' to a minority interest in a body of 500 representatives.

* For the country as a whole, however, he had a different description a few months later, writing to a friend of Yaba Higher College days that, 'The short-sighted gospel of tribal capitalism being preached and practiced by the Maja-Gbadamosi-Awolowo and Azikiwe-Ojike-Mbadiwe schools of thought must be replaced in due course by a more robust and broader-based Nigerian Capitalism if we are sincere in our desire for a strong and Unified Nigeria able to take her place among the comity of free nations.' (Adelabu to G. C. Nonyelu, 22 June 1951, A.P.)

A further failure to provide workable organizations to deal with a serious problem is found in his provisions for the Northern Districts. Referring to what he called the 'Tug-of-War between the ancient rights of Ibadan Town and the liberal yearnings of the subordinate out-lying Districts', he pronounced empires to be 'as ridiculous as Tails' and urged Ibadan to become more of a leader and less of a ruler in dealing with District towns. He then prescribed what he called a federal pattern for their councillors, chiefs, courts, executive structures and tax systems, which would lead them from 'subordination to association'. For them he also provided a place in the structure of Councils. The Territorial Council would consist of 150 representatives and meet twice a month, although it lacked both executive and administrative authority which would still have to be sought from the Central Council, thus merely perpetuating precisely the conditions which caused the delays and interventions in their affairs against which the District towns now protested.

Adelabu also prescribed a restructuring of the relations between the chiefs and their followers. To lead them toward a more modern, industrial and socialist life the reformer must put on 'the humble robe of the Missionary. Otherwise a destructive revolution of an ignorant mob led by mischievous demagogues looms large on the horizon.' The remedy for the 'antithesis' of the physical necessity of industrial modernization to the spiritual attachment of the people to their chiefs was the gradual removal of power from the chiefs while willingly paying 'for the maintenance of the outward pomp and pageantry'. Calculating precisely thirty-six per cent of the political power as the chiefs' diminished share, granting the rest to commoners, he then provided a remunerative position for every chief in the city, with council positions for an additional ninety mogajis and ten heads of immigrant ethnic groups. To implement this deceptive continuation of the colonial government's policy of depriving the chiefs of power, he also subordinated the chiefs' exercise of it to the elaborate series of interlocking and overlapping councils which would make it impossible for the chiefs to exercise any real legislative or executive authority. They were, however, to continue to dominate the tax collection system and the courts, where only a minority of court members would be literate. In 1954, as we shall see, the diminution of the chiefs' legislative and executive authority and the defense of their judicial and fiscal prerogatives were major aspects of Council policy under Adelabu's chairmanship.

Beyond this already elaborate structure he also proposed a Staff Council made up of the one hundred most senior departmental employees of the Council, and a panel of the one hundred 'most useful experts' who could be called upon to give 'sound, expert advice on technical problems and informed and balanced views on constitutional issues'. Many of these experts on the problems of Local Government Socialism were to come from foreign companies and religious bodies, curious as it seems.

These various councils and panels working together toward Local Government Socialism would change society from communalism to socialism, from agriculture to industry, or as he put it most interestingly, from 'the fetish grove to Fifth Avenue'. Together they would foil the attempt of the capitalists and the intelligentsia 'to capture all political power from the bewildered and decadent but harmless' chiefs. The local government of Ibadan ought therefore to establish a bus system, a printing works and a cinema, and subsidize other local industries. He even went so far as to urge that Ibadan should become an inland seaport by means of a canal cut through Ijebu Province from the Atlantic, a straightline distance of some 70 miles traversing an elevation of some 700 feet. In short, the reformed Council should dominate the local economy, for 'A Government is either the commander or the servant of financial interests.'

All the plans, all the councils and committees and the panels of experts required personnel to operate them. Although Adelabu still viewed Ibadan essentially as a native administration operating within a centralized colonial government, he mentions local–central relations only with regard to the role of the Administrative Secretary, discussed below, and never in relation to finance, provision of experts or policy control. There is no discussion whatsoever of the role colonial administrators were to play in the future or to whom they were to be responsible, since he accepted their presence as given and fixed, even though the colonial administrators themselves knew that basic changes in their authority would and should occur before their era closed.

More curious than his failure to discuss the colonial rulers was his specific job assignment for virtually all of the significant Christian and commercial leaders against whom the Master Plan spoke with such unabated vituperation. For example, he urged that T. A. Oyesina, Dr Agbaje, S. A. Oloko, and Akinpelu Obisesan should be among the new Territorial Councillors, all chosen, apparently, in the old colonial style, by appointment rather than by election. The Executive Council, chosen in part from the chiefs and in part from the Territorial Council, would apparently also be composed of appointed members, whether by the Hayley Committee or central government we cannot tell, and would include Obisesan as its Chairman, Adelabu as the Vice-Chairman and eight other councillors whom he listed by name. Court presidencies were provided for none other than Salami Agbaje, as well as Chief Akinyele, D. T. Akinbiyi and J. L. Ogunsola, an intriguing list in that the last three were appointed court presidents in 1954 over Adelabu's bitter and unsuccessful protest that the traditional order was being subverted on behalf of the Christian establishment. The list of members for the various committees reads as a veritable Who's Who of the privileged few. The Ayorinde brothers and their cousin T. S. B. Aribisala, Y. S. O. Ishola, the former councillor and successful contractor, T. L. Oyesina, lawyers Agbaje, Akinloye and Esan, and such businessmen as E. A. Sanda, Y. O. Carew, A. Allen and K. O. S. Are all had their places, with their qualifications and experience neatly listed by Adelabu to justify their selection. After all, as his sixth primary canon of practicability had prescribed, 'No segment of the population must feel so frustrated or ill-treated as to become a permanent cog in the wheel of progress.'

The role of the Administrative Secretary and his own fulfilling of it are only briefly discussed. On the one hand, largely in justification of the intrinsic organic unity of the scheme, he argued that 'if the plan is accepted in its entirety effective co-ordination is bound to result naturally and with a minimum of effort...'. On the other hand, he urged that 'The success of the new experiment we are about to launch depends more on the apt choice of the right person to fill this most important professional/political post than on all other factors combined.' His own experience he listed as ex-Government co-operative inspector, ex-manager at U.A.C., critic, merchant, landlord, socialist, and General Secretary of the Egbe Omo Ibile. Presumably this would suit him for the post. 'The sheer extensiveness and onerousness of the Secretary's clerical duty is incomparably great...He is to be the Public Relations Officer and Interpreter between the most turbulent and complicated Native Authority in Nigeria and the Regional Administration.' Such duties Adelabu could perform. 'All those who have the patience, the courage, the understanding and the good fortune to accompany me on this perilous journey into the Immortal Future will give unanimous unstinted support to my MASTER PLAN. *It Is Right.*'

Adelabu's reaction to the Hayley Reform Committee, then, was not to petition against it, like Obisesan, Oyesina, Akinloye and the rest, but rather to attempt through his Master Plan to use it to secure for himself the long-coveted Administrative Secretaryship. Perhaps almost immediately he sensed that the Master Plan was an ineffective weapon, for on 23 April, in his role as a leader of the Egbe Omo Ibile, Adelabu appeared outside Hayley's office with a letter addressed to him, saying, 'As it is your declared policy to meet all sections of the populace and to exchange views with all shades of opinion we hope you will seize this opportunity to interview a body that represents well over three-quarters of Ibadan Town and Environs.'[16] Since Adelabu was waiting outside with 500 followers, according to Hayley's own estimate, it seemed to Hayley that the opportunity, in the interests of public safety, should indeed be seized. The confrontation consisted of 'a string of complaints and grievances against the Butcher Commission & a refusal to cooperate in Reform unless or until the Olubadan's suspension is ended'.[17] Hayley apparently decided that he could master the situation. He said he was interested in the future, but not in the past, whereupon Adelabu announced that the Egbe Omo Ibile would not be attending the meetings of the Reform Committee. With this the meeting ended, and on the next day the Egbe, the Maiyegun League and the Iyalode's Section withdrew their members and their co-operation from the Committee's formal work.

This initiative, of course, quite discredited Adelabu with Hayley, but it perhaps served to re-establish him as the spokesman for groups which in April had protested the suspension of the Olubadan through Fred Anyiam rather than himself. While Adelabu persisted in his preoccupation with local solutions to the problems before the Hayley Committee, national political parties were concentrating on the opportunities presented in the new national constitution.

It will be remembered that in January 1950, during the height of the Agbaje agitation, the Ibadan Conference had laid down the outlines of what later came to be known popularly as the 'Macpherson Constitution' after the Governor of Nigeria, Sir John Macpherson, who in August 1948 had initiated the process which led to its adoption. Under this Constitution (which was not actually promulgated until 29 June 1951), elections were to be held throughout Nigeria for the first time to choose Members for the Houses of Assembly which were to be established in each Region. These were in their turn to select from their Members the Members for a House of Representatives for the whole of Nigeria. Moreover, both in the Regions and at the center, ministerial portfolios were to be given to Nigerians, thus taking the important first step in the national devolution of power by the British, with Nigerian independence as the ultimate goal.

In response to this situation, a new political party, the Action Group, led by Obafemi Awolowo, invited civic leaders to 'devise plans for organizing the people of the Western Region so that they may be able to play an influential and effective role in the affairs of Nigeria under the New Constitution'.[18] As the first public announcement of the new party put it on 21 March 1951, if elections were to be held in each Region, and if Executive Councils including Nigerian Ministers were to be set up there, 'One inescapable result' followed – 'there must be a powerful nationalist organisation in each Region'.[19] The Action Group's first conference was called for 28 and 29 April to meet at Owo to elect officers.

The need for 'political or labour parties' had already been strongly stated in a *Defender* editorial on 7 March. It was not the N.C.N.C.'s intention, however, that the party representing the West should be any other than itself. On 2 April the editor of the *Defender* attacked the Action Group as speaking only for 'the Oyo, Ijebu and handpicked Egba intelligentsia'. 'It is a comedy of national error', he went on, 'if the Action Group is allowed to exist without the membership of other Westerners.' In fact, the Action Group was already taking steps to extend itself into the non-Yoruba parts of the West. On 4 April the Benin Provincial Action Group was formed, and on the 10th the party constituted itself in Warri Province, while on 14 April these two sections came together to form the Mid-Western Action Group, with Anthony Enahoro, formerly a journalist with Dr Azikiwe's newspapers and later to become one of Adelabu's most formidable opponents, as its Secretary.

The regional elections were not to be direct ones with large electorates, but indirect ones through electoral 'colleges'. This meant that in each administrative Division the largest number of electors would be involved at the primary stage, when all taxpayers (in effect adult men) would be entitled to vote for those who would go to the Intermediate College, who would in turn vote for some of their own number to form the Final College, which would choose the actual Members of the Western House of Assembly for the division – six of them, for example, for Ibadan Division. Although fewer and fewer men would be involved at each stage, some sort of organization was still needed by the parties in order to contact the members of the electoral colleges and, if necessary, to mobilize public support in order to put pressure on them to choose the right men.

The need for party organization was as keenly felt in Ibadan as elsewhere, and both parties had some embryonic support in Ibadan among the resident strangers. Obafemi Awolowo himself had his law practice there, with Abiodun Akerele from Oyo, and a number of the most prominent founder-members of the Action Group were residents in the town – J. O. Adigun and Akintunde Sowunmi, joint editors of the *Morning Star*, one of the smaller and short-lived local newspapers, and the latter the General Secretary of the Native Settlers' Union, S. T. Oredein, General Secretary of the British-American Tobacco Company Workers Union, and Ade Akinsanya, Managing Director of the African Press. Similarly, as we have already noted, friends and supporters of Dr Azikiwe were to be found among the native strangers, men like Oshilaja Oduyoye, 'the Bread King of Ibadan' as he was called, or Adesegun Odunmbaku, an Egba lawyer, or A. J. Nicholson Sangster, Manager of the West African Club at Oke Padre. Theoretically, the N.C.N.C. should have enjoyed a considerable advantage over the Action Group in Ibadan, as elsewhere in the West, since it had been in existence since August 1944. However, this was not the case. Organizationally the N.C.N.C. suffered from a great weakness, since until May 1951 it was made up not of individual members but of affiliated organizations, which meant that it did not build up any branches of its own, capable of imposing direct discipline on their members.

In the circumstances, it is not surprising that the N.C.N.C. had not impinged very greatly on the fabric of Ibadan life by early 1951. No important channel existed by which it could do so. In 1949 the Ibadan branch of the Nigerian National Democratic Party, its affiliate, had functioned sporadically, but had made no real impact. The Zikist Movement, the militant wing of the N.C.N.C., had had an Ibadan branch until its suppression by the Government in April 1950 (its Chairman, Adebayo Asaya, will figure prominently in our story later), but it showed no particular militancy. There was in 1951 a branch of the National Church of Nigeria and the Cameroons, an N.C.N.C. satellite, but it seems to have been made up entirely of Easterners resident in Ibadan. Some of the special pressure groups thrown up by the nationalist movement in the late 1940s had also made an appearance in Ibadan: Oshilaja Oduyoye, who was also nicknamed 'Local Bustamante' after the colorful West Indian leader, was prominent on the local Anti-Colour Discrimination Watch Committee. Such groups, however, were not confined to N.C.N.C. supporters; Awolowo and Abiodun Akerele had played a prominent part in the Ibadan branch of the National Emergency Committee formed by the Nigerian Youth Movement and N.C.N.C. after the Enugu Colliery shootings in November 1949. Nor, as we have seen, was Azikiwe's *Southern Nigeria Defender* a much greater asset to his party than was Awolowo's *Nigerian Tribune* to the Action Group. Both papers were largely read by strangers, both had denounced Adelabu and his associates, and neither had supported the Olubadan or the city against the administrators or the demands of the Northern Districts.

Above all, Ibadan itself, as opposed to its stranger element, was ill-suited to become a hotbed of nationalist politics. The city had retained much of its earlier social structure, and if colonialism had altered the political structure, it had not put Ibadan's slowly modernizing polity in the hands of non-Ibadan men. The nationalist groups of the early 1920s, whose leaders had often been non-Ibadan men, had collapsed, and since in contrast to other Yoruba towns Ibadan's brightest sons had not gone to Lagos, with the coming to power of the Ibadan Progressive Union the city had its own modernizing if sometimes parochial leadership.

In its attempts to penetrate Ibadan, the new Action Group was in the worse position, however, since men like Awolowo and Akintunde Sowunmi were known as particularly militant spokesmen for the Settlers' Union, while J. O. Adigun was General Secretary of the Egbe Irepodun, the organization spearheading the demand for the separation of the Northern Districts. Nevertheless, it was necessary for both parties to enlist support among the sons of Ibadan as well as among the native strangers if they were to win the forthcoming elections, and in seeking this latter support the two parties in effect committed themselves to taking a stand upon those issues which most concerned Ibadan – reform of the Native Authority, the position of the strangers, and the Northern Districts' agitation.*

In May 1951 both the N.C.N.C. and the Action Group began to organize in Ibadan. The former was first off the mark and made the most determined effort, following now a new policy of establishing itself on the basis of direct, individual membership and its own local branches. On Saturday, 12 May, a meeting in the West African Club, summoned by a group calling itself the N.C.N.C. Reception Committee, was attended by prominent individuals, representatives of such strangers' organizations as the Benin Federal Union and the Ibo Union, and of local associations of bricklayers, laborers, tailors, shoemakers and barbers, the object being to prepare for a visit to Ibadan by Azikiwe and other N.C.N.C. national leaders on the following Monday. Also present, speaking for the Egbe Omo Ibile, was Adegoke Adelabu. If any national or regional political party was going to establish itself firmly in Ibadan, it would be a great advantage to have the support of the Egbe, grandly claiming as it did to speak for about 150 different organizations, of which the Maiyegun League alone claimed 20,000 farmers as members. In the month since he had submitted his memorandum to the Hayley Committee the Egbe's General Secretary had shifted his attention to broader horizons, and had now realized the importance of making a link with one of the major parties.

Adelabu had had some contacts with the N.C.N.C. since his return from Lagos in 1946. When Nnamdi Azikiwe visited Ibadan in December 1946, he stayed in the house of Chief Saka Adebisi, Adelabu's friend, and Adelabu had gone with Chief D. T. Akinbiyi and his son to greet him there. When F. U. Anyiam became Political Adviser of the Maiyegun League in November 1949 he provided another link with the N.C.N.C. Extraordinarily, the N.C.N.C. apparently never attempted to exploit this link for its own purposes, but Anyiam and Adelabu were personal acquaintances. Moreover, in the context of Ibadan local issues, it was easy to oppose the leaders of the new Action Group, men like Awolowo, S. L. Akintola and J. O. Adigun, who were associated with the demands of the Native Settlers' Union and the Northern Districts. Personal ambition also no doubt served to place Adelabu in the N.C.N.C. camp in 1951, since even as early as May he may have had

* This is not to suggest that Ibadan was in any way different in this respect from other places in the Western Region in 1951. Everywhere it was basically local issues which determined stands, party affiliations and election results.

his eye on a seat in the new Western House of Assembly and was more likely to be nominated by that party than Awolowo's.

In his speech at the meeting on 12 May Adelabu firmly committed the Egbe Omo Ibile to supporting the N.C.N.C., simultaneously making his own personal commitment to that party. He associated parochialism with the new Action Group, which had avowedly come into existence in order to speak for the Western Region rather than to operate on a national level. On these grounds he pledged the support of the Egbe Omo Ibile for the N.C.N.C., while not forgetting to refer to Ibadan as the 'largest native city in Central Africa' and to pay tribute to the suspended Olubadan. At the end of his speech he moved to broader themes, beyond the boundaries of Nigeria itself, asserting that 'the foundation of a sovereign independent Republican West African States Union stretching from the Gambia to the shores of the Congo and taking her rightful place in the United Nations Organization, is our goal'.[20] Thus, just as he was about to embark on his national political career, he seemed genuinely repelled by the regionalism dominating Nigerian politics by 1951.

Whatever a man's leanings, however, throughout Ibadan and the Western Provinces rapidly shifting circumstances made it extremely difficult at this time to know just where he could find support or even enemies to attack. We have seen how uncertain personal ties could be. Equally uncertain were the supposedly more formal institutional arrangements. In Ibadan, for example, it was announced in the Council on 14 May, that under the new Nigerian constitution which was shortly to create the Western Region from the Western Provinces, the Ibadan delegation 'for electoral purposes' was to be chosen by two electoral districts, namely Ibadan and its immediate rural areas, and this arrangement antedated, and was quite out of step with, the general re-organization recommended by Butcher.

The announcement was made on the day that Azikiwe at the head of the National N.C.N.C. delegation made a triumphal entry into Ibadan to attend the previously arranged meeting. They went in procession to Mapo Hall, where a mass meeting presided over by Bello Abasi was held after the conclusion of the Council meeting and the closing of Council offices. Speaking in Yoruba, Azikiwe seized on the announcement made at the Council meeting and pledged the N.C.N.C. to resist the splitting-up of Ibadan Division, offering to mediate between Ibadan and the Northern Districts, and also between the Ibadan community and the Native Settlers. For the Ibadan side Adegoke Adelabu again pledged the support of the Egbe Omo Ibile and the Maiyegun League for the N.C.N.C. Thus the new, re-organized N.C.N.C. was launched in Ibadan, when after some delay it incorporated into the battlelines of the emerging national party system some of the cleavages left in the community by the Agbaje dispute, to which Adelabu had contributed. The delegates remained until the 16th, meeting various local leaders privately, and then left to continue their tour in Ilesha.

As a follow-up to this visit the N.C.N.C. Ibadan branch met on 25 May at the West African Club to elect its officers. Oduyoye was made President, with Odunmbaku as his Vice-President and Sangster as General Secretary. George H. Cowan, the new editor of the *Southern Nigeria Defender*, became Publicity Secretary. Thus the major offices went to non-Ibadans. Ibadan sons were represented by the Olubadan, who became Patron of the branch, and by Adegoke Adelabu, who became Assistant Secretary. With a duly constituted branch the N.C.N.C. was now free to put all its energies into its recruiting drive; four days after the visit of the delegation it had claimed a registration of 11,500 members.

In contrast, the efforts of the Action Group were much more modest. Since many of its most prominent founders were not Ibadan sons, and were strongly associated with the Native Settlers' Union and the agitation for the separation of the Northern Districts, the memories and associations which helped to put Adegoke Adelabu in the N.C.N.C. camp were also undoubtedly of great importance in determining the attitude of Ibadan people at large to the Action Group. It behoved the new party, then, to tread lightly.

The Action Group did have one important point of contact with some of the most prominent sons of Ibadan through the Egbe Omo Oduduwa. This Yoruba cultural organization had been founded by Obafemi Awolowo while he was a student in London, and refounded in Nigeria after his return. When it was formally constituted at Ife in June 1949, S. A. Akinfenwa, one of the leaders of the Ibadan Citizens' Committee, became a Vice-President. Other important I.C.C. and I.P.U. members such as Akinpelu Obisesan, the Rev. E. A. Alayande and T. L. Oyesina joined its Ibadan branch. Since the relations between the Action Group and the Egbe, after some hesitation on the part of the latter, had become very close by May 1951, the Ibadan branch of the Egbe might have become a recruiting ground for party members.[21] Three Ibadan men had in fact attended the Owo Conference of the Action Group in April. These were the Rev. E. A. Alayande, S. O. Lanlehin, an accountant at the Union Trading Company and well known in local affairs, and A. M. A. Akinloye, the young barrister who had appeared at Adelabu's side on behalf of the chiefs in the Agbaje Inquiry. Having earned distinction both academically and as a student leader in London, he had returned to Ibadan amid the fanfares of the local press and a round of receptions in late 1950.

It was Akinloye, in fact, who gave the main speech at the Action Group's first Ibadan rally on 21 May in Mosley Hall, and it was reported that he 'expressed his pride in being a staunch member of the Group right from the time of inception'.[22] When a divisional conference elected officers on the following day, however, he was not among them; indeed, no Ibadan man was elected to office, and only two – Akinfenwa and Dr A. S. Agbaje – to the committee of eleven members. In fact, by this time Akinloye and S. O. Lanlchin were planning to start a new party of their own, and one of their associates in this plan was Adegoke Adelabu, a prominent member of the N.C.N.C.

The justification of this coming together of members of the two major parties in the Ibadan Peoples Party, with Akinloye as its President and Adelabu its Vice-President, came in Akinloye's speech at the I.P.P. inaugural meeting on Saturday, 16 June, in Mapo Hall.[23] There he pointed out that existing Ibadan organizations were not purely political, being concerned also with social and cultural activities; that there was a need for a purely local political party, not linked to any national organization; and that no already existing body was able to bring literates and illiterates together for common action. For in spite of their protestations, neither the Action Group nor the N.C.N.C. was clearly enough related or committed to Ibadan issues and political personages to render much aid in the solution of Ibadan problems or in winning the forthcoming elections. The I.P.P. was the creation of a group of Ibadan sons who wanted to have their own party in order to maneuver between the major parties in the coming elections. Ironically, most of its founders, such as A. M. A. Akinloye, son of the trader, Akandi Akinloye, and Moyo Aboderin, son of I.P.U. Councillor, J. C. Aboderin, represented not 'the grandchildren of the old nobility', with whom Adelabu identified himself and who, as we saw in Chapter 3, Adelabu thought would be the important new force in Ibadan politics, but the second generation of the educated 'self-seekers' of the 'new nobility'. It was among this group, however, that the need was seen for organization and the necessity of drawing far more people into political life than ever before, something which the I.P.U. and the I.C.C., with their 'elitist' overtones, could never do.

Neither, for that matter, could the Egbe Omo Ibile, whose following among the illiterate population of the city lacked sufficient educated leaders to be able to maneuver in the new, complex world of national and regional politics. Perhaps only Adelabu could have provided such a leadership (as he was to do later with the Mabolaje), but at this stage he could not dispute Bello Abasi's control over the Egbe.

Furthermore, although Adelabu seemed to have turned his back on it, the Master Plan had not been withdrawn when the Egbe Omo Ibile left the Hayley Reform Committee, and its support of Butcher's proposals, its insistence upon compromise and British fair play, and its acceptance of the loss

96

of the Northern Districts were unlikely to endear it to the Egbe. Although members of the Reform Committee have told the authors that they never saw the Master Plan, on 29 May, following the eleventh of the Committee's fifteen meetings and presumably with Hayley's permission, it was suddenly announced over the radio that the General Secretary of the Egbe Omo Ibile had filed a memorandum with the Committee. On the following day Bello Abasi for the Egbe, Yesufu Mogbonjubola of the Maiyegun League and officers of several of the other constituent groups of the Egbe wrote to Hayley that Adelabu had acted 'in his private capacity' and that they would not approve any reforms until the Olubadan had been restored to his office.[24] On the strength of this, although he had originally invited statements from individuals as well as groups, Hayley put the Master Plan back in the file. In his view, 'It was a lot of nonsense anyway.'[25]*

On 16 June 1951 the separation issue was discussed at a rally of the Ibadan Peoples Party, attended by 200 people and presided over by Obisesan at Mapo Hall.[26] On 18 June, the issue of separate elections in the Northern Districts was discussed at a special meeting of the Reform Committee called to consider the problem out of the order of the agenda. The committee members decided to prepare a memorandum charging Government with 'conspiracy' with the Northern District chiefs for separation. On 23 June, however, Hayley reported to the Committee that the Districts were unhappy about the ceaseless disputes in Ibadan, about their contribution to Ibadan chiefs' salaries and about the selection and posting of Council staff. He could see no compromise with the insistence of the Districts upon separation and he was reminded, he said, of Ibadan's insistence in 1934 upon separation from Oyo. T. L. Oyesina responded that he was now convinced that the higher authorities were against Ibadan, and with the Ibadan leaders now clearly uniting against a hard Government position the meeting ended.

During this period, Bello Abasi seems to have been uncertain about his relations with the new I.P.P. On 17 June, the day after the inaugural rally of the new party, he informed Adelabu of his dismissal as member and General Secretary of the Egbe since he had become a member of the I.P.P. and it was not possible to serve two masters at once.[27] Less than a week after its inaugural meeting, the *Defender* was speculating in its editorial about the relations of the I.P.P. with the I.P.U. and the Egbe, asking, 'Is the Ibadan Peoples' Party out to seduce the membership of these older organisations or to

* Interview with John Hayley in New York, August 1965. The *Defender* on 12 June 1951 gave another (unfortunately anonymous) opinion: 'A European correspondent describes Mr Adelabu's draft constitution as being "one of the most competent efforts at real reorganisation of an administration on modern lines".'

co-operate with them?'[28] The day after, it suggested that the Egbe would not link with the I.P.P. and that the former's Secretary (i.e. Adelabu) was at the meeting on 16 June only in his private capacity. Finally, the claim by Abasi which it published on 27 June, that the Egbe was the 'mother party' of the I.P.P., hardly settled the question one way or another.

For Adelabu, the realization that his Master Plan was not being seriously considered, sharpened by the repudiation of him by Abasi as a spokesman of a major political group, drove home the fact that he must continue to search beyond the Administrative Secretaryship for employment. Nor at this time did a place in a party organization offer sufficient certainty of election to the House of Assembly and a Member's salary to provide a living. Late in June we therefore find him applying for the advertised post of Clerk to the Ikeja Native Authority, and early in July for that of Chief Clerk to the Town Council in far-away Port Harcourt, in the East.[29]

Early in July the I.P.P. leaders decided to clarify the position of their party with relation to the national parties. On 3 July they published a press release in both the *Defender* and the *Tribune*, quoting from the 'Aims and Objects' of the party: 'To co-operate with truly conscientious national political parties for the overthrow of imperialism and the realisation of immediate self-government for Nigeria.' Point 4 of the release also pointed out that 'Whereas the individual members of the Ibadan Peoples Party can join any of the National Political Parties, the I.P.P. as such is not a member of any National Political Party. The urgency and the extent of the local problems dictate this expediency.'[30] This formula no doubt suited Akinloye, Lanlehin, Adelabu and others very well. It left them free to belong to the Action Group or the N.C.N.C. as individuals while at the same time the I.P.P. as a party could concentrate on local issues and building up a following in Ibadan. The co-operation formula could be used to maneuver between the national parties if this became necessary. While this formulation was helpful in maintaining local autonomy and establishing a working group to prepare for the elections, it was contrary to the hopes of the national parties who had attempted to take sides in local issues and gain direct membership.

In fact, I.P.P. leaders were already working on local issues in keeping with their declared position. On 25 June, a committee reviewed the draft memorandum charging the Government with 'conspiracy', during the course of which a portion of the draft was replaced with one composed by I.P.P. leaders Akinloye and Adelabu 'which added to its fineness' according to Obisesan.[31] On 9 July a mass meeting was held at Mapo Hall to protest against the suspension of the Olubadan and the prospect of the separation of the Northern Districts. It was upon the latter topic that Adelabu was deputed to speak, and while he spoke as a leader of the I.P.P. there were also speeches from B. A. Adeoye, a local contractor and Adelabu's successor as Secretary of the Egbe Omo Ibile, and three members of the Citizens Committee. The final resolution cited the Treaty of 1893 and referred to British policy as that of 'Divide and Rule', 'intended to weaken the people's resistance to imperial bondage', while a boycott of the coming elections was threatened.[32] The resolution was passed without opposition.

The Government's response to this rising storm was to announce to the Council on 12 July the creation of a separate Oyo Province and the separation of the Northern Districts, to be known as Oshun Division, which, together with the new truncated Ibadan Division were to make up Ibadan Province. As Obisesan recorded, 'The Council received the news with great shock & sorrow and said nothing before bidding the Resident goodbye.'[33]

Hayley was aware of the sentiments and proprieties involved and, as his remarks in the Annual Report of 1951 show, Government had made its choice. As Hayley wrote, the approaching national elections made it necessary to adopt the new divisional structure quickly. Had there been time to explain to the Hayley Committee and the Council, 'much of the ill-feeling which subsequently arose might have been averted. Pressure of events, however, precluded such consultation...'[34] Thus the proposed Macpherson constitution was already shaping the Nigerian political system. The forthcoming elections would reinforce existing local arrangements, and since these were not desired by the administration they were changed by fiat in spite of the elaborate consultative process set in motion elsewhere. The immediate reaction to the announcement of 12 July was the formation of a 'quadruple alliance' among the I.C.C., the I.P.U. (though these two were almost identical), the Egbe Omo Ibile and the I.P.P., which now claimed 2000 members in the city and many more in the rural areas. This alliance soon took for itself the title Greater Ibadan Unity Grand Alliance.*

On 14 and 16 July further mass meetings were held at Mapo Hall to protest the creation of Oshun Division. The first was addressed by Obisesan, Lanlehin and Adeoye, representing the different groups making up the Alliance. The main business of the second meeting was to pass a resolution, which asserted that the Governor of Nigeria 'had done violence to well-established history and tradition' and demanded a policy of non-co-operation with the British administration, which it called on the chiefs to support. This was indeed an issue which bound together all Ibadan people, rich and poor, literate and illiterate, the new elite and the chiefs, in a common sense of outrage at this affront to the historical dominance of their city. Popular

---

* Its Working Committee included Chief Adebisi, Chief Obisesan, E. A. Adeyemo (Treasurer of the Native Authority), B. A. Adeoye, and V. O. Esan, S. O. Lanlehin, R. Ola Oke, Moyo Aboderin and Adegoke Adelabu of the I.P.P.

feeling became intense, and speakers at the meetings predicted worse to come. On 18 July a campaign fund was opened to fight the separation.

The Grand Alliance campaign was continued at the second meeting of its Working Committee, on 21 July, attended by two chiefs from the Northern Districts who joined in approving unanimously the immediate publication of a press release, which appeared as the 'Greater Ibadan Unity War Release No. 1'.[35] At the same time the Grand Alliance took steps to improve its organization. Sub-committees were set up to deal with Finance, Co-ordination, Secretariat, Propaganda, Publicity and Legal matters.[36]

Such activities could not escape official observation of course, and on 27 July the Acting Resident invited the Council to meet him and warned them, as Obisesan recorded, 'against fresh development on the Agbaje affair & suggested many things'. 'Members', Obisesan also noted, 'assured him that only a bastard would try to re-open the agitation.'[37] Although the old enemies of the Agbaje agitation attempted to continue the Grand Alliance campaign, they were undermined by Government's intervention in the issues which bound them together.

Since the Governor had resolved the separation issue a few days before the final meeting of the Hayley Committee on 15 July, that recommendation of Commissioner Butcher did not require the acceptance of its members, which, in face of popular feeling on the matter, they would scarcely have been able to give. One other matter caused bitter debate. After spirited defenses by Ogunsola and others of the prerogatives of the junior chiefs and mogajis, particularly in regard to their 'right' to collect taxes, it was agreed that their powers should be diminished in favor of a wider extension of the franchise and the increased power of the Administrative Secretary, which the Reform Committee roundly endorsed. To get around the question of filling that post, the Committee also agreed that it should be held initially by a European officer seconded to the Council's employment (rather than Government's) until the post could be filled by a Nigerian. Having agreed to these positions concerning the Council and its executive direction, the Reform Committee then also agreed that the chiefs generally should no longer dominate both the Council and the court system, and while awaiting the final report of the Brooke Commission which was inquiring into customary courts throughout Western Nigeria, the Council agreed to a separation of executive and judicial functions which would not entail a loss of salary to the chiefs.

Thus, when it came to the final decision, the majority of the issues which were the legacy of the Agbaje agitation were settled, in principle at least, with surprising speed, and along some of the lines which Adelabu had welcomed in his Master Plan. Moreover, the agreed reforms met with considerable approval throughout Ibadan, not only from the educated men who were concerned with 'good government' but even from the chiefs and mogajis, who were quite prepared to cast off some of their burdens in exchange for an assurance that their financial perquisites would be continued. Even the issues which did not come before the Reform Committee, the suspension of the Olubadan and the Northern separation, were to peter out as matters of profound popular discontent by the end of the year, when wider issues began to engulf Ibadan. The fact was that as a result of the 'bloodless revolution' into which Adelabu and the others had stumbled, Ibadan was forced to turn its face away from the preservation of its traditional ways of doing things to a consideration of its place in the new world of Nigerian party politics. Certainly local issues were to continue to be extremely important, perhaps decisive, as when, beginning in 1952, the chiefs and mogajis began to fear that losing their responsibilities meant also losing their perquisites. As we will see, it was to some extent upon their resultant discontents that Adelabu (who had advocated such an extinction of traditional authority in his Master Plan) was to build his political power. Yet all of this was to be in a new context in terms of regional and national affairs, and Ibadan was to discover that, like all revolutions, its bloodless one was a beginning, not an end.

CHAPTER 5

ADELABU ENTERS NATIONAL POLITICS

> I knew that Nature was busy with the selection, on the spiritual plane,
> of the few who would lead in the Struggle ahead.
> Adegoke Adelabu, *Africa in Ebullition*, 1952

In mid-1951 Ibadan's 'bloodless revolution' had been accomplished in principle only; its effects were still future events. The national political parties were in the first stages of establishing a foothold in the city, and the whole organizational situation was extremely fluid. Thus, only a month after the Greater Ibadan Unity Grand Alliance was formed the seeds of its decay began to creep in and divisive issues appeared. It was announced on 18 July that the primary stage of the elections to the new House of Assembly would be held on 13 August, with seventy quarters in the city and a special area made up of the 'stranger' areas, the Reservations and the University College electing ninety-six men to the Intermediate College. Energies and attention were diverted from the Alliance's campaign concerning Ibadan's grievances to the election, as each quarter sought to decide on its candidates. Where possible a contest was avoided, as in Oke Are quarter, where on 28 July the quarter head and elders met to select its allotted three men, to pass unopposed to the Intermediate College. When it was pointed out that this would mean that there would be no voting, the chief who presided over the meeting countered that any of the three who failed to come up to scratch could easily be eliminated at the next stage. This process of indirect election was spread over more than two months and since the number of electors involved at the last two stages was small, great emphasis was placed on maneuvering by the organizations involved to ensure that the six new Members of the House of Assembly finally elected would be acceptable to themselves. The I.P.P. leaders in particular were determined that they be well-represented, and after 1 August, when they concluded their membership drive with a claimed 4000 members in the city, they were ready to give the elections their full attention. Their party could by no means claim a mass membership, but it included most of the younger and more active educated men, like Adelabu, and the separation issue had furnished them with contacts with the chiefs and the mass of the people.

Nevertheless, the Working Committee of the Grand Alliance hoped to nominate six candidates at the Final College acceptable to all its constituent bodies, in order to avoid internal conflict. As soon as the primaries were over, with Adelabu duly elected to the Intermediate College from Oke Oluokun, speculation began about the final candidates. On 15 August the *Defender* suggested that these would be Adelabu, Akinloye, T. L. Oyesina, E. A. Sanda, J. M. Johnson (Manager of the Mobil Petrol Mart) and W. Mosley (another local businessman). Thus in this list the I.P.P. and I.P.U.–I.C.C. were equally represented, while the last two nominees were native strangers. The inclusion of these two, with Johnson at least known to be an N.C.N.C. member, coupled with the fact that in its report the *Defender* spoke of these six as the candidates of the N.C.N.C. Grand Alliance, raised once again the question of the links between the Ibadan local organizations and the national parties. It seems certain, in fact, that at a meeting of the Alliance's Working Committee late in July or early in August it was decided to co-operate with the N.C.N.C. Adelabu later stated the voting to have been 28 to 2, the dissidents being Akinfenwa and the Rev. Alayande, the most open Action Group members of the Committee.[1] In the light of the Alliance's concern with the issue of Northern Separation and the part played by prominent Action Group leaders like S. L. Akintola and J. O. Adigun in leading the agitation for the establishment of Oshun Division, this decision is not surprising. Insofar as it committed the I.P.P., as a member of the Alliance, it was to have great significance later.

Still the Alliance's chief concern during August was not its relations with the national political parties but the attempt to agree on six final candidates. On 29 August, a meeting was called at Mapo Hall of all members of the Intermediate College. On behalf of the I.P.P. Akinloye denied that his party had already agreed on a full slate of six candidates to be chosen only from its members, but by this stage of the meeting it was becoming obvious that no common agreement would be reached on final candidates. Adelabu therefore proposed that discussion be postponed until after the intermediate election on 10 September, and Dr A. S. Agbaje, speaking last, recommended that a committee be set up to discuss the matter, and this suggestion was accepted.

The committee failed to meet, however, apparently because the I.C.C. and Egbe Omo Ibile refused to nominate representatives to it, and on 1 September two senior Chiefs, the Otun and Osi Baloguns, intervened in an attempt to patch up an agreement, inviting the Quarter Representatives and the four organizations (the Egbe, I.C.C., I.P.U. and I.P.P.) to a 'reconciliation meeting' on the 4th. This was a complete failure, and the reasons can perhaps best be seen in a 'Political Bulletin' entitled *The So-Called Big Men of*

Ibadan, which the I.P.P. and Egbe Omo Ibile circulated afterwards. This explained that

During the discussion at the Peace Meeting between Ibadan Political Parties at Mapo Hall, one of the apologists for the Old Regime made the astounding statement that Ibadan should send only big men into the Western House of Assembly ...Who is a big man? Is he the oldest man, the richest man, the tallest man, the man with the largest number of children, wives or native gowns or the occupant of the most imposing mansion?

The Bulletin went on to ask, 'Is bigness in a prospective member of the Western House of Assembly to be measured like the heaviness of a forest log, the weightiness of a bag of cocoa or the bulkiness of the jungle elephant?' and added that

If the answer be in the affirmative away with voting, election, electoral college and all the other cumbrous provisions of the New Constitution. All you need at Mapo is the cocoa exporter's 10-ton scale to pick out the six heaviest tax-paying *Citizens* of Ibadan to go into the Western House of Assembly.[2]

The Bulletin, which can safely be presumed to come from the hand of Adelabu, demonstrates why the Greater Ibadan Unity Grand Alliance failed to preserve its unity in an electoral situation. Its division was not over party loyalty but over the local issue of who was to control the government of Ibadan itself. For years the group of educated, wealthy, Christian and now aging men which included Obisesan, Sanda, Adeyemo and Akinfenwa had dominated Ibadan. Now another group, some of them better educated like Akinloye, more of them Muslim like Adelabu and Adeoye, less wealthy perhaps, but much more willing to engage in party politics with the chiefs and the mass of the people, had emerged to challenge this dominance, linking the I.P.P. and the Egbe Omo Ibile to do so. The forthcoming reform of the Native Authority meant that open conflict was imminent, and in a sense the nominations for the final election to the House of Assembly were the first round of that struggle.

On Monday, 10 September 1951, the Intermediate College met. The 152 rural and urban members elected in the primaries met with 22 chiefs and Councillors from the Native Authority to elect 85 of their number to go to the Final College. Some 167 of them signified their wish to go forward, and of the 85 elected, 75 were known to be I.P.P. supporters. The 'Big Men' had suffered a crushing defeat, and among those eliminated were Sanda and Obisesan, the two Members of the old House from Ibadan Division, Oyesina, Dr Agbaje and the Rev. Alayande. Among those who went forward were Adelabu and Akinloye.

The I.P.P. now set about drawing up a list of six final candidates, in conjunction with the Egbe Omo Ibile. Four of these seemed generally agreed upon – Akinloye, Lanlehin, Moyo Aboderin and Adegoke Adelabu. The others were much disputed. A general feeling was growing that the Christians had dominated Ibadan politics for too long, and a new 'Ibadan Muslim Party' had begun to circulate leaflets to this effect.* Bello Abasi, eager that the two open places on the list be filled by Muslims, pressed the candidature of two of his associates, B. A. Adeoye, who had recently been a member of the Ibadan N.C.N.C.'s delegation to the party's Kano Convention, and S. D. M. Busari, a clerk in the Native Administration. When the list was considered again on 16 September, the four were accepted without trouble, but the last two places had to be left open. The I.P.P. then completed the list without further consulting the Egbe, choosing two Christians, D. T. Akinbiyi and S. A. Akinyemi, a retired Police Inspector who was now the Manager of the Ibadan General Service Company. Thus Adelabu saw the tables reversed on Bello Abasi.†

On Monday, 24 September, the eighty-five members of the Final College from the city met the thirty from the rural areas to elect the six Members of the new Western House of Assembly from Ibadan Division.[3] There were twenty-one candidates, but it was the six I.P.P. men who won, with the following votes:

M. Aboderin	82	A. Adelabu	61
A. M. A. Akinloye	81	D. T. Akinbiyi	61
S. O. Lanlehin	67	S. A. Akinyemi	59

The solid bloc of I.P.P. votes had held together sufficiently to elect its men, though individual factors obviously counted for something, with two candidates out-distancing the rest, and Adelabu tying with his old patron. No matter where he was placed in the top six, however, he was now a legislator, entitled to place 'Honourable' before his name, and, perhaps most important from his point of view, to the salary of £300 a year that went with the office, not to mention the unofficial advantages, pecuniary and otherwise,

* The Muslim Party held its inaugural meeting on 30 July. It was supported by the Chief Imam, Muili Ayinde, and by Adelabu's friend, Councillor Oke, but it enjoyed only a brief existence.
† The Egbe's version of the story, as given by Bello Abasi in an interview in April 1966, was that four of the six nominations had been allocated to the I.P.P. and two to the Egbe. It was originally intended that an oath of support for the six men chosen was to be taken at the Ibadan Central Mosque, but the representatives of the I.P.U., which had also agreed to accept the six, never appeared. Finally, the Egbe and the I.P.P. swore a Yoruba traditional oath with kola nut and alligator pepper, but the I.P.P. broke it.

that might result from his enhanced status. With two-thirds of his working life gone, Adegoke Adelabu was thus launched upon a political career.*

Not that there was any time for resting upon laurels. The elections to the new Native Authority Assembly were scheduled for 22 October, and they were obviously going to be a bitter struggle between the I.P.P. and the I.C.C., with the latter trying to revenge its defeat in the regional elections and supported now by the disappointed Bello Abasi and the Egbe Omo Ibile. In the first week of October the I.P.P. launched an intensive campaign. Adelabu was very active in this, taking as his main platform the accusation that the Citizens' Committee had been instrumental in getting the Olubadan suspended, and had advocated the separation of the Northern Districts, an accusation which, if generally believed, would certainly win the local elections for the I.P.P. On 6 October, Adelabu, Aboderin and Adegoke Akande (a trader and contractor who had contested against the I.P.P. official candidates in September) held a meeting at Olugbode Quarter. One of the crowd was E. A. Sanda. After Adelabu had spoken, Sanda took up the main point of his speech, which was an attack on the role of the I.C.C. on the lines already mentioned, asking whether or not it was true that at the time in question I.P.P. leaders had themselves been members of the society thus accused. In reply Adelabu again attacked the I.C.C. and Egbe Omo Ibile, and again alleged that the former had petitioned for the suspension of the Olubadan and for Northern separation. Sanda asked to see the relevant document, and was joined in this request by Chief Salami Olugbode, who was chairman of the meeting. Adelabu refused, the crowd became excited, and his supporters then stoned Sanda and his car, chasing him away. The incident, comparatively minor though it was, heralded similar incidents to come, and it announced to the old guard that a newer, rougher, less dignified star had appeared in the firmament.

A last attempt to reconcile the I.P.P. and I.C.C. was made at a meeting at Mapo Hall on 11 October, with Chief Salawu Aminu, the Ashipa Balogun, in the chair. The prime matter at issue was the allegation against the I.C.C., made especially by Adegoke Adelabu, that it had petitioned for the separation of the Northern Districts. The I.C.C. leaders were confident of their position, believing that Adelabu had over-reached himself and could not produce a relevant document. In a good-humored speech E. A. Adeyemo offered to give £500 to anyone who could prove the allegation. Some of

---

* Though it can hardly be said that he never looked back. In November 1951 and again in September 1952, he applied for posts with the Ibadan N.A., first as Chief Tax Clerk, then once again as Administrative Secretary; either of these jobs would effectively have prevented him from following an elective political career. (B. K. Cooper to Adelabu, 13 November 1951 and Adelabu to I.N.A., 13 September 1952, A.P.)

those present were nervous, remembering perhaps what had happened to
E. A. Sanda at Olugbode Quarter on the 6th; Chief Olugbode himself, Chief
Yesufu Kobiowu, the Ekerin Balogun, and Alhaji Y. S. Ola Ishola (who the
day before had resigned from the I.P.P.) urged that the alleged petition
should not be read at the meeting, but should first be shown to a committee
of chiefs. This would have covered up for Adelabu, and Sanda, who was also
present, protested that 'If you do not allow the reading of this petition, it
means you, the Chiefs and Mogajis, are either concealing falsehood or trying
to shade our opponents' fault.'[4] The chairman asked for a copy of the petition for examination outside the meeting. Adelabu, with his back to the wall,
had to refuse, but gave what he called 'reference headings' for the consideration of the chiefs. With this they had to be content, and the meeting came
to an inconclusive end. On the next day it was announced that the Native
Authority elections were to be postponed indefinitely, since the Hayley Committee had been unable to agree on the number of electoral wards, and in the
following decline of campaign activity Adelabu was saved from further embarrassing attentions. The issue which over the next three months brought
him into increasing prominence was the relation to the national parties of
the I.P.P. following its electoral victory.

Since elections to the House of Assembly were still to be held in Lagos,
where five Members were to be directly elected on 21 November, and in
Benin Division, where the election had been postponed because of disturbances, there was considerable doubt as to which party would hold a majority
of House seats. The N.C.N.C. had been sure that a majority of the Final
College victors were committed to it, while the Action Group had sought to
make sure that they would in fact declare for the new Western party once
elected. On 26 September the *West African Pilot* had claimed thirty-seven
for the N.C.N.C., Action Group twenty-eight and Independents seven. On
the 28th, however, the *Nigerian Tribune*, in an editorial entitled 'The Strife
is O'er...', claimed forty-two of the seventy-two known results as Action
Group victories. In this situation the final commitment of the six I.P.P.
Members was of great importance. For about two weeks after the final
election the policy of most of the six seems to have been to deny a close
affiliation with any party, but rather to talk of co-operation, giving the impression that they would stick to the original decision of the Grand Alliance
and support the N.C.N.C., rather than the Action Group. The *Tribune*
quoted Akinloye on 26 September as saying that 'the I.P.P. is an independent political party, NOT affiliated to the N.C.N.C.', and as pointing out that
the I.P.P. contested the election in Ibadan in its own name, not as an ally of
anyone.*

---

* This is true. Only the Action Group and the I.P.P. had officially filed lists of their

On the other hand, the *Defender* on the 29th, reporting an interview with S. O. Lanlehin, represented the party as much more committed to the N.C.N.C. Lanlehin was quoted as saying that 'The I.P.P. is an independent party, though not affiliated to the N.C.N.C., which pledges its co-operation with the nation-wide organisation – N.C.N.C. There was no time the I.P.P.'s successful candidates stood on the platform of the Action Group neither was there any plan or desire to co-operate with or affiliate to the Action Group.' Lanlehin was also reported as having resigned from the Action Group. On 1 October the *Defender* described the I.P.P. as 'an annex of the N.C.N.C.'. On 2 October the *West African Pilot* published a declaration of allegiance to the N.C.N.C. which it said had been signed by all six Ibadan legislators.

If the *Pilot* correctly represented the facts at this time, Adelabu's commitment to the N.C.N.C. was no doubt genuine, but it was becoming increasingly doubtful for the other five, for by the second week of October they were moving rapidly towards the Action Group. Already on the 6th one of the founder-members of the I.P.P. had announced in a letter to the *Tribune* that he was leaving the N.C.N.C. and joining the Action Group, and this was evidently a straw in the wind. On the 11th there were significant developments. The *Tribune* and the *Daily Service* each published a photostat copy of the signatures of thirty-nine Members of the new House of Assembly under a declaration of allegiance to the Action Group. None of the six Ibadan Members had signed, but this list now made it quite obvious which way the wind was blowing. The attraction of being on the winning side was very great, and, moreover, the party which would form the new Government of the West could hold out the inducement of ministerial portfolios, one of which might well go to an I.P.P. legislator. The *Defender* certainly had little doubt about this, for on the same day it published a letter by 'Omo Oke' accusing Akinloye, Lanlehin, Aboderin and Akinbiyi of going back to the Action Group, and suggesting that their example might well be followed by Akinyemi and Adelabu.

From this point onwards the *Defender* reversed its attitudes towards the I.P.P. and the I.C.C. On 18 October, in an article entitled 'History of IPP Men to Be Given Soon: IPU Digs Out 1920 Files', it declared that 'Political circles observe that the IPP has not been fair to the "old brigade" sons who had rendered voluntary services in the cause of the nation.' In this article a particular target was made of Adelabu, accusing him of ingratitude to his former patrons:

Making references to personalities who are sincere, a quiet-natured trader said that in the case of Mr. Adelabu, the IPU had been very generous to him.

candidates in the Final Colleges; the N.C.N.C. had not done so, remaining content to declare that most of the candidates supported it.

The IPU (Study Circle) contributed to his scholarship while Adelabu was at the Yaba Higher College.

That was when the UAC offered him feepaying scholarship, but was not responsible for maintenance and clothing.

Members of the I.P.U., he said, paid a guinea or more each to finance Adelabu's education. On the 19th the *Defender* again returned to the attack, reporting Bello Abasi as saying that the I.P.P. was committed by virtue of its membership of the Grand Alliance to something more than just co-operation with the N.C.N.C., and complaining that 'The type of politics the IPP is trying to introduce is exactly the type that will ruin Ibadan.' He also accused the I.P.P. of being 'very cunning and disrespectful to the elders of the town'.

On Saturday, 20 October, the I.P.P. held one of its weekly general meetings at Bere Court No. 1 to discuss statements of allegiance which the N.C.N.C. had now asked to be signed by all those supposedly elected as its supporters. That morning the *Defender*, reversing the line it had taken towards Adelabu on the previous two days, described him as the only one of the six I.P.P. legislators who had not crossed to Action Group, and George Cowan commented in his editorial that 'it is a cock-fight between one man and five of his colleagues. That man is Adegoke Adelabu, an unadulterated N.C.N.C.er, who is reputed to be made of tougher moral stuff than lucre or promises of ministerial posts can buy.' The meeting was inconclusive. Adelabu attacked the I.C.C., which had just launched a campaign in connection with the local elections, meeting with a rough reception in the process. Akinloye called for extra effort now that these elections had been deferred. It was reported that the executive had called an emergency meeting the day before to consider the new hostility being shown by the *Defender*. However, no concrete decision was taken on the most important question of the allegiance to the N.C.N.C. The excuse was used that there had not been sufficient time for discussion since the allegiance forms had arrived, and that opinion was divided. Akinloye, obviously playing for time, again promised co-operation with the N.C.N.C.*

The fact was that the I.P.P. was now incapable of a collective decision, and the question of party allegiance was resolved individually. On the 26th the *Tribune* published a new list of forty-five Action Group Members of the House of Assembly, and this time Moyo Aboderin of Ibadan was included. On the 30th it announced that Lanlehin, the I.P.P. Treasurer, had also declared for the Action Group. On 5 November the I.P.P. published a press release in the *Defender* which attempted to preserve a myth of collective

* He repeated this promise again in an interview with the *Defender*, which it reported on the 23rd.

action. Aboderin and Lanlehin were said to have declared for the Action Group on their own initiative, and were on the other hand prepared to accept the party's collective decision on co-operation with the N.C.N.C. The other four legislators had signed pledges of co-operation prepared by the executive, but not, significantly, the formal N.C.N.C. pledges of allegiance. However, the I.P.P. was irrevocably split. Adegoke Adelabu and his supporters apparently ceased to attend its meetings after that on 20 October, and from this point on we can really speak of two I.P.P.s, Adelabu's and Akinloye's, the latter faction being the larger and including the other four Members.

This had been a crucial period for Adegoke Adelabu, and, looking back on it a few months later, he saw how important it was. Having become so far involved in politics that he had been elected to the new House of Assembly, he was then faced with a tremendous decision. With the advent of party politics, with the future development of Western Nigeria obviously to be dominated by the conflict between the N.C.N.C. and the Action Group, should he stick to his original commitment to the former or join his five fellow-Assemblymen on whatever path they chose? As he put it in his book:

Before me lay a great decision which would dictate the tenor of my future political career. It was significant. Either to line up with the other wavering five, maintain our solidarity and save our local party from disintegration; or to redeem my solemnly pledged word of honour, follow my convictions against all odds, contribute my quota to the Unity of Nigeria, and assure Freedom to the suffering millions of my countrymen.[5]

He did not find the decision easy to make and he turned to an analogy to the Yoruba rejection of the child in favor of the mother to express his dilemma.

I had many sleepless nights. I was torn between two loyalties. The Ibadan People's Party is dear to my heart. It is the child of my creation. It is the Army of Young Progressives against an opulent reactionary Old Brigade. But Nigeria is dearer to my heart. She is my mother, the Author of my beginning. It is only in her timely freedom that the unbroken line from Adam, of which I am just a link, can be kept unbroken. If I sit idly by, while the ship of state is sunk by the enemy, I, and all other passengers, will go down to the bottom of the sea with her. If my child dies and I live long enough I may bear another. If my mother dies I shall go through life a wandering orphan. My mind was made up. The tarred road of expediency leads to ultimate destruction. The thorny road of principle leads in the end to salvation.[6]

Thus the issues and the electoral organization which had originally given birth to the I.P.P. were absorbed and transcended by the new situation created by the holding of elections and the beginning of the devolution of power by the British. The elections were fought in Ibadan — as they were throughout the country where there was any contest at all – on local issues. Considering the state of development of the political parties, with the N.C.N.C. just beginning a complete re-organization and the Action Group scarcely launched, nothing else was possible. The crux of the matter, from the point of view of the future political development of Nigeria, was the choice of party allegiances made by the new legislators. In the East and North the decision proved relatively simple. In the former, the N.C.N.C. had no effective challenger, and all but a handful of Members of the new House of Assembly supported it. In the North the new Northern People's Congress, which came into existence at the end of September 1951 after the primary elections had been held, was nevertheless created in time to ensure that those men finally elected were all at least passive sympathizers of the new party. Only in the West was the issue in doubt and a real choice open to the new legislators.

Why did Adelabu make the choice he did? On one level the answers are all reasonably explicit in the quotations already given. Laying down 'The Faith of a Nationalist' late in November, he made the answers clearer.

I am not in the N.C.N.C. because I believe its leader, Dr Nnamdi Azikiwe is an indispensable superman or because I, for one moment, underrate the unique contribution of the Yorubas to Nigerian progress.

I am in it because from a dispassionate and realistic survey of the National political scene, I am convinced beyond all reasonable doubt that judging from ideology, quality of leadership, past performance and capacity for growth and adequate competence, the National Council of Nigeria and the Cameroons is the only Party that can deliver our beloved fatherland from the yoke of British imperialism, organise a democratic Republican Socialist West African Commonwealth dedicated to the welfare of the masses and put West Africa in her rightful place in world politics.[7]

On another level one can see that it was not merely his ideas which distinguished him from his five colleagues. He had been an odd man out in the leadership of the I.P.P., neither an established Ibadan figure like Aboderin, Akinyemi, Lanlehin or Akinbiyi, or someone who had scaled the academic heights like Akinloye. He was valuable to them because of his energy, the fluency of his tongue and his pen, and his wide range of contacts, but they had found him difficult to work with and never really trusted him. In this respect, an interesting picture of him was painted by Chief Akinbiyi in a two-part article published in the *Nigerian Tribune* late in December.[8]

For the sake of peace in the party we had to brook a lot of insults from Mr. Adelabu. . .He would often rise in the midst of a meeting, with Mr. A. M. A. Akinloye, LL.B., B.L., in the chair, and yet have the audacity to say that there was none who was as bookish or as intelligent as he in the party. This is not an occasional practice, it is a regular one known to all the regular members of the I.P.P. Everything that Mr. Adelabu does is none such, he is *sui generis*...We had learned to tolerate his garrulity and insolence because outside the fold he would be dangerous with our political rivals closely pressing upon us at the heels, and with the gullible masses of Ibadan who are ready to swallow any false doctrine. Thanks to the few discerning elders both in the I.P.P. and in the masses. They have often impressed me that they realise that an old ass knows more than a young colt. Would to God that our erring brother Adelabu realise that all liberty that transgresses the rights of another is a despotism...It will be fair that I make a formal acknowledgement of Mr. Adegoke Adelabu's valuable contribution to the I.P.P. He is highly intelligent and dynamic. But he needs curb his egoism which often distorts his vision and which tends to make him self-contradictory.*

Here we can see the reverse side of Adelabu's almost boundless self-confidence – the adverse effect which it could have upon those who felt themselves to be his equals or his seniors.

Nevertheless, it was this quality which also sustained him in adversity, clearing his vision to make a decision which immediately brought him to the public attention, for along with his stand on principle, he saw that to stand alone as the strong man of the N.C.N.C. in Ibadan would mean not eclipse but in fact greater prominence than was to be obtained as one of six Action Group Ibadan legislators, the most important of whom was bound to be Akinloye.

It was also fortunate for Adelabu that he was taking the decision which earned him special attention from the N.C.N.C. while the party was attempting to consolidate the re-organization which had been set in train in May. In his report to the Kano Convention at the end of August the National Secretary, Kola Balogun, had claimed an enrollment of 50,000 individual members in four months, grouped in about 150 branches.[9] By early November the Ibadan members of the party could see local evidence of this national

---

* Akinbiyi also sent this article to the *Defender*, which published it with some changes but under the title 'I Defend Myself', which caused him to complain in the *Tribune* on the 22nd that 'The title, "I Defend Myself" is opposed to the spirit of my article, because rather than take up a defensive attitude, I am writing to educate the public.' His tone toward Adelabu also became more acerbic. He called him an 'unprovoked Zikist hireling who is not satisfied with prostituting his own intelligence and selling his manhood; but who, with his malicious wits and uncharitable temper is besmearing honest and conscientious fellow citizens with the mud'. The *Defender* gave back as good as was given. In its editorial on the 24th, entitled 'How Dare you Akinbiyi!', in which Adelabu's pen can perhaps be discerned, it commented that 'No wonder the Stygian torment which the title "I Defend Myself!" has generated on the wandering mind of Akinbiyi. For, wherever is it known that political turncoats and jelly-fish have a defence to make for treachery?'

growth. When the Ibadan party executive met on 9 November, it was in the knowledge that the new Western Provincial Headquarters had just been opened in Oke Bola Street, and present at the meeting for the first time was a newly-appointed permanent party organizer.

The following day Adelabu travelled to Lagos for a conference of the Western Region N.C.N.C. in the Tom Jones Memorial Hall on the 11th and 12th. This was Adelabu's first appearance outside Ibadan as an N.C.N.C leader, and it was crowned with success. When the conference elected the new Western Provincial Working Committee, which was to be responsible for the Western Region, he became its Secretary. Such were the fruits of his sudden rise to political prominence, emphasized perhaps by the fact that he was one of the few Assemblymen among the forty delegates. In the late afternoon of the 11th he also spoke at a party rally in Campos Square, sharing a platform with such well-known figures as Kola Balogun and A.B.I. Olorun-Nimbe, the Mayor of Lagos, and being fortunate enough to get his speech over before heavy rain brought the meeting to an end. The *West African Pilot* reported him as assuring the crowd that the Action Group did not control the new House of Assembly, and that all six I.P.P. legislators were N.C.N.C. supporters, which he must have known to be untrue.[10] During the conference itself he urged the delegates (according to his own report) to concentrate on Nigerian independence, not on winning political power, noting that if inspiration, organization and sacrifice were needed in the independence struggle he could see signs of the first but little of the other two. He also urged the party press to devote less space to Lagos and more to the hinterland.[11]

When Adelabu returned to Ibadan after a stay of two weeks in Lagos, he could feel well-pleased with his progress in his new political career. His statement that he had 'captured the imagination of the masses as the Strong Man of Ibadan and the Authentic Voice of the West' was exaggerated, but he had been elected to an important office in the Western wing of the party and had obviously captured the attention of the party leaders. Once back in Ibadan he was again caught up in the struggle between the two factions of the I.P.P. His article, 'The Faith of a Nationalist', was published on 1 December, the same day the other five Ibadan Assemblymen made their first public avowal of their Action Group allegiance by attending a rally of that party at the Ibadan Boys High School, provoking Adelabu to write a long article, 'A Stab in the Back', published in the *Defender* two weeks later.[12]

The first part of this article reviewed the equivocating allegiance of the other five I.P.P. leaders to the N.C.N.C., challenging them to deny that they had been elected because it was generally believed that they were ready to co-operate with the N.C.N.C. In the second part 'all patriots' were called upon 'to rise up like one man and save the good name of Ibadan from calumny and ignominy' by joining hands 'to discipline or destool any disloyal representatives we have mistakenly enthroned'. The third part is the most interesting, for it represents the first attempt by Adelabu to extend his views on Ibadan and its local issues into a general view of the new political conflict emerging in the Western Region as a whole. On the other hand, it represents what was to be his lifelong tendency – to see all issues ultimately in terms of his position in Ibadan. Thus he claimed in his article that

The irreconcilable antipathy of the trueborn Ibadans to the Action Group is not based on sentiment or personal animosity.

It has its roots deep in factual reasons of historic ethos and psychological congeniality. It is a fundamental antithesis between two philosophies, two ideals, two ways of life.

These ways of life were those of the Ijebu Yoruba (Obafemi Awolowo's people) and the Ibadan Yoruba. The former he characterized as 'petty, aggressive, boastful, parochial, individualistic, combative, self-assertive and intensely jealous of better-favoured people', the latter as 'co-operative, patient, large-hearted, compromising, instinctively communalistic, slow to mobilise for a fight, but irresistible in action'.

Adelabu was making, then, the link between the Action Group and the Ijebus which came to be part of the political stock-in-trade of the party struggle in the West. The fact that not only Awolowo, but S. T. Oredein, A. A. Akinsanya, S. O. Shonibare and other founders of the Action Group were Ijebus gave some basis to the belief that the new organization was an 'Ijebu' party. The Ijebus were unpopular in other parts of Yorubaland, with a reputation as 'smart operators', and in Ibadan memories went back to the days before 1893 when the Ijebus had stood across the trade-paths to the sea and Ibadan's supplies of guns and powder. It proved convenient, therefore, for Adelabu now and in the future to arouse Ibadan feeling against the 'Ijebu' Action Group, and put less emphasis on non-Ijebu leaders of the Action Group like S. L. Akintola, from Ogbomosho, or Bode Thomas from Oyo.*

Adelabu had become the most prominent N.C.N.C. leader in Ibadan, and parts of the stranger element and the N.C.N.C. newspaper now rallied to his cause. On 17 December the *Defender* published a letter by J. G. D. Onwuka,

---

* It was probably about this time that Adelabu also planned a long biographical article on Awolowo entitled 'Obafemi Awolowo – Apostle of Disunity, By Adegoke Adelabu – Man of Destiny', in which the Action Group leader was to be characterized as 'The Upstart', 'The Ascetic', 'The Robot', 'The Confusionist', 'The Capitalist' and 'The Villager'. (Manuscript notes, A.P.)

a leading member of the Ibo community in Ibadan, headed 'Adelabu – Man of Iron Will', which stated that 'the chiefs and commoners, old and young, must be grateful to God for having sent a man Adelabu whose dynamic principles in leadership are superb'. He had demonstrated his leadership two days before when he had organized an N.C.N.C. rally at Mapo Hall, which was to have been addressed by Dr Azikiwe and the four other N.C.N.C. Assemblymen for Lagos, who had swept the board in the election three weeks before. At the last moment the five were prevented from leaving Lagos, and the crowd at the meeting had to be content with speeches from Adelabu himself and from J. Sale Sule, the President of the N.C.N.C. Western Working Committee. However, a week later another rally was held, this time attended by Azikiwe, and other N.C.N.C. luminaries.*

Part of the struggle within the I.P.P. which was an element in the N.C.N.C.'s concern with Ibadan was the fact that the Native Authority elections had still to be held, and Adelabu had still to decide on his tactics in regard to them. With the I.P.P. now divided, the I.P.U.–I.C.C. and Egbe Omo Ibile became more active. On 15 December, the same day as the N.C.N.C.'s rally, they held a joint mass meeting at Mapo. A resolution was passed, requesting the reinstatement of the Olubadan by 1 January, even if the reformed N.A. constitution was not in force. This was signed by the Balogun, ten other senior chiefs, the Quarter Representatives and the Iyalode and other women chiefs. On the 18th a delegation waited on the Senior District Officer to press this demand. As might have been known to some civil servants, the Government, as it announced the following day, had already decided to reinstate the Olubadan, thus giving the I.C.C. and the Egbe Omo Ibile something very tangible which they could claim as achieved largely by their efforts. Adelabu and his cohorts were clearly upset over this development, going so far as to give over £50 to the Olubadan to reassure him of their support, and contemplating a boycott of Ladimeji who they felt was countering their influence with his father.[13] Nevertheless, when it was announced on the 28th that the local elections would be held on 31 January in the forty urban wards finally decided on by the Hayley Committee, the political balance in Ibadan had already swung back from the I.P.P. to its rivals. Adelabu was quick to perceive this, and to realize that at the local level his best hope now was to bring his faction of the I.P.P. back into alliance with his former allies.

The problem was that they were pitted against each other at the Regional

* The *Tribune* reported on the 24th that 'All the NCNC could claim that evening as their audience were a collection of Ibo Civil Servants and their neighbours all in Western shirts, and shorts or trousers'; Adelabu was not the only one writing in terms of cultural divisions.

level where the first meeting of the new Western House of Assembly was scheduled for 7 January. This would be the final test of strength of the two opposing national parties and their Ibadan adherents. On 5 and 6 January a conference of the N.C.N.C. Assemblymen was held at Mosley Hall. It was claimed that forty-one attended. If this was so then almost half of them knew secretly that at the final reckoning they were with the Action Group. Nnamdi Azikiwe was still apparently full of confidence; in typical vein he cited Dickens, Seneca and J. R. Lowell, declaring 'we have won resounding victory in the Western Provinces, by firmly entrenching the N.C.N.C. as an undisputed majority party in the House of Assembly'.[14] As Adelabu recorded, events in the N.C.N.C. ranks on the eve of the opening of the House scarcely bore out Azikiwe's optimism, and the next few days were to bring him a series of cruel shocks.

Far into the previous night manoeuvring, negotiation, bargaining, pleading, persuasion, remonstration, argument, threat and ultimatum went on at fever pitch. Party leaders, party whips, party executives, party managers, party members, Obas, and friends ran helter and skelter. Oaths, imprecations, swearing on juju and promises rent the air. Wives lay lonely, awake on beds, expecting distressed husbands undergoing inhuman ordeal. Tired private secretaries were rudely woken from slumber to type out impromptu undertakings to do or not to do certain acts. The Battle of Wits swayed to and fro as the night gradually rolled away.[15]

The victors were revealed at the opening of the new House of Assembly on Monday, 7 January 1952, attended by the pomp and circumstance usual on such occasions. The First Battalion of the Nigeria Regiment provided a guard of honor, opening prayers were offered by Bishop Akinyele, and there was an address by the Lieutenant-Governor, Sir Chandos Hoskyns Abrahall. The Action Group, however, was intent on demonstrating their victory. Entering behind their leader, Obafemi Awolowo, and wearing their party badges, the forty-nine Action Group legislators insisted on sitting in one bloc, although the official seating arrangements would have mixed together N.C.N.C. and Action Group Members for this formal occasion. On the following day three more N.C.N.C. Members 'crossed the carpet' and joined the Action Group, reducing the N.C.N.C. to twenty-seven. Thus it was clear that the Action Group would possess the posts of Ministers of the Western Region Government. Awolowo was to become Leader of Government Business and Minister of Local Government, while Azikiwe, Adelabu and their minority of N.C.N.C. associates would form the parliamentary Opposition.

When the N.C.N.C. met to survey its ravaged ranks, Adelabu claimed to have turned them into a determined band with precisely the egoism which had alienated his I.P.P. colleagues.

At this juncture arrived the supreme moment of my life, thus far. At a private meeting, when discussions were definitely taking a defeatist turn, I got up. In a few well chosen sentences of deep emotion and biting sarcasm, I asked, 'where are the fanatical ideologists, the resolute crusaders, the heroic martyrs? They have been squeezed out by the well-tailored and pleasant mannered. Without them the Liberation Movement is doomed to failure. As a revolutionary socialist, I see in the present debacle a heaven-sent opportunity to purge our ranks, purify our creeds and rededicate ourselves to the service of Nigerian Freedom. Without a rude setback to the slow onward march of our forces, Revolutionary Risorgimento will not oust Progressive Reformism. I advise all those who seek material gains and the spoil of office to move over into the other camp whilst there is still time. So far as I am concerned if Dr. Azikiwe and myself alone are left, I will go on fighting to my last breath. I am very happy.'

The effect was electric. Speaker after speaker got up and reechoed my sentiments. Joy and cheerfulness replaced gloom and despondency.[16]

From that fateful Monday and Tuesday, then, emerged a hard core of N.C.N.C. legislators who remained loyal to their party. Most of them were from the Mid-Western provinces, Benin and the Delta, which were the non-Yoruba areas of the West. Adelabu, as one of the few Yorubas who had resisted the blandishments of the Action Group, was thus made even more prominent.

The defections on the 7th and 8th were not the only blows which the N.C.N.C. was to suffer at this traumatic time. At the meeting of the Assembly on 8 January those Members who wished also to sit in the central House of Representatives in Lagos put their names forward. The Assembly was to select from among these the specified number to go to the center. The N.C.N.C., which controlled all five Lagos seats, felt it essential that Nnamdi Azikiwe should go to the center, and the constitutional provision being that only two of the Lagos Assemblymen were to be chosen, the two candidates decided on by the N.C.N.C. were Azikiwe and Adeleke Adedoyin. When the moment came to sign the nominations book on the 8th, however, Olorun-Nimbe, who had recently been re-elected Mayor of the Lagos Town Council by its N.C.N.C. majority on the understanding that he would not attempt to go to the House of Representatives, suddenly put himself forward as well, whereupon the remaining two, T. O. S. Benson and Haroun P. Adebola, followed suit. Had the N.C.N.C. controlled a majority in the House, it could have selected the center representatives from Lagos regardless of the Lagos delegation's internal confusion, as a matter of party discipline. However, since the Action Group was in fact in the majority, it could now decide which two Lagos members remained in the contest. Although Benson and Adebola withdrew, Olorun-Nimbe would not. On Thursday, 10 January, therefore, he and Adedoyin were elected to the House of Representatives by the Action Group majority, with fifty-one and sixty-seven votes respectively; Dr Azikiwe got twenty-seven, and Adelabu, as a candidate for one of the Ibadan Division seats, received only twenty-five.[17] When the House adjourned, a meeting at the Catering Rest House managed to persuade Adedoyin to resign from his new position and in the middle of the afternoon he announced that he would do so, apparently on the understanding that in return Olorun-Nimbe would relinquish the Mayoralty of Lagos in his favor. Olorun-Nimbe balked at this, and next day Adedoyin announced in the newspapers that he had withdrawn his resignation. Nnamdi Azikiwe was still denied the opportunity to go to the center.*

The Action Group was exultant. The *Nigerian Tribune* published an article on 14 January entitled 'The Ruins Of An Egocentric Politician' which gloated over 'the plight of Nnamdi Azikiwe last week, when the remnants of his thunder-struck disciples led him out of the Western House in a gloomy procession'. For his part, Adelabu took heart from the reception accorded to N.C.N.C. Members outside the House by a group of students from the University College – 'Spurned by our corrupt contemporaries, we were the hope of a Greater Tomorrow.'[18] Nevertheless, it could not be denied that this thwarting of Nnamdi Azikiwe was a severe blow to the N.C.N.C., and, as will be seen later, to the Macpherson Constitution.

On 18 January the House met again to vote its approval of the list of new Ministers, submitted to it by the Lieutenant-Governor, but drawn up by him in consultation with the Action Group leaders. The N.C.N.C. minority did not make an issue of these nominations; Awolowo's was approved, for example, by sixty-eight votes to four, with six spoiled ballot papers. Only A. M. A. Akinloye, who now appeared to be getting his reward for declaring for Action Group by being made Minister of Agriculture, was objected to seriously by the N.C.N.C.† Adelabu declared that 'Of all the people proposed I think Mr Akinloye holds the unique distinction of being the man most likely to be denounced by his people because of his inconsistency.'[19] Akintola ironically commiserated with the N.C.N.C., declaring that the 'lachrimal gland of this side of the House is unfortunately dry otherwise we would have

---

* Accounts of this incident may be found in Sklar, *Nigerian Political Parties*, pp. 116–118, and Anyiam, pp. 22–3. Both accounts take events to their conclusion, which it would be chronologically inconvenient to do here. Olorun-Nimbe was expelled from the party for his actions and Adedoyin left it for the Action Group in 1953.

† Akinloye denied that his ministry was a pay-off, stating that the I.P.P. as a local electoral machine was not a suitable instrument for the organization of legislative activity within a regional context and that the ministerial salary represented a considerable loss to him rather than a reward, considering his earnings of £7000 as a lawyer the previous year. (Interview with A. M. A. Akinloye, July 1963.)

shed some tears for them upon the loss of such a valued member'.[20] Akinloye's nomination was finally approved by fifty-four votes to twenty-two.

Adelabu had meanwhile to turn his attention to Ibadan affairs. The first meeting of the House of Assembly had set the seal on the rift in the I.P.P. and on 14 January the *Defender* announced the formation of an I.P.P. (N.C.N.C.), with Adelabu as its President; most of its other officers and committee members were comparatively young and unknown men. On the 15th the newspaper carried an article by Adelabu, 'Dividing Line In The IPP', the draft of which he had begun to scribble in the House of Assembly a week before, on his copy of the official program.* In this article he denounced the five for aligning themselves with Obafemi Awolowo, 'the man whose party bifurcated Ibadan greater republic, destooled the Olubadan and vowed to pass legislation allowing the whole of the much coveted land of Ibadan to be grabbed away by native settlers', and declared that 'In the year 2052 Ibadan will recall their names with unspeakable horror, virtuous indignation and merited and well-deserved contempt.'

On the same day both factions of the I.P.P. held meetings, that of the I.P.P. (N.C.N.C.) being enlivened by the appearance of A. M. A. Akinloye, who apparently had confused the two and come to the wrong meeting! When Akinloye finally arrived at the proper place his faction proceeded to expel Adelabu and J. A. Ajuwon, the Propaganda Secretary of the I.P.P. (N.C.N.C.) from their I.P.P. on a variety of charges. The last of these was 'Secret Co-operation with the I.P.P.'s Political opponent, the Ibadan Citizen[s] Council and the Egbe Omo Ibile.'[21] Adelabu now claimed an alliance of his section of the I.P.P. with his former opponents against Akinloye, who had himself met with representatives of the I.C.C. and Egbe on the 13th in an attempt at reconciliation. It was announced that Adelabu's I.P.P., the I.C.C. and the Egbe had now reconstituted the Greater Ibadan Unity Grand Alliance to contest the local elections at the end of the month. On Saturday, 19 January, a mass meeting of the Alliance at Mapo Hall heard Adelabu move a vote of no confidence in the five Assemblymen, supported by Bello Abasi and the Iyalode. At the same meeting, after speeches by Bello Abasi and B. A. Adeoye, the Alliance's allegiance to the N.C.N.C. was renewed. On the part of the I.C.C. component of the Alliance, this unlikely decision was almost certainly an unofficial one, made by the one I.C.C. officer involved in this meeting of the Alliance. As it was, the revived Alliance was largely the creature of the I.P.P. (N.C.N.C.) and the Egbe, of more value to them than to the I.C.C., as the election returns were shortly to show.

On 31 January Ibadan went to the polls to elect a Native Authority

* The draft is in the Adelabu Papers.

Assembly which was to act as an electoral college selecting members of the Council. Of an estimated 80,700 tax-payers eligible to register, only 6304 had done so during the period allotted in the second week of January; no one had registered at all in the new ward NW 7. Modern electoral politics had only begun to touch the surface of Ibadan, as in all other parts of Nigeria except Lagos and Calabar. There was no contest in 10 wards where Assemblymen were returned unopposed, no electors or Assemblyman in one ward, and 119 candidates contested in the remaining 29 wards, with a total of 61 elected seats to be won; Adelabu was not a candidate. Some 3954 electors actually voted (62.7%), and although the allegiance of some of those elected was uncertain, the Grand Alliance, counting I.C.C. supporters as its own, claimed about 40 Assemblymen as its supporters. On 4 February, when the newly-elected Urban Assemblymen met with ten junior chiefs and mogajis and fourteen elected members from the rural areas to select from among their number thirty-nine new Native Authority Councillors, the I.C.C. was able to control well over half of the Assembly, from which majority it proceeded to elect all thirty-nine Councillors. Thus the attempt to revive the Grand Alliance collapsed in face of continuing I.C.C.–I.P.U. control of local affairs. Both the I.P.P. (N.C.N.C.), which had failed its local government test, and the I.P.P. (Action Group) were left without local control.

The local elections may be regarded as bringing to a close a momentous year for Adelabu, one beginning in March 1951 in penury facing a thwarted career and ending in March 1952 facing a new life as a politician. Succeeding through force of circumstances and his own abilities in projecting himself upon the national scene through his chosen party, the N.C.N.C., Adelabu still had far to go. Within the N.C.N.C. he was a bright young man, a rising star, but he still ranked far below men like Ojike or Balogun and still had no basis of power of his own. In an article written just after his death, the editor of the *Daily Times* claimed that 'In an excited mood at the opening of the Western House of Assembly in 1952, he told me in an off-the-record remark: "I shall shake this House and I am determined to seize power in this Region." '[22] Nevertheless, whatever his ambitions, he was still not even master of Ibadan in 1952, although the fact that he could on the other hand no longer be ignored is borne out by the concerted effort his enemies made to discredit him during the second half of January. The *Nigerian Tribune* published five attacks on him in eleven days, accusing him of being Azikiwe's chief 'hireling' in Ibadan, criticizing his role in the Agbaje Agitation, and drawing attention to his ingratitude to his early patrons and to Akinloye. A letter in the issue of the 25th complained that Yoruba towns were being infiltrated by Ibos and asserted that Azikiwe wished to become

Mayor of Ibadan, with 'The irrascible rascal who goes by the name Adelabu' as his Deputy. An article on the 29th predicted that

The fall of Dr Nnamdi Azikiwe started in Ibadan. His utter ruin will come in Ibadan, will be ushered in by an Ibadan, and probably that man will be none other than Hon. Adegoke Adelabu. Zik has not known his man yet. He is rating his capacity for political intrigue too cheaply.

As we will see in later chapters, there is a sense in which this prediction was uncannily accurate, or almost became so. On 1 February Tunde Alaka, a relative and friend, but not a political supporter, of Adelabu, took up the same point in a much more balanced article on 'Ibadan Affairs', claiming that 'Adelabu has probably more brains than Zik. This will be the first time that Zik is working with one of the best brains Ibadan can produce, but with him who has not the folly of character.' And Alaka concluded with a prediction about the new star in the political firmament which, as will become apparent, could with a few changes of tense almost stand for his epitaph:

If Adelabu will only cultivate the 'unpleasant' habit of being sincere, of not thinking of self alone, of not being susceptible of doing anything for money, I think he stands a good chance of leading the country.[23]

CHAPTER 6

THE POLITICAL MIND OF ADELABU, 1952

> It is sheer impudence for over-dressed half-wits who have never read
> Thomas Paine, who have never heard of Robert Ingersoll, who confuse
> Thomas Jefferson with Marshal Joffre, to whom the name of Voltaire,
> of Rousseau, of Diderot, of Zola and of the Mills Brothers conjure no
> visions of heavenly bliss to poke their nose into the Freedom Forum.
>
> Adegoke Adelabu: 'The Case for a
> Militant Nigerian Nationalism', 1952

The elections of 1951 launched Adelabu upon his political career, and the
events of January 1952 brought him to some prominence in the N.C.N.C.
Yet, as we have seen, he was drawn into national politics if not by accident
then without any real intention. Insofar as his ambition before 1951 could
be termed political at all, it was strictly within the context of Ibadan affairs
and the intrigue necessary to secure for himself the post of Administrative
Secretary to the Native Authority. However, as part of his involvement, he
had written a number of newspaper articles and other documents in which
he began to rationalize his own position in terms other than personal ambition. Gradually during 1950 and 1951 he evolved a view of himself and his
role in public affairs, so that when, early in 1952, he found himself a national
figure of some standing, his evaluation of his new position was based upon
some store of existing ideas. He made a determined effort at this time to
analyze more closely the decolonizing nation of Nigeria and his own role in
politics, publishing a book, *Africa in Ebullition*, in May, and later that year
drafting a long speech, 'The Turning Point', which was more an essay on
the political situation in late 1952 than the text of a speech. At no other
period in his life had he time to produce so extended a reflection upon what
was happening in Nigeria.

Adelabu liked to portray himself as a man of ideas, but one who only at a
late date had sought to make them public. Only in 1950 had he published
his first newspaper article, 'Ibadan at the Crossroad: Plain Talk on Current
Affairs', which, he claimed, had proved a sensation.[1]

Already in that article, written while his political ambitions were still
limited to Ibadan, Adelabu can be seen assuming another of his favorite pos-
tures, that of the fearless critic and champion of principles:

I am in private life cheerful, urbane, and almost docile. But when it comes to a matter of principle I am forthright, uncompromising and almost brutally frank. I am a literary and sociological surgeon dissecting the body politic with the scalpel of Truth...Democracy is not government by an obedient, melodious chorus but by discordant shouts and mannerless yells.[2]

In January 1951, at a time when, as we have seen, his fortunes seemed at a very low ebb, he published a two-part article which considerably extended his claim to act as a social critic. Appearing in the *Nigerian Tribune* under the title 'Man, Ponder Over These Things' on 26 January, and concluding as 'Man, Think On These Things' on the 30th, he reviewed the world after fifty years of the twentieth century had passed, and presented the future as a choice between 'Universal Peace through a World Government' and 'Total Annihilation by Atomic Fission'. Referring to the power of the U.S.A. under Truman and the U.S.S.R. under Stalin, he painted a grim picture of the possible future.

Ponder what horrible fate awaits you if one of two frail mortals now living should give the deadly signal. Your flourishing cities will be wiped out, your homes ruined and blown to smithereens, your farms and countryside laid waste, your neighbours mutilated in millions.[3]

However, there was a choice. If the world were to be unified under one government, no matter whether capitalist or communist, 'Mankind will enter the age of everlasting holidays.' But, at the moment of writing, 'We are on the threshold of Extinction or the Millennium.'

War, Sex, Adventure, Science, Art, Mysticism and philosophy have offered themselves separately as idols claiming the adoration of man. They had all been discredited through failure to satisfy the inner cravings of the human soul.

Man recoiled from unbridled war as barbarism, sex as animalism, adventure as piracy, science as heartlessness, art as degeneracy, mysticism as day-dreaming and philosophy as mere abstraction. Effete separately, these seven schools of experience are the seven concrete aspects of Serial Organic Reality.

In this situation, what remedy was there? This was to be achieved by listening to 'a few courageous fools or grinning iconoclasts like Shaw, Wells or Adelabu', and the author had no doubt as to who was the greatest of these:

I am humbler than Shaw, physically stronger than Gandhi, more cultured than Stalin, older than Jesus, more educated than Shakespeare, more worldly-wise than Socrates and better tailored than Lincoln.

Moreover, Adelabu was determined to be heard. As he put it:

I will deliberately offend your stupid sense of decorum and consciously outrage your childish sensibilities; I will shout at the top of my voice. You must get up from slumber, perceive your house on fire and act before the conflagration consumes you.

And if he was heard, what might be the reaction? The article ended with a typical flourish.

Hardly known at the beginning of this half century, if we live to tell the tale at its close, I may become its symbol. Already I can hear a thousand rancorous voices threateningly exclaim, with clenched fists and set teeth, 'THE SUPREME ARROGANCE OF THE INTELLECTUAL SNOB'. Exactly.

This article has been quoted at length for a number of reasons. It shows clearly Adelabu's style of writing and of thought, broad in viewpoint despite his lack of travel, and always searching for synthesis and underlying patterns, usually in terms of the number seven. Above all, it shows the strength of his egotism and self-confidence, and his appreciation of these qualities in himself. Considering the situation in which he found himself at this time, we may regard it as a manifesto, as a public statement of his confidence in his own ability to survive, prosper, and make a name for himself.

Late in 1952, when the frustrations of being in political opposition had become apparent, Adelabu began to grope toward a new view of himself in politics. His cousin and political opponent, Tunde Alaka, who was now in London studying to become a lawyer, had seen *Africa in Ebullition* and had written to request a copy and permission to review it. In this letter he paid tribute to Adelabu's talents, pointing out that 'in spite of our political differences we have always recognised the innate worth of each other', and avowing that 'Not even in my bitterest moments against you have I ceased to harp on the same old note – that you possess a fund of potentials which only need some direction.'[4] This provoked a characteristic though good-humored effusion from his cousin.[5] Opening his letter by hailing Alaka as 'My young Uncle', Adelabu went on to point out that 'you are my junior in all things save an incurable propensity for proffering uncalled for advice'. 'I value you', he went on, 'as a study specimen of the Oscar Wilde–Byron type about whom I have read much and you little. You "cling" to me because even a drifting ship needs a reliable compass and chart for putting in at ports for revictualling.'

After treating his hapless cousin to more of the same commentary, he brought the letter to a close:

Look here, Tunde, you see I have pulled your legs with 1000 poisoned darts without bitterness and without malice. I have sworn never, never to take you seriously. You are a stupendous joke! The human weaknesses of your class are the cause of my distinction and willl be the reason for my immortality. Nature is ten times over-generous to Nigeria. It takes her 300,000,000 trials to produce one Gandhi and only 30,000,000 trials to evolve one Adelabu. My kingdom is no more of this world. With the Sword of the Spirit I shall liberate Nigeria from British Rule for the benefit of her 30,000,000 inhabitants. That achievement will outlast all buildings in stone and words and echo down the centuries.

Yours meekly but defiantly,
A. Adelabu

It is obvious from this letter that Adelabu, once involved in national politics, was rapidly able to extend his view of himself as a critic to the conviction that he had a mission. In doing this, in adopting the role of the nationalist whose mission was the liberation of Nigeria, he had to push his ideas to a point further than he had taken them before, and one at which he was somewhat uneasy about his position.

Adelabu had arrived, in fact, at a time in Nigerian history and at a point in the development of his own life when he was somewhat out of phase with the persons and the attitudes critical to change. He had usually viewed his personal relations with individual Europeans with some pleasure, rather than as the stuff of anti-colonialism. He had not been caught up in the nationalist emotion aroused by Nnamdi Azikiwe in the 1940s as had many other young men, and in 1944, at the age of twenty-nine, when the N.C.N.C. was founded, he was preoccupied with career and family, unlike such men as Kola Balogun, who was twenty-two, or Anthony Enahoro, who was twenty-one. They might be considered his juniors in the Yoruba value system, which placed emphasis on deference to age, and they had not made definite commitments to careers as he had, but they were nevertheless gaining seniority over him in the political movements they had entered before Adelabu had made his basic political judgements. Thus he tended to view his general position in terms of his basic relations with his employer, as when, in a letter in which he admittedly had the strongest possible incentive to portray himself as a friend of the United Africa Company, he wrote of the deterioration of labor relations as a result of the activities of Nduka Eze, the Marxist union leader and nationalist:

In 1945 Nduka Eze was an unknown junior clerk in the singlet factory...Men of my class who escaped zikification [*sic*] during adolescence were then the steadying influence preventing the [U.A.C.] Workers' Union from falling into the control of the extremists.[6]

While he had complained of the white man's influence on his own education and on Salami Agbaje's career, it was not until March 1951, in the unpublished article 'Ibadan Has Turned Over a New Leaf', that he specifically attacked imperialism.

Once projected into the Western House of Assembly and decisively committed to the N.C.N.C. he found his previous localism unsatisfactory and sought to portray himself much more definitely as a nationalist. In search of a personage to emulate, he added Nnamdi Azikiwe to his pantheon of model world figures. Thus he described the impact of 'Zik' on Nigeria in 1937:

Then one day a strange thing happened. A cargo boat docked at Lagos. There stepped on shore a middle-aged African. He was tall and stately, neatly dressed and bespectacled with the agile gait of an athlete, the firm chin of a fighter, the fine hands of an artist, the sonorous voice, and the radiant smile of a suave diplomat, the penetrating gaze and majestic personality of a prophet and a leader. Nnamdi Azikiwe! Merchant of light and Hero!...He shed the light and our people found the way.[7]

Regarding himself as the equal of Azikiwe and the others, however, he asserted in another unpublished article drafted in 1952 that 'I am a ferocious debunker, an irreverent iconoclast, an intolerable intellectual snob and therefore dangerously un-Zik-ified [*sic*].'[8] Along with his view of himself as world luminary and critic of the follies of mankind, as well as a locally-involved politician, he felt himself to be a rather special kind of nationalist. As he wrote in the same draft:

I am a militant nationalist but I am neither a wild-eyed blood thirsty communist-anarchist nor an eccentric rabble-rouser. I AM RESPONSIBLE. I am a comfortable middle-class entrepreneur, the recipient of a modest income, the lord of my castle, a satisfied husband, a good father, the head of a household and a pillar of society. I am firmly rooted in the soil and I have a very big stake in political stability.[9]

Thus, he went on to sum up, 'Environment and Circumstances incline me to Complacent Conservatism, Conviction and Duty compel me to Militant Radicalism. I AM A PARADOX.'[10]

In approximately a year from April 1951, Adelabu had moved from a rather mild Ibadan-centered nationalism to one which involved him in a statement of a whole theory of history. For, in his view, the individual really had no choice in the stands he took, but rather was the product of historical circumstances. As he put it, almost at the end of the autobiographical section of his book,

Politically, as a West African in 1952, I am a radical socialist and a fanatical nationalist. This means that in other circumstances, I could have been other things. If I were an Englishman, I would be a Conservative; if French, a De Gaullist; if Russian, a Communist; Indian, on the left-wing of Congress; German, a Nazi; American an incurable capitalist and South African, a racial bigot.[11]

This being the case, it was important to know whether history itself followed any particular pattern of development. Adelabu held that it did, but by 1952 he had arrived at a form of determinism all his own. In his view, the 'Evolutionary Cosmological Scheme of the Universe' was based upon the significance of the number seven. To this proposition he devoted the last paragraph of his book:

There is a coherent Philosophy...which I hope to live to propound and amplify in all its ramifications. I am sure it will do for intellectualism what Einstein's General Theory of Relativity has done for Physical Science. That philosophy is built around the esoteric number seven, 7777777. In some mystical, mysterious, magical and mathematical way, a series of Seven Cycles seem to be at the very foundation of the Universe.[12]

From this principle, Adelabu deduced that there had been seven significant events in the history of the universe – the birth of the sun, then of the earth, the beginnings of life on earth, the appearance of mammals, the establishment of civilization, the first landing of Europeans on the West African coast and the declaration of protectorates by the European Powers 'over various portions of our country'. 'Today', he went on, 'we are on the threshold of the Atomic Age. Whither Nigeria in five years time?'[13] Between each of these seven significant events and the next were seven significant intervals of time, beginning with five billion years between the appearance of the sun and that of the earth.

Seven important geographical areas, making up the 'Sociological Context of the World', formed the counterpart of the Evolutionary Cosmological Scheme of the Universe. These areas were North America, South America, Europe, the Middle East, Asia (including Russia), the Pacific and Africa. The last he subdivided into four parts, North, East, South and West. Each of these areas had its own particular history, culminating in special political forms for individual countries. England was distinguished by Socialism, the U.S.S.R. by 'Soviet Communism', China by 'Agrarian Peoples' Communism' and Australia by 'Adolescent Orthodox Liberal Democracy'. Nigeria was bound to follow the same pattern of evolution, for

It is these Revolutionary Movements...that compel us to become a People Renascent; to ASSERT, to DEMAND, to SNATCH, and, if necessary, to SMASH our way into FREEDOM, into Self-Determinate Sovereign National Independence.[14]

Nigeria, then, had to become independent within the next five years – 'Self-Government for Nigeria by 1956 is a Cosmological Imperative.'[15] It was to this end that Adelabu had now dedicated himself.

In examining Adelabu's ideas on the nature of History it would be absurd to pretend that they had any deep intellectual content. He was not even one of the large group of Nigerian political leaders who had university degrees, and often were lawyers by training. Despite his efforts and ambitions Adelabu never succeeded in joining that magic circle of 'been-to's', those who had been to Britain or the U.S.A. for their higher education. What ideas he had were acquired from experience, and from his wide, though unsystematic reading. He had put together his theory of historical development from a patchwork of reading, including (to cite some items from the bibliography in his own book) Wells's *Outline of World History*, Van Loon's *Story of Mankind*, R. G. Ingersoll's *Lectures and Essays*, Sir Arthur Eddington's *The Nature of the Physical Universe*, and Bernard Shaw's *Intelligent Woman's Guide to Socialism*.[16] To this he added the idea of predestination – derived presumably from his Islamic faith – and also his concern with numerology, particularly with the significance of the number seven. The source of this last concern cannot be traced; probably its origins are to be found in popular Muslim beliefs. In this, as in the whole of his mental make-up, Adelabu was 'a living laboratory of my age', at the last resolve still rooted in traditional culture, but a product also of the highest level of Nigeria's colonial educational system which had stimulated him mentally without apparently offering him a sufficient challenge. Adelabu's problem was that of the extremely intelligent pupil in a system which by its very nature was unable, and probably unwilling, to cater for his needs, and who lacked the resources to go abroad for the university education from which he might have benefited greatly.

Be that as it may, whether the source of his ideas was a feeling of personal deprivation or some wider perspective, once launched upon his political career, he was determined that his country should be free. What was needed to redeem her from her bondage was not one, but seven revolutions.[17] First came the Intellectual Revolution, 'a planned predetermined concerted effort to disregard, disobey and violate the accepted rules and regulations of Formality and Orthodoxy'. Once this was accomplished 'The mentally emancipated...become malleable stuff in the hands of the chosen Revolutionary Political Leadership', and the Political Revolution could be carried out and independence won for Nigeria. The Economic Revolution must follow next, for 'A free People without assured means of Livelihood are not really free', and to achieve this there must be 'a balanced agricultural-industrial economy'. At the same time there must be a Social Revolution, to which Adelabu attached great importance, for 'political freedom unaccompanied by a Social Revolution is a sham and a snare. It will be the replacement of a White Officialdom by a Black Oligarchy. The new condition of the masses will be worse than their old situation.'[18]*

* This passage is a remarkable foreshadowing of events in Nigeria between indepen-

From these first four revolutions the last three, Cultural, Ethical and Spiritual Revolutions would result. The first two of these taken together would restore the pride of the African in himself, in his traditional culture, and in his traditional moral values, which had been corrupted by 'European Materialism'. The Spiritual Revolution is the least easy to understand. Adelabu described it as 'the most real but the least substantial', and 'the sum-total of our achievements in all other fields', and concluded that

It is fate. It is destiny. It is all-in-all. It is endowing Mother Nigeria with the WILL-TO-BE. We shall ride to Freedom on its crest.[19]

However confident Adelabu may have been that the tide of History was with him, when he wrote these words none of the seven revolutions had yet taken place, though he had high hopes that his book would considerably advance the Intellectual Revolution. Indeed, the independence movement seemed, as he looked at it in 1952–3, to be declining rather than riding to Freedom on the crest of the Spiritual Revolution. In both *Africa in Ebullition* and his draft speech written later in 1952, 'The Turning Point', there is a strong sense of 'the Revolution Betrayed'. The book opens with an introduction which describes and analyzes the N.C.N.C.'s failure in the 1951 elections in the West, when it saw itself robbed by the new Action Group of the victory of which it had been confident. This Adelabu described as 'a Blessing in Disguise', giving the party an opportunity and incentive to reconsider and reassert its fundamental principles, which *Africa in Ebullition* was, in fact, an attempt to do. In his speech he set himself the task of reviewing the history of the party over a broader perspective, seeking to find the point at which the tide turned against it, and pointing out that 'A Party without constructive criticism lacks the toughness of fibre, the fighting stamina and the dynamic poise needed for sustained political warfare.' 'The Party', he went on, 'must be extolled above its leadership, the Country above the Party and Freedom above Friendship. A desperate disease requires a desperate remedy. Hence, I have called this the Turning Point.'[20]

In Adelabu's view, then, the N.C.N.C. was suffering because it had deviated from its basic principles. As he put it,

When we abandoned our principles our good fortune deserted us. The Struggle for Nigerian Freedom started with the enunciation and PRACTICE by the leadership of the correct ideology...Then at an unfortunate hour during our painful journey to our goal temptation came. We succumbed to the lure of the flesh, the sweet cadence of expediency, the alluring comfort of material goods, the glittering prizes of good society. From that moment failure dogged our steps.[21]

dence and the military coup in January 1966, and a refutation of the myth sedulously fostered in Britain and the United States of Nigeria as the model of democracy in Africa.

Tracing the course of events since the foundation of the party in 1944, Adelabu singled out the general strike of 1945 as 'the first test for the New Ideology', and concluded that 'it emerged triumphant':

The momentum generated by the Victorious Strike swept the Liberation Army into the Nigeria Wide Tour and the London Delegation. Once again victory. But the first signs of the corroding malady reared its head. There was bickering, quarrelling, fault-finding and misunderstanding.[22]

At this stage it was the 'militant youths', 'the first graduates from the school of the new ideology', who saved the day. Active in the labor movement and dominating journalism, 'They lashed and scorned social respectability, scoffed at Religion and avoided family bondage. They missed the degenerate genteel culture of the Higher learning and were destitute of the social polish of the Upper Crust. They were virile, able, daring, blunt, disciplined, honest and steel willed – ideal vanguard for a Revolutionary Movement.'[23] Adelabu singled out certain successes of the Zikist Movement (for it was to this that he referred) in 1949–51, and described the period from the publication of Herbert Macaulay's pamphlet 'Justitia Fiat' in 1921 to the speech by the Zikist leader Osita Agwuna, 'A Call for Revolution', in October 1948, as 'one upward Curvature of Success for the leadership of Nigerian Freedom'. In this portrayal, the activities of the nationalist youth paralleled Adelabu's description of the role of the 'Youth' in Ibadan during the Agbaje agitation, when they 'in fifteen months of whirl-wind campaign extorted political advancement which threw into insignificance the result of 17 years of slow motion by the Old Brigade'.[24] On the national level, however, the successes and exertions had led to the 'Great Betrayal of the Youths Militant', which, along with the electoral failure in 1951, marked the nadir of the N.C.N.C.'s progress – 'The Betrayal of Youths Militant and the Election Tragedy at Ibadan are the Alpha and the Omega of one and the same Story.'

If the Revolution had been betrayed, then who were the traitors? Who were the enemies of the liberation movement? The leading contender for the title of foremost enemy was, of course, the British administration, but Adelabu's attitude towards the colonial rulers of Nigeria early in 1952 was still a mixed one. We have seen this manifested in his early life, particularly in his education and business relations, and it can now clearly be seen extending into his politics. Although he denounced the British as Imperialists who must be forced to surrender their control over Nigeria, Adelabu also went out of his way in his book to pay tribute to what he regarded as the British achievements in his country: 'I make bold to assert that the Nigerian Connexion with the Protecting Power has not been an unmixed and continuous tale of woes and miseries.'[25] Asserting that 'We are privileged to take a cooling draught from the thousand-year seasoned wine of British Culture, British Ideals and the British Way of Life', Adelabu paid tribute to 'the services of the British men and women to our country', especially the missionaries, 'honest and sincere' administrators, and 'skillful and conscientious' technicians. 'Too many narrow-minded enthusiasts', he concluded, 'in an impatient and misdirected if well-meaning endeavour to storm the citadel of Imperialism, accuse all white men of coming to our shores for solely predatory purposes. To this view I do not subscribe. The case for Freedom can be better put without distortion or exaggeration.'[26] At this point we are reminded again of Adelabu's good relations with many individual Europeans, and of the importance in his early life of men like Powell, Richardson, Haig and Booth.

The Action Group was another obvious potential target, although not as much in his book as one might expect. Writing there, his main charge against it was that it had intervened in the West for purely material motives:

The Action Group cannot by any stretch of the imagination lay pretended claim to be a political party or even a nationalist organisation. Its name accidentally is more sincere than its leadership, its handful of power-thirsty followers and its larger impromptu mob of middle-class mercenary fellow-travellers. It is a Group who have ganged up hastily and temporarily for a specific Action – the cashing-in on the Colossal Bribe offered in the form of empty fake Ministerial Appointments to noisy and troublesome agitators, by the Imperial Government in Nigeria.[27]

On the other hand, he could envisage for it ultimately a positive place in the Nigerian political system:

I should have liked to see the Action Group, under a more auspicious title, as a national Liberal-Conservative Movement with branches all over the country, instead of burying its head in the sands of the Western Region and playing into the hands of our common enemy, the Imperialists. It would then be serving a useful and necessary national purpose as the Rallying Point for the Aristocracy of Birth, Wealth and Individual Excellence, and the other natural stabilising forces of Society...A Parochial Regional Party is a curse. A Liberal Reformist party for the conservation of our heritage is a desideratum.[28]

In his draft speech he made a few references to the Action Group directly, but his attitude to it had begun to harden. From his point of view, nothing it had done seemed to indicate that it was going to give up its parochialism and regionalism. Now he labelled it 'Reaction Triumphant', and 'the Party of Arrogant Tribalism'.[29] By late 1952, his real enemies seemed to him to be those who stood for tribalism and regionalism, seriously menacing the unity of Nigeria for which the N.C.N.C. stood. The policy of his party in this respect had changed completely in 1951, when, at its Kano Convention, it had come out for a unitary system instead of the federal form it had advocated since 1944.* This was primarily as a reaction against the Macpherson Constitution, which the N.C.N.C. interpreted as an attempt to weaken the nationalist front by introducing the regional principle and decentralizing the measure of political power which that constitution offered to Nigerians for the first time. Already in *Africa in Ebullition*, Adelabu had distinguished between the Imperialist, manufacturer of 'Pakistanic Constitutions' and fosterer of 'balkanisational tendencies', the Isolationist, who personified the Northern Region, and the Tribalist.[30]

Two other enemies of the Revolution remained to be distinguished. One of these was the group of men which Adelabu felt had become prominent since 1951, which had in fact been given its opportunity by the Macpherson Constitution, tribalism and regionalism, and which had tended to find its natural home in the Action Group. Some of its members were the traitors who had gone over to that party after the elections, his five fellow-legislators from Ibadan and the rest. In more general terms, they were the opportunists and place-seekers, 'materialists who regard Nigerian Freedom as an entertaining and paying hobby'.[31] It was their influx in 1951 which had made Nigerian politics a competition for jobs, money and other benefits, pushing all questions of principle into the background. He painted his most vivid word-picture of them under the heading 'The Nouveau Riche' in the draft article 'The Case for a Militant Nigerian Nationalism':

These pot-bellied plutocrats are mainly deserters from the Liberation Army or innocent political greenhorns recently rescued from lowly retirement in outlandish villages. By their continuous processions in new hats, gay ties, fashionable suits, shining limousines, the New Look and all the gaudy paraphernalia of the 'nouveau riche' they impress none but fools. Rather they parade their immaturity in juvenile joy over mechanical gadgets and irresponsible pre-occupation with tremendous trifles. They are a pleasure to small children, an entertainment to young girls, the envy of the Junior Service, an embarrassment to their soberer supporters, an eyesore to the intelligent public, the laughing stock of veteran nationalists and just the keg of gunpowder needed to set fire to the seething discontent of the oppressed masses of Nigeria.[32]

Behind all these others, however, lurked yet another enemy, and this the most dangerous of them all. In his book Adegoke Adelabu singled out the Apartheid policy of the Nationalist government of South Africa as representing the ultimate challenge. In 'The Turning Point' he developed this

---

* For a discussion of the N.C.N.C.'s stand on federalism in the period 1944–51, see Coleman, *Background to Nationalism*, pp. 324–5 and 347–9.

theme further. Regionalism, he claimed, was 'an excuse to prolong our bondage until Apartheid creeps slowly from the South. . .until the burning light of Freedom once more relapses into the everlasting doom of a New Slavery'.[33] It was in the name of opposition to Apartheid, then, that the campaign for Nigerian independence was to be waged, for 'by conniving at the atrocities' of that system 'Britain has forfeited her right to continue her tutelary role anywhere in Africa.'[34]*

Thus, in the period after his entry into national politics Adelabu analyzed the situation in Nigeria and tried to relate it to a view of the nature of History and of the imperatives which made it essential that his country be free. It was the N.C.N.C., of course, which was to be the principal instrument of the liberation of Nigeria from British rule. In his book, Adelabu commented that 'The National Council, as its name clearly shows, is a Nationalist Front. It is the common platform for nationalists holding a variety of shades of political belief.'[35] It was his stated hope, however, that 'the National Council will gradually purge its ranks of right-wing pseudo-capitalists and become a genuine Radical Socialist Party of workers, peasants and left-wing intellectuals'.[36] In order for it to do this, two things were of vital importance, the principles adopted by the party, and the nature of its leadership. In his opinion, by 1952 principle was becoming of more importance as the cement which held a party together than its leadership. As he put it, 'The Age of Personalities in Nigerian Politics is passing away. We must inaugurate the Age of Principle.'[37]

It was this which Adelabu felt to be his own special mission – to launch the Intellectual Revolution and restore Principle as the guiding light of Nigerian politics, raising the level of discussion above the sordid level reached in 1951–2. In this respect, he was concerned with his role as an 'artist'. As he wrote in 'The Case for a Militant Nigerian Nationalism':

As a politician I fight for the masses. Most of them are incapacitated by complete illiteracy from pleading their own cause. But as an artist I refuse to write down to the semi-literate uninformed public.[38]

* It was perhaps also in this context, and at this time, that he toyed with the idea of founding a 'West African Socialist Party', with its headquarters in his own house, the Taj Mahal, with the object of creating a federal union of West Africa made up of twelve constituent states, five of them parts of the former Nigeria. The twelve states were to be the Western, Eastern, Northern, Central and Cameroons (all former parts of Nigeria), Togoland (there is no indication whether or not this was to include French Togo), Dahomey, Ghana (he used the Nationalist name, rather than the Gold Coast), Liberia, Sierra Leone, Senegal and the French Sudan. There seems little reason for leaving out the Ivory Coast, Upper Volta, French and Portuguese Guinea and Niger – except for shaky geography – and the territories listed here do not form a contiguous area.

The most important product of his artistry, the statement of principles which was to be (to quote its subtitle) 'A Handbook of Freedom for Nigerian Nationalists', was, of course, his book, *Africa in Ebullition*. This he regarded as the product of sixteen years spent as a 'free-lance thinker, an economic adventurer and a political firebrand'. It was in his book that he sought to extend his discussion of principles to explore the relationship between principles and ideology, maintaining, in fact, that the latter was the medium through which the former governed political action, and that it was the possession of an ideology which distinguished a Party (which he wanted the N.C.N.C. to become) from a Front (which he held it to be in 1952).

The concept which he put forward as the future Ideology of the N.C.N.C. was Radical (or Revolutionary) Socialism.* As early as March 1951 he had described himself as a Socialist in an unpublished article:

True to the type of all native intellectuals who have grown from the soil of their fatherland, I am a Communalist – that rare West African replica of Churchill in England, Lincoln in America, Mao Tse-tung in China and Stalin in Russia. If this means anything at all it means that I am a Socialist (West African brand). I believe that our Communal Peasantry Economy should be gradually built up into a modern Socialist Industrialistic Economy without any intermediate stage of unbridled Capitalism.[39]

He did not develop his new concept of Radical Socialism in any detailed way to relate it to current Nigerian conditions. His discussion in his book of necessary reforms in the educational system, changes in agricultural policy and the need for industrialization was conducted without any specific refer· ence to it. In his chapter on 'The National Income', which takes as its main theme the need for a redistribution of the country's wealth, he did remark that 'The objective of Radical Socialism which this irreverent revolutionary enquiry is out to advocate and popularise is the relegation of the rich few to their rightful places in the background...'[40]

In 'The Turning Point' he developed this further, stating that in using the term Socialism,

The Intellectual Ideologist must enter into a pact-unto-death with the masses – Proletarians, peasants and petty traders – for the precipitation of the Political-cum-Economic-cum-Social Revolutions. The People and not a Ruling Caste shall inherit the State Property.[41]

Nevertheless, it is somewhat difficult to see Adelabu, who had spent so much time and effort attempting to make his way in the world of private enterprise, as a Revolutionary Socialist. There is no reason to doubt the

* The first term is used in *Ebullition*, the second in 'The Turning Point'.

genuine nature of his sympathy for the masses, the 'Silent Millions' as he called them, 'known by their wants, distinguished by their disabilities and conspicuous by their incapacitations', whose condition he eloquently and indeed movingly described in his book.[42] On the other hand, his ideas on Socialism were unsystematic, and tended to suggest a compromise with capital rather than revolution. Although he described the economic ideas in his book as being drawn from 'Marxian Socialism', he apparently had no direct acquaintance with any Marxist writings as one of his visitors noted with surprise.* As he himself explained – though in somewhat different terms – he preferred to express his radical sympathies without subjecting himself to the discipline of adherence to a particular doctrine:

An over-dose of doctrinaire socialism without a judicious admixture of progressive conservatism, of orthodox liberalism, and of that centre-stabilising process, leads inevitably to communism, to totalitarianism, to regimentation and to fanatical, ideological and doctrinal intolerance of opposition.[43]

Taken all in all, Adegoke Adelabu's treatment of 'Principle' or 'Ideology' as a necessity for the N.C.N.C. if it was to function effectively as a political party is incomplete. *Africa in Ebullition* had been written, he claimed, in order to remedy 'the atrocious absence of a written literature of the N.C.N.C. Principles'.[44] In discussing his analysis of the progress of the N.C.N.C. from 1944 to 1951 we have seen the great importance he attached to ideology and to its exponents, the 'militant youth', but it is difficult to perceive the content of that ideology, to discover if it meant more than the will to freedom. In a sense, Adelabu's concept of ideology does not accord with his more metaphysical propositions on the nature of History and its laws of development, which would seem to raise the question whether in fact the N.C.N.C. had need of any conscious ideology, if its historical role was as an expression of 'Nature's Universal and Immutable Law of Accelerated Motion'. Apparently, however, he did feel that there was some room for chance, or free will, or some such random factor; otherwise he would not have felt it necessary to fill the N.C.N.C.'s ideological vacuum and restore the principles sapped by the events of 1951–2. It is unlikely that he ever even considered the possibility of there being contradictions in his views. At this level of discussion, after all, he was to all intents and purposes self-taught, and his reading had been unsystematic and undirected, a fact which is reflected in the writing of his longer pieces, themselves often loosely constructed.

Similarly, his views on leadership, that other basic need of a political party,

---

* In a letter offering to exchange a volume of Lenin for one by Disraeli which the writer had left at Adelabu's house. Frustratingly, the letter is now incomplete, and we do not know who wrote it. (Unknown to Adelabu, 11 May 1952, A.P.)

contain conflicting elements. Views on the leadership of the N.C.N.C. in 1952 – as indeed for the whole of Adelabu's political career – meant in effect views on Dr Azikiwe. We have already seen the decisive importance in the development of the modern Nigerian nationalist movement which Adelabu attached to the return of Azikiwe in 1937, and we have also seen that he felt that he had himself escaped 'zikification', unlike many other younger men. Thus, while he expressed his admiration for the N.C.N.C. President, he tended from his first entry into politics to bracket himself with Dr Azikiwe as if they were equals, rather than leader and follower. He described their meeting in May 1951, when the N.C.N.C. leader made his triumphal entry into Ibadan, as one of 'two kindred souls', a 'Spiritual pact between East and West'. Speaking of the dark days in January 1952, when many N.C.N.C. members were defecting to the Action Group, he pointed out that 'only one man, besides myself, remained calm, serene, unmoved and unmovable. The Colossal Figure, the Massive Frame, the Gargantuan Edifice named Nnamdi Azikiwe stood between British Pakistanisation of Nigeria and Nigerian Unity.' 'What an experience', he went on, 'to be near a great man in a moment in history!'[45]

'The Turning Point' is perhaps even more revealing, for Adelabu intended this for his party comrades, not for public consumption.* Certainly he paid the customary – almost ritualistic – direct tribute to his party President:

Our leader is a child of Destiny, the Appointed of God, A Credit to our Race, the Common Property of all, the Hope of Millions, the Architect of our inevitable Victory, the Saviour of the Black Man and the Redeemer of our Country.[46]

On the other hand, in analyzing the failings of the N.C.N.C., he was highly critical of the leadership of the party. Declaring that 'THIS IS A TIME FOR STRAIGHT TALK', he intended to exhort his audience to 'place the blame squarely, frankly, directly and fearlessly where it rightly belongs at the very door of our leadership'.[47] In the circumstances of 1952 it is difficult to construe this as anything other than an indirect attack on Dr Azikiwe.

In this light, it is scarcely surprising to find that when Adelabu turned later in his speech to suggestions for restoring the fortunes of the party he made it one of his major recommendations that a new kind of leadership be evolved.

We must evolve a new leadership based solely on Heroism. Our new leaders must be men and women who are prepared to suffer for the cause of Freedom, who are prepared to endure loss of their properties and incomes, curtailment of their per-

---

* It must be remembered that quotations are taken from a first draft, and we have no detailed account of what was finally included in the speech when it was delivered.

136

sonal liberty, loss of their personal comfort and social position, to face privation, starvation and imprisonment, to lose contact with their home and families, to fight without hope of reward, if necessary to die but never to surrender or compromise. Presumptions to leadership based on birth, wealth, academic degrees, social prestige, professional status, oratorical powers and favouritism and preferment must be abrogated.[48]

Already in his book he had stated the need for what he called 'Spiritualistic Nationalists', those, in other words, who would carry forward the Spiritual Revolution. These would emerge as a result of a process of natural selection at the particular historical moment when they were needed, and Adelabu believed that the crisis in the N.C.N.C. in January 1952 marked that point. Writing about those who remained faithful to the party at that time, he described how

I noticed in the physiognomy of our thinning ranks, a common similarity of features – the compact build of the man of principle, the taut nerves of the athlete, the dreamy eyes of an idealist, the fine hands of an artist, the agile gait of a fighter, the ringing voice of leaders, and the restful composure of the faithful. . .I knew that Nature was busy with the selection, on the spiritual plane, of the few who would lead in the Struggle ahead.[49]

Later in the book, in a more extended discussion of this new type of leader, he contrasted them with the Materialists and the Intellectuals. Only the Spiritualistic Nationalists, 'the exquisite flowering of human genius', 'the reincarnated soul of their race', would be capable of forcing the British to grant freedom. The British would not be able to stand against them, for 'you cannot offer pecuniary inducements and positions of profit to men–gods who have deliberately chosen the Avenue of Poverty as the shortest route to the Hall of Virtue in the Square of Contentment'.[50]

There is no doubt that Adegoke Adelabu regarded himself as one of these specially-chosen leaders; indeed, in his description of the N.C.N.C. loyalists he seems almost to be drawing an idealized pen-portrait of himself. In his draft speech, 'The Turning Point', he includes himself as a matter of course among the '21 nationally acknowledged nationalists who are also very influential leaders of opinion in their various ethnic groups', who were to be grouped together as the 'Liberation Committee' which was to lead the nationalist movement into the next phase of its campaign.[51] Headed by Dr Azikiwe, this was to include 'the happy warriors, men and women, young and old, learned and simple, fluent and tongue-tied, who have refused to compromise, to surrender or to bow down to adversity'.[52] Not all members of the Committee needed to be drawn from the ranks of the N.C.N.C., for it must be 'a War-Time Coalition Cabinet representative of all regions from all walks of life'. These individuals were to be asked to serve by Dr Nnamdi Azikiwe, and Adelabu suggested twenty-one names, although he stressed that it was their representative character which mattered, not the actual persons named, so that there could be 'one or two adjustments'. For the East he chose Azikiwe, Mbonu Ojike, Osita Agwuna and Nduka Eze, with Eyo Ita and N. N. Mbile to represent the minority groups there. The West was to be represented by Kola Balogun, Adegoke Adelabu, Oged Macaulay and H. P. Adebola, with H. Omo-Osagie, Owetomoh Oweh and J. Sale Sule from the ethnic minorities. Abba Maikwaru, Aminu Kano and Habib Raji Abdallah would speak for the North, with Abubakar Zukogi and two others referred to as 'Belo' and 'Bida' from the Middle Belt.* Lastly, to represent the women of Nigeria there would be Mrs Funmilayo Ransome-Kuti from the West and Mrs Margaret Ekpo from the East.†

These, then, were the men and women whom Adelabu presumably felt to represent the cream of nationalist leadership, the potential 'Spiritualistic Nationalists' who were to lead the Political Revolution; indeed, his idea of a Liberation Committee was in a sense an attempt to create a revolutionary High Command, 'a core of responsible, incorruptible, ironsides rallying round their heaven-sent leader in the supreme crisis of their Nation'.[53] His

---

* Eze, the Marxist trade union leader, was not in fact from the East, but was a Western Ibo from Asaba. Ita, an Efik from Calabar, was the leading figure among the N.C.N.C. Eastern Ministers, Mbile was one of the most pro-N.C.N.C. Cameroonian leaders, favoring close links between the Cameroons and the East. Adebola was a trade union leader who had been elected as one of the Lagos Assemblymen in 1951. Oweh was a prominent Urhobo supporter of the N.C.N.C. from Delta Province. Sule, an Itsekiri and also from Delta Province, was a rather elderly teacher and President of the Western N.C.N.C. Maikwaru, Aminu Kano and Zukogi were leaders of the Northern Elements Progressive Union. Abdallah had been one of the most militant leaders of the Zikist Movement. 'Belo' is probably Bello Ijumu, a Yoruba from Kabba, another N.E.P.U. leader. 'Bida' is almost certainly Abderahman Bida, the Nupe pharmacist who was one of the N.C.N.C.'s strongest supporters in the Ibadan Sabo.

† In what at this stage could be little more than a flight of fancy, Adelabu also drew up a government for an independent Nigeria on the back of a page of his draft speech. He gave himself the portfolio of 'Economics', and allotted most of the rest to potential members of his Liberation Committee: Defence went to Aminu Kano, Transport to Abdallah, Communications to Zukogi, Works to 'Bida', Justice to Balogun, Education to Mrs Ransome-Kuti, Agriculture to Omo-Osagie, Health to Oweh, Information to Ojike, Labor to Eze, Local Government to Ita, Foreign Affairs to Mrs Ekpo, and Land to S. A. George, a Yoruba living in the Cameroons who had been a leader of the 1945 general strike and was a Member of the Eastern House of Assembly from that area. In a nomination which apparently caused Adelabu much thought, since the original note was crossed out and then restored, Dr Azikiwe was listed, not as Prime Minister, but – rather curiously – as in charge of 'Coordination'.

emphasis, however, reflecting his views on his own social position, was less on revolutionary zeal than on experience and responsibility. As he put it:

We shall not repeat the miscarried plan of our valiant Zikists. The enthusiastic but untried youths of the N.C.N.C. Youth Association may be good battalion commanders.* The Command of the Army of National Liberation can only be entrusted [to] the Veteran Corps of the Old Brigade. Any shortcut of using frantic school-boys is suicidal. I for one will be no party to it.[54]

It was not only the central direction of the N.C.N.C. which was to be reorganized. The whole party would have to be revamped, and there was no mystery about the principles involved. Adelabu approached the problem in a manner befitting a former U.A.C. manager. 'A full-time, well paid, well trained Administrative Service must be founded,' he urged, 'who shall regard political organisation as their vocation. We have no leisured class able to devote their spare time to party work. Politics as a hobby is slip shod, half-hearted, perfunctory and dilatory. We must recruit a hierarchy of secretaries, clerks, inspectors and managers, with good salary scales, attractive promotion prospects and a decent Bonus Scheme.'[55] To do all this the party must have money, for 'No human activity in the modern world can be carried on without funds.'[56] He therefore suggested the establishment of a 'Liberation Fund' of £25,000 to meet expenses.

Once it was properly led, financed, and organized, the N.C.N.C., Adelabu believed, would be in a position to take decisive action first against the British, behind whom lurked Dr Malan and the Afrikaner Nationalists. The action which Adelabu urged first was a program of civil disobedience against the British. This was to be entirely non-violent, along the lines of Gandhi's *satyagraha*, since 'Our enemies have all the coercive forces', and 'We have nothing but our indomitable spirit.'†

The party's second decisive action was to be taken electorally against the Action Group, whose emergence had become 'the stumbling block to the realisation of our Ideal of One Nigeria' and had shifted the political center

---

* The N.C.N.C. Youth Association was founded in January 1952, in a belated attempt to fill the gap left by the banning of the Zikist Movement almost two years before.

† The example of the Indian nationalist movement was obviously of great importance in Nigeria. Obafemi Awolowo has described how as a young man he obtained Indian pamphlets from 'an enterprising gentleman of Ijebu extraction in Lagos', and how by 1932 he was 'a fanatical admirer of the Indian National Congress, and of three of its illustrious leaders – Mahatma Gandhi, Pandit Nehru, and Subha [sic] Bose'. (*Awo*, p. 160.) At least two prominent personalities in Ibadan in the late forties and early fifties – Alhaji Fakmagandhi and Omilabu Gandhi – had gone so far as to incorporate one well known Indian name in their own. We may also note again Adelabu's identification of himself with the same person, as in the letter to Tunde Alaka quoted on p. 125. This whole subject deserves further research.

of gravity from Lagos to Ibadan. Adelabu therefore gave his view of the strategy to be adopted.

The East is our Home, the West our Battleground, and the North our Prize. Any party that captures a majority in East and West will be able to dictate terms to the North where in any case the spread of education and enlightenment will soon break the stranglehold of Fulani Feudal Autocracy.[57]

To this end he proposed the expenditure of £5000 on men and transport in 1953 to provide the Western N.C.N.C. with an adequate organization. This would have to be drawn from the Liberation Fund, which might also have to subsidize the West in 1954; from 1955 onwards he hoped that the regional party would be self-supporting.

Thus Adegoke Adelabu sought during 1952 to present his party not merely, in his own words, with 'a new ideology or system of thinking' but also with 'the course of practical steps to take'. It is typical of the man that he should have done this so soon after committing himself to a career in national politics. He did not follow up *Africa in Ebullition* and 'The Turning Point' with other theories or analyses. Instead, from about mid-1953 onwards he was to become more and more involved in the practice of politics, and he was to see the N.C.N.C. increasingly troubled by the very weaknesses he had diagnosed – lack of money and professional organizers, the absence of an ideology capable of transcending local interests, chronic indiscipline and the calling into question of the party's leadership. His involvement in all these issues will form a major part of the rest of our story.

CHAPTER 7

IN SEARCH OF A POLITICAL INSTRUMENT

Arguments have nothing to do with the actual achievement of freedom.
Adegoke Adelabu, May 1953

Although Adelabu was now a spokesman for his community in the Regional legislature, there were two severe limitations on his influence, neither of which he was to overcome as a legislator. He could not hope to match the prestige and influence of Regional Minister of Agriculture A. M. A. Akinloye or even that of the other four Ibadan legislators, who could speak with all the authority of the governing party. Nor did he have organizational backing in his constituency, since his faction of the I.P.P. was virtually inert after the elections to the Native Authority Council in February. Organizational uncertainty also marked his relationships within the N.C.N.C. Although he was Secretary of the party's Western Working Committee and had won considerable acclaim in its ranks as the only I.P.P. legislator to remain loyal to its cause, he was neither a nationally known figure nor was he esteemed by the party because of the votes he could garner or the seats he could deliver. As he came to realize with increasing clarity, advancing his political career and acquiring a share of the political power the British were willing to hand over to Nigerian politicians depended upon the ability to win votes and organize dominant parties. Although he had acted to some extent on this realization in the 1951 elections, and although both political parties were anxious to exploit existing contacts and make new ones to prepare for the expected extension of the franchise and direct elections, Adelabu spent a long and futile year testing the role of an opposition legislator as an efficacious political instrument and criticizing the organizational instruments created by others outside the legislature as useless.

In Ibadan neither the Action Group nor the N.C.N.C. could hope to prosper unless it could strike deeper local roots. The efforts by N.C.N.C. leaders in the first months of 1952 to make an impression on Ibadan were aided by the presence of Dr Azikiwe and a number of his lieutenants in the city during sessions of the House of Assembly. Thus Azikiwe took the chair at a lecture-meeting on 19 February for an address on 'The Spirit of the

North' by Aminu Kano, President-General of the Northern Elements Progressive Union, the radical party which had failed to capture any seats in the Northern House of Assembly. Adegoke Adelabu was chosen to introduce the speaker, and thus had his first meeting with the Northern politician who was to be associated with him in a dramatic stand upon principles more than five years later.

Although lectures by prominent men were frequent during 1952, they tended to appeal to the already converted and the native strangers, who were inadequate substitutes for properly organized branches engaging the loyalties of the mass of local citizens. Adelabu was well aware of this. As he wrote in his draft report to the Western N.C.N.C. conference in November, 'The Turning Point':

Efforts to use the Western Working Committee as an organising Committee for Ibadan branch were insistent but failed for obvious reasons...The illiterate and semi-literate masses in Ibadan today will fight shy of any local political organisation with obvious non-indigenous local leadership...It is a physical fact which only patient political education and time will correct.[1]

When the Ibadan branch of the N.C.N.C. elected new officers in the first week of March, native strangers were once again prominent: Oduyoye was re-elected President, and Abderahman Bida, from the Sabo, the First Vice-President. Possibly in response to this, for it was only two weeks later, a number of Ibadan sons from the Egbe Omo Ibile called what was described as a 'representative meeting' of the N.C.N.C. on 22 March; at the meeting were L. Ade Bello and Y. S. Ola Ishola, the Egbe's Secretary. They set up their own committee to press forward with the organization of branches in the urban wards, and just over a month later it was claimed that some twenty wards now had branches, with elected officers on the pattern of the N.C.N.C. 'Chapters' in Lagos.[2] It was intended to set up an 'Ibadan headquarters cabinet' elected by the ward branches, and the Egbe group also managed to persuade N.C.N.C. National Headquarters to appoint L. Ade Bello as full-time Organizing Secretary for Ibadan. To mark their progress Ishola and Bello Abasi called a public meeting on 26 April; this was attended by such celebrities as A. C. Nwapa, the N.C.N.C. Central Minister of Commerce and Industries, Oshilaja Oduyoye, Abderahman Bida and D. K. Olumofin from Akoko, who was rapidly emerging as one of the most active N.C.N.C. Assemblymen.

A further devolopment at this time was the inaugural meeting at the house of Alimi Adeshokan, a rapidly rising cocoa merchant who in 1954 was to become a Councillor, of an Ibadan branch of the N.C.N.C. Youth Association on 19 April. With members at first in only one ward of the city, it began to expand to others after a visit by a touring delegation from the Lagos branch and the holding of a rally in May, but something less than a mass base was ever achieved, for by November it still claimed only forty-five members in the whole of Ibadan.[3]

Adelabu was virtually – and probably deliberately – excluded from these organizational developments. After the election of new officers for the N.C.N.C. Ibadan branch in March he held no office in the local party, and his involvement seems to have been rather a mediatory one as Western Secretary; as he put it towards the end of the year, 'I have used all my tact to avert a crisis.'[4] It was not to be expected that he would be associated closely with activities sponsored by his former allies, Ishola and Abasi. Moreover, he believed that they were adopting the wrong approach in taking the N.C.N.C. Lagos organization as a model. Ibadan was a different case, requiring different methods. 'The clerical/trading/artisan/literate class who form 80% of Lagos only form about 5% in Ibadan and less in other places. Lectures fetch but limited returns, street campaigning little or nothing. The Lagos way will not succeed.'[5] He was thus in full agreement with the editor of the *Defender*, who in May denounced 'Zik-In-Town N.C.N.Cers' and demanded an end to 'empty debates and club house piffles on nationalism'.[6]

During 1952, Adelabu's only formal place in Ibadan politics was as leader of a feeble faction of the I.P.P., which with the Ibadan Citizens' Committee and Egbe Omo Ibile still maintained the Greater Ibadan Grand Alliance. Nevertheless, the Citizens Committee alone controlled the reformed N.A. Council, and this particularly highlighted for its members the problem of the relationship of the Ibadan Native Authority with the Regional Government. Some Councillors, including A. S. Agbaje, S. A. Oloko and Salami Akinfenwa, were already Action Group supporters, and in June it became apparent that there were tensions within the I.C.C. between the Action Group faction and the rest. The Council was accustomed to inviting Government Ministers and officials to discuss problems of cocoa trees, development and education. On 3 June, Minister of Local Government Obafemi Awolowo attended a special meeting of the Council. A. M. A. Akinloye joined him, without having been invited according to a broadside released by the Alliance. When Akinloye insisted on speaking, twenty-eight of the thirty-nine I.C.C. Councillors staged a pre-arranged walk-out; those who remained included Agbaje, Oloko and Akinfenwa. The release, 'Why the Ibadan N.A. Councillors walked out', claimed Akinloye was forcing the I.P.P. on the Council, whereas Awolowo was present in response to an invitation. Those who stayed were thus not simply supporting Awolowo, but refusing to continue doing battle with Akinloye and the I.P.P. group which had joined the chiefs in the Agbaje agitation.

When the Alliance threatened disciplinary measures against the dissidents, nine of them published a letter claiming that they had a 'special reason' for staying to hear Akinloye, presumably their affiliation with the Action Group.[7] Nevertheless, at a Council meeting on the last day of June, the I.C.C. suspended the membership of Agbaje and Akinfenwa for six months and another of their group for three. No minutes were kept of this meeting, but it is referred to in the minutes of 16 June when the standing rules of the Council were suspended to consider the aborted meeting 'as a matter of urgency'. A Special Committee including Chiefs Akinyele and Ogunsola and Councillors S. A. Oloko, Dr Agbaje and E. A. Sanda was appointed 'to deal with this matter' but no report of this Committee is to be found. Apparently it met with failure, for the matter was taken up outside the Council (and also outside the Alliance) in a meeting on 29 August arranged by Bishop Akinyele between representatives of the Alliance and Obafemi Awolowo and Akinola Maja, the Lagos businessman known as 'Father of the Action Group'. As a result of this meeting the Councillors were reinstated in the I.C.C., and, moreover, it was claimed that the differences between the Alliance and five I.P.P.–Action Group legislators had been settled. It appeared as if the Alliance was now swinging toward the Action Group. This was denied by Alliance leaders, who claimed that the role of Maja and Awolowo was only mediatory; T. L. Oyesina, for instance, stated that 'Dr. Maja's mission was a peaceful one and has only succeeded in bringing the four organizations in Ibadan together which were hitherto scattered as a result of the misunderstanding.'[8]

This assertion was in contradiction to the already open secret that an important section of the I.C.C. was now definitely aligned with the Action Group; the Ibadan party could not put off the decision on its relations with the national parties for much longer, however useful the Alliance might be as a holding operation against the day when hopefully the whole I.C.C. and the I.P.U., its parent body, might declare for the Action Group. On Sunday, 21 September, the I.C.C. met without the other Alliance members at Mapo Hall to consider a motion to allow individual members to affiliate with any political party of their choice. Oyesina and S. A. Oloko now proposed as a counter-motion what Oyesina had presumably delayed doing until he felt he could succeed in delivering these groups corporately to the new national party, namely that the I.C.C. should now so act. Although this was defeated, the acceptance of the main resolution clearing the way for individuals to declare their personal allegiances in the end proved to be sufficient, for the majority of the I.C.C. members did now come out for the Action Group, providing an important reinforcement for the five legislators and giving the Regional governing party a nucleus of members with organizational experience in the regional capital and formal control of its Council.

It is important to remember that the efforts of political parties to organize themselves during the period 1951–2 took place within a general context of similar efforts in other spheres to establish working groups through which Nigerians and Ibadans could channel their energies in dealing with the increasingly complex nature of emerging Nigerian society. Yet throughout this year stressing the building of organizations in Ibadan, Adelabu's political role was an ineffective one. During the first half of the year his main political arena was the floor of the Western House of Assembly, not the streets and markets of his native city. The House met only three times in 1952, in January, February and July; during each sitting he was one of the most active of the N.C.N.C. Members. Numbering only twenty-five, just under a third of the House, the N.C.N.C.ers had to fight hard to play the role of a parliamentary Opposition offering constructive criticism and alternative policies to those of the Action Group Government. If the majority of them contributed nothing except their votes, this was equally true of the Action Group Members, and was to remain true for both sides throughout the coming years. Yet on the N.C.N.C. side, Dr Azikiwe, H. P. Adebola the Lagos trade union leader, Festus Sam Edah the jovial businessman from Warri in the Mid-West, and Adegoke Adelabu strove to give meaning to their part of the proceedings of the House. Adelabu's first contribution from the floor, on 18 February, was, indeed, a defence of the right of Private Members of the House to introduce their own bills, and not leave this function solely to the Government.

On Thursday, 21 February, he rose during the debate on the second reading of the Appropriation Bill to make his first major speech. It was not a total success. He first referred to this 'unique occasion' following upon 'a century of twilight under the tutelage of the British Crown'.[9] He then embroidered on 'the evolutionary cosmological scheme of the universe we live in' and dealt at some length with some matters of policy. Officials, he said, must 'grasp the all-important fact that the four pre-requisites are Education, Agriculture, Industrialisation and the Africanisation of the Civil Service'. At this point, without having considered the Government's budget for the coming year which was the matter at hand, he was forced to sit down, the thirty minute limit for all speeches having expired. Azikiwe himself asked for his time to be extended, but the President of the House, W. M. Milliken, a British official, ruled that 'His time is up.'

This speech Adelabu used, almost verbatim, as a major part of *Africa in Ebullition.** In his next major speech, five days later, in the debate on the

* The speech is reproduced with only minor changes on pp. 26–37 and 47–60 of the

145

Development Estimates, he began to discuss issues with which he wished to be identified, particularly those which would cast him in the role of champion of the rural poor. His main target was the Development Officer, a post for which he had once applied himself, for 'many of these people that call themselves Development Officers are imported. They are so far away from the people and with the greatest amount of goodwill in the world, they are absolutely useless.'[10] Any program for rural development must fail unless constant contact was maintained with the farmers, and he called for more electricity, piped water and schools for the rural areas.

Although he was obviously enjoying his part as a legislator, he was already casting about for a wider audience, for even before delivering his first major speech he had decided to turn it into a book. The well-known Tika-Tore Press in Lagos offered to print 10,000 copies for £687, but this was obviously far more than Adelabu could afford.[11] The book was finally produced by the Union Press in Ibadan. Under this agreement, 5000 copies were to be printed, at a cost to Adelabu of £187. 10. 0d., of which £150 had to be paid in advance. He also had to supply the paper and the cardboard for the covers. On 15 March the *Southern Nigeria Defender* carried a front-page advertisement for *Africa in Ebullition*. There was a crisis which delayed publication, caused by the author's failure to deliver the promised paper, and although on 3 May he gave a public lecture which included readings from the book, it was not until the end of that month that it was on sale.

Adelabu was proud of his book. In a typical passage he described it as

an Ode to Liberty, a Guide to Nationalists, a Handbook of Freedom, a Grammar of Politics, a Revolutionary Manifesto, our Book of Revelation, an Encyclopaedia Nigeriana, the Voice of the People, a Challenge to Imperialism, an Indictment of Colonialism, an Abrogation of Gradualism, an Invitation to Youths, a Call to Arms, the Sacrament of Patriotism, a Psychoanalysis of the Nation, a Dissection of our Soul, an Answer to our Detractors, a Reaffirmation of Faith, a Plea for Unity, an Appeal for Understanding, a Rededication to the Struggle, a Bill of Rights, a Declaration of Independence, an Appreciation of Heroism, a Supplication for Sacrifices, an Atonement for Renegation, a Monument to Martyrdom and a Pact with Death.[12]

His estimate of potential sales was correspondingly grand. He spoke of selling 1,000,000 copies in twelve months, including 100,000 each in Nigeria, the U.S.A., China and the U.S.S.R., and a like number in South Africa, Kenya, Uganda and Tanganyika. Sales would be facilitated by its publication not merely in English, but also in French and Arabic, and in

book. Adelabu thus added much autobiographical and other material to what became a book of 113 pages. Even then, the printer did not find it possible to include his carefully prepared index of over 500 items, a copy of which is in his papers.

Hausa, Igbo, Yoruba, and Efik for the Nigerian market. At five shillings a copy, he calculated that this would bring him £200,000 minus cost of printing (at 3d. a copy) and paper.[13]

The reality proved very different. His plans for distributing the book were hopelessly impractical. The Rational Bookshop in Ibadan took one hundred copies, to be sold at 20 per cent commission, and presumably sales were best in the author's native town.[14] In general, however, his sales record book and various letters from agents which have survived reveal a gloomy picture.

A few of the more politically aware appreciated *Africa in Ebullition*. The author distributed some copies at the N.C.N.C. Convention in Lagos in August 1952, and in October Adelabu received a letter from Abubakar Zukogi, one of Aminu Kano's most active lieutenants in the Northern Elements Progressive Union, who had seen one of these. Zukogi was optimistic about the book's future, commenting that: 'You may not realize that your book is a rare gem and that in the near future it will be so popular and no nationalist will miss it in his library.'[15] But despite a Foreword by Nnamdi Azikiwe and the intrinsic merits of the book itself, the Nigerian reading public failed to respond to the author's exhortation on the back cover:

> Do you believe in Freedom for Nigeria in 1956?
> Are you prepared to deny yourself two bottles beer
> and pay the Price of Liberty?
>   OF COURSE, YES ! ! !
>   THEN BEG, BORROW OR
>   SAVE BUT BUY THIS BOOK
> 201 Doses of Poison for Imperialism
> 35,000 Shots of Dynamite for Liberty
>   for only
> 5/-   FIVE SHILLINGS

Five shillings might only have been the price of two bottles of beer, but it was more than a day's pay for a Government-employed laborer. In the end, Adelabu recorded a total sale of only 720 copies. Even without the commission to dealers this represented a return of only £180, not enough to cover his payment to the Union Press. Seven years after his death, a room in the Taj Mahal was still stacked with cases full of Poison for Imperialism and Dynamite for Liberty.*

His book, however, was but part of his effort to develop a public position for himself after his failure to emerge from the Agbaje agitation as a hero

---

* Adelabu kept a record book of his own sales and complimentary copies in his own hand, and remained convinced that his book was a potential financial asset. As late as mid-1957 he was still hoping to make £1000 from it in the coming year.

either of any of the Ibadan political groups or of the general public. During 1952 he succeeded in having his speeches in the House of Assembly reported in the *Defender*. After February, his picture began to appear frequently and in March the issue which carried the front page advertisement for *Africa in Ebullition* cautiously noted that it was 'understood' that Adelabu, the President of the reformed I.P.P., was 'gaining popularity daily with the youths and masses'.[16]

On 14 July the Western House of Assembly sat again, and for the next two weeks energetically debated a series of legislative measures and policy proposals made by the Action Group Government. Adegoke Adelabu, with a major statement of his views now in circulation, once again took an active part, and became better acquainted with some of the men who were to be his close political associates in future years. On the N.C.N.C. benches was T. O. S. Benson, a Yoruba lawyer from Ikorodu, near Lagos, a founder-member of that party (acting as Leader of the Opposition while Nnamdi Azikiwe indulged his interest in sport by attending the Olympic Games in Helsinki). D. K. Olumofin was also prominent, as were Haroun Adebola and Festus Sam Edah, the latter joined by such voices from the Mid-West as Dennis Osadebay, lawyer and poet, a Western Ibo from Asaba and another founder of the N.C.N.C. Similarly, on the Government benches were ranged some of Adelabu's future political adversaries: Obafemi Awolowo, now Minister of Local Government, staid, serious, a Methodist teetotaller, personally as well as politically in sharp contrast to Adelabu; Anthony Enahoro, a former disciple of Zik, who, like Adelabu, was a short man and shared his quickness of wit; and S. L. Akintola from Ogbomosho, Central Minister of Health, a wily opponent and crowd-pulling orator with his curious high-pitched voice.

Awolowo and his colleagues were faced with two main problems at this time: implementing the reforms which they had stated to be their policy before being elected, and finding a suitable relationship with the British officials who still held the key bureaucratic positions in the Departments and the Administrative Service in general. It was especially irksome to the new Nigerian Ministers, not only in the West but in the other Regions and at the center as well, that they had no direct control over the mainly expatriate civil servants in their Ministries, this being in the hands of the British heads of Departments. Added to these constitutional and administrative problems were the personal difficulties of a very sensitive situation, in which Nigerian politicians, given access to the seats of power for the first time, and forced to learn the routine of committee meetings and file-keeping were now also having to work with the 'imperialists'.*

* As witness the remark of one British official about his own Minister, S. L. Akintola,

The July meetings of the Western House of Assembly took the first steps toward reforms aimed at self-government.* Pride of place went to the Local Government Bill and the associated Native Authorities (Employment of Staff) Bill. For many years the reform of the Native Authority system in the West had been one of Obafemi Awolowo's main concerns; in 1947, while a law student in London, he had published a book, *Path to Nigerian Freedom*, which set out his views on this matter in some detail. Now, as Minister of Local Government and supported by a comfortable majority in the House, he was able to do something about it. The main proposal was far-reaching in its implications: it was that a system of local government councils should be set up, the majority of whose members would be directly elected on a tax-payer franchise; traditional chiefs might be members, but were never to number more than one-third of the total. The two bills together would provide the basis for a modern, democratic local government structure, but at the same time they implied a decisive shift of power from the traditional chiefs to the modern elite, and an extension of party politics through the medium of the new councils in a way which would bring the parties much more closely into contact with people's everyday lives.

Although the new system of local government this legislation brought into being provided the legal structure of the Ibadan Council which Adelabu was to control after March 1954, in 1952 he was involved in his party's opposition to it in the legislature. On 15 July he spoke in the debate on the second reading of the Native Authority Staff Bill, objecting to the provision for control by the Minister of Local Government over the appointment and dismissal of senior officials of the local councils, describing it as 'a hidden tool to bludgeon the Native Authority employees, to show them that the Minister for Local Government is all in all, that unless they toe the Action Group party line they must be ready for the consequences'.[17] The Opposition's main complaint about the Local Government Bill was that they had not had time to study it properly and weigh its implications, since it had only been published on 26 June. Led by T. O. S. Benson, they attempted to have the Second Reading deferred for three months. Adelabu spoke on the amendment, pressing for the deferral. The Opposition's delaying move was beaten in one of the few actual voting divisions in the House by fifty-two votes to twenty. In the debate on the Second Reading Adelabu spoke

in a personal letter to an expatriate colleague. 'As you well know there have been times when S. L. A. has nearly "driven me round the bend" and it was to me a real relief to be able to come across and seek your counsel and get matters back into their true perspective.' This sort of close contact between British officials was often a help in expediting matters, but could be a source of natural suspicion to new Ministers.
* There is an interesting assessment by Awolowo of his position at this time, and a discussion of his government's reforms in *Awo*, pp. 259–74.

again, quoting David E. Lilienthal's *Tennessee Valley Authority* and De Tocqueville's *Democracy in America*. Presciently he raised the problem of a situation in which one political party controlled the Regional Government and another a local council, and how the former might react to this – 'I want this point to be quite clear. We are reaching a state where we are giving much wider powers to party politicians than we gave to imported expatriates who had no axe to grind except to do their job and to retire on pensions.'[18] Although it might be held that this was a somewhat naïvely stated view of the role of the colonial administrator, he was again highlighting the problem of the transfer of power by a Colonial Office which was becoming increasingly concerned with withdrawing its direct control.

After four days of debate the two bills were passed by the House on 21 July, though in order to become law they had to receive the approval of the Central Council of Ministers and the Governor in Lagos, since Nigeria was not yet a true federation, with a division of legislative powers between centre and Regions. For the remainder of the sitting the Western House of Assembly devoted most of its time to considering various ministerial policy papers. Adelabu spoke in the debates on those for agriculture and education, once again acting as the representative of the peasant farmer; all Members of the House, he said, should live with the farmers for thirty days each year, just as Muslims fast for thirty days, in order to know at first hand the sufferings of the poor. A little later in the same debate he struck what was for him, despite his avowed Socialist beliefs, an unusually radical note, when he spoke of the heed to control the activities of foreign business enterprises – 'It is going to lead to revolution if the people find that the fruit of their labour is going to be reaped by people from overseas just because they bring some capital into this country.'[19] When the House debated the Government's proposal to provide free and compulsory primary education starting in 1955, Adelabu indicated that he was in full agreement with this. To deal with this problem, he argued, there were two essentials: compulsory, free primary education from the age of five, and a guarantee that at least fifty per cent of all new schools should be built in the rural areas, the last demand bringing the very rare tribute of applause from the public in the gallery. A policy of austerity must be followed to pay for all this, with limits on the salaries of Ministers, legislators and senior civil servants.

The assumption of his new role as legislator and as spokesman in the House for the underprivileged, without doubting the sincerity of his views, was, however, but one of his concerns. There was also the problem of projecting his political personality, for which debates in the House were not a very satisfactory medium. They did not receive very extensive press coverage and the attention paid him by the *Southern Nigeria Defender* dwindled after

March. Even then, as he had pointed out in his speech on educational policy, the illiterate masses took no interest in debates in the legislature, nor, as he was learning, in his new book, despite his wild optimism about its sales.

The House of Assembly was an unsuitable instrument with which to build his political career for yet another reason. His ebullient personality and his own special political style were ill-suited to the almost ritualistic, and to him cramping, maneuvers of the parliamentary system. Adelabu made some small effort in these early debates to make the appropriate courteous gestures, praising S. O. Awokoya, the Minister of Education, as capable of drawing up an educational plan for the whole world, and even congratulating A. M. A. Akinloye on his plans for Agriculture. However, in a clash with Obafemi Awolowo on 28 July, his biting tongue revealed his more natural pugnacity. The House was debating a bill to extend the life of the Lagos Town Council, in order to give time to apply the provisions of the new Local Government Act before elections were held there. The N.C.N.C. was opposed to this, on the general ground that no reform of Lagos local government (which it controlled) was needed. Supporting this line, Adelabu referred to Remo, Awolowo's home Division, 'a place nobody likes to live in, simply because those people who substitute intelligence for wisdom have had an unbridled power in that area to put into practice their nefarious philosophy of life'.[20] The Action Group leader took exception to this, and the incident ended with Adelabu lashing out at the 'fascist principles' of the Western Region Government.

By the end of the year, Adelabu was showing signs of disillusionment with his role as a member of the legislative Opposition. Reviewing the Opposition's performance in his draft speech, 'The Turning Point', he noted the National President's absence in Helsinki 'during the session to debate grandiose but empty Policy Papers and Reactionary Bills of Repression mis-named Reform Bills'. The Opposition fought these measures, yet was defeated, and for this Adelabu placed much of the blame on the leadership in the House of T. O. S. Benson, objecting to the way he had been chosen. Nor had the return of Dr Azikiwe improved matters, for with that 'we have once again sunk into a state of impotent stupor'.[21]

The floor of the House, then, was not the best arena for a man of Adelabu's temperament, nor was it the place from which he could win a following. There was, in fact, little hope elsewhere either. We have already noted that during 1952 Adelabu's activity in the Ibadan branch of the N.C.N.C. tended to diminish, rather than grow. The same applied to his membership of the Western Working Committee. Indeed, after the N.C.N.C. Western Conference, which was held at the Opera Cinema in Ibadan on 22 and 23 November, at which he delivered a version of his Secretary's report, 'The Turning

Point', he even ceased to hold that office, being replaced by Y. S. Ola Ishola.*
Oshilaja Oduyoye continued as President of the Western Working Committee with J. O. Fadahunsi of Ilesha as First Vice-President, and Chief
Humphrey Omo-Osagie from Benin as Second Vice-President.

Adelabu was experiencing the same disillusionment with party work that
he had felt in the legislature. In the draft of his report he observed 'quite
frankly' that 'your Working Committee have not been able to do anything
at all commensurate with the requirements, the possibilities or the potentialities of the role the N.C.N.C. ought to play in the Western Region of
Nigeria'.[22] Everything was lacking – paid staff, office equipment, means of
publicity, transport, and above all money.

During the previous month, indeed, Adelabu's attention had turned away
from party politics altogether, and focused once more upon the post of
Administrative Secretary to the Ibadan Native Authority. On 20 October the
Defender carried a leading article on the need for such an appointment, since
B. K. Cooper, the administrative officer then filling the position, was about
to go on leave. On the 23rd the same newspaper regaled its readers with the
rumor that D. M. O. Akinbiyi, the son of D. T. Akinbiyi, Adelabu's old
schoolmate and currently Deputy Town Clerk of Lagos, was anxious for the
job, and that 'An honourable member of the Western House of Assembly
will contest for that post with Akinbiyi.' In fact, Akinbiyi ultimately did not
apply, and although Adegoke Adelabu's name was among the six applicants,
when the Staff Committee of the N. A. Council met at the beginning of
November it selected Victor O. Esan, an Ibadan son and a lawyer, to take
the position. Once more Adelabu had been disappointed.

With Adelabu's interest in a political career with the N.C.N.C. floundering, that party entered into a long, internal crisis which was to occupy it for
the greater part of a year. Adelabu took no direct part in this, not being yet
eminent enough in the party to become involved of necessity, while personally the crisis appeared to him to be an argument unrelated to either important philosophical or practical organizational problems. Still, it is essential to
pay some attention to the crisis in order to understand more fully the nature
of Nigerian politics at this time.†

We have already noted that the Action Group during 1952 experienced
strain in co-operating with the British administration to make the constitu-

---

* Unfortunately, we do not know whether Adelabu contested for the office against
Ishola or stood down completely. If he contested he almost certainly had the votes
of the Egbe Omo Ibile–N.C.N.C. delegates against him, and Ishola was probably
better known to many non-Ibadan delegates through his links with the Muslim
Congress of Nigeria.

† Another account may be found in Sklar, *Nigerian Political Parties*, pp. 118–25.

tion work. Indeed, in December, the stresses thus produced culminated in that party's decision at its Benin Conference to boycott all social and ceremonial contacts with the Governor, Sir John Macpherson. Similar stresses at the same time were throwing the N.C.N.C. into crisis – an interesting commentary on the relative internal cohesion of the two parties.

Conflict arose in the N.C.N.C. between those who wished to try to make the Macpherson Constitution work, despite its rapidly emerging limitations, and those who were still reluctant to co-operate with the British. In another of its aspects, this was a clash between those who had no office under the new constitution and who claimed to put the party's interest first, and the N.C.N.C. Ministers in the East and at the center, supported by some of the parliamentarians. In yet another aspect this tended to be a conflict between those with a long association with the N.C.N.C., often dating back to its foundations in 1944, and those, like A. C. Nwapa, Central Minister of Commerce and Industries, who were comparative newcomers to the party. None of these interrelated conflicts might have become open, had it not been for the equivocal and embarrassing position in which Nnamdi Azikiwe, the National President of the party, found himself in 1952. As we have seen, he had confidently expected to win the election in the West in 1951, as well as in the East, and then to be sent to the House of Representatives in Lagos, there to become a Central Minister. However, when his party became the minority in the Western House, the Action Group majority would not send him to Lagos. Condemned to be Leader of the Opposition in the Western Legislature, Azikiwe lost interest in making the constitution work, a feeling which brought him into conflict with Nwapa and his colleagues in Lagos, and with Eyo Ita and his ministerial colleagues in the East.

On 30 September, Azikiwe's *West African Pilot* published an attack on Nwapa, only days before the meeting of the National Executive Committee of the N.C.N.C. at Port Harcourt at which Azikiwe argued that those holding public office under the auspices of the party should obey the decisions of party leaders or resign. However, the motion calling for non-co-operation in making the Macpherson Constitution work was defeated by Nwapa's partisans, the eastern legislators forming the largest bloc at the meeting. Adelabu was not in attendance. Azikiwe and the other officers of the party's Central Working Committee summoned a Special Convention of the N.C.N.C. for December to meet in Jos in the North, on 'neutral' ground where the eastern legislators might be less dominant. The rest of the party in the East was unreliable, but in the West, including Lagos, it was strongly for Azikiwe.* The new Youth Association and its President, F. S. McEwen,

* It was reported at the Jos Convention that telegrams had been received from 67 branches, 21 in the West, 26 in the East and 20 in the North; according to the

manager of the Lagos City College, which was owned by Azikiwe, were particularly active on the N.C.N.C. leader's behalf. The Ibadan branch of the Association on 21 November held a public debate on the resolution 'That the new constitution be given a fair trial', which was lost by 160 votes to 50.

On 8 December the Special Convention opened in Jos. The Western Working Committee was represented by Oduyoye and Ishola, but not Adelabu. On the other hand, only two of the seventy-four N.C.N.C. Eastern legislators attended, all but one of the Eastern Ministers were absent, as were the three N.C.N.C. Central Ministers (Nwapa was in Britain for a Commonwealth Economic Conference). With Dr Azikiwe's supporters thus given a clear run, the decisions of the Convention were scarcely surprising. The Macpherson Constitution must be revised. A new electoral system, with universal adult suffrage and direct elections, must be adopted. The Central Ministers, opposed by Mbonu Ojike, K. O. Mbadiwe and Kola Balogun (who had just arrived dramatically from Kenya, where he had been refused entry to appear as a defense counsel at the trial of Jomo Kenyatta), were to be expelled from the party. Party organization was to be centralized by abandoning the regional Working Committees, and in the future the party was to be run from National Headquarters, under the direction of a National Executive Committee made up of the seven National Officers and thirty-five others, and a Central Working Committee made up of the National Officers and seven others.*

By the New Year Nnamdi Azikiwe was ready to carry the struggle into the East, the center of opposition to him. On 3 January he took the chair at a joint meeting of the N.C.N.C. Eastern Parliamentary Party and the Central Working Committee: only forty-one people were present, including all the Eastern Ministers and the four Central Ministers, Endeley, Nwapa, Arikpo and Njoku. The last three agreed to withdraw, and a discussion lasting eight and a half hours followed, the meeting finally accepting the Jos decisions and re-affirming its loyalty to Azikiwe. Although less than half the

Defender of 17 December, 90 per cent of the Western branches opposed the Port Harcourt N.E.C. decision to support the constitution, 75 per cent of the Northern and 50 per cent of the Eastern. It should be noted that the Northern N.C.N.C. is proportionately heavily over-represented here.

* The winding-up of the Regional Working Committees did not involve any drastic change of personnel or loss of influence by their members. Regional Officers were automatically included among the 35 ordinary members of the new N.E.C., thus filling 21 of the vacant places and leaving only 14 new names to be chosen. The members from the West, therefore, automatically included J. O. Fadahunsi, Y. S. Ola Ishola, W. A. Mosley, Adesegun Odunmbaku, and Oshilaja Oduyoye; D. K. Olumofin and Dr Ikejiani were among the additional group selected.

Eastern legislators had thus directly expressed their support, the N.C.N.C. President now sought finally to assert the control of the party over those elected to public office. On 29 January he secured letters of resignation from all nine Eastern Ministers, which were to be submitted to the Lieutenant-Governor of the East by the Central Working Committee as a sign of the party's supremacy. At the moment they signed the Ministers seem to have believed that their names would automatically all be put forward again for office after this; overnight they learned differently, and Eyo Ita and five others withdrew their letters of resignation on the 30th before they had even been delivered.

The details of the crisis which followed, lasting several months, need not concern us here.* The six Eastern Ministers refused to budge, and constitutionally they were not required to, despite the vote of no confidence which followed. Ita was expelled from the N.C.N.C. and was joined by two of the Central Ministers and some others who resigned to form the opposition National Independence Party. The N.C.N.C. majority in the Eastern House delayed the budget, which had finally to be passed by the direct authority of the Lieutenant-Governor. At length, in May, after a special amendment to the Constitution, the Eastern House of Assembly was dissolved and a new election set. If further proof of the difficulties of the Macpherson Constitution was needed, the necessity of amending it in face of an intolerable situation certainly provided it.

In fact, by May 1953 the Constitution was virtually a complete anachronism. While the N.C.N.C. was engaged in its internal conflict, the Action Group had stolen its thunder as the chief exponent of Nigerian Nationalism. On 31 March, Anthony Enahoro, selected by the Western House to go to the center, proposed a motion in the House of Representatives in Lagos which demanded independence for Nigeria in 1956, a date first put forward by the N.C.N.C. at its Kano Convention in 1951 and adopted by the Action Group at its own Benin Conference in December 1952. Both southern parties, then, were able to support Enahoro's motion. The Northern People's Congress, however, was not. That party had made no commitment to independence at any date; indeed, it was feared that independence would mean the withdrawal of the British, leaving the North at the mercy of the energetic and better-educated southerners, who already dominated the lower levels of the mercantile and administrative structures in that Region. Until the N.P.C. leaders felt sure of their ability to control their own Region and its bureaucracy they would never entertain the thought of fixing a firm date for independence, and in that they were completely in agreement with the views of

* For these see, in addition to Sklar as cited above, Kalu Ezera, *Constitutional Developments in Nigeria*, 2nd edn. (Cambridge: University Press, 1964), pp. 159–64.

the Colonial Office. On 31 March, then, the N.P.C. legislators, led by the Sardauna of Sokoto, tried to replace the date 1956 in Enahoro's motion by the nebulous phrase 'as soon as practicable'. The motion in the end was never put to the vote. Watched by Nnamdi Azikiwe from the public gallery, the N.C.N.C. and Action Group Members walked out, led by Obafemi Awolowo and K. O. Mbadiwe. Moreover, the four Action Group Central Ministers also resigned in protest at a previous decision by a majority of the Council of Ministers that none of them should take part in the debate or vote.* For their part, the N.P.C. Ministers and Legislators went home to the North, amid the jeers of the crowds which gathered in Lagos and at stations along the railway line.

Another fatal flaw in the Constitution was thus revealed. The Central Ministers, chosen theoretically to represent Regions rather than parties, were unable to support their own party policies because of the doctrine of collective responsibility. For the time being the N.C.N.C. and the Action Group came together against the Constitution and in the name of independence in 1956. Thus, on 5 May, Adelabu found himself in the unfamiliar position of supporting a motion moved by an Action Group Member in the Western House of Assembly, which had resumed its session the previous day. On 4 May the first Nigerian to take office as President of the House had, in a suitably symbolic fashion, received a copy of Erskine May's *Principles of Parliamentary Practice* from Oliver Lyttelton, the Colonial Secretary, then visiting Nigeria. Now the House was to debate a motion approving Enahoro's call for self-government in 1956, commending the gesture of the Action Group Central Ministers and their supporters in walking out, reaffirming confidence in the four who resigned, and declaring that their names would be re-submitted if nominations to the vacancies were requested. Dennis Osadebay from Asaba seconded the motion on behalf of the Opposition, and both sides of the House were given an opportunity for a display of nationalist fervor.

This was an occasion which Adegoke Adelabu relished and his ebullient rhetoric built up. History, geography, science, economics, psychology, philosophy and religion, he declared, 'Law, art, morals, time, space, nature and peace', all together demonstrate the vital importance of freedom.

Give a plant plenty of water and an abundance of mineral foods but deny it air and sunshine. It will die. The Human spirit requires for its culture the sunshine of liberty and the air of freedom. The vast systems of protons, atoms, molecules, moons, planets, stars and universes are all dancing the everlasting rhumba of freedom.[23]

* See Sklar, *Nigerian Political Parties*, pp. 125–8, and Ezera, *Constitutional Developments*, pp. 164–7, for a more detailed account of these events.

Then, after more in this vein, he suddenly turned the whole speech on its head. 'Arguments', he announced, 'have nothing to do with the actual achievement of freedom.' What he had been saying was 'monumental tom-foolery', in which he had indulged 'in order to demonstrate its absurdity and its futility'. 'I have out-fadded the faddists', he declared. 'Even though I can talk I have no belief in mere talking. Arguments are irrelevant, ineffective, puerile and unproductive. Sir Winston Churchill, Mr Oliver Lyttelton, Sir John Macpherson, the whole British imperial hierarchy know all these plati-tudes to perfection and yet they withhold the freedom of our country.'[24]

How then was independence going to come? This was the message Adelabu really wanted to deliver.

We are setting our foot on the road to freedom. That road leads through strain, through struggle and through sacrifice. We are already in the beginning of the strain. Day by day the strain will increase. Imperialism will never give way. Let us be clear, certain and positive about that. More links of collaboration will snap. When we have thoroughly marshalled our forces, we shall give the signal for mass action. That is the beginning of the struggle.

And in the end? Pressed by the President to finish, he presented his alterna-tives – either 'One fine, bright, sunny, glorious day, Nigeria which slept in slavery, will wake up in freedom', or 'Malanism will overrun the whole of Africa and condemn our forebears [sic] to eternal slavery.'[25]

This speech was an important one for Adelabu, second only to his maiden speech just over a year before, and there is no doubt that he felt it to be such.* Not only was it an oratorical performance which in style and delivery few of his fellow legislators could match, containing a shift of mood and a deliberate self-mockery of which possibly only Anthony Enahoro might also be capable, but it was in addition an important statement of his view of the process of decolonization. He would not himself have seen things in these terms. Nevertheless, what he was saying was that the attainment of indepen-dence was a process of struggle, not of co-operation, and that if it became the latter then independence itself would be compromised. It was a view of the political process as conflict which he was to retain throughout his life, and which was to bring him into open conflict with Nnamdi Azikiwe and the N.C.N.C. not long before his death. It was ironical that this statement of his views should have been made in the Western House of Assembly, where Nigerian politicians were learning to become Westminster parliamentarians. The process of decolonization as bargaining between Nigerian leaders and the Colonial Office had already succeeded; the time of struggle, a time when

* A revised copy of this speech in his papers suggests that he thought of publishing it, as he had his first major speech, either as a long article or a pamphlet. For some reason this was not done.

men like Mokwugo Okoye and Osita Agwuna had gone to jail for saying in public not much different from what Adelabu had said, was past. Insofar as conflict was to be employed, it was among Nigerians. Only ten days after Adelabu's speech, a visit to Kano in the North by an Action Group campaign team provoked bloody fighting between northerners and southerners living there. Just over a week after that, the Northern legislature passed an 'Eight Point Programme' which virtually amounted to a threat of secession by that Region. This was itself a response to the announcement by Oliver Lyttelton in the British House of Commons on 21 May that the Nigerian Constitution was a failure and would have to be redrafted 'to provide for greater regional autonomy'. With a Constitutional Conference thus to be held in London, the process of decolonization by debate was moving forward a further stage.

When Adelabu spoke in the House of Assembly on 5 May, however, he too had already taken the struggle elsewhere. On 6 April, the Ibadan Tax Payers Association was formally organized. It was Adelabu's personal political instrument, an instrument to marshal the forces of public participation which he had found neither in his national political party nor in the regional legislature. He had, in fact, set his feet firmly on the streets of Ibadan, and within a year he was to be its master.

CHAPTER 8

TOWARD THE MASTERY OF IBADAN

Practical experience has shown that N.C.N.C. ideology is too abstract and highbrow for the masses in various localities to digest or understand in significance. Too make it useful as an instrument for arousing local enthusiasm it must be related to realities intimately connected with the people's daily lives.

Constitution of the Ibadan Taxpayers Association

Nineteen fifty-two was a disappointing year for the weaver's son from Oke Oluokun. Neither in the House of Assembly nor in the organization of the party as it was being built by his colleagues had he found an instrument which could guarantee him a lasting source of employment or the reputation and power of a public figure, goals which had been substituted for that of studying law in England. While it was true that the Western House was no 'clubhouse piffle', Adelabu was not a member of the governing party club. Nor did he prefer to be a member of someone else's club within his own party, a sentiment shared by a number of his party peers. Realizing he would never achieve the Administrative Secretaryship and legal career for which he still retained some hope as late as September 1952, he dismissed the close of his first year in public office and looked toward a more hopeful future:

Welcome my good fortune 1953. Heaven knows how much I need you for the good luck of the New Year to redress the balance of the old so that all enmeshed in one stupendous success we may rise together as one nation.[1]

The new year had not begun auspiciously in Ibadan from Adelabu's point of view. On 1 January, V. O. Esan assumed the coveted post of Administrative Secretary to the Council, and on 4 February a new set of Councillors chosen from the Ibadan Assembly, which was still controlled by the I.C.C., took office. However, as events were to prove, Adelabu was to find in this particular Council the perfect foil for his ambitions. Throughout the year, as the Council dealt with the critical problems related to the Hayley reforms and the Local Government Law of 1953, it was to discover to its great embarrassment that, for the first time in Ibadan's colonial history, an opposition campaign could be mounted from outside against the Council which could effectively negate its deliberations and intentions. As succeeding issues came upon the Council agenda – tax reform, court reforms, the selection of a new Balogun, the control of trading on Lebanon Street – Adelabu articulated the voices of opposition into a chorus large enough, but only just large enough, to gain him control of the Council in March 1954, not as Administrative Secretary, but as its Chairman. It is therefore important at this point to look in some detail at the work of the Council of 1953–4 since it demonstrates how his strength rested on a set of issues and events of which he took skillful advantage. It also offers the opportunity ultimately to compare the work of the earlier I.C.C.-controlled Council with the work of his own Council and its successor.

Of all the issues, taxation contributed most directly to Adelabu's assertion of himself as a leader in 1953. The search for civic revenue in Ibadan had long served to tax the patience and sense of humor of the collectors far more than the money-purses of the citizenry. For the Council, taxation had been a matter of financial life and death year after year; but for the taxpayer and tax-evader the tax season resembled a game more than a civic duty. As a rule of thumb, some official observers have suggested that twenty-five per cent of those who ought to pay tax avoided doing so, and that seventy-five per cent of those who paid understated their liability. Failure to pay tax has not been a cause for a guilty conscience. On the contrary, it has been freely admitted to and boasted about. Some people have felt the Council has no right to collect taxes, which have been universally decried as exorbitant. They have felt much of the money to have been mis-spent and, because enforcement has been so much a matter of chance, it has had an arbitrary aspect which made it close to discriminatory to be forced to pay at all.

Direct taxation was introduced in Ibadan in 1918. During the cocoa harvest season, when money was more plentiful, the chiefs were obliged to collect from their followers on the assumption that they would know better than professional tax collectors whether an individual might be in his urban compound or rural farms. The Government took from thirty to fifty per cent of the proceeds and the Council the remainder, from which a ten per cent rebate, later reduced to five per cent, was paid to the chiefs to induce them to collect as much as possible. While rebate was a significant part of Ibadan's political economy, it did not represent remuneration to the collectors which could without qualification be considered part of their incomes. As forty-one junior chiefs and mogajis reminded the District Officer in 1942, it was necessary to send messengers by lorry and rail to outlying villages and these messengers had to be fed and paid.[2]

To catch evaders, a practice known as 'tax raiding' was begun in the late 1930s. Compounds or streets were cordoned off and all those caught without tax receipts were forced to pay or bribe their way free. Furthermore, the courts in which tax cases were heard were presided over by the chiefs who were also tax collectors. It was an early practice, encouraged by the British, to close the courts in order to allow the collection of tax to proceed.

The system operated on the assumption that everyone cheated. Evasion was practiced not only by the poor, or by those who rebelled against taxation as a new thing not sanctified by tradition. In 1939–40 the Assistant Commissioner of Income Tax for Ibadan compiled a list of 170 non-Nigerians who had left Ibadan without paying their income tax to the Nigerian revenue service. The list included administrators, military officers, railway employees, and missionaries.[3] If Europeans with determinable salaries did not bother to pay, how could one expect traders to declare their incomes honestly or poor people to pay willingly?

There were a number of inconclusive attempts to improve matters until 1951 when, as we have seen, the Butcher Commission which inquired into the charges against Chief Agbaje also looked into the efficiency and administration of Council activities, including that of tax collection. One of the bluntest charges made by Butcher was that

Tax collection should be reorganized on a territorial basis and should no longer be the perquisite of the Junior Chiefs and Mogajis. Not only would such a reform bring in a great deal of extra revenue without necessarily altering the incidence of tax, but it would remove a fruitful source of corruption. I submit that all the evidence shows that the Junior Chiefs and Mogajis have gravely abused the privilege of being tax collectors, and should no longer be allowed to do this work *ex-officio*.[4]

Accepting his report, Government established a territorial system for the collection of personal tax for the 1952–3 season, using as tax areas the wards which the Hayley Reform Committee set up for Council elections. Each area had an Assessment Committee of six residents, whose duty it was to register all taxpayers resident in their area and to estimate the income on which they should pay. The committees were supervised from the Council offices by a Chief Tax Clerk, who had under him a Tax Clerk for each unit. Months before collection began, a number of junior chiefs and mogajis protested the new arrangements, but in September 1952, as the tax collection season was about to begin, the new Olubadan, Igbintade, who had been installed in July, announced to the chiefs and mogajis that he had accepted the new system. During the following week eight mogajis were fined a total of £410 for obstructing tax collection.

Although the new system boosted revenue with its higher assumed incomes and rates of taxation, the figures for taxpayers (Table 1) show that evaders were not necessarily being netted. The Assessment Committees were appointed by the Council and, whatever the make-up of the Council, members of the minority party were to complain annually and bitterly of discrimination and harassment. The rebate was now paid to the committee and, with the bribes paid to avoid high assessment, constituted a ready source of remunerative patronage for the parties.

TABLE I   *Tax in Ibadan 1952–7*

Year	Payers	Tax paid (in pounds)
1952–3	122,816	103,000
53–4	113,905	153,000
54–5	116,477	149,000
55–6	112,440	165,000
56–7	114,000	202,000

Source: Annual Report for Ibadan District Council, 1958, in PADID 3278/S.1.

The sense of grievance over these administrative reforms was heightened when, on 30 December 1952, it was announced that the capitation tax was to be increased from 12s. 6d. to £1. 2. 6d. with 10s. 6d. to be used for health and education programs imposed on local councils by the Regional Government. The new levy would affect about 85,000 persons then paying the minimum flat rate. Obafemi Awolowo himself came to the Council in January 1953 to explain the necessity for the new measure, and two weeks later Adelabu attacked it in the House of Assembly. The first organized protest against the increased tax came at a mass meeting on 1 February at Mapo Hall, sponsored by the Egbe Omo Ibile, of which Bello Abasi was still President. Present also were Abdulahi Elesinmeta of the Maiyegun League, representatives of the Chief Imam and the Iyalode and several of the mogajis and individuals who were later to be associated with Adelabu's anti-tax campaigns.[5] If such a tax were to be imposed, they argued that the Council, not the Regional Government, should decide how it was to be used. It should be remembered that the reconstitution of the Council under the 1953 local government law had been foreseeable since the July 1952 House of Assembly debate on the bill requiring direct election of the majority of the Council members. According to the conveners of the meeting, 5,000 persons were in attendance. The February meeting is interesting because, first, it demonstrated the popularity of an anti-tax campaign in the name of strengthening local institutions; second, it provided further proof that leaders of political groups could unite with at least some representatives of the so-called traditional sector of the society; third, it introduced an issue which was to emerge in every following election; and, fourth, Adelabu was not present.

A second development, that of court reforms, was also under way and, as we shall see shortly, court and tax reform were to converge, creating a political opportunity which Adelabu began to realize in April.

The Brooke Commission, which had been set up to consider reform of the courts in the Western Provinces, had visited Ibadan early in September 1950. At that time there were 51 courts in Ibadan Division, which had heard a total of 21,992 cases in the previous year, 16,413 of these being civil cases, overwhelmingly divorce suits. Although the smallest court in the Division had heard only 13 cases in the year, the principal city court at Bere had heard 6385 cases. These local courts administered what the British, under the system of Indirect Rule, referred to as 'customary' law, and were presided over by chiefs. It was accepted in the Ibadan Council at this time that the city's practice of including at least one literate chief on each court panel, sometimes numbering ten members, should be extended in principle to all Division courts.[6] Lawyers could not appear in these courts. Their domain was the Magistrates' Courts which had jurisdiction in the case of more serious crimes or civil cases involving relatively large sums of money.

The report of the Brooke Commission was not publicly available until the latter part of 1952, but confidential draft copies of it had already been circulated to the administrators. With its guidelines in mind, District Officer Hayley was able to warn the Council that their own slowly emerging guidelines for reform were not in keeping with those which Government would eventually approve from the Brooke Commission.[7] Thus, by early 1953, most of the conclusions of the Brooke inquiry were unofficially known to the Councillors and plans were advancing for their implementation in Ibadan. Early in February 1953 the Resident was informed of the Regional Government's intended lines of development for Ibadan, which included reconstituting the Ibadan Native Court of Appeal, the highest local court, which served as an appellate channel between the Ibadan courts and the Supreme Court. According to the lines laid down by the Chief Justice and approved by the Regional Government, the Ibadan Court of Appeal should have

a single Judge (assisted by 'traditional' assessors) with professional qualifications, of good repute, of sufficient age and standing to command respect and sufficient experience to hold the balance between customary law (including procedure) and his professional bias toward English law and forms.[8]

Such a post, he urged, could be easily filled by a pensioner, a retired court registrar or administrative officer, who would not only be satisfactory but inexpensive.

Hayley gained acceptance of this proposition on 20 February 1953 at what he termed a 'private Session' of the Native Authority Council, although it was presided over by the Olubadan. A select Committee, created to spell out these reforms in more detail, accepted the judicial-executive separation principle and the idea that other judges and assessors should be recommended by the Chief Judge.

This proposal was supported by the colonial officers on the one hand, in the name of efficiency, and by the chiefs on the other because age and illness meant that they could not keep up with Council and committee and court duties, all rapidly increasing. The only conditions insisted upon by the chiefs were that justifying reasons for their loss of their judicial positions be advanced which would protect their prestige, and that no decrease in salary and perquisites would result. It was also understood by the chiefs that their vacated positions on the courts would be filled by junior chiefs and mogajis whose increasing sense of corporateness, sharpened by their loss of tax powers, had to be taken into account by the senior chiefs as they tried to avoid intrigues against themselves and as they sought popular support for their waning traditional powers. For these reasons, the senior chiefs, after meeting with the Select Committee on 4 March 1953, began to suggest alterations. Their suggestions could, however, only lead to a continuation of the inefficient administration of the courts, a strengthening of the 'executive' control of the Olubadan over them, and a weakening of the ability of a literate judge to act without the influence of Olubadan-appointed illiterate assessors.

This reactionary movement had taken shape at a meeting on 5 March, at which time the proposed reforms were explained, apparently for the first time, to the junior chiefs and mogajis. The following day, in a letter addressed to the Olubadan and the senior chiefs, and apparently to Bello Abasi of the Egbe Omo Ibile as well, they explained their own reservations. The essence of their fear was that the family structure was under attack. Legal cases at that time were first dealt with by the mogajis and, when this proved inadequate, they went on appeal to the courts run by the chiefs, even as a man went from his mogaji to a chief in political matters generally. Now the chieftaincy houses were to be shorn of this function, which would pass to lawyers and literates.[9]

Important as these tensions were in Ibadan at this time, we must note that the style of the petition was hardly that of Adelabu. His espousal of the cause of the junior chiefs and mogajis at the time of the Agbaje dispute had no more established him as their spokesman than as an articulator of the I.P.A. policies. Adelabu became involved because court reform was not an isolated problem in Ibadan, but part of the general restructuring of affairs inherent in the Hayley Reforms and the 1952 Local Government Bill, which offered a more general entrepreneurial opportunity for a new type of politician. These reforms were intended to be part of the movement towards self-government which took as one of its premises a diminution of the chiefs' powers, in this case through the device of separation of powers and closer centralized control over the problems with which the courts dealt.

The result was a temporary alignment of interests of the traditionalists, who urged that the courts 'belonged' to the Olubadan and the chiefs, and members of the Ibadan Assembly looking toward the next Council election, who urged that no further steps be taken until a representative elected Council was formed to take them and until the Brooke Commission recommendations could be applied to all of the Western Region, rather than in 'discrimination' against Ibadan. Both groups were agreed, then, in delaying reform.

By this time the outlines of the Brooke Commission recommendations were reasonably well known, and it was felt with great certainty that Government would enforce them without bothering to consult or inform those most affected. As the junior chiefs and mogajis put it in yet another petition on 27 March, 'It is true that in every country progress is required... but we resent any progress... which will snatch away or deprive us of our age-long heritage...'[10] They urged the retention of the Olubadan as President of the Appeal Court, although the Olubadan was willing to pass this duty on to the Otun Balogun, Isaac Akinyele. Even more than in the Agbaje agitation, the court reforms and the long delay in the release of the Brooke Commission Report were serving to create a unified working group among the mogajis.

Thus, by the end of March 1953, two very significant conflicts, over tax and the courts, were taking shape. The issues had been defined, partisanship had been established and the identification of working coalitions had been made. It is at this point and not before, as closely as can be determined, that Adelabu entered the scene in a decisive manner.

While prior discussions and arrangements had undoubtedly taken place earlier, the Ibadan Tax Payers Association was born at a meeting on 6 April 1953.[11] Apparently present on invitation, the founding members recognized Adelabu as President without the formality of an election. Notable among those present were two persons who had attended the meeting of 1 February chaired by Bello Abasi to protest changes in the tax system. These were Abdulahi Elesinmeta, a well-known Alfa, and Yesufu Mogbonjubola, a cocoa farmer, the Chairman and a member of the Maiyegun League who had both been jailed in December 1949 for their activities. These two were also elected to the Council in 1954.

Also attending the inaugural meeting were Bello Konipe and Obadara Atanda, both Maiyegun League members. Further organizational experience was brought by L. Ade Bello, inveterate organizer of the Oke Badan Improvement Party, the Ibadan Welfare Association, the Community of Ibadan Citizens, and the Egbe Omo Ibile, and Buraimo Alao, a leader of the Ibadan Textile Traders Association. In addition, Ibadan Assemblymen S. L. Akano and Samuel Lana, clerk in the ministry of Education and Councillor L. A. B. Lawal, a transporter, joined the Association from the beginning. All contested successfully for the N.C.N.C. in 1954. Thus the Tax Payers Association initially combined participants in the recent cocoa and tax issues, a variety of persons with organizational and political experience and at least eighteen of the men who would enter the Council with Adelabu.

It should be noted that there were no mogajis present at the inaugural meeting of the I.T.P.A., as far as we can determine, although illegible signatures in the membership registers may conceal a few. Moreover, those entrusted with recruitment were not mogajis but the leaders of several earlier Ibadan political associations, who were literate and therefore capable of keeping the planned membership ledgers and financial records, and who presumably knew of other persons who might join such a group. The members were listed by electoral wards, not by compounds or by political societies, in keeping with the need to have ward organizations rather than 'tradition', communal spirit or political clubs as the basis for contesting the local elections in 1954.*

The constitution of the Association consisted of three parts, dealing with policy, organization and finance.[12] The political policies dedicated the Association to a local government 'democratic in constitution, efficient in service and conducive to the progress of the whole community'; it recognized the 'special position' of the chiefs and urged that in Ibadan democracy 'must be built around the framework of our Chieftaincy System'; and declared that the Ibadan 'cultural and moral codes of social behaviour are a noble heritage from the past'. 'We may purify, modernise, adapt and codify them', the document went on, 'but the social utility of their essence must be preserved secure from the desecrating encroachment of shallow amateur iconoclasts'. Finally it declared that the I.T.P.A. was a local organ of the N.C.N.C.

The policy for education proposed adult evening schools to eradicate illiteracy. The policy for development stressed that the city must be supplied with better roads, water, electrical, postal and transportation facilities, parks,

---

* Volumes I, III and IV of the Membership Register are in the Adelabu Papers. They have spaces for 6738 names, with some 400 empty, so that 6000 members by 29 January 1954 is a safe estimate. Only 30 are recorded as paying their 3d. weekly dues.

pools, markets and orchards, while the rural areas required 'modern mechanised technique, the supply of high yield strains of seeds, the provision of rural credits, efficient marketing organisations and extension service and frequent shows and exhibitions shall be the order of the day'. In contrast to Adelabu's Master Plan of 1951, no mention was made of industrial development or joint government–private enterprise projects.

The social policy of the I.T.P.A., as spelled out in its Constitution, continued these liberal themes. It urged free education for all to 'ensure a rigidly casteless society distinguished by Social Mobility'; it noted that 'no nation can rise above its womanhood' and that 'motherhood shall cease to be a drudgery and become a happy vocation and honoured national service' and emphasized the necessity of health facilities and maternity clinics, orphanages, reformatories, asylums and homes for the infirm, maimed and aged, maintained at public expense. It also urged public honesty in an attack on the traditional political order: 'In contra-distinction to the perquisites attached to the office of Chiefs and Mogajis we shall educate public opinion to see the evils of bribery and corruption in order to see it drastically curtailed and ultimately abolished.' Finally, it guaranteed that religious belief must remain 'the sole affair of private individuals'.

The organization of the Association provided for an Annual Convention which could elect and impeach its President, who must be 'a highly educated native of Ibadan, not below the age of 35 and of reputable character'. (Adelabu was at least thirty-seven.) The President was empowered to appoint the members of the Central Executive Committee, and also to dismiss them or abolish their posts. The hiring and firing of all employees were under his control, and he was to direct the Association's secretariat. In fact, the only control exercised over the President was to be his election by chapter delegates 'at the rate of one per 100 financial registered members'. Since the Central Executive Committee, appointed by the President, could expel any members of the Association for disobedience, disloyalty, treachery or any other serious offense, and since 'financial membership' was never realized, this control was meaningless. Regulations 'for the detailed work of Association' were to be made by the President, and amendments to the Constitution, 'if agreeable and with the President's assent', might be sent to the Annual Convention for ratification.

The Association's financial matters were equally under the President's control. Revenue was to be derived from fees, subscriptions, levies, donations, fines, grants and bequests and its expenditure was to be made merely 'on the instruction of the President'.

The Constitution, then, was clearly the work of the Association's first president, Adegoke Adelabu. It elaborated a confusing set of Committees, reminiscent of the organizational chart of the 'Master Plan' and like the 'Master Plan', placed power in Adelabu's hands. It also continued a number of themes with which he had been concerned earlier, many of them not policies so much as elements of a good life for Ibadan. It was at once a declaration of purpose and a statement of morality, and it was more these things than a practicable guide toward the foundation of a new organization.

This document was probably prepared for the first meeting of the Association. It reflects too clearly the sole image of Adelabu to allow of the interpretation that much give and take among co-founders had brought it into being; and in blaming 'the evils of bribery and corruption' on the chiefs and mogajis who had demonstrated their skills in these areas to Adelabu during the Agbaje agitation, it suggests they had not yet made their appearance in the Association. This event appears to have come about shortly after the first meeting. A meeting of the Association on 22 April heard a request by four mogajis, suggesting they had the support of the Olubadan's and Balogun's lines of chiefs, to be accepted into the Central Working Committee of the Association.* They apparently also requested membership on the 'finance committee', although no such committee had been included in the Constitution.[13] They were readily accepted into membership but, since the places on the Executive Committee were already filled, the mogajis were listed separately as the party's mogajis. It thus appears that the Maiyegun League members and the rest of the Association were happy to welcome the mogajis. They represented a concern with traditional politics not represented among the founders, having been among the thirty-two mogajis signing the petitions of 6 March and 27 March protesting court reforms, petitions with which Adelabu was not involved. It thus appears that the idea that co-operation might be mutually useful occurred simultaneously to a small minority of the less important mogajis and to the Association, each of which had been organizing separately at this time.

The rapid evolution of the Association was demonstrated sometime between 27 April and 4 May in a leaflet distributed by the Central Executive Committee, the Yoruba version of which gave the name of 'Mabolaje' to the Association. Akere's Compound, a few hundred yards down King George V Avenue from Mapo, was given as the address of the Headquarters and Secretariat. The leaflet was signed by four mogajis, listed, as we have just seen, in addition to and separate from the ten Executive Committee members allowed by the I.T.P.A. Constitution. Warning all patriots that 'enemies within and without have hatched a seven point conspiracy against the republican freedom and communal liberty of Ibadan state', the leaflet enumerated

---

* There is considerable doubt whether Mogajis Arijemogba and Oluwa were from recognized chieftaincy houses; Oriare and Olowu were.

eight 'facts about the disabilities of Ibadan'. No less than four of these 'facts' dealt with chieftaincy, including the courts, the council and the tax system.

HERE ARE THE FACTS ABOUT THE DISABILITIES OF IBADAN

1. The abrogation of Ibadan Suzerainty over the Northern District of Ibadan or Oshun Division.
2. The subjugation of the Olubadan and Senior Chiefs in the Local Govt. Executive.
3. The Divorce of the Junior Chiefs and Mogajis from the Machinery [of] Tax Collection.
4. The planned Elimination of Traditional Chiefs and Mogajis from the Native Judiciary.
5. The continued Deprivation of the Farming Community of their livelihood through the cutting out of Cocoa Trees.
6. The intended imposition of hardship on Landlords by the introduction of property Rating.
7. The abolition of Native Chieftaincies and the Native Court System.
8. The possible separation of Ibadan Rural Areas from Ibadan Township by the creation of Rural Council(s) under the new Local Government Law.
   If you are a true-born son of Ibadan
   If you are a patriot and Freedomite
   If you are a tax-payer and voter
   If you want to relieve present distress and prevent coming disaster
   Rally Round our Olubadan, the Traditional Chiefs and Mogajis
   Enrol with your Babaoguns and join the
   IBADAN TAX PAYERS ASSOCIATION*

At about the same time, on 30 April 1953, the *Southern Nigeria Defender* also published the first press release of the Association, the spokesman for which noted that they approved territorially organized tax collection, since there was nothing in it to prevent junior chiefs and mogajis from continuing to serve if they were chosen to do so. The majority of the Ibadan taxpayers, they asserted, in absolute contradiction to their concern with corrupt mogajis and chiefs in their Constitution, had 'confidence in the ability and honesty of Junior Chiefs and Mogajis to play a vital role in our machinery of local government including tax collection and will put them on the job with their votes'. Having defended the chiefs and mogajis, the Association then attacked the existing I.C.C.-controlled Council as 'the imposition of the rule of a minority clique who have not got the backing of the masses' and as 'people

---

* 'Babaogun' was a term originally meaning 'father of the war-boys' (*baba omo ogun*), i.e. war captain. By 1953, it was used to mean anyone who acted as a spokesman or intermediary with higher authorities, often in a pejorative sense.

with vested interests who regard the Ibadan Native Authority as their private monopoly'. Looking to the courts and the future, the release also asserted that

The question of Court Reform is for the Court chiefs who will be affected by any proposed reform and for the new democratic and representative Native Authority Council which the new Local Government Bill will call into being.

These documents, then, clearly represent an evolution from the early organizational meeting of the Tax Payers. At that time it had not been foreseen that any mogajis might be included and the Executive Committee of ten, as fixed in the Constitution, had already been appointed.*

From the beginning, the I.T.P.A. had at least the tacit support of Olubadan Igbintade, who had been installed (from his title of Osi Olubadan over the Otun Olubadan, who was next in line but sick) on 11 July 1952 at a time when he was already in his eighties. In his first year of office he distinguished himself largely by converting from Yoruba religious adherence to Islam in March 1953, an act which put him in step with the public religious practices of a broader group of his subjects. With his support, it was easier to enlist the aid of some of his junior chiefs and mogajis to the cause of the I.T.P.A. On 3 May, a 'combined Meeting of the Senior Chiefs, Junior Chiefs, Mogajis, Village Heads' and the Central Executive Committee of the Association met again at Akere's compound to discuss the 1953 Local Government Act which had become active in the Western Region on 26 February and which would eventually be applied to Ibadan. At this time the possibility still existed that the area governed by the Council would be divided into its rural and urban components. This was the basic concern of the letter sent from this meeting to the administrators and the Council. Accepting the creation of territorial tax units, they urged that under the new law the existing rural–urban unity should be retained. Ibadan town was one with its rural areas: '...every farmer maintains a home at Ibadan and regards his farm tenement as a temporary work-camp'. In further but contradictory justification of this principle, the letter went on to urge that

The rural people have no previous experience of local Government operations. Their best training ground will be for their first elected representative to sit along with more experienced city representatives in a comprehensive assembly to familiarise themselves with the procedure.

* President: Adegoke Adelabu; Vice-Presidents: Obadara Atanda, Yesufu Mogbonjubola and Popoola Iyanda; Secretary: S. Olanrewaju; Treasurer: Bello Konipe; Propaganda Secretary: Abdulahi Elesinmeta; Publicity Secretary: Salami Tolorunioshe; Executive Committee Members: Mustafa Akanni and Tiamiyu A. Eniafe. Mogajis Arijemogba, Olowu, Oluwa and Oriare were added after 22 April 1953.

While they insisted that the new Council should be 'completely democratic', they also insisted that it was 'the firm determination of the whole Ibadan Community that the office, dignity, powers, rights, Prerogatives, and Paramountcy of the Olubadan shall be maintained intact'.[14]

The Ibadan Council met on 4 May. Councillor S. A. Akinfenwa, after the rules had been suspended, reminded his colleagues that he had brought the 'Mabolaje Society' to their attention at their previous meeting on 27 April; since then its leaflet had come to his attention and he read it to the Council. After a short discussion, the Council unanimously resolved that junior chiefs and mogajis should not meet with the Association in the future 'for discussion of any matter' and that any chief or mogaji 'who was found in such an intriguing meeting in future would no longer be recognised either as a Chief or Mogaji'.[15]

On the following day, however, Hayley received a copy of the Tax Payers' leaflet and the letter from them reporting their meeting of 3 May, which was signed by eighty persons, of whom twenty-eight were junior chiefs and mogajis and six were senior chiefs, including Ashipa Olubadan Olugbode, Ashipa Balogun Akinyo, the Seriki and Iyalode Abimbola. It was an impressive set of names and while it neither represented the majority of the chiefs and mogajis nor meant that the signatories were necessarily members of the Association, it was to cause a great deal of consternation in the Council. It is interesting to look at the chiefs and mogajis who signed this letter, along with the signatories of the petitions of 6 and 27 March against court reform and the possibility of Chief Akinyele's appointment as Chief Judge. Careful examination of signatures reveals that although the protesting chiefs were sufficient in number to cause concern to their opponents, neither they nor Adelabu had been able to recruit and organize even a third of the total in the protest.

The same was true for the mogajis. Some of those who signed the 3 May letter and one other came from such important houses as Bioku, Mosaderin and Oderinlo. Many of them, however, came from smaller, politically less important houses, and, in at least two instances, there is doubt whether the signatories were mogajis at all, in the sense that they came from one of the perhaps 175 lineages in Ibadan recognized by this time as having the right to be considered for chieftaincy titles.* Of this number, forty-six would be

---

* It was impossible to locate an authoritative list of recognized mogajis in Ibadan in 1963. This figure was arrived at by adding those in Olubadan Akinyele's *Iwe Itan Ibadan*, recent Chieftaincy Committee Minutes, and a document prepared and used by chiefs and mogajis during the 1961 local government election. It probably leaves out a few, but it undoubtedly also includes a number who have little hope of gaining titles although their right to be considered for titles is acknowledged. It represents a growth in recognized mogajis corresponding to the growth of population since 1893.

serving at any one time in the two major lines and an additional eight in the Seriki's line; special titles reserved to a few houses and vacancies would account for a few more so that at any given time perhaps 110 heads of lineages might be referred to as mogajis rather than as chiefs. The twelve mogajis who signed the 3 May letter thus represented but a small fraction of this group. While Adelabu was to speak grandly of 'the junior chiefs and mogajis' who supported him, and while some observers have accepted this, it was at best but a tenuous hold on the so-called traditional sector of Ibadan politics.[16]

Nevertheless, in face of what was construed to be a new threat, an emergency meeting of the Council was called for Wednesday morning, 13 May. After prayers by Chief Akinyele, the subject of the Tax Payers Association was introduced by Senior District Officer Hayley. Taking the leaflet first, Hayley assured the Council, particularly the chiefs, that the eight 'facts' enumerated in the leaflet were untrue: the chiefs were not subjugated in the present Council for they had agreed to it; the removal of the junior chiefs and mogajis from tax collection had nothing to do with politics; the issue of court reform was not yet resolved, and chieftaincy and the court system had not been nor would they be abolished. When he had gone through the entire list, Hayley informed the Council that he had received the letter signed by the chiefs and mogajis. 'He would like to know' the Minutes record, 'what the Council proposed to do to inform the townspeople of the truth regarding these matters.'

It is interesting to note at this point that according to the Minutes no other person had yet spoken; the initiative had seemingly been entirely that of the Senior District Officer. John Hayley had now been laboring for two years reforming the tax, court and electoral structures of the Ibadan Council, and he was anxious to see these reforms instituted before the application of the Local Government Law to Ibadan would give a popularly elected Council power to decide such matters for themselves. It was nevertheless clear that his remarks had found an attentive audience. A number of Councillors now spoke, calling for various sanctions against the Tax Payers Association, the junior chiefs and mogajis, and even the Olubadan. Finally, Chiefs Akinwale, Aminu and Kobiowu urged that the senior chiefs who had signed the petition 'through ignorance and misrepresentation of matters' be forgiven; after 'serious warning' the chiefs did apologize and were pardoned.

Adelabu was clearly delighted at this reaction to the I.T.P.A. In rapid succession he prepared two statements, neither of which was published, scorning the Council. The *Tribune* had carried the rumor in early May that the Council elections would be held in July 1953 and Adelabu linked this with another report that the Councillors had attempted a reconciliation with the

Olubadan in preparation for the election. These two events, Adelabu pronounced, marked a turning point in Ibadan politics. After only two months, the Tax Payers Association had 'compelled the reactionary freebooters' in the Council to surrender, he declared in 'Ibadan Tax Payers Battle for Democracy'. 'The volte face from swaggering bravado to cringing obsequiousness has been most shameful.' He charged them with threatening arrest of Association members, sending the leaflet to the Crown Counsel, threatening the Olubadan and chiefs with suspension and deposition and 'dangling the Will-o'-the-Wisp of Local Autonomy before loyal farmers'. The latter referred to the plan under consideration by the Action Group and the Regional Government, with the support of some administrative officers, to divide Ibadan District's rural and urban wards into separate Council areas, with powers specifically designed to meet their particular problems.[17] All of this must fail, Adelabu continued. The Association would continue to hold meetings, the chiefs were not yet deposed, and the Crown Counsel had not yet done anything about the leaflet. In what he hoped would be a public taunt at his opponents, Adelabu wrote

The Ibadan Tax Payers Association is the Army of Ibadan Democracy on the March. We plot against no one. We hate nobody. But any conceited Chief or Councillor who constitutes himself an obstruction to our onward March of Progress will be ground into powder. We issue this solemn and last warning to all doubting Thomases to reorientate their political thinking to the changed circumstances of mid-1953. We are already the strongest political Party in Ibadan today. Our figures of enrolment will astonish all snail-pace gradualists. We have a leadership imbued with dynamic energy and indomitable courage our followership is a multitudinous horde. We shall sweep the polls in the coming election. Woe betide any futile effort at resistance!!!![18]

This he immediately followed with another raucous set of jibes against the Councillors in a piece entitled 'Much Ado About Nothing'.* Their activities were 'tainted with Uncle Tomism, Childishness, Unreasonableness, Highhandedness, Bigotry, Mischief and Intimidation' but his specific charges were mainly related to problems of chieftaincy. Why, he asked, when the Oni of Ife, the Alake of Abeokuta and the Odema of Ishara all co-operated with political parties, should the Ibadan chiefs be an exception? 'I am sure Mr Obafemi Awolowo will be the last person to countenance local autocrats

* This is also in his papers in typescript, and includes many of the phrases from 'Battle for Democracy', cited above, which had by this time perhaps already been rejected for publication. Adelabu produced a whole series of typescript articles in the middle months of 1953 which were not published. It is possible that he made no attempt to do so, heavily involved in street-campaigning as he became, and that he tended to lose interest in these effusions once he had finished them.

belabouring our Obas and Chiefs for exercising their democratic right of giving their moral and political support to parties with policies and programmes acceptable to them.' What had John Hayley had to say to the Ibadan chiefs, he wished to know, in the Chieftaincy Committee meeting prior to the Council meeting at which they had been forced to apologize for 'exercising their constitutional right of freedom of association. . .'?* Stating again that the I.T.P.A. obeyed all laws and was not engaged in an anti-tax campaign, Adelabu warned the administrative officers 'to steer clear of this domestic skirmish between two political parties'.

Adelabu's warning to the administrative officers was also a more general warning that the I.T.P.A. was mounting a full-scale attack upon any of the bastions of the Ibadan Native Authority in which a victory might strengthen the Association's chances of controlling the new local government through the elections which were expected at any time. His assumption that a number of the existing Councillors would stand again was to be born out in March 1954 when the elections were actually conducted, but his attacks upon them and their policies in 1953, both direct and indirect, aroused such immediate response on their part that he was able to turn the Council into one of his best publicity sources while crippling many of its policies sufficiently so that in 1954, upon his assumption of office, Adelabu himself could determine many of them as he saw fit.

One such instance lay in the problem of taxation. We have seen above how the Council was forced to consider, as had virtually all Councils before it, some methods of improving the tax base and tax collection procedures. At just the time when the inauguration of the Tax Payers Association was announced, news was received by the Council from Lagos that rents there had risen an astronomical 400 per cent since the first evaluation and that a re-evaluation in order to raise rates was under way. A tax on houses had first been proposed for Ibadan in 1948, but the news was not interpreted by the Ibadan Council as an indication of how lucrative a source of revenue property rating might be, for suddenly on 26 May, the Finance Committee passed a resolution, later accepted in the full Council, stating that it was 'inopportune' to introduce property rating 'at present' and that the matter should be 'left in abeyance'. Thus the same Councillors who had once favorably considered the system and argued for its acceptance, 'despite all advice and very considerable pressure' from the District Officer brought to a

---

* From the Council Minutes of 13 May 1953: 'On the 6th instant [Hayley] met the Chieftaincy Committee to discuss the [Mabolaje Society] and also the question of the leaflets distributed in the town and district by the Mabolaje Society. At that meeting it was decided that a special meeting of the Council should be convened and the Junior Chiefs and Mogajis invited to attend.'

halt a program which seemed on its way to success. There were hard political reasons for this shift. First, the 1952–3 tax season had proven unexpectedly successful so that a fiscal surplus was actually on hand. Second, the Councillors had now come to realize that the houses which many of them had constructed in reponse to the post-war housing shortage would be hit by the tax, a fact which the Lieutenant Governor commented on when reading the Ibadan Provincial Annual Report for 1953.

Unfortunately, some of the most influential members of the Council are among the biggest property owners in Ibadan and they are determined to resist the introduction of a system that will increase their own contribution in proportion to their interest.[19]

Curiously linked to this was the opposition to the proposal from the chiefs, who persisted in thinking that a tax on lineage-owned land was involved, which would cause an increase in their taxes, when, in fact, the proposed shift of the tax burden to rented properties would have lowered the rate of income tax. It was against this background that the anti-tax platform, on which Adelabu encouraged his followers to believe he stood, rapidly gained substantial public support. By word of mouth and through informal communication channels the idea was spread that Adelabu, if elected, would abolish or lower taxes. Under the circumstances, what position would the body of illiterate taxpayers-cum-electors take? The Councillors in 1953 felt they knew the answer. Tax reforms had hitherto increased tax rates without fail, and the best way to deal with the tax issue was not to be associated with it in any way at all. With the approach of the local election, it was necessary for them to get off the property rating platform as quickly as possible.

Although the *Defender* on 17 June carried an official denial that local government elections in Ibadan were imminent, it is hardly surprising that the I.T.P.A. continued its efforts toward recruiting members, improving its internal organization and attacking its opponents. At a General meeting of the Association held on 13 June at Akere's compound, Adelabu announced that 1705 members were already inscribed, a figure whose validity is somewhat questionable in light of the fact that on 27 June the Association took delivery of only 1500 membership cards from the Kibo Printing Works of Oke Padre Street. Also of interest was the assertion of strength by the Association mogajis, who demanded and received from President Adelabu an accounting of expenditures to date, during which it was revealed that a balance of £8. 1. 4d. was on hand.[20]

A letter in June from the Association to the Administrative Secretary of the Ibadan Council and the Senior District Officer further demonstrates the attempts of the I.T.P.A. to attack the existing order and hopefully to change it prior to the anticipated elections. Protesting that the existing forty wards into which the city was divided did not correspond with the distribution of population and that the allocation of only fourteen seats to the urban population resulted in their gross under-representation in the Council, the letter, with a confusing use of terms, proposed a new total of fifteen 'constituencies' demarcated along the city's main roads and extending into the rural areas. In each of the nine urban 'constituencies' there would be two three-member 'wards', in either of which a resident of the constituency could stand for election. Each of the six rural constituencies would be made up of six single-member wards, making a total of ninety elected members of the Council. Under this new system, which allowed some freedom to political parties to allocate candidates on a non-residential basis and to create slates which might sweep all three urban ward seats for a single party, the electorate would for once be given 'a chance to vote for party principles as against parochial personalities'. Such a scheme, the letter urged, would meet with 'universal acceptance', although Adelabu and his associates of course knew that the 'parochial personalities' against whom they inveighed were the I.C.C. members, some of whom had successfully opposed a similar scheme brought before the Hayley Committee, all of whom had been elected under the existing forty-ward system and some of whom intended to run under it again.

The I.T.P.A. also knew of the plans under consideration to divide the District into its urban components, where the I.C.C.–I.P.U.–Action Group consortium might expect to do well, and its rural components, where Adelabu's ties with the Maiyegun League and their own disinclination to conduct 'bush' campaigns could work against them. The I.T.P.A. urged that electoral rules be established at least two months prior to the actual date of the election to allow the parties and the electorate to assimilate and act upon them, and they made a statesmanlike offer to meet with a committee of the existing Council to discuss 'any obscure points needing elucidation' in their proposal. Foreseeing the reception this suggestion was bound to receive, and recognizing the contradictory value of a discrediting attack upon the existing Council, they at the same time urged that a Management Committee of traditional chiefs and the Senior District Officer should replace the Council during the electoral period.

Although there is some doubt that the letter was ever sent, it had undoubtedly served to clarify the workings and opportunities of an electoral system through discussion among the stalwarts of the Association gathered around Adelabu. Their campaign was now in full swing and to those who preferred the more gentlemanly process of selection by arrangement and agreement that had characterized the 1952 elections, it must have seemed threatening indeed. Between 25 June and 25 July, I.T.P.A. campaign meetings were held in various wards of the city every Tuesday, Thursday, Friday and Saturday, and beginning on 26 July they were held almost daily. The early meetings were presided over by the mogaji or chief in whose compound they were held, while the later meetings, in the central parts of the city, often at large intersections or markets, were presided over by Adelabu himself. The *Defender*, which now viewed the N.C.N.C. cause as best furthered through Adelabu, carried frequent reports of the Association's activities and published its news releases with great regularity. As the Council prepared to select the committees of tax assessors in each ward for the 1953–4 tax season, the *Defender* publicized the Association's position that junior chiefs and mogajis not already assigned to court duties should be appointed to such committees and that members should in no case be chosen without the knowledge of the taxpayers.

So menacing indeed was Adelabu's new organization that it was considered repeatedly in the chambers of the Ibadan Council itself. On 13 July, after two weeks of I.T.P.A. campaigning, the 'intriguing propaganda' being spread by 'Mr Adelabu, some Chiefs, Mogajis and others' against the tax program of the Council was brought to its attention. The Olubadan was forced to state that such propaganda was being distributed without his knowledge, that he had no connection whatsoever with the campaign the I.T.P.A. had under way and that his bellman would announce throughout the city his lack of connection with Adelabu. It was apparently unknown at this time that the Olubadan was scheduled by Adelabu to preside over an Association rally on 1 August in Mapo Hall itself. A special Committee, including Chief Salawu Aminu and Councillors Akinfenwa, Oyesina and Sanda was appointed to examine the contact with the I.T.P.A. of Mogajis Akere, Arijemogba, Tajo, Oluyole and Ibikunle, all recent I.T.P.A. recruits, the last of whom was scheduled to preside over a rally the following day, and Chiefs Akinyo, Ayuba and Solagbode, who had chaired a meeting only two days earlier. It was further agreed that the chiefs and mogajis 'should show the cause why they would not be disciplined for their intrigue against the Constituted Ibadan Native Authority by inducing people to break the law and not to pay tax'. Any chief or mogaji who took part in such intrigues should be suspended or removed from his office.

The Tax Payers Association promptly denied inciting any intrigue and threatened legal action against those who alleged that it did, calling 'childish' the Council's attempts to restrict the chiefs 'in the enjoyment of political rights granted to their brother Obas and Chiefs all over Nigeria'.[21] The Council then attempted to take the wind out of the sails of the I.T.P.A. by siding with the chiefs in their fears over court reforms. Thus, twenty-five

Ibadan Assemblymen, having read the report of the Select Committee on court reforms and taking note of the impending application of the Local Government Law, argued that 'any reform of the Ibadan Town Courts should be suspended until a more representative Council is formed'. Court reform, they urged, was not as pressing a problem as the creation of the new Council and, as the Assemblymen were to argue on the entire range of issues before them (including tax), a new Council might deal quite differently with such an issue.[22] On the other hand, the Council also attempted to keep the chiefs under closer surveillance by resolving that the Chieftaincy Committee should henceforth hold all its meetings at Mapo Hall rather than at the House of the Olubadan.[23]

The Select Committee's report had also been sent to all Members of the Western House of Assembly, and the former I.P.P. (now Action Group) legislator Moyo Aboderin joined the Councillors in proposing a delay, noting that the Brooke Commission Report had not yet been officially released and urging that nothing be done until it was and its recommendations applied to the whole Region.[24]

While such serious concern with his campaign in the Ibadan Council was a welcome indication of his success against his enemies, and although he wrote early in July of 'The Victory of Truth', Adelabu had since June been confronted by much more dangerous counter-measures, threatening his campaign at a more popular level.[25] On 21 June a new local party, the United Muslim Party, had come into existence at a meeting at the Central Mosque; among those present were Bello Abasi, Alhaji Y. S. Ola Ishola, and Councillors A. B. Inakoju and Salami Akinfenwa. Already, just over a week before, the Chief Imam, Muili Ayinde, had raised the issue of religion in politics in his message on the occasion of the festival of Id el Fitr, when he warned the faithful that they should not sell their votes 'to black masters who want to have Muslims under their feet forever', a distinct and clearly understood warning against the I.C.C.[26]

Adelabu immediately sensed the danger of this coming together of some of his enemies in an organization which might blur the line of battle between N.C.N.C. and Action Group which he was anxious to preserve. Moreover, he was alarmed by the potentialities of the United Muslim Party as a rival of the I.T.P.A.–Mabolaje in gaining popular support on an issue – the feeling of relative deprivation on the part of Ibadan Muslims – which might prove as effective a vote-getter as anti-tax agitation. The U.M.P. was the result of a change of tactics on the part of the Action Group. Anxious to increase its support in Ibadan it was in search of issues and men as media through which this could be done. Hitherto it had found support primarily among I.C.C. leaders who could make no appeal to the masses; in Bello Abasi it hoped it had found the solution to this problem.* He could bring to it his reputation and long experience in Ibadan politics; in return he was to get the new office of Babasale (Patron) of the Muslims in Ibadan, which would give him the rank of chief. Throughout the century various people had held the title of Babasale of the Christians and had sat as advisers in court cases involving people of that faith to prevent violations of its observances by non-Christian court members. Now the new position was being suggested as a pretext for giving Abasi a court position and the salary attached thereto.

All this drove Adelabu to a fury he never again reached in his campaign. Denouncing the new party as a 'Political move by a clique of Ibadan Muslim Ideological Masqueraders', Adelabu argued that 'all over the civilized world the dividing line in politics is not based on religious creeds but on political Ideologies'.[27] 'The United Muslim Party is an organisation with no recognised ideological paternity. It is born out of legal wedlock. It is the mental product of confused political chameleons...' At this time he revealed that the Tax Payers had already selected their own candidates, of whom forty-nine were Muslims and five were Christians. Referring to the largely Christian I.P.U., he argued that although 'a few selfish Christians cheated the Muslims of their right' there was no valid excuse to exclude all Christians from a political party; because they had been included in the I.T.P.A. proportionately to their strength in the general population, it was therefore a secular organization. Furthermore the new U.M.P. in proclaiming Muslim solidarity had left out the element of 'Christian team work' and emphasized 'extreme individualism...a notorious Muslim vice'. 'In order to create a stable political Party you need not only Muslim courage and combativeness but also Christian discipline and fortune.' N.C.N.C. members who joined the Muslim Party that accepted Action Groupers were traitors to the cause of the N.C.N.C. and Adelabu promised to fight them exactly as he fought all Groupers.

Islam had been politically significant from the beginning of Ibadan. In 1916 a separate quarter, the Sabongari (more popularly 'Sabo'), had been created on the outskirts of the town for the largely Muslim immigrants from the North on the insistence of the British, against the opposition of Ibadan landlords and trading partners of northerners. One of the results was that variations in Muslim practice now also had geographical focus and organizational differences, since mosques in the different parts of the city were controlled by different sets of Alfas and Imams. An attempt had been made in

* This had required some change of heart on the part of Action Group leaders, as shown by Awolowo's letter to the Resident of Oyo Province on 27 June 1950: 'It is a well known fact that the Abasis, particularly those that were close to their late father the Olubadan, are not in the good books of all those in authority in Ibadan.'

1942 to halt this separatism and Olubadan Fijabi made another attempt in 1951 to stop the separate Friday prayers of the Sabo group. In 1951 the view of the Sabo was that expressed in 1942 by Sabongari Chief Sarkin Zungeru, '...the more mosques, the more keys to Heaven'. In 1948 a further issue had been added to the complex pattern of intra-Muslim relations in Ibadan, when the Chief Imam of the Central Mosque requested that a Babasale of the Muslims be appointed. The Maiyegun Society, among others, protested this as unnecessary in a town where 'everyone' was a Muslim anyway and in September the Chief Imam was informed that his request had been refused.[28]

In 1951 Sarkin Zungeru wrote to the Sultan of Sokoto, seeking advice on the separate mosques issue. The Sultan sent a memorandum on the criteria for separate mosques to the Secretary of the Northern Provinces, who in turn sent it to his counterpart in the Western Provinces, through whom it was transmitted to the Resident of Ibadan in August 1951. The matter had been made more urgent by the encroachment into Ibadan of the militant Tijaniyya sect from Senegal through Lagos which, drawing support from both the Sabo and from Ibadan Muslims, insisted on praying apart.* The activities of the Tijanis drew indirect support from the attitude of the colonial authorities toward the issue of separate Friday prayers in the Sabo. To halt this practice, the Acting Resident stated in October 1951, would have been to interfere in something which had been going on for twenty years.[29] Thus there was official, colonial sanction of what was portrayed as religious freedom and separation of religion and politics.

The separate prayers issue came to a head in August 1953 through Alfa Sunmonu Lanase, a Yoruba Tijaniyya adherent whose challenge to the authority of the Chief Imam led to street fights late in that month.[30] On 4 September Adelabu warned the Senior Resident of 'possible communal upheaval' if the separate Friday prayers of the Alfa were allowed to continue.[31]† In his letter Adelabu now portrayed himself as 'the special spokesman of the grievances of the Ibadan Muslim Community to the higher authorities': this was a position which he could hardly avoid claiming if he were to outflank the U.M.P. and indeed appear to represent the masses of

---

* Abner Cohen in his *Custom and Politics in Urban Africa* (London: Routledge and Kegan Paul, 1969), pp. 153–6, gives details of how the issue affected the northern community in the Sabongari.

† A threat of riot might have carried some weight at this time. In the villages of Eruwa and Lanlate, a widespread refusal to accept tax assessment notices had developed. John Hayley and B. J. Cooper had gone with a battalion of police to investigate when rocks were thrown, Dane guns fired and the police broke. Cooper was hospitalized and later received the M.B.E. Hayley wrote, 'I shudder to think what can happen if incidents such as this arise at more populous places...' (Resident's Report to Civil Secretary, 5 September 1953, PADID 3140/S.1.)

Ibadan. Though he called for armed intervention to halt the violence he predicted and perhaps hoped for, his protest came too late. On 7 September the Council approved Abasi as Babasale of the Muslims, and on 1 October it was announced that the dispute between Lanase and the Imam had been resolved.[32]

Adelabu did all in his power to resist this encroachment on his own new use of religion in politics, for now the defense he had made of the Imam was irrelevant. On 10 September he delivered letters to the Resident and the *Defender* protesting against Abasi's selection. To the Resident, citing Akinpelu Obisesan as an authority, he urged that elected councillors should 'avoid direct interference' in issues of Chieftaincy titles.[33] He also enclosed a statement, 'The Babasale of Ibadan Muslims Chieftaincy Dispute', in which he charged that the creation of a Muslim chieftaincy was merely a trick to quiet protest over the recent creation of an honorary line of titles to be given for service to the community, the senior title of which had been given to Bishop Akinyele on 22 May. The following day a similar but sharper line was taken in a long lead article in the *Defender*, 'Taxpayers Oppose New Title as Travesty on Ibadan Traditional Chieftaincy.'[34]

On 18 September, Bello Abasi was formally installed as Babasale of Ibadan Muslims. Olubadan Igbintade stayed away, but the impressive ceremony still went ahead in the Central Mosque, presided over in the Olubadan's absence by a Christian, the Otun Balogun Isaac Akinyele. The presence of many notables provided a powerful demonstration of the Action Group's ability to fuse together Muslim leaders, prominent Christians, I.C.C. Councillors and even traditional elements in the winning over of a man, Bello Abasi, in whom the N.C.N.C. had placed much hope. From this point onward, the Action Group could feel that it had established its presence in Ibadan.

It was against this background, then, and in spite of requests that nothing be done about court reforms until the release of the Brooke Commission Report, that Leader of Government Business and Minister of Local Government Obafemi Awolowo informed the Ibadan Council on 23 September that he wished to meet with them on the morning of 26 September to discuss the proposed court re-organization. According to a newspaper report of this meeting, Awolowo stated he had come to make 'investigations'; stressing that it was possible for him to act without consulting the people of Ibadan at all, he said that he did not wish to do so, in the interest of good will.[35] This was an extremely strong position to take for a man who was best known to Ibadan in his recent capacities as leader of the Native Settlers and supporter of the Oshun separation, all the more startling in view of the less authoritarian stance taken in recent years by the colonial officers.

Awolowo's principal argument was a legal one. The creation of a system of local government whereby local councils were responsible administratively to a Minister and a Cabinet Government meant the elimination of the dual roles of the colonial administrative officer. Previously the administrator had served as supervisor of the customary courts and channel of appeal in customary cases through to the Resident and the Lieutenant-Governor. Now that administrative tasks were to be exercised under the direction of the Ministerial Government, it was necessary to make all appealed cases amenable to the laws and rules of the single appellate process that culminated in the Supreme Court. This required literate judges under a Chief Judge appointed by Government for customary courts. Awolowo did not deny that literate judges might be even more corrupt than illiterate ones; what was necessary was that records be kept and communications properly formulated. As indicated in the first chapter of this book, the chiefs of Ibadan in the early part of the century had refused to allow their sons to be educated, since they saw in education a deterioration of the moral fiber of their society. Now in a time of still-illiterate chiefs, this calculation was coming home to roost in the person of the Ijebu politician. As Adelabu himself had foreseen in 1936, 'The next generation will not tolerate illiterate chiefs.'

The various Members of the Western House of Assembly from Ibadan, including Adelabu, were present at this session. Protests were heard that the reforms did not originate from a representative body and that it was dangerous to appoint rather than elect a Chief Judge. Adelabu argued that the 'Native Courts' 'belonged' to the Olubadan, the chiefs and the mogajis, and to do away with their control of the courts would bring 'chaos' to the city. What Awolowo sought was the elimination of the concept of 'Native Courts' which 'belonged' to anyone, in the old Indirect Rule sense, and the substitution of a more rational structure which would have as its basis the 'territorial' view that a man should be subject to the laws of the area in which he resided. The aged Olubadan, when pressed for his views, stated, perhaps as faithfully as he could remember, that he had not been informed of the Council's discussions of the reform, in spite of the fact that his mark appeared on several of the documents already quoted. The meeting ended without any further agreement or removal of the misconceptions.

After attending the morning Council meeting, the Olubadan appeared at a rally in Mapo Hall held that afternoon to honor the beginning of the Western N.C.N.C. Conference called for 26 and 27 September. Adelabu had suffered a sharp defeat. At the rally he could see the Olubadan lending whatever traditional dignity was still his after the morning's confusion, but he had also to address the gathering (on 'The Essence of Leadership') with Bello Abasi in the chair. That same evening the 'Self-Government in 1956' dance at the West African Club was held 'under the distinguished patronage of Chief Bello Abasi, Babasale of Ibadan Muslims', a tribute with which the N.C.N.C. sought feebly to save its face in Ibadan and paid by Adelabu's most reliable public medium, the *Southern Nigeria Defender*. At this point the N.C.N.C. could not afford publicly to admit Abasi's defection, while he seems to have been content to pretend that his installation as Babasale had made no difference to his political alignment.

Adelabu's humiliation was great, but the Olubadan was under even greater stress. His position was already made difficult by the fact that the new ward tax committees had been announced only a short time earlier, and no mogajis were on them, casting doubt on the ability of the traditional ruler of Ibadan to provide for his own.[36] After much preliminary discussion an Extraordinary Council meeting was called on 8 October, at which a resolution was passed charging him, although he was absent due to illness, with deliberate falsehood in denying to Awolowo any knowledge of the Council's court reform plans, refusing to co-operate with the tax program until forced to do so, and supporting 'outside influences'.[37] As pressure mounted against him, he was forced to declare in a *Nigerian Tribune* release on 15 October that he had not known the rally on the afternoon of 26 September was an N.C.N.C. meeting, that he had stayed only fifteen minutes, and that 'I want to state publicly that I do not support N.C.N.C. or Adelabu in the confusion that he is creating in my town.'

Given these circumstances, Awolowo's Government must have concluded that the time was ripe to press its case for reforms of the Ibadan courts, and sometime early in October the Ibadan Resident was informed that Awolowo felt that the court reforms should be implemented not later than 1 January 1954. Since no date had yet been announced for the elections, it was clear that the reforms were to precede them.[38] In an accompanying press release, the structure of the new courts was laid down. The Judicial Court of Appeal would have a single literate judge assisted by two assessors, to be appointed by the Resident. The judge of the Judicial Court would be the Chief Judge and in the first instance it would be Otun Balogun Akinyele, who would also advise the Resident on the appointment of all other judges, who must be literate, and their assessors, one of whom should be literate. While this was being protested by the Ibadan Welfare Committee, the Ibadan Band of Unity, a Select Committee of the Council and some of the Chiefs, the death of Balogun Salami Agbaje was suddenly announced.*

Agbaje's death opened the way for Otun Balogun Akinyele to become

---

* We were told that the death of Agbaje, who was a Muslim, was caused by *juju* and was related to his failure to perform the weekly washings with sheep's blood of Opa Balogun, his staff of office, and his description of the object as 'smelly'.

Balogun, presenting him with a very difficult decision about taking the title. Only a week prior to Agbaje's death, the Council had passed a unanimous vote of confidence in Akinyele as Chief Judge-designate, so that it was not a question of his political support within the Council. The problem lay in the traditional sector. An important symbol of the office was the staff of Oranyan, the Yoruba god of war, which had allegedly come to Ibadan during the nineteenth century, when Ibadan chiefs served as generals of the army of the Alafin of Oyo. This fetish object required a weekly bath in the blood of a freshly slain sheep and, although the pacific Isaac had been prepared to accept his position in the military line of chiefs, as head of the Christ Apostolic Church in Ibadan and a devout Christian he could not bring himself to observe this sacrifice. A compromise was therefore reached. A new staff was made for him with an aluminum cross on the head of it and he appeared at his installation before 5000 persons with it in his hand. He was supported in this action by the new Otun Balogun, Salawu Aminu, who, being an equally devout Muslim, had no desire to maintain the tradition of the Balogun's staff should he accede to the office. This promotion also virtually committed Akinyele to the acceptance, should it come to him, of the Olubadanship.

With Isaac Akinyele, a man of strong and independent will, waiting in the wings, Igbintade, upon whom Adelabu rested some hope, looked particularly weak. Thus, although Adelabu charged in November that the Olubadan had been 'intimidated and coerced' into an unwilling 'marriage under duress' wth the 'fascist' Action Group, having lost the battle against the court reforms and the creation of a Babasale of the Muslims and having failed to see any mogajis placed on tax committees, he now had to take a somewhat different line. The Association would continue to oppose unjust laws, but its members would obey them only until they had taken office, when 'in all spheres every objectionable law, bill, measure and rule shall be constitutionally repealed'. Thus the Association could still be viewed by its followers as having the intention to repeal the 'unjust' tax measures of the existing Council. Until this had occurred, however, it was the responsibility of the colonial power 'to maintain law and order and to prevent political party administrations from instituting a totalitarian regime by misusing the State power to suppress their political opponents'.[39]

At this same time, the Council continued to play a strong hand, the Finance Committee on 27 November and the Staff Committee on 7 December approving the fiscal and personnel aspects of the court reform, and the Council itself on 14 December voting to withdraw recognition as mogajis from the heads of the Oluyole and Oderinlo lineages who had aligned themselves with Adelabu. Throughout the campaign the Action Group's local leaders devoted most of their efforts to dealing with the repercussions of Adelabu's campaign upon the Council's work. In the forthcoming elections, however, these efforts would almost certainly count for less than those devoted to party organizational work. At the end of 1953 neither the Action Group nor the N.C.N.C. had any perceptible party organization in Ibadan, and both parties were generally conscious that at all levels their machinery left much to be desired. As early as January 1953, a group of N.C.N.C. supporters in Ibadan had written to Nnamdi Azikiwe and other party leaders, including Adelabu, pointing out what was needed. There were three essentials. First of all, there must be constant contact with party supporters – 'The present system of occasional lectures to some crowds and then leaving them to themselves without [a] shepherd is anything but adequate.'[40] Second, to remedy this situation, there must be fulltime professional organizing secretaries. Third, to make all this possible, there must be a regular supply of large sums of money: the writers of the letter suggested that it should be possible to recruit half a million dues-paying members throughout Nigeria in a year, thus ensuring £50,000 from the sale of party cards and £300,000 from their monthly contributions of one shilling. The diagnosis made by these N.C.N.C. supporters was undoubtedly correct; constant contact, fulltime organizers and adequate funds would have ensured N.C.N.C. strength – or for that matter Action Group strength – in many localities where there was potential support for the party. Over the next years these issues were to be discussed repeatedly within the ranks of the N.C.N.C., but the party never proved able to grapple successfully with its organizational problems.

From the point of view of its overall administration, the Action Group was in little better shape in the period 1952–4.[41] At the Warri Conference of that party in December 1953 it was reported that 181 branches had been founded in 1951, but that only 81 could be considered active. In June 1953 the party had launched a Trust Fund campaign to raise £150,000 but in the first six months only £14,000 was donated. When in October 1953 a Party Manager was appointed, he diagnosed the major problems as lack of finance and apathy on the part of Action Group legislators and set out with the help of three Organizing Secretaries to do what he could in the West.[42]

In Ibadan, Action Group Branches were founded in November 1953 in the rural areas of Amurire, Gbeduge, Gegede, Amosun, Folara and Akinboade.[43] Within the city, a number of personalities also attempted to place themselves closer to the electorate and strengthen party ties. A. M. A. Akinloye, for example, had already demonstrated his realization that a politician must woo his constituents more closely by holding an elaborately publicized house opening in June to celebrate his change of residence from Mokola, a stranger-dominated part of the city, to a new house in the heart of the traditional sector at Oje, which would henceforth be his constituency. The recruitment of the I.P.U. leaders, begun earlier by T. L. Oyesina, was completed early in 1954 when Obisesan notes that they gathered for photographs.[44]

On 4 December 1953, the *Tribune*, voice of the Action Group, reported that the Ibadan local elections would be held on 16 March 1954. Adelabu now turned to the establishment of a formal tie to his own national party. On 26 December, at the usual meeting place of the Tax Payers Association in Akere's Compound, the Ibadan N.C.N.C. Grand Alliance held its inaugural meeting. In addition to Adelabu, signatories to the invitation to attend this meeting were Elizabeth Adekogbe, wife of the Asistant Registrar of Co-operative Societies and President of the Women's Movement of Nigeria, of which Adelabu had become Patron in May 1953, Dr Ikejiani, prominent leader of the Ibadan Ibo Community (and family physician to Adelabu), Oshilaja Oduyoye, representative of non-Ibadan Yorubas and N.C.N.C. leader in Ibadan since May 1951, D. K. Olumofin, a particularly active N.C.N.C. member of the Western House of Assembly who was a manager for the Shell Oil Company in Ibadan, Adebayo Asaya, like Olumofin a Yoruba from Akoko Edo in Ondo Division, a printer who had been President of the Ibadan branch of the Zikist Movement until its suppression and who was already demonstrating his campaign meeting talents. Thus Adelabu called on a heterogeneous selection of elements of the national party to join him. Since the failure of the attempt to build a network of 'chapters' in the city in 1952, there had really been no N.C.N.C. organization in Ibadan, other than the ancillary youth wing. The party had been kept alive by prominent individuals, many of them native strangers. Adelabu had now built his own organizational basis and was making an alliance with the N.C.N.C., not by negotiating and agreement with the national party as such but by co-opting individuals.

Certainly the concerns of the Alliance, as given in the 'Ibadan NCNC Grand Alliance War Communique No 1. The Battle for the Soul of Ibadan', were entirely focused upon local issues aimed at the activities of the existing Council members.[45]

Seven features have characterised the policy of the new Council since its inauguration. They are (*a*) The Humiliation of our Senior [and] Junior Chiefs. (*b*) The subjugation of the Olubadan. (*c*) The persecution of the Mogajis. (*d*) Arbitrary Assessment of Artisans, Petty-Traders and small farmers. (*e*) The enactment or proposal of obnoxious bye laws. (*f*) Disregard and contempt for public opinion. (*g*) The shameless victimisation of political opponents.

Referring to the Tax Payers Association, the Communique stated that it had come into existence in response to these features and the need for 'an effective, militant local political party'; had this not been the case, illiteracy, lethargy and complacency would have had no other outlet and would have resulted in 'rioting and other illegal activities'. Now the Grand Alliance had come into being in order to transcend all other local parties. 'So far as the NCNC masses are concerned there are only two parties in the coming election, NCNC and the Action Group.' Evidence of the distinction between the Association and the Alliance in the minds of its founders can be seen in the fact that new membership volumes were drawn up at this time for the Alliance.* In fact, the next instrument which Adelabu used against the Council was neither the Association nor the Alliance, illustrating his total opportunism in regard to issues and organizations, even those of his own making.

It will be remembered from Chapter 1 that Lebanon Street and New Court Road are the major commercial streets of the city. In 1951 these streets were made one-way for motor vehicles. No discipline on other forms of traffic had yet been imposed. During the post-war boom the number of 'petty traders' and 'hawkers' increased greatly, particularly in Lebanon Street; anyone with a few pounds, or even a few shillings, of capital, could establish himself in trade, moving around shaving pennies off the retail prices offered in the shops. When the Lebanese returned to Ibadan after the War, a few acquaintances and relatives of influential chiefs and Councillors were allowed to sell their goods in front of the Lebanese stores where they bought their wares wholesale. At night, they left their bundles locked safely in the Lebanese shop. By 1952, however, they had entirely filled the space between shop front and road with their racks and shelves. Lebanon Street is only 2100 feet long and New Court Road is 3800 feet long. By 1952, 3000 petty traders, hawkers, and squatters divided this space among themselves.

Although the Lebanese now began to complain, the administrative officers dared not enter the dispute for fear of appearing to side with the Lebanese, just as they had sided with the Ibadans against the Ijebus. The answer found by the administrative officers was the proposal of a new bye-law which dealt specifically only with traffic control rather than with the question of trespass by prohibiting hawkers from engaging in their activities within fifty feet of the center of important streets and within five feet of the gutter on smaller streets. Since fifty feet in the crucial cases of Lebanon Street and New Court Road went far into the space immediately in front of the Lebanese shops, some relief was also provided for shopkeepers in the guise of traffic control.

* The authors were permitted a brief examination of volumes B and D of this four-volume set by Chief Akere, who had them in his possession. They were last used on 17 July 1957.

The degree of public involvement increased as knowledge of the action spread. A group of traders, Lebanese and Ibadan, who had permanent shops on Lebanon Street, came to complain that police control on the street was inadequate.[46] A dozen of the squatters in turn charged that 'the sheer molestation recently received from the Syrian-Lebanese Traders including most African shopkeepers...who malignantly conspired together against us...' had forced them to ask for land at Dugbe to set up their own market.[47]

By 21 September 1953, however, enforcement had already displaced many persons. A 'heavy assembly' of them from the Ibadan Textile Traders' Association gathered outside Mapo Hall that day during a Council meeting. In face of this, the Council resolved that the Street Trading Rules as applied to Lebanon Street, New Court Road and Onireke Street near Ogunpa Motor Park should no longer be enforced until 'suitable market places' had been provided by the Council for the traders on these streets. The police were to be asked to stay execution of the Rules.[48] The Council decision was conveyed to the Senior District Officer who responded in anger.[49] The police had been put in an awkward position which would probably make them less enthusiastic about enforcement in the future. The man-in-the-street had been taught that 'if an unpopular measure is passed by the Native Authority, all that is necessary to have it suspended is for a noisy demonstration to be organized at Mapo Hall'. Later in November, under great administrative pressure, the Council agreed that enforcement could proceed once again. Publicity would be given that the Rules would be enforced as of 1 January 1954. Police were ordered to be ready to prevent traders from returning on 2 January and to be on duty thereafter for a week to prevent 'filtering back'.[50] On 28 December 1953, however, two days after Adelabu formed the 'Grand Alliance' of his local party with the N.C.N.C., he and Barrister E. Ola Fakayode, a native of Ibadan and an N.C.N.C. leader, but not one of the founders of the Alliance, took up the cause of the 'Ibadan Street Traders' Association' (apparently the Textile Traders under another name). From that time, Lebanon Street became a party matter.

On 28 December, Fakayode requested an opportunity for the Traders' Association to learn from the administrative officers of the advantages and disadvantages of the rules which were shortly to be enforced, and, on the same day with Adelabu, Buraimo Alao, leader of both the Tax Payers' and the Traders' Associations, and 5000 others arrived at Mapo for an interview. Adelabu and Fakayode spoke with District Officer Lewis while the 'street traders' waited in the Mapo Compound. They opposed, they stated, the restrictions about to be enforced upon street trading and requested that they once more be postponed, this time until the existing Council had been replaced in the election to be held in March. The new Council, according to a note of this interview which Adelabu signed, could then amend the Rules, as the Commissioner who later inquired into Adelabu's Council put it, 'in deference to public opinion'.[51]

As with many of his other causes, Adelabu's championship in this case was paradoxical. From 1949 to 1951, as we have seen, he had rented a textile shop on Lebanon Street from a Lebanese, Anthony Younan, and in 1955 he was to become a full partner with Anthony's son, Albert, in a general merchandise and transport business. How these relationships affected his ability to lead an anti-Lebanese movement is not clear. Perhaps by this time the street traders were beginning to hold the Council's administrative officers more responsible than the Lebanese for their fate. Indeed this was encouraged by the Lebanese who, by refusing to take trespassing suits against the squatters, left full initiative and responsibility in the hands of the District Officers. In various ways, such as the granting of eighty-four lock-up stalls to the Traders' Association by the Council the day after Adelabu's visit, the impression of this responsibility was confirmed, to Adelabu's credit, if not that of his political organization, which had not been formally involved.

The enforcement actions of the police were promptly undertaken in January. Adelabu at this time was campaigning heavily to win the impending Council elections for his party, and he did not attempt direct opposition to the street trading rules.

Nevertheless, Adelabu had taken upon himself the leadership of a battle in the streets, one which had vastly irritated the police and the administrative officers and which had shown again that the vacillating Council responded more to public pressure or administrative remonstrances during an election year than to its own principles. In the process, Adelabu had undoubtedly led his largest public group and had become a channel through which the market women of Ibadan could express their demands. This was particularly important since the market women of the area came from all over the city and were in touch, through their families and customers, with virtually the entire female population.

At the end of 1953 it appeared, if only for a brief moment, as if the Council might yield on reform of the Courts, as well as on Lebanon Street, and be forced to consider the reforms as a matter that should be resolved entirely within the context of the struggle for power through elections. On 27 December, the day after the formation of the Alliance, a sub-Committee of the Assemblymen whose views had been solicited resolved that the selection of the Judges and assessors should indeed be postponed until after the elections. The Council, however, with Obafemi Awolowo at its heels, could not afford to accept this resolution.

Adelabu, by this time absorbed in daily street campaigning for the approaching election, did not respond to this indecision by some members of the Council until early in February, when he called again for its dissolution so that the Council could not complete the local implementation of the reforms. In particular he urged that the selection of judges and assessors was a task which democracy required should be done by a truly representative local government, rather than alone by Chief Akinyele. This misrepresented the selection process somewhat, in that technically Akinyele was supposed to propose a list of judges and assessors from which Government would select those to serve. However, the District Officer had already made clear to Government what his views of Akinyele's nominees would be.*

At Akinyele's insistence, Awolowo attended a special meeting of the Council on 5 March to clarify the ground rules which Akinyele wished to apply and which Government had agreed to accept regarding the nomination of judges and assessors.[52] At this meeting the Minister assured the chiefs that the literacy tests for judges need not apply to them as assessors and would not affect chieftaincy succession; nor did any illiterate need to fear that he was thereby disqualified from the Olubadanship.[53] When Akinyele then urged that the senior chiefs whose names he had not listed as assessors should be paid a sum in compensation for the court allowances they had been drawing to that date, he was suddenly welcomed as the protector of tradition. The chiefs, now willing to exchange the exercise of power for the perquisites of office, no longer opposed the reforms of the courts and no longer looked to Adelabu to protect their 'traditional' rights. Although it was too late to select and install the judges and assessors before the election, it was now certain that Adelabu could not prevent this from happening after the new Council was formed.

While Adelabu was unsuccessful in stalling the forces aligned against him in the matter of court reform until it could become the business of his Council, the issue had illustrated that the decolonization process, as far as he and his Alliance and the entire city of Ibadan were concerned, was much more complex than a simple nationalist attack upon the colonial power. Not only were many more participants involved, but each of them was also uncertain of himself and therefore unable to act in a predictable manner with the others. This was just as true of the colonial power as of the rest, for the administrative officers frequently found themselves shifting their values, un-

---

* '...my views are...that the opposition hope that they will form the new council and they wish themselves to make the nominations of the proposed judges and assessors. I should myself prefer to rely on Chief Akinyele's recommendations rather than on any Council's view, however honest, upright and distinguished the individual members of that Council might be.' (District Officer Lewis to the Resident, 19 January 1954, Ibaprof 1, 1109 vol. IV.)

able to control other participants and uncertain as to how to deal with the changing rules of decolonization and the technical problems of modernization. This was a situation in which the actions of a number of different individuals – chiefs, politicians, administrative officers – which were usually unco-ordinated, produced a varying set of reactions. In a bewildering, even kaleidoscopic, dialect of decolonization these actions and reactions were beginning in 1953–4 to move Ibadan (and, on a national level, the whole of Nigeria) along paths which would end in a new political system. The general trend was punctuated occasionally by events which, more obviously than any others, moved the system in its new direction. Such an event was the election of the new Ibadan District Council in March 1954. We have already seen Adelabu preparing for this organizationally and taking stands upon issues of significance for his native city. It is now time to turn to the final stages of the campaign.

By the turn of the year, the N.C.N.C. was holding campaign meetings daily and sometimes twice daily, visiting a village for a morning meeting and returning to the city for a meeting at a market, street intersection, or major compound at 4.00 p.m. A regular team of campaigners travelled together continually, including Adelabu. Frequently they had the benefit of the company of the Olubadan's messengers who were paid, uniformed employees of the Council placed at the Olubadan's disposal, a campaign artifice bitterly resented and frequently protested against by the incumbent Councillors. Campaign meetings were typically begun with a prayer by Alfa Elesinmeta, followed by speakers in various combinations but always including Adelabu and, in the outlying wards of the city, representatives of the ethnic groups, such as the Ibo or Hausas living there. A ballot box was frequently brought along to instruct new registrants in its use and to help them identify the N.C.N.C. symbol, a picture of a cock rooster, which would be prominently displayed on the N.C.N.C. box at the polling booth to help the illiterate find the box belonging to the candidate of his choice.*

Campaign messages, in addition to the discussions on the courts, chieftaincy, taxation and the vices of opponents, attempted humor and often referred to the money the Action Group candidates were spending, 'We

---

* Voters were not called on to mark ballot papers in any way, as it was agreed that this was not possible with a largely illiterate electorate. Each candidate was allocated a ballot box, therefore, in each polling station and these were placed in a booth there. The voter entered the booth alone and placed his or her ballot paper in the box of the chosen candidate unobserved. This method was adopted for virtually all Nigerian elections until the collapse of the First Republic in January 1966. For an exception to this general rule see K. Post, *The Nigerian Federal Election of 1959* (Oxford University Press, 1963), p. 342, note 3, and for some general criticisms of the method, ibid., pp. 341–4.

chop [eat] Awolowo's money, but we love Adelabu.'* Abuse was common but not unending. J. A. Ayorinde, an independent candidate, listened to an Adelabu tirade at a meeting in the ward where Ayorinde was contesting, only to have Adelabu halt his speech and order the crowd to be quiet. 'A benefactor is here', he said, and then going to Ayorinde, 'Uncle, I am in politics and you are not. Please go home.'

Most important was the joyful affection this man of diminutive stature earned from the schoolboys who carried 'portable Ade' through the streets, from his followers who happily called him Penkelemesi, a corruption of the taunt of 'peculiar messes' he and his Action Group detractors frequently exchanged, and from the hangers-on who took his automobiles (while he sat in the market allowing his 'mamas' to feed him) and drove around the city singing his praises until the fuel ran out.

For all his insistence upon his self-importance when presenting himself as a job applicant or nationalist, when in the compounds of Ibadan, he made his achievements and status those of the masses. As a commentator put it a year later:

Adelabu went a little farther; he not only described his political opponents as 'the peculiar messes of the Action Group'; he created himself the 'peculiar man of the masses' by walking round town bare-footed and by eating with 'the people' from the same dish. What would you say about a 'book-man', a former U.A.C. manager, a motor magnate who does not consider himself as one of the detached *elite*, but as one of the illiterate masses whose only recommendation is 'this is my fatherland'?[54]

In addition to campaign meetings and his own captivating personality, Adelabu could now count entirely on the support of the *Defender*, which on 31 December published 'Election Communique No. 2, Party Principles Against Pompous Personalities'. In it, Adelabu emphasized, as he had done in House of Assembly Debates in 1952, that the N.C.N.C. was a party of high principle and performance, while the Action Group relied on tribalism, arrogance, technique and chicanery. These latter charges he expanded into a third, vitriolic communiqué.

The editor of the *Defender*, writing a column of political commentary under the pseudonym 'Ariel', also played his part, and rose to new heights of vituperation during the campaign. On 4 January, Ariel warned that he had been observing Ibadan from the roofs of Mapo and the United Africa

* People who were Grand Alliance candidates at this time stated in interviews that total electoral expenses of £35 to £50 were sufficient for illiterates to defeat literate Action Group candidates who spent up to £150. Costs rose in later years; the local elections of 1961 probably cost Action Group candidates as much as £300.

Company headquarters, and the pockets of the politicians, and that he would use *juju* against the unrighteous and see to it that those who 'dance bend-bend in the election Konga' would be dismissed. A few days later, shifting his attack on the British administrators, he asked, '...Mr. District Officer, what the hell are you doing about this election business?'[55] This boisterous journalism continued throughout the campaign.

It was a style entirely in accord with tactics employed by Adelabu himself as the campaign entered the final weeks. On 11 March the *Defender* carried his letter of 5 March to the Superintendent of Police, alleging the Action Group had hired hooligans to 'cause bodily harm' to him and possibly to kidnap him. On 14 March public disturbances broke out following a Grand Alliance rally at Mapo Hall. Nnamdi Azikiwe was present to introduce the candidates, while Olubadan Igbintade presided. The chamber was so full that Adelabu could not bring the crowd to silence and they satisfied themselves with singing songs. Afterward, 'portable Ade' was carried toward his home on the shoulders of his admirers. As the mob followed its leader, it came to constitute an unlawful assembly, since such street demonstrations were illegal without explicit, written police permission. In the process, a number of persons were shoved and probably beaten, and the police brought the first of many charges of unlawful assembly against Adelabu, Elesinmeta, and Mogbonjubola as a result of the affrays that occurred at Bere Square.

On 17 March, Adelabu put the final touch to the campaign plans. At a meeting at Akere's compound, each candidate of the N.C.N.C. signed a pledge of allegiance agreeing to:

...abide by all instructions and decisions of my party. If the party is satisfied at any time that I have failed in my duty of absolute loyalty to my party I agree to be expelled from the party and shall henceforth forfeit my seat in the Native Authority Council.

It shall then be the duty of the party to arrange for a bye election to fill the vacancy caused by the forfeiture of my seat.*

In addition, in the presence of two signed witnesses, candidates were obliged to sign their name or impress their thumbprint with their party membership card number on a blank sheet of paper, adequate precaution against any eventuality. Most of them were political unknowns and, in a number of cases, Adelabu specifically refused to allow persons of some stature and reputation to contest with the N.C.N.C. symbol. By election day, the N.C.N.C. was able to field thirty-nine urban and nineteen rural candidates. As we have seen, eighteen of these were drawn from founding members of

---

* Copies of these documents are in the Adelabu Papers. It should be noted that reference is still being made to the 'Native Authority Council', which in fact was to cease to exist as such.

the Tax Payers Association. Beyond this, Adelabu was probably able to enforce his selection of candidates because others lacked a sufficient organizational base from which to resist him and because of his campaign techniques. In interviews with several candidates of other groups who had more standing than Adelabu's choices in their wards prior to the election, they told how, when they attended N.C.N.C. campaign meetings, Adelabu would spot them in the crowd, call them 'Groupers' and 'thieves', even though they might have been Independents, and order that they be chased away and beaten. Candidates fleeing for their lives hardly represented the best protectors of the interests of the voters.

If Adelabu was thus able to select and defend his candidates, his relationships with Oba Sunmonu Igbintade II, Olubadan of Ibadan, remained uncertain. Only two days before the election, the *Daily Service* carried a story of a meeting of Central and Eastern N.C.N.C. Ministers with the Olubadan. Igbintade, it claimed, had appealed to Azikiwe to tell the British that they did not want an African government. Zik made the best of the embarrassing situation the Ibadan patriarch thrust upon him, assuring him that the Ministers before him came not as a political party but indeed as members of Governments, that they were close to the Governor himself and that nothing could happen in Ibadan that the N.C.N.C. and the Governor did not discuss.[56] Adelabu had written in 1951 that it would be necessary to withdraw the reality of power from the chiefs while leaving them with perquisites and pageantry. The withdrawal was a slow one and, as we shall see below, the Olubadan continued to embarrass his supporters in the following federal election.

On 17 March, the eve of the urban election (the rural wards were to poll a week later), top Action Group officials also came to Ibadan for a final appeal. In his speech, Awolowo seemed to assume defeat in assuring his listeners that the policies of his regional government would continue to prevail in spite of the N.C.N.C. challenge locally.[57]

The Action Group had also put up a battery of thirty-nine urban and nineteen rural candidates, relying heavily upon those long associated with the Progressive Union and the I.C.C., some of whom had had previous Council experience. With Awolowo behind them, they appeared to offer a serious opposition to the Alliance. What is astonishing is the degree to which the Action Group and the N.C.N.C. failed to impress on the other candidates, persons who presumably would have more political sophistication than the average elector, the importance of belonging to one of the major parties. The Ibadan scene at this time was one of conflict among highly fractionated and diffuse groups and interests. There were eighty urban candidates and twenty-eight rural who were not drawn from the Action Group or Grand Alliance.

Polling day in the city, Thursday, 18 March 1954, was a wet one, but by 10.30 p.m., when the results for the urban wards were announced, there was no cause for depression on the part of the N.C.N.C.–Mabolaje Grand Alliance. As Table 2 on page 196 shows, the declared results that night, giving the Grand Alliance thirty-five of the forty-three urban seats, revealed that the N.C.N.C. Cock would would henceforth crow from Mapo Hall, assuming that the Alliance won some rural wards on the 25th and was supported by some of the nineteen traditional members of the new Council. Enthusiasts showed no hesitation in proclaiming complete victory for the Alliance. The *Defender* announced that the Olubadan had 'conquered his enemies'; Kola Balogun, the N.C.N.C. National Secretary, sent his congratulations to the Olubadan and Adelabu, and one candidate who had won as an Independent hastened to assure the public that 'whatever happened I am an NCNCer to the core'.[58] On 25 March, as can be seen in Table 2, the Alliance victory was fully confirmed.

Adelabu's Grand Alliance had thus succeeded in using the contacts of the N.C.N.C. and the Mabolaje in the city to make some sort of showing in almost every ward, though noticeably less strongly in the eastern sector, where Christian families had always tended to reside. There were no Alliance nominations in four of the ten East wards. (See Map 3 for the urban ward boundaries.) They had conducted a vigorous campaign and won an overwhelming number of the urban seats. Nevertheless, the victory was not as sweeping as it first appeared. Most wards had been carried either with a minority of the total votes cast or by a small margin; the Alliance vote in the city, 13,685 to 12,330 for all its opponents, was only 52.6 per cent of the total.* Action Group had managed to find candidates in most urban

---

* There are certain obstacles to comment on any aspect of these elections. Detailed results for the urban wards were published in the *Nigerian Tribune* for 19 March 1954 and the *Defender* for the 20th, and for the rural wards in the *Tribune* for 21 March, and some further details, such as the number of registered electors, appeared in the *Defender* on 27 March. However, there are several inaccuracies in these newspapers; in addition to altered figures one urban candidate is omitted altogether and so is the whole result for one rural ward. The figures used here are calculated from the manuscript notes of results made on a master copy of the list of wards and candidates kept at Mapo Hall. The official figures given for registered electors, a total of 186,916 (which we believe breaks down as 120,303 for the urban wards and 66,613 for the rural) is a mystery. The franchise was based on the payment of tax, and officially 113,905 people paid their taxes to the Ibadan Council for 1954 (Chief Tax Clerk to Senior Divisional Adviser, 4 January 1957, PADID 547 s.8, vol. 1). J. P. Mackintosh, in *Nigerian Government and Politics*, states that no exact registration figures are available and quotes an estimate of 150,000 (p. 344). The official figures have been used in the calculations made here. Authorities also differ about the result of this election: Mackintosh for some reason omits the rural

TABLE 2 *Results of the Ibadan District Council Elections, March 1954*

	Grand Alliance			Action Group			Others			Polling		
	Urban	Rural	Total	Urban	Rural	Total	Urban	Rural	Total	Urban	Rural	Total
Votes	13,685	4670	18,355	4892	856	5748	7438	2288	9726	26,015	7814	33,829
Poll (%)	52.6	59.8	54.3	18.8	11.0	17.0	28.5	29.3	28.7	21.6	11.7	18.1
Seats	35	16	51	5	9	14	3	5	8	43	30	73

wards, but was weaker in the south-west part of the city than elsewhere. (Three of the four wards in which the Action Group failed to make nominations were in the south-west sector.) Its final showing was embarrassingly bad for a governing party. Only four urban seats could be claimed by its adherents, all in the eastern wards, two unopposed and two won on minority votes.

In the rural areas, it would appear that the parties had found it less easy to make contacts. Ten of the thirty seats were uncontested, two of these falling to the Alliance, six to the Action Group and two to other candidates. In the nineteen contests where the Alliance did field a candidate, however, only three of them were defeated and the Alliance won a larger proportion of the poll than in the urban wards.

As in every election in which many candidates sought the same seat, the winners tended to compile lower scores than in straight contests. As we have noted, this was an extremely fragmented contest, especially in the urban wards, which had 158 candidates for 43 seats as opposed to 66 for 30 rural seats. In all, twenty-three symbols were used, ten of them by lone individuals, and there were six groups of five or more candidates. In the urban wards there were eleven straight fights, but nearly two-thirds of the wards had four or more candidates; in two wards there were eight candidates, and seven in three others. This meant that a third of the seats were won on a minority vote, and nearly half the candidates got twenty-five votes or less. In the rural wards there were twelve straight fights, but six of the remaining eight contested wards had four candidates each and one had five. However, only three rural seats were won with minority votes, though nearly a third of the candidates who actually faced a contest got less than twenty-five votes. In this complex situation, the multiplicity of small voting combinations and Independents disappeared before the major parties. However complex the electoral process which produced it, a famous victory had been won by the Grand Alliance. The Grand Alliance's explanation was that the Ibadan masses had shown their support for the party of the common man and rejected the party of the elite; after all, the old I.P.U.–I.C.C. had now largely gone over to the Action Group, transferring to the newer party the animosities felt towards Ibadan's educated, Christian leadership. On the other hand, in an article published just after the urban election, Obafemi Awolowo explained the results largely in terms of the limitations the Action Group had put on the power of the chiefs and mogajis. The 'large' percentage of the tax paid in Ibadan had gone to the mogajis, he argued, and the Action Group

wards altogether, while Sklar, *Nigerian Political Parties*, p. 297, says that the Alliance won 56 elected seats. There is a high probability that the results given here are more accurate.

had corrected this by removing them as tax collectors, while the N.C.N.C. had promised to restore them and urged a reduction from the present flat rate of twenty-five shillings to the previous seven shillings. The Olubadan had campaigned for the N.C.N.C., but, Awolowo reminded his readers, he would no longer be president of the court system.[59]

The facts hardly bear out this interpretation, providing no real evidence that the influence of the chiefs and mogajis had any great bearing on the voting patterns. We have seen in Chapter 1 that most Ibadans probably did not belong to the chieftaincy structure. Nor were voter turnouts significantly heavier in the older, central wards where the more influential mogajis lived. More particularly, there is no evidence that the mogajis chose to throw their weight behind the Alliance; if they had, its vote would presumably have been greater than it actually was. There was in fact no reason for them to have done so. They had not lost merely the courts and the collection system, the opportunity to control which had come within the lifetime of many of them, but political opportunity generally. Most of them would never become senior chiefs, and their power was waning, nor could most hope to fare well in the rough and tumble of electoral politics which would lead to the seats of power in the new structure. What was already clear from months of association with and observation of Adelabu was that he, not one of them, was the head of the Mabolaje and that he, not a representative of the traditional order, would attempt to take power in March 1954. Only three of the Alliance's thirty-nine urban candidates were mogajis and they were not necessarily an electoral asset.

Although the Action Group's explanation for its defeat may be rejected, the sort of reason for its victory given by the Grand Alliance is scarcely more acceptable. Despite the sweeping nature of the Alliance victory in terms of seats, its performance in terms of the number of people it had been able to mobilize to the point of voting for it was scarcely impressive for a party which claimed to represent the masses. The 18,355 votes cast for the Alliance in all represented 54.3 per cent of the total, but only 18.1 per cent of the electors bothered to go to the polls (21.6 per cent in the urban wards and 11.7 per cent in the rural, voting in the latter being much reduced by the uncontested seats).* The Alliance's total vote, therefore, was only about 9.5 per cent of the possible total, hardly justifying a description of the I.T.P.A. (Mabolaje) as a mass or communal party.

Three factors had helped to bring Adegoke Adelabu and his associates to power in Ibadan in March 1954. First, and of lesser importance, the British

---

* The effect on the rural poll of uncontested wards was reinforced by the fact that these had an average of 3049 electors, while the contested wards had an average of 1806.

'first past the post' system, with single-member wards and no element of pro-portional representation, gave them twelve seats with only a minority of the votes in those wards. Adelabu's second and most substantial asset in March 1954 was the energy and opportunism he brought to bear over the previous eleven months in combining enough of the existing groups and leaders of Ibadan's organizational life into a supporting following at the time when a grant of powers was to be made on the basis of numbers. The web of con-tacts which he and the others had spun, in some cases over a decade or more, provided for the mobilization of sufficient votes. They had campaigned over many months, first as the bold enemies of an uncertain Council, then as the patrons of groups excluded by that Council from the political process, and in the last weeks in the streets, the market-places and the compounds of Ibadan.

They had a third asset. In an election in which relatively few people voted, and where the ability to pull together a few hundred supporters could mean victory in a given ward, the sort of men nominated by the Grand Alliance were often able to present an image which could attract enough support for the purpose. This asset was, as much as anything, a result of the contrasting image of their opponents. Table 3, for example, shows the pro-portion of Christians nominated by each party. The Action Group in par-ticular was thus identifiable in the minds of many voters with Christianity

TABLE 3 *Percentage of Christian Candidates, March 1954*

	Urban	Rural	Total
Grand Alliance	8.0	26.0	14.0
Action Group	44.0	63.0	50.0
Others	31.0	36.0	32.0
Total	28.0	44.0	32.0

and its attendant characteristics, literacy and relatively high status. Although it is not possible to collect complete data, it would appear that in as many as nineteen urban contests an illiterate Grand Alliance candidate defeated one or more literates. Table 4 on page 200 shows the occupations of candi-dates. From this it can be seen that the Action Group, at least in the urban wards, drew a significantly higher proportion of its candidates from the occupational groups marked by literacy and participation in modern eco-nomic and administrative pursuits (i.e. businessmen, business managers, professionals, government employees, and clerks). Other groups and indi-viduals had a similar pattern. In contrast the Grand Alliance had as the core of its list the ten farmers who stood in urban, rather than rural wards, thus demonstrating the closeness of the ties between the city proper and its rural

TABLE 4 *Occupations of Candidates, March 1954*

	N.C.N.C.		Action Group		Others	
	Urban	Rural	Urban	Rural	Urban	Rural
Farmers	10	9	2	12	7	14
Traders	8	–	7	2	29	4
Petty traders	4	2	2	–	1	–
Contractors	4	–	4	–	7	–
Craftsmen	3	2	1	1	5	1
Produce company employees and buyers	4	4	4	2	4	3
Businessmen	3	–	5	–	6	2
Salesmen	–	–	–	–	3	–
Business managers	–	–	2	–	1	–
Government employees	–	1	6	–	3	–
Clerks	–	–	2	1	8	–
Co-operative secretaries	–	–	–	–	3	–
Professionals	–	–	2	–	1	1
Educationists	–	1	–	–	1	1
Pensioners	–	–	2	–	–	1
Others	2 alfas 1 legislator	–	–	1 Chief	1 storekeeper and 1 journalist	1 Village Head and 1 Associate Judge

extensions as expressed through the traditional lineage structure. It seems likely that, although the influence of the mogajis themselves was not particularly apparent in this election, the ability to exploit kinship ties more skillfully was a definite asset for the Mabolaje/Maiyegun section of the Grand Alliance.

By the last week of March 1954, then, the final act of the 'bloodless revolution' had been played out. The I.C.C.-controlled Council, urged on by the Action Group Regional Government and the British administrators, had played its part in translating the new laws on local government, chieftaincy, and courts into real terms in Ibadan. It had initiated action, too, in other matters, such as taxation and the control of the Lebanon Street traders. All these were fitting activities for men whose entry into the politics of Ibadan via the I.P.U. had been made as radicals and reformers whose mission had been to change the old, externally dominated Native Authority system of Indirect Rule into a modern, local government. In the process, however, they had experienced their own 'iron law of oligarchy', they had come to be disliked by many people as a result, and they had failed to see that the wider scheme of colonialism could not be replaced by localism when both the colonial power and Nigerian political leaders viewed the colonial system as the basis for a new regional and national system. Adegoke Adelabu, their own protégé, but someone who had never been fully recruited into their ranks, had perceived their weaknesses and exploited them in order to complete the bloodless revolution by driving them from power. It now remained for him to tackle the problems which they had left behind as their inheritance.

CHAPTER 9

WIDENING HORIZONS

I want to find out from you as from today whether the Self-Government has been given to Ibadan People. Are we under British control? If not you will please set us free.

Olubadan Igbintade to the Senior
District Officer, June 1954

In the nutshell I gathered that the regime I grew up to know is gone and I became embarrassed on being unequivocally told what the implication of self-rule is.

Akinpelu Obisesan, November 1953

Adelabu was about to become the most powerful man in Ibadan. Under the new local government law the traditional rulers of Ibadan, with the exception of Chief Akinyele in his capacity as Chief Judge, were constrained to advise and consent; they could no longer insist or withhold. This had long been a policy goal of the colonial administrators, and with it accomplished, they too were surrendering considerable authority. Nevertheless, and to the benefit of the new power-holders, they could be expected to carry on the daily tasks of administration and policy preparation, even though they could no longer overrule the Council, which was now the local authority in Ibadan of the Western Regional Government and not a native authority controlled by colonial rulers. Furthermore, in his selection and control of his party's candidates for the Council, Adelabu had asserted a strong control over that body.

His ability to control the wider, regional situation was a matter of much greater doubt. Immediately after the election, Azikiwe by telegram had pronounced it a 'brilliant victory signalling the beginning of the end of tyranny in the West. This is shape of things to come.'[1] Nevertheless, from the point of view of most N.C.N.C. supporters, the Action Group was still master of the Region and principal author of change there, and thus the most severe threat in the new political and constitutional circumstances in which Adelabu now found himself. In its 20 March issue, the *Defender* warned of the future through 'Ariel'. He had hidden, he claimed, in the pocket of a defeated 'top ranking Grouper during a secret meeting' and heard him boast that the Regional Government would use its power to dissolve the Council should the N.C.N.C. be returned. 'John West', the *Tribune*'s equivalent of 'Ariel', had already on 18 March taken up Awolowo's eve of election threat and predicted the dissolution of the Council should Adelabu win, and in her letter of congratulations to Adelabu Mrs Adekogbe also warned that the Regional Government 'may, on any pretext, dissolve the Council'.[2] On 22 March, the *Tribune* advised the N.C.N.C. Councillors 'to search their own consciences', for 'if they choose to continue their fraudulent and corrupt practices in the new Council as did their colleagues in the old Lagos Council they can rest equally satisfied that the Council will be dissolved in the interest of good government'.

Similar concerns were expressed by others, some of them more explicitly related to Adelabu's ability to control himself and his Council. As N.C.N.C. First Vice-President J. O. Fadahunsi, a successful transport magnate from Ilesha, wrote, 'Now it is one thing to win a victory but it is the other to maintain it. You are now elevated to a position you never attained before – to control the affairs of the largest city in central Africa, is no joke.'[3] Fadahunsi, who in 1963 was to become Governor of the Western Region, went on to advise Adelabu to arrange lectures for his inexperienced Councillors by N.C.N.C. leaders experienced in local affairs; he urged him to establish an advisory committee of N.C.N.C. men resident in Ibadan (mentioning Olumofin, Oduyoye, Asaya and Ishola) to comment on policy and to gain their co-operation; and he warned Adelabu to give 'full recognition to the elected and traditional members who are not members of our party'. Lastly, he admonished that 'Corruption in all forms be avoided.'

Adelabu had in fact already taken steps in this direction. As in April and December 1953, these steps foresaw a structural re-organization of the party, a re-organization which is difficult to analyze because former and conflicting organizational patterns were not rejected and because the use of the new structures was both intermittent at best and generally unrecorded. On 20 March the first meeting of the 'Parliamentary Council' was held at the party secretariat at Akere's compound.* Its membership was to include the elected Councillors, party mogajis and 'active party leaders'. This meeting

---

* There were probably no more than two meetings of this new body. Minutes of that on 20 March were kept in a ledger which was among Adelabu's papers. The minutes were signed by him as having been approved on 27 March, but if approval was given at a meeting, no minutes were kept. The next set of minutes in the ledger are for an 'NCNC Grand Alliance' meeting on 10 July 1954, described as 'the usual weekly Meeting of the Grand Alliance which contained about 500 taxpayers...that attended their Central Working Committee...'. (These weekly meetings in fact persisted until Adelabu's death.) The next page in the ledger is headed 'NCNC Grand Alliance Central Working Committee', but there are no entries. The rest of the ledger is blank, with many pages at the end torn out.

first heard a report from Adelabu of his recent visit to the Olubadan, who had invited him to his house after hearing rumors that if Adelabu became Chairman of the Council 'he may not allow the Olubadan as President of the Council to exercise his powers, and thereby, deprive him. . .of his existing rights'. Adelabu reported he had denied this to the aged and somewhat confused ruler, who then, according to Adelabu, 'warned him to refrain from these three Social Evils: (1) Drinking (2) Women (3) Going out in the Dark'. Adelabu reported he had promised to abide by this advice.*

Adelabu had also proposed to the Olubadan, who agreed, that 'Reliable Chiefs' should sign 'a pledge of Loyalty' to the Olubadan, that 'Unreliable people living in the Palace, who are supposed or suspected to be agents of Confusion, [were] to be driven away from the Olubadan's Palace' and that the Olubadan would consult with Adelabu 'regarding any request or frequent hearsay'.

After stressing 'the need for General neatness and decency' and warning that 'bribery and corruption' should not be 'a passport to richness', Adelabu declared the function of the Parliamentary Council to be the preparation of the agendas and discussions of the Ibadan Council, all of which 'must definitely be finalized' at the party Secretariat. A general policy discussion followed. Adelabu mentioned the need to amend the law regarding petty traders at Lebanon Street, a suggestion that town planning should be encouraged was defeated, and a discussion of tax assessment 'and of Promise that has been made to the People' followed. Exactly what was said is obscure. The minutes only record, 'There was a lot of argument on this, but nevertheless the do's and dont's on this matter is absolutely confidential for recording in this book.'

On the following day still another new party body, the 'Cabinet Executive Committee' of the Grand Alliance, held what appears to have been its only meeting. It was attended by three recognized leaders, in addition to Adelabu. J. M. Johnson, Samuel Lana and E. O. Fakayode were well-known and were to continue their relations with Adelabu in one way or another in the next few years. Of the other three, A. S. Asuni was a founder of the Tax Payers Association and a newly-elected Councillor, but the other two are totally obscure. It would appear that Adelabu was again demonstrating his desire for complete control of the Grand Alliance by ensuring that, although the national party was represented, he and his unquestioning adherents would carry the day if it came to a vote.†

* It was most unusual for Adelabu to report to his followers in this way. Possibly he had been accompanied to the meeting with the Olubadan by others at the meeting on 20 March and was under some constraint to report.
† Even then, it might be assumed that Adelabu's control would have been secured by

Nevertheless, there is no indication that there was any dispute at the meeting. Concerns similar to those discussed the previous day were aired. It was agreed that 'the present level of I.N.A. revenue' should be maintained by preventing tax evasion by the rich, requiring disclosure of all sources of income, and by introducing a 'Pay As You Earn' scheme for wage and salary earners. Related to this was to be a 'war on bribery and corruption in all departments and activities of the I.N.A.'. Another major concern was the provision of 'various social amenities' which 'are now shamefully lacking in the town and district'. Area Committees were to be set up in every urban and rural ward to look after their general welfare and to submit requests for improvements to the Council through their elected representatives. Lastly with regard to matters of policy, it was resolved that 'no progressive measure shall be taken except with the consent of the people', while on the other hand 'it shall be a cardinal principle of the party to recognise and respect traditional dignity and status of all Native title holders'.

An elaborate new organizational structure was also agreed on without apparent consultation with the rest of the party. The Parliamentary Council was described as 'the Supreme Organ' of local government, and was presumably intended to be the real center of debate about policy. On the other hand, two 'Special Committees' were envisaged, a Political Committee to deal with 'purely political matters and affairs affecting the Party', and the other, the Executive Committee, to deal (despite its name) with 'party governmental policy'. It is difficult to see how these two could have been prevented from overlapping in function with the Parliamentary Council, and in any case the Political Committee apparently never came into formal existence. The other twelve committees, dealing with matters such as Staff, Health, Education and General Purposes, were presumably intended to be committees of the District Council, rather than of the party.

Questions of finance, discipline, the press, and relations with the Council staff occupied the remainder of the meeting. The party was to provide Adelabu with a car, the office at Akere's compound was to be fully equipped and staffed, and an overdraft account or a loan was to be secured from the N.C.N.C. There were to be fines for failure to attend meetings, disclosing of party secrets was to be punished by expulsion, and the Central Working Committee of the Alliance, which was continued, was to be generally responsible for dealing with 'any act of disloyalty'. Disciplinary action was to be taken also against 'sabotage' by any member of the Council staff, whose co-operation and 'efficient and faithful services', however, would be matched

the inclusion of such better-known Mabolaje figures as Abdullahi Elesinmeta, or Obadara Atanda. Once again, minutes of only one meeting exist for this body, in a 'Minute Book' in the Adelabu Papers.

by equal co-operation on the part of the Alliance and concern with staff welfare. Lastly, the meeting instructed the new Executive Committee to attend to the need for good publicity in all the affairs of the new Council, and resolved that the Committee should meet 'regularly'.

At a ceremonial meeting in Mapo Hall on Thursday, 8 April 1954, Acting Resident N. E. Whiting presented the signed Instrument establishing the Ibadan District Council to Adegoke Adelabu in the presence of the Councillors and chiefs who had just elected him Chairman. An attempt had been made by an Action Group Councillor to have Otun Balogun Salawu Aminu elected Chairman, an attempt which, if successful, would have placed a chief, with two more senior chiefs above him, in the difficult position of presiding over a group of freely elected commoners divided on party lines. This motion was defeated seventy to twenty, and, after prostrating to Olubadan Igbintade, 'gorgeously dressed in costly native attire and heavily turbanned in white, Mr Adelabu mounted the dais to take his seat as Chairman amidst another loud and sustained ovation'.[4] The District Officers were present, but Obafemi Awolowo and Chief Akinyele were conspicuously absent when Adelabu proceeded to deliver a ninety-minute speech.

Adelabu's Inaugural Address, as it was reprinted in serial form in four issues of the *Defender*, repeated the lines of Council policy formulated in the two party meetings prior to his election as Chairman.[5] It was in the familiar septuple form and stated that his Council would co-operate with the regional authority, maintain the high level of the Council's revenue, declare war on bribery and corruption, provide for an equitable distribution of social amenities, protect chieftaincy institutions, provide for a genuine democracy of the people and institute a regime of rule by consent. Since it was given in English and apparently from the manuscript later handed to the *Defender*, the Address might have been an occasion for Adelabu to spell out systematically and at some length his political thought as it had evolved since 'The Turning Point' in 1952. In fact, it was rambling and disconnected and any discussion of it imposes more organization on it than exists in the original. While it was considerably more realistic than the 'Master Plan', it lacked that document's incisive views on the nature of Ibadan politics as well as the ringing ideology of *Africa in Ebullition*.

One interesting aspect was the sharp awareness, hinted at in his earlier House of Assembly speeches, of the critical role of the Regional Government in local affairs.

It is as fatal for us as a derivative authority to adopt obstructionist tactics in our dealings with our principal agent as it is for the regional authority to put on the arrogant robes of pontifical almightiness in their dealings with us...

Concerning revenue, Adelabu was more preoccupied with dispelling myths than with spelling out policy. He dismissed as 'two ridiculous misconceptions' the allegations that the N.C.N.C. had promised to abolish territorial tax collection or that they would reduce the flat rate to seven shillings per head. These 'obnoxious suggestions' were 'a slander on our political responsibility'. However, he did not intend to raise taxes either. A study was needed, for a 'colossal sum' of money was being lost through inefficient collection, evasion by the rich, and bribery, while small traders, artisans and peasant farmers 'are being arbitrarily assessed on imaginary incomes which they never see'. Given efficient assessment and collection procedures, he argued, the present £350,000 revenue could be increased in the three years of the Council's life to £700,000 without increasing rates. We shall see the consequences of these views in the next chapter.

The new funds available from improved tax procedures should be earmarked to provide better rural water supplies and rural health centers; a new Standing Committee for Rural Development would be created to assure a more equitable distribution of such services and the 'overdue municipalization' of the Ibadan Bus Service (owned by defeated former Councillors T. L. Oyesina, S. A. Oloko and others) would allow its routes to be extended into rural areas.

As for corruption, the N.C.N.C. was the party of 'the common man' and included Councillors from the 'middle and lower strata of society'. While it was true that 'in any herd there must be a few black sheep', his Council, the 'handwork of the toiling masses' would declare total war on bribery and corruption.

Turning to the chiefs, he supported the 'paramountcy' of the Olubadan as 'inviolate' and stated that the chiefs and mogajis should 'take their customary places in the native scheme of things'. More specifically, in a pledge which he was almost immediately to violate, he promised that the Council, especially its elected members, would not interfere directly in chieftaincy matters.

He also attempted to earn the goodwill of the native strangers, and waved an olive branch at the Native Settlers Union suggesting that Ibadan belonged not only to the natives but to all residents, Yorubas and fellow Nigerians. Restrictive practices, particularly in regard to land policy, would 'only engender hatred from our co-nationalists'. Indeed, Ibadan had a special place not only in Nigeria but in that wider West African context to which Adelabu often referred.

Far-seeing men of vision in public life are looking eagerly forward to the evolution of a West African States Union stretching from the shores of the Gambia to the basin of the Congo.

Where else can the capital of such a federation be located than the ever-fortunate and always-blessed City of Ibadan?

In closing, he thanked the British administration which had 'carried the onerous burden for the order and good Government of Ibadan' and acknowledged (without a bow to the chiefs, who in any case did not understand his English address) that the previous Council had born 'the brunt of the inevitable friction attendant on the transference of power from traditional Chiefs into the hands of the elected commoners', and instituted the 'more efficient' system of territorial tax collection, even though they had 'failed to carry the masses with them in their progressive measures'.

It was a lengthy and bravura performance, and one listened to with care by friend and foe alike. Obisesan called it

a speech powerful in tone and substance; many wise things were embodied in it and some were superfluous and high-sounding if not nonsensical. He replied to N.C.N.C.'s critics; he stated what his council meant to do on taxation and of making the Mogajis to have a part in connection of tax and finally threatened the boycott of the proposed reform of native courts.[6]

It was the last matter referred to by Obisesan – the setting up of the new courts under Chief Judge Akinyele – which became the first issue faced by Adelabu as Chairman of the Ibadan District Council. Before he could apply the high principles enunciated at the party meetings and in his Address he found himself embroiled in a last-ditch attempt to prevent what had become a *fait accompli* in the last days of the old Council.

When Adelabu turned in his Address to the question of the reform of the native courts, he charged that the new law had been introduced without any public demand or prior consultation and in spite of the fact that the Assemblymen of the previous Council had insisted that its implementation be delayed until the direct election of a representative legislative body. The most critical of his remarks were directed against Chief Akinyele. His appointment with the power to recommend other judges and assessors was 'most scandalous, objectionable and unacceptable'; such power should reside in the hands of the Olubadan. Chief Akinyele was 'a staunch Action Grouper', who could not 'escape the human and natural tendency to pack the benches with his party henchmen and supporters'. This, Adelabu asserted, was precisely what was in store. For two years, he continued, the people of Ibadan had 'suffered in silence under a reactionary regime that makes no bones of its contempt for public opinion'. The only remedy now was to suspend the court reforms 'forthwith in deference to duly accredited public opinion'.

Thus Adelabu made the downfall or the maintenance of the courts a matter of party policy for all concerned. Prominent on Chief Judge Isaac

Akinyele's list of new judges were D. T. Akinbiyi, Akinpelu Obisesan, J. L. Ogunsola, Mogaji Osunware and O. H. Adetoun. Although Akinyele, with admirable lack of personal feeling, had included at least four of those who had signed the petitions protesting his choice as judge and Balogun in March 1953, the most prominent of his nominees, Akinbiyi, Ogunsola, Adetoun, Osunware and Obisesan, were drawn from the I.P.U.–I.C.C. group which had dominated Ibadan for so long. In part this was inevitable, since these were the literate and experienced men who were needed for the new judge-ships; Mogaji Osunware, who had been to the Bale's School, was one of the few traditional title-holders who could have been chosen. Nevertheless, all five (and Akinyele himself) were known to be either members of the Action Group or its supporters – Akinbiyi was one of its legislators – and this was bound to raise the cry of political bias.

The day after the inauguration of the new Council, the Chief Judge and his new colleagues (who had known of their appointment for some days) met with the Senior District Officer: '. . .to discuss the threat contained in Mr. Adelabu's speech of yesterday and not contrary to my expectation, Mr. Lewis assured them of Government resolve to handle whatever situation might arise'.[7] By the time of this meeting, however, a second problem had arisen for Government in addition to that of the intransigeance of Adelabu, whose temper cannot have been helped by the fact that on the same day he was found guilty in the Magistrates Court for his part in the Bere Square affray, fined £15, and bound over for a year on a bond of £50. On 30 March, Chief Justice Adetokunboh Ademola of the Supreme Court of Nigeria had granted an order *nisi* to an applicant on the grounds that the judges of the Ibadan Judicial Council (the old appellate court, now to be replaced) who had heard his case had also been members of the Native Authority Council, one of the parties to the case, and had been present when the latter Council dis-cussed the case.[8] In granting the order the Chief Justice in effect instituted the principle of legislative–judicial separation, a ruling which applied with equal force to Obisesan, Ogunsola, Mogaji Osunware and Akinyele him-self, the first three being elected members and the last an *ex-officio* member of the new Council. Chief Justice Ademola actually attended the meeting on 9 April, and the matter was discussed. Commenting on this in a minute written after the meeting, Senior District Officer Lewis urged that 'it would be a great pity' for the Council to lose the services of the four, and that a way be found to make an exception in their cases.[9]

At the time of his Inaugural Address it is most unlikely that Adelabu was aware of the decision by Chief Justice Ademola, or he would almost certainly have raised the issue it involved. He sought, rather, to attack Chief Akinyele in an indirect way by manipulating the Chieftaincy Committee, one of the committees of the new Council which were set up on 12 April. As we will see in the next chapter, these were one of the main ways by which the new Chairman intended to impose his will: in this particular case he imposed it to the extent of breaking the law. It was intended that the Chieftaincy Committee be composed of the Senior Chiefs, who were thus to preside over all questions involving their own ritual and promotions and those of the junior chiefs and mogajis. Nevertheless Adelabu took advantage at this point of the fact that the Chieftaincy Committee was in some insufficiently specified sense a committee of the Council to appoint its members rather than taking them *ex officio*. Thus he made himself Chairman, added four junior chiefs and mogajis, two elected and two co-opted Council members and excluded Chiefs Akinyele and Aminu and the Seriki, leaving only the senior chiefs among its members who were amenable to his direction.

One of the first tasks with which this Committee was faced was a motion in the Council on 15 April, moved by L. Ade Bello, that 'in order to get the Regional Authority to respect the Council's views on Ibadan Proposed Native Court Reforms' the Chieftaincy Committee should hold an emergency meeting to consider disciplinary action against any chief guilty of disloyalty to the Council's position on the court reforms. This was followed on 16 April by a telegram from the Council to the Resident of Ibadan claiming that the Council unanimously disapproved the reforms, that a judiciary beholden to a party was intolerable, and that the situation was 'critical'.[10]

By the middle of April the new Chairman was not only expressing his displeasure at the selection of the new judges by indirect attacks on Akinyele's authority. He and his associates had also lit upon the issue raised by Chief Justice Ademola's decision on judicial–legislative separation. As the *Defender* argued on 13 April, the issue was the fundamental constitutional principle of whether the judges who adjudicated should at the same time be members of the Council which legislated. While not doubting the integrity of the nominees, the *Defender* went on,

In the interest of justice and for the preservation of democracy for which many have suffered and died, it will be necessary that these judges and others of their rank who may be so connected, resign their legislative posts at once and renounce forthwith their affiliation to any political party. Otherwise, let them refuse the judgeship offered them.

A follow-up had been made in the middle of April in the form of a Council committee sent to the Lieutenant-Governor to protest the court reforms. With this question now made a party issue the Government had to find an answer, and Obafemi Awolowo, as Minister of Local Government, chose to give it at the ceremonial installation of the new judges on 21 April.

The Resident of Ibadan was directed to invite all regional Ministers, the Civil Secretary of the Region and other senior civil servants, administrative officers, magistrates, 'and any other distinguished persons'. The Minister also indicated that he would like the new judges to go directly to their courts from the ceremony, before there was any time for a popular demonstration against them.* Furthermore:

In view of the public and political interest attaching to these reforms, the Minister wishes to draw your attention to the desirability of suitable police arrangements being put in hand in order to guard against any possibility of disturbances.[11]

Under the circumstances it was hardly surprising that Adelabu, the other Alliance leaders, and the senior chiefs who had begun to look to Adelabu as they faced an increasingly uncertain future, were absent when Awolowo, in the company of Government and civic leaders and an entourage of the Egbe Omo Oduduwa led by notables from Lagos, installed the new judges. In his address, Awolowo went to painstaking lengths to explain the necessity for the courts and their procedures. He particularly emphasized that the establishment of the courts was a prerogative of the Regional Government and that the appointments of senior personnel in the employment of the Council, such as court members, had to be approved by Government. Any consultation with the local Council was a matter of courtesy, not obligation.

Awolowo had been forced to modify his earlier position on separation of the judiciary from the other organs of the Council, and although he was able to maintain Akinyele in his position as head of the courts and as chief, the elected Councillors, Obisesan, Ogunsola and Osunware were obliged in mid-April to resign their Council seats. The court reforms had indeed been put through with some haste. It had not been ensured that the financial means, or even the pencils and stationery, would be available until long after Awolowo had initially insisted that the courts be opened. Nevertheless, by the end of April, they were functioning and there was nothing further that Adelabu could do about it, mortifying though it was to have what he regarded as bastions of Action Group influence operating in his city but outside his control. Defeated over the first issue which he chose to raise as Chairman of the Council, he had extra cause to ensure that he would be able to keep the administration of Ibadan tightly under his own control. Even before the end of April he had begun to devise various ways of doing this.

In the first place, he had had himself elected Chairman of every standing Committee of the Council. These committees met from one to four times between the monthly meetings of the Council and it was here that the basic

* In fact, the first court to open, at Mapo, did so on 26 April under police guard and without trouble.

governmental work was done. For each meeting, an agenda and the appropriate supporting documentation were prepared by a member of the Council staff; meetings were also attended by such officers of the Council as the Secretary, the Treasurer, the Registrar of Lands, the Health Officer or the Town Engineer, depending on the nature of the Committee's business. Decisions of the Committees, in the form of resolutions, were then brought before the Council at its next scheduled meeting. Control of the Committee processes was thus of utmost importance and Adelabu controlled them entirely. As Chairman, it was his duty to propose for the Council's approval the membership of these Committees. This meant, of course, having the initiative in assigning Councillors to positions where rewards of office were to be gained from the services they performed on behalf of constituents in getting official approval for their applications for butcher's licenses, market stalls, water standpipes and contracts to provide goods and services. It was also the Chairman's prerogative to appoint 'co-opted' members to these committees, that is, persons from outside the Council whose expertise, concern, and leadership could be put at the Council's service.

These appointments provoked a crisis in the ranks of the Alliance, details of which are unfortunately obscure. Certain N.C.N.C. leaders were omitted from the Council committees, including Oduyoye and Olumofin, who had been recommended as advisers by J. O. Fadahunsi in his letter of 27 March. Apparently those who were excluded protested to the national leaders of the party, since on 13 April the N.C.N.C. National Treasurer, Festus Sam Edah, telegraphed Adelabu from Sapele:

Disturbing news from Ibadan party circle frightfully alarming. Seriously requesting you close ranks immediately and yield to majority decisions on Council arrangements etc. Arriving Ibadan next week. You must prevent playing into enemies hands.[12]

Whether Edah in fact came to Ibadan to mediate, and if so the extent to which the final list of co-opted members represents a compromise, we do not know. The incident is important, even if obscure, because it shows how from the early days of the Grand Alliance Adelabu was determined to have control not only over its I.T.P.A. (Mabolaje) wing but over the Ibadan N.C.N.C. members as well.

In addition to co-options to Council committees, Adelabu had the appointment of tax assessment committees as another means of employing the party faithful. There was one of these committees to each ward since these served as the units of tax administration, made up of residents of the ward. It was presumed that persons who knew the whereabouts and incomes of their neighbors would be able both to assess and ensure payment. To select those who knew their neighbors best, however, also required some considerable personal knowledge of the ward, and the opportunity of distributing this patronage therefore fell to the Councillor. Occasionally, as with J. M. Johnson, the Councillor himself served as the Chairman of the ward tax committee. This provided him with an opportunity to control quite directly a very real interest of his constituents, for, without prejudicing Adelabu's Council, the power of the tax committee to determine assessable income and even to fail to inscribe taxpayers on their rolls was a power whose magic no Ibadan Council has ever overlooked. Ten members were appointed to each of the 43 urban committees and, although the lists for the rural committees are incomplete, perhaps 1000 persons in all were involved in the Council's business and with the party's approval in this manner.

Adelabu's hand in the Council was again strengthened in July when bye-elections were held to replace Obisesan, Mogaji Osunware and Chief Ogunsola, who had been appointed court presidents. In the first case we know that Adelabu took a personal part in having his candidate elected. Obisesan had worked to ensure family support for a candidate of his choosing and had addressed the 'Hausa Community' in his village of Akanran on his behalf. On election eve, however, he noted that he was being 'vigorously challenged' by Adelabu and on election day, 30 July, Obisesan recorded that the Hausas, and the villages under the Obisesan family's authority, had all turned to Adelabu, giving Obisesan 'a routing defeat'.

Not all of Adelabu's attempts to control personnel went so smoothly, as indeed we have seen in the case of his attempts to control the personnel of the reformed courts, which ended in his total defeat. The greatest difficulties came with the Council's own staff. The Council employed approximately 1000 persons at this time, the largest categories being 250 akodas or messengers, 200 police, 200 at the Adeoyo Hospital and clinics, and some 200 clerks. Throughout the first months of his Chairmanship, letters of application arrived daily for jobs as clerks, nurses, tax collectors, and guards.* Staff had been one of the gravest administrative problems of the Council since the institution of bureaucratic procedures in 1893. No Annual Report, no handing over notes from one administrative officer to the next, no Council, failed to comment on the need for improving staff quality. Administrative officers serving in Ibadan in 1954 and 1955 were also keenly aware of the inadequate staff Adelabu had inherited from the 1953 Council, and there is no doubt in their minds that, particularly among the clerks engaged in collecting tax and among the akodas, Adelabu pursued a vigorous policy of retiring the aged and the incompetent. Among the akodas, who were

* Some 250 of these letters prior to 20 July 1954 survive in the Adelabu Papers.

occasionally engaged in vigorous physical activity, many older men were subjected to a medical examination and retired when found wanting.

However laudatory this may have been from the point of view of efficiency, coming from a Chairman of Adelabu's vigor and willingness to get on badly with those of whom he disapproved, it was bound to cause distress among heads of departments who were responsible for getting the Council's daily work done while staff changes were being rumored, threatened or actually made. Principal among the heads of departments thus concerned was Treasurer E. A. Adeyemo. Born in 1906 of a chieftaincy house in Ibadan, Adeyemo had worked as a clerk in civilian life before entering the Nigerian Regiment in which he was promoted to sergeant while serving in Burma during World War II. In January 1947 he became the Council's Assistant Treasurer, and in due course Treasurer. On 31 May 1954 he expressed his concern about Adelabu's staff policy in a letter to the Council Secretary, stating his belief that the Council was pursuing a policy bound to strain council–employee relations.[13] In June he took his complaints directly to the Minister of Local Government and urged that the 'sabotage of the efficient administration of the Finance Section of the Ibadan District Council and [Adelabu's] determination to destroy all the Council's employees who are not members of his political party is a serious case worthy of your timely interventions'.[14] The Treasurer reported to Awolowo that at the first meeting of the Finance Committee Adelabu had forbidden him to associate further with certain of his friends and stated that as Chairman he controlled all staff matters, for '. . .the days of District Officers' and Residents' interference and intervention are gone'.

Not all of the Treasurers' complaints were taken seriously by the Resident, who reminded Awolowo's Permanent Secretary that Adeyemo had been an active member of the Ibadan Progressive Union and that a change in political masters was bound to bring recriminations when 'local government servants indulge in party politics. . .'.[15] Some of his complaints, however, did receive considerable attention. One was that Adelabu had demanded and accepted £25 and several presents of meat in order to get a clerk of the Council promoted. This charge was investigated by the police in 1954 and again by the Nicholson Inquiry into the whole of Adelabu's administration, both of which failed to establish a sufficient case to bring a criminal charge against Adelabu. Underlying this charge were not only the fears that corruption of this nature might be infiltrating the staff, but the personal fears and activities of the Treasurer. Former administrative officers who served on the Council at this time have recounted Adelabu's interest in and command of tax and fiscal questions from the first days of his Chairmanship. Adeyemo's call for a commission of inquiry on 24 June 1954 to look into the activities of the Chairman and the Council as a whole is thus best seen against this wider background, more especially since it was also obviously being supported politically from outside the Council. Thus, a few days after Adeyemo's letter to the Minister, his old friend and I.P.U. associate, T. L. Oyesina, the former Councillor, organized fifty residents of his ward to call on the Government to dissolve the Council.[16] Nevertheless, serious charges by men with more than politicking at stake continued to come in (Assistant Treasurer S. I. Amole claimed to be under substantial pressure as well).[17] Since Adeyemo took the lead in asserting the claims of others, it was decided in Staff Committee on 14 July that he should be interdicted in his authority. Although the Council was empowered to take such a step, at the request of the Government this order was rescinded at an emergency meeting of the Council on 26 July.

Part of Adelabu's method of control was simply to do as many jobs as possible, and it was this inability to trust others and to delegate responsibility to them that led to much of the conflict with Adeyemo. Thus, in addition to controlling the Staff Committee to whose appointments Adeyemo objected, as Chairman of the Tax Committee Adelabu was also the Councillor in Charge of Tax, which made him Chairman of the Assessments Appeal Board, a task previously undertaken by Chief Ogunsola with considerable distinction and grief. Along with this onerous responsibility Adelabu had also accepted the remuneration attached to the office. *The Daily Service* (never, of course, his friend) claimed in June that as Councillor in Charge of Tax, Council Chairman and Chairman of the Central Assessment Committee (another of his offices), Adelabu would receive £830 per annum in 'salary'.[18] While the propriety of accepting a salary from the Council was later to become a serious issue, for the moment Adelabu was attacked by his enemies for using the powers and prerogatives of the Council to his personal benefit.

Certainly Adelabu's insistence upon performing so many tasks for the Council, the accepting of money for expenses and in lieu of other earnings, and his refusal to placate his detractors, made it difficult for him to consider many of the problems before the Council in a manner which would keep the intensity of personal and party differences low. The *Defender* quoted him as stating at the Council meeting on 1 May that he could put matters on the Council agenda as he saw fit, but it must be recognized that part of this insistence upon his own personal ability to guide the business of the Council was determined by his keen awareness that the world in which the Council existed was a shifting one and that the Council would have to work hard to preserve an adequate place for itself.[19] This awareness, however, did not always lead him to rational or justifiable positions. Thus, in the case of the

Ibadan Prison, Adelabu argued that the Council's control over it was a matter of native law and custom. To relinquish it to the Central Government would be a violation of a trust. This was, of course, historical nonsense since the first prison in Ibadan had been built by Captain Bower, the first British Resident. While the Central Government, anxious to standardize prisons throughout the country, argued that the expense of the prison was a wasteful drain on local revenue, the Chairman of the Ibadan Council also knew that it provided many jobs and many opportunities for local contractors to sell supplies.

A more serious dispute lay in the area of education. Adelabu had frequently opposed the Regional Government's education scheme and the imposition of increased taxation, to be collected through local councils, to finance it. Control by an Action Group Minister over what was becoming Ibadan's largest local government service meant not only differences about the nature of education, but also disputes concerning control over teachers, school buildings and supplies. If the program was to be implemented, Adelabu at least wanted the construction of the necessary new schools in the hands of his own Tenders Committee, which could guarantee that contractors who were party members or those who would reliably reward members of committees dealing with contract matters, would do the Council's business. In June 1954, however, the Regional Government decided to take control over the building of new schools in Ibadan.

A mass meeting of the Grand Alliance was called for Sunday, 13 June, at Mapo Hall to discuss this issue. During the course of it, a number of Action Group leaders led a crowd of their supporters to Mapo, with 'apala' drummers playing and singing 'Baba eniti o ba ko bi akuko, ope ni yio pa o' – 'Anybody who dares crow like a cock will be smashed by the palm tree.' Alliance supporters gathered round the Taj Mahal after abandoning their meeting at the request of the police, and in the evening the police themselves threw a cordon round the house.[20]

The following day, Resident H. K. Robinson and the Senior Superintendent of Police discussed the problem. It was the Resident's feeling that 'political feeling in Ibadan needs careful and tactful handling' and that it would be a pity if meetings and processions had to be banned 'for they provide a useful outlet for steam, and there should be no necessity [of banning them] if your officers handle matters carefully'.[21] On 16 June, the Council met to discuss the school problem. A statement by Councillor Akinfenwa alleging that certain contractors had given £25 to certain Councillors as rewards for school construction contracts caused an uproar, and when Adelabu proposed a motion condemning Government for its decision to remove the building program from the Council's supervision, the fifteen

Action Group Councillors and five rural chiefs walked out. They were met outside by hoodlums who attacked two of them, a brawl between N.C.N.C. and Action Group members and adherents ensued, Adelabu's own aide was beaten and the riot squad was called. Concerned with the violence and apparently quite uncertain as to what was happening generally was Olubadan Igbintade, who wrote the following day to the Senior District Officer to protest 'too much of Political riots' and to ask that the courts be closed.[22] In fact the Resident himself banned further political meetings that day to give tempers a chance to cool and on 21 June yet another case of party political violence was heard in the Magistrate's Court. Still, the Resident was anxious to keep political expression free and on 22 June the ban was lifted. On 24 June, as we have already seen, Treasurer Adeyemo, stating that life was no longer safe in Ibadan, requested the Government to institute an inquiry into the Council's activities.

From the beginning, then Adelabu's Chairmanship was full of turmoil and strife. There had been no 'honeymoon' during which he might settle into his new political house before having to face domestic strife or public scrutiny, nor indeed had he sought one. From the outset, the strain of holding together the various and often independent personalities with which he was now involved led him into political trouble.

Furthermore, he was rapidly discovering the high cost to himself of the acquisition of power – the financial burden which he assumed in return for the opportunity to enforce his will. In the years of his rise to power in Ibadan he had employed a small group of personal retainers to do his leg-work.* As Chairman of the Council he was accompanied everywhere by aides, messengers and bodyguards, all of whom had to be supported. He had purchased one car late in May, since the local party failed to do so, and a second in August, and they required maintenance and drivers in addition to the cost of their original purchase. Wherever he moved with this now formidable entourage he was an object of public attention and the drummers and beggars who demanded a gift from the great man's purse could not be left unsuccoured, at the risk of showing he was no better off than one of them. At his home, the clerks and typist which he employed to prepare his speeches and press releases, and the telephone bills with an increasing number of long distance charges, proved further drains on his income.

This set of calculations became increasingly clear to him as the early

---

* Of those whom we know were employed during 1952 and 1953, one died, one became a revenue collector, another a correspondence clerk and another a forest guard for the Ibadan Council, while L. A. Lawal became a member of the House of Representatives in 1954 and Adebayo Adeyinka was Divisional Secretary for the N.C.N.C. for Ibadan before he too entered the House in 1954.

months of his Chairmanship merged into the early months of the campaign for the federal election scheduled for the end of 1954 as part of the process of introducing a new constitution for Nigeria. As head of the victorious party in the Ibadan elections earlier in the year, and as a bitter foe of the Action Group, he could not sit idly by and observe such an important event; neither the expectations of his followers, who depended on him to demonstrate leadership, nor his own re-awakening interest in national events, would allow that. Moreover, it must have seemed to him that if he were elected a federal legislator, a considerable enhancement of his income would follow, and it is probable that he was setting his sights considerably higher, upon the glittering prize of a federal Ministry.

The years 1953 and 1954, during which a new Ibadan emerged from the old, were also years in which a new Nigerian political system took shape. As we saw in Chapter 7, the stresses and strains of trying to make the Macpherson Constitution work had culminated in Anthony Enahoro's motion of March 1953 demanding independence for Nigeria in 1956. We also saw that Adegoke Adelabu, as a Member of the Western House of Assembly, joined in debate in supporting this motion. The crisis which Enahoro's motion produced resulted in a Constitutional Conference in London in July and August 1953. Leaders of all the Nigerian political parties, administrative officers, and representatives of the British Government, led by the Secretary of State for the Colonies, met and discussed the future shape of Nigeria. The N.C.N.C. and Action Group at that time worked in temporary alliance to seek a federal constitution and independence for Nigeria in 1956, while the Northern People's Congress sought a much looser, 'confederal' arrangement giving virtually all powers to the regions, and opposed all talk of independence in the near future. On the second question, the most to which the British Government would agree was that each region would be given wider powers of control over its internal affairs ('regional self-government') in 1956 if it asked for it, and also that the whole question of independence would be reviewed in that year. This in turn reassured the Northern leaders, who accepted the federal system, in the knowledge that given a great degree of control over their own region they would be able to buttress their position there against encroachments from the south.

The biggest stumbling block at the London Conference proved to be the question of the future status of Lagos, which the British, the N.P.C. and the N.C.N.C. all wished to separate from the West, making it the federal capital and giving it the status of an autonomous territory. This the Action Group bitterly opposed, and the London Conference ended with the issue unresolved. In October Obafemi Awolowo sent a telegram to the Colonial Secretary, Oliver Lyttelton, threatening the secession of the West over this issue; the reply was that such an attempt would be regarded as the use of force, and resisted. The Action Group backed down, after a tense period which, among other things, destroyed the temporary alliance with the N.C.N.C.

A further session of the Constitutional Conference in Lagos in January 1954 settled the final details of the new constitution, and also decided to separate the Southern Cameroons from the Eastern Region, giving it a degree of autonomy. The new constitution, which was to come into force on 1 October 1954, gave the Northern, Western and Eastern Regions most legislative powers, including exclusive control within their own territories over such vital matters as education, agriculture, justice (though with a right of appeal to the Federal Supreme Court), and local government. The civil service, the judiciary and the various public boards and corporations were to pass under the control of the regional governments. In the case of the Marketing Boards, this meant access to relatively large sums of money (especially in the West) earned by the sale of Nigerian raw materials abroad in the prosperous early 1950s, while a new system of revenue allocation for the whole federation in effect left each region free to develop its own economy.

In sum, the new constitution of 1954 marked a decisive shift of power from the center to the regions, as well as a decisive step by Britain in withdrawing control by the administrative officers over the governments of the regions, which from 1 October were each to be headed by its own Premier.

The Colonial Office still retained many powers, ranging from such matters as complete control over foreign affairs and defense and the ability to declare a state of emergency if required, through forms of control which stemmed from the detailed supervision of British personnel; thus in the mid-1950s the judiciary and the senior levels of the civil service were still in effect under British control, as were the police and the army. The important fact, however, was that the decision had been taken to transfer these gradually to Nigerian control, and the appointment of a new Governor-General of the Federation, Sir James Robertson, who had presided over much of the decolonization process in the Sudan, and of new Governors for the Regions, represented the selection of new men for a new task.

The results of this shift of power were to have profound effects upon the career of Adegoke Adelabu. We have already noted that in less than half a year after his rise to power in Ibadan he had begun to feel its irritations and show an interest in new horizons. By the end of the year he had projected himself upon a much wider screen, but at the same time had entered into a set of relationships beyond the confines of Ibadan which were continually to affect his ability to handle his commitments, both in that city and elsewhere.

In order to understand these relationships, it will be necessary to go back a little in time.

As early as mid-1953 he had begun to involve himself in the politics of Oyo, thirty miles to the north of Ibadan. There party politics had been established on the basis of a struggle for power between the Alafin, Alhaji Aderemi II, aged, illiterate, and determined to keep his traditional authority intact, and the new educated men, led by Chief Bode Thomas, who sought to take control of local affairs through party politics and the new local government structure.* A lawyer of considerable intellectual ability, at the age of thirty-two Thomas had been one of the founders of the Action Group, and, some said, the brains behind Obafemi Awolowo. Friends of Thomas at first, the Alafin and his son, the Aremo, had turned against him in resentment at the curtailment of their power; on a celebrated occasion in April 1953 the Aremo struck the lawyer, and for this was banished from Oyo by the Action Group-controlled Divisional Council. Oyo gradually split apart, partly along lines of traditional rivalry with the town, some of the sub-ordinate hierarchy of chiefs and the northern part of the kingdom tending to support the Alafin, and the majority of the chiefs and southern Oyo backing Thomas and the Action Group. Nor was it only the chiefs who were divided; some of the educated men feared Thomas also, and in August 1953 formed the Egbe Oyo Parapo, led by P. A. Afolabi, a Catholic headmaster.

The Parapo soon moved into alliance with the N.C.N.C., taking the Alafin, whom it championed, with it. Adegoke Adelabu also began to fish in these troubled waters. Although he claimed descent through his father from a former Alafin, his main contact with Oyo affairs was possibly through Alhaji N. B. Soule, a Lagos merchant with whom he became friendly in 1952. Around the middle of 1953 a group from the northern Oyo Division town of Shaki, calling itself the Egbe Mabolaje, sought organizational help from the I.T.P.A. (Mabolaje) in Ibadan, itself only founded the previous April. In September, the Central Working Committee of the I.T.P.A. (Mabolaje) agreed to help start a Tax Payers Association in Shaki, supplying it with membership cards and lending it an organizing secretary 'to put you through the initial stages of the foundation of your Association'.[23] A campaign team from Ibadan also visited Shaki on 12 and 13 September. Bode Thomas died suddenly on 20 November 1953 – there were dark mut-

* For another account of Oyo politics at this time, see Sklar, *Nigerian Political Parties*, pp. 235–8. Also of great interest is the report by R. D. Lloyd, appointed as sole commissioner to hold an inquiry after the riot on 5 September 1954. This report was never officially published, but fortunately it was printed in the *Daily Times* on 8 June 1955.

terings of poisoning – but the local Action Group, led now by Abiodun Akerele, Awolowo's Ibadan law partner, continued to harass the Alafin.

The involvement of Adelabu in Oyo affairs in 1953 was similar to his involvement in Ibadan in that he put himself forward as the champion of traditional authority against the programs of the Action Group government and its local agents, especially in regard to tax increases. Nevertheless, he was also attracting attention outside Ibadan among men who were very far from the conservatism of traditional authority by the role which he claimed as a man of the people and the champion of the poor. These contacts came at a time when he was beginning to rise in the ranks of the party.

By January 1954, some months before his electoral victory brought him to a new prominence in the N.C.N.C., he had begun to show a greater interest in the party than at any time since late 1952. Buoyed up by his local organization, the Mabolaje, which was capturing the political initiative in Ibadan and had taken the N.C.N.C. there into partnership with itself in the Grand Alliance, in January 1954 he traveled to Enugu in the Eastern Region as one of the Ibadan delegates to the Fifth Annual Convention of the N.C.N.C.

The sessions of this assembly, held from the 6th to the 10th, were very important ones for a party which had passed through grave internal troubles in 1952–3 and was now trying to refurbish its machinery. At an early session Adelabu was made a member of the Policy and Programme Committee set up to make recommendations on the party's future strategy, and on 9 January he was elected to the National Executive Committee for the first time. This was doubtless a recognition that, with the formation of the Grand Alliance, he had become the most prominent son of Ibadan in the N.C.N.C.

Against the background of these personal successes, he painted a very optimistic view of the achievements of the Convention in an interview with the *Southern Nigeria Defender* on his return to Ibadan. 'Our dear Leader Dr. Nnamdi Azikiwe', he declared, 'had gone through the fire of battle and has been definitely reborn. The old fire has witnessed his fighting physique, pungent speeches and wise determination to preserve party unity against external detractors and internal divisionists.'[24] Azikiwe had, in fact, offered to retire from the leadership of the party during his Presidential Address. As we have seen, he had returned to the East for the election there the previous month, and was now to be Minister of Local Government and in effect leader of the new N.C.N.C. Regional Government. Thus he declared in his Address:

Now that your President is to be saddled with responsibility of State matters, one wonders whether the time has not come for the election of another nationalist to carry on this great task. It may not be my business to tell you what to do in this particular respect, but I am urging you to bear this factor in mind and help me in easing the situation in any way possible.[25]

In the election on Saturday 9 January, however, he was re-elected National President, with J. O. Fadahunsi as First National Vice-President, Mbonu Ojike as Second National Vice-President, and Kola Balogun as National Secretary once more.

Both Azikiwe in his Address and Balogun in his Secretary's Report laid stress on party organization and finance. Azikiwe particularly emphasized the need for strong central control of the party, which was 'absolutely necessary for the integration of party ideology and the enforcement of discipline'. 'There is only the N.C.N.C.', the National President insisted, 'and there is only one machinery through which it works and that machinery is the National Secretariat.'[26] With the approach of the 1954 federal election, the first major test of party support since 1951, the Action Group and the N.C.N.C. had to pay attention to their organizational capacity to make contact with potential voters. In the Eastern and Western Regions far more electors were to be involved than in 1951, with direct elections instead of electoral colleges. The London Constitutional Conference had left the matter of the franchise up to the Lieutenant-Governors and Governments of the Regions, and the East had decided on universal adult suffrage and the West on a taxpayer suffrage which meant in effect votes for men only. In response to this, the N.C.N.C. Convention's Finance and Organization Committee, reporting on 8 January, recommended that the party's organization should be based on six 'sectors' (the West, East, North, Middle Belt, Cameroons and Lagos), with an Organizing Secretary in charge of each. In Lagos a new Principal Organizing Secretary would combine the affairs of the capital with his overall supervision of the party structure. The committee also came up with a comparatively realistic estimate of the party's revenue and expenditure for the forthcoming year. Basing its estimate of revenue mainly on a levy to be made on the salaries of all N.C.N.C. Ministers, legislators and members of public boards, it suggested that an income of £10,305 might be possible. Expenditure, mainly on the salaries of party officials, whose pay scales were now fixed for the first time, was reckoned to be £11,250. The balance was to be covered by donations from wealthy supporters, the party having been carried through 1953 primarily by a donation of £5000 by Dr Azikiwe at the Jos Convention in December 1952.

These suggestions were adopted by the National Executive Committee at a meeting at the end of January (although the six-fold division of the country never in fact became operative). At that meeting appointments were also made to the new organizational posts – Osita Agwuna became Principal

Organizing Secretary, Mokwugo Okoye Eastern Organizing Secretary, and Adesanya Idowu Western Organizing Secretary. All three had also been elected to the National Executive Committee at the Convention. Thus, the militants who had once led the Zikist Movement were now brought back into important positions in the party hierarchy and, in effect, given the job of putting its machinery into order ready for the struggles ahead. This 'come-back of younger insurgent ideologists who had been squeezed out by career-ists and their being taken into the National Executive Committee to give that body virility and striking punch', was hailed by Adelabu as another triumph of the Convention.[27]

On the other hand, a further claim by Adelabu, and a significant decision taken by the Convention, revealed a latent tension which in less than a year was to bring internal strife to the party again and lead to the elimination of the radicals. The N.C.N.C. Ministers and legislators had been boycotting all official cocktail and dinner parties, which its more militant members felt to be 'some of the devices used in corroding and softening the temper of nationalists'.[28] The majority of the Policy and Programme Committee were for continuing this boycott, but K. O. Mbadiwe, its Chairman, argued against this in a minority report to the Convention:

In times such as these when the NCNC party has stepped into power in the Eastern Region, it is very highly desirable that we become circumspect and reason-able in all our actions. I am not suggesting that we should in any way dampen the ardour of our struggle but I am saying that the present struggle has shifted into a new scene. We can do a lot by our psychological relationships with the British Government to achieve the objective which is dear in the heart of everybody.[29]

In a highly significant gesture, the Convention in fact accepted Mbadiwe's minority report, rather than that of the Committee. Adelabu in his interview claimed this 'determination to rescue the party from mere sentimental talk of freedom, to go into the field and fight for freedom through parliamentary and other constitutional means', as another achievement of the Convention. It was in fact a long way from his call for 'mass action' and 'struggle' in the debate on self-government in 1956 in the Western House of Assembly only eight months before and, indeed, a long way from continuing the boycott, to which he had apparently agreed along with the majority of the Convention's Policy and Programme Committee. The fact was that the N.C.N.C., and Adelabu with it, was becoming increasingly involved in helping Britain to bring to an end its political control of Nigeria, rather than forcing it to do so. Co-operation was part of the price the N.C.N.C. was now willing to pay for liberty. The abandonment of the call for indepen-dence in 1956 at the 1953 London session of the Constitutional Conference meant that the session due to open in Lagos on 19 January would be dedicated to the detailed problems of the transition to a federal system, which would allow each major political party its greatest access to power at a regional level, and thus considerably affect the perspectives of the parties as elements of the political system.

Adelabu's Inaugural Address as Chairman of the Ibadan District Council on 8 April 1954, prolix and ill-organized as it appears in the reading, nevertheless attracted further attention to him as a nationalist, although it also marked the assumption by him of considerable responsibility within the laws designed for decolonizing local government whose adoption he had opposed. In the audience on that day was Dr Sanya Onabamiro, an expert on parasitology and Lecturer at the University College. Onabamiro had been attracted by socialist ideas while a student in London, and after his return to Nigeria had become a member of the United Working People's Party, a small group of Marxist-oriented intellectuals which maintained a shadowy existence during the early 1950s.* About the time of the Ibadan elections the U.W.P.P. had decided to dissolve itself, leaving its members to join other parties of their choice. After hearing Adelabu's speech, Onabamiro, who was an Ijebu, not an Ibadan man, immediately wrote to him applying for membership in the N.C.N.C. 'What impressed me most in this speech', he wrote, 'is your statement of your Party's aims and policy.' He continued:

I gather from your speech of today, which I believe I am right in taking as an official exposition of your Party policy, that this Party, the N.C.N.C. is now back where it has started, i.e., standing for *the unity of the Country* and concerned only with the *welfare* of the masses of the people.

I see therefore a close identity in views and belief between you and me and, as such, would deem it an honour to be admitted into the membership of your Party so that I may be able to play my part within the scope of the Party's constitution in the great struggles lying ahead.[30]

Thus, Dr Onabamiro's considerable energy and undoubted organizational ability were henceforward at the disposal of the Western N.C.N.C.†

The attention of other men of socialist leanings was drawn to Adelabu now that this self-confessed champion of the poor was in a position of power. On 13 April Mokwugo Okoye, former Zikist Movement militant and now

* For the U.W.P.P. see Sklar, *Nigerian Political Parties*, pp. 270–1.
† The announcement of Onabamiro's adherence to the N.C.N.C. brought him under heavy attack from the Action Group newspapers, which claimed that he hoped for nomination by his new party in the forthcoming federal elections, and hinted that he was a Communist. He indignantly denied both charges in a letter published in the *Defender* on 12 April 1954.

Eastern Organizing Secretary for the N.C.N.C., wrote to him about the general state of the party.

It is gratifying to know that in spite of detractors and the opportunist deviations in our work, there are still progressives in our ranks who can speak and be heard ...one can only hope that the doubting, disillusioned progressives outside our ranks will come to respect this new force in the NCNC and decide to come to work with us for the great cause of freedom and socialism.[31]

On the previous day Nduka Eze, once a United Africa Company clerk under Adelabu, militant trade union organizer of the 1940s and early 1950s, had written to warn him against 'bourgeois elements' in the N.C.N.C. and give his own advice.

Very many people will prefer [sic] advice to you at this stage. Very many of them will come forward and claim to be your friends and comrades in arms. But I know you can distinguish all. I find myself incapable to advise you than to remind you that you need constantly to refer your mind to the careers of great talents and exquisite minds of past history. You need also to have by you expositions of the lives of renowned revolutionaries like Lenin and Stalin. By this I do not suggest an adoption of their political philosophy of Communism but I only want to remind you that in their efforts to erect a new society from the rottenness of a Czarist regime, they led a revolutionary life which is worthy of reference.[32]

Eze also asked Adelabu to give a public lecture in Lagos. The Ibadan leader's answer gave an interesting measure of his attitude to his new fame – he asked for a share of the proceeds from the lecture. Eze's radical sensibilities were wounded. He wrote back to say that he would suggest this to the Lagos Executive Committee, but 'I suggest to you that your conception of the whole matter looks irregular. You are the honoured guest, and I could have wished you leave everything to the judgement of your hosts. What is material is the popular support the party is building for you and I will not advise you that you introduce any element of hitch.'[33]

The lecture, entitled 'Spirit of New Democracy' was given on 4 May and was apparently a success. The whole incident is indicative of Adelabu's attitude to politics. He was not without principles – indeed, as we shall have occasion to see, he was more firmly wedded to 'ideology' than the other N.C.N.C. leaders. On the other hand, he was ambitious, he wanted power and money, and politics was a way of getting these. Moreover, he had to be the master of any group with which he was associated, and individuals as tough-minded as Okoye or Eze would have been impossible colleagues for him. He did not regard himself as one of the group of radicals in the N.C.N.C., but this was not because he was lacking ideas about the purpose of politics. His failings were rather of the personal kind to which another letter of advice, which he received at this time from a son of Ibadan, referred:

One secret I have for you is that people who are well educated admired your intelligence and you are ranked higher than some of our so[-called] leaders. But this should not make you to forget to back that praise up with good behaviour which is characteristic of Ibadan people.

It is not possible to please everybody in this world. But try your best.

Read your Quran regularly, and lecture your followers the art of politics. Above all watch your step and God will be your guidance. Keep away from useless women. They can easily mar one's career.[34]

Concern with Adelabu's career was also shown by a group of men in Lagos who were to be of great help to him. Some of these were sons of Ibadan, like Fasasi Adeshina, a labor contractor to whom he was related by marriage, who had taken an interest in him since his Yaba College days. It also included a number of men, some Lagosians, others long resident there, who were stalwart supporters of the Nigerian National Democratic Party (or 'Demo', as they liked to call it), the N.C.N.C.'s ally in Lagos, and major contributors to its coffers. Adeshina himself was one of these, another was E. J. Ogundimu, a trader and Lagos traditional chief, another Jasper Sofidiya, a trader originally from Abeokuta. Most important of all from Adelabu's point of view was Alhaji Nuruddeen Badaru Soule, a very wealthy trader of Oyo origin, who had moved to Lagos by way of Porto Novo in the 1920s. Alhaji Soule had first met the rising young politician in 1952 and had taken a fancy to him; henceforward he was to treat Adelabu almost as his own son, providing him with important financial support. As Adelabu's career developed, Soule and the others showed an almost proprietary interest in it.

Neither Adelabu's supporters nor he and his fellow party officers had been able in the months since the Enugu Convention to establish a network of local party branches sufficient for the work of the coming elections. When the National Executive Committee met on 4 July at Akere's Compound in Ibadan to consider the campaign, it had before it a report by Osita Agwuna, the Principal Organizing Secretary, who commented:

I have discovered that outside the municipality of Lagos and the large cosmopolitan towns, the N.C.N.C. is not properly organised at all. In the hinterland, especially in rural districts, the villagers are NCNC-conscious but they have not been organised into groups of active members.[35]

The key posts of Regional Organizing Secretary had been created by the Enugu Convention, 'but from January this year, when the party started to create these offices, to this day, efficient administration and co-ordination has not been enhanced to any appreciable degree'.[36] Agwuna suggested two reasons for this. First, the Convention had failed to define the role of the Secretaries and emphasize their personal status as elected members of the National Executive Committee. Second, friction had arisen between the new officials and Kola Balogun. It is obvious that Balogun, understandably, regarded these new officials as his subordinates, while they preferred to think of themselves as a separate and independent part of the N.C.N.C. hierarchy. 'There should be less dictation and less direct interference from the National Secretary', wrote Agwuna in underlining this point, asking that all Organizing Secretaries should be responsible to and take orders from him alone.

With these tensions in effect rendering the attempted re-organization of the N.C.N.C. fruitless, it was left to local branches (where they existed) or groups of local sympathizers to do what they could. The affairs of the N.C.N.C. in the West were under the general direction of the Western Organization Committee, set up after the January Convention, with T. O. S. Benson as its Chairman, Adesanya Idowu as its Secretary, Elizabeth Adekogbe as Treasurer and Adegoke Adelabu as Publicity Secretary, and this acted in effect as the Election Committee for the coming campaign. On 3 and 4 July a conference of the Western N.C.N.C. was held at Akere's Compound to discuss arrangements for the federal election, including the pious hope that £20,000 could be raised as a fighting fund. This was no more realistic than the hope that the N.C.N.C. machinery could be over-hauled in time, a hope which was itself dispelled by the report which Agwuna presented at the N.E.C. meeting timed to coincide with the conference. In the circumstances, the Western Election Committee was forced to fall back towards the end of August on the expedient of appointing prominent party members in each locality as 'Zone Leaders', making them personally responsible for the campaign in their area. The Region was divided into ten Zones, excluding Lagos, which was to become a separate Federal Territory on 1 October. Ibadan and Oyo Divisions were grouped together as one Zone, with two Leaders, Adegoke Adelabu and H. O. Davies.*

Thus, as the local initiator of a successful N.C.N.C., Adelabu, by his two separate but mutually supportive roles as a party officer and as Chairman of

---

* Davies, the lawyer who had been prominent since the late 1930s as a leader of the Nigerian Youth Movement, had refused to follow most of the Movement's leaders into the Action Group in 1951, forming instead his own Nigerian People's Congress. In 1954, he applied to affiliate this tiny Lagos group with the N.C.N.C., and this was accepted by the N.E.C. meeting on 4 June. Thus Davies's appointment as a Zone Leader and later adoption as an N.C.N.C. candidate in Oyo (where he had family connections through his mother) were related to his reputation as a veteran politician rather than his seniority in the N.C.N.C., which supposedly had a rule demanding at least two years' membership in the party as a qualification for nomination as a candidate.

the Ibadan Council was drawn into the vortex of the federal election. To keep abreast of the flood of demands upon him, Adelabu was forced to set an exhausting pace for himself, one faced by no other N.C.N.C. leader, in that Adelabu was responsible for the administration of the largest city in the country. In Ibadan, the N.C.N.C. Mabolaje Grand Alliance victory in March had been won because Adelabu was able to establish a series of contacts at the right moment, rather than through a smoothly-functioning and widespread ward organization. The big organizational effort of the Alliance came in July and August, after Agwuna's report, with a particular effort in the eastern wards, where the Alliance had conceded to the Action Group in March.

The Ibadan branches of the functional wings of the N.C.N.C. itself were also active at this time. The Youth Association had apparently been taken under the care of the editor of the *Defender*, and met regularly at that newspaper's offices at Ogunpa. Early in July the Women's Section formed an Ibadan branch, and the *Defender* proclaimed in an editorial, significantly entitled 'Sleeping Giant is Up', that 'the women section of the NCNC, Ibadan Branch, has come to stay'.[37]

These efforts by the N.C.N.C. were not without failures and great confusion among Adelabu's followers and those who might have at least been disposed to oppose the Action Group. The Olubadan, for example, was obviously bewildered by the piling up of events in 1953–4 – the extensive discussion of reforms in Ibadan local government, the implementation of some of these, the many tensions this caused, the elections, and the constitutional changes which were due to come into force nationally on 1 October 1954. In his letter of 17 June to the Senior District Officer quoted above, he went on to ask clarification of the whole position: 'I want to find out from you as from today whether the Self-Government has been given to Ibadan people. Are we under British control? If not you will please set us free.'

The Olubadan's control of Ibadan was again called into question in the first week of July when a man died from a severe beating administered by masqueraders at the annual Egungun festival, during which the custodians of the traditional masks roam the streets dressed in these and costumes of raffia to represent the spirits of the dead, and occasionally beat the onlookers with whips. The Grand Alliance was avidly courting the masqueraders, both for publicity purposes and as handy agents to inflict beatings on opponents who might be caught in the street. This event occurred less than two weeks after the Resident had dropped the ban against processions, which he had called a 'useful outlet for steam', although they were now being used by a party to undermine the Olubadan's authority.

The smoldering campaign against Chief Akinyele also broke out into the open again. A number of the senior chiefs were becoming increasingly alarmed at the prospect that Isaac Akinyele might quite soon succeed the aged and feeble Olubadan Igbintade, and they resented his victory in the court reforms. On 6 July, they charged Akinyele with disloyalty to the Olubadan. His reply on 13 July, even though he offered to surrender his posts if the Olubadan and the Council formally requested him to do so, failed to mollify his attackers.* Moreover, the Finance Committee, like all the others under Adelabu's personal chairmanship, now joined in the new onslaught on the Balogun. It took the view that it, and not the Chief Judge, was the proper authority for recommending salaries and special benefits, and on 2 August the Olubadan and Senior chiefs 'withdrew' their recommendations of 1953 in which they had originally supported the idea of some kind of court reform. They had made nine recommendations, they noted, and only one, that of Chief Akinyele's appointment, was accepted. However, they had made the recommendations to be considered together, and since this was not done they now disavowed any responsibility for the reforms.

Whatever the difficulties of the N.C.N.C., the Action Group was much less well placed to organize in Ibadan. It had few Councillors around whom to build ward branches, and the men who supported it were the educated and well-to-do, like Dr A. S. Agbaje, its local Chairman, who had little time (and perhaps little inclination) for such leg-work, and who tended to live in the outer, more modern, less densely populated wards. In consequence, it seems to have followed two tactics. First of all, it sought to display its strength as the Regional governing party. Thus, on 5 July, hard on the heels of the N.C.N.C. Western meeting, a ceremony was held at Bere Square to mark the beginning of the enrollment of school children for compulsory primary education which was one of the most-publicized reforms of the Action Group Regional Government. Obafemi Awolowo, Moyo Aboderin, A. M. A. Akinloye and a number of other Ministers attended the ceremony. So did Adelabu, as behoved the Chairman of the District Council, but though he shook hands all round he ostentatiously left after fifteen minutes, perhaps mindful of the violence that occurred on 16 June, the last time the Action Group and the N.C.N.C. had met at Mapo Hall.

Action Group's second tactic was to win over prominent individuals whose prestige might be influential with the electorate. At the end of May, Lawani Latorera's faction of the Maiyegun League declared for it and expelled Alfa

---

* 'Olubadan is my father', he declared, 'I love him, and I believe he loves me too.' Regarding his titles, he wrote, 'The posts were offered to me, I have never striven for them...The three most Senior Chiefs and Chief D. T. Akinbiyi urged and begged me to take the post as I was unwilling to take it; and after all what I feared then did come to pass now.' (Chief Akinyele to the Olubadan and Senior Chiefs, 13 July 1954, PADID 26/S.3.)

Elesinmeta, Bello Konipe, Obadara Atanda and Yesufu Mogbonjubola. On 20 August, the *Defender* carried the news that Mrs Adekogbe, leader of the Women's Movement of Nigeria and Treasurer of the N.C.N.C. Western Organization Committee, had defected to the Action Group. On the following day it confirmed that Alhaji Y. S. Ola Ishola had committed himself to that party. The Action Group was also busy in a less public way. Akinpelu Obisesan recorded in his diary on 24 August that he had attended a meeting at Chief Akinyele's house with the rest of the judges and most of the assessors of the customary courts, at which 'political affairs were discussed also Action Group election support'.

On 16 August the Action Group had published its election manifesto, 'Forward to Freedom', and on 22 August it formally launched its campaign at a rally in Lagos, displaying its powers of organization by announcing the names of forty of its forty-two candidates in the West. Its candidates for the four seats in Ibadan Division were T. L. Oyesina, Y. S. Ola Ishola, S. O. Durosaro and S. O. Ladipo, former stalwart of the I.C.C. and Manager of the Kajola Trading Company. Dr Agbaje and E. A. Sanda, contrary to public expectations, were not nominated. It was to be another two months before the N.C.N.C. candidates for Ibadan were known.

In the last week of July the Western N.C.N.C. had begun its electoral campaign in earnest, with its Ibadan leaders no doubt considerably cheered by the three victories during those days in bye-elections to replace J. L. Ogunsola, Akinpelu Obisesan and Mogaji Osunware, the new judges, on the District Council. On 27 July Adelabu went to Ilesha to campaign, the next day T. O. S. Benson visited Abeokuta, and on the 31st Benson, H. O. Davies and Oshilaja Oduyoye carried the word to Ile Ife. The issues on which the N.C.N.C. chose to fight in the West were in effect an attack on the legislative record of the Action Group since it came to power in the West at the beginning of 1952, even though this was a federal, not a regional, election, and the tenure of the Government of the West thus not in question. The N.C.N.C. bitterly attacked the raising of capitation tax by the 'Health and Education Levy', and promised to reduce it from 10s. 6d. to 2s. 6d., denounced the introduction of free compulsory primary education as premature, pledged itself to pay a 7s. 6d. minimum daily wage to government laborers, instead of the 5s. 0d. which the Action Group Government had instituted, and rejected the new local government and chieftaincy laws as damaging to the authority of the natural rulers of the people. The N.C.N.C. campaign was not co-ordinated and left much to the initiative of local leaders and candidates, many of whom were even more sweeping in their promises than the party was in its public declarations.*

* For a discussion of the election campaign see a two-part article 'The Parties and the

Adelabu, in spite of his party responsibilities, only campaigned once outside Ibadan. We have already suggested the various strains he was under at this time and there was a report that he may have been drinking heavily.

It was thus not surprising that the Grand Alliance campaign in Ibadan did not really get under way until the last week of August, when Adelabu and others threw themselves once more into the long round of meetings and speeches. Adelabu opened the campaign on Tuesday 24 August. The platform adopted, which was to be that of the whole effort in Ibadan, was a variant of the N.C.N.C.'s approach throughout the region, but more largely an attempt to exploit local themes. He promised a taxation policy designed to relieve the burden on the poor, the re-adjustment of street rules to permit women to trade along Lebanon Street and New Court Road (promises still unfulfilled since the March election), the 'restoration' of the mogajis and an increase in the salaries of district chiefs and the car allowances of the city chiefs. The relevance of these local themes to electoral success, and indeed to such important national questions as independence, was revealed the next day in a remarkable drama at the palace of the Olubadan.

The opposition of some groups to independence was reinforced at this time by the activities in Ibadan of Miss Adunni Oluwole, a formidable lady from Mushin, in Ikeja Division, who had founded the Nigerian Commoners Party to oppose the rapid transfer of power to Nigerians at the price of the 'dictatorship' of some of them over the others. During August Miss Oluwole made a determined effort to win over the Olubadan. On 25 August she visited him dressed in prison garb, to emphasize what she feared would be the nature of self-government. Present were Chief Kobiowu, the Otun Olubadan, Chief Akinyo, the Ashipa Balogun, some other senior chiefs and also Adegoke Adelabu, who reacted strongly to the intrusion. After a chase through the courtyard and backrooms, Miss Oluwole was caught and brought struggling to the Olubadan's feet, denounced and sent away. The aged Igbintade then had to attempt to mend his fences. Pointing to Adelabu he assured the assembled company that 'I could have died by now of sorrow but for this my good son who restored my royal dignity. God forbid that I disown him and his party.'[38]

Adelabu now paused in his campaign to strengthen the hand of the Olubadan by continuing his vendetta against Akinyele. Adelabu had excluded the Balogun and his Otun from the Council's Chieftaincy Committee, which he filled with more amenable chiefs and Councillors. This Committee, with Adelabu's backing, now undertook to support the Olubadan in invest-

Federal Elections', *West Africa*, 15 and 22 January 1955. The anonymous correspondent was in fact P. C. Lloyd, at that time a Research Fellow at the West African Institute of Social and Economic Research, University College, Ibadan.

ing with new titles ten chiefs in the lines of the Seriki and the Balogun. Balogun Akinyele did not participate in approving their promotions and indeed had not been informed of them. This meant, of course, that shares of the various fees required for their approval had not been given to Chief Akinyele and those in his line who remained loyal to him, as required by customary law. Chief Akinyele called a meeting to discuss this threat to his authority, which Adelabu dismissed as insignificant since Akinyele was not a member of the Chieftaincy Committee.[39]

Adelabu's manipulation of the Chieftaincy Committee was taken up in the September meeting of the Council, when an Action Group member moved that the existing committees be dissolved and that Adelabu surrender his office as Chairman. The motion was made by S. L. Akano, who had won on the N.C.N.C. platform and had reportedly switched to the Action Group at this time. Confusion reigned. The next day Osi Balogun Bello Akinyo felt compelled to deny that he had accompanied Chief Akinyele to the Senior District Officer to 'report' Adelabu.[40] In addition, an emergency meeting of the Central Working Committee of the Grand Alliance was called at which two party Councillors, one of them Akano, were suspended from the party for 'gross disloyalty'.[41]

As was so frequently the case when chieftaincy politics and party politics mixed in Yorubaland, violence was once more increasing. In April, May and June 1954, a series of anti-tax riots swept the towns of northern Oyo, including Shaki. On 25 August, as the situation in Oyo Division grew more tense, a number of the most important Yoruba chiefs (including the Oni of Ife) and other senior men met with Akinola Maja, the President of the Egbe Omo Oduduwa, and agreed to send Sir Kofo Abayomi to see the Alafin to try to persuade him to drop his support for the N.C.N.C.; it was also claimed later that Sir Kofo advised the Alafin not to allow Adegoke Adelabu to come to Oyo.* Alhaji Adeniran, however, took no notice of his fellow chiefs. In that same month the Oyo Divisional Council suspended his salary as its President, and this drove him closer to the N.C.N.C.–Egbe Oyo Parapo Alliance and to Adelabu. It was in August or September 1954 that he gave his daughter, Omoriyeba, to the Ibadan leader as his wife. On 5 September occurred the most serious clash of the campaign in the West, in Oyo.[42] On that Sunday, H. O. Davies led a campaign team to Oyo town. At about midday they were

---

* As early as the previous November, Akinpelu Obisesan and Bello Abasi had tried to mediate between the Alafin and the Action Group. 'Mr. Belo Abasi, the Ibadan Muslims Babasale, came to see me to discuss Alafin's crisis; at 6 p.m. we met Hon. Mr. Awolowo on Mr. Abasi's suggestion...The Minister condemned Alafin as one utterly unfit to be in his office...On his advice we motored to see Alafin at Oyo who rebutted Mr. Awolowo's accusation and swore if [i.e. denied that] he had done all that people alleged he had done.' (Obisesan Diary, 2 November 1953.)

attacked by a mob of Action Group supporters. Fierce fighting broke out, leaving six dead and many injured. The police eventually got the situation under control, but just before 5.00 p.m. Adegoke Adelabu arrived from Ibadan with a number of private cars and five trucks full of men. He was met outside the Police Station by the Acting Resident, J. H. Beeley. Adelabu claimed that he had come for the campaign meeting and was told by Beeley that he was too late. Adelabu was to persist with this story and later was even to claim that the whole riot had been planned in order to give the Action Group a chance to assassinate him. If this was the case, it seems strange that he did not arrive until some five hours after Davies and that he came so well defended. It seems more probable that after the riot had broken out he was telephoned by someone in Oyo and asked to bring reinforcements. In any case, he now insisted on his right to hold another meeting. The Acting Resident refused, Adelabu and his retinue refused to go home, and at last tear-gas bombs were thrown by the police to disperse them. The Chairman of the Ibadan District Council, his cars and his truck-loads of men drove off at great speed down the Ibadan road, colliding with and severely damaging a taxi-cab on the way.*

The immediate result of the events of 5 September was an order from the Western Regional Government suspending the Alafin from office and forbidding him to live in Oyo Division. The old man, victim of political changes he barely understood, first took refuge with the Owa of Ilesha and later moved into a house in that town. (Later still he was to live with Alhaji Soule in Lagos.) He was never to return to his kingdom. From now on he lived on the charity of others, his son-in-law included, and on the hope that if the N.C.N.C. could only gain control of the Regional Government he would be restored.†

The campaign in Ibadan was also marked by violence in the first week of September, much of it seemingly initiated by Action Group supporters, the result perhaps of a feeling that they were on the losing side.‡ On 6 September Festus Edah and T. O. S. Benson, visiting Ibadan for the campaign, were

---

* In November 1955 the Ibadan Magistrates' Court awarded the owner of the taxi damages of £62.5.8d. and twelve guineas costs in a civil suit brought by him against Adelabu as a result of this incident.

† Already by the end of 1954 the Alafin had been forced to borrow £1000 from Dr Azikiwe on the security of a house he owned in Oyo, and needed £100 for conveyancing fees before the loan could be completed. (Alafin to Adelabu, 4 January 1955, A.P. The date on the letter is actually 1954, but this is obviously a slip of the pen.)

‡ They were also under considerable provocation. On 28 August the Acting Senior Superintendent of Police wrote to Adelabu asking him to stop his followers shouting 'Ole, Ole' (thief, thief) at their opponents, and on 8 October he wrote again to complain that N.C.N.C. propaganda vans had disturbed Action Group meetings with their loudspeakers. (Letters in Ibaprof 1, 26/S.4, 1.)

attacked, and on the 8th Benson's car was stoned outside Obafemi Awolowo's house.

On 8 September, the day of the second incident involving Benson, the Acting Resident, D. A. Murphy, held a meeting attended by the Senior District Officer and Assistant Superintendent of Police for Ibadan Province, the Senior Superintendent of Police for Ibadan and Oyo Provinces, D. K. Olumofin and C. N. Ekwuyasi for the N.C.N.C., and an Action Group delegation made up of O. Agunbiade Bamishe, the Party Manager, T. L. Oyesina, and S. L. Durosaro. It was necessary, Murphy told his audience, to study the 'mechanics of peace'. It was agreed that there would henceforth be no more processions before or after meetings, that meetings would disperse immediately, that no processions would be directed against persons or houses, that the Senior Superintendent of Police would arrange for uniformed police to attend meetings for which he had granted permits, and finally that there would be no permits granted for rival meetings at the same day and time.[43] On the 9th a second meeting was held in the office of the Acting Lieutenant-Governor, attended by Abafemi Awolowo, S. L. Akintola, Festus Edah, T. O. S. Benson, the Oni of Ife, the Chief Justice of the Western Region, Adetokunboh Ademola, and W. M. Milliken, now the Acting Civil Secretary of the West. They accepted the decisions of the previous meeting and also agreed that parties should not book the same place for rallies on consecutive days in order to allow others its use. At the end of the meeting the four political leaders signed a joint 'peace' declaration of their agreement.

In fact, the violence (which was to increase substantially as the election campaign progressed), the confusion of the Olubadan and others in the traditional order, and the emergence of groups opposing Nigerian independence, were all symptomatic of the tensions caused by the very rapid change occurring in Ibadan, the Western Region, and Nigeria as a whole. Structures and values were being replaced by new ones, old sources of legitimacy rejected and new ones sought, without hard and fast rules governing how all this was to be done. Involved in this was the competition of the major parties for the power which was gradually being transferred to them by the British, perhaps the central fact of this piecemeal process. Thus the growing violence, for example, was not a sign of a system in decline, of an attempt by the British to resist nationalism or the last desperate attempts of the chiefs to maintain control. Rather, it was symptomatic first of the intense inter-party competition at this time, and second of an attempt to define the limits within which political action was to be taken, in a situation where neither the British nor anyone else was laying down adequate rules of conduct.

By this time, however, Adelabu's own attention was turned toward another issue of the campaign in Ibadan, his promise to alleviate the burden of taxation upon the poor. There is in fact no indication, despite the preoccupation with tax in the local government election campaign, that Adelabu once in office intended to lower tax rates, or that the administrators thought he would. Rather, both seemed concerned in the early months of his chairmanship with problems of tax evasion by the wealthy. As we have seen, the Alliance 'Cabinet' at its meeting on 21 March did agree to impose a Pay As You Earn scheme, and early in September the Secretary of the Council, V. O. Esan, also recommended this method of collection, which had been successful in Lagos.[44] It was only later discovered that the payment of such tax proceeds into the Ibadan Treasury was not permitted under the tax laws of the Western Region in 1954, and Adelabu had to turn to some other way of assuring revenue without alienating the mass of his supporters.

In July 1954 the Council agreed to examine the question of property rating.[45] On 18 September, the *Tribune* carried the misleading statement that the Council had already decided to make a special assessment on modern houses of the type that many former Councillors owned; among the first to protest were property-owning former Councillors who in 1953 had first considered and then rejected the idea. T. L. Oyesina protested that 'without giving thought to the economic life in Ibadan, the N.C.N.C. councillors qualify as the greatest enemy of Ibadan people' [46]

Protest came from other quarters as well. On 25 September, the Ibadan Parapo, the Welfare Committee and the 'Ibadan Band of Unity-Grand Alliance' held a mass meeting to protest house rating, a bye-law requiring compulsory registration of births and deaths, and the lack of respect the Council was showing to the senior chiefs; the Council, they charged was not consulting with the people and should withhold such measures until the people were more 'fully educated'.[47] In spite of this pressure, the Finance Committee on 30 September resolved that 'the principle of localised property rating be endorsed'.

The principle, however, was a purely political one. Adelabu's real interest, as was revealed at this meeting, was to tax the buildings of the University College, government and Railway Corporation buildings, the structures of the Nigerian Tobacco Company, and the business firms along Lebanon Street and New Court Road owned by the Lebanese and Europeans.[48] This selective approach had a number of political advantages to it. In the first place, insofar as the scheme was to be directed primarily against properties owned by the Regional and Federal Governments, there was little reason for the masses of electors to become worried about it. While it was certain that both Governments would refuse the scheme, an open refusal by them would help confirm Adelabu as the leader of the masses against the Regional Government. To tax commercial structures on Lebanon Street and New

Court Road also put Adelabu in a favourable anti-Lebanese position just at the time when the petty trader issue on Lebanon Street was again hotly debated. This also put the Government in a nice dilemma: either back Adelabu's obviously discriminatory tax scheme or appear to support the Lebanese.

Rumors that tax reforms were to be made led to some disquiet in the town which Adelabu used to good advantage. On 20 October he was able to persuade the Regional Broadcasting Service to announce that only government properties and the buildings of the foreigners in the Lebanon Street area were to be taxed, thus seeming to have Government's approval for a position which it in fact did not support at all. Since the Council could not undertake such a program without Government's approval, Awolowo and his colleagues now merely adopted a position of silence and delay; nothing more was communicated to the Council until after the election.

Obafemi Awolowo had particular occasion to wish to thwart Adelabu at this time, since Penkelemesi had just inflicted a considerable humiliation on his old enemy. On 4 October the Action Group leader was ceremonially installed as the first Premier of the Western Region, following the coming into force of the new constitution three days before. The Action Group, through a body organized by Dr Agbaje somewhat grandly called 'the Ibadan Community', had sought permission to hold a celebration at Mapo Hall on the afternoon of the 4th, following a morning church service at St Peters at which Awolowo had read the second lesson. A letter from the Council, which was only written on 2 October, refused permission, but the Action Group arrived at 1.45 p.m. anyway, in a triumphal procession met by Local Government Police barring the gate. The Police gave way, however, when they saw official cars in the procession and admitted it to the compound although not to the Hall itself. The Action Group supporters demonstrated their wrath, as on 13 June, by dancing round the Hall and singing abusive songs. The Action Group's insistence upon arriving during office hours was matched by Adelabu's reason for refusal to grant permission; the Council sub-committee on schools, which he said would be using the Hall, in fact met that morning.

It was now a month to polling day, which in the West had been set for 11 November. On 13 October the lists of electors used for the local elections in March were posted in Ibadan as preliminary lists for the federal election. During the following week, applications from those wanting to add their names and objections to any names already listed were heard, and on 28 October the final lists were displayed. Despite the fact that people tended to register (and vote) together in groups from the same compound, the lists were compiled for each polling station in alphabetical order, a stroke of

Western rationality which considerably slowed down the voting process on election day.[49] Nevertheless, the administration of the election was in general greatly helped by the experience gained in March. Not only were the electors' lists from then available for use now, but the ballot boxes constructed by the Nigerian Tobacco Company and the polling booths made by the Public Works Department were still on hand. Moreover, Resident Murphy, Senior District Officer Lewis and District Officer Bey, who had supervised the March election, were also in charge in November. Better organized than in March was the vast contingent of polling officials – some 1413 senior and junior police and government employees, bank clerks, commercial employees, and members of the Boys' Brigade.

The filing of candidates' nominations was to close on 1 November, with each one depositing £25, to be forfeited if he garnered less than one-eighth of the total votes cast in his constituency. We have already seen that the Action Group made its list of candidates known long before this, an advantage in that it gave them a chance to make themselves known to the electorate. As the day approached, it became apparent that, in contrast to the March elections, the contest in Ibadan was to be monopolized almost completely by the Action Group and the N.C.N.C.–Mabolaje Grand Alliance. In the last seven months almost all local parties and political clubs had identified themselves with the two major parties. A few of those individuals who had hesitated to do this attempted to intervene as the Ibadan Parapo Party, forming an alliance with the Nigerian Commoners Liberal Party, a fusion of the organization led by the redoubtable Miss Adunni Oluwole and another which opposed the idea of independence in 1956.*

There was one other candidate not sponsored by one of the major parties – Oshilaja Oduyoye, standing as an Independent in Ibadan North. Oduyoye, the old N.C.N.C. stalwart, once known as 'Local Bustamante', who had perhaps been more responsible than any other man for getting the N.C.N.C. started in Ibadan, had not even been included as a co-opted member on a Council Committee. He now found himself opposing the official Grand Alliance candidate, J. M. Johnson, in the federal election. The *Southern Nigeria Defender* greeted the full list of N.C.N.C. candidates with something approaching rapture when it was officially published on 2 November,

---

* Yet another such party, the Nigeria Peoples Influential Self Government Fiasco Party met a sad fate in the 1954 election campaign. It had urged its supporters to vote for the symbol of the Crown, without having received official permission to make this royalist identification. When told that it would have to use the officially recognized Blue Lion instead, the party withdrew from the electoral race, having apparently spent its entire campaign fund of £200 in familiarizing its supporters with the Crown. The Ibadan Parapo also wanted to use the Crown, but finally agreed to accept a Yellow Lady. (PADID 3224/S.1.)

237

'Who but die-hard snivellers will have the impudence to speak of this galaxy with infamy?'[50] Nevertheless, in Ibadan the choice of the Grand Alliance had not been easy, and it was not until a meeting at Akere's compound on 26 October, running late into the night, that Johnson, Adebayo Adeyinka, L. A. Lawal and Adelabu were selected.

Adegoke Adelabu had now decided to go to the center, to the House of Representatives in Lagos, and he was also determined to be the sole arbiter of who went with him from Ibadan; he wanted only men who would follow his lead. It was this determination which brought out the latent conflict within the Grand Alliance, between those who felt themselves to be first and foremost members of the N.C.N.C., and those who were Adelabu's men. Already by the beginning of July, Oduyoye and D. K. Olumofin had begun to hold separate meetings of N.C.N.C. supporters, who were denounced as a 'scandalous minority clique' by the Grand Alliance.[51] The strength of the N.C.N.C. Grand Alliance in Ibadan lay in the Mabolaje, and this was an instrument of Adelabu's creation. It was Penkelemesi who could get the necessary votes in Ibadan. The national N.C.N.C. had to recognize this, to appreciate that he was indispensable, given its inability to organize effectively in its own right. T. O. S. Benson and F. S. McEwen sent a telegram to Adelabu pointing out that 'While we regret that Oduyoye was not selected to contest election on NCNC platform please note that NCNC parent body does not sponsor Oduyoye.'[52]

On Thursday 11 November 1954, Ibadan, together with the rest of the Western Region, went to the polls. A polling station had been planned for each 500 electors, although in retrospect the Senior District Officer felt that one station for each 1000 electors would have been sufficient.[53] Each party was entitled to a poll watcher sitting opposite the polling officer in each station, and T. L. Oyesina, with typical Action Group preparedness, provided 324 poll watchers for the whole township. The N.C.N.C. left its candidates to find their own watchers. In the circumstances, however, there was little for them to watch. The day proceeded 'in a friendly atmosphere with good will and patience expressed by all parties', according to the S.D.O.[54] This was fortunate, for the Regional Electoral Officer's telephone was out of order most of the day, and the police 'striking force' intended to quell disturbances could hardly have arrived anywhere from its 'central' position promptly enough to save life, limb or ballots had the need arisen. There were few complaints of violence or electoral fraud. The *Nigerian Tribune* did allege belatedly on the 15th that the houses of Alhaji Ishola and A. M. A. Akinloye had been attacked by N.C.N.C. hooligans, but Lewis's report failed to mention this.

When the count was completed, the N.C.N.C.–Mabolaje Grand Alliance had won all four seats in Ibadan proper. Full results are shown in Table 5. The N.C.N.C. lost Ibadan West (out-of-the-way Ibarapa) to the Action Group, but by only 156 votes. Adegoke Adelabu had beaten S. O. Ladipo by 5085 to 1256 in Ibadan South. The Grand Alliance claimed to have carried 71 wards out of the 73. The Action Group had not been utterly smashed, but it had certainly been humiliated. Moreover, this was true not merely in Ibadan Division but in the Region as a whole. When all the results were in, the N.C.N.C. had won 22 seats, with 208,401 votes, and the Action Group 19 seats, with 139,573 votes; the remaining seat was won by the Commoners Liberal Party.* All ten seats in the Mid-West had gone to the N.C.N.C., mainly through the judicious exploitation of anti-Yoruba feeling. Of the thirty-two seats for Yorubaland, twelve fell to the N.C.N.C., which won seats in Oyo Division (one out of two), Oshun Division (two out of five),

TABLE 5   *Ibadan Federal Election Results, 1954*

	N.C.N.C.		A.G.		Others		Total
	Votes	(%)	Votes	(%)	Votes	(%)	votes
Ibadan East	4089	86.9	617	13.1			4706
Ibadan North	5559	65.0	2868	33.5	126	1.5	8553
Ibadan South	5085	80.2	1256	19.8			6341
Ibadan Central	4699	68.6	2064	30.1	83	1.3	6846
Totals	19,432	73.5	6805	25.7	209	0.7	26,446

Ondo Division (one out of two), Ekiti Division (one out of two), Egba Division (two out of three) and the one for Ilesha Division, in addition to the four Ibadan seats. The poll was low, less than a third of the qualified electors having voted (and in Ibadan only a sixth), but those that did had demonstrated convincingly that there was considerable dissatisfaction with the Action Group Government. What the N.C.N.C. lacked in organization it had managed to make up by exploiting the widespread discontent with the Education and Health Levy and all the other disadvantages the Action Group suffered as a governing party which had not yet established itself.

The N.C.N.C. could scarcely believe its own good fortune: on 15 November and again on the 18th the *Defender* published the same editorial, warning against a repetition of the 'carpet-crossing' in 1952. It was not until 16 November that Adelabu's supporters in Ibadan demonstrated their joy by turning a visit to the city from the Governor-General (as he had become

---

* The N.C.N.C. had not contested four seats. The unopposed candidate for Egbado North first claimed that he was N.C.N.C., giving the party 23 seats, but then changed his mind.

under the new constitution) into a victory celebration when Adelabu, 'dressed in his Muslim costume' and on horseback, led a crowd estimated at 10,000 from Oke Oluokun to Kings Barracks to meet Sir John and Lady Macpherson.[55] Nevertheless, Adelabu had already comprehended the political reality which underlay the N.C.N.C.'s triumph in the West – victory in a federal election had not the slightest effect on his enemy's control of the Regional Government. On 27 November, after taking the chair at a public lecture by Dr Onabamiro on 'The Role of Youths in the Present Struggle', he declared in his summing-up that 'the headquarters of the Western Region must be wrested from the hands of fascists'; 'I will demand from Chief Obafemi Awolowo', he said, 'the key of the Western Region.'[56] There was no response from Awolowo – now not only Premier, but holder of an honorary chieftainship title – who knew that he had only to sit back and weather the storm.

Moreover, the Grand Alliance had little reason for long-term optimism at the end of 1954. Admittedly they had won the four Ibadan seats, with an impressive percentage of the total votes cast. Since the March local election they had raised their share of the total from 54.3 to 73.5 per cent. Action Group had also improved its position, however, from 17.0 to 25.7 per cent; the share of the Independents and small parties had, of course, dropped by the 28 per cent the major parties had gained. On the other hand, if any of the Grand Alliance leaders looked closely at the voting figures – and there is no reason to suppose they ever did – they might have had cause to ponder. Their improved percentage of the poll was on a reduced total vote, 26,446 in November compared with 33,829 in March. In terms of actual persons voting, the Grand Alliance in seven and a half months, two and a half of them taken up with strenuous campaigning, had been able to secure only 1077 more supporters; Action Group had done almost as well, gaining 1057 more votes. If the Alliance had won any new supporters beyond this thousand, it had been at the expense of a parallel loss of existing support. There is no sign here whatsoever of a mobilization of the masses of Ibadan behind a populist leadership.*

* Thus there is little evidence in 1954 that the Mabolaje was a party based on 'communal participation', which was Sklar's description, based on observation in 1957–8. (*Nigerian Political Parties*, p. 475.) If it was, only a very small proportion of Ibadan people had come to regard it as 'an extension of a social order into which [the individual] had been born and to which he attributes spiritual or mystical significance'. As we saw in Chapter 1, Ibadan in the nineteenth century never established a communal feeling capable of overriding all cleavages, and the changes brought about by British administration, Christianity, education, commerce, and Islam contributed significantly to the heterogeneity and conflict one would normally expect in a mid-twentieth century city of well over half a million people.

The years 1953 and 1954 had been ones of great change in Ibadan, as indeed throughout the Western Region, but this was change which had not yet worked itself out, had not yet produced structures which could be seen to be viable or to have an acceptable basis of legitimacy. In the minds of the few people who were politically conscious at all, therefore, there was at this time often a great uneasiness. The rash of small parties opposing the very idea of independence and the preparatory changes which it entailed was one symptom of this. Another was the victory of the N.C.N.C. in the West in the federal election in November, part of which was Adelabu's second triumph. The N.C.N.C. and its leaders were able to exploit the association in the popular mind of the Action Group with the new and often inconvenient measures which it had initiated since 1952 – reform of local government, of the courts, of chieftaincy, and of education, and the great rise in taxation which had accompanied these. By instinctively putting itself on the side of conservatism (a conservatism which Adelabu himself neither felt nor demonstrated in his actions), the N.C.N.C. was able to win itself a victory which organizationally it had certainly not earned.

Conversely, from this point onward, the Action Group set itself to consolidate its hold on the administration of the West, hoping that in time its reforms would become acceptable, and even popular. The new constitution of 1954 gave it the wherewithal to do this. The greatly increased control which the regional governments had now acquired over the civil servants, judiciaries, public corporations and boards in their areas of jurisdiction gave them weapons which they were able to use in many different ways over the next few years to improve their control. The end of 1954 can be taken as a watershed in our story. Not only did Adelabu personally begin to face a series of new problems and new situations, but in Nigeria as a whole politics began to bite deeper, the parties began to look more and more to the winning of power before independence, the new breed of professional politicians began to come into their own. There was no place now for a man like Akinpelu Obisesan, in his time a radical and reformer. Late in November 1953 he talked for over two hours to H. K. Robinson, the Resident of Ibadan, and recorded that:

He made me to know what ministerial government meant. In the nutshell I gathered that the regime I grew up to know is gone and I became embarrassed on being unequivocally told what the implication of self-rule is.[57]

Henceforward we will be examining at close quarters what the implication of self-rule was for Adelabu, for Ibadan, for the Western Region and Nigeria as a whole in the period up to his death.

CHAPTER 10

THE USES OF POWER

> You will have seen from the evidence already given before you that every-thing revolves around the intriguing personality of Adegoke Adelabu. This is because I am the architect, the planner, the field commander and chief administrator of this unique, social-religious transformation.
>
> Adelabu at the Nicholson Inquiry,
> September 1955

By November 1954 Adelabu had expanded his political activities across nearly the full range of the Nigerian political system. Although he was often to shift the emphasis of his involvement, he now had an effective political instrument in his chairmanship of the Council and after mid-January 1955 his national political responsibilities were increased greatly. Concurrently with his expanding duties in these two spheres, during 1955 Adelabu was also to experience an increase in the expectations others had of him as a party leader. All of these activities, in addition to those devolving upon him as head of a large and rapidly growing family, were eventually to overburden him greatly by the end of 1955, the point at which this chapter closes. They also illustrate how in the process of attempting to ensure a place for himself in the political system, Adelabu was to discover the ramifications of being in opposition to a party which was gaining increasing control over a decoloniz-ing political system. Unlike his previous confrontation with an establish-ment, that of the Ibadan Progressive Union in 1952–4, in this case Adelabu found that the rules were fixed rather than shifting and that the means of controlling the system were more, not less, in the hands of his opponents.

Although the distribution of power within the regions was not affected by the federal election of 1954, at the center, where it seems that even the N.C.N.C. was surprised by its victory, a curious situation resulted. Under the new Constitution, the Federal Government was to be made up of three Ministers from each Region, nominated by the party winning the majority of seats in that Region, and one from the Southern Cameroons.* As previ-ously, it was assumed that the three major parties would be represented and would form a coalition. The Action Group, however, by failing to win a

---

* Under the previous constitution, each Region had been entitled to four Ministers.

majority of the Federal seats from the West, also forfeited to the N.C.N.C. the privilege of nominating that Region's Federal Ministers, giving that party the opportunity to nominate six of the ten Ministers, since in the Eastern elections it had taken thirty-five of the seats against seven for the Action Group–U.N.I.P. Alliance. An extra complication was caused by the fact that in the Northern Region, which still followed an indirect electoral college system as in 1951, the federal election lasted into December, delaying the formal establishment of the Federal Council of Ministers.

While the country waited on the North to vote, it was clear that the N.P.C., which was certain to win there, would have to co-operate in the Federal Council with the N.C.N.C. and that the Action Group would be absent.* When the Northern results were finally declared, the N.P.C. had 89 of the 92 seats, making it by far the largest party in a House of 192 members. On 1 January 1955 the Sardauna and two of his Regional Ministers arrived in Lagos for talks with the out-going northern Central Ministers. While they were there a 'courtesy' call was paid on them by the out-going N.C.N.C. Central Ministers, led by K. O. Mbadiwe; perhaps at this time, the assurance was given that the N.P.C. would not refuse to participate in the new Government, even though it meant co-operating with an N.C.N.C. majority in the Council of Ministers. On 7 January, the Executive Committee of the N.P.C. met in Kaduna under the chairmanship of the Sardauna and agreed to accept the situation in which there would be six N.C.N.C. Federal Ministers. By this time Dr Azikiwe had already taken the train from Enugu to Lagos, passing through Zaria in the North, then Ibadan on the 7th, stopping at Abeokuta later that same day where he consulted with Western N.C.N.C. leaders. The following day he proceeded to Lagos where a joint meeting was held of the N.C.N.C. National Executive Committee and its new federal legislators to select the party's six Ministers. This did not prove easy and the meeting lasted for seven hours. While the out-going Ministers from the East (K. O. Mbadiwe, Raymond Njoku and

---

* The Sardauna of Sokoto had traveled on 17 November to see Chief Awolowo. What took place between them is obscure. Their positions had been much closer to one another than either had been to the N.C.N.C. during the Constitutional Conference in London. Moreover, the N.C.N.C. felt that the North, along with the other Regions, should be broken up into smaller units, whereas Chief Awolowo did not as yet hold this view. (For later developments in his position see page 383.) A third reason for the N.P.C. to prefer the Action Group was that the N.C.N.C. was in alliance with the N.E.P.U., the northern opposition party, while the Action Group had not yet taken much part in northern politics. On the other hand, the Sardauna must have had some hostility to the feeling on the part of some of the Action Group that the Yoruba Divisions of Ilorin and Kabba should be allowed to leave the North and rejoin their Western brethren. (The single seat won by the Action Group in the North was in Kabba Division.)

Mathew Mbu) were to continue to serve, those from the West were another matter: none of the N.C.N.C. leaders from that Region had experience of ministerial office, so none was automatically marked out as a choice. On the other hand there were several important claimants: T. O. S. Benson, with his experience as Leader of the Opposition in the Western House; H. O. Davies, new in the party but respected and with great political experience; Kola Balogun; Adelabu, the new rising star of the Western N.C.N.C.; Festus Okotie-Eboh (the new name which F. S. Edah had taken in September 1954), the leading spokesman of the Midwestern N.C.N.C.* In the end it was Okotie-Eboh, Balogun and Adelabu who were chosen, with Benson becoming Chief Whip for the Government and Davies Deputy Leader of the N.C.N.C. Federal Parliamentary Party as lieutenant to Mbadiwe.† There had been opposition to the choice of Balogun from some of the older men in the Western N.C.N.C., on the grounds of his brusque and abrupt manner, a characteristic of a 'youngman' not likely to endear itself to his Yoruba elders. A promise of more circumspection on his part had placated them, though even then it is probably significant that he was given only a relatively junior ministerial position.

Also on 8 January there was a joint meeting in Kaduna of the N.P.C.'s federal and northern legislators which approved as N.P.C. Federal Ministers Abubakar Tafawa Balewa (already with three years' experience as Central Minister), Muhammadu Ribadu, a powerful and conservative aristocrat from Adamawa, and Inuwa Wada, an able politician from Kano. The N.P.C. was careful to explain, however, that they were entering the Government as required by the Constitution, rather than joining the N.C.N.C. in a freely chosen political alignment. On 9 January the party's Executive Committee issued a statement that 'the Northern People's Congress will not enter into any form of alliance with any political party which has its roots and origins in the South or with a party which is Southern dominated'.[1] That evening the new Northern Ministers arrived in Lagos in a charter plane from Kaduna and about two hours later the composition of the new Council of Ministers was formally announced by the Governor-General from Government House. In his first public pronouncement on the new Government, Adelabu declared that by 'its realistic interpretation of the Constitution' the N.P.C. had shown 'that it is a party to be reckoned with in the making of any objective plan in Nigeria'.[2] The force of this statement was to be demonstrated in his personal career in the future.

* This change of name was a political asset in the chief's Warri constituency, linking him more closely with an important family in the Benin River area.

† H. O. Davies was later unseated by an Action Group electoral petition against his victory in Oyo North.

His two electoral victories in Ibadan in 1954 had taken him from being a virtually powerless, though prominent, member of the Opposition in the West to control of the administration of the biggest city in tropical Africa, and now to the national importance of a Federal Minister. They had also fulfilled for the first time his desperate hopes for an adequate income. He had been drawing approximately £75 per month for sitting fees from the Ibadan Council, but as his other obligations increased his financial liabilities had waxed correspondingly, while the number of meetings he actually attended and for which he was entitled to remuneration declined. Now he calculated the income he thought would be his as Federal Minister: £3200 salary, £1700 in various allowances to cover entertainment, upkeep of his new ministerial house at 15 Alexander Road in Ikoyi, drivers and operating his ministerial car, £500 in fees (presumably from the Ibadan Council) and £600 in 'profits', perhaps from a business venture he was contemplating in Ibadan.[3] This would give a total of £6000, almost a seven-fold increase over the previous year. On the other hand, he budgeted £900 in vehicle maintenance in expectation of his increased travel, £600 on social obligations, £480 on food, £360 on 'drinks', £120 for light, £60 (a mere 1% of his income) on taxes and nothing for upkeep of his ministerial house although he was to receive £350 for it. His expenditures as he calculated them, subtracted from his income, would give him 'savings' of £3000 per annum. Although his salary was in fact to be £3000 and his allowances from the Federal Government only £900 as against his expectations of £1700, he was nevertheless justified in his new sense of economic security.

This in turn meant that he could feel free to play the role of family man with greater intensity. We do not know how many wives and children he had by the end of 1954; already in November 1950 he was claiming a total of eighteen. With a larger, and growing, number to care for, his assured income from the beginning of 1955 onward gave him the chance to be the 'lord of my castle, a satisfied husband, a good father, the head of a household and a pillar of society' which he had claimed to be in 1952. Among his papers for the next few years are to be found a number of daily domestic schedules, scribbled on scraps of paper or the backs of envelopes. Thus one, which may, however, date from an earlier, more leisurely time, reads: '1. Waking up. 2. Household Clean Up. 3. Breakfast. 4. Lunch. 5. Relationship with Servants. 6. Siesta. 7. Visitors. 8. Demeanour. 9. Requisition. 10. Pocket Money.' Another, probably written in late 1955, includes the removal of his wives to another part of the house, and (probably a related matter) the problem of wives bathing in the servants' quarters. A third, possibly dating from early 1957, mixes family matters with politics in its twenty-seven items, including house cleaning, completion of the rebuilding of part of the house, the purchase of cloth, finding accommodation for one of his political clients, and a mysterious libel suit.

Nevertheless, at the end of 1954 and throughout the following years such personal concerns were dependent upon Adelabu's political fortunes, and in January 1955 he had reached the political summit.

On 10 January the new Council of Ministers at its first meeting decided on the allocation of portfolios which was announced the next day. Abubakar Tafawa Balewa was to have Transport and Works, Mbadiwe Communications and Aviation, Ribadu Land, Mines and Power, Njoku Trade and Industry, Okotie-Eboh Labor and Welfare, while Adegoke Adelabu became the proud possessor of the title of Minister of Natural Resources and Social Services. Mbu, Balogun, Inuwa Wada and Victor Mukete (the Kamerun National Congress Minister from the Southern Cameroons) were to be without specific portfolios for the present.

The nature of the portfolios of Federal Ministers was, of course, determined by the division of legislative powers between the center and the Regions, defense and foreign affairs still lying in the hands of the British Government. As we have already noted, the balance of power in the 1954 Constitution had swung in favor of the Regions, so that such vital matters as Local Government, Chieftaincy and Agriculture were their sole preserve. Education was also very largely a Regional matter, the exceptions to this being post-secondary education, and primary and secondary schools in Lagos, which was now Federal Territory. These educational responsibilities thus became Adelabu's: he had to oversee the University College of Ibadan and the development of its new Teaching Hospital (to be one of the biggest in West Africa), and a number of other teaching and research institutions. Medical and health services in Lagos, fisheries, veterinary and forestry services were also in his portfolio, which was thus a very wide and diverse one, a fact which occasionally earned derisory comment from Action Group Opposition Members in the House of Representatives, but it did include matters of direct concern to the welfare of the ordinary people of Nigeria, the 'Silent Millions' whose cause he had pleaded in his book and in the Western House of Assembly. He now had a chance to put some of his principles into practice.

The instrument at hand for implementing his principles was his Ministry, housed in the old Secretariat and overflowing into the old Legislative Council building in the government quarter on Lagos Island. Since his portfolio also represented an amalgamation of subjects previously divided between the Ministries of Health and of Lands and Natural Resources, or in the hands of the chief Secretary (scholarships for higher education) it was also necessary to make organizational alterations within the new Ministry. The senior personnel operating this system were all British: a Permanent Secretary, C. J. Mabey, a Private Secretary, J. Blackwell, and two (from February three) Senior Assistant Secretaries. In addition there was a junior Nigerian staff of clerks and typists. Unlike some politicians who experienced racial tensions with their bureaucrats, Adelabu's capacity for good relations with Europeans saw him through. His expatriate civil servants appreciated his intelligence and his capacity to perceive with great speed the essentials of a problem. In time, a real affection developed between some of them and their Minister; they sympathized with him in his political troubles and brought him presents when they returned from leave in Britain.

As a Minister, Adelabu's main public arena was the House of Representatives. Here he had to expound policy and answer criticisms from the Opposition, a new experience for him, one perhaps made easier by the fact that his Permanent Secretary, as did those of the other Ministers, sat with him on the Government bench.

The first meeting of the new House, from 12 to 18 January 1955, was largely devoted to dealing with matters left over from the previous Government's period of office. Thus the first matter affecting his Ministry, a Bill relating to the University College Hospital which came before the House on the second day, was moved by the Acting Chief Secretary and only seconded formally by Adelabu.

Yet, while he was becoming acquainted with the personnel and problems of his new position in Lagos, his responsibilities in Ibadan were being correspondingly neglected. He had missed four meetings of Ibadan Council committees of which he was still Chairman and the second session of the Western Planning Committee of the N.C.N.C. He had been made Chairman of this Committee which had been set up after the federal election as an adjunct to the Organization Committee, a position which presumably lent him new influence in the party. Sanya Onabamiro was its Secretary and such well-known figures as T. O. S. Benson, Kola Balogun and H. O. Davies were members. At the second meeting of the Planning Committee on 14 January, the familiar question of party organization was faced once again. At this meeting it was decided to retain the system of Zonal Leaders, since (as was confirmed at a later meeting) much of the success of the federal election was due to their '...exploitation of the fullest [of] issues which were purely local'.[4]

Curiously, although he was Chairman of this Committee, Adelabu allowed it to meet on a day when as Minister he would be attending the first meeting of the Federal House. It was thus rather his responsibilities as a husband and father which brought him back to Ibadan to celebrate the birth of a son on 20 January, interrupting his first weeks in office as a fledgling Minister.

Once back in Ibadan he again shifted the emphases of his activities somewhat. On 1 February, he and Albert Younan entered into a partnership as 'General Merchants and Transporters' for a period of two years.[5] Profits were to be divided on an equal basis of shares, but the firm was to be known by Younan's name alone and he was authorized to sign checks on behalf of the company. This enterprise, as far as we can determine, did not occupy much of Adelabu's time during 1955 but it was to play a more significant part in his life in 1956.

On 1 February he also resigned his position as Chairman of the Tax Committee. This, with his request on 2 February that Council meetings be shifted from Tuesday afternoon to Saturday mornings to 'lessen the conflict with my duties in Lagos', revealed his new awareness that it was physically impossible to be in all the places where his attendance was required.[6] His resignation from the Tax Committee, however, coming at the most critical time of the tax collection season, was in fact typical of his response to his responsibilities when they became boring or overburdensome. He simply left them in midstream.

During the first week of February he once again became intensely involved in Ibadan chieftaincy politics. In spite of a warning, by no means the first, from Minister of Local Government F. R. A. Williams in January that Councillors were not competent to appoint or remove chiefs, early in February 1955 the Chieftaincy Committee to which Adelabu had appointed Councillors made promotions partly contravening the established rules.[7] It appeared that Adelabu's chiefs were advancing to greater control of the chieftaincy structure, a development Adelabu welcomed, given his preoccupation in Lagos.

On 8 February, however, Olubadan Igbintade died. Already about twenty-eight years old when colonial rule came to Ibadan, installed Olubadan on 11 July 1952, he had spent the last years of his life in the turbulence of the return of power to the hands of Ibadans and other Nigerians, and he died at the age of ninety.

If Igbintade's advanced age had prevented him from being the strength to the N.C.N.C. which Adelabu might have hoped, he was at least preferable as Olubadan to Isaac Akinyele, the most senior chief in the Balogun's line, whose turn it was to nominate, since Akinyele openly supported the Action Group and was firmly and publicly accepted by the British administrators. Balogun Akinyele's record was beyond reproach and it would be necessary to convince the administrative officers and Government to the contrary should someone else be selected. Otun Balogun Aminu's record was equally faultless; although he was not literate and had not been as involved in modern activities as had been Akinyele, he presumably also would have been acceptable to Government. However, Aminu was Akinyele's firmest supporter among the chiefs. It was not surprising then that Adelabu chose to intervene on behalf of an anti-Akinyele candidate, Osi Balogun Akinyo. The third chief in the line, he had backed Adelabu since the beginning of the anti-Akinyele protests along with Aderogba and Solagbade and was legally, if not customarily, eligible for the Olubadanship.

At a meeting of senior chiefs on 11 February, Akinyo's nominator (the Ashipa Balogun) explained why Akinyele was not minimally acceptable. He had refused during the 1954 Egungun celebrations (in which a man had died) to receive masqueraders; he had refused to keep the Balogun's staff in his house and to make sacrifices to it and had manufactured a substitute of his own design; he was averse to accepting the gifts of the Sango priests, the cult of iron and fire; furthermore, he had not shown 'any desire to become Olubadan', saying that he could at any time 'resign his post as Chief'. Akinyele then took the initiative, asking if anyone knew of any 'allegations of corruption, stealing, hatred and disloyalty to the Chiefs and people of Ibadan against him and the house unanimously replied in the negative'. Chief Akinyele did not deny the charges about the fetish worshippers and his staff, but he declared that 'he had made a promise in writing that he would satisfy all the conditions required by their custom'. Akinyele now requested a response from the Olubadan's line and the meeting was adjourned to give them a chance to confer.[8]

At 10.30 on 12 February, in the District Officer's headquarters, Otun Olubadan Kobiowu again presided over a meeting of the Kingmakers.[9] D. A. Murphy greeted them and left. Chief Akinyele's letter promising to observe tradition was read and he gave his assurance that 'he had consulted God and obtained his sanction'. Kobiowu then announced that the Olubadan's line stood unanimously for Akinyele. Coupled with the vote of the Iyalode, the Kingmakers had thus voted six to three for Akinyele and against Bello Akinyo, Adelabu's candidate.

The decision of the Kingmakers to select Akinyele was conveyed by letter to Resident Murphy, who promptly approved it; a copy of his letter of approval was given to Adelabu at the Senior District Officer's house. Within two hours, however, it appeared that Ibadan already had an Olubadan, and he was not Isaac Akinyele. According to Murphy, Adelabu, after learning of Murphy's decision, decided to install Akinyo as Olubadan of Ibadan at Oja'ba Market at 6.00 p.m.

Adelabu arrived at Oja'ba in a car with four followers. A crowd estimated at 3000 gathered, some carrying stones, iron rods and broken bottles. Rev. Alayande arrived in his car, which was beaten by the crowd, whereupon he left the scene. Then J. A. Akinlotan, the Action Group Divisional Organizing

Secretary and 'the real Grouper', arrived in his car. From his perch on top of someone's shoulders, Adelabu shouted, 'There are the bastards; Ijebu slaves, beat them and kill them.' Some rioting occurred and Adelabu was criminally charged with five others, including one of his Councillors, for taking part in a riot, unlawful procession, and damaging the car of Akinlotan. Commenting on the 'installation' and the mob, D. A. Murphy later noted, 'It is obvious from the speed and passion with which it was carried out, it was done without the knowledge of the vast majority of the people of Ibadan and District.'[10] His response was prompt. On the radio on the 13th, he announced that Government's recognition of Akinyele was 'final, irrevocable and in accordance with the law. Any other installation is bogus and anybody taking part in it exposes himself to the risk of prosecution.'[11] From the other side the *Defender* on 13 February stated that people it had contacted thought Akinyele had been fine as Chief Judge, but would be 'a square peg in a round hole' as Olubadan.[12]

To forestall any further public demonstration against Akinyele, Chiefs Kobiowu and Akinwale Mato obtained a court injunction on Sunday evening ('goaded' into so doing by top-ranking Groupers according to the *Defender*) restraining Adelabu and Akinyo from further activities until Akinyele's installation. Adelabu suddenly left for Lagos, satisfying himself with a telegram to the Governor and a speech in Isalegangan Square charging that the entire procedure by which Akinyele was selected was illegal. Akinyele's friends were gathering. Obisesan promptly wrote out a check for £100 and W. N. Chidiak, the Lebanese transporter, gave Obisesan £100 for the Olubadan-elect's expenses.[13] Nor was the Action Group found wanting, although their gift of £150 and the arrangement to buy a new car apparently were embarrassing.*

The Council in an emergency meeting on 17 February with L. Ade Bello in the chair attempted to continue Akinyo's cause by resolving that having won the majority of votes in the Balogun's line he was entitled to be recognized as the Olubadan. They also rejected a counter-motion stating Akinyo's installation was irregular and unconstitutional by fifty-six to six. Nevertheless, Akinyele's installation proceeded without further incident on 18 February and Obisesan enthusiastically reported that 20,000 persons were in attendance.[14]

---

* Again from Obisesan: 'Had discussion with Olubadan about political state of Ibadan. He revealed that Action Group Hierarchy through Dr. Maja & Mr. Ajao gave him £150 gift during his installation & that his present Chevrolet car was bought for him on arrangement to sell his old car, pay certain amount & begin to pay installment until the whole is paid. He said that this kind of kindness did not allow him to decide what to do because it appears that people are tired of existing.' (Obisesan Diary, 18 April 1955.)

The question remained as to what should be done with 'Adelabu's Olu-badan', the unhappy Akinyo left to his own devices by Adelabu's retreat to Lagos. The Government's plan was that Akinyo should be ordered to appear before Murphy who would tell him to stop appearing as Olubadan, to pay homage to Akinyele, to return the paraphernalia of the office which he had seized and to make a public acknowledgement of loyalty to Akinyele. Should he not do so by 4 March, he would be suspended by the Governor under the Appointment and Recognition of Chiefs Law.[15] On 3 March Akinyo duly appeared. In a ceremony that was photographed and recorded on tape he stated that he sincerely regretted that 'mischief makers' had caused opposition to Akinyele and that he was 'determined not to allow people with political axe to drive wedge in future. . .'[16]

While interrupting his apprenticeship as a Minister from 20 January to 15 February, Adelabu had also neglected his duties as Chairman and member of the Ibadan Council. On the 18th, the Chairman absented himself from the installation of the new Olubadan. He stayed in Lagos a little over two weeks at this time, preparing White Papers on Education and Lagos Medical and Health Services for the approaching meeting of the House. On Friday 4 March, he returned to Ibadan in anticipation of the Council meeting the following day. At the conclusion of this session, Adelabu had the pleasure of letting his Ministerial Private Secretary witness his re-election to the Chairmanship of the Council.* At the same time, however, the Council passed a resolution postponing until April all Committee meetings except those on tax in an attempt to take the pressure off Adelabu, who by 8 March was once more back in Lagos.†

His presence in Lagos was necessitated by the second and most important meeting of the year of the Federal House of Representatives, lasting from 8 March to 7 April. This was the Budget meeting during which the new Government's policy papers were debated and financial appropriations sought for the coming year. The Action Group Opposition, led by S. L. Akintola, was determined to give close scrutiny to the Government and especially to its N.C.N.C. Ministers, and Akintola, as the previous Minister of Health, was especially vigilant as far as Adelabu was concerned. His attack began on 10 March, after the House had heard Abubakar Tafawa Balewa and Muhammadu Ribadu deal with their programs. Referring scornfully to the Government as 'the glee club' and the 'mutual admiration club', Akintola announced that 'the time has come for the monotony to be broken'.[17] He severely lambasted the N.C.N.C. Ministers who, he claimed,

---

* The re-election came as a simple resolution and no vote was recorded.
† In fact, several committees had to meet in order not to delay Council business; other Councillors substituted as Chairman for Adelabu.

were in a majority in the Council of Ministers but were making no effort to implement their election promises on such matters as 'Nigerianisation' of the civil service, the expansion of university education, minimum wages based on the cost of living, or rent control.

Adelabu's first major speech came in the course of Government's response and much of it consisted of a description of his Ministry's responsibilities and a report on the activities of the various bodies under its control. This part of his speech, prepared by his civil servants, he read, and was challenged for doing so by the Opposition. Good-humoredly he answered them: ministerial statements might be read, with the Speaker's permission, but 'If there is any member of the Opposition who thinks he is a better debater than myself let him say so, and I shall be pleased to meet him at a place he chooses.'[18] Concluding his written statement, he urged that all research work must be directed to improving the quality and productivity of agriculture. Then he began to extemporize on his favorite theme, the need for rural development – 'We are not going to have unbalanced development, with the big towns having the best amenities of life at the expense of the peasants – cocoa farmers, groundnut farmers, palm produce farmers.'[19] Akintola was wrong, he asserted, in saying that the proposals on health and education had no originality:

We are not going to have half-baked teachers who put our children through a mock system of education. We are certainly not going to have mud houses for hospitals and to get untrained people to come and give them treatment. All these things require planning. We have provided the money. These plans will go forward with all vigour, and we will be able to report to the House that what we have put down on paper is within the financial capacity of the Government of the day to execute the programme.[20]

With this attack by implication – as his audience knew it to be – on the Action Group Government's policies in the West, Adelabu survived his first major parliamentary test as a Minister. He apparently stayed on in Lagos during the next week of debate, although he made no speeches. We at least know he was absent from obligations in Ibadan where he missed four meetings of Committees of the Ibadan Council and the next session of the N.C.N.C. Western Planning Committee. When it met again in Ibadan on Friday 11 March J. O. Fadahunsi deputized for him as Chairman.

Nevertheless, in his absence, he was selected as a member of one of ten Working Teams on party policy, his responsibility being to produce a Policy Paper on Health, in collaboration with Dr Ikejiani and Prince Adeyinka Oyekan of Lagos. The Committee also heard a report from Secretary Onabamiro that a Regional Organizing Secretary had been appointed – Adebaya Asaya, former Zikist leader in Ibadan.

By the end of the third week in March Adelabu's intentions of returning to Ibadan on the 20th, a Sunday, had been made known in a *Defender* article reporting allegations that plans had been made to assassinate him (and to plant Indian hemp on N.C.N.C. members) by Action Groupers.[21] Weighing more heavily on his mind, however, were the criminal proceedings taken against him as a result of his alleged part in the affray at Oja'ba during the installation of Chief Akinyo. Convinced that this was an attempt on the part of the Action Group Regional Government to embarrass him as an N.C.N.C. Federal Minister, he went so far as to threaten to refuse the N.C.N.C. whip in the House unless the national party rallied round him. On 23 March he and the other three Ibadan Grand Alliance legislators wrote to his five N.C.N.C. ministerial colleagues calling for a 'firm and resolute stand' on the part of the Ministers and the N.C.N.C. Federal Parliamentary Party, 'right up to the edge of the destruction of the present Federal Government set-up'.[22] While recognizing that Adelabu had already received a great deal of moral support from the leadership of the Federal Party, the letter noted that 'what is needed is readiness to sacrifice everything by precipitating a Constitutional crisis'. The N.C.N.C. Ministers must call an emergency meeting of the Council of Ministers to discuss the legality and constitutional propriety of the summons against Adelabu. Otherwise the four Ibadan legislators would refuse the N.C.N.C. whip 'for as long as, and until, these issues are determined'. For the time being, in fact, K. O. Mbadiwe and his colleagues were able to persuade Adelabu not to go to these lengths and to accept the fact that he must go to trial. In their turn they apparently assured him the best possible legal representation.

During this time in Ibadan, he also saw his new business partner, Albert Younan, who on 28 March requested permission from the Federal Government to import a new automobile for their business. By 30 March, he was again in his seat in the House. On that day he came under heavy attack again during the debate on Head 55 of the Appropriation Ordinance, providing for an expenditure of £478,590 on Education in the coming financial year. A severe critic was Jaja Wachuku, winner of a gold medal for oratory in his days at Trinity College, Dublin, and a leading light of the Eastern N.C.N.C. until the ministerial crisis of 1953, when he followed Eyo Ita out of the party and into the U.N.I.P., winning a seat for that party in Aba Division in the federal election. Now he berated Adelabu. Queen's College, supposedly the best girls' grammar school in Lagos, was 'an apparition'. Too many expatriate teachers were employed at too great a cost at the Yaba Technical Institute (a successor to the Higher College). The University College at Ibadan was not taking enough students and was putting too much emphasis on fine buildings – 'It is not a mansion, Sir, that makes the university, it is the product of the university and in a country like our own we can lecture under trees.'[23] S. L. Akintola then took up the refrain, dwelling particularly on the situation at Yaba and the alleged heavy cost of training there.

Adelabu quickly squashed the former Minister of Health by pointing out that until October 1954 the Yaba center had been under the control of the Western Region Government and thus Akintola's own party. He was fast learning the tricks of the trade of being a Minister and dealt with Wachuku's points with some aplomb, though possibly with more rhetoric than argument, as when he claimed that the number of university students was being deliberately kept low to preserve standards – 'We do not want in Nigeria that kind of Degree awarded in India which has no recognition whatever beyond the boundary of India.'[24] However, to give him his due, he did go on to point out that the real bottleneck in producing graduates was not in the University College, but in the secondary schools which prepared students for the university.

The day after this strenuous debate, however, Adelabu received word that a storm which had been pending for nearly a year had finally broken. As usual, bad news from Ibadan came while he was in Lagos.

We have already seen that Adelabu was scarcely made Chairman of the Ibadan Council in April 1954 before the demand for its dissolution began. This demand reached the official level during the 1954 federal elections, when the Acting Minister of Local Government interviewed some councillors and chiefs who sought the dissolution of the Council and the formation of separate rural and urban Councils.* The *Defender* regularly carried rumors of an inquiry and even of the dismissal of the Council; on 30 November 1954 it reported that a 'fault finding committee' consisting of Dr Agbaje, A. M. A. Akinloye and Anthony Enahoro, Minister of Home Affairs, had been set up to consider the dissolution of the Council and that it was being encouraged by 'a senior chief'. In mid-December it was rumored that the Action Group Government might even set up a Government-appointed provisional council to replace the elected N.C.N.C. Council and that some of the present Councillors had already 'been bought over'.[25] We do know that Chief Akinyele, probably the senior chief referred to above, and Akinpelu Obisesan had close and frequent contact with Government Ministers. On 24 December, Awolowo directed Akinyele and several other judges and chiefs to submit a complaint to the Minister of Local Govern-

* S.N.D., 5 August 1954. The Minister referred to was Chief J. F. Odunjo, Minister of Lands, who, according to the *Daily Service* of this date had been appointed by Awolowo to probe allegations of bribery and corruption following the appeal of 7 June to dissolve the Council.

ment and while we do not know the nature of the complaint, Obisesan was satisfied with the results.[26] On 28 December, Minister of Home Affairs Enahoro forebodingly suggested that the Council's method of acquiring property for new schools could expose it to court actions. Thus considerable warning had been sounded for the announcement on 31 March 1955 that a Government fact-finding Committee was already at work investigating allegations of bribery, corruption, and failure to meet tax collecting obligations, or, as the *Defender* put it, seeking justifications for dissolving the Council.[27]

There was little Adelabu could do at this point about the storm in Ibadan since the Federal House was in the middle of the Budget session and the most important parts of his own Ministry's business had yet to be presented. His major performance came on 6 April when he rose three times to seek approval of three different White Papers. The first was on education in Lagos where it was intended to introduce universal, free primary education by 1957, and secondary school places for a quarter of those leaving primary school. Once again, of course, this was intended as a criticism of the Action Group primary education scheme in the West.[28]

The second policy paper laid out plans for the development of health and medical services in Lagos where there was only approximately one hospital bed for every 1300 people (in Britain the ratio was 1 bed for 200), and to expand 'difficult case' maternity facilities for the entire Federal territory of Lagos.[29] To train doctors and nurses Adelabu's third policy paper of the day asked for a further £650,000 for the completion of the University College Hospital at Ibadan.

After 6 April, and the approval of his policies, Adelabu spoke only once more at this meeting of the House. Matters in Ibadan were growing increasingly disturbing and on 19 April F. R. A. Williams, Minister of Justice and Local Government, confirmed that a formal inquiry into Council affairs would be conducted, an outcome that was already accepted by the N.C.N.C. in Ibadan as inevitable.* A Commissioner, to be appointed by Williams, would inquire into alleged failures to act in conformity with the provisions of the local government law, corruption, nepotism, and interference with tax assessment and collection.[30] A mass meeting of the N.C.N.C.–Grand Alliance was held at Mapo by the party leaders to denounce the inquiry.[31] On the other hand, the inquiry was hotly welcomed by the Action Group. The Lagos *Daily Service*, which castigated the N.C.N.C. for maintaining in Ibadan 'a damnifying spectacle of graft, corruption, malpractices, and gang-

---

* Thus D. K. Olumofin: 'Knowing the chronic diseases of the Action Group, the Party-in-Power, in the Western Region, namely, intolerance, victimization, oppression, vindictiveness, coercion and fascism, no one is surprised...' (S.N.D., 22 April 1955.)

sterism reminiscent of the notorious Hitlerite era. . .', stated that although the Western Regional Government had thus far been timid about investigating such abuses, it was high time that they did so.[32]

Crucial among the problems referred to by the *Daily Service* was that of tax and in a sense it combined all the other charges. The simple fact was neglect. During the early months of the 'tax season', in October and November 1954, when new staff was being hired and trained, forms printed and the duty to pay was being publicized, Adelabu was busy with the federal electoral campaign. After the election, on 22 November and again on 28 December, he was absent from meetings of the Tax Committee. After 31 December, the legal deadline for tax payment, when less than ten per cent of the tax had actually been collected and the difficult business of extracting taxes from the citizenry was at its height, Adelabu was in Lagos at his Ministry, from 7 to 20 January. On 1 February, he simply relieved himself from direct responsibility by resigning as Councillor in Charge of Tax and devoted a solid week to his attempt to prevent Chief Akinyele from becoming Olubadan.

On the other hand, however, the Regional Government, both collectively and individually, had contributed a share to the failure of the Ibadan Council to improve its tax collecting program. Late in October 1954, D. A. Murphy had asked the Ministry of Local Government if the Council could employ a sliding rate against income tax, a proposal which would have affected the taxes paid by all government employees resident in Ibadan. Quite promptly, on 12 November, a negative answer was given.[33] In February, Acting S.D.O. Balmer informed the Resident that no Regional Minister resident in Ibadan had yet paid his tax.[34] Chief Awolowo himself did not pay his 1954 tax until 7 March 1955, and then only after a special note was sent to him warning of court action against offenders.[35]

The Council discussed these problems at its March meeting, at which Adelabu was re-elected Chairman for the coming year. The new Councillor in Charge of Tax, A. S. Asuni reported that only £113,000 had been collected as against £130,000 at the same time the previous year, a year which had already experienced a slow-down in payments due to Adelabu's election campaign.[36]

In 1954–5 the number of taxpayers had increased from 113,905 in the previous year to 116,477, but revenue had not increased correspondingly. It will be remembered that at the meeting of the 'Parliamentary Council' of the Grand Alliance on 20 March 1954 some discussions of tax questions had been deemed 'absolutely confidential' and not recorded in the Minutes, and in his Inaugural Address in April Adelabu had spoken of the small traders, artisans and peasant farmers as being 'arbitrarily assessed on imaginary incomes they never see'. Although 2572 new taxpayeres had been added to the rolls in 1954–5, they had all been added to the minimum assumed income roll, while another 13,286 persons previously paying on incomes above the minimum assumed income, £24 in that year, had been downgraded to the minimum.[37] According to Adelabu, however, he had perceived this process and the new tax clerks had been assigned to the ward committees to halt it. Nevertheless, he complained that the absences of the Chief Tax Clerk due to illness and of the Secretary and the Treasurer who were on leave, and 'the inefficiency and disloyalty' of the staff, many of whom had been hired by the Staff Committee of which he was Chairman, had undermined a specific order given by him forbidding any tax assessment committee to reduce the assessment of any taxpayer. The situation had been made the worse by the Free Service Bureau, operated by Regional Minister of Lands A. M. A. Akinloye, which encouraged taxpayers to protest their assessments and offered free legal aid for court appearances in regard to tax.

Careful comparison would probably show that Ibadan was no more delinquent in its tax habits than many other so-called developed cities. However, the consequences for Ibadan are different since it is not a wealthy city in terms of its ability to acquire modern services. It must tax an economy only now rising above a subsistence level in order to purchase services and equipment priced according to the ability of rich nations to pay. Evasion in Ibadan simply means a shortage of money in the Treasury, a shortage which may lead to breakdown of Council services.

It was indeed such a breakdown which Adelabu's enemies charged had occurred, and it was interesting that the Commissioner appointed by the Minister of Local Government late in April, only shortly before the N.C.N.C. was to hold its Annual Convention, was D. M. O. Akinbiyi, who was qualified to explore tax matters by his position as Town Clerk of Lagos. While the *Defender* noted that the Minister had been Chairman of the Lagos Council until recently, and that the Commissioner's father was 'a known Grouper', the *Daily Service* reported that Williams had denied that the younger Akinbiyi was listed on the Action Group party register or that friendship was relevant to the discussion. Adelabu's own response seems peculiarly restrained. He prepared a statement, but it was calm in tone and seems not to have been published. In 'Democracy on Trial' he urged that if the Inquiry were not to be 'a mere preliminary skirmish in the inevitable 1956 Western Region elections', the Governor, not the Minister, should appoint the commissioner, who must not be in the employ of the Government.[38] Should this not be acceptable, he would welcome either dissolution and a new election, or a plebiscite. Perhaps Adelabu's attentions were drawn elsewhere, indeed to an event already pending when Government announced the inquiry into the Council.

On 5 May, the N.C.N.C. was to meet in Ibadan for its Annual Convention and it was to go through yet another internal crisis, one stemming from strained authority patterns and personality and ideological differences. Roughly speaking, the lines were drawn between the moderates and the radicals in the party. The latter group, familiar with Adelabu's personality and militant nationalist statements during the past three years, expected Adelabu to be with them in their struggle against the moderates who controlled the party as a whole. Yet in this instance, as we shall see, Adelabu failed ideologically from the radicals' point of view, while he remained attentive to the moderate forces controlling the party, the national Government, and whatever forces he might hope to enlist in resisting the increasing attempt of the Regional Action Group Government to undermine him.

We have already noted that in January 1954, in attempting to reorganize the party, the National Executive Committee had appointed a number of the former Zikist Movement radicals to key positions in the new structure. We have also seen that by July of the same year tensions were beginning to emerge between the new officials and Kola Balogun, the N.C.N.C. National Secretary. There were several reasons for this. First, the appointment of Osita Agwuna, Mokwugo Okoye and Adesanya Idowu to the new posts of Organizing Secretaries raised problems of defining their authority as compared with that of the National Secretary. Second, there were profound ideological differences regarding the involvement of the N.C.N.C. in the process of decolonization. At the Enugu Convention in January 1954, the N.C.N.C. had begun to consider its attitude toward the colonial system during the process of transfer of political power to Nigerians. Agwuna, Okoye and their supporters were suspicious of close collaboration with the British and the compromises which this might involve. They looked back with nostalgia to the Zikist Movement and its militantly nationalist and anti-British stance, and were inclined to trace back all the recent tendencies which they deprecated to its banning in April 1950. As one of them put it in August 1954,

What did Nigeria gain from the banning of the Zikist Movement? It gained the notorious Macpherson Constitution, the demise of the National Emergency Committee that united the nationalist movement, the disintegration of the Nigerian Labour Movement, the Ibadan debacle in which our Party Leader suffered a nasty humiliation, the new Constitution with its odious regionalist trend and the present instability, uncertainty and rugged materialism that saturate our national life.[39]

The N.C.N.C.'s involvement in the constitutional and institutional processes of decolonization, Okoye believed, was corrupting the party.

258

The close involvement of the radicals in party affairs had obviously been a shock for them. In practical terms, Okoye claimed in August 1954 that only £60 had been handed over to him as Eastern Organizing Secretary out of the £1446 budgeted for the Eastern Headquarters of the N.C.N.C., and that he had spent money for rent and electricity out of his own pocket.[40] Kola Balogun and Mbonu Ojike, the N.C.N.C. Second National Vice-President, had also resisted the attempt by Agwuna, and more especially Okoye, to act as focal points for those critical of tendencies within the N.C.N.C. Okoye's attempts to bring the complaints and allegations of the rank and file to the notice of Eastern Ministers had earned him a rebuke from Ojike, who pointed out that it was not Okoye's job to 'play the role of a petition writer'.[41]

In this dispute, Ojike and Balogun represented the majority of N.C.N.C. leaders who were concerned to bring the party into line with British policy, at least enough to allow the N.C.N.C. to inherit as much as possible of the power in the new political system. This group included Nnamdi Azikiwe. He had come out against the Macpherson Constitution of 1951 and in so doing had precipitated the internal crisis which beset the N.C.N.C. in 1952–3, but his opposition to it had not been based upon an objection in principle to working with the British. Rather he condemned it because from his own personal point of view it was an inadequate vehicle for power; its workings had barred him from election to the House of Representatives and a Central Ministry. Indeed, he had been prepared to accept the Macpherson Constitution insofar as it allowed him to return to the East at the end of 1953 and become a Minister there. Finally, he was at least temporarily prepared to accept the federal Constitution which came into force on October 1954, even though it ran counter to the N.C.N.C.'s previous policy of a united Nigeria.

Less than six months after the Enugu Convention Ojike and Balogun had begun to move against the radicals. The two asserted that they had proof that Okoye and Nduka Eze were Communists and 'were trying to turn the N.C.N.C. into a Communist Party'.[42] The Principal Organizing Secretary raised these matters in his report to the N.E.C. meeting on 4 July. This report also reveals a third reason for the tensions between Agwuna and Balogun at this time: personal relations between them were also extremely bad.*

* The fact that both of them not only had offices at 23 King George Avenue, Yaba, the N.C.N.C. National Headquarters, but also lived there – Balogun on the top floor with his family – had increased the strain between them. Agwuna complained that 'From morning till night, the whole Secretariat rooms and premises are noisy. Disturbances due to shouting, loose banging of doors, sliding, shifting, and dropping of boxes and

When the National Executive Committee met at Enugu on 2 and 3 August 1954, Mokwugo Okoye was summoned to answer charges against him made by Ojike and Balogun. His attitude was one of defiance:

...if free expression of opinion in party meetings and uncompromising hatred of opportunism, careerism, chicanery and incompetence are calculated to bring the name of the N.C.N.C. to ridicule, while erratic conduct of its affairs, crudity, financial frauds, commandism, and sabotaging of party cadres' efforts and dampening of mass enthusiasm together with the unscrupulous perversion and flouting of the Party Constitution, Policy and Programme (which are the stock in trade of our prime accusers, Messrs. Ojike and Balogun) do not – then I plead guilty to the fantastic charges brought against me and the sooner I sever my connection with the Party the better.[43]

Following this uncompromising answer Okoye was suspended from his membership of the N.E.C. and his duties as Organizing Secretary for the East. The pressures continued. Adesanya Idowu was suspended from his duties as Western Organizing Secretary. Osita Agwuna held on to his position, however, and in November was elected to the Federal House of Representatives from Awka Division.

In February 1955 Balogun and Agwuna clashed again, provoking a letter from the former Zikist to Balogun in which he claimed that 'I am not in the mood for recriminations. My mind moves towards regions of serenity and nobler actions. You want to draw me into controversies at a time my endeavours are geared towards construction.'[44]

Nevertheless, despite Agwuna's philosophical mood, it was obvious that the 1955 Annual Convention in Ibadan would bring a final battle. At the preliminary meeting of the National Executive Committee on 2–3 May, Okoye (whose suspension had been lifted) tried unsuccessfully to introduce a motion of censure on Mbonu Ojike for interfering in N.C.N.C. nominations during the federal elections. This charge was also carried, with many others, in a document, 'An Appeal to the NCNC Convention Delegates', which was being circulated at this time. Signed by Okoye, Agwuna and two N.C.N.C. leaders from the Mid-West, J. E. Otobo and F. M. Yamu Numa, and claiming the support of fifty-six other members of the party, this appeal

other weights on the upper floor of the building, with the offices directly below... make any serious and concentrated thinking and organisational planning difficult and at times impossible.' According to Agwuna, indeed, he had more than noise to contend with: 'I have to mention that both day and night of nearly every day in the week, urine and water are carelessly allowed to drop from the upper floor on to the rooms below, soiling beddings, clothes, furniture, files, papers, etc. Mrs. Balogun has always expressed regret for these occurrences, but it always seemed she is incapable of preventing the incidents which continue to recur with increased frequency.' ('Report of the Principal Organising Secretary...July 4, 1954', p. 5.)

attacked the 'willing collaboration with Imperialism and the betrayal and sacrifice of the Party's forward elements'.[45] Balogun, Ojike and their supporters, however, dominated the National Executive Committee, and the session ended in the expulsion of Nduka Eze from the party for 'disloyalty', the suspension of Adesanya Idowu, and an order to Agwuna to apologize to Balogun and obey his instructions in future.

On Thursday, 5 May, the Convention proper began. The morning was given up to Nnamdi Azikiwe's Presidential Address, 'Our Heritage of Democracy', which took as its main theme an analysis of the position of the N.C.N.C. as a governing party in the Eastern Region and a coalition partner of the N.P.C. at the federal level. He referred to the inherent problems involved in a situation in which Nigerians were being given Ministerial responsibility, while the British Governor-General and regional Governors still held substantial control over civil servants. 'I must here pay tribute', he went on, 'to those civil servants, white and black, who have been upholding the best traditions of the British Civil Service: by giving their best in advising Ministers, by becoming impersonal when it comes to party politics, and by helping the Ministers of any party in power to formulate and implement the policy of the current Government.'[46]

In reviewing the party's achievements in the East, Dr Azikiwe re-asserted its devotion to its principles, which had been called into question by his left-wing critics:

As a party whose aim, among others, is the achievement of a Socialist Commonwealth, we have begun in earnest to tackle the fundamental problem which must confront any Government, representing such a political organisation. Our first task, as Socialists, is to control the means of production and the media of exchange. Realising the difficulties in creating a Socialist society in the midst of capitalistically inclined compatriots and expatriates, we decided that our first move is to devise a means of co-existence with the economic forces at work. We, therefore, established two giant public corporations, the Finance Corporation, and the Development Corporation – to expand our economy by stimulating and diversifying investments, in order to achieve an equilibrium in the interests of producers and consumers.[47]

After some remarks upon the subject of federalism and the Bandung Conference of non-aligned nations then being held, he turned finally to a direct attack on the radicals, describing them as a 'microscopic minority' of 'irresponsible elements, mercenary characters and cantankerous individuals who thrive on confusion'.[48]

Not surprisingly, the Convention turned its afternoon session into a direct assault on the radicals. A demand was raised for an open trial of Agwuna, Okoye, Otobo and Yamu Numa. The National President asked for a trial by committee, and when this was refused by the assembly, vacated the chair, leaving J. O. Fadahunsi to preside. For their part, Otobo and Yamu Numa, led by Adeniran Ogunsanya, a lawyer from Ikeja, denied all knowledge of critical views, even of the document which carried their names. This plea was accepted. After arguments from both sides, the voting was 212 to 6 against Okoye and 193 to 3 against Agwuna.[49]

Thus, when it came to a showdown, the radicals had virtually no support among the more active members of the party. Throughout this bitter clash, Adelabu was with the majority. As we have seen in earlier chapters, in 1952 and 1953 he regarded himself as a nationalist and tended to sympathize with the Zikists, though he never identified himself completely with them. As he moved closer to the corridors of power, however, he became more prepared to work with the British and less concerned with the more dramatic gestures of nationalism – though he continued to regard himself (as did Nnamdi Azikiwe) as a nationalist. As a Federal Minister he almost automatically aligned himself with his colleagues, Kola Balogun and K. O. Mbadiwe. Balogun in particular seems to have looked to him as a more likely ally in the Western N.C.N.C. than T. O. S. Benson; in the National Secretary's report to the Ibadan Convention, for example, he proposed attaching greater weight to the Western Region Planning Committee headed by Adelabu than to the Organization Committee, of which Benson was Chairman. At the Convention, then, Adelabu made no gesture of support for the radicals. As Okoye wrote to him reproachfully a few years later, 'You have always floated above party factions and when you did come down it was to ally with the right [ist]s – I did not like it much.'[50]

Since January, Adelabu, Mbadiwe and Balogun had been colleagues in the Federal Government, and now they were to become colleagues as officers of the N.C.N.C. On the morning of 6 May the Convention heard the reports of the National Secretary, Treasurer and Auditor, and set up a Finance Committee to consider ways of raising funds, and a Legal Committee (under H. O. Davies) to undertake the defence of party members. At 7.00 p.m. the delegates met for what was to be a twelve-hour session. The first main item of business was to elect new Officers. Nnamdi Azikiwe was offered the Presidency for life, but refused, and was then re-elected unopposed. Vice-President J. O. Fadahunsi, however, was challenged and defeated by Adelabu who had two electoral victories and a Federal Ministry to his credit within the past year. As the *West African Pilot* put it, 'One of the sensations of the elections was the elevation of Hon. Adegoke Adelabu from Floor Member to First National Vice-President.'[51] Now the most important man in the party hierarchy next to Zik himself, he was truly part of the innermost circle, a colleague on equal terms with Ojike, Balogun, Festus Okotie-Eboh and

Kofi Blankson, who were returned to their respective posts as Second National Vice-President, National Secretary, National Treasurer and National Auditor. Moreover, he could now definitely be regarded as out-ranking T. O. S. Benson, elected to the new post of National Financial Secretary, and his ascendancy in the Western N.C.N.C. over men like J. O. Fadahunsi, Okechukwu Ikejiani, Sanya Onabamiro, Dennis Osadebay, Babatunji Olowofoyeku and Isaac Shodipo, all elected to the new 36-member National Executive Committee, was further reinforced.

When the Convention broke up, then, the radicals had finally been defeated. The final major act of the Convention had been to fix the age limit of membership of the N.C.N.C. Youth Association at twenty-five, thus making it impossible in the future for senior party members to use their position in that body to make it a center of opposition to the party leadership. Nevertheless, the immediate effect of this ruling was to force the resignation of some of Dr Azikiwe's most loyal supporters, Mbazulike Amechi, the Association's Secretary-General, and F. S. McEwen, its President-General, though the latter was compensated by his election on 6 May to the post of National Publicity Secretary.* At the same time Adegoke Adelabu, self-confessed champion of the poor, socialist and militant nationalist, had crowned his meteoric political career with a place among the party's foremost leaders.

Not that it must be supposed that his highly individualistic approach to party affairs was dramatically changed as a result. Only a few days after his election as First National Vice-President the Ibadan leader again came into conflict with the 'Lagos leadership', this time with McEwen, the new National Publicity Secretary. Shortly after the Convention, Adelabu issued a press release on Ibadan affairs without first clearing it with McEwen, though he had apparently read it to Mbadiwe over the telephone and had been advised by him to pass it through 'the normal Party Channels'.[52] Such actions on the part of N.C.N.C. leaders were not rare, but this time McEwen chose to make an issue of it, by releasing his own statement disassociating the N.C.N.C. from Adelabu's views. Adelabu was furious, and wrote a long letter to McEwen on 11 May, seeking to put him in his place.

The party leadership resident in Lagos, not excluding Honourable Mbadiwe, must learn to take spontaneous actions if they mean to dent Action Group armour, and the quicker any of us who has not adjusted to this new order of the day, of combining collective responsibility with individual initiative, adjusts himself, instead of a sit-tight policy in the prerogatives of office, the better for team work in the party as a whole. It is because in the past key-men have not been too willing

* Adeniran Ogunsanya, the Chairman of the Lagos branch of the Association, also lost his membership as a result of the new ruling.

to concede minor procedural deviations in order to achieve strategical advantages that spectacular results have been the exception rather than the rule in Lagos.[53]

McEwen replied on the following day, in hurt tones, confessing himself 'very much embarrassed indeed' by Adelabu's letter.[54] The affair was concluded with a letter from Mbadiwe on 16 May in which he sought to soothe McEwen's ruffled feelings by assuring him that 'I know that no harm was intended and I want you to take it in that spirit.'[55]

Adelabu's elevation in the party hierarchy had thus not affected his independence of mind or his determination to treat Ibadan as his own private preserve, and the whole incident brought home once again the dependence of the N.C.N.C. in the West upon local notables, who were often its Zonal Leaders, and over whom it had very little real control. The Ibadan Convention had agreed to set up Working Committees in each Region in an attempt to systematize and improve the whole organizational structure of the party, but in the West this proved no easy task. As was usually the case, the difficult problem arose of striking a balance of power between various personalities. At a meeting of the Interim Western Working Committee on 22 May Adelabu was elected its Chairman and Dr Onabamiro its Secretary; this was no doubt satisfactory to Kola Balogun, who was keeping the minutes of the meeting, but it can hardly have appealed to T. O. S. Benson.[56]

Suddenly, however, Abelabu's very power base was severely threatened. Early in June, the rumour circulated that Akinbiyi had been dropped as Commissioner, perhaps to be replaced by Ibadan Supreme Court Puisne Justice R. Y. Hedges.[57] It appeared that the inquiry might gather new momentum. On 10 June, however, much worse news was revealed. On that day, according to Adelabu, he received a letter addressed to him a week earlier by the Permanent Secretary of the Ministry of Justice and Local Government.* The Permanent Secretary informed Adelabu that his Council seat was now vacant and that a bye-election to fill it would be held in due course, since Adelabu had not observed a ruling requiring ministerial authorization to retain it from April 1954 to February 1955, while he was Councillor in Charge of Tax and for which he received remuneration.[58] Adelabu's reply carefully probed the questions of fact and law involved and then took up the challenge.[59] Since the Minister's decision came five months after Adelabu had resigned the position, Adelabu first pointed out that there was nothing in the local government law dealing with this point to suggest retrospective application. Second, he pointed out what seems to be the gravest charge

* The letter was addressed to him at his ministry in Lagos, although he was in Ibadan on 4 June attending a Council meeting. Why it was not sent to Mapo Hall or his house, and whether, as Adelabu claimed, it was first given to the party manager of the Action Group, we do not know.

against the Government. Under the local government law during the time when Adelabu had been Councillor in Charge of Tax, it was the Local Government Adviser, not the Minister, who was authorized to determine whether a person might retain a position at the disposal of the Council. Precisely this question, Adelabu asserted, had been discussed with him by Local Government Adviser D. A. Murphy, at which time Adelabu claimed he had persuaded Murphy that in approving the estimates of the Council in which the authorization was made, he had granted his approval to Adelabu's position as tax councillor. Not until 19 May 1955 had the authority to grant this approval passed to the Minister under the 1955 local government law. Finally Adelabu denied that he had held an office 'in the gift or disposal of the Council', but merely received the sitting fees attached to the duties involved and paid to all Councillors as recompense for time taken from other forms of employment and expenses. After all, it would have been impossible to have been Councillor in Charge of Tax and accept the remuneration attached to the post without being a Councillor.

Adelabu also jibed at the Minister (a distinguished lawyer) in terms suggesting he had not forgotten his own blighted hopes for a legal career. The only reason for writing his protest was to show 'that other people can be learned and nimble of wit without wearing wig and gown'.* Since he had no hope of appealing to the Minister's reason, sense of justice or conscience, he now took 'great pleasure' in informing the Minister that he intended to contest the bye-election to be held on 3 August to fill his vacated seat.

At a Council meeting on 14 June, his lieutenants moved to fill the gap caused by his absence. L. Ade Bello and A. S. Asuni nominated J. M. Johnson as Chairman, who after his election declared it to be 'an interim measure'. His policy would be to implement Adelabu's policies.[60] This he very quickly had an opportunity to do when the question of the courts and the chiefs came up once again. Olubadan Akinyele's resignation as Chief Judge was still pending the selection of his successor, and a further judgeship had become vacant. Akinyele on 7 June had led the chiefs in protesting the rumor that had gone through the town 'like lightning' that two lawyers would be appointed by the Regional Government to the vacant posts.[61] The Council's response was heavy-handed but not immediately effective. During this period Akinyele and several other chiefs had refused to attend Council meetings, fearing the indignities that might be heaped upon them and protesting their continued exclusion from the Chieftaincy Committee. In June, L. Ade Bello therefore began working on a scheme to halt their salaries. Adelabu was thus without his Chairmanship and his seat in his own

* The style of this letter, its layout and its professional typing, suggest that it may have been prepared by Adelabu's lawyers rather than by himself.

Council and not in charge of the efforts to assert the Council's authority against the chiefs, when a conference of the Western N.C.N.C., agreed on at the meeting on 22 May of the Interim Western Working Committee, met at Ilesha on Saturday 18 June. The Ibadan leader took the chair, but when the 200 delegates voted for the office of Chairman of the new Western Working Committee, Benson was elected, with 77 votes, to 66 for Fadahunsi, 22 for Adelabu, and 4 for H. O. Davies.[62] It was, in fact, the first warning by the party that he must master his house in Ibadan if he were to continue to be given power and responsibility within the N.C.N.C. By late June 1955 the new Working Committee was in a position to begin picking up the organizational threads in the Region. In addition to Benson as Chairman, Chief Oweh from the Mid-West had been elected Secretary unopposed, Dr Onabamiro standing down to allow this, and J. O. Fadahunsi had been made Treasurer. Adelabu and all National Executive Committee members from the West sat on the new Committee as of right, and each administrative Division not otherwise represented also elected a delegate. At the Ilesha meeting resolutions had been passed supporting the creation of a Mid-West State and an alliance with the Benin-Delta Peoples Party and promising to seek every constitutional means to restore the Alafin of Oyo to his throne. These aims – and any others – would be achieved only if the Working Committee could develop an effective campaign machine in the West. An election to the Western House of Assembly was due in 1956 and, as Adebayo Asaya, the Regional Organizing Secretary, warned in a report to the Committee in July, the chances were that 'if our party fails in 1956, that is the end of N.C.N.C. in this Region'.[63] Asaya pointed out the continuing lack of a properly-staffed headquarters, permanent local organizers and funds. It remained to be seen what could be done to remedy the situation.

Not that Adegoke Adelabu was to have much opportunity – or even much inclination – to devote himself to party matters during the latter half of 1955. Troubles came thick and fast for him in those months.

On 19 July, as he had promised Rotimi Williams earlier, he recontested his Ibadan council seat. Moyo Aboderin opposed him for the Action Group, contending that the Chairman's ward remained the least developed in the city. The bye-election campaign was no less bitter than its predecessors. The *Defender* complained regularly of victimization, false ballot papers and imported voters. Street violence also re-appeared.

Election day was clouded by an event which both reflected and increased political bitterness in Ibadan. While Adelabu was observing polling, he was served by a uniformed messenger of the Council in the company of Action Group supporters and the editor of the *Nigerian Tribune* with a subpoena to appear at D. T. Akinbiyi's court. Angered by such an intrusion on his electoral activities, and claiming that the day he was ordered to appear conflicted with a meeting of the Federal Council of Ministers, Adelabu immediately left for the court, being joined by a band of excited children and L. Ade Bello, who was standing on the balcony of Mapo Hall. When the crowd reached the court, abusive songs and gestures followed and Akinbiyi, supported by his clerk, later testified that Bello had slapped Akinbiyi on the face. Adelabu had allegedly called Akinbiyi an Awolowo slave.

It was true that by nightfall he could point to his fourth electoral victory, a resounding 513 to 167 defeat of Moyo Aboderin.[64] His enemies were hardly thwarted, however, for on the complaint of his old patron D. T. Akinbiyi, he and L. Ade Bello were charged with contempt of Akinbiyi's court and Bello with assault. On 22 July Adelabu again came to Mapo Hall where he refused to resume the Chairman's seat and delayed the proceedings until his private chair had been brought from the Taj Mahal. Having made his point, Adelabu was re-elected to the Council Chairmanship. The Council then passed a motion removing Akinbiyi as a court judge on the ground that they paid his salary, although in fact only Government had the power to appoint and remove. Thus Adelabu's grip was somewhat firmer when on 25 July he and Bello pleaded not guilty at the Ibadan Magistrate's Court to the charges Akinbiyi had brought against them.

On 29 July it was ruled that the two politicians had a case to answer and hearings were scheduled to begin on 2 August. Adelabu's troubles were beginning to pile up. On 30 July the newspapers carried the announcement that Mr E. W. J. Nicholson, Town Clerk of the Council of Abingdon, England, had been appointed Sole Commissioner to inquire into the allegations of corruption and maladministration of the Ibadan Council. With this news in hand, Adelabu and L. Ade Bello appeared before Judge Kester at the Onireke Magistrate Court, defended by Ganiyu Agbaje, the younger brother and law partner of Mojid Agbaje. D. T. Akinbiyi appeared as a witness for the prosecution since the Regional Government was bringing the case as an assault against one of its public officials. The contempt charges rested on the question of whether the court was properly constituted and in session or whether Akinbiyi was simply present in the court room as a private person at the time the insults had been offered. Only a few days after the beginning of the trial, a tragic event took place of which the prosecution made the best possible use. A fire had broken out in a Lagos school, which came under Adelabu's jurisdiction as Federal Minister of Social Services and Natural Resources. Eight children died in the disaster and there was talk that the fire stemmed from faulty construction under contracts let by Adelabu's Ministry. While the *Daily Service* argued that the Lagos incident had occurred because the Minister was also busy as the Chairman of the Ibadan

Council and that he should give up the latter post, Crown Counsel in the Akinbiyi case suggested the slapping incident had occurred because Adelabu was not sufficiently occupied by his duties as a Federal Minister.[65] Under these highly political circumstances, defense counsel took a legalistic approach, demanding that Akinbiyi's court records be submitted in evidence. It was thus established that for the day in question they did not record his name or those of assessors assigned to his court, necessary steps in opening a day's legal proceedings. Agbaje argued therefore that since court was not in session no contempt could have occurred. While waiting for Magistrate Kester's decision, the Nicholson Inquiry into the Council's affairs was postponed until 29 August.

On 25 August both leaders were found guilty as charged; Adelabu was sentenced to two months' hard labor and L.. Ade Bello was convicted of common assault and given six months at hard labor as a 'deterrent punishment' without the alternative of paying a fine. It was, Magistrate Kester said, 'the most shocking case of its kind that I have ever heard'. For a Federal Minister and a member of a local government council to have brought a court into disrepute 'is an outrageous offence which cannot and should not be tolerated in any civilised country or state'.[66] Both men promptly appealed, bringing to two the number of cases outstanding against Adelabu, since he and seven others involved in the riot at the installation of 'Adelabu's Olubadan' were now required to appear for the Preliminary Investigation into the unlawful assembly charge arising from that incident. Government had announced on 27 August that the Council inquiry would begin on 30 August and now a further delay was required. As though Adelabu were not already busy enough, the Federal House of Representatives was in session from 17 to 30 August in Lagos. Adelabu spoke there on 24 August against allowing the Western Regional Government to establish corporations which could not be taxed by the Federal Government and then hurried back to the Preliminary Investigation on the 25th, leaving his Parliamentary Private Secretary, D. C. Ugwu, and Kola Balogun to answer for his Ministry in debate. Trial was set for 9 November and Adelabu and the others were released on £50 bail.

No doubt mindful of their tempestuous colleague's threats at the end of April, the N.C.N.C. Federal Ministers now rallied round the beleaguered Ibadan leader. While on a visit to London, Chief Okotie-Eboh contacted Dingle Foot, an eminent barrister and elder brother of Hugh Foot, Chief Secretary to the Nigerian Government from 1947 to 1951, who had been instrumental in bringing the Macpherson Constitution into being. Representations were made to Dingle Foot that the Action Group was attempting to influence the judiciary to persecute Adelabu, and that a lawyer of his standing was therefore needed to lead the counsel for the defense in the two cases.

Foot agreed to appear, and further liaison was maintained with him in London in September by an expatriate official of Adelabu's ministry, who had to travel to Britain on government business.

On 2 September, Commissioner Nicholson opened his Inquiry in the hall of the Western House of Assembly. He had been warned that 'an atmosphere of intense bitterness' might prevail, but the distance between the Secretariat grounds where the House of Assembly met and the center of town was good insurance that disturbances would not mar the proceedings.[67] A total of 43 witnesses were to appear, led by 17 lawyers and supported by '138 exhibits. . .a large number of files, minute books, tax assessment records and other documents'.[68] Adelabu himself was not to appear until two weeks later and in the meantime a related but independent chain of events had taken its course in Lagos.

On 6 September, the fact that an inquiry into allegations of corruption against Adelabu, who was in one of his capacities a Federal Minister of Nigeria, was discussed by the Governor-General, Sir James Robertson, K. O. Mbadiwe and Abubakar Tafawa Balewa. It was agreed that Mbadiwe would see Adelabu and tell him that the public interest required that he should apply for leave from his Ministerial duties. It had apparently been the Governor-General's original intention to request Adelabu to go on leave, but his colleagues persuaded Sir James to save Adelabu's face by allowing him to make the request himself. The Governor-General would then grant a leave of two months, during which time Kola Balogun would act as Minister of Natural Resources and Social Services. At the end of this period the Ministry would be divided, and Balogun, who had previously been without a specific portfolio, would become Minister of Research and Information, taking responsibility for Public Relations from the Chief Secretary and Natural Resources from Adelabu, who would thus be left as Minister of Social Services.

The same day Mbadiwe telephoned Adelabu's Permanent Secretary and requested him to get in touch with his Minister in Ibadan and ask him to come to see Mbadiwe at his house in Lagos not later than 8.00 p.m. on the 7th, as there was a message from the Governor-General 'of the utmost importance'.[69] The Ibadan leader tore himself away from the Inquiry hearings and came down to see Mbadiwe. Three points arising from what Mbadiwe told him caused him particular concern. First of all, he was anxious that his Ministry should not be divided until he had returned from his leave, lest this be interpreted as showing a lack of confidence in him at a critical juncture in his career. Second, he wanted it made clear in the announcement that he was going on leave at his own request, and not that of the Governor-General. Third, he wanted to make the announcement himself, rather than this being done by the Office of the Council of Ministers. It was apparently also his suggestion that the period of leave should be for six weeks, not two months as originally suggested.

It would appear that Mbadiwe agreed to Adelabu's points at their 7 September meeting, and asked his colleague to remain in Lagos until the necessary Press Notices had been drafted. Adelabu, who could not stay away from Ibadan so long at this crucial time, left on the 8th without telling Mbadiwe, who on 9 September wrote a letter of reproach, enclosing two draft Press Notices prepared by the Chief Secretary, one amended by himself. Balogun, he said, had agreed to the amendments. It was hoped to make an announcement on the 12th, and to that end Adelabu was to meet the Governor-General on the 11th.[70]

On reading the drafts Adelabu took great exception to them, and with some cause: one made a bald announcement of the division of Ministry and the new portfolio for Balogun, the other, even as amended by Mbadiwe, made no mention of Adelabu himself requesting leave, leaving the clear impression that the Notices came from anyone but himself. In a reply to Mbadiwe he made these points, and went on to observe that

I will gladly make any personal sacrifices to save our great party which is more important than any individual member of it, but I respectfully submit that the present proposals as outlined in that draft statement will not only deliver me bound into the hands of my political enemies but will do grievous harm to the party as such.[71]

'Once more I assure you, old Rock of Gibraltar', he concluded, 'of my absolute devotion to our great party and its worthy leadership.'

In the next few days that devotion was to be tried further. The meeting with the Governor-General was not a satisfactory one from Adelabu's point of view, and on the 12th someone leaked the news to the press that his Ministry was to be split and some of his responsibilities given to Kola Balogun.[72] Finally, on 15 September the *Daily Times* carried the notice of the granting of six weeks leave of absence to him by the Governor-General, with Balogun acting for him while he was away. Thus, none of his objections to the draft Press Notices had materialized, nor was he revealed in quite as embarrassing a position as he had feared. The Action Group newspapers, which already could watch him as he appeared before the Inquiry, and which had been warned that the campaign for the early dissolution of the Council led by the *Nigerian Tribune* was viewed in an ill light by Commissioner Nicholson, refrained from any comment.

When opening speeches before Commissioner Nicholson were made on 2 September, a clear indication of the changes in Ibadan's political structure during the less than two years of Adelabu's mastery of the city could be found in the groups and their representatives who appeared before it. The Action Group minority members of the Council were represented by three lawyers, as were the twelve senior chiefs who were members of the Council. The Ibadan Taxpayers Association had briefed another trio. Government was represented solely by Crown Counsel B. A. Adedipe, while Mojid Agbaje and E. O. Fakayode represented the Council. Shortly after the hearings began, a national team of N.C.N.C. lawyers joined them, led by H. O. Davies and including H. U. Kaine, J. M. Udochi, B. Olowofoyeku and T. O. S. Benson. Totally missing were the many societies and trading guilds of the Butcher Inquiry and the Hayley Committee. This was a conflict between the authorities of two levels of government speaking through the best legal talent their parties could muster. In fact, most of the work during the hearings was conducted by A. O. Lawson, representing the chiefs but speaking also for the Action Group as complainants, and Mojid Agbaje, representing the Council but also its individual N.C.N.C. members. Agbaje had appeared before in such a hearing, during the inquiry into his father's fitness as a chief, when he found himself ranged against Adelabu. This time, in Nicholson's words, he handled the case on Adelabu's behalf 'not only with tact and skill but with a disarming friendliness of manner'.[73]

On 3 September, the serious business began. The first witness was S. A. Akinyemi, charging that he had been forced to pay Adelabu a bribe to receive a promotion, followed by Treasurer E. A. Adeyemo, who had waited over a year for his hour, with the day's hearings concluded by testimony from Victor Esan, the Council's Administrative Secretary and holder of the post Adelabu had once coveted. Day after day, evidence and exhibits poured in. Councillors, contractors, chiefs and administrative officers testified for a total of twenty-seven sessions, lasting until 4 October.

The substance of the Inquiry covered a wide range of subjects, the most important of which we have already discussed in examining Adelabu's administration of the Council. Nicholson's Report ran to 131 pages and it is therefore not necessary to follow this Inquiry in great detail.* A few items are nevertheless worthy of special notice. In the first place, monetarily the charges against Adelabu and the Council are strikingly small individually and in the aggregate. In four cases involving jobs for his followers, Adelabu was accused of demanding a total of £70 and thirty shillings worth of meat. In another case involving L. Ade Bello as Chairman of the Council's Tender Board, the Inquiry revealed that ninety-two chairs had been purchased in 'a barefaced attempt to defraud the Council of...£57 10s...'.[74] Adelabu dis-

---

* We do not have the verbatim record as in the Butcher Inquiry, so that little can be added to Nicholson's summation.

missed the implications of this testimony in a statement that he was worth
£20,000 and the owner of a house worth £15,000, a blatant lie in total
contradiction of the facts and his further testimony about his tax payments.

Nevertheless, the point remained that the Commission was attempting to
establish whether standards had been breached, whereas throughout his
entire life Adelabu had been concerned with the basic conditions that allowed
any kind of action at all in a rapidly changing system. Nicholson's own view
was that Ibadan and Nigeria were still in the process of approximating the
standards of public conduct that he fondly believed prevailed in such a developed and honest country as England, and that in these circumstances one
should be lenient toward shortcomings. However, Nicholson viewed Adelabu
as a unique phenomenon and not a person caught up in the uncertainty of his
times, a view which Adelabu for his part did his best to inculcate in Nicholson.
Nicholson found Adelabu to be a 'remarkable man' and speculated as to
what might have happened had Adelabu found employment with the Council
at an earlier date. He noted that he seemed 'to exercise a certain fascination
over Europeans as well as Africans', but that many of his qualities brought
with them 'dangers which he has not had the strength of character to
avoid'.[75] He commented on his 'wonderful command of English', his 'great
ability' and 'ready wit', his 'organizing ability, and his capacity to sway
masses of people' and his 'sincere desire' for the success of the Council and
the improvement of the masses of Nigeria and Ibadan. Yet, 'with some regret' Nicholson found him, quoting John Dryden,

> For close designs and crooked counsels fit,
> Sagacious, bold and turbulent of wit,
> Restless, unfixed in principle and place,
> Unpleased in power, impatient of disgrace.[76]

He concluded his sketch of Adelabu by saying that 'If he could learn to
control his overweening personal ambition and his desire to dominate his
fellow men he might yet render great service to Nigeria, perhaps either as a
Federal Minister, in which capacity he is surrounded by men of equal calibre,
or in some other way.'[77]

Ironically, it was an analysis which Adelabu might well have accepted,
or indeed have written. The problem was the context, a context in which the
rules, the sources of power and the men who held power were constantly
shifting; in this context, to be held responsible for the petty complaints
brought against him, violations of the law though they might have been, was
to suggest that Adelabu limit himself to 'the duller but none the less important tasks of a Chairman of a District Council'.[78] This would have been
to restrain Adelabu from engaging in the burning issues of the times, and

the conflicts into which they continually drew him. It is a superb comment on the final results of the British belief in and attempt to create local governmental institutions as the basis upon which a national political life could be built that Nicholson commented that the Chairmanship of the largest Council in black Africa might best be left to leaders 'of less but sufficient ability and suitable temperament such as, for example, Mr. J. M. Johnson or Mr. S. Lana'.[79]

Another point of considerable interest is that Nicholson found fault with a number of the administrative officers who presided over the last years of Ibadan's control by British authority. D. A. Murphy, for example, was found to have misinterpreted the law governing conflicts over the selection of a new Olubadan. Nicholson thus held that Murphy should have submitted the selection of Olubadan Akinyele to the Governor for 'due inquiry'.

Commissioner Nicholson ended his public inquiry on 4 October, leaving Adelabu to live with the expectations of his findings. On 24 October, he resumed his duties at his Ministry in Lagos, but after mid-September he had in effect ceased to function in this capacity. Although he remained a Member of the House of Representatives until his second election to the Western House of Assembly in May 1956, he spoke again in the national legislature only once, to announce his resignation from his Ministry. His total contribution to the business of that legislature was thus about a dozen speeches, most of them very brief.

We have on record Adelabu's own estimation of himself as a Minister, in a brief 'Autobiography' intended for public consumption:

Since taking Ministerial office the Honourable Adelabu has brought to the matters which fall in his portfolio that same determination which made him so successful in his deliberations with the Ibadan District Council. In his Ministry he is far from being a 'rubber stamp' but makes himself thoroughly acquainted with all the aspects of his Ministry which cover so many departments and subjects. Unafraid of long hours and determined to give of his best to the people who have placed their confidence in him he does not spare himself in the many duties which befall him.[80]

Unfortunately, this is a misleading picture. Certainly he was no 'rubber stamp', and he was determined to have his own way in Lagos, as he was in Ibadan. The problem was that the two offices – Chairman of the Ibadan District Council and Federal Minister of Natural Resources and Social Services – were more than any one man, even one of Adelabu's energy, could tackle at the same time. On 17 February 1957, for example, when he should have been at a Conference on Natural Resources in Lagos, he was neither there nor in Ibadan at an emergency meeting of the Council. K. O. Mbadiwe and L. Ade Bello appeared in his place. The truth is that he was not a good Minister. By preference, he spent his time in Ibadan rather than Lagos, appearing in his Ministry usually only when there were meetings of the Council of Ministers, or when business in the House affecting him was due to come up, or when there were important visitors from abroad to see. He trusted his British civil servants (which fortunately, in fact, he could do) with a great deal of responsibility, telling them what principles he wished to have embodied in a given White Paper – as with that on Education – and relying on them to do this, even to the extent, it is said, of going into a meeting of the Council of Ministers to explain a White Paper without reading it first.

He disliked life in Lagos, taking as little part as possible in the cocktail and dinner parties which were part of government life. None of his wives spoke English or had the western education necessary to be the 'knife and fork wife' who could entertain for him or appear in the company of sophisticated European and Nigerian women. In consequence, none of them came to live at his ministerial residence.

He also drank heavily during office hours at this time, a sign of the pressures upon him during 1955, adding the spirits to Coca-Cola to disguise them. It was an offense against his Muslim faith and something which his followers would deny, but it was obvious enough to his northern colleagues particularly, who observed him attending meetings of the Council of Ministers not completely sober.

By the beginning of September 1955, then, Adegoke Adelabu was becoming an embarrassment to the N.C.N.C. His electoral victories in Ibadan during 1954 had brought him into greater prominence in the party and involved him more and more in its affairs. His activities now brought credit or discredit to his party as well as to himself and could no longer be ignored or lightly excused.

Furthermore, he was no sooner back in his Ministerial office in Lagos when the Regional Government levelled another blow at his control of traditional politics in Ibadan. In a letter dated 25 October, the District Officer informed Council Secretary Esan that a new Chieftaincy Committee for the Ibadan Council was to be established under the Western Region Appointment and Recognition of Chiefs (Amendment) Law (W.R. No. 16 of 1955). Esan promptly invited the senior Ibadan chiefs and the five village heads of the Ibadan District to an inaugural meeting which was held on 9 November. In attendance were Akinyele and his supporters from the Olubadan's line, Chiefs Kobiowu, Akinwale, Olugbode and Irefin, as well as Chief Aminu, the Balogun, and J. L. Ogunsola, the Ekerin Balogun. Iyalode Abimbola, newly-installed, was also present. Absent were the other three principals of the Balogun's line – Akinyo, Aderogba and Sholagbade – and Seriki Adeleke. As Esan explained, the new committee was henceforth to be 'the Constitutional body to deal with all Chieftaincy matters'. Expressing sentiments voiced by several others, Olubadan Akinyele

...greeted and congratulated all members of the re-organised Chieftaincy Committee and warned them against bribery and corruption which, he said, often made sound decisions difficult if not impossible. He was glad that matters affecting Chiefs were to be handled exclusively by a Constitutional body of Chiefs, i.e. the Chieftaincy Committee and not by ordinary men.[81]

Adelabu's next tribulations followed close on this. On 5 November Dingle Foot arrived in Nigeria, and on 9 November the Ibadan Assizes began hearing the case against Adelabu and seven others regarding the Oja'ba Market incident. Four of the defendants were discharged on the second day, and on the third day Adelabu, while giving evidence, denied being present at Oja'ba on 12 February. The case against him was obviously tinged with politics; one of the prosecution witnesses was Omilabu Gandhi, J. A. Akinlotan's successor as Action Group Organizing Secretary for Ibadan, who during the trial actually announced his resignation from that party. This kind of circumstance was obviously a great asset for Dingle Foot in his defense. On 14 November he made his final submission, lasting ninety-five minutes. Adelabu showed his confidence in his counsel by going to sleep during the speech on a hot afternoon, and had to be awakened by the judge and sharply reminded to pay attention. On Tuesday, 15 November, the Chief Justice of the Western Region, Sir Adetokunboh Ademola, acquitted and discharged Adelabu and four others, finding that the prosecution had failed to prove its case.*

A week later he had even greater cause to rejoice. On 22 November, in the appeal against the sentence for the Akinbiyi affair, the defense again brought in the British lawyer Dingle Foot, supported by four other Nigerian barristers, including T. O. S. Benson, B. Olowofoyeku and E. A. Fakayode, only the last being an Ibadan. Chief Justice Ademola now ruled that the lower court had erred in law by finding that Akinbiyi's court was properly constituted; since it was not, he dismissed the contempt charges against both L. Ade Bello and Adelabu, after subjecting them to a severe admonition:

...it would appear, drunk with power, they disgraced the high office they fill by their behaviour...It is bad manners and the worst form of irresponsibility on the part of a Minister of State to attempt, in any way, to bring a Court of Law into

* The remaining three defendants were sentenced to fines of £50 each, or three months imprisonment, for damaging the car of the Action Group.

disrepute or try in any way to scandalise it, merely because the Judge of that court holds a different political view to his.[82]

Ademola upheld the findings and sentence for assault against L. Ade Bello, however, and since the lower court had not given him the option of imprisonment or a fine, Bello was faced with imprisonment. L. Ade Bello promptly appealed to the Supreme Court and was released on £200 bail. His appeal rested on a question of law, asking the Court to find that Chief Justice Ademola had erred in law in holding that the Magistrate's Court had adequately directed itself to the onus of the proof. Since Adelabu was free, however, Akinbiyi took the initiative of appealing Ademola's action to the Federal Supreme Court, which left Bello under a severe threat until late May 1956, when the case was finally resolved. Adelabu was also left under a cloud, politically as well as legally, as he learned when the Governor commented to him on the criticism made by the Chief Justice.

On 3 November, a week after they had learned of Government's insistence upon a new Chieftaincy Committee, but a week before its inaugural meeting, another meeting was held at Olubadan Akinyele's house at Alafara. S. Ade Ojo, Chief Ogunsola and Obisesan were present. Obisesan records they agreed to institute arrangements 'to put things right at Ibadan'.[83] It was known in Ibadan that this committee was meeting and that it had in fact the appearance of a shadow government.

Although the sessions of the Inquiry were over and the court cases had been brought to a successful conclusion, Adelabu remained in Ibadan, ignoring his Ministerial duties and his N.C.N.C. colleagues. On 14 December, K. O. Mbadiwe wrote to 'My dear Adel' formally handing over to him the leadership of the N.C.N.C. Federal Parliamentary Party while Mbadiwe was in the East, and also reproaching Adelabu for his absences from meetings of the N.C.N.C. Ministers on the 12th and 13th, the latter 'despite the fact that I specially informed [you], and again telephoned your house'.[84] With an apparent feeling of foreboding Mbadiwe ended with the remark

I leave with prayer in my heart that the Almighty God show us the way, if we must discharge our obligations to this mighty nation.

The feeling of unease was soon to prove entirely justified.*

---

* Adelabu was also displaying possible signs of strain at this time. On 21 December the *Daily Times* carried a curious allegation by him that two days before 'an Ibadan politician' had sent eight men to see him late at night at his Ikoyi residence (he had by then moved down to Lagos), and that he had had to call the police to get rid of them. He also claimed that he had been receiving anonymous telephone calls asking whether he had left for the East.

CHAPTER 11

A TIME OF TROUBLES

I have often said this: that the battle for the West is a single handed combat between me, Adegoke Adelabu, and Obafemi Awolowo.

Adegoke Adelabu, October 1955

On 28 December 1955, the Western Region Government announced that it had received the draft report from E. W. J. Nicholson. On 16 January 1956, the *Report of the Commission of Inquiry into the Administration of the Ibadan District Council* was published in Ibadan. In his findings, the Town Clerk of Abingdon gave it as his opinion – according to his terms of reference – that there had been no 'general failure' of I.D.C. affairs, and no 'substantial failure' by the Council to levy rates or to act in conformity with the Local Government Law.[1] The Commissioner also found it 'regrettable' that the *Nigerian Tribune* should have begun to campaign for the dissolution of the Council as soon as it was inaugurated, and 'unfortunate' that A. M. A. Akinloye, although a Minister, should have taken 'an active personal part' in the campaign against the Council.[2] On the other hand, the Report found that eleven 'substantial separate failures in administration' had occurred, of which four were 'gross' failures. The Commissioner was inclined to give the benefit of the doubt to the Council as a whole, and instead to lay the responsibility at Adelabu's door.

Just as the energy and ability of the Chairman of the Council contributed to its achievements, so his lack of integrity, his excessive interference and his domineering conduct brought about almost all its failures.[3]

Worse than this, however, from Adelabu's point of view, was the finding that there had been 'six instances of corrupt or dishonest acts by the Chairman of the Council, Councillor Adelabu, and/or Councillor L. Ade Bello'.[4] Three other N.C.N.C. Councillors were also held to be guilty of corruption. The *Report*, moreover, not only identified the crime, but suggested as punishment disqualification from membership of a local government council for three years for anyone found guilty of corruption or 'acts conducive to maladministration'.[5]

In a press statement issued on 16 January and attached to the *Report*, the

Action Group Government accepted nearly all of its findings, including the recommendation on disqualification, and noted that the charges of corruption had been placed in the hands of the Attorney-General. Now, indeed, Adegoke Adelabu had been delivered into the hands of his enemies. An opening had been given to his Action Group foes to dispossess him from his chairmanship of the Ibadan District Council. In the press statement the Government called on the I.D.C. 'to dissociate itself from the wrongful acts referred to by the Commissioner by removing from the Council the unfortunate influences which have damaged its good name and administration'.[6] The first reactions to the *Report* by prominent members of the N.C.N.C.–Mabolaje Grand Alliance revealed them in some disarray. According to the *Daily Times* of 17 January Adelabu himself had refused to comment, but Mojid Agbaje and E. O. Fakayode were quoted as saying that they accepted the *Report*, and S. L. A. Elliott, the Alliance Secretary, called it 'a balanced document with which all reasonable and unbiased people must perforce agree'. On the 19th, however, the same newspaper reported that L. Ade Bello had described the document as prejudiced. Ominous signs of dissension were appearing among Penkelemesi's supporters.

The first blow, in fact, fell upon Adelabu's other position of power, his Federal Ministry. The day after the *Report* appeared, Governor-General Sir James Robertson wrote to him:

I have been greatly distressed to read the findings of the Nicholson Commission on the Administration of the Ibadan District Council and to see in that Report the very serious criticisms made against you. Coming so soon after the previous criticisms made by the Chief Justice of the Western Region in recent legal proceedings to which I called your attention only a month or two ago, the findings of this Report seem to me to make it incumbent upon you to consider most seriously and carefully your position as a Federal Minister.[7]

Sir James then went on to list the various findings against Adelabu, and to offer his opinion as to the correct course of action to be followed:

These are grave findings indeed. It may be that you feel disposed to challenge them. There is not, of course, a prescribed channel of appeal against the findings of a Commission of Inquiry as there is against the findings of a Court of first instance (although even there I understand there are limits set on the extent to which findings of fact may be challenged) but I think it is my duty to say clearly to you that in the United Kingdom no Minister who had been so criticised by a Commission of Inquiry would remain in office, whether or not he accepted the competence of the Commission or the validity of the findings. He would immediately resign and try to rehabilitate himself outside the Government. The first reason for his so doing would be the general tradition of honesty and competence which all politicians in the United Kingdom now feel bound to honour. A Minis-

278

ter so impugned would not wish to continue in office while he sought to remove the doubts which such findings would be bound to raise in the minds of the people of the country about his fitness for his post. The second reason, however, is the principle of collective responsibility for acts which he did in his personal capacity but which would, if he remained a Minister, inevitably reflect on him in his Ministerial capacity and so on his colleagues. In Nigeria we are trying to build up a parliamentary democracy on the lines first adopted by the British Parliament and it is my considered opinion that it would be right for you if you really have this aim for the future of Nigeria, to resign your membership of the Council of Ministers.

It is evident from this passage that the Governor-General had a very clear view of his own role in the decolonization process. The remodelling of Nigeria's political institutions, begun in earnest in the late 1940s, implied also a re-definition of the rules of conduct for participants in the working of these institutions. The British, having allowed Nigerians into their hitherto exclusive game, now wished not only to have the sole right to mark out the court, but also to act as coach and umpire combined. Sir James Robertson had come to Nigeria in 1955 in order to play these last roles during the final stages before independence. Now, anticipating what Adelabu's reaction to this lecture on the ethics of ministerial resignation might be, he hinted that the rules could be invoked against a faulting player:

I fully appreciate that to do this will be hard for you, but I believe you are sufficiently patriotic to do the right thing for your country, and also to agree that you should not weaken the Council of Ministers by remaining a member of it in these circumstances. I am ready to see you at any time to discuss this question with you, but I hope you will not take too long in making up your mind on your course of action.

Adegoke Adelabu's first reaction to what amounted to a request for his resignation was indeed to resolve to fight it. He prepared two drafts of a long reply to the Governor-General, in which he claimed that the Nicholson Inquiry was part of a series of personal attacks upon himself, both on his reputation and his life. To the second he added two documents. The first, entitled 'J'Accuse: The Visit to England by the Western Region Minister of Local Government and Justice', declared that 'Like Andrew [*sic*] Dreyfus, I, Adegoke Adelabu, shall wait patiently no matter how long, until justice is done and my good name is cleared from this violent character assassination.' In it he alleged that on this visit (in November 1955) Chief Rotimi Williams had exerted pressure on E. W. J. Nicholson to influence his findings. The other document offered sixteen detailed criticisms of the *Report* itself. The basis of the problem, he seemed to feel, lay in the nature of the Nigerian federal system 'I honestly believe, Sir, it has not been possible

279

within the present Nigerian constitutional set-up of co-ordinate governments to afford me that degree of protection which my federal Ministerial status warrants.'⁸ Moreover, the fact that the balance of power lay on the side of the regions meant that the Action Group Government of the West was able to protect A. M. A. Akinloye, who had also been found wanting by Nicholson: 'A Minister of the Crown who has committed an act bordering on high treason which strikes at the very foundation of the government is being protected in his Office on the specious plea of the peculiar local political conditions.'*

Yet, at the final resolve, Adelabu was curiously ambivalent in his attitudes, seeming to contradict himself within the same draft. At one point he rejected the Governor-General's advice:

Possibly in my precarious position I have no other defence than that of 'public opinion' but in the face of all that I have said above, Sir, and much against my natural inclination and any conventional moral obligation, I find myself not justified to act on your advice which, although given in good faith and with the best intentions, would be tantamount to handing myself over to the absolute power of my political enemies.⁹

Earlier in the same letter, however, he had commented that 'Most distasteful and anguishing as this advice may be – as it affords a grievous, temporary set-back to my promising political career – I admit that if I were in your position I would feel compelled to take similar steps.' Moreover, at the end of the letter he did actually offer to resign:

Constitutionally I appreciate that the allocation to me of a Portfolio is a subject altogether within your discretion. In order to save Your Excellency from the unpleasant and possibly inevitable duty of relieving me of my Portfolio I offer to surrender my duties as Minister of Social Services so that my present Ministry will not suffer from my pre-occupation with other and engaging public affairs.

Taken as a whole, these draft letters seem to reflect the genuine confusion of his first responses to this new turn of events and the prospect of the loss of his ministry. On the one hand his automatic reaction was to fight to keep his office and the political prestige it carried; on the other his apparently quite genuine commitment to behaving as a Minister ought to behave,

---

* This was a typical piece of dramatization by Penkelemesi. The original passage reads: 'Mr. Akinloye undoubtedly played a big part in the campaign against the District Council over the assessment and collection of taxes, and personally tried to persuade the Minister of Justice and Local Government to intervene in this respect. This was not the only sign of his enmity, and I regard it as unconstitutional for a Minister of the Crown to take part in, or lend his support to, any campaign for or against an individual local authority.' Nicholson Report, p. 123.)

according to the theory of parliamentary government, enabled him to see the Governor-General's point of view. There is perhaps a suggestion of a possible compromise in the last passage quoted above, a hint that he might be asked to hand over his specific responsibilities, rather than resign his position as a Minister altogether, but more than anything else, these letters read like those of a man facing a difficult choice and uncertain what to do.

In the end his decision was to fight or, rather, to make his party fight for him. A meeting of the Grand Alliance Executive Committee, including the chiefs and mogajis, at Akere's Compound on 18 January heard him report on the contents of the Governor-General's letter of the previous day. The meeting then resolved to request the N.C.N.C. Federal Parliamentary Party to 'take a firm and resolute stand against the loss of Hon. Adegoke Adelabu as a Federal Minister'.[10] If this were not done, the Mabolaje would sever its alliance with the N.C.N.C. and become an independent political party, the 'Taxpayers' Association Ibadan Branch', with the four Alliance Members of the House of Representatives withdrawing from the N.C.N.C. Federal Parliamentary Party.

The N.C.N.C. Federal Parliamentary Party also met, at K. O. Mbadiwe's house in Lagos, on 18 and 19 January, to decide what line it was to take concerning the party's First National Vice-President, now that his conduct had been called into question. Before the meeting on the 18th, Mbadiwe announced to the press that this party was still studying the Nicholson Report, but events were catching up with it. That day the *Daily Times* had called for Adelabu's resignation, editorializing that 'Like Caesar's wife a Minister must be above suspicion.' Public interest was of course great. Hundreds of N.C.N.C. supporters from Ibadan were reported to have gathered outside Mbadiwe's house at Ikoyi to await the party's verdict. Much to the embarrassment of the N.C.N.C. it was facing a potential crisis in the East as well. In that region, Dr Azikiwe as its Premier was awaiting the report of a Commission of Inquiry into official corruption in which Mbonu Ojike, Second National Vice-President of the N.C.N.C. and Eastern Minister of Finance, was involved.

On 20 January the *Daily Times,* under the banner heading 'Ojike Grossly Corrupted His Office', carried the news that the Ikpeazu Commission of Inquiry in the East had found Mbonu Ojike guilty of misconduct, and on the 21st Dr Azikiwe, as Premier of the Region, requested Ojike to resign from his government. In the case of Adegoke Adelabu, however, the party had not yet made up its mind. The Federal Parliamentary Party had failed to come to an agreement at its session and had contented itself with issuing a statement which declared that '. . .it is the N.C.N.C. that will withdraw Mr. Adelabu by resignation from the nation's service if circumstances warrant such withdrawal, and will not allow dictation from any quarters'. The statement cited the criticism of Akinloye by Nicholson and once again attacked the treatment of the old Alafin of Oyo by the Action Group Government of the West. 'The N.C.N.C. will make its stand', it concluded, 'and when it has spoken the nation will take note.'[11]

Then, on 25 January, K. O. Mbadiwe issued a statement to the press. Adegoke Adelabu, he said, had handed over his letter of resignation to the Governor-General at 7.30 p.m. on the 24th, two and a half hours after the Parliamentary Party at another meeting had agreed to this action. The statement did its best to save Penkelemesi's – and the party's – face. His conduct as a Minister, it pointed out, was not before the Nicholson Inquiry, nor was this resignation a confession of his guilt. If the *Report* had not mentioned corrupt motives the party would not have allowed him to resign, but the Council of Ministers was 'a most delicate organisation', 'fingers cannot be pointed at it', and so 'Mr. Adelabu as well as his party had made the necessary sacrifice so that Nigeria may reach the pinnacle of democratic government.' 'The first year of the Adelabu era closes', it went on, 'only to open a magnificent page of a second Adelabu era.'[12]

It was imperative for the N.C.N.C. to make its position clear, for that very day, Wednesday 25 January 1956, Adegoke Adelabu had stood up in the House of Representatives and announced not only his resignation from the Federal Government but also his renunciation of the N.C.N.C. Party Whip. In thus publicly severing his connection with the party he showed how reluctantly he had agreed to resign. His letter to the Governor-General on the 24th had enclosed a document setting out his views on the Nicholson Report, and only grudgingly admitted to being a letter of resignation:

If, after reading the attached papers, you still feel justified in asking for my resignation. I should be grateful if you would kindly take such action as may be necessary, accepting this letter as my formal notice of resignation from the Council of Ministers.[13]

Sir James Robertson had shown no hesitation, verbally accepting the resignation immediately on 24 January and following this up with a letter on the following day. 'I am glad', he wrote, 'that you have decided to follow the tradition that a Minister should resign when a finding derogatory to his honour and reputation has been made by a Court of Inquiry, even if he does not accept the findings.'[14] There can be little doubt that Adelabu had responded only with reluctance to the arguments which were uppermost in the minds of his N.C.N.C. colleagues. It was essential to prove to the Colonial Office that they had learned to jump through the Westminster hoop. A visit to Nigeria by the Queen and the Duke of Edinburgh was imminent (they were due to arrive in Lagos on 28 January), and no unseemly clash between the party and the Governor-General must be allowed to mar this, the overt sign that Nigeria was on the road to independence. For the sake of the party, then, the other N.C.N.C. Ministers felt that Adelabu should resign. For their part, the Northern People's Congress Ministers quite naturally left this decision entirely up to their coalition partners. In any case, some of those close to Adelabu at this time believe that his drinking had affronted his northern Muslim colleagues, especially Abubakar Tafawa Balewa, so that they were not sorry to see him go.

Adelabu yielded, but made his real views plain by refusing any longer to observe N.C.N.C. parliamentary discipline. K. O. Mbadiwe's statement on 25 January, therefore, while reminding the Ibadan leader of the legal help given to him by the N.C.N.C. in the past, sought above all to put the best possible interpretation on his action:

Mr. Adelabu's declaration of being independent is understood. He is awaiting his party's stand. He now knows it – Adelabu must be retained for the service of Nigeria. His magnificent gesture to save Nigeria embarrassment at this period of the Queen's visit has elevated him to a status of a hero of Ibadan, a crusader of his party and a lover of his country.[15]

A few days later Nnamdi Azikiwe also wrote him a private letter, expressing his regret at the need for Adelabu to resign his Ministry and his renunciation of his association with the N.C.N.C. The loss of the services of both Ojike and Adelabu had obviously saddened the party's National President. Thus he wrote:

It grieves me to be a witness to all these incidents and they make one ponder whether party politics is worthwhile in a nation in the making. I make the above remark bearing in mind what both of us, in association with others, went through during the early days of the Macpherson Constitution. Indeed, it was stormy and excruciating at that time, and one should have wished that the present situation had not developed.[16]

The remainder of the letter was intended, nevertheless, to bid farewell to the N.C.N.C.'s First National Vice-President rather than to persuade him to remain in the party:

I want you to know that I endorse the statement which the Honourable K. O. Mbadiwe, N.C.N.C. Parliamentary Leader in the House of Representatives, made immediately after your resignation. That expresses the feelings of those who are now to be numbered among your former comrades-in-arms but who, I can assure you, still hold you in high regard and feel for you in your hour of trial.

I am not in a position to persuade you to remember that old friends are usually the best, because the privilege to pick and choose friends depends upon many factors and personal conviction has a lot to do with the final decision made.

So long as you still believe in the ability of Nigerians to scale the heights of self government and to support the cause of justice and fair play in the governing of those entrusted to their care, so long, must I assure you, Mr. Adelabu, that we are in the same boat sailing towards a common objective.

With kind wishes,
Believe me to be,
Sincerely yours,
Nnamdi Azikiwe,
Premier

Penkelemesi had in fact returned to his beloved Ibadan furious with the N.C.N.C. and its National President because of their failure to support him in refusing to resign from his Ministry.* By the time he received Dr Azikiwe's letter, however, he had cooled down. On 28 January a meeting of the Mabolaje passed a resolution to return 'to the fold of the N.C.N.C.', 'expecting the Party to take immediate and energetic measures to fight the cause of Ibadan on all fronts'.[17] A delegation from the N.N.D.P. in Lagos had come to Ibadan to make peace, giving assurance 'that in co-operation with all Yorubas concerned they were certain of securing justice for Ibadan'. Adelabu, always close to the senior members of the Democratic Party, allowed their arguments to prevail with him, and at the meeting on the 28th announced to the crowd that he was still a member of the N.C.N.C., to be greeted with the 'usual revered applause of Zeek-Zeek'.[18]

By the end of January the Nicholson Report had thus had its first effect upon Adelabu's political career, forcing him to give up his position as a Federal Minister. By the end of February, Penkelemesi was facing his second crisis resulting from the Nicholson Report, centred this time on his chairmanship of the Ibadan District Council. We saw at the beginning of this chapter that the first reaction to the *Report* on the part of the Western Region Government was to call on the Councillors to purge themselves of their guilty associations with their Chairman and four of their other colleagues. We also saw that signs of dissension appeared immediately in the Grand Alliance ranks. On 4 February the Ibadan District Council set up a committee of fourteen to study the Nicholson Report, including such stalwart supporters of Adegoke Adelabu as S. L. A. Elliott, Yesufu Mogbonjubola, Isau Lawal, A. O. Adesokan and Adebayo Adeyinka. Matters seemed to be under control, but on 22 February a great split in the ranks of the Grand Alliance

---

* An oft-repeated story has it that on his arrival by train he was met at the station in Ibadan by N.C.N.C. supporters shouting the customary 'Zeek! Zeek!' Angrily he forbade them ever again to use Azikiwe's nickname in this way, but in the future always to shout 'Ade! Ade!'.

became apparent. On that day it was made public that a motion demanding the removal from the Council of Adelabu and the four others criticized in the Report, signed by three Action Group, one traditional and twenty-eight N.C.N.C. members, would be placed before the Council at its next meeting on 3 March. A release by Elliott the following day tried to represent this motion as merely a request for an emergency meeting of the Council, signed by 'a few innocent Council members', and claimed that the 'domestic misunderstanding' among the N.C.N.C. members of the Council had been 'amicably settled'.[19] The critics of Adelabu stuck to their guns, however, and on the 24th re-affirmed their intention of going ahead with the motion; perhaps rather unkindly they also reminded Elliott of his acceptance of the *Report* when it first appeared.

Within Government, plans were drawn up for the dissolution of the Council on the premise that the Council would fail to purge itself of the unsatisfactory members. The committee of the Council was not expected to submit a report to the Council on 3 March which would be satisfactory to the Government. On 18 February officials of the Ministry of Local Government discussed the matter with the Governor, and on 27 February with Awolowo. At this meeting Awolowo reviewed a draft letter of dissolution and a list of provisional Councillors drawn up by the Minister of Justice and Local Government, F. R. A. Williams, who wished to have the Council dissolved before the meeting scheduled for 3 March, since he feared the delay might create the opportunity for further political difficulty.[20] This Awolowo rejected, on the advice of administrative officers who thought this precipitous; among these was Local Government Inspector Murphy who had taken care to inform Awolowo on 20 February that the Council had already collected £130,000 of its estimated £155,000 tax. 'Assuming that the momentum is maintained, this looks good.'[21]

On Sunday 26 February, the national N.C.N.C. intervened in the affairs of its Ibadan ally. A large delegation arrived in Ibadan, headed by Dr Mbadiwe, and including Chief Festus Okotie-Eboh, T. O. S. Benson, H. O. Davies, Chief Isaac Shodipo, Tunji Olowofoyeku, Dr Ikejiani and N. B. Soule. A mass rally scheduled for 2.00 p.m. was cancelled and, instead, closed meetings were held in the Committee Room in Mapo Hall with Elliott and sixteen Grand Alliance Councillors in attendance. Adelabu was obviously angry. The *Defender* stated the next day that he had only attended the meeting on N. B. Soule's persuasion, and when he spoke he bitterly attacked E. O. Fakayode, whom he blamed for the revolt of the Councillors against him and declared that people must never vote for the lawyer again.

Late that night Mbadiwe and Adelabu spoke to the crowd outside Mapo Hall. Adelabu, the former declared, was still the N.C.N.C. leader in Ibadan, while Penkelemesi himself announced that the twenty-eight had withdrawn their signatures from the offending motion. Whether this was true or not – and there is some doubt – the revolt in the Grand Alliance was certainly not over. On Friday 2 March, the *Defender* published an open letter addressed to Adelabu, signed by Olowofoyeku, Ikejiani, Fakayode, D. K. Olumofin, Sanya Onabamiro and A. J. Nicholson Sangster. This began by acknowledging the Ibadan leader's courage in standing by the N.C.N.C. at the beginning of 1952 and his 'stupendous energy in turning the tables over the enemy at Ibadan within the short space of a couple of years'. The result of this had been promotion to high office, but now the Nicholson Report had called Adelabu's position into question and, having already been advised by the N.C.N.C. leaders to resign his Ministry, he must now review his position in the Ibadan District Council. Only Adelabu and the four others had been called into question – if they went the N.C.N.C.-controlled Council could go on. Yet, the letter continued, Adelabu was opposing the resolution calling for the removal of the five, and insisting on the collective responsibility of all the Councillors – 'in short, you are using precisely the same technique that you employed to bully and threaten the N.C.N.C. Federal Parliamentary Party in connection with your membership of the Council of Ministers'. 'What we utterly fail to understand', the six signatories sadly remarked, 'is why you, a great builder, could so smugly contemplate the destruction of your own handiwork.'[22]

Thus, in a situation of crisis, the latent cleavage always present in the Ibadan Grand Alliance, between the N.C.N.C. proper and the Mabolaje, had again emerged. At the time of the 1954 federal election campaign, when this cleavage first became public in the context of the nomination of candidates, it had been only a comparatively minor revolt by a section of those who regarded themselves as N.C.N.C. rather than Mabolaje members. Now, in March 1956, the discontent was given voice by three leaders of the Ibadan N.C.N.C., Fakayode, Ikejiani and Nicholson Sangster, and three prominent members of the Western wing of the national party, Olowofoyeku, Olumofin and Onabamiro. As educated men, regarding themselves as leaders of the party in their own right, they were not prepared to submit to Adelabu's controlling the Grand Alliance in the same autocratic manner he used with the Mabolaje. Their interpretation of the position of the Ibadan District Council at this point differed from his. Adelabu identified the Council with himself: his loss of the chairmanship would mean the end of Grand Alliance control of the Council. To his opponents it appeared possible to preserve control without Adelabu. As they pointed out in their open letter, the Action Group Regional Government was not likely to dissolve the Council after the resignation of the five and, even if it did, there would be time to resolve on a suitable course of action after such an eventuality had arisen. Adelabu, then, must resign from the Council, and if he did not his critics were prepared to take action:

If you disregard our advice which we have offered not only to preserve the life of a Council but to safeguard your own political career we shall be obliged to table a Motion before the National Executive of the Party to determine what the attitude of the Party should be to your continued membership in it.

The immediate reaction of Adelabu and his supporters to this public ultimatum was one of defiance. On 3 March, the day after the letter was published, the *Daily Times* printed a statement by S. L. A. Elliott in which he referred to a decision by the 'parent NCNC', to which N.C.N.C.–Mabolaje Grand Alliance would adhere, that the five Councillors should sit tight. They would henceforth, Elliott claimed, 'regard with contempt the malicious effusions of a few party renegades who have no *locus standi* in the issue'.

That same day, 3 March, the Council met to hear the Committee's report. The meeting dragged on for hours, and was a confused affair, with Adelabu and other Councillors frequently appearing on the balcony to greet the crowds gathered below. Adelabu had some difficulty in persuading the Councillors that as Chairman he could overrule a motion calling for the removal of himself and the other four whose conduct was in question, but in the end he was successful. The shift in opinion was marked by the departure of J. M. Johnson, Penkelemesi's close supporter and keen socialite, who left saying that it was now safe to go to the races.

On 5 March the editor of the *Southern Nigeria Defender*, Effiom E. B. Effiom, an Efik from the East, who had already made his position clear by publishing the attack on Adelabu, took up the cudgels. In his editorial that day he declared that the Mabolaje leader should give second thoughts to what he was doing – 'Let premium be placed on the interest and welfare of a majority of the people of Ibadan over that of a few Councillors.' Just as the stage seemed set for a major schism between the native sons of the city, as represented by the Mabolaje, and the native strangers, as represented by the N.C.N.C. proper, the Action Group Regional Government removed the whole basis of the dispute.

On 5 March, the day Effiom published his editorial, Chief Awolowo's Government, which had received a report on the Council meeting on the 4th, dissolved the Ibadan District Council, taking the Nicholson Report as the necessary excuse to use its legal powers to break Adelabu's hold on the administration of his native city. On 8 March the appointments of the new Provisional Councillors were made. On 13 March the Provisional Council was inaugurated by F. R. A. Williams. It promptly elected as its President and Chairman Isaac Akinyele, holder of its highest traditional office. 'To-day', Akinpelu Obisesan happily recorded in his Diary, 'the Olubadan truly became the Ruler of Ibadan.' A few days later, in order to secure the initiative among traditional forces thus gained, Akinyele and Obisesan 'agreed to organise a political society, [The] Sons of Ibadan Chiefs Society'.[23]

Disorder reigned among the Mabolaje and its supporters. The *Defender* continued to castigate Adelabu and the Council for their obstinate refusal to dissociate themselves from the corruption with which the Nicholson Commission had charged the Chairman and the four other Councillors.[24] The 'uncompromising attitude' of the Chairman and his 'total disregard for the NCNC policy of National Service' had caused him to play into the hands of his enemies. The *Defender* had warned Adelabu that the Action Group would have its pound of flesh, and now it had it. Indeed, the N.C.N.C. newspaper went so far as to say that dissolution may have been justified under the circumstances.[25]

It was also becoming clear that the Acton Group would take pleasure in salting the N.C.N.C. wounds. Williams had refused to allow further elections until 1958, giving the appointed Council a two-year life tenure. And on 16 March, the obvious fact was announced that all new Council Committees would be dominated by Action Group members. It was even suggested a few days later that Akinyele might appoint an entirely new line of Balogun chiefs in order not to have to deal further with his fractious subordinates.[26]

These local problems against the background of the national disputes in which Adelabu was involved seriously threatened the N.C.N.C.–Mabolaje Grand Alliance, even if only temporarily. On 13 March, E. A. Fakayode in denying that the Ibadan N.C.N.C. would boycott the actions of the Provisional Council also gave notice that the local branch of the national party was considering its position in regard to the Alliance. 'The object of separating the Ibadan branch of the NCNC from another party, Mr. Fakayode said, is to ensure discipline within the party, and to disassociate the party from false and malicious campaigners.' Two days later, the *Defender* reported Adelabu himself as saying that his party, the Mabolaje Society, although it still claimed to be an ally of the N.C.N.C., might not adopt the Cock as its symbol, and it carried an appeal from Adebayo Asaya to the party faithful to buy N.C.N.C. membership cards. At a going-away party held that day for the *Defender*'s editor, Effiom E. B. Effiom, who had been appointed Editor of the *Nigerian Spokesman* at Onitsha, D. K. Olumofin was in the chair and Adebayo Asaya was present, but Adelabu was absent.[27]

Almost exactly two years after his famous victory in the local elections, which had been the real launching-pad for his rise to political prominence,

Adelabu was virtually back where he started, uncrowned king of the streets of Ibadan but with no public office except that of an ordinary legislator, and although still First National Vice-President of the N.C.N.C., hardly able to wear that mantle easily. Moreover, on 16 March he and one of his body-guards were charged with corruptly demanding and receiving bribes, a charge arising from the Nicholson Report. Refusing a summary trial and thus forcing the holding of a Preliminary Inquiry, they prolonged the hearings on through March and into an adjournment until 13 April, amid complaints by the prosecution of interference with its witnesses. Finally on 21 April they were committed for trial, and, agreeing this time to a summary trial, a date was fixed for 4 June. Adelabu thus found himself in legal jeopardy without even the comfort of office.

Not the least troublesome effect of his double loss of office was that upon his income. During 1955 his official income had been between £375 and £400 a month, depending on the amount of fees drawn from the Ibadan District Council. From March 1956 his salary was merely the £66. 13. 4d. he drew as a federal legislator. Moreover, in the following months he was continually troubled by demands for payments of various kinds: £75. 14. 11d. to reimburse the Government for his ministerial salary and allowances for the last week of January 1956 which he had received in advance, £1121. 19. 9d. as the balance of a loan which he had taken to buy a car; £102. 12. 0d. for items found missing from his ministerial house when the Public Works Department repossessed it, and £5. 17. 6d. for a ministerial briefcase he had lost. As late as August his former expatriate subordinates were forced to write reminders to him about these sums, accompanied by personal notes of apology for thus troubling him. In the same month he was threatened with legal proceedings by the Union Trading Company's Motor Department in Lagos unless he paid them his bill of £65. 1. 8d. As late as August 1957, S.C.O.A. (Motors) of Ibadan, through their lawyer, Adelabu's party comrade T. O. S. Benson, were demanding settlement of a bill for £13. 5. 6d., payment of which had first been called for in April 1956.[28]

Despite all these troubles, Adelabu, with his great resilience and energy, had begun only a week after the dissolution of the Ibadan District Council to devise new ways to win power. Apparently confident that the threatened split in the Grand Alliance would come to nothing – a confidence that proved justified – he turned his attention instead to preparing an onslaught on the Provisional Council. In an issue which he had once used against the old I.C.C.-controlled Council, the threatened eviction of the traders from Lebanon Street, a weapon was ready to hand. Two days after the Action Group Government had announced the dissolution of Adelabu's Council, the Provincial Adviser (as the Resident was now called) wrote to the

Minister of Local Government strongly recommending that the new Council should not approve the proposed bye-laws against the Lebanon street traders. It would be better to let matters alone, he felt, since the general public was pleased with the dissolution and those traders already evicted had made no protest.[29]

On 13 March, the day the Provisional Council was inaugurated, Adelabu scuttled the last point. He led five hundred market women to the House of Assembly at Agodi, where they confronted Minister Akinloye 'on their stomachs', in the traditional pleading posture. Akinloye thought it expedient for a dozen of them to confer with the Minister of Local Government immediately and Chief Williams advised them to draw up a petition to the new Council.[30] Adelabu had thus served notice of his intentions, and he used the opportunity of the delay in the court hearings of the Nicholson charges for further campaigning, this time in the villages around Ibadan.

He also had his eye on powers beyond those of the Ibadan Council. For the last six months, throughout all the anxieties of the Nicholson Inquiry and the crises which followed the publication of the Report he had been at least intermittently concerned with the new regional election which he believed would be held in the West sometime early in 1956. As one of the most important leaders of the N.C.N.C. in the region he was, of course, certain to take an interest in it, but the personal rivalry which he felt towards Obafemi Awolowo made the election all the more important to him. The Nicholson Inquiry and its aftermath must have served to confirm to him that the Regional Government represented the key center of power which must be captured, since all his troubles with the Ibadan District Council and, through these, the loss of his Ministry, had stemmed from the fact that although he controlled Ibadan politically he was ultimately answerable as Chairman of its District Council to an Action Group Minister of Local Government. If he could win control of the West, all the levers of power which the British were preparing to hand over would fall, not into the hands of Awolowo, Akintola and the rest, but into the grasp of the Western N.C.N.C. leaders, not least of whom was Adegoke Adelabu. For this it was worthwhile virtually to ignore the attacks of his colleagues and to balance his sense of betrayal by Dr Azikiwe and other N.C.N.C. leaders against the prospect of an N.C.N.C. electoral victory in the West.

Indeed, Adelabu was casting himself in the role of a future Premier of the Western Region long before his federal ministry was greatly in jeopardy. Probably sometime in October 1955 he drew up a list of '14 Significant Intervals' in his own political career.[31] (The date of the election was then unknown, though he himself believed that it would be held in February 1956.) Beginning with the 'Statutory Birth' of the I.D.C. on April 1954, his list progressed by way of such events as his election as Chairman, his becoming a federal Minister, his removal from the post of Chairman in June 1955, his 'Comeback' (which he labelled 'Conquest A.G.'), and the beginning and end of the Nicholson Inquiry, to 30 June 1956, which he triumphantly labelled in capital letters, 'PREMIER'. After this, at short intervals, were to come 'CONSTITUTIONAL REVIEW' and 'NEW NIGERIA', with last of all, on 31 March 1957, the end of the term of office of the Ibadan District Council elected in 1954.*

Convinced that there was some predestined pattern leading him to power in the West (again with a multiple of the mystical number seven involved), he felt free, probably at about the same time, to draw up two different lists of governmental and other appointments he intended to make after his victory. Only six men were thought worthy of portfolios in both lists – Adelabu himself as Premier, E. A. Fakayode, D. C. Osadebay of Asaba Division, E. C. Ekwuyasi from Benin, A. Dahunsi from Oshun and Chief Isaac Shodipo from Egba.†

Nevertheless, the decision to dissolve the House of Assembly and call an election lay in the hands of Chief Awolowo, the Premier, since the British Governor of the Region, Sir John Rankine, would almost certainly feel bound by his recommendations, unforeseen circumstances aside. The life of the legislature elected in 1951 did not legally expire until January 1957, as Chief Awolowo reminded his audience and the general public in a speech to the Egbe Omo Oduduwa Conference in October 1955. Certainly there was cause to believe that the election would be held much earlier. The next constitutional conference, which would consider the question of internal self-government for the regions, and a date for the independence of Nigeria as a

* There are many mysteries about this list. Thus, if Adelabu in fact believed that the election would be held in February (on the evidence for this see p. 292), why did he give the end of June as the date when he would be Premier? Another curious feature of these '14 Significant Intervals' is that they have no detectable significance, for they run in no discernible mathematical series. Adelabu, a devotee of numerology, apparently hoped that they would, painstakingly working out the number of days in each interval in an attempt to find such a relationship.

† Unfortunately, there is no indication which of these lists – if either – represented the final fruit of Adelabu's thoughts. (Both are to be found in the portion of note-pad referred to above.) Their bases were different, one being drawn up as a list of offices to be filled, the other as a list of people to be assigned offices. One of them carefully allocated portfolios, Parliamentary Secretaryships and Chairmanships of Corporations and Boards on a provincial basis, Ibadan providing three Ministers and the Chairman of the Western Region Production Development Board. One final point to be noted is that two of the six men who appear on both lists (Ekwuyasi and I. Shodipo) ultimately did not contest the election (though Shodipo's son did) while Fakayode would scarcely have been rated so highly by Adelabu by the time of the election.

whole, was expected to be held in August or September 1956.* If the Action Group delegation could go to the conference with the mandate of a recent and decisive victory in the West behind it, the authority with which Chief Awolowo and his colleagues would be able to speak would be correspondingly increased. It was reasonable to suppose, therefore, that the election would be held before the middle of 1956. In fact, by the end of October 1955 Adelabu had become convinced that it would be called as early as the following February. In a document entitled 'Grand Election Conspiracy in the West' he asserted this, stating that 'it is my duty and my responsibility to expose the diabolical plan of the Action Group Government of the Western Region to steal an election march over my party'.[32] He then gave in detail ten reasons why he believed that the Action Group was planning an early election and complained that the Action Group had used its majority on the special parliamentary committee set up to delimit new constituencies to gerrymander them in its own favor, that the process of the registration of electors, due to begin on 1 November, would discriminate against N.C.N.C. supporters, and that the local government officials who would administer the election were mostly Action Group supporters. Moreover, he alleged, N.C.N.C. Western leaders (including himself) were being persecuted in a 'planned, premeditated attempt to handicap the NCNC by crippling its leadership through rigged-up civil and criminal cases'.[33]

Adelabu's prediction proved incorrect, however, since for a number of reasons the election was not held till May. First of all, in January and February Nigeria was to enjoy its State Visit from Queen Elizabeth II and the Duke of Edinburgh, and it was unlikely that the administration – or, indeed, the Action Group government – would welcome a turbulent, even violent, election campaign during this period. Second, Chief Awolowo was planning to visit Europe, the U.S.A. and Japan on an economic mission between 12 March and 15 April and would, no doubt, prefer to fight an election with the prestige of this behind him. Probably decisive in the timing of the election were the administrative problems of preparing the final Register of Electors.[34] The franchise for this election was to be much wider than those of 1951 and 1954; in particular, women could now vote in large numbers for the first time.† Thus, a completely new Register had to be compiled on the principle of voluntary registration (since automatic registration was

---

* On 6 July 1956, Chief Awolowo stated during a debate in the House of Assembly that the Secretary of State for the Colonies had indicated in a despatch to the Governor-General in March that he hoped the Conference might meet in the week beginning 17 September.

† Broadly speaking, electors could now qualify as taxpayers resident in an area for at least two years, or as natives of the area who were either twenty-one or older, or had paid tax there for the previous year.

administratively impossible), with time allowed for revision of the Preliminary Lists of names once these had been compiled and duly published. In fact, all this, along with printing the final Register – which proved unexpectedly complicated – took from 1 November 1955 until 30 April 1956. On 2 May Chief Awolowo announced the dissolution of the House of Assembly, with the election to be held on the 26th, the first Saturday after the lapse of three weeks from the dissolution required by law.

Whatever the uncertainties about the actual date of the election, the N.C.N.C. in the West had known for months that it was coming. As early as August 1955 Sanya Onabamiro had written a memorandum to Kola Balogun, the party's National Secretary, giving his views on the procedure to be adopted in nominating candidates when the time came.[35] At the beginning of October the first definite organizational steps were taken, though Adelabu was not present when the National Executive Committee met in Ibadan and Lagos on 1 and 2 October. To direct operations, it decided to set up an Election Council, consisting of all members of the N.E.C. itself, all members of the regional and federal legislatures, all members of the three working committees, the twenty Western Zonal Leaders, the Administrative Secretary of the National Headquarters (Chief Gogo Abbey) and the Principal Organizing Secretary in the West (Adebayo Asaya). Even allowing for overlapping between these categories this would have meant an extremely unwieldy body and, in fact, most responsibility for the organization of the campaign devolved on the Chairman of the Western Working Committee, T. O. S. Benson, the lawyer from Ikorodu who had been a stalwart of the N.C.N.C. since soon after its foundation, and Sanya Onabamiro. At this session of the N.E.C. Onabamiro was elected to the new post of Election Secretary, with J. O. Fadahunsi of Ilesha as Election Treasurer. From this point on, a stream of letters and directives were to issue from the indefatigable Onabamiro, who used his house at the University College as his headquarters, despite the fact that he was not able to get a telephone installed there until early May.

The organization of the N.C.N.C. campaign – known as 'Operation 80' from the number of constituencies – was the responsibility of the Zonal Leaders, as it had been in 1954. These twenty men were prominent figures in their home areas, and often regional and national leaders as well; thus Adelabu was Leader for the Ibadan Zone, Balogun for Oshun and Festus Okotie-Eboh for Warri and Western Ijaw. In the case of Egbado, F. S. McEwen, its Zonal Leader and N.C.N.C. Publicity Secretary, had no connection with the area, but it was apparently felt that none of the local party men was of sufficient stature to hold this position. Adelabu was thus potentially involved in the election as a national party leader who looked forward to becoming Premier as a result of it, and as a Zonal Leader of one of the party's main areas of support in Yorubaland. His commitment would thus appear to have been complete and yet, looking at the period October 1955 to May 1956, as the N.C.N.C.'s creaky machinery lurched into action, his part seems curiously ambivalent. From 15 September to 24 October he had been forced to take leave from his ministry and had spent the time testifying before the Nicholson Commission, preparing for further hearings in the Akinbiyi case and mulling over the threat to his position as Federal Minister by his party cohorts. This may account for his apparent reluctance to become too involved in the activities of the N.C.N.C. Early in October, for example, Election Secretary Onabamiro wrote to ask him to be an author of one of the series of pamphlets which the National Executive Committee had commissioned at its meeting at the beginning of the month. These were to be devoted to such subjects as 'The Tyranny of the Action Group Government's Electoral Regulations', 'The Treatment of Chiefs by the Action Group Government' and 'Cases of Victimisation by the Action Group Government'. They were to be between 1500 and 3000 words in length and were to be published in both English and Yoruba in an attempt to reach as wide a public as possible. The Election Secretary ended his letter with a cry to battle: 'Please take this matter as one of urgency. The Battle for the West has been launched. The N.C.N.C. all over Nigeria require all hands – all capable hands – on deck!'[36] Yet Adelabu was not moved. A month later, with only five days before the completed pamphlets were required, Onabamiro again wrote asking for his co-operation, pointing out that three of the eight titles planned (including two of those mentioned above) had not yet been taken up, but to no avail.[37] Adelabu wrote no pamphlets, and, indeed, the whole series failed to materialize.

Again, with regard to the registration of electors, the Election Secretary had occasion to prod Adelabu. Throughout November offices were open in the Registration Areas into which the eighty regional constituencies had been divided (for example, 96 Areas for the ten wards in Ibadan South, the seat which Adelabu was to contest). Here would-be voters could exchange an official application form for a card which would serve as proof of registration. Wide publicity was given to this operation by P. H. Balmer, the British official serving as Electoral Commissioner, and his staff. There were notices in newspapers, pamphlets and posters for the literate, and broadcasts, loudspeaker vans and even special songs for the illiterate. The main effort, however, devolved on the political parties, for it was in their interests to get as many of their supporters onto the register as possible. As Kola Balogun put it in a letter to Adelabu early in October, 'Western Regional Election is a national issue and can only be tackled effectively by a very solid registration campaign. The Party must march forward. It is imperative.'[38] At first registration went slowly, and T. O. S. Benson grew alarmed at the failure of the N.C.N.C. to get its supporters to register. On 17 November Onabamiro therefore wrote at Benson's behest to Adelabu, pointing out that the estimated number of eligible electors in Ibadan Division was 450,000 and that only about 50,000 of these had registered by the 12th.[39]* Moreover, Benson estimated that these were divided equally between N.C.N.C. and Action Group. When registration ended the total figures had picked up considerably and, in all, 195,587 people (108,639 men and 87,948 women) were finally registered in Ibadan Division; still this represented only about 50 per cent of the estimated potential, falling behind the figure for the region as a whole of 55 per cent.

At the beginning of November the N.C.N.C. set another important process in train – the selection of its candidates for this crucial Western election. On 27 October the Election Council, which had been set up at the beginning of the month, met in Mapo Hall. It decided that it must

...ensure that the process of nominating candidates is gone through all over the Western Region in a uniform pattern and done in a way to reduce to the very minimum such acrimony and misunderstanding that were usually features of Election nominations in the past.

Zonal Leaders were therefore instructed to set up Nomination Selection Committees at either the Constituency or the Divisional level (grouping together several constituencies), and to act as chairmen of these themselves, unless they were candidates for the party's nomination. Anticipating the usual keen competition for the party's official nomination, the Election Council also decided that appeals by the unsuccessful were to be heard at the next meeting of the National Executive Committee on 9 December at Enugu.

These plans for the early resolution of conflict over nominations did not come to fruition. The N.E.C. meeting was delayed and when it did meet on 22 and 23 December it set up a special Elections Appeal Committee. Adegoke Adelabu was not at the meeting; as we saw in Chapter 10, he was by this time at loggerheads with the N.C.N.C., threatening to refuse the party whip in the House of Representatives. Nevertheless, he was made a member of the Appeal Committee, which was chaired by Benson, with Onabamiro as its secretary, and which also included Kola Balogun, Festus Okotie-Eboh and nine other Zonal Leaders. The new Committee was scheduled to meet in Ibadan on Saturday 21 January 1956, after a meeting

---

* The official estimate of potential electors in Ibadan Division would have put the total at rather less, about 391,000.

of the Western Working Committee, for which its members would in any case have to gather. Some hopeful prospective candidates did actually travel to Ibadan on that day, gathering at the District Council School Room at Mokola in the hope that their appeals would be heard. In fact, the hearing had already been cancelled and the nominating process became greatly prolonged. The N.C.N.C.'s hopes that the 'acrimony and misunderstanding' of previous elections could be avoided proved false. In such constituencies as Warri East, Asaba South and Egba East the dispute over N.C.N.C. nominations proved bitter and prolonged and the whole process dragged on, in some cases even into May.[40]

Similar disputes arose in Ibadan Division, despite the party's wish to establish selection committees, because Adelabu was determined to keep the choice firmly under his own control, as in previous elections. The situation had changed since 1954, however, when he incurred only the resentment of Oshilaja Oduyoye. Adelabu was able to maintain his control over the Mabolaje itself in 1956, working with such faithful lieutenants as Alfa Elesinmeta and Mogaji Akere. The N.C.N.C. half of the Grand Alliance, on the other hand, included men who had emerged to prominence in the party since 1954, who were much less likely to accept Adelabu's word uncritically, and who, in fact, had already strongly opposed him when he refused to resign the chairmanship of the Ibadan District Council. Aspiring candidates from this latter group were Onabamiro (anxious to contest in Ibadan South West or North West and seeking to balance the fact that he was not a native of the Division with his more than twenty years' residence and his building of a house there), and Fakayode, who led an appeal to the party when Adelabu released his list, which included Adelabu, L. Ade Bello and Mojid Agbaje, but not Fakayode or Onabamiro.[41]

In this embarrassing situation, representing a rift in the Ibadan Grand Alliance, the first attempt at a settlement came from Nnamdi Azikiwe; on 26 April he stopped at Ibadan on his way to Oshogbo for a meeting of the National Executive Committee preparatory to a pre-election Special Convention of the N.C.N.C. Although he arrived for the meeting two and a half hours late, he had not been able to secure an agreement and the N.E.C. therefore set up a committee to resolve the Ibadan nominations dispute with J. O. Fadahunsi as chairman and K. O. Mbadiwe, Festus Okotie-Eboh and Gogo Abbey as members. This committee directed Adelabu to submit a list of ten names, from among which with great tact the committee chose as the eight final nominations Adelabu's original list with only one change, the inclusion of E. O. Fakayode.[42] It was also agreed that the Ibadan candidates should be described simply as 'N.C.N.C.', not as 'N.C.N.C.–Mabolaje'. Even then, Adelabu apparently hoped to exercise personal control over the

Ibadan legislators, just as he had been able to do with the Ibadan Alliance
Councillors. He drafted an agreement, to be signed by all eight of them, that
they would deposit undated letters of resignation from the House of
Assembly with the mogajis and Elesinmeta, which would be used against
them if they either crossed to the Action Group or failed to 'join with the
[Grand Alliance] in preserving for Ibadan the leadership of the Western
Regional Government', or did not join the Alliance in restoring the prestige
of the mogajis and chiefs 'by securing an Olubadan of Ibadan who shall be
the choice of the Mogajis and people of Ibadan'.[43] It does not seem, however,
that Adelabu was able to enforce such an agreement upon his colleagues.

Adelabu was also rather curiously involved in a dispute over nominations
in Oshun Division. The N.C.N.C. Zonal Leader there, Kola Balogun, was
not particularly popular in his own area, Oshogbo District. In February 1956
the five most important officers of the N.C.N.C. branch there complained
about Balogun's part in the process of nomination to Adelabu and asked
him 'to use your offices in persuading this overambitious young man to stop
all the fuss and retrace his steps if actually he wished to claim any leadership
in Oshun'.[44] Adelabu took this invitation to intervene to the extent of supporting independent candidates against the official N.C.N.C. nominees in
Oshun West and Oshun Central and, in the latter case, the ultimate result of
this intervention was to split the N.C.N.C. votes sufficiently to let in the
Action Group candidate. It is rather difficult to understand Adelabu's
motives in thus interfering in another Leader's zone and in doing so in a
way which could only weaken the N.C.N.C. Admittedly, at this time his
disenchantment with that party was considerable and there may have been
in his actions an element of personal hostility towards Balogun because of
his involvement in Adelabu's loss of his federal Ministry. Whatever his
motives, the repercussions of his actions continued for some time after the
election. The committee headed by O. Bademosi, the Zonal Leader for Ondo,
which during June investigated the reasons for the N.C.N.C.'s defeat in the
election, took note of the complaint of the unsuccessful official candidate in
Ondo Central that his defeat had been caused by Adelabu's intervention and
Balogun's allegation that the Ibadan leader had trespassed into his Zone. The
final verdict of the Bademosi Committee on this incident was a judicious one
though hardly favourable to Adelabu: 'It is quite possible that an amicable
solution would have resulted but for the alleged patronage of Bello Adeyemo
and Layonu by Hon. Adegoke Adelabu. Cognizance must be taken of this
accusation.'[45]

The Action Group was also having trouble with its nominations. Two
Action Group regional Ministers, S. O. Awokoya (Education) and E. A.
Babalola (Works), found when the time came that their local parties were for

various reasons unwilling to re-adopt them. When the party executive refused to impose them on their localities, first Awokoya (on 21 April), then Babalola, resigned from the party, being joined by its Publicity Secretary, Oladipo Amos. Accusing Chief Awolowo of 'dictatorship', Awokoya seems to have flirted with the idea of joining the N.C.N.C., but then launched the new Nigerian People's Party. This nominated five candidates in the election, four of them in Ibadan, the other being Awokoya himself in Ijebu West; all five lost their deposits.

As the election approached, indeed before the date was even known, the problem for both parties became increasingly one of gearing up their organizational machinery for the most effective possible campaign. The Action Group, alarmed by the defeat it had suffered in the Western Region in the Federal Election of November 1954, had devoted considerable effort to refurbishing its organization. Throughout the West it had sought to use the establishment of new local councils as a means of recruiting influential men into the party by seeking out those who were elected as Councillors. The party's bureaucracy was given a new stimulus by the opening of the permanent party headquarters in Ibadan in June 1955, and particularly by the efforts of the Principal Organizing Secretary, S. T. Oredein, who spent some time in Britain during 1955 studying party organization there.

For the N.C.N.C. money was the perennial problem. Since 1954 that party and the Action Group had been able to use their increased control over regional governments and public boards to bolster their positions. Each had deposited public funds in banks which were affiliated to the party, and secured overdrafts for it, and each was able to use the prospects of patronage of various kinds (usually the granting of government contracts) to solicit donations from wealthy supporters.* Thus the Action Group was in a strong financial position in the West in 1956. The Western N.C.N.C., however, had no comparable resources and could not rely on substantial help from National Headquarters in Lagos, since the party's financial affairs were largely decentralized. At a meeting of the Western Working Committee held on 21 January, it was decided to spend £16,680 on the party organization in the region, over £15,000 of this being intended for the salaries of field staff, including eighty constituency secretaries at annual salaries of £120 each.[46] At the National Executive Committee meeting held before the Special Convention at Oshogbo on 26 and 27 April a report on 'Financial Policy' by Chief Okotie-Eboh, the party's National Treasurer, proposed an expenditure of £52,588 on the election (in addition to what the Western Working Committee had agreed on). The estimated income to balance this

---

* A more detailed discussion of the banking aspect of this trend, with particular reference to the East, will be found in the next chapter.

was only £12,700, including £8000 from the compulsory contributions which successful candidates for the party nominations were expected to pay. Although the party had spoken as early as the previous October of spending £50,000 on the election, it seems certain that it was not, in fact, able to meet the demands of Chief Okotie-Eboh's report, and that even then its election expenses substantially increased its debt to the African Continental Bank, controlled by Dr Azikiwe.* Complaints about the lack of party vehicles continued from the local branches, and there were disputes over the use of those that were available. Above all, the party continued to show its major source of organizational weakness, the absence of a permanent staff at the local level. Letters of appointment went out to the new Constituency Secretaries on 30 April, to take effect from the next day, but this left just over three weeks to polling day, during which period they were to get the measure of their constituencies (often very large, with poor communications) and in addition to organizing the election campaign were supposed to set up new village branches.[47]

In the absence of the advantages to be gained from a continuous organizational effort, beginning long before the actual election campaign was launched with the dissolution of the old House, the N.C.N.C. was forced to place its greatest emphasis upon hard campaigning by its leaders.

As Sanya Onabamiro made clear in a circular letter in mid-October 1955, it was intended that Adelabu should in effect be restricted in his campaigning to the area where he was most powerful and best known. The leading role was filled by the President of the N.C.N.C. himself, Dr Nnamdi Azikiwe, who in the second and third weeks of May 1956 held more than forty meetings in all parts of the Region.[48] His First Vice-President contented himself in the main with campaigning around Ibadan, with occasional forays elsewhere – to Ijebu Ode on 12 May, for instance, where the appearance of the Lion of the

---

* Some notion of the financing of N.C.N.C. branches at this time can be derived from two school note books in the Adelabu Papers, one labelled 'Espences [*sic*] Book', the other untitled, which enable us to put Chief Okotie-Eboh's plans into some sort of perspective. The first book lists contributions from various ward branches in Ibadan made on 13 March 1956, a total of £5. 2. 0d., along with 'Petty donations' of £1. 9. 0d. Interestingly, this is described as 'Cash with Mogaji'; it will be remembered that the mogajis had sought to act as custodians of funds at the inception of the I.T.P.A. (see p. 168). The only expenditure recorded in this book is 3s. 3d. for gasoline. The second book lists two individuals in ward SW 2 who had each given £2. 2. 0d. on an unspecified date, and a contribution of £2. 10. 0d. from SW 4 on 10 March, with 'Petty Contributions' totalling £5. 7. 0d. 'Repairs to van' had cost £7. 4. 6d., gasoline 10s. 0d., and 'Transport' (taxi fares?) 1s. 6d., leaving a balance of £4. 5. 0d. This sort of petty financing from local resources probably meant more to the party eventually than the larger sums irregularly doled out to Zonal Leaders by National Headquarters.

West (another nickname he had acquired) and his entourage sparked off fighting between N.C.N.C. and Action Group supporters.

This situation did not fail to arouse comment among Yoruba supporters of the N.C.N.C., more especially since the Action Group took as one of its main themes the fact that N.C.N.C. was really an 'Eastern' (indeed, Ibo) party whose only interest in winning the election in the West was in order to gain access to that Region's wealth, which it would then funnel off for use in the poorer East.[49] The presence of Dr Azikiwe and other Eastern N.C.N.C. leaders in the West during the campaign was held to prove this allegation and the argument had enough effect on the electors to alarm the N.C.N.C. In one of the memoranda submitted to the Bademosi Committee after the election it was observed that

...non-Yorubas accompanied our National President when conducting the Campaign meetings in the different parts of the Region. Crowd pullers like Adelabu, Fadahunsi at least ought to have accompanied the tourists. The impression of this mistake suggested in some circles that Ibos would in fact dominate the West if the N.C.N.C. won the election.[50]

Another, taking a rather different tack, gave as one reason for the party's defeat its failure 'to use Adelabu to tour the whole of the West to campaign and dispel all the propaganda about his character and behaviour commonly referred to in villages and hamlets where Daily Papers are not in circulation'.[51]

Despite the incident at Ijebu Ode and a few minor clashes elsewhere, the campaign was far less violent than might have been expected in a situation where the Action Group was trying to revenge its defeat in the federal election less than two years before, and the N.C.N.C. was hopeful of wresting the basis of its power away from the party which it sincerely believed had obtained it by fraud and bribery in 1951. In Ibadan itself the authorities feared widespread violence, a fear which seemed to be justified when, on 16 April, one of Penkelemesi's parades through the streets of Ibadan led to a street fight at Isale Ijebu, during which J. A. Akinlotan, once more the Action Group's Organizing Secretary for Ibadan, had his car damaged and was himself injured. When some of the suspected participants were taken to a police station for questioning a further fight broke out there. The police came to look for Adelabu at his house, but could not find him, and it was not until the 18th that they arrested him and charged him with assault and malicious damage. His release on bail by the Magistrate's Court allowed him to go on with the election campaign.

On 19 April the Olubadan and the Provincial Adviser, D. A. Murphy, called a meeting of local party leaders to discuss means of keeping the peace.

300

The Action Group delegation was led by Dr A. S. Agbaje, brother of Mojid and Chairman of the Ibadan branch of the governing party, and O. Agunbiade-Bamishe, the Party Manager; the N.C.N.C. group was led by D. K. Olumofin and E. O. Fakayode. Adegoke Adelabu did not attend: he was appearing in the Magistrate's Court. The political leaders agreed that the ban on political meetings in Ibadan should continue, that an attempt should be made to reduce the amount of drumming and dancing (often intended to be provocative to one's opponents), that bodyguards no longer be used while there were no meetings and their numbers controlled by the police after this, and that the 'Peace Declaration' of September 1954 be republished and observed.[52]

On 3 May the parties met again with the Provincial Adviser and Senior Divisional Adviser. Adegoke Adelabu was there, along with a number of his closest followers, and the Action Group delegation was led by A. M. A. Akinloye, himself a candidate for Ibadan North East. The peace having been kept since the last discussions, it was agreed that public campaign meetings could now be allowed, provided they ended before 6.00 p.m. Adelabu and Akinloye signed an agreement to that effect and in a broadcast version of this urged people not to carry 'sticks, stones or weapons of any kind'.[53] Thus the electoral proprieties had been observed, though the administrative officers and police continued to leave nothing to chance. The Acting Senior Superintendent of Police for Ibadan and Oyo Provinces made plans for the Local Government Police to tour the streets on election day, and for the Nigeria Police detachments to be kept as a reserve. A new sensitivity to politics seems apparent in the Senior Superintendent's circular:

Every effort must be made to avoid giving the impression that the police, especially the Nigeria Police Force, are biased in favour of any particular political party and to this end members of the Force should try to avoid carrying on conversation with any members of the public and leaders of political parties.[54]

The day after the second peace meeting the Action Group manifesto appeared, emphasizing, as is usual with the manifestoes of parties in power, what it claimed to have achieved and what – under twenty-one headings – it intended to achieve in the next five years. A week later the N.C.N.C. manifesto appeared, representing the party in power as hopelessly corrupt and inefficient, and listing, under fourteen headings, what it would achieve if given power.[55]

The last weeks of N.C.N.C.'s 'Operation 80' saw Adelabu more involved in party affairs than in previous months, and once more on the wrong side of the law. Following the incident at Ijebu Ode on 12 May, he was charged with disturbing the peace but, in the excitement of the campaign, it was not for some days that the police could find him to execute their warrant of arrest. During that time there were demonstrations in Ibadan against the issuing of the warrant and an appeal to the Governor who refused to intervene. Adelabu then surrendered himself to the police and, having been allowed bail, returned to the last week of the campaign. Already on bail following the Isale Ijebu affray on 16 April, he now had the prospect of yet another trial in front of him.

Thus it was that on Tuesday 22 May he began his party political broadcast on the Western Nigeria Broadcasting Service with the words, 'This is Adegoke Adelabu, first National Vice-President of the N.C.N.C., speaking to you from Ibadan. I am still hale, hearty, safe and secure. This gives the lie to Mr. Obafemi Awolowo's lying propaganda that I have been in hiding or arrested.' This broadcast was the last of the three allotted to the N.C.N.C., with a similar number for Action Group, Dr Azikiwe having spoken on 20 May, Chief Awolowo on the 21st, and S. L. Akintola followed Adelabu on the 23rd. His half-hour oration saw Adelabu back to his old form. Describing the Action Group as 'the Yoruba edition of the American Ku Klux Klan that wants to masquerade under the venerated generic terms of a political party', he waxed almost lyrical in his description of the 'four years Reign of Terror' into which he claimed it had thrown the Western Region.[56] Under these conditions, 'The farmer cannot go the daily round of his farm plot without returning with maimed limbs and splashes of clotted blood. The humble worker cannot go to his factory with any sense of security without becoming an ambulance passenger and a hospital casualty.' Under the rule of the Action Group:

Uniformed party brigades who are paid fabulous sustenance allowances have become a regular feature of party political warfare. The import of matchets has risen, not through any increase in the agricultural population but to replenish the stock of war implements stocked by a political party, and more iron rods now go to fashion fighting tools than into the building trade.

Accusing the Action Group of favoritism in such matters as the granting of government loans and scholarships, of investing over a million pounds of public funds in 'a private bank', and of forcing civil servants, judges and local government officials to toe the party line, he moved from an attack on the double standards which that party applied in local government, condoning all corruption in Action Group-controlled councils, to a general attack on the misrepresentations of Chief Awolowo and his party. Indignantly denying that the N.C.N.C. was dominated by the Ibos, he pointed out that its leadership was 'the most assorted heterogeneous and supra-tribal cadre of the Nigerian nation as it is in reality', and that if any group dominated it, it was the Yorubas. In actuality, what the N.C.N.C. was primarily concerned with was Nigerian unity, for 'a country is one big family'. Attacking the view that the wealth of the West should be used only for the benefit of the West, he pointed out that:

The Nigerian economy is an inter-dependent unity. We need northern man-power in case of war, eastern strategic materials like coal and oil in a balanced economy and the agricultural export crops and the talent of the West for an emergent Nigerian nation.

Somewhat paradoxically, he then settled down to a discussion of 'the Yoruba Chieftaincy System', since 'it is my duty as a full-blooded Yoruba of the Yorubas to educate the mongrels from the outlandish fringes of Yoruba-land'. Claiming that all Yorubas should venerate the Alafin of Oyo, as the direct descendant of Oduduwa, father of the Yoruba people, Adelabu attacked the Action Group for interfering with the traditional chieftaincy. 'Those of us who are Yoruba NCNCers', he pointed out, 'are more attached to the substance of Yoruba royalty than the strained beggars for Obas' political support who have turned them into brokers and Commission Agents. Our stand is that Obas, like Constitutional Monarchs, should be above party politics.' Only in this way could the 'traditional dignity and prestige of our Obas and Chiefs' be maintained.

In conclusion, he turned to 'the positive programme of the NCNC', which he treated in very general terms – 'rehabilitation, continued and even progress and the modernisation of our mainly agricultural economy'; the restoration of 'peace, order and tranquillity'; and the 'absolute guarantee of the fundamental human freedoms'. Adding a few more specific items, such as the diversification of export crops and the establishment of village and small-scale urban industries, he appealed

...to all voters of the Western Region, men and women, to follow the shining examples of the people of Ibadan, dethrone your oppressors the Action Group, and vote solidly and en masse for the party of the masses; the National Council of Nigeria and the Cameroons, NCNC.

While it would be idle to suppose that Adelabu's broadcast, or any of the others for either party, had a great effect on the way in which people finally voted, we can glean from his speech not only something of his own style and temperament, but also much of what the election campaign was about. This election was the first to test the Action Group's control of the Region since 1952, and the first to be fought on an almost universal adult suffrage. The Action Group had had more than four years in which to implement its reforms and eighteen months in which to consolidate its position, using the new powers given to the regions in 1954. The reforms, especially those concerned with local government, chieftaincy and courts, had brought about considerable changes in the structure of government of the region, and the consolidation of political power since the Federal Election of 1954 meant that the new institutions, and the rules under which they operated, were now probably irreversible. Adelabu had set himself the task of winning control of this apparatus from his old enemy Chief Awolowo so that never again could he be thwarted as he was over the dissolution of the Ibadan District Council. In so doing, he was calling on the Western electors to reject the Action Group on the grounds of its record in administering the region. He was also raising the wider issues of the relations between the regions and the center and of party to tribe, issues which were important even though this was a regional, not a federal, election. Just as Ibadan affairs could no longer be conducted without reference to regional questions, so these last years of colonial rule were calling into question the whole operation of the emerging political system in terms of the balance of power within the federation.

The N.C.N.C.'s major fear was that it might be 'cheated' in 1956 as it had been at the end of 1951 by 'carpet-crossing' to the Action Group on the part of men elected as N.C.N.C. candidates. A week before polling-day Sanya Onabamiro wrote a circular letter to all candidates, giving them detailed instructions on what to do on the day itself, and particularly what to do when elected:

As soon as the result is declared, if you win the seat, take a car or jump on any motor vehicle you can find and *come straight away to Ibadan where the National President, Dr the Hon. Nnamdi Azikiwe will be awaiting you to have an important consultation with all the successful N.C.N.C. Candidates.*

This is to be taken as a serious PARTY ORDER to you. If any NCNC Candidate wins the Election and does not come to present himself before the National President of the Party at Ibadan within 24 hours fears would be entertained concerning the loyalty and integrity of that Candidate. Remember that the N.C.N.C. won the Election in 1951 but we lost it again to the Action Group because disloyal members who won the Elections on the Platform of the Party allowed themselves to be bought over by the Action Group.[57]

On Saturday 26 May between the hours of 9.00 a.m. and 5.00 p.m., 1,291,174 people cast valid votes, some 68 per cent of the registered voters in 78 of the 80 constituencies. In Egba North and Ondo North-West the Action Group candidates had been returned unopposed on 14 May, when it was found that on a technicality the nominations of the N.C.N.C. candidates were invalid; naturally this greatly upset the N.C.N.C., though it is unlikely that they would in fact have won in either constituency. The first result was declared two and a half hours after polling ended, and by 5.00 p.m. on Sunday sixty-nine results were known. Already by about 1.00 p.m., however, it was known that the Action Group would have an overall majority, and when the last result was declared on the morning of 29 May (in some constituencies the ballot boxes had to be brought into the counting center by canoe or on the heads of porters) the Action Group had forty-eight seats and the N.C.N.C. thirty-two, the minor parties and Independents being completely unsuccessful. Action Group had gained 48.3 per cent of the votes, N.C.N.C. 45.3 per cent, S. O. Awokoya's new N.P.P. got only 0.2 per cent of the total vote, and other minor parties and Independents the rest. The British 'first past the post' system had shown its usual bias in terms of the relation between votes gained and seats won.

In the non-Yoruba constituencies of the Mid-West, the N.C.N.C. had fared extremely well, winning sixteen of the twenty, but they had won only sixteen of the sixty Yoruba constituencies. As can be seen in Table 6, seven of these were the gifts of the Grand Alliance in Ibadan. As in 1954, the Grand Alliance had cause to be well satisfied; it had won each seat convincingly and again taken nearly three-quarters of the total votes cast. A more massive intervention by minor parties and Independents had trebled their 1954 share of the poll, but it was still minute. The Action Group had made no progress whatsoever; indeed, their vote had dropped two per cent. A higher proportion of the electors had voted this time, nearly two-thirds compared with about one-sixth in 1954, but these newly-mobilized voters had not proportionately been attracted to the Grand Alliance in any significant numbers since 1954: its vote had increased by only one per cent, less than the gain by the minor parties and Independents, despite the chance to consolidate organizationally in the eighteen-month interval, and another election campaign. There is, indeed, no real indication that the Alliance, beset by the problems of its leader, had made much organizational effort since 1954. Ibadan's masses still remained to a large extent outside political participation, showing less readiness to register as electors than the rest of the Region, polling less heavily on election day, so that only about forty-six per cent of those who had registered actually turned out to vote for the Alliance.

Nevertheless, despite all these limitations, Ibadan was still squarely in the N.C.N.C. camp. Elsewhere in Yorubaland the party had won the two Ilesha seats, three of the five Oyo seats and one each in Egba, Egbado, Ondo and Ife Divisions. The eighth Ibadan Division seat, Ibadan West, which had never been within the Mabolaje orbit, was lost, and a number of prominent N.C.N.C. individuals fell by the wayside, the most important of them being T. O. S. Benson; D. K. Olumofin and A. Dahunsi were also defeated. From the point of view of individual defeats, however, the Action Group in its

TABLE 6 *Ibadan Regional Election Results, 1956, excluding Ibadan West (Ibarapa)*

	N.C.N.C.		A.G.		Others		Polling	
	Votes	(%)	Votes	(%)	Votes	(%)	Votes	(%)
Ibadan Central	11,828	79.3	2776	18.6	309[a]	2.1	14,913	70.9
Ibadan North West	13,728	73.8	4624	24.9	242	0.8	18,594	69.6
Ibadan North East	6625	61.8	3941	36.8	149	1.4	10,715	54.5
Ibadan East	12,713	70.4	4396	24.4	938	5.2	18,047	59.2
Ibadan South East	14,369	75.6	4428	23.3	205	1.1	19,002	56.7
Ibadan South	11,390	81.3	2449	17.5	168	1.2	14,007	56.5
Ibadan South West	8985	76.9	2694	23.1	–	–	11,679	61.0
Totals	79,638	74.5	25,308	23.7	2011	1.8	106,957	61.6

[a] Divided among three candidates.

turn had cause for dissatisfaction; four of its former Ministers (in addition to the N.P.P. dissidents) had been defeated. Most satisfying of all from Adelabu's point of view must have been his own victory in Ibadan South, with the highest percentage of all of the N.C.N.C. candidates, and the loss of his seat by A. M. A. Akinloye, soundly beaten by L. S. Salami, a young produce-buyer in Ibadan North East.*

Nevertheless, whatever individual satisfaction Adegoke Adelabu and the Western N.C.N.C. might have, the fact remained on Tuesday 29 May, with all the results now in, that Action Group had won the election and remained in control of the Region. For two days Adelabu had known that despite his personal faith in his destiny, he was not now to be Premier of the West. The fact that the N.C.N.C. had fared much better than in 1951, and that none of its thirty-two Members yielded to any temptation to cross to the winning side, was small comfort to him or to the party.

Of not much greater comfort to him, in the circumstances, was the dismissal by the Federal Supreme Court on that same day, 29 May, of Chief Akinbiyi's appeal for a reversal of the High Court decision of November 1955. Three British judges, presided over by the Chief Justice of the Federation, Sir Stafford Foster Sutton, heard the submissions of the various parties, with Dingle Foot again appearing for Adelabu. Their decision was that Akinbiyi in his personal capacity could not appeal the case, since in law the Regional Government, on whose behalf he served as a judge, was the 'person aggrieved'. Had the Inspector-General of Police brought the appeal it would have been a different matter.[58] Thus, by reason of a technicality, Adelabu was finally freed from the menace of one of his brushes with the law. L. Ade Bello was not so fortunate. His appeal against the decision of the High Court of the Western Region was dismissed, and his sentence of six months imprisonment confirmed. Elected a legislator only a few days before, he now disappeared behind prison bars.[59]

When the N.C.N.C. legislators gathered in Ibadan on 30 May – as Onabamiro had instructed – for their Parliamentary Party meeting with Dr Azikiwe, they were in a bitter mood. Adelabu had already set the tone for the meeting in a statement published in that morning's *Southern Nigeria Defender*. Alleging electoral fraud, rowdiness and undue influence by the Obas and Chiefs on behalf of the Action Group, he declared that that party should resign and hand over to the N.C.N.C., or else call a new election. At the meeting itself the National President took up the theme of a rigged election, making the allegation once again that constituencies had been

* The defeat of these four and the defection of Awokoya and Babalola left Chief Awolowo with only two of his former elected Ministers, Anthony Enahoro and Chief C. D. Akran, a fact which gave the N.C.N.C. some gloomy satisfaction.

gerrymandered, and also laying emphasis on the fact that Action Group had won less than fifty per cent of the total vote, and had taken few seats outside Yorubaland.[60] It was obvious that the N.C.N.C. was not prepared to accept the result of the election without a fight, and it was to fall to Adegoke Adelabu to lead it. At the meeting on 30 May he was selected to lead them in opposition by the N.C.N.C. Members of the House of Assembly, with J. O. Fadahunsi as Deputy Leader, J. E. Otobo (of Urhobo Division) as Secretary to the Parliamentary Party, Mojid Agbaje as Assistant Secretary, V. I. Amadasun (of Benin Division) as Chief Whip and E. O. Fakayode and Frank Oputa Otutu (from Aboh Division) as the other Whips. From now on Adelabu was to return to the role he had played in 1952–4 – a leader of the Opposition in the Western Region. Now, however, he was *the* leader, the defeat of T. O. S. Benson in particular leaving him unrivalled in the popular imagination. Foiled in his bid for control of the regional government, the Lion of the West had now to accustom himself to a very different role from that which he had imagined playing after 26 May.

It was a role which he did not relish. Opposition had no attraction for him. Only a position of power was worthwhile, to be able to sit in the Premier's Office at Agodi, the Ministerial buildings all around, their civil servants at his beck and call, his hands firmly upon the levers of power which could make themselves felt throughout the region – the local government councils, the customary courts, the various boards and corporations. From the end of May onwards, his thoughts were turned almost exclusively to one aim – dislodging the Action Group by any means possible and replacing it with his own party, putting himself in Obafemi Awolowo's place. The remainder of his life, rather less than two years, was to be devoted to this cause.

CHAPTER 12

ADELABU IN OPPOSITION

...whilst you have the ballot box, the school room, the legislative houses, the bench and the bar...you have got but faint shadows of tolerance, fair play, sense of justice, goodwill...It is, therefore, all the more necessary when any territory is clamouring loudly for self-detachment from Whitehall, on the basis of its inventory of visible political property, that a stock be taken of its spiritual endowment, which is the lubricant of democracy.

Adegoke Adelabu, December 1956

The Colonial Office is impervious to gentility and etiquette. There is only one language the Colonial Office speaks and understands. As a political party we must now speak in such a language and we shall be heard.

Nnamdi Azikiwe, July 1956

During the latter half of 1956 and the entire year of 1957, a three-cornered struggle took place in the West over the conditions under which self-government would be granted to that region as part of the foundation of emerging Nigerian independence. Of the three major interests involved, the Action Group triumphantly claimed to have had its mandate to rule renewed by the people and it sought further to entrench itself in power in the West, using it as a base for the extension of its influence into the East and North. The N.C.N.C., which controlled the East and was a partner of the Northern People's Congress in the Federal Government, sought the removal of its sworn enemy from the seat of power in the West at the earliest possible opportunity.

The position of Her Majesty's Government and the British administration in the Western Region was more complex. Until the granting of internal self-government to the Nigerian Regions, which was expected – at least for the East and West – at the forthcoming constitutional conference, the Governors of the Regions were to retain considerable power over the activities of their governments. They presided at meetings of the regional executive councils and took an active part in the formulation of policy and decisions. Moreover, they could reject the advice and veto the proposals of the regional Premiers and their Ministers. An active and interested Governor could, therefore, in effect control the conduct of government in the Region if he wished. On the other hand, it had been decided by the British Government in the late 1940s that its control was gradually to be withdrawn, and steps had been taken in the constitutions of 1951 and 1954 to initiate this process. Moreover, by mid-1956 another constitutional conference was planned for the near future. There is no reason to believe that Sir John Rankine, the Governor of the West, was in any way opposed to these developments. Indeed, his appointment in 1955 was a sign that the rapidly changing old order required changes in personnel. There is also reason to believe that he was very much committed to the view that the extension of full Nigerian control over the processes of government must be pushed forward, even if this meant a deterioration – in the eyes of some of his British subordinates – in administrative efficiency and honesty. He was accordingly unlikely to interfere with the Action Group Government unless he could be shown very good cause to do so. Yet to the N.C.N.C. he represented one of the last levers of power which their political rivals did not control and by appealing to his sense of the proprieties of the Westminster parliamentary system they hoped to use him as a weapon against the Action Group. The political struggles of the next months were consequently not merely those of nationalists against imperialists, but complex three-cornered affairs, with the Opposition N.C.N.C. attempting to push a liberalizing and withdrawing British Governor into siding with them rather than with the Government party into whose hands the Region's political power was rapidly falling.

The opening move was made at 11.00 a.m. on Saturday, 2 June 1956, when a delegation of five men waited upon Sir John Rankine, the Governor of the Western Region. Adegoke Adelabu, J. O. Fadahunsi, P. A. Afolabi, Mojid Agbaje and E. O. Fakayode had come to present a petition to the Governor, following up the meeting of the N.C.N.C. Western Parliamentary Party a few days earlier, which alleged such irregularities in the conduct of the recent election as the gerrymandering of constituencies, the disallowing of the two N.C.N.C. candidates, biased officials, the absence of police at polling stations to prevent intimidation of voters, and some eighteen anomalies in the process of voting itself. It also urged the Governor to 'exercise immediately' his 'discretionary powers as custodian of peace, law and order if the imminent danger to public tranquillity is to be averted'. Danger was to be found in the question of the exiled Alafin of Oyo, the current situation in the local government of Ibadan, and the 'hanging threat to the civil liberty of HER MAJESTY's subjects and their properties throughout the Western Region'.[1] The secession of the West from the Federation (rumored periodically as a possible move by the Action Group), the creation of new Mid-West and Central Yoruba States out of the Western Region, and the question of

310

regional or central control of the police and the judiciary were listed as three issues which, in view of the forthcoming constitutional conference, should be removed from 'the arena of public controversy'.

The latter part of the petition more specifically attacked the Action Group. It requested the consideration of direct rule by the British administration until the constitutional conference in September, either with or without a bi-partisan Caretaker Cabinet, if the Action Group failed to 'come to terms with the Opposition Political Parties backed by 52% of the electorate'. Furthermore, it asked for the appointment by the British Government of a Royal Commission of Inquiry to examine first, the 'general Administration of the Action Group Government during the past 4½ years', and second, the 'system adopted during the last regional Parliamentary Election with the constitutional implications arising therefrom whereby it might never be possible for any alternative parliamentary democratic government to emerge as distinct from the present party in power'. The document which the N.C.N.C. delegation presented to Sir John Rankine thus laid down the lines of attack which the Western Opposition was to develop in one form or another during the struggle of the next eighteen months.

For the moment, the Governor accepted this request for crisis politely, with the assurance that it would be given due consideration, while Adelabu and the other N.C.N.C. leaders continued other party business. On the 5th, the National Executive Committee meeting in Lagos appointed the members of the Bademosi Commission of Inquiry, some details of whose report we have already seen, 'To inquire into the failure of the NCNC at the recent election in the Western Region.' Between 11 and 22 June this Commission held forty-one interviews throughout the Region, in addition to accepting memoranda (including a long one from Sanya Onabamiro, just off to Britain on leave from the university). Adelabu appeared twice before the Commission, on 13 and 21 June, seeking as Zonal Leader to explain the party's defeat in Ibadan West, and also his interference in Kola Balogun's Oshun Zone.

On 18 June Adelabu scored a personal triumph, with the announcement of his acquittal by the High Court on the charges arising from the Nicholson Report, Dingle Foot, appearing for him yet again, argued that the politics of the witnesses so hopelessly tinged the evidence that there was no real hope of arriving at the truth, and the judge, bound by stricter rules of evidence than the Nicholson Inquiry, found accordingly. On the same day the case against Adelabu in connection with the Isale Ijebu affray was dropped. The Lion of the West took advantage of these victories to respond to a personal attack on him by the Action Group on the 12th, an attack which appeared to be based on knowledge that the Governor would not act on the N.C.N.C. petition of 2 June.

On 12 June, following discussion of the matter at a meeting of the Action Group Parliamentary Party ten days before, Chief Anthony Enahoro wrote a circular letter to N.C.N.C. Members of the House concerning their selection of Adelabu as Leader of the Opposition.[2] Enahoro, one of the few Action Group Mid-Westerners to be elected, had retained his portfolio as Minister of Home Affairs in Chief Awolowo's new government, and was also Leader of the House. A capable parliamentarian, whose pugnacity matched that of Adelabu, he was now making the first move in what was often to be a personal battle across the floor of the House.

While conceding to the Opposition the right to choose its own leader, Enahoro argued that the Government must also concern itself, in order to preserve the good name of the legislature, 'lest on the eve of self-government, the impression were unfortunately to be given to the outside world that freedom, when granted, would result in a deplorable lowering of moral standards in the public life of this region'. Enahoro went on to point out that the position of Leader of the Opposition was in fact that of an alternative Premier, and therefore 'I hope you will agree that it would be palpably wrong for an Opposition to select as its Leader in the Legislature someone whose character and morals might be called in question and whose public life was not a shining example of moral probity.' If the Opposition did make such a selection, the Government was not bound to acquiesce, and in this case it would have to take account of the Nicholson Report and the Akinbiyi affair. He described Dennis Osadebay, the former Opposition Leader, as 'a trusted and respected member, with whom I and my colleagues did not find it difficult to co-operate'. In this light,

I would respectfully invite you, therefore, to reconsider the appointment of Mr. Adelabu as Leader of the Opposition, preferably before the first meeting of the new Legislature. I would like to add, with much regret, that if you were to find it impossible to reconsider your previous decision, I on my part could not undertake, as Leader of the House, to advise Government and the Government Party to accord the Leader of the Opposition, as hitherto, the recognition and co-operation generally due to him.

Adelabu was clearly stung. Blaming his legal problems on the Action Group, he publicly declared,

At the age of 42, the dastardly attempt to ruin my political career by the godless party that has imposed itself through treachery and fraud on the people of the Western Region has failed.

I am saved to contribute my humble quota towards the progress of my beloved country.[3]

Nevertheless, he went on,

It is a matter for great regret that with the just, fair, and tolerant British still among us wielding the substance of political power, persecution and oppression characteristic of the dark ages of despotism are still allowed to hold sway unchecked in this transitional era from colonialism to self-government.

With the first meeting of the new House of Assembly scheduled for Monday, 2 July, the N.C.N.C. Parliamentary Party met on 30 June and 1 July to discuss the heavy-handed attempt by the Action Group to influence its choice of leaders. It was in a somewhat edgy mood that the N.C.N.C. gathered on the Opposition benches of the House of Assembly on the morning of the 2nd. Crowds of N.C.N.C. supporters had gathered outside, brought out perhaps by a rumor that as many as sixteen Action Group Members were going to defect to the N.C.N.C. They cheered their own leaders, jeered at the Action Group, and even mocked some of the chiefs, gathering for a meeting of their House, before being dispersed by the police.

Once convened, the Assembly elected as Speaker the sole candidate, R. A. Doherty, a respected lawyer who had been Speaker of the last House, and who, contrary to British practice, was not an elected Member of that or of the new one. As Leader of the N.C.N.C., Adelabu pronounced Doherty acceptable to them, but complained of not having been consulted about his candidature. Enahoro, adopting an attitude similar to his views on the leadership of the Opposition, denied the N.C.N.C. had any right to be consulted on this matter, and Doherty was elected unanimously without a division of the House. In view of what had seemed to the N.C.N.C. to be very dubious behavior in January 1952 and his subsequent defection to the Action Group, it was rather more surprising that Adeleke Adedoyin, who had been elected in Remo South, was unanimously chosen as Deputy Speaker.

The next three days were marked only by small thrusts and parries. On the 3rd, J. O. Fadahunsi refused to serve on the Committee of Selection, because the N.C.N.C. had not been consulted on its membership and Adelabu absented himself from the House and ignored an invitation to lunch with Chief Awolowo, which Dennis Osadebay accepted. On the 4th, during the debate on the Speech from the Throne, Opposition Members complained about several matters (the proposed Mid-West State, the allocation of seats between Divisions and partisan electoral officers, and elections to the Ibadan District Council) not immediately germane to the debate but very much in the thoughts of the N.C.N.C. leaders.

On Friday 6 July, the first real conflict came when Adelabu seconded a motion by P. A. Afolabi, the Member for Oyo East and staunch defender of the exiled Alafin, 'That the Western Regional Government do refrain from employing threats, intimidation and victimisation in their dealings with

313

people and organisations who do not support the Action Group Party.'[4] In contrast, Afolabi urged, 'During the past eighty years, Great Britain has set us a model of good, democratic and Christian Government.'

Taking victimization as his main theme, Adelabu seconded the motion in a speech claiming that members of the police, laborers working for various Action Group-controlled local councils, and even expatriate administrators had been persecuted because of their N.C.N.C. sympathies. Finally he revealed the purpose of the Opposition motion of that morning. 'We, the thirty-two members of the NCNC Opposition...in order to clear our good name' of complicity in regard to the 'cruel, wicked, inhuman, heartless, callous, abominable and brutal treatment' given to the Alafin of Oyo, the Mid-West state, Ibadan local government and in being a minority party with a majority of the popular vote, would 'forthwith cease co-operation with the Action Group government by non-participation in the debates in this honorable House until these four problems are resolved according to accepted democratic principles'.[5] The Speaker having put Afolabi's motion to the House, the Opposition walked out of the chamber.

The N.C.N.C.'s second attempt to force a crisis in the Western Region was less an appeal to those present at the debate than to the British Government, an appeal repeated on 7 July in a telegram to the Secretary of State for the Colonies in Westminster, Alan Lennox-Boyd, repeating the four questions and the terms of Adelabu's peroration. Pressure was also brought through Fenner Brockway, a Member of Parliament long known for his championship of colonial peoples, who on 19 July wrote to the Secretary of State, seeking his intervention at the request of P. A. Afolabi on behalf of the Alafin.

On the morning of 6 July after the N.C.N.C. walk-out, the Action Group Members were left with the chamber to themselves and they made the most of the opportunity to abuse the Opposition and its Leader. Afolabi's motion, with due regard for parliamentary procedure, was rejected and the Minister of Justice and Local Government announced that that very day an order of deposition was being served on the Alafin. His banning from his former kingdom would also remain in force. With this demonstration of the Government's strength of purpose, the House adjourned *sine die* at 12.20 p.m.

The N.C.N.C. could now only hope for some positive British reaction to their move. On 13 July they requested the Governor to grant them an interview. Two weeks later they received an answer which was cool, although constitutionally correct. Writing on behalf of the Governor, the Acting Deputy Governor informed them that the most appropriate place to raise these matters was in the House of Assembly. Moreover, he understood that the Opposition had made no attempt to approach the individual Ministers concerned. 'In the circumstances,' the letter concluded, 'since the normal constitutional methods for the ventilation of such matters remain unused, His Excellency considers that no useful purpose would be served by granting the interview requested.'[6]

Another door was closed when the Secretary of State, on 30 July, wrote to Brockway that the case of the ex-Alafin 'is a matter for the Western Region Government and I take the view, with which I think you may agree, that it would not be right by reason of the stage of constitutional development reached in the Western Region, for me to intervene'.[7] The N.C.N.C. had to wait three months for its own reply, which then came through the Governor of the Western Region and not directly from Westminster. On 8 October the Deputy Governor wrote to Adelabu to inform him that such communications should not be sent directly to the Secretary of State, but should be forwarded in triplicate through the Governor. The Secretary of State had consulted the Governor about this matter, 'but in view of the fact that you have failed to make proper use of the constitutional means at your disposal for the ventilation of your grievances he sees no reason to intervene'.[8] As if the question were merely a procedural one Adelabu now sent the same telegram in triplicate to the Governor for transmission to Lennox-Boyd and again received only a dusty answer from the Deputy Governor: 'Since the Secretary of State has already replied to your communication, no useful purpose would appear to be served by repeating it.'[9] Thus the Western N.C.N.C.'s first major onslaught on the Action Group Government petered out in face of the British administration's unwillingness to respond. Adelabu and his colleagues found themselves in the extremely frustrating situation of being involved in a process of decolonization which they desired, but which included the handing-over of political power to their arch-enemies. In these circumstances, their view of the decolonization process began to be modified. As P. A. Afolabi put it in a letter to Fenner Brockway, 'The constitutional development in the Western Region to which the [Secretary of State] referred [in his letter of 30 July] cannot and must not be allowed to take precedence of, or trample under foot, British sense of justice, equity and fairplay!'[10]

Between the Opposition walk-out from the Assembly on 6 July, however, and the Governor's final answer more than three months later, an issue had arisen which called into question the whole N.C.N.C. strategy of attempting to use the British administration as a lever against the Action Group. In addition to failing to respond to N.C.N.C. pleas, the British had ordered a probe into the affairs of the African Continental Bank, Dr Azikiwe's creation and the financial mainstay of the N.C.N.C. From ignoring the party, they now appeared to be passing to a positive attack upon it. In order to understand more fully what was happening, it is necessary to look at certain events which had occurred in the period 1954–6.

In Chapter 9 we saw that the constitution of 1 October 1954 had altered the economic structure of the Federation by increasing the allocation of revenue to the Regions and establishing regional marketing boards to replace central ones. With the N.C.N.C. and Action Group in control of the regional governments of the East and West respectively, both parties began to use their control of regional finances to strengthen the position of their associated banks. Thus in December 1954 the N.C.N.C. Government of the Eastern Region deposited some of its funds in the African Continental Bank, and in March 1955 the Action Group Government deposited Western Region funds in the National Bank. Even more decisive was the direct Government investment in these banks, the Eastern Region Finance Corporation deciding to invest £877,000 in the African Continental Bank on 20 May 1955 (a crucial date, as we shall see) and the Government of the West investing £1,000,000 in the National Bank in October.[11]

The main justification for such actions was that the regional governments were thus supporting indigenous banks, which had always found it difficult to compete with the greater financial reserves of the foreign-owned banks, particularly the Bank of British West Africa and Barclays D.C.O. Moreover, the expatriate banks had always been notoriously reluctant to grant credit to Nigerian businessmen.[12] This argument had been endorsed in the report of a mission from the International Bank for Reconstruction and Development in September 1954, which, however, also stated that 'On the basis of its observation of the Nigerian political scene the mission fears that decisions regarding transfers of government deposits to African commercial banks would not always be free from party-political motives.'[13]

Concern with corruption in the East became official in August 1955 when Dr Azikiwe, as Premier of the Region, was instrumental in establishing an inquiry into corruption in public life, headed by Chuba Ikpeazu, an Ibo lawyer from Onitsha. As we have seen, the most prominent individual to become involved in this inquiry was none other than Mbonu Ojike, Adegoke Adelabu's colleague as Vice-President of the N.C.N.C., and Finance Minister of the Eastern Region. What would in any case have been a difficult situation was made worse by the fact that the issue was linked with the struggle between the natives of Onitsha and settlers from other parts of Iboland for control of the local government of that town, a struggle which had already caused serious internal disputes in the Eastern N.C.N.C.[14] On 19 January 1956, after casting the deciding vote on his own commission, Ikpeazu publicly declared Ojike to be guilty of the corrupt practices of which he was accused. On the 21st, Nnamdi Azikiwe requested the resignation from his

Ministry of his chief lieutenant in the East. (Seven days later he endorsed the resignation from his federal Ministry of his chief lieutenant in the West, with results which we have already seen.)

For Nnamdi Azikiwe this was one of the crises of his career. Judged by the proprieties of British public life, he had acted quite correctly. Judged by the standards of his (and Ojike's) nationalist past, and of their personal friendship, the verdict of some members of the N.C.N.C. was less favorable. E. O. Eyo, an Ibibio who had been one of Dr Azikiwe's staunchest supporters in the crisis of 1952–3, and who in January 1956 was Government Chief Whip in the Eastern House of Assembly and Chairman of the Eastern Region Development Corporation, was one of those upset by this incident. What finally prompted Eyo's action is not completely certain, but it seems that attacks on him from various quarters in the N.C.N.C. – in evidence given before the Ikpeazu Commission, for example – made him feel that he was not being given enough support by his party's President. In April 1956 he accordingly asked to be relieved of his two offices and then filed a motion for the current session of the Eastern House of Assembly which accused Nnamdi Azikiwe of grave impropriety in sanctioning the investment of government money in the African Continental Bank, of which he was the founder and principal shareholder. Eyo subsequently amended this motion to include a demand for a commission of inquiry into this matter.

The motion was never debated, the Speaker of the Eastern House ruling it *sub judice* because of a libel suit which Dr Azikiwe initiated against Eyo, but the mere allegation was enough to provoke a crisis. The N.C.N.C. was placed in a most embarrassing position. First, it had to fight the Western election campaign under the shadow of the allegation. Even more important was the reaction of the British Government. We have already seen that at this period the Colonial Office was still closely involved, through the Regional Governors, with the day-to-day administration of affairs in Enugu, Ibadan and Kaduna since the regions were not yet internally self-governing. The Secretary of State for the Colonies had, therefore, to take a stand on Eyo's allegations. His choice was, on the surface, a simple one. By refraining from intervention, he could leave the position of Azikiwe and the N.C.N.C. unthreatened and prevent a serious deterioration of relations between the colonial administration and one of the major Nigerian political parties. However, this would have meant a public, though tacit, acceptance of the view held by many senior British officials that the standards of public morality and integrity demanded in the government and administration of the United Kingdom could not be expected in Nigeria.

The British Government, however, had been committed publicly to the view that the conventions as well as the institutions of parliamentary government could be set up in Nigeria since December 1951, when the Secretary of State (then James Griffiths), with ministerial positions being created for the first time in Nigeria, sent out a circular laying down the rules of ministerial conduct with regard to the matter of conflict of interests which was now raised in the case of Nnamdi Azikiwe.[15] While in London in November 1955, the Eastern Premier had assured Lennox-Boyd that he no longer had any direct connection with the African Continental Bank, and that he had no prior knowledge of the terms of the investment agreement of 20 May between the Finance Corporation and the African Continental Bank. The fact still remained that with 28,000 ordinary shares he was the biggest individual shareholder in the Bank and that as a result of the investment of Government money in the Bank the value of each share had risen in effect from nothing to 14s. 10d.[16] Most important of all, perhaps, was the fact that the agreement of 20 May was signed only two days before the expiration of the three-year period set by the Banking Ordinance of 1952, during which banks in Nigeria had to qualify for licensing by ensuring that their cash holdings were not less than thirty per cent of their customers' deposits. Before the agreement to invest the Eastern Region Finance Corporation's £877,000 the African Continental Bank's liquidity ratio had been only about eight per cent, and without this investment it would have failed to qualify for a license and been closed. These facts led Lennox-Boyd on 24 July 1956 to announce in the House of Commons that a public inquiry into E. O. Eyo's allegations would be held, and that in consequence the expected constitutional conference would not after all be held that year.

In July 1956 Adelabu and the Western N.C.N.C. Parliamentary Party, embroiled in their first major attempt to induce the Colonial Office to intervene on their side against the Action Group Government of the West, with their own party apparently under attack by the British Government because of its conduct of affairs in the Eastern Region, saw this as nothing less than a hypocritical attempt by the British Government, probably in collusion with the British banks which had interests in Nigeria, to destroy indigenous Nigerian banking and delay the constitutional progress of Nigeria toward independence. Much was made by the N.C.N.C. of the fact, for example, that on his retirement from the Colonial Service Lord Milverton, who as Sir Arthur Richards had been Governor of Nigeria from 1943 to 1948, had become a director of the Bank of British West Africa.[17] There can be little doubt that there were expatriates in prominent positions, both in business and the administration, who would have been glad to see the N.C.N.C. and Dr Azikiwe in particular publicly humiliated and politically weakened. At present there is no evidence available which would enable us to judge

318

whether or not the motives of the British Government went beyond its desire to impose a particular set of standards on the Nigerian political system at a particular stage in its development. Nevertheless, at the very least the Colonial Office created an unfortunate impression of partiality in the minds of N.C.N.C. supporters by its blank refusal to listen to any of that party's complaints about the Action Group Government of the West, strident though they may have been, and by its apparent eagerness to pillory Nnamdi Azikiwe.*

On Thursday, 26 July, the National Executive Committee of the N.C.N.C. met at Onitsha. Dr Azikiwe and those members who were Eastern Ministers were at a meeting of the Government's Executive Council considering Lennox-Boyd's announcement in the House of Commons of two days before, but Adelabu, Ojike, Balogun, Osadebay, Fadahunsi, Benson and Mbadiwe and two other federal Ministers, Raymond Njoku and Aja Nwachuku, were present. In the absence of Dr Azikiwe the chair was taken by Adegoke Adelabu during the morning session. The discussion naturally centred on the African Continental Bank crisis. On 16 June Dr Azikiwe had announced that he was contemplating resignation from the Office of Premier of the East, declaring that 'I am not prepared to take dictation from the Governor or from the Secretary of State for the Colonies.'[18] In his absence and that of the other Eastern Ministers at this meeting, however, it was now decided that he and the other Eastern Ministers should not resign but should submit themselves to the inquiry into the relations between their government and the bank. Adelabu also reminded the audience that the N.E.C. 'was the N.C.N.C. policy-making body who must resolve all issues and solve all problems confronting the party'.[19]

Thus some of the leaders of the party, including those from the West, were avoiding a militantly nationalistic line for one which might by precedent constrain the British to institute a similar inquiry in the West. The other party concerns of Oyo, the Mid-West State (which it was agreed must be considered before the West became self-governing) and the walk-out from the Western House, which the Western representatives now promised was

---

* P. A. Afolabi pointed out in the course of a petition on the Ex-Alafin drafted in August, commenting on Lennox-Boyd's answer to Fenner Brockway that the Governor-General had no jurisdiction in this matter: 'If we are to accept this doctrine in the devolution of power dictated by the 1954 Constitution we would be doing ourselves more harm than good by accepting an interpretation of our Constitution which will surely militate against Your Lordship's [*sic*] recent action against the Prime Minister of the Eastern Region by the appointment by you of a Commission of Enquiry.' ('Petition to the Secretary of State for the Colonies Through His Excellency the Governor-General of Nigeria on Oba Hadji Adeniran Adeyemi II, C.M.G., the Alafin of Oyo [now in exile]', typescript, 31 August 1956, p. 3, A.P.)

not intended to be permanent, were also discussed before the noon adjournment.

That afternoon, Mbonu Ojike, who remained active as a vice-president of the party although he had resigned from his ministry on Dr Azikiwe's instructions, chaired a session at which a statement on the Bank crisis was approved and a special committee was created under Benson's chairmanship to review the case of the Alafin.* On the following day, the party met at the Broadway Cinema in a Special Convention, the second general assembly of the party in four months, which perhaps accounts for the low attendance.† A motion was passed supporting the relatively cautious stand of the N.E.C. on Dr Azikiwe's resignation and submission to an inquiry, but with rank-and-file members of the party present, the meeting took a rather more militant turn than the previous day's N.E.C. sessions. Adegoke Adelabu in his brief speech as chairman of the meeting, called for moral and financial support for the leadership of the party and described the crisis as 'a British device to delay our political and economic independence'.[20] The National President also delivered 'an impressive laudable and soul-stirring address' entitled 'We are Passing through the Crucible'. Weeping, he declared that:

I am no longer prepared to drift with the wind of a political party on an uncharted sea of politics. Our great party must sail against the wind or surrender the mantle of national guidance to a more virile and militant political party. The Colonial Office is impervious to gentility and etiquette. There is only one language the Colonial Office speaks and understands. As a political party we must now speak in such a language and we shall be heard.[21]

A motion was then carried calling for a boycott of Sir Clement Pleass, the Governor of the Eastern Region, and of the Bank of British West Africa by all N.C.N.C. supporters. Also passed was a motion proposed by the party's Principal Organizing Secretary in the Northern Region which attacked Sir Clement and his Attorney-General for their 'non-co-operative attitude towards the elected Government of the eight million people of the Eastern Region'.‡ It also demanded that the British Government recall these two officials and urged the party's regional and federal Ministers and members to adopt an attitude of 'non-fraternization and non-co-operation' with the two officials until they were recalled. Finally, Dr Ikejiani's motion to expel E. O. Eyo from the party for life 'and with ignominy' was accepted.

* Ojike was not to serve the party for much longer, as he died on 28 November 1956.
† In particular there were few delegates from the West, although the Ibadan N.C.N.C. Youth Association was represented, along with branches in Asaba and Benin Divisions.
‡ The Eastern N.C.N.C. had already clashed with Sir Clement Pleass in April 1955, the basic issue being who had ultimate control over the conditions of service of expatriate officials.

The Convention then heard the report from the committee dealing with the ex-Alafin, which recommended the immediate reference of his deposition to the party lawyers, the investigation by the N.C.N.C. federal Ministers of the possibility of a federal commission of inquiry into the affair (commissions of inquiry being on the concurrent legislative list), and the establishment of yet another special committee on the Alafin issue 'in order to obviate isolated efforts'. Finally it was decided to contact British Members of Parliament in order to prepare the ground for the discussion of various Western issues at the constitutional conference when it finally was held.

On his return to Ibadan, having found Sir John Rankine's refusal of an interview waiting for him, Adelabu continued throughout August to give his main attention to the commission of inquiry into the African Continental Bank, the appointment of the members of which was announced on 4 August. He was spurred on by Obafemi Awolowo, who on 19 August issued a statement in which he gave an account of the relations between the National Bank and the Western Region Government, stressing the fact that neither he nor any of his Ministers was a shareholder in the Bank, and that it was operated as a business concern, not for political purposes.[22] Declaring himself and his party to be 'neutral' in the struggle between the Colonial Office and the N.C.N.C., he nevertheless decried the irrationality of the party's 'Zikism' and spoke of the need to avoid any action which might jeopardize the granting of regional self-government at the next constitutional conference. The latter part of his statement listed the misdoings of Dr Azikiwe and his lieutenants, among them Adegoke Adelabu, who thus found the Nicholson Report once again thrown in his face.

Adelabu replied to this with characteristic vigor in a release entitled 'Awolowo – Greatest Saboteur of Nigerian Nationalism'.[23] He dismissed with scorn Awolowo's account of his own relations with the National Bank, pointing out that even if the Action Group leader had never had an overdraft from the Bank,

. . .he has failed to tell us whether the same can be said of his Parliamentary Secretaries, party branch and party-controlled Council Chairmen, party Newspaper establishments, the numerous army of contractors, importers, exporters, transporters, Insurance Houses, industrial concerns and dubious publicity practitioners who form the backbone of the party and contribute so compulsorily generously towards the party endowment funds.

Similarly, he went on, with its claim to be 'neutral' in the present struggle

The Action Group is an opportunistic mushroom political party owing its emergence to the treacherous propensities of tribal regionalists in league with tenacious British imperialism and its avowed and unabashed policy of 'divide and rule'.

Awolowo's attack on Adelabu himself also provoked an indignant reply from 'a victim of Action Group intolerance and persecutions whose probity has been attested by the Highest Court set up by his own government', along with a threat to 'seek remedy at law for this gruesome libel'.

Finally Adelabu came to the point that had been on his mind since the meeting in Onitsha which he had chaired in Azikiwe's absence. Citing the relations among the Regional Government, the National Bank, the Action Group and the Amalgamated Press, and pointing out that the N.C.N.C. had accepted the need for a commission of inquiry, he urged that now the Action Group should do the same. Adelabu had learned, however, through the failure of the N.C.N.C motion in the Western House of Assembly, the walk-out and the approaches to the Governor and the Secretary of State, that the Action Group would not submit itself and its supporting institutions voluntarily to an inquiry, and that a massive case would have to be made to persuade the British Government to initiate one. He now undertook to make such a case, just as the hearings of the Tribunal on the African Continental Bank were beginning under the chairmanship of Sir Stafford Foster-Sutton, the Chief Justice of the Federation.

He took time, however, to keep alive the running attack he maintained against the Ibadan Provisional Council. The *Defender* was indeed acting as a watchdog generally over the new Council's activities.

The Ibadan Provisional District Council...has been most indolent and like its Godfather, the AG, very intolerant and unco-operative. As a result of this unpardonable attitude of the nominated council the town looks awfully neglected, dirty and untidy. The Councillors apparently interested only in sacking Akodas and demolishing market stalls built by NCNC members and supporters, had no time for the welfare of Ibadan as a town.[24]

Late in August Adelabu convened the N.C.N.C. Ibadan Members of the House of Assembly to urge the Minister to make the duration of the Provisional Council a short one so that the Local Government Law could be applied equally in all parts of the Region.

On 14 September Adelabu called together virtually the same group of men for a meeting of the N.C.N.C. Parliamentary Party in the N.C.N.C. headquarters at Mokola. Only ten of the thirty-two N.C.N.C. Members attended, half of them being from Ibadan. No meeting of the House was scheduled so that few Members were in Ibadan and it appears that the party meeting was called on short notice. L. Ade Bello, of course, was still in prison. Adebayo Asaya, the Principal Organizing Secretary for the party in the West was present. No one raised the question of a quorum, and Adelabu, arriving an hour late, turned their rather desultory discussion in a more vital direction.

Addressing the meeting on the boycott of the House of Assembly, he raised the question of the desirability of its continuation, in view of possible changes in circumstances.[25] Mojid Agbaje, no doubt by pre-arrangement, then suggested putting a motion before the House calling for a commission of inquiry into the affairs of the Western Region Government.* Adelabu pointed out that the Government would probably wish to avoid calling a meeting of the House before the constitutional conference, which he apparently thought would be only slightly delayed by the Foster-Sutton Tribunal, and that therefore pressure would be required to force a meeting to debate a Private Member's Motion from the Opposition. Three things he thought must be brought to light – the 'Administrative Atrocity of the Action Group Western Region Government', the 'Scandal in the Financial Policy of Western Government' (primarily the investment of government funds in the National Bank), and 'Wide scale practice of Bribery and corruptions'. All this was agreed to, and a committee made up of Agbaje and two absent Members, E. O. Fakayode and Babatunji Olowofoyeku, was instructed to draw up a motion. A 'Fact Finding Committee' to collect information for use in the debate was also to be established.

The meeting also discussed replacing Adelabu in the Federal House of Representatives and in his Ministry, which had not yet been given to anyone else, and the matter of his salary as Leader of the Opposition. True to the threat of non-recognition made in Anthony Enahoro's letter of 12 June, and because he had in fact boycotted legislative meetings, Government had withheld his monthly salary of £140. The Secretary of the N.C.N.C. Parliamentary Party was now instructed to write officially to the Clerk of the House seeking an explanation.

On 18 September a new file, number NC/WR/298, was opened at party headquarters, with the title 'Royal Commission of Enquiry'.† On the 19th a circular letter was sent out to Zonal Leaders, N.C.N.C. federal and regional legislators and members of the Western Working Committee, informing them of the decision taken on the 14th and asking them to act as agents for the gathering of material which might be used in making a case against the Action Group government.

While waiting for a response to this letter, Adelabu celebrated the sort of victory over his enemies which he enjoyed most. L. Ade Bello had been released early on good behavior from the Lagos prison and on 23 September he

* This tactic had been used before, in December 1955, after Adelabu had gone to the center, when D. K. Olumofin had proposed a motion calling for a commission to investigate allegations of bribery and corruption in the political life of the West. On that occasion the Action Group majority had ensured its defeat.

† Adelabu took personal possession of this file, and it was found in his personal papers.

returned to Ibadan. The *Defender*, with understandable enthusiasm, reported that 200,000 N.C.N.C. supporters led him from Moor Plantation at the edge of the city to his home behind the slaughter slab at Oranyan. Traffic was disrupted for two hours as he and Adelabu, mounted on white horses, paraded through the city to show the Government that even imprisonment could not suppress them.[26] The next day, these two, with Alimi Adesokan, Adebayo Adeyinka, Yesufu Mogbonjubola and Abdulahi Elesinmeta, marched to the office of the Senior Divisional Adviser (with 'several hundred supporters' according to him) demanding an interview with the Deputy Governor to request a new election. Although the *Defender* claimed 50,000 had joined them to sit quietly on the grass outside the office while Adelabu made a seven point presentation inside, Akinpelu Obisesan estimated the crowd at 500. This was serious enough in itself. Obisesan feared 'that things politically will become topsy turvy' and the police took precautions against such an intimidating force. There was no doubt that even a deposed Adelabu could command a considerable response in Ibadan.[27]

The circular letter of 19 September in fact received only one direct response, which spoke vaguely of 'nepotism' and 'organized corruption' in the writers' Action Group-controlled local council.[28] Another information-gathering device was a rather mysterious body known as the 'Investigation Bureau', initially set up with loans of £5 each from Adegoke Adelabu and an N.C.N.C. supporter from Oyo and apparently under the direction of Adebayo Asaya.[29] It seems to have contacted a person who was able to supply the party with copies of items from the confidential files of the Western Region Production Development Board. Adelabu also received an undated and unsigned letter from someone in Idi Oro, Lagos, claiming to be employed in the Accounts Branch of the National Bank, who asserted that 'Chief Awo received £500 per Annum as Director of Amalgamated Press Ltd.' and that 'his account was credited with £60,000 for his successful bringing £2,000,000' to the National Bank.[30] The writer promised to give the exact details of the relevant ledger entries later. The Investigation Bureau apparently followed up this letter, since its statement of account contained an item of £3. 10. 0d. for 'Investigations' at the Idi Oro address, but their informant presumably either got cold feet or was unable to produce the documents, since no evidence for either of these allegations was ever produced, nor indeed was the second and most damaging of them ultimately even made by the N.C.N.C.

The most interesting response to the letter of 19 September was not to the request for information, which met with virtually no success, but a questioning of the method of investigation itself. On 26 October Nnamdi Azikiwe, doubtless very mindful that he was about to give evidence before the Foster-

Sutton Commission, wrote to Adebayo Asaya urging caution. The channel of communication between the National President of the N.C.N.C. and its Western Wing is in itself revealing. Azikiwe had not been consulted in advance about Adelabu's plans; the initiative had come purely from the Lion of the West, who viewed his section of the N.C.N.C. as completely free to launch such a campaign, although, coming on top of the inquiry into the African Continental Bank, it would necessarily involve the whole party in a bitter battle with the Action Group and complicate the delicate relations with the British Government. Moreover, Adelabu had not even seen fit to write a personal letter to his National President explaining the action being taken, leaving it to the Regional Principal Organizing Secretary to send Azikiwe a copy of the ordinary circular letter. Now the National President replied in like form, writing not in personal terms to Adelabu, but formally to Asaya.[31]

He made his intention plain from the beginning of the letter. He would 'bear in mind' the request for data, 'but may I respectfully call your attention to the need for absolute accuracy in whatever allegations you may be disposed to make against the Government of the Western Region'. Dr Azikiwe then ran through the main items which it was proposed to raise. Administrative appointments in the Civil Service were made by the Governor on the advice of the Public Service Commission – 'So long as you bear this in mind then you will be safe.' He reminded Asaya that the Western Government in fact had the statutory power to depose Obas and Chiefs so that it could only be attacked if it had done something 'extraneous to the spirit and letter of the law'. The investigators would be 'well-advised' to 'obtain incontrovertible evidence to prove to the hilt your allegation that the Lagos, Ibadan and Asaba Councils were dissolved on grounds which are not justifiable'. He then warned that if financial discrimination by the Action Group against such N.C.N.C.-controlled councils was to be proved, there must be 'sufficient and conclusive evidence'.

The National President of the N.C.N.C. then turned to two matters about which, as chief witness before the Foster-Sutton Tribunal and as a former Minister of Local Government and now Premier of the Eastern Region, he was very sensitive.

You have also alleged diversion of Government funds into the National Bank for party political purposes. In the absence of concrete facts, please note that it will be very difficult to prove any Government diverting Government funds into any particular bank for purely Party political purposes. I take it that you have your facts straight? You have also mentioned the Finance Corporation and other statutory bodies. Facts must be obtained in order to justify any allegations when put to the strict proof.

He also warned them of his own experience.

You talk of wide-range practice of bribery and corruption in Local Government and statutory bodies. From our experience in the Eastern Region, it is very difficult to prove bribery and corruption in Local Government bodies. Port Harcourt, Aba and Onitsha are cases in point, and where we succeeded in proving same our Attorney-General advised us that we cannot prosecute them in the Courts of Law.

In conclusion, Dr Azikiwe made a general observation on tactics, based directly upon the recent experience of the party in the East:

If we are going to debate such a Motion we must marshal our facts and after they have been put to the strict test, which could survive the rules of evidence in any judicial tribunal, then we can go ahead and make a case for the Government Party to answer.

'I would not like you to feel', he concluded, 'that I am discouraging this Motion; rather, I only want us to be sure that if the world must take us seriously then the premises upon which our conclusions are based must be fool-proof.'

Adelabu had not sought this advice from his National President, and he certainly would not have welcomed more active interference. This was his own personal campaign. He had become without question the dominant figure in the Western N.C.N.C. at its regional conference in Abeokuta on Sunday, 21 October, when he was elected Chairman of the Western Working Committee in place of T. O. S. Benson, who had led the party to defeat in the regional election in May and been personally defeated by S. O. Gbadamosi, a prominent Action Group businessman. More and more the party looked for direction to Adelabu.

He soon gave proof of his determination to exercise the same sort of personal control over the party throughout the region as he sought to wield in Ibadan. On 23 October, only two days after his election at Abeokuta as Secretary of the Western Working Committee, the indefatigable Sanya Onabamiro submitted a memorandum to his new Chairman on the reorganization of the party in the West. Adelabu's notes on this are very revealing.[32] Onabamiro, for instance, drew attention to the need for a proper Liaison Committee between the Parliamentary Party and the Western Working Committee: Adelabu commented that the Chairman of the latter (namely himself) was quite sufficient as a liaison between the two, while the officers of either were entitled to attend both. Onabamiro proposed tighter control over the issuing of press releases by members of the party and that only the National President, National Secretary, National Publicity Secretary, the Chairman of the Western Working Committee and Western Principal Organizing Secretary should be allowed to make such statements.

Adelabu responded that it was 'absurd' that the National President and Secretary should make statements about the Western N.C.N.C. Control should rest in the hands of the Chairman. Here we can see once again the dislike of 'Lagos' which Adelabu had shown since his earliest days in the party, and his desire to treat the West as an autonomous unit of the N.C.N.C., into whose affairs the national officers of the party would intrude only by invitation, not by right.

In order to ensure better co-ordination between the elected officers of the party and its permanent officials, Onabamiro suggested that the Principal Organizing Secretary should be under the direction of the Secretary, not the Chairman, of the Western Working Committee. Adelabu's notes again emphasized the role of Chairman as being responsible for this co-ordination, and summed up the relationship between the three in the formula: 'Sec[retary] custodian decision – Chairman generator – P.O.S. executive organ'. Moreover, since the Abeokuta Conference had elected only the regional officers of the party, and not the ordinary members of the Working Committee, he also claimed the right to nominate these, pending a proper decision by a competent body.[33] He concluded by making extensive additions to Onabamiro's proposed agenda for the first meeting, adding, for example, a 'Chairman's policy speech' and a review of the walk-out from the House.

Adelabu was, however, genuinely concerned with improving the efficiency of the party's organization in the Region, proposing a new financial system and the recruitment and training of professional organizers, but as was so often the case with the N.C.N.C., these organizational good intentions in the end came to nothing. Although the feeling had not yet been publicly voiced, the party in all regions was sinking into the doldrums, experiencing that gradual drop in morale which was to culminate in its openly splitting into factions in April 1957.

Rather than attending to organizational work, in November 1956 the Lion of the West, dominant in his own wing of the party and still confident that one day he would rule the whole Region, was seeking his goal by preparing an all-out assault on the Action Group. In the middle of that month his spirits were given a great boost when within a week three of his wives each gave birth to a son. As he proudly announced in the *Defender*, 'As if to confirm the oracles of the NCNC and to uphold the prophecy of genuine nationalistic ascendancy as envisaged by the NCNC, I have been blessed in rapid succession with three baby boys.'[34] The motion demanding a Commission of Inquiry into the affairs of the Western Region Government, which was to stand in Mojid Agbaje's name, had been completed and on 13 November it was sent to the Governor for his prior warning. This time, however, in addition to pressure applied on the Governor as a means of communication with the Secretary of State for the Colonies, the motion was also sent to Hugh Gaitskell, Leader of the British Labour Party and Leader of the Opposition in the British House of Commons and to Lord Ogmore, a former Labour Minister and the solicitor who had been used to brief the two British lawyers who appeared for Azikiwe during the Foster-Sutton Tribunal hearings, which ended on 16 November. Adelabu's hope was that the Opposition in the Westminster Parliament would rally to the aid of its fellow Opposition in Ibadan and exert pressure more directly upon the British Government.

It now remained to plan the debate on Agbaje's motion. In an undated draft entitled 'Strategic Plan for Debate of the Motion for a Royal Commission of Enquiry' it was laid down that speakers would deal with topics in the context of one province of the region; Adelabu, for example, was to deal with the subject of Local Government and Chieftaincy in Ibadan Province, and Fakayode with the Judiciary and 'Lawlessness' in Ijebu Province. In all, 105 specific cases were to be cited, the object of the Opposition being to make a *prima facie* case sufficient to force the British Government to order a tribunal of inquiry, which, with its power to obtain evidence compulsorily, would reveal the final guilt of the Action Group Government.

It eventually proved impossible to adhere to this plan, the response to the request for information being too poor to permit the evidence on any one subject to be drawn from only one province. Agbaje's motion was therefore framed in very wide terms, and it was arranged that he should be seconded by Olowofoyeku, with Adegoke Adelabu speaking third for the Opposition and making the main speech. Considerable attention was paid to Agbaje's presentation. J. O. Fadahunsi proposed that it should be prepared 'by a selected few among the best brains in our party especially those around Ibadan', suggesting Adelabu, Onabamiro, Ikejiani, Olowofoyeku, Fakayode and Agbaje himself; certainly some if not all of these had a hand in its preparation.[35]

A week before Christmas 1956, the Western House of Assembly met to hear the Opposition's challenge to Government. In Ibadan, things could be said to be going well from Adelabu's point of view. The Provisional Council had determined not to enforce the trading rules on Lebanon Street which 'at present might tend to aggravate the unrest and uproars prevailing in the town'.[36] The *Defender* could continue to decry the destruction of market stalls by the Council and public attention was called to the continuing use of violence in the streets by a newspaper headline 'It's free-for-all fights weekend in Ibadan'.[37] The most intriguing trouble for the Council occurred in the first week of December, as the tax season began, when a number of employees of the Treasury Department set fire to the main building in an attempt to destroy tax records. Things were thus at least running against his local antagonists in Ibadan and Adelabu's confidence had been greatly increased at the end of November by the ruling of the Ijebu Ode Magistrate's Court on the 27th that he had no case to answer with regard to the charges arising from his visit there during the election campaign in May.* This proved, he declared, that 'we have a judiciary determined to dispense justice without fear or favour'.[38] The Action Group, with its majority in the House, was also confident, and Chief Awolowo and his lieutenants had shown no hesitation in calling a session whose main purpose would be to debate Mojid Agbaje's motion. On Friday, 21 December, shortly after 9.00 a.m., Agbaje rose to propose

That this honourable House calls on the Western Region Government to pray Her Majesty's Government in the United Kingdom, through His Excellency the Governor of the Western Region, to institute forthwith a Royal Commission of Inquiry into the activities of the Western Region Government, with reference to the following matters of urgent public importance and interest:

(1) The management and administration of Statutory Boards, Corporations, Government equipments and the use the Action Group Government has made of these to foster party political purposes.

(2) The Investment of two million pounds of public funds in the National Bank of Nigeria Limited between 1952 and 1953, and the subsequent phenomenal increase in loans and/or overdrafts to members and supporters of the Action Group, the Party in power in the Western Region.

(3) The relationship between
    (*a*) The National Bank of Nigeria and the Amalgamated Press Limited – a business organization in which top-ranking members of the Action Group have financial interests.
    (*b*) The National Bank of Nigeria Limited and the Action Group.
    (*c*) The National Bank of Nigeria and the Mutual Aids Society Limited.
    (*d*) The Amalgamated Press Limited and Chief Obafemi Awolowo, Premier of the Western Region, and other persons of note who are members or supporters of the Action Group.
    (*e*) The circumstances leading to the transfer to the Amalgamated Press Limited, of the sum of £100,000 of public funds.

(4) The loan policy of the Government of the Western Region.

(5) The policy of the Government of filling posts in the Civil Service of the Western Region with Action Group Supporters mainly.

---

* For the incident in question see pp. 299–300 above. This still left him with one case pending, since in July he had been recharged with assault in connection with the Isale Ijebu affray. Successive adjournments dragged the case out until 29 December, when the prosecution finally withdrew its case and he was discharged, having thus survived four legal actions unscathed during 1956.

(6) The award of public contracts in the Western Region with tremendous bias in favor of Action Group supporters.

(7) The tendencies of the Action Group Government towards fascism and dictatorship in practically every aspect of its activities.

(8) The allocation of Parliamentary Seats in the Western Region.

(9) The unwarranted deposition of Obas and Chiefs by the Government, and

(10) Partiality practiced by the Regional Government in its relationship with Local Councils.[39]

Like a shotgun, this motion was designed to scatter its charges over as wide an area as possible. Thus it ranged from specific instances to such broad accusations as 'fascism and dictatorship'. This was to have considerable bearing on the course of the debate and the ultimate success of the tactics of the Opposition.

Following the terms of his motion, Agbaje's speech covered a wide range of subjects. He began by denying that his motion was in any sense a reprisal for that of E. O. Eyo in the Eastern House, a sentiment which the Action Group Members, at least, were likely to take with a pinch of salt, since their party had supported Eyo in his quarrel with the N.C.N.C.

The various public boards and corporations of the Western Region, Agbaje claimed, had been used 'not in accordance with the objects and purposes for which they are created, but principally to foster Action Group Party political purposes'. The Production Development Board had 'been turned into gold mines or oil fields where members of the Action Group can prospect'.[40] As an example he cited the case of the appointment of Alfred Rewane, Chief Awolowo's personal political secretary, as a Special Commissioner for this same Production Development Board. This use of material which can only have been purloined from the files of the Board ran Agbaje into trouble. He quoted a letter which he claimed the Governor had written about Rewane's appointment:

It seems to me that the appointment of a Special Commissioner with powers to take executive action and to sack people on the spot cannot do other than have a most unsettling and undesirable effect on staff and will tend to destroy the authority and the sense of responsibility of management. Altogether it seems to me to savour far too much of a Soviet Political Commissar.[41]

This brought Anthony Enahoro to his feet to challenge him on a violation of Standing Order of the House number 27(7): 'Her Majesty's or the Governor-General's or the Governor's name shall not be used to influence the House.' On the Speaker's request Agbaje was then made to give a reference for this letter, which he was not officially supposed to have seen, and passing on to other matters he again attempted to quote the Governor.

Agbaje's speech was not a brilliant one, and it was obvious that the Action Group was fully prepared to fight back. Nevertheless he continued his prepared brief, touching on the affairs of the Finance Corporation and the Local Loans Boards, then raising the question of the alleged investment of £2,000,000 of public funds in the National Bank. 'Our contention is that the investment has been made from public funds with no other purpose than to strengthen the financial stability of the Action Group and to support financially Action Group party men.'[42] He laid emphasis on the allegation that a loan of £100,000 had been made by the Bank to the Amalgamated Press, which published the main Action Group newspaper, the *Daily Service*, and also dwelt on what was to be one of the most important issues of this whole struggle, namely Chief Awolowo's relation to the Press.

Babatunji Olowofoyeku, N.C.N.C. Member for Ilesha Central, spoke next, seconding the motion. He focused upon the National Bank. Why, he wanted to know, unless there was something shady about the transaction, was the investment of public funds in the Bank not announced at the time?

Since the generally accepted *credo* in all civilized countries today is nationalism, the economic aspect thereof no less than the political aspect is a common fighting slogan of political parties in all colonial territories. It is therefore strange that the Premier, noted for his brilliance of intellect, unmatched sagacity and unparalleled courage in giving frontal attacks should disdain to proclaim even from the house tops the happy news of the salvation of the Western Region from the shackles of British banking monopoly.[43]

The Member for Ilesha Central then indulged in a series of speculations about the affairs of the National Bank. Approximately three-quarters of the £4,000,000 advanced as loans by the Bank, he alleged, were in fact public funds, and these loans were used for political purposes. Recipients of such loans were obliged to pay ten per cent to the Action Group account, or else their checks were not honored by the Bank. Contractors (among them, Olowofoyeku alleged, Bello Abasi, 'the old man who ran from the NCNC to join the Action Group') were given overdrafts in return for donations to the party. The Action Group had spent a quarter of a million pounds on the 1956 election, and similar sums in 1954 and on local elections. Where had it all come from, he wanted to know? Further, he alleged, the investment of one million pounds in the Bank at an announced 4 per cent interest was in fact at 6 per cent, with the difference going to the Action Group. Olowofoyeku rounded off his speech by referring to Chief Awolowo's position as a director of the Amalgamated Press, which he maintained had been held by the Premier at least as late as October 1954 with a fee of £1500 a year. However, he conceded just before he sat down, he had heard that the Premier had resigned before the Press was given a government contract to print part of the electoral register in 1956.

Fittingly the next person to speak was Obafemi Awolowo who rose to move 'That this House has full confidence in the Government of the Western Region and supports its policy in every aspect.' He supported his motion with a twenty-five minute analysis of Agbaje's original motion. Items 1 and 4–10 were regional matters, and if they were submitted to a Royal Commission, 'this honourable House would be abdicating its hard-won authority over matters which the Constitution of the land has vested in this Region for the exclusive use of its Legislature and Government'.[44] The Secretary of State had set up the Foster-Sutton Inquiry because the issues involved related partly to federal and partly to regional matters. 'In other words, if the matters in issue had been purely Regional, or exclusively Federal, the Secretary of State would not have interfered in the way he did.'[45] Although items 2 and 3 of the substantive motion were of a mixed federal–regional character, they were far outweighed by the eight items of an exclusively regional character.

So wide was the scope of Agbaje's motion, Awolowo felt, that it implied 'an Inquiry into the activities of this Government in all its ramifications':

To approve this Motion is to agree to the institution of a Commission of Inquiry the terms and scope of which would be without parallel in a democracy. Indeed, by such an approval, this honourable House would not only be setting up something worse than a Spanish Inquisition, but would also be lending its support to a wicked, ruthless and relentless campaign of character denigration which is designed to gratify the evil and malignant dispositions of a breed of politicians who have thus far found it absolutely impossible to take defeat in elections in a sporting spirit.[46]

Amid frequent interruptions, Chief Awolowo went on to review the early history of the National Bank in the light of the credit policies of the expatriate banks. He gave an account of deposits made by the Western Region Production Development Board in the Bank since November 1952, with long-term deposits totalling £1,500,000 and a fluctuating amount of short-term deposits. He then became completely personal. It was 'astonishing' to hear that Government financial relations 'should be advertised to the whole world' from Adelabu, 'who claimed at one time during the Nicholson Commission of Inquiry that he was worth not less than £20,000 before he became a Minister, [but who] never took the trouble to present his Bank Book before the Nicholson Commission'.[47] When he was interrupted by P. A. Afolabi, he called him 'an Oyo man...led by the nose by an Ibadan man'.[48]

The achievements of his government on the other hand were considerable, as shown in testimonials from the Wall Street finance house of Kuhn, Loeb and Company, the Canadian Minister of Health and the Vice-Chancellor of the Federal German Republic. Amid shouts of 'God save the Queen' from the Action Group Legislators, he quoted a complimentary reference by Queen Elizabeth II to the Western Region with the arch aside that Standing Orders forbade the actual use of the name of 'the revered and beloved author of this immortal passage'. He then defended the appointment of Alfred Rewane to the Production Development Board, citing J. M. Johnson, the new N.C.N.C. Federal Minister, as an example of someone with fewer qualifications holding a job with a higher salary and allowances.

As for the bank, the recent expansion of loans to Nigerians depended on Government's investment of public funds to create a source of credit – 'but whether the Bank's borrowers are members and supporters of the Action Group or the N.C.N.C. I do not know, and I am not entitled to know. The relationship between the National Bank and the Action Group is pure and simple, one between banker and customer', and the Opposition was 'extremely impertinent, meddlesome, and mischievous' to want to know what went between such partners.[49]

Chief Awolowo next reviewed in detail his relations with the Amalgamated Press of which he had become an honorary director in June 1953, his own African Press (publisher of the *Nigerian Tribune*) having merged with the Service Press (publisher of the *Daily Service*) to form the new company. He had disclosed these interests to the Governor of the Western Region. In March 1955 he had sold most of his shares, and on 20 December of the same year he resigned his directorship, selling his remaining shares in June 1956. Thus, it was after his resignation but before his final sale of shares that the Amalgamated Press had been given a contract to print lists containing 1,226,398 of the names on the electoral register, at a cost to the Region of £43,475. 14. 6d., a printing company in the United Kingdom being given the other lists and charging just over £26,390. With great emphasis the Premier repeated these figures, with the comment that he was doing this 'for the benefit of the ex-students of the Yaba Higher College who cannot do simple arithmetic', a hit at Adelabu which earned 'boisterous applause' from the Government side of the House.[50]

The policy of the Western Government in granting loans through its various agencies was the Premier's next topic. Denying that this was influenced by party motives, he cited examples of loans given to N.C.N.C. supporters (including one to J. O. Fadahunsi's Ijesha United Trading and Transport Company) and of Action Group supporters who had defaulted on loans and had action taken against them (including one of his own former partners in the African Press). While three of his present Ministers had been given loans, they had all subsequently repaid them without any favored treatment.

It was the allegation of tendencies toward 'fascism and dictatorship' upon which Chief Awolowo waxed most eloquent. Describing this as the 'height of hypocrisy', he gave his own view of the present tactics of the Opposition:

Every organ of Government, every decent phase of our society, has been assailed by the N.C.N.C. terror gang. Even the judiciary, which we all regard as sacrosanct, and as the bulwark of the liberty and security of the citizens and of all that is brightest and best in any community, appears to be wavering now in the face of a series of concentrated and skillfully planned attacks.[51]

Chief villain of the piece, of course, in Awolowo's view was Adegoke Adelabu, and the Premier continued with a reference to the comments of the Lion of the West on the decision of the Ijebu Ode Magistrate's Court at the end of November:

The Courts of this Region have several times been accused of all manner of evil things. A few days ago, however, the Leader of the Opposition paid a glowing tribute to the impartiality and incorruptibility of the judiciary in the Western Region. I do not know what the members of the Bench themselves think of this piece of eulogy, coming, as it did, from one who has consistently conducted himself in defiance of law, order and constituted authority.

Some people may regard this tribute as a compliment to the Bench; but there are others who see in it a very strong evidence of a deflection from the path of rectitude and impartiality on the part of a thoroughly intimidated judiciary.

Whatever views may be held for or against, it will now, I believe, be generally agreed that the Western Judiciary, far from being under the influence of the Executive, is not altogether free from the mortal dread of an unscrupulous class of politicians.[52]

When the Premier sat down, Adegoke Adelabu rose to answer. He began his speech on a moderate note. He was not seeking an action in a court of justice, which could inflict punishment, but a commission of inquiry which might encourage the 'repentance that comes from remorse, self-correction and self-adjustment'.[53]

Adelabu's main appeals were directed less at the Action Group than to a British Government seeking to establish institutions which would permit the withdrawal of direct control over the regions, and then over the Federation as a whole. The Action Group was pressing hard for regional self-government, but 'Have you ever seen a trade where the apprentice demands a master's certificate without submitting to the master's tradesman examination test?' One motive of the Action Group might well be 'an attachment to the sacred principle of liberty', but the desire for regional autonomy could also be 'a shameful attempt to lock the door against any investigation into their administrative atrocities and financial scandals'. In this context he went on to state clearly one view of the process of decolonization:

One aspect of the development of self-government institutions in the British dependent territories is that written codes of public conduct which took many centuries to evolve in Great Britain and other European countries have been asked to keep pace in growth with the physical apparatus of democracy which has been transplanted overnight. The result is that whilst you have the ballot box, the school room, the legislative houses, the bench and the bar, the church and the mosque, the press and the soapbox, and a Premier and a Leader of Opposition, you have got but faint shadows of tolerance, fair play, sense of justice, goodwill, alert, responsive and responsible public opinion, civic sense of duty and genuine patriotism.

It is, therefore, all the more necessary when any territory is clamouring loudly for self-detachment from Whitehall, on the basis of its inventory of visible political property, that a stock be taken of its spiritual endowment, which is the lubricant of democracy. Otherwise those opposed to the Government of the day will only be exchanging white benevolence for black fascism.[54]

While Adelabu's distinction between formal institutions and actual practice was simplistic, it was in keeping with his purpose of forcing the British Government to listen to him before it surrendered formal authority. It was his intention at that time, he admitted, 'not to prove the allegation...but to make out a *prima facie* case'. This was partly because of the functional nature of the House of Assembly, for 'a Legislature can never be a proper tribunal for the establishment of judicial facts. The setting, the actors, the procedure, the time-table, the rules of attendance, the theatrical and rhetorical atmosphere and the general method of approach are unsuited to sober fact finding.' Although he did not admit explicitly the impotence of the minority Opposition against the majority, he urged that the decision to hold an inquiry rested 'solely, squarely and unequivocally on the Colonial Office, acting through its agent, the Governor of the Western Region'.[55]

After the luncheon adjournment, the debate became a rough and tumble affair as Adelabu, continuing his speech, was frequently interrupted. One of Adelabu's most frequent adversaries, Chief Rotimi Williams, the Minister of Justice and Local Government, occasionally joined the fray. A huge man, standing well over six feet and weighing more than three hundred pounds, he added dramatic contrast to 'portable Ade' and the solemn, bespectacled, schoolmasterly Awolowo. As *ad hominem* references increased, the style of debate and Adelabu's own speech suffered in consequence. Asserting that the onus of proof was on Chief Awolowo to show that he was only an honorary director of the Amalgamated Press and did not share in its profits, he was interrupted by the Premier and countered that 'I have not gone for law, but I can argue lawyers out.' Commenting on the Nicholson Inquiry he pointed out to the Government that as a result of it 'I am now a bone in your throats', and being again interrupted he proclaimed triumphantly that 'If you knew better you would have left me in Lagos!'[56]

The interruptions mounted to a storm as Adelabu produced one of the items of evidence collected by the Opposition. It was a copy of an internal audit report on the Production Development Board which found serious fault with some of its procedures and expenditures, and Adelabu claimed possession of 'thirty-three files here all full of evidence of this nature', which in his own administrative experience with the United Africa Company seriously indicted the Government. Taunted with having been dismissed from U.A.C., he retorted, 'I was never dismissed. I worked there twice, when I first left them and went back on my own will, I was received back with open arms.'[57]

With the House perhaps temporarily exhausted by these passages of arms, Adelabu was then allowed to discourse for some time on the National Bank, and, uninterrupted, to attain something of his old eloquence. 'The simple, the candid and the only truth', he asserted, 'is that the diversion is in no sense an achievement, but the nocturnal consummation of a diabolical crime committed with all the artistry and ingenuity of a twentieth century Machiavelli.' 'Were the diverted funds', he wished to know, 'made available to the generality of the tax-payers of the Western Region, or were they used solely to enrich the coffers of the supreme pontiff and his lieutenants and a handful of supporters?'[58]

However, the Leader of the Opposition was not to have such an easy time for long. Referring once again to Chief Awolowo's relations with the Amalgamated Press, he alleged that the Premier had been paid £1500 annually as director's fees, and further that the letter of resignation of December 1955 had been backdated by Awolowo. 'How do you know?' demanded the Premier. 'Because you will not agree to produce it', Adelabu answered. 'You think that by the power that has come to your hand that you can do anything with impunity. You cannot.' As to the printing of parts of the list of electors by the Press, 'Thousands of NCNC names were omitted. Who knows what happened in the night over the original draft?[59] Having shifted his ground yet again back to the National Bank, he responded to an interruption by Rotimi Williams with a flood of reproach:

Mr Speaker, I refuse to be bothered by the interruptions of people who cannot take their cup when it is their turn. I have taken mine and I come here purified. There is a Government Front Bencher here that is frightened, terrified, annoyed.

He is stamping his feet because the judiciary has refused to toe a political party line. He is issuing empty threats, that because cases have been decided in a certain way, and politicians have used their divine liberty to express their satisfaction about the way the judiciary is being run, issuing empty threats that they may be afraid. If they are not afraid of the Government of the day, enthroned in power, entrenched behind money gotten by all means, how can they be afraid of the Opposition which is not yet in power?[60]

After this, a repetition of the various allegations about loans, contracts and 'kickback' led up to one of Adelabu's most typical pieces of rhetoric.

Chief Obafemi Awolowo, the Premier in the Action Group Government, who enjoys posing as a paragon of moral excellence, is the architect, the planner and the chief of brigandage before whose achievements all previous records of Tammany Hall practices pale into insignificance. You search in vain the Roman records of the exploits of Ancient Consuls at the height of the Roman Imperial Plutocracy, the latter day achievements of the notorious American City Government in Chicago and New York, the fabulous private wealth of Goering, Mussolini and Peron of South America, and you are astounded to find what has happened in the Western Region is unmatched if not in scale at least in intensity and ramifications.[61]

In the last part of his speech, he turned to a long list of specific charges: the Action Group had been able to spend £250,000 on the last election against N.C.N.C.'s £4891; because of the National Bank's loans policy, 'Five million pounds of tax payers' hard-earned money has gone down the drains in the sacred name of nationalism'; certain people, among them Moyo Aboderin and the Oni of Ife, owed huge sums to the Bank. The material for an inquiry was abundant, he asserted – 'This paper I am holding contains 105 specific charges, but I am not going to bore the House by reading through. . .I want to end up.' Met with shouts from the Government benches of 'Don't end up, carry on', he concluded by citing again the Butcher, Storey, Lloyd, Nicholson, and Foster-Sutton Commissions – 'In all cases they have always ended by bringing to light many facts and many data which should have been hidden from the public if such Inquiries were not made.' It was his hope that the Government would have second thoughts and offer itself up to such an inquiry.[62]

When Adelabu sat down, after a speech lasting in all more than three hours, the debate was virtually finished. The principal speakers had raised all the issues, so that the thirteen speakers who followed could do little except repeat their leaders' arguments. Nor, for that matter, was the immediate result of the debate in any doubt; when the House divided in a vote on Chief Awolowo's amendment it was carried by forty-eight votes to twenty-seven, five N.C.N.C. Members failing to vote.

Much of this debate is interesting as an example of the style and relevance of parliamentary debate in pre-independence Nigeria. It also portrayed the bitterness which a number of the Action Group speakers felt toward Adegoke Adelabu. His irreverence, the pungency of his speech, the unmasked contempt which he often displayed toward them, drew upon Adelabu abuse which was never hurled at any other Member of the House.

The debate and the defeat were in fact part of the necessary ritual for the N.C.N.C., which knew it would be defeated in the short run, but still was confident that in the long run the Secretary of State would have to take action. Adelabu thus wrote to the Governor of the Western Region, Sir John Rankine, two days after the debate, taking the next step in the N.C.N.C. offensive.[63] The letter was intended to underline certain features of the debate, by pointing out that 'Apart from the incontrovertible PRIMA FACIE case which we made against the Government', Chief Awolowo had himself made 'three factual admissions' of great significance. First of all, he had admitted that he had remained a director of the Amalgamated Press after taking office at the beginning of 1952 until the end of 1955. This contravened the code of conduct laid down in the Secretary of State's dispatch of December 1951, and Adelabu maintained the Governor should therefore request Awolowo's resignation from the Premiership, and if he refused dismiss him. Second, it had been admitted that about £60,000, which the N.C.N.C. held to be public funds, had been invested in the Action Group's Amalgamated Press by the National Bank.[64] Third, under Awolowo's Premiership the Press had been given the contract to print part of the list of electors 'in clear abuse of his high office and in great prejudice to NCNC chances in the said elections, hundreds of thousands of whose supporters' names were deliberately omitted'. Thus the Opposition was in fact narrowing the scope of their original attack to concentrate on implicating Chief Awolowo personally, seeming to have accepted his judgement that the British Government was hardly likely to agree to conduct a 'Spanish Inquisition' into the whole range of activities of his Government. However, the Secretary of State might agree to investigate the conduct of a particular individual, just as Dr Azikiwe's conduct had been investigated by the Foster-Sutton Tribunal.

For the moment Adelabu tried not to overplay his hand, contenting himself with the relatively mild threat that the Opposition would boycott the Western House of Assembly and that the 'other co-ordinate Governments in the Federation of Nigeria may not agree to sit side by side with the delegation of the Action Group Western Government at the Constitutional Conference table until the Western Region Government's reputation which is now under a frightfully heavy cloud is cleared'. Indeed, he took care to point out that 'No breath of scandal affected Your Excellency or any of your expatriate Civil Servants in the several grave allegations so far made', though he continued by pointing out that 'We trust Your Excellency will not give public opinion a wrong impression of Your Excellency's stand on this momentous issue, by mis-using your office to impede that course of justice which is the pride of the British people.' Adelabu's main request for the moment was that this letter and copies of the record of the recent debate should be forwarded to the Secretary of State. He took care, however, to send an advance copy by cablegram to Alan Lennox-Boyd himself, and other copies were sent to the Governor-General, the Federal Council of Ministers, the Premier and the Executive Council of the East and North, the Leader of Government Business and Executive Council of the Southern Cameroons, all Members of the various Nigerian legislatures and the Nigerian Press. Copies were also sent to Members of the British Parliament. Adelabu was determined on maximum publicity, and he was determined also to enlist allies in Britain to help him put pressure on the British Government. As we saw earlier, he had sent copies of the original motion to Hugh Gaitskell and Lord Ogmore; now he sought to extend his contacts much further, to include about 160 British Members of Parliament who might be interested.* To this end, he also planned to make contact with a wide range of newspapers and journals in the United Kingdom, including in the final list *The Times, Daily Herald, Daily Mirror, News of the World, Daily Worker*, the *Western Independent* of Plymouth, *West Africa, International Affairs*, and *The Political Quarterly,* though there is no evidence that this plan was actually put into effect.[65]

Meanwhile, the most immediate need was to keep up the pressure in the Western Region. The N.C.N.C. newspapers, particularly the *Southern Nigeria Defender*, had given full coverage to the speeches of the main N.C.N.C. speakers in the debate, and had published Adelabu's letter to the Governor. However, more than this was needed. On 8 January 1957, J. O. Fadahunsi wrote to Adelabu on the next step to be taken.[66] Noting that 'There may be no reply forthcoming from the Governor or the Secretary of State to our letter of protest against the attitude of the Government towards the motion', he suggested that something must be done 'to set the ball rolling'. He felt that Adelabu should lead an N.C.N.C. delegation on a tour of the Region, suggesting the last two weeks of February as a suitable time for this, and noting that 'This will surely arouse public interest and

---

* A manuscript list in an unknown hand of some of these in the Adelabu Papers includes 'Mr Hugh Gaskin', 'Sir Frank Sokscise', 'Mr. Malliuo' (Mallalieu?), 'Mr. Frank Brookway' (Fenner Brockway?) and 'Mr. Regionald Bevan' (presumably Reginald Bevins, but since all the rest are Labour Party men this may be a confusion with Aneurin Bevan!).

create some panic in the Action Group circle.' The letter is also interesting for another reason, for it shows the uneasy relationship between Adelabu and some other Western leaders of the party whom he had pushed into second place with his return to the Western legislature. Thus, Fadahunsi in the latter part of his letter remarked rather plaintively,

Please note that I should be much disappointed if you give me no reply to this letter in time. It may be acceptable or not, I just need a reply. If you have planned to take any better step, I should be pleased to know.

The letter concluded with the reproachful comment that 'It appears that our publicity machinery has not been doing much since we left Ibadan. Will you please help and see that we rise to the occasion.'

Adelabu was not prompt to answer this letter, the sentiments of which can scarcely have appealed to him. His failure to answer until eleven days later, however, was the result of his absence in Lagos, whence he traveled on 8 January to stay with N. B. Soule and lead the N.C.N.C. during the last week of the campaign for the election to the Lagos Town Council on the 15th. His contacts with the N.N.D.P. in Lagos had always been close, and it is an interesting comment on this relationship, and on his growing prestige in the N.C.N.C., that he should have been asked to lead a vital campaign in which the N.C.N.C.–N.N.D.P. alliance was trying to wrest control of the federal capital from the Action Group. In his eve-of-election appeal he gave seven reasons why the Action Group should be rejected.[67] Although he seems to have had his usual impact on the campaign (his car was attacked on polling day), he failed to lead his party to victory, the Action Group winning by the narrow majority of twenty-three seats to nineteen.

Fresh from his rebuff, Adelabu replied to Fadahunsi. Aggrieved by the complaint about lack of publicity, he pointed out that he had himself spent £22. 12. 8d. on the cablegram to the Secretary of State and other postal expenses.[68] With regard to the tour of the West, he was planning to travel to London with the ex-Alafin and a representative of the Mid-West, but Fadahunsi might lead such a campaign in his absence. This proposed trip is something of a mystery, and may possibly have been an idea which Adelabu had on the spur of the moment: from the composition of the group, it would presumably have been intended to raise wider issues than the proposed Commission of Inquiry, including the creation of a Mid-West State. In any case it never took place.

A clue to this proposed trip may perhaps be found in a circular letter to N.C.N.C. branches sent out by Adebayo Asaya on 17 January. This referred to a fund of £50,000 which the Action Group was supposed to have raised to send a delegation to London, and Adelabu's idea may have been for a counter-delegation. The main purpose of the letter, however, was to give party members an account of events to date, claiming that 'documentary records' to be presented to the Commission now numbered 201, and more were coming in to be added to the original 105. The N.C.N.C. branches were asked to call general meetings to discuss the steps taken so far and to signify their approval. They were also asked to register their replies, since the Action Group had supposedly insinuated its agents into post offices so that 'N.C.N.C. letters cannot move freely in the Western Region.' Few branches took the trouble to answer, and those which did usually seized the opportunity to raise some special local concern. Thus one branch in Egbado Division in supporting the party leaders' actions in the campaign for a Commission of Inquiry also requested the appointment of its own full-time Organizing Secretary, and another for the constituency. Another branch near Agbor declared that 'Mid West State is a burning fire in the mind of us all.'

The interests and enthusiasm of the rank and file members could only be kept up if something definite appeared to be happening. By the beginning of February party branches had discussed the situation, and those which were going to reply to Headquarters had done so. Adelabu and Asaya continued to make plans for stepping up the campaign, hoping, for example, to get copies of the debate of 21–2 December printed for general distribution. As February wore on, however, the fatal weakness of the Opposition's position re-emerged. They could do nothing unless the British Government was prepared to act, and no sign had come from the Secretary of State. Nor, for that matter, had there been any sign from the Governor of the Western Region, except for a three-line note written on 29 December to acknowledge receipt of Adelabu's letter of the 24th.

On 26 February Adelabu's patience came to an end. In another letter to Sir John Rankine that day, he commented bitterly that 'Your Excellency's questionable silence has dismayed, scandalized and horrified Nigerian Public Opinion', and pointed out that 'I have given your Excellency such a long rope in order not to afford your Excellency any excuse for lack of time for matured consideration of the grave issues involved.' He demanded 'catagorical answers' to a string of seven questions, particularly in regard to the extent to which the Governor had been in contact with the Secretary of State. Since it was now known that the delayed constitutional conference was to be held in May, Adelabu also stressed the need to settle this matter before the delegates left for London. Moreover, he intended to go beyond exhortation.

It is my unpleasant duty as Leader of the Opposition speaking on behalf of 40% of the popular legislative house and 52% of the electorate of the Western Region, to deliver this 48 hour ULTIMATUM expiring at noon, Sunday 3rd March 1957, that your Excellency shall cause an answer to be given to my 2-month-old letter

341

so as to afford our supporters, groaning under Action Group misrule and corruption, an opportunity to map out our next line of positive action to secure justice and liberty under the protection of Her Majesty.[69]

Last, the Governor was informed that copies of the debate had been sent to all members of the British Parliament 'and other appropriate institutions in the United Kingdom, the Commonwealth and the United Nations Organization'.*

It was not only Adelabu's patience which was exhausted. Finance was also becoming a serious problem. On 28 February Adebayo Asaya submitted a statement of account to Adelabu. Nearly six hundred packets had been sent out, each containing a copy of Agbaje's motion, material published in the *Daily Times* and *West African Pilot*, and copies of Adelabu's letters to the Governor of 24 December and 26 February; this had cost nearly £26, and the total expenses to be met were £27. 5. 3d. Asaya asked permission (which was granted) to use a back payment of £28 for four months' ten per cent donation of salary, which had just been made by an N.C.N.C. legislator, to cover this.[70] Efforts to secure financial help from the N.C.N.C. National Headquarters had met with no response. As early as the previous December, Asaya had written to T. O. S. Benson to ask for his help in securing £200 for 'petty cash', pointing out that expenses of over £80 incurred up to then had been met by Western Headquarters and by Adelabu and other N.C.N.C. leaders personally.[71] In his letter at the end of February Asaya was still complaining that 'at present there is no assistance from the National Headquarters'.[72] Adelabu had yet another reason to be angry with the 'Lagos' leadership of the party. In mid-February he had arranged with F. S. McEwen to have copies of the debate in the Western House printed by Zik's Enterprises, one of the companies founded by Dr Azikiwe. This had not been done in time for the debate to be sent out with the other materials, despite a promise of delivery in two weeks, and this failure provoked an angry telegram from Adelabu to the company on 28 February.†

Adelabu's anger was no doubt compounded on 3 March when the period of his '48 hour ultimatum' expired with no response from the Governor. A joint meeting of the N.C.N.C. Western Working Committee, the Western Parliamentary Party and the Western members of the N.C.N.C. Federal

---

* This was a statement of intent rather than actuality. Only 162 British Members of Parliament were contacted, and nothing was sent to the United Nations.

† Apparently the order was never executed, presumably because the company was not sure of the Western N.C.N.C.'s ability to pay the bill. For further details on the relations between Zik's Enterprises and the N.C.N.C. see Post, *The Nigerian Federal Election of 1959*, pp. 58–9.

Parliamentary Party had been called for noon on that Sunday to consider Sir John Rankine's reply or his failure to make one. Allowing for duplication of roles, some sixty people would thus have been eligible to attend the meeting, but in fact only fourteen (including Adegoke Adelabu) did so, with Adebayo Asaya also in attendance. The distance to be travelled by some delegates, especially from the Mid-West, may in part account for this. Probably more significant in discouraging attendance was the fact that a smallpox epidemic had been raging in Ibadan since the beginning of the year, requiring the emergency vaccination of about a quarter of a million people and claiming over a hundred deaths by mid-March. It is still curious, however, that so few of the N.C.N.C. legislators attended the meeting. The only federal Member was S. L. A. Elliott, who had been elected unopposed to Adelabu's old seat, and only four regional Members attended beside Adelabu. The absence of Ibadan legislators other than Elliott and L. Ade Bello is particularly strange. There is some indication that at this stage many of the Western N.C.N.C. were cooling towards the campaign for a Royal Commission. On 3 January 1957 it had been announced that the constitutional conference, originally scheduled for September 1956 and delayed by the Foster-Sutton Tribunal, would be held the following May. On 6 February the Colonial Secretary declared that it would convene on 23 May, and this date was finally confirmed on the last day of February. The presence of only two representatives from the Mid-West at the N.C.N.C. meeting on 3 March probably indicated that the energies and attention of the absentees were now being concentrated on the attempt to prepare the case for a separate Mid-Western Region.

What the meeting on 3 March lacked in numbers it made up in vehemence. P. A. Afolabi's motion of no confidence in the Governor, with a request to the Colonial Office to recall him, was unanimously accepted. Twelve reasons were given for thus censuring the Governor, including his failure to intervene in the allocation of seats between Divisions, his sanctioning of the deposition of Obas and Chiefs, and his failure to invoke his reserved powers under the constitution against the Action Group government. He was rebuked for his 'lack of restraint in attending backwood feasts and drink parties in Awolowo's hometown village of Ikenne', 'his allowing himself to be terrified, cowed, brow-beaten and bullied by the strong personality of Premier Awolowo', for 'careerism', 'lack of administrative experiences', 'weak personality' and (perhaps most serious of all) his 'unBritish character in that his soul does not rebel against injustice and foul play'.[73] Finally, the minutes of the meeting recorded:

The sum and substance of our reaction to Sir John Rankine's gross negligence of his constitutional duties is to declare a holy crusade on bribery and corruption and British hypocrisy of divide-and-rule. To effect much needed redress in the present state of affairs, in Western Region, the leadership of the NCNC in the Region are ready to pay the penalty of leadership by submitting voluntarily and willingly to imprisonment for their militancy. We call on the people of the Western Region to brace up for any necessary sacrifices in order to achieve our common objective of liberty and justice under the reign of law.[74]

Various measures were decided on as part of the 'holy crusade'. A policy of 'non-fraternization' with the Governor was to be followed by N.C.N.C. legislators at official ceremonies, and N.C.N.C. local councillors were to walk out of meetings when their councils were visited by him. A press campaign was to be launched, with articles bearing such titles as 'What the Governor has condoned', 'Have we a Governor in the Western Region?', and 'Double-face Lennox-Boyd'; these were also to be translated into Yoruba and circulated as pamphlets.

A much more militant program of 'Positive Actions' was also proposed, with prayers, fasting, mourning, the closure of markets, a transport strike, the boycotting of schools and government institutions, a refusal to buy British goods, protest meetings and 'peaceful demonstrations'. Interestingly enough, the emphasis at the meeting was less upon using all these measures to force a Commission of Inquiry than on forcing the Governor to declare the last regional election null and void, so that another could be held, with a different distribution of seats, before the constitutional conference could meet in May and grant self-government to the Region.

Nevertheless, it was the Commission of Inquiry which formed the main theme of Adegoke Adelabu's next letter to the Governor. On 4 March, the day after the ultimatum to the Governor had expired and the N.C.N.C. meeting had decided to launch a holy crusade, the Deputy Governor wrote to Adelabu on behalf of Sir John Rankine. While assuring the Leader of the Opposition that a copy of his letter of 24 December had indeed been sent to the Secretary of State, the Deputy Governor also pointed out that in the Governor's opinion the charges made in that letter and the second one had been 'fully ventilated' in the House of Assembly, 'when detailed replies to all the allegations were made on behalf of the Government'.[75] Moreover, Chief Awolowo's amendment had been carried by forty-eight votes to twenty-seven, so that 'In the circumstances, and since the Motion for a Commission of Inquiry was defeated, it is not clear on what grounds it would be appropriate to set up a Royal Commission of Inquiry as suggested.'

This letter provoked Adelabu's longest effusion yet. Already, as his contribution to the 'holy crusade', he had begun a 'fast of penance' immediately after the meeting on 3 March.[76] The amendment to Agbaje's motion was invalid, he replied on 9 March, because it had never been properly seconded, and was thus contrary to Standing Order 23. Since the Action Group was obviously not going to vote against itself it was 'fatuous' to take a stand on the number of votes cast in the House; a 'higher authority' must always order such an inquiry, and *prima facie* an incontrovertible case had been made. However, Adelabu went on, 'In order to help your Excellency to resolve this equivocation and vacillation between your sense of duty and your well-known temperamental addiction of being bound by dictation from the Minister-Members of your Executive Council, I will narrate briefly 14 strange events which have occurred since the debate in the House.' Among the events which Adelabu then went on to list was the fact that that P. H. Balmer had 'silently vacated' the office of Electoral Commissioner; that the Opposition had not been consulted on the composition of the Western delegation to the constitutional conference; and that 'Seven months after illegally withholding the stipend of the Leader of Opposition belated recognition has now been accorded in such a way that the public cannot but infer that he is being induced by offer of monetary reward to relax his effort for the demand for a Royal Commission of Enquiry.'

The Leader of the Opposition then went on to hint that the whole decision might in fact be taken out of the hands of the Governor. Warning him that 'Nigeria and the World at large are watching your Excellency', he declared that: 'The Governor-General may be obliged to act in accordance with the wishes of the Central Legislature as conveyed to him in advice to be tendered by his Ministers.' There is no evidence available at present, however, to suggest that any serious attempt was made by the N.C.N.C. federal Ministers to raise this issue with the Governor-General, and if Adelabu discussed the matter with Nnamdi Azikiwe when he met him in Onitsha on 12 March, a few days after writing this letter, nothing came of it. For the moment, all Adelabu could do was to exhort the Governor to action (citing 'a great English Statesman, Lord North' in the process) in the name of the 'great and good name of British Justice and Fairplay'. He went on to draw a parallel between the African Continental Bank Inquiry and the position of the National Bank, which for 'exactly similar reasons' should be investigated, and to remind Sir John of his power, under Section 64 of the Nigerian Constitution Order in Council of 1954, to override decisions of the House of Assembly 'in the interest of public order, *public faith* or *good government*'.* Toward the end of his letter he again adopted a somewhat minatory tone:

I have demolished the false premises on which your arguments are based by skirmishing in the landscape when you should have taken the total picture into consideration. I have placed afresh before you for your perusal the main charges, allegations and admissions. I have warned you against taking advice from the

* Emphases Adelabu's.

wrong quarters on a matter where your own discretion should be the decisive factor. I have shown you how this matter may be taken from your limited jurisdiction with great loss of face. I have shown the reserve powers vested in you by the constitution.

In conclusion, your Excellency, I reject as unreasonable, unrealistic and dangerously prejudicial to the long association, in Nigerian minds, of Great Britain with a high sense of Justice and Fairplay your preliminary evasive and equivocal ruling that you are not clear on what grounds it would be appropriate to set up a Royal Commission of Enquiry as suggested.

The letter ended with a flourish – the statement that the Opposition would publish 'next week in Nigeria and London' documentary evidence that Chief Awolowo, contrary to his own statement in the House, was still involved with the African Press and the Amalgamated Press on 18 December 1956. Attached to it was an appendix, 'What Sir John Rankine has condoned', containing ninety-nine points, most of them now familiar to that official. Copies of this letter were to be circulated rather more widely than before in Nigeria, with individual copies to senior British officials in addition to the Governor-General, and to seventy-six British Members of Parliament, and *The Times*, *Daily Express*, *Daily Herald* and *Daily Mirror* of London.

This sort of distribution cost money, however, and on 11 March Adebayo Asaya submitted another statement of account, this time for £18. 11. 2d., of which £13 was for postage to the United Kingdom. Because of the difficulty in getting copies of the debate printed, the Western N.C.N.C. had also had to buy twenty copies of the official record, at a cost of £4. 0. od. In his accompanying letter, Asaya pointed out that 'we are hopelessly in dire need of postages and other expenditures on the despatch of documents to Europe and Nigerian legislatures,' since 'at present there is no assistance from the National Headquarters, Lagos, on the Royal Commission activities'.[77] Again he had to ask permission to use a back-payment of a legislator's ten per cent donation which had just come in to cover the latest bills.

On 12 March the Lion of the West appeared on the same platform with Dr Azikiwe in a campaign meeting at Onitsha for the election to the Eastern Region House of Assembly, called for 15 March as a result of the report of the Foster-Sutton Tribunal, which had been published on 16 January. The report recognized that Azikiwe's main concern had been to use the African Continental Bank to liberalize credit terms for Nigerians, but it also commented that as a Minister his conduct 'has fallen short of the expectations of honest, reasonable people'.[78] Even before the report was published the N.C.N.C. Eastern Ministers had recommended to their Premier that he should call an election, rather than resign, believing (correctly as it transpired) that the Eastern voters would take little notice of the Tribunal's verdict. On 18 January a joint meeting of the National Executive Committee and the Eastern Working Committee had endorsed this advice (Adelabu had not attended), and so the election had been called. Now, in the last days of the campaign, Adelabu put in a brief appearance at the nearest point in the East to his own region, just across the Niger from Asaba by ferry. We do not know exactly what transpired at this meeting, but Azikiwe did declare publicly that his government would not sit down at the constitutional conference table with the Action Group government of the West unless a Commission of Inquiry had been conceded. Adelabu, in his speech, went out of his way to scotch rumors that he had been boycotting the Eastern N.C.N.C.'s campaign, and stated that 'crisis acts as a cement to the unity of the NCNC', and ('with thunderous ovations') that 'the NCNC under Dr Azikiwe was "more united now than ever before" '.[79]

Although Adelabu issued a press release on his return to Ibadan triumphantly drawing the attention of the public to Dr Azikiwe's pronouncement, it seems unlikely that he was deceived by it into thinking that he would now have the full support of the party. Moreover, there was another letter from the Deputy Governor waiting for him, stating even more firmly the line taken in the letter of 4 March:

...in His Excellency's view having regard to the present constitutional position the proper forum in which the allegations made should be fully discussed and disposed of is the House of Assembly where the force of public opinion can be brought to bear. In His Excellency's view it would be only when it can be shown that there has been no proper opportunity for public debate, or when the replies given on behalf of the Government can be shown by satisfactory evidence to have been incorrect in important material respects, that any question of the exercise of His Excellency's reserve power would arise. Even then His Excellency would have to be satisfied that it would be in the public interest to have further investigation before he would consider taking the very drastic step of overriding the decision of the Legislature of the country.[80]

Now was the time for Adelabu to produce the evidence on the relations between Chief Awolowo and the Amalgamated Press to which he had referred in his letter to the Governor on 9 March, and which he had threatened to publish. On 20 March he sent to Sir John Rankine a copy of a letter on Amalgamated Press stationery, dated 18 December 1956, which included Chief Awolowo's name among the printed list of directors at its head. The Governor taxed the Premier with this, and then, more than five weeks later, sent the last letter of the series to Adelabu.[81] In this he stated that Chief Awolowo had pointed out that the use of stationery on a particular date was not proof that the list of directors on the printed letterhead was still valid on that date. Moreover, the Action Group Leader had produced documents to prove that he had resigned his directorship in December 1955. Finally, the Governor passed on the verdict of the Secretary of State: having considered the submissions of the N.C.N.C., he, the final arbiter, in fact had nothing to add to the Governor's letters of 4 and 13 March.

Long before receipt of this letter, however, Adegoke Adelabu had in effect given up this phase of his campaign for a Royal Commission of Inquiry into the activities of the Western Government. Early in April he did obtain from the Registrar of Companies in Lagos a list of directors of the National Bank, the African Press and the Amalgamated Press covering the period at issue. This source of information (curiously, he had not tapped it earlier) yielded nothing except confirmation of Awolowo's resignation from his directorship of the Amalgamated Press on 20 December 1955. Now there was nothing more to be done. Lacking the support of his own party, and with little hope by this time of a change of heart on the part of the Governor and the Secretary of State, there was nothing he could do but tacitly admit temporary defeat. At this point it is worthwhile examining in general terms the stands of the various elements involved in the campaign, which had occupied Adelabu for seven months.

The position of the Action Group leaders was clear. Confirmed in power in the West by the election of May 1956 with a majority in the House of Assembly sufficient to defeat any motion launched by the Opposition, they needed only to retain the confidence of the Governor, and through him of the Secretary of State. This could only be threatened by the case made by the Opposition, and it must be recognized that in the circumstances this was not particularly strong. As we noted earlier, the Opposition began in the original motion by adopting a 'shotgun' technique, hoping that if they made many allegations some of them would strike home and prod the British administration into action. Adelabu gradually realized that the Governor was not impressed by this technique, and that the British tradition favored an inquiry into the conduct of persons with ministerial responsibility – as with the Foster-Sutton Tribunal and Dr Azikiwe – rather than a general inquiry into the whole range of activity of a government. Unfortunately for him, when he tried to narrow his focus to an attack on the probity of Chief Awolowo, the *prima facie* case he was able to make was not as strong as that made by E. O. Eyo against Nnamdi Azikiwe. Above all, Awolowo had never been a director of the bank into which his government had put public funds, and which had then invested money in the party press of which he was a director. As a result, he was not directly placed at the center of the financial complex underpinning the Action Group as was Dr Azikiwe in that which supported the N.C.N.C.

We have repeatedly emphasized the fact that the final decisions on whether action was to be taken against Azikiwe and Awolowo rested with the British Government, or more particularly with its local representatives, Sir Clement Pleass in the East and Sir John Rankine in the West. Adelabu fully recognized that this was so, hence the long letters which he sent to Rankine in support of his case, and hence, too, his appeals to 'British Justice and Fairplay', trying to speak in a language which he thought the Governor might understand. Though he presented an ultimatum, and though he and some other N.C.N.C. leaders threatened 'Positive Actions' as sanctions, the threatened action was in fact never taken. The days of militant nationalism had ended with the Zikist Movement early in 1951, as Adelabu, despite his view of himself in 1952 as a 'Spiritualistic Nationalist', came to learn. From that year onward, the Nigerian leaders had in effect agreed to construct a political system for an independent Nigeria in collaboration with the British Government and its local administration, and the quarrels over matters of detail which had periodically arisen had not affected the main outlines of this arrangement, which Adelabu had apparently accepted. The most serious threat to this 'unwritten agreement' had in fact come from the action initiated against Nnamdi Azikiwe by Alan Lennox-Boyd's appointment of the Foster-Sutton Tribunal, which many Nigerians felt had been undertaken too readily. Sir John Rankine and through him the British Government might be accused of favoring Obafemi Awolowo unduly in contrast, but Rankine's position was plain. He was concerned with making the unwritten agreement work, with co-operating with the Action Group Government of the West, to the best of his ability; thus his 'well known temperamental addiction of being bound by dictation from the Minister-Members of your Executive Council' to which Adelabu had referred in his letter of 9 March. It would only be in response to a much stronger case than the Opposition was in fact able to present, therefore, that he would be likely to take action against the Premier of the Western Region.

Similarly, if we look at the actions of Nnamdi Azikiwe and the N.C.N.C. as a whole during this period, we can see that they too were bound by the unwritten agreement to participate in the interchange between Nigerian political parties and the British administration which was to lead to independence – what might be termed the 'dialectic of decolonization'. The agreement at the Onitsha Special Convention of the N.C.N.C. in July 1956 that Azikiwe should submit himself to an inquiry indicates this. So also does Azikiwe's letter to Asaya in October, advising extreme caution in the proposed attack on the Western Government.* To stir up further conflict at that

* It is an extremely interesting comment on this whole episode that once the period of decolonization had come to an end, and there was no longer a 'dialectic' because the

juncture, in particular to risk a clash with the British administration at a time when the hearings of the Foster-Sutton Tribunal were being held and its report prepared seemed most unwise from the point of view of Azikiwe and the Eastern and Federal N.C.N.C. leaders. Hence, the failure of the party to support Adelabu with money, or in the House of Representatives. The publication of the Tribunal's report and the onset of an election in the East in the early months of 1957 only served to reinforce these attitudes. Moreover, with the postponed constitutional conference finally announced for May, the attention of the N.C.N.C. gradually became fixed on this to the exclusion of all else. Here was to be the supreme opportunity to right all wrongs; all matters of contention could be settled there. In particular, from Adelabu's point of view, this was the arena in which could be fought the next round against the Action Group. His last onslaught had foundered on the rocks of the Governor's adamancy; in London, with the whole weight of the N.C.N.C. definitely behind him, he could get what he wanted. In the circumstances, he was prepared to change his tactics.

British had withdrawn their direct presence and left the Nigerian parties in open confrontation, the successor to the British, the Federal Government, did intervene in the West and hold a general inquiry into the financial affairs of the Action Group. Weakened by an internal conflict which became open in May 1962 and gave the N.C.N.C.–N.P.C. Federal Government an opportunity to intervene, the Action Group found itself a year later dispossessed from the Western Region, with its financial dealings publicly exposed and its leader on trial (and subsequently imprisoned) for plotting the forceful overthrow of the Federal Government. For the crisis of May 1962, see John P. Mackintosh, 'The Action Group: the Crisis of 1962 and its Aftermath', in Mackintosh *et. al., Nigerian Government and Politics.* For Action Group finances see the *Report of Coker Commission of Inquiry into the affairs of Certain Statutory Corporations in Western Nigeria, 1962* (Lagos: Federal Ministry of Information, n.d. but 1963).

CHAPTER 13

TO LONDON AND BACK

The Nigerian Delegation to the Conference lost because it accepted battle with Lennox-Boyd on Lennox-Boyd's own grounds and conditions. Lennox-Boyd like a clever general drew the line of battle and baited the Nigerian delegation into accepting battle on his own grounds.

Chike Obi, July 1957

Between the end of March and the end of July 1957, the period covered in this chapter, the tri-cornered struggle between the N.C.N.C. Western Opposition, the Action Group Government and the colonial power was waged as part of the entire process of decolonizing Nigeria. The struggle began in the Western House of Assembly, shifted to meetings of the N.C.N.C. and of the regional Premiers in Lagos, moved next to the stately setting of Lancaster House in London and ended aboard the M.V. *Apapa* at sea. The struggle was thus escalated to levels where Adelabu had no more control over events, indeed often less, than many other men. In this chapter the thread of his life is more intensely woven into the entire tapestry of Nigerian events than ever before. He was to discover more clearly than ever the close but discordant relations between the local, the regional, the national and the colonial levels of Nigeria's political system, and he was to discover with equal clarity that he had as yet created no firmly founded political house of his own. For a moment, then, the biography (as was the life itself) is taken up by the broader events, events which at once demonstrate the dilemmas of many of Nigeria's other founding fathers.

On Monday 25 March (he had exactly a year to live) Adelabu announced at the first meeting of the new session of the Western House of Assembly, that in view of the forthcoming Constitutional Conference, which would give his party the chance to place its continuing concerns before the British Government, the N.C.N.C. Opposition was ending its boycott of the proceedings of the House, first called in July 1956 although ignored for the purposes of Mojid Agbaje's motion in December. Anthony Enahoro, the Leader of the House, took the opportunity to congratulate 'the saner members of the Opposition on compelling their Leader to see reason'.[1]

The following day, Adelabu spelled out his new position in more detail.

351

Briefly he noted that the Commission of Inquiry had gone unmentioned in the Governor's Speech from the Throne, he referred to the letter listing Obafemi Awolowo as one of the Directors of the Amalgamated Press, which he had sent 'last week' to the Governor, and he declared again that the issue of an inquiry had been raised with the Federal Council of Ministers.[2] Nevertheless, the purpose of his presence was to shape by advocacy and opposition the background against which the Constitutional Conference would take place. A constitution for the Mid-West, he declared, must be agreed on before the delegates left for London. If the West itself was to become self-governing, certain 'safeguards' must be built into its constitution, especially a Council of State, made up equally of Action Group and N.C.N.C. members, which would appoint the Governor, the Chief Justice, the newly-created Attorney-General, the Chairmen and members of the Public Service Commission and a new Local Government Service Board, and other officials. The Opposition, he said, 'want the Government to lay down a system which would make political influence impossible, even when Dr Chike Obi's Dynamic Party takes over power in this Region'.* (At this there were Government shouts of 'There will be no opponents then!') The chiefs, too, must be kept out of politics – 'In my own way of thinking, as one hundred per cent Yoruba man, I want all our Obas and natural rulers to feel like Her Majesty the Queen of Great Britain, that they are the fathers or mothers of all their people.'[3] He ended his speech with a warning that the Opposition would 'fight every inch of the ground to see that nothing is now, at this stage, written into our statute book which will make it possible for the Government of the day to go about victimising some classes of our people'.[4]

The main business of this session, in fact, was to consider three Government bills on local government, riot damages and public order. The basic provision of the first of these was further to reduce the powers of the administrative officers in local government. The other two bills would increase the Government's control over disturbances and their aftermath, in particular the ability to make collective assessments to pay for damages. Chief Awolowo and his party were anxious to get these measures onto the statute book before the Constitutional Conference met, and it was to these that Adelabu had referred at the end of his speech on 26 March. Yet he was not present, much less fighting, on the 27th when the Riot Damages Bill went to a division on the second reading and was passed by forty-six votes to twenty-nine. He appeared on the 28th for the debate on the Local Govern-

---

* The Dynamic Party had been founded in 1952 by Dr Chike Obi, an Ibo from Onitsha in the East who by 1957 was a Lecturer in Mathematics at the University College of Ibadan. Its official doctrine was 'Kemalism' (after Kemal Ataturk) and it favored authoritarian measures. Its membership was very small.

ment Bill, making what was for him a rather pedestrian speech. Possibly he felt somewhat constricted while marking time for the Constitutional Conference rather than leading some dramatic attack upon the Action Group Government, for at the end of his speech he took another position in terms reminiscent of the Ibadan Taxpayers Association decision in 1953 to tolerate the Ibadan Council's policies until they could be overthrown by the new Council in 1954.

Nevertheless on 29 March J. E. Otobo introduced an Opposition amendment to postpone the second reading of the Public Order Bill for six months and Adelabu spoke on behalf of it, contrasting the Action Group administration unfavorably with the British colonial system. Not surprisingly, the Bill passed into law.

Adelabu's new role as a 'responsible' Leader of the Opposition was somewhat irksome. His opponents delighted in making it more so. The Government and its supporters found a golden chance to bait him on 1 April while the House was in Committee to discuss the Appropriations Bill for the budgeting of the administration of the Region during the next financial year. In the discussion on Head 326, the expenses of the Legislature, an Action Group Member, R. A. Olusa, moved that the salary of the Leader of the Opposition be cut from £1680 a year to £1000. He remembered that 'on this very floor, he told us that it would have been better for us to leave him there in Lagos, but since he has come here he would be here to be a pain in our neck. Is he to be paid for being a pain in the neck to somebody?'[5] This sally was received with 'prolonged laughter', but Adelabu kept his temper and assured the House that when the N.C.N.C. came to power he would give Chief Awolowo a salary as Leader of the Opposition not much less than that of the Premier. He also reminded the House that he had not been paid his own salary for seven months after his election to lead the N.C.N.C. Opposition, and Anthony Enahoro, speaking next, assured him that this was not deliberate, a statement which Adelabu might have been forgiven for doubting. Enahoro again drew laughter at Adelabu's expense by pointing out that when the N.C.N.C. leader did draw his arrears, 'I am informed (and I do not know whether it is true) that he had such a good time on these arrears that he was not quite well and he had to declare a fast.'[6] The picture he drew of Adelabu as a legislator was an accurate one.

He is in my view a person who has not the inclination or the patience for democratic processes or for constructive work...you hardly ever find him at the Committee Stage when the constructive work is being done. He comes here, he delivers a flamboyant speech and then walks out until he has another opportunity of lashing at the Government. In fact, I hardly expected him to turn up this morning because we are working very hard this morning on these Estimates.[7]

353

When Olusa finally withdrew his motion it was with a malicious reference to Adelabu's drinking habits, the withdrawal being partly 'in view of the soberness. . .(laughter, laughter. . .) with which the Leader of the Opposition responded'.[8] Nevertheless, the session ended on a jocular note, with the Premier thanking the Opposition for their constructive attitude, and Adelabu congratulating the Government on its new Public Health Bill. 'I wish the Ministry of Health continued success, so that when we go to London, other delegates will, by observing our health, know that we have the best public health service in the whole of Nigeria.'[9] By the conclusion of the Session in the first week of April, then, Adelabu's attention was fixing upon forthcoming events in London. The Western N.C.N.C. delegates were to be Adelabu, Babatunji Olowofoyeku and Dennis Osadebay, with Otobo and P. A. Afolabi as advisers. All were to leave on 7 May, but while Afolabi, Osadebay and Olowofoyeku were to travel by sea, Adelabu and Otobo wished to fly. Since they would arrive almost two weeks before the others, they requested the Government to pay the agreed daily allowance for delegates earlier than originally planned, while all five requested advances on their salaries as legislators for May and June.[10]

Money had in fact occupied much of Adelabu's attention during February and March. His own financial problems were now less acute, since at the end of January the Western Government had at last paid him his arrears of salary as Leader of the Opposition, £487. 14. 10d. in all, but the loss of his Ministry and Council chairmanship and the salaries and perquisites that accompanied them were lasting demonstrations of the uncertainties of the political life to which he had become almost entirely committed. Looking back on his party's ability to guarantee him either security or success from the point at which he knew he would go to London, there was little reason to believe that this would improve in the future. It is important to look back with him at this point to see what had been happening to the party and how this shaped Adelabu's divergent views and uses of the London episode.

Part of the party's trouble was also financial, the hardy perennial problem of the N.C.N.C. and a problem with which the Chairman of the Western Working Committee had to deal even while still involved in the campaign for the Commission of Inquiry. Adelabu had therefore set up a new Regional Finance Committee, under the chairmanship of Chief S. J. Mariere, who saw in this departure promise that 'the N.C.N.C. has come to stay'.[11] At a meeting of this Committee on 23 March a draft set of Estimates of party revenue and expenditure for 1957–8 was approved, causing Adelabu to praise the Committee for its 'sense of responsibility, sincerity, economical aptitude and foresight' in preparing 'a commendable, reasonable and workable Estimates, first of its kind in the arena of our Party's history both in the Region or in the National Headquarters'.[12]

An expenditure of £16,440 was envisaged; £2436 for routine administrative costs at the Regional Headquarters and £14,004 for the expansion of field staff and their transport, including the purchase of seventy-eight motor cycles. The proposed expenditure on field staff and transport was indeed essential if the party was to consolidate and expand its strength in the Region, as the 1956 election had proved. In addition to this planned expenditure the party had outstanding debts of £361. 3. 4d.*

On paper, projected revenue was enough to cover expenditure and leave a surplus of £726. 6. 9d. In fact, this revenue relied on the flimsiest of presumptions, as did any enthusiasm about the estimates. It was hoped to raise £500 by collections and donations, a dubious proposition for a party which could offer no governmental patronage in return. A proposed monthly precept of £6 levied on each N.C.N.C. constituency branch organization would have raised £5760, but this presupposed both a higher level of local organization and willingness to pay than had previously been demonstrated even for elections. The Estimates also foresaw £367. 10. 0d. income from that half of the fee of one guinea paid annually by each branch to National Headquarters to which the Regional Party was entitled. The Estimates calculated on 700 branches when something like 100 would have been more realistic.† Equally optimistic was the hope of selling 200,000 membership cards, which would raise £2500 but which depended on the willingness of National Headquarters to allow Ibadan to keep half of the 6d. cost of the card.‡ Indeed, the indulgence of 'Lagos' was to be craved much further, since the National Executive Committee was expected to grant £4000 from the National Consolidated Account.

Potentially, the most reliable source of income for the Western N.C.N.C. was a levy of ten per cent made on the salaries of its Western and federal legislators, Ministers and Parliamentary Secretaries. In 1957–8 it was expected that this would total £5508. Previously, this entire levy had been

---

* In the original draft a further £2299. 17. 4d. was shown as owed to the firm of S.C.O.A. in Lagos, and it was noted that this figure stood at over £6000 until reduced by National Headquarters. The remainder was a sum owed on several vehicles, but it was noted on 23 March that 'we are not in possession of the cars'.

† This estimate is based on a list of files handed over by Adebayo Asaya to Adelabu on 1 August 1957. In his speech to the N.C.N.C. Kano Convention in June 1959, Dr Azikiwe said that there were 126 branches in the West at that time. (*West African Pilot*, 6 June 1959.)

‡ Adelabu had already contracted with Zik's Enterprises, Ltd, for Western N.C.N.C. membership cards to be printed separately at a reduced rate of 1½d. each, but it was apparently felt by National Headquarters that this was too radical a departure, and the contract was cancelled.

paid into the National Account, from which only £73 a month for staff at Western Headquarters was returned. Now an arrangement was sought with Lagos similar to that obtaining for the Eastern N.C.N.C., which retained sixty per cent of its levy. Everything depended, however, on the parliamentarians' willingness to pay, and this was a matter of considerable doubt. As early as July 1956 the N.C.N.C. Accountant had complained to Adelabu that 'payment of these subscriptions to the Party by those concerned has not been encouraging'.[13] In August Adelabu authorized Adebayo Asaya, the Regional Organizing Secretary, to collect dues from the Western legislators for June, July and August, and at their meeting on 14 September the N.C.N.C. Parliamentary Party agreed to formalize the levy procedure, but this did not mean that most of them actually paid it regularly. In March 1957 Asaya rendered a statement of account for the period June 1956 to February 1957 during which the thirty-two legislators should each have contributed £63 to party funds.[14] In fact, only six of them had done so; eighteen owed the whole amount, three owed £42 and four owed £14. Among the leading lights in the party were some of the worst defaulters. Adelabu had not paid anything while his salary was being held back, which was reasonable, and had contributed for June–October once his arrears were paid, but even he had contributed only part of the November levy and nothing since, so that he was £24 in arrears by March 1957. (He then paid only on the basis of an ordinary legislator's salary, £70 a month, not on his £140 a month as Leader of the Opposition.) Where the party should have collected over £2000, it had only collected £636.

The final comment must be that made by Adebayo Asaya in submitting further accounts in August:

> ...in the statement, you will find the sincerity of each member's financial support to the Party, you will also find the seriousness of the Opposition to take over the Government in the nearest future. These are the personalities we look up to in the Region as Leaders, people you think are prepared to sacrifice everything to bring N.C.N.C. dream into reality in ushering N.C.N.C. government into this Region, but alas they could not afford to pay £7 out of £70 to the party, judge them.[15]

Asaya might be excused some bitterness. A faithful and hard-working servant of the party since his appointment in February 1955, in March 1957 he wrote to Adelabu, 'My patience is running out, because there is a limit to human endurance.'[16] By that time the party owed him £151. 3. 3d. contributed out of his own pocket to keep things going when the party coffers were empty, as well as £183 arrears of salary! At its meeting on 23 March the Finance Committee, though praising his 'hardwork, efficiency and honest effort', found itself unable to increase his salary from £360 to £480 a year and on 19 April Asaya wrote to his National President, then in Lagos for a party convention, resigning his post as from 31 July.* As he explained, 'I have been occupied with the jobs of the party so much that my printing establishment has gradually and lastly collapsed. With this age of 43, I would wish to live [leave?] a sound establishment after my existence to enable my children to go on in life without difficulty.'[17]

Adebayo Asaya's disillusionment was part of a creeping demoralization in the party, represented in the West by the general lack of realism and responsibility in financial and organizational matters and failure to attend meetings. The Finance Committee meeting which had approved the Estimates was attended by only four of its fourteen members, and an important meeting of the Yoruba Publication Committee (another of Adelabu's pet projects) was attended by only three of its fifteen members, even the chairman being absent 'without reason and excuse'.[18] Certainly there was no single cause for the malaise which gripped the party by April 1957, but more important than any other was the crisis in the leadership of the party.

The N.C.N.C. national leaders were talented men with capabilities similar to Adegoke Adelabu's. From Yorubaland came men like T. O. S. Benson, Sanya Onabamiro and Kola Balogun, from the Mid-West Dennis Osadebay, Festus Okotie-Eboh and J. E. Otobo, from the East others like K. O. Mbadiwe and M. I. Okpara. They did not find it easy to work together. Some were more concerned with their own regional 'fiefs' than with the party as a whole; Adelabu was often at odds with 'Lagos', Osadebay's prime concern was the establishment of a Mid-West State (Region) which he would be likely to dominate, while Okpara had built his career firmly upon his position in the Eastern Region. Mbadiwe, Balogun and Okotie-Eboh, known to the radicals as the 'Ikoyi clique' from the area in Lagos where they lived, were engrossed in federal politics, concerned since 1954 with maintaining the coalition with the Northern People's Congress and preserving an N.C.N.C. interest in what went on at the center. They were mistrusted as compromisers. From this collection of men with its congeries of overlapping and conflicting interests in 1956, we shall see a very significant faction gradually developing by the middle of April 1957.[19]

Above all the rest loomed Nnamdi Azikiwe, whose importance to Nigerian history is as clear as it is insufficiently studied. He has been characterized by an American observer as 'a persuasive teacher, an effective propagandist, an able formulator of principles, an astute political tactician, a rugged antagonist, an inspiring personality, but a less than dedicated organizer'.[20] With

---

* Asaya may also have had political ambitions of his own. He was attempting to revive his old Akoko Freedom Party in his home area, with a view to contesting the local elections in 1958.

the last of these it is possible to agree unreservedly. As teacher, propagandist and formulator of principles there is no doubt that Dr Azikiwe was of great if sporadic importance in the period 1937–48, when more than any other man he articulated the growing desire for independence. After 1951 he was more frequently called on to be organizer, political tactician and antagonist, and he was frequently less than astute or rugged. He was badly out-manœuvered in the elections of 1951 and their aftermath, finding himself first of all politically hamstrung in the Western House of Assembly, then isolated as Premier of the East, instead of creating, leading and defending his party at the center where he was so greatly needed. Nnamdi Azikiwe is not a single-minded man, imbued with a sense of personal mission to which all other considerations must be bent. He is not a Lenin or Nkrumah. He has a sensitivity, a nervousness, an artistic or perhaps an actor's temperament which at times brings him almost to the point of collapse, accompanied by threats of resignation and fears of assassination.* By the beginning of 1957 his dislike of political in-fighting had led him to withdraw as far as possible from the hurly-burly of life within the N.C.N.C. Such a withdrawal was not possible, however, for the National President of the N.C.N.C. was involved with the party's other leaders.

These leaders were ambitious men. While paying respect to Azikiwe's undoubted personal ability, his role as the founder of the N.C.N.C., and his popularity with the masses, especially his own Ibo people, they were not always prepared to defer to his wishes. From his point of view, their abilities and ambitions made them a difficult group to handle, and it seems that by early 1957 it was his inability to handle them and the party's haphazard organization that were at the root of the N.C.N.C's troubles. A number of Azikiwe's lieutenants had come to feel that they could not trust him under the pressure of the crises confronting the party to give them without fail the support they expected from their leader. The example of Mbonu Ojike, whom he had forced to resign from ministerial office, was much in their minds. The case of Adegoke Adelabu, whose own resignation from federal office had been endorsed by Azikiwe only a week after Ojike's, seemed to bear out this view. Certainly it had convinced Adelabu that his National President could not be depended on, and this feeling must have been re-inforced by the events of the campaign for a Commission of Inquiry in the West. Kola Balogun, too, had come to feel that his efforts in the thankless task of party organization were not sufficiently appreciated or supported by his leader.

* As in July 1945, during the general strike, when he fled from Lagos to go into hiding in Onitsha, alleging that 'unknown persons' were plotting to kill him. For this incident see Coleman, *Background to Nationalism*, pp. 285–8.

During the first months of 1957 the breakdown of party leadership became inextricably linked to the forthcoming Constitutional Conference. The Conference had originally been expected in September 1956, and the National Executive Committee of the N.C.N.C., at its meeting in December 1955, had created a Select Committee to prepare the party's policy at the Conference. Adelabu was not a member of the Committee (he was not at the N.E.C. meeting), but Ojike, Balogun and Mbadiwe were.* The postponement of the Conference because of the inquiry into the affairs of the African Continental Bank left all the political parties with a much longer period than originally expected to think over their proposals, however, and when the invitations went out from N.C.N.C. National Headquarters on 4 April 1957, to a Special Convention of the party on 19 April which was to elect new officers and ratify the party's proposals for the future constitutional development of Nigeria, the situation had changed in more than one respect.

In this context, perhaps the most significant change of all was the attempt by the leaders of the three major parties to come together and agree on a common front which they could present in London. The initiative for this seems to have come from the Sardauna of Sokoto, President of the Northern People's Congress, who early in 1957 invited the Action Group to take part in an exchange of ideas.[21] Such an approach by the N.P.C. in itself represented a most important shift of opinion. In 1953 that party had refused to go along with the others in asking the British Government to grant independence to Nigeria in 1956, and in doing so had brought on a major constitutional crisis. Now the N.P.C. was sure enough of its own control of the administration of the Northern Region, and its political strength in the federation as the party controlling the biggest bloc of seats in the House of Representatives, to be prepared to negotiate with the other parties. It was also ready to come to a mutual agreement on a date for Nigerian independence. Overtures were first made to the Action Group; the bitter enmity between the two parties was to develop later, and N.P.C. suspicions early in 1957 were directed rather toward the N.C.N.C., since that party was the ally of the northern governing party's chief enemy, the Northern Elements Progressive Union. On 3, 10 and 17 March meetings were held at Ikorodu, not far from Lagos, between S. L. Akintola for the Action Group and Abubakar Tafawa Balewa for the N.P.C. The Sardauna was anxious to broaden the basis of the talks,

---

* Dr Azikiwe was to have been Chairman of the Committee, though in fact he does not seem to have acted in that capacity, and J. M. Udochi from the Mid-West was its Secretary. The other members were R. A. Njoku, an easterner and Federal Minister of Transport, E. O. Eyo, B. C. Okwu, E. C. Akwiwu and E. Emole, also easterners and the last a regional Minister, W. B. Egbe and C. N. Ekwuyasi from the Mid-West, and T. O. S. Benson, H. O. Davies, D. C. Osadebay, and S. D. Onabamiro from the West and Lagos.

however, and on 26 March all three parties came together in support of a motion in the House of Representatives calling for independence in 1959. On 4 April the Sardauna visited Dr Azikiwe in Enugu and invited him to attend a 'summit conference' of the three Premiers in Lagos; the N.C.N.C. leader agreed and asked Adelabu, Mbadiwe and Okpara to accompany him.[22] A preliminary caucus meeting of the N.C.N.C. representatives was held at the Ibadan Catering Rest House on 14 April, while Dr Azikiwe was passing through on his way to Lagos. On the 15th there was a meeting of the Premiers' advisers (Mbadiwe and Balogun for the N.C.N.C., Akintola for Action Group, and Abubakar Tafawa Balewa and the Makaman Bida for the N.P.C.) to settle an agenda.* This same day an informal N.C.N.C. caucus also met and arrived at many contrary positions. The Premiers' 'summit conference' followed on the 16th and 17th. On the 18th, the National Executive Committee of the N.C.N.C. met before the Special Convention of the entire party on the 19th.

The exact degree of unanimity achieved at the Premiers' conference on 16 and 17 April is now difficult to establish. All three parties sought Nigerian independence in 1959, but the Eastern and Western governing parties wanted immediate regional self-government while the North preferred to delay regional self-government to coincide with national independence. Not surprisingly the advisers, and later the Premiers, were unable to agree whether regional self-government or independence for the whole Federation should be considered first in London, Azikiwe being more concerned with Nigerian independence. The other major item of potential disagreement related to the carving of more 'states' or units of the federation out of the existing three regions, and the possible revision of already existing boundaries between regions. The N.C.N.C. advocated the division of the three regions into fourteen new states, or possibly the transformation of the existing administrative provinces into federal states which would have meant more than twenty such units.† The N.C.N.C. hoped thereby to create a

---

* Thus it was Kola Balogun and not Adelabu who in fact represented the Western N.C.N.C. as one of Azikiwe's advisers. The reason is unknown to us, but may be related to the fact that Adelabu had not been a member of the party's Select Committee on the forthcoming Constitutional Conference, and was therefore not as familiar with its discussions as Balogun.

† The Select Committee set up in December 1955 listed the fourteen as Bornu–Adamawa, Kano, Sokoto, Zaria–Katsina, Benue–Bauchi–Plateau, Niger–Ilorin–Kabba to replace the existing North; Owerri–Rivers, Onitsha–Abakaliki–Afikpo, and Calabar–Obubra–Ikoma–Ogoja to replace the East; Ibadan–Oyo–Ondo, Abeokuta–Ijebu–Colony, and Benin–Delta to replace the West; Lagos Federal Territory; and the Cameroons (it was not specified whether this was to include both the Northern and Southern Cameroons). ('National Council of Nigeria and the Cameroons Constitu-

stronger central government able to exert fuller control over weakened regional ones, not a decentralized system. As Sanya Onabamiro put it in a memorandum to his party's leaders a few days before the Premiers' conference,

This for us, therefore, is the moment for a serious dedication to the theoretical stand which the N.C.N.C. took many, many years ago. That is, *that Nigeria is and should remain one Country, comprising many states*, minimum number, eight, and *having a strong Central Government* capable of maintaining the unity of the Country and of keeping within bounds the separatist tendencies of tribally minded Regional politicians.[23]

The Action Group position was quite different. That party had come out at its Regional Conference in October 1955 in favor of two new states, the Mid-West, to be carved from the West, and the Calabar–Ogoja–Rivers (C.O.R.) State from the East. At that time the party rejected the idea of carving a Middle Belt State from the North but by early 1957 had swung around to giving it lukewarm support. The Action Group also wanted a change of the boundary between the Northern and Western Regions in order to allow the Yorubas of the Ilorin and Kabba Divisions of the former to join their brethren in the latter. The N.P.C. simply opposed any changes in the composition or boundaries of existing regions. Thus the three parties seem to have reached agreement on 16–17 April, not on whether or which new states should be created, but solely on the procedure to be followed should a 'State Boundary Commission' be appointed by the Secretary of State.[24] (Even this measure of agreement was not long to survive the arrival of the delegations in London.)

Adegoke Adelabu was entirely in agreement with his party in wanting independence for Nigeria in 1959, in regarding this as more important than the question of regional self-government and in supporting the principle of a strong central government and weak regional ones, provided that the central government was controlled by the N.C.N.C. It is on this question of the creation and purpose of new states that his position and that of his followers becomes complex. In part the question was raised within the party because of its inadequacies, discussed above, and the attempts of its ambitious leaders to derive something for themselves from the party's confusion. As Chairman of the Western Working Committee and Leader of the Opposition in the Western House of Assembly, Adelabu was committed to supporting Dennis Osadebay and the Mid-West State Movement which he had founded in May 1956 in seeking such a state, creation of which was fast

tional Conference Committee: Proposals to be placed before the National Executive Committee', p. 6, mimeographed, n.d., A.P.)

becoming the major political issue in the Mid-West. Support for the separation of the non-Yoruba peoples from the West had begun to develop during
the great constitutional debate of 1948–50; with the backing of the Oba of
Benin the Benin–Delta Peoples Party had been founded in September 1953
to campaign on this issue, and, finding themselves unsuccessful in local and
federal elections, the majority of its leaders had merged with the Action
Group. Now Osadebay's Mid-West State Movement was seeking to harness
the enthusiasm for separation on behalf of the N.C.N.C.*

The proposed Central Yoruba State affected Adelabu more directly. The
originator of the idea seems to have been S. O. Ajai, an Ijesha, who had gone
into business in Owo after a period as a civil servant. In August 1955 he had
sent a circular letter to Adelabu, Balogun, Fadahunsi and others, arguing
the need for a 'North-West' or 'Ibadan' state, in part because of 'the beastly
scare of Ijebu domination which is gaining ground through the ignorance of
our natural Rulers and which makes every Western citizen to groan'; he also
urged that an Ibadan State Party be set up in alliance with the N.C.N.C.[25]
A meeting of interested people at Ilesha was cancelled due to the advent of
local government elections, and after sending around another circular, Ajai
went to Ibadan to see Adegoke Adelabu on 27 October 1955. He later
claimed that the Lion of the West spoke in favor of a separate Ibadan state
at a meeting of the N.C.N.C. Western Parliamentary Party that same day.[26]

Ajai continued his campaign in a letter dated 28 March 1956 sent to the
Daily Times, the *West African Pilot* and the *Southern Nigeria Defender*
urging that the 'North-West State' be put on the agenda for the forthcoming
Constitutional Conference. Since Adelabu hoped the N.C.N.C. would win
control of the whole Region he did not advocate the division of Yorubaland
during the election campaign. Having lost, however, he immediately demanded such a state in the N.C.N.C. petition to the Governor shortly after
the election. The campaign for the Royal Commission of Inquiry tended to
push this issue into the background again, since Adelabu once more hoped
to force another election and win control of the whole region. With the
failure of that campaign, he again urged a new region, now referred to as
the 'Central Yoruba State' and composed of Ibadan, Oyo and possibly Ondo
Provinces. Early in 1957 he set in motion plans for a 'Central Yoruba State
Movement'. He still did not give up all hope of a Commission of Inquiry
and, as he made clear in his speech in the House of Assembly on 26 March,

---

* The first organization to concern itself with this issue seems to have been the
Reformed Benin Community Organization, founded in or just before October 1948.
In April 1951, Anthony Enahoro called a conference on the subject at Sapele. In
1952–3 there was a short-lived organization called the Central State Congress, which
was replaced by the B.D.P.P.

he also intended to press for constitutional 'safeguards' as a necessary pre-condition for regional self-government in the West. Nevertheless, the idea of a Central Yoruba State was also an attractive one, especially in terms of his own personal power, and in his speech in the House on 28 March he had proclaimed it as the corrective to all the ills of the Action Group regime. In an area containing the major N.C.N.C. strongholds of central and northern Oyo Division, Ilesha Division and Ibadan itself, he could win a majority in any election and so become Premier of this new unit of the federation. More-over, with the Mid-West State also in being, and controlled by the N.C.N.C., his old enemy the Action Group would be confined to a residual region made up of Ijebu, Colony and Abeokuta Provinces.

By implication, of course, Adelabu's views did not really accord with the N.C.N.C.'s desire to see the creation of fourteen or more units whose reduced powers would be subject to much stronger central control than was the case under the constitution of 1954. Adelabu was not hoping to become Premier of a region with restricted powers. The Central Yoruba State represents a great narrowing of his vision at this point. Gone were the Union of Socialist States of West Africa and *Africa in Ebullition*; behind him were his days as a Federal Minister; victory in the Western Region, even in the whole of Yoruba-land, now seemed beyond him. Politically, though not administratively, he still held sway in Ibadan, however, and there is a sense in which the Central Yoruba State, his new, more limited hope for power in 1957, was Ibadan writ large, a personal fief which only marginally would be the domain of either the N.C.N.C. or the independent Nigerian government. In addition to his personal and, in a sense, alternative business plans, Adelabu thus had two chief concerns as a member of the N.C.N.C. delegation to London. The first was to try to loosen the Action Group's grip on the West as a whole. The second, if that failed, was to secure the establishment of his new region. The Constitutional Conference which was to meet at the end of May would be the arena for his latest triumph.

On 15 April 1957 some of the delegates and party leaders who had come to Lagos caucused in the house of Alhaji N. B. Soule to discuss the mandate to be given to the London delegation. (Soule himself was apparently not present.) This meeting is of great interest for it brought together for the first time as a discernible group those ambitious and dissident elements of whom we have spoken above as moving toward a faction within the party. Among them were the two main leaders of the revolt against Nnamdi Azikiwe's leadership, Kola Balogun and K. O. Mbadiwe, fresh from the adviser's meeting of that same day, and seven others who with them were to sign the famous 'Zik Must Go' letter in June 1958. Adegoke Adelabu was also there, along with P. A. Afolabi, D. K. Olumofin and H. O. Davies.

The Mid-West was strongly represented (by Chiefs Omo-Osagie, Okotie-Eboh and Oweh). From the East were Aja Nwachukwu, Adelabu's successor as federal Minister of Education, D. C. Ugwu, formerly Adelabu's Parliamentary Secretary, and U. O. Ndem, Mbadiwe's Parliamentary Secretary. To complete the assembly were O. Bademosi, Balogun's Parliamentary Secretary, Chief Adebowale, the ex-Olobi of Ilobi, and a strong group of the Lagos N.N.D.P. members whom we have already noted as being close to Adelabu.*

The decisions taken at this meeting naturally reflected the special interests of those attending. It was minuted, for example, that the Mid-West State was to be 'regarded as a Fait Accompli'. While this faithfully echoed the words of the proposals of the N.C.N.C.'s Constitutional Conference Committee, it did not accord with what was in fact decided at the Premiers' meeting held on the next two days when, as we have seen, it was decided to refer all questions of new regions to a 'State Boundary Commission'. The meeting on 15 April was also out of line with what was emerging as official party policy in listing among the topics 'on which there should be no compromise' the position that all residual powers under the constitution should be vested in the central rather than in the regional governments as in the 1954 constitution. In fact, the policy put before the N.E.C. meeting three days later was that there should be no change in the list of subjects under federal jurisdiction. Similarly, the ideas of the unofficial meeting on the electoral franchise ran counter both to the original proposals of the Constitutional Conference Committee and to what was to be ratified on the 18th. Adelabu, Mbadiwe and the others were in favor of uniform electoral laws for the whole federation. The Constitutional Conference Committee, however, had been more sensitive toward the religious susceptibilities of the Muslim leaders of the North:

The peculiar situation in the North where Islamic religion restricts the right of certain married women to vote is recognised. Religious freedom is one of the recognised fundamental human rights and we are willing to accommodate the North by exempting such married women as could not exercise franchise under Islamic religion.[27]

The proposal which emerged after the Premiers' meeting was even more

---

* Chief Adebowale, a minor natural ruler from Egbado Division, had been deposed by the Action Group Government of the West and his case had been championed by the N.C.N.C. The Lagos Group included G. B. Akinyede, a lawyer who acted as secretary of the meeting, Fasasi Adeshina, E. J. Ogundimu, M. A. Cole, J. S. Sofidiya, and E. A. Ladega. Balogun, Mbadiwe, Bademosi, Ndem, Afolabi, Davies, Akinyede, Adeshina, Ladega, and also Alhaji Soule, were among those who later signed the 'Zik Must Go' letter.

conciliatory toward the views of the Muslim leaders of the Northern People's Congress, for the final proposal put before the National Executive Committee recommended universal adult suffrage in the South and in the North the vote only for men without even a qualified female franchise.

The gathering on 15 April was quite explicit on another matter on which the final proposals put before the N.E.C. were silent, no doubt reflecting the failure to agree at the Premiers' meeting. This was the question of internal self-government for the regions, and on this Adegoke Adelabu had his way. The N.C.N.C., it was held, should oppose self-government in the West unless the Royal Commission of Inquiry into the affairs of the Action Group Government was held first. A rather curious attempt was made to distinguish between a request for internal self-government made by a region and one made by its elected representatives:

It must be appreciated that the promise given in 1953 was to the effect that any Region that desires self-government shall have it, the promise is not that any Government or any political party that asks or desires. A Party that has not ⅔ in the house and which has less than 50% of the electorate supporting it cannot speak for a region.[28]

It is noteworthy that by this time Adelabu still had not understood that the Colonial Office regarded the election of 1956 as giving a mandate to the Action Group to speak on behalf of the whole Western Region. He does not seem ever to have appreciated the basic feature of the process of decolonization – that the abdicating colonial power, having decided with whom it would negotiate, was very loath to abandon that dialogue and initiate another. It is also interesting to see that at this point Adelabu's main emphasis was again upon winning control of the whole of the Yoruba West, and no mention was made of the proposed Yoruba Central State.

K. O. Mbadiwe was also able to lay a foundation for his personal ambition in getting the meeting to agree that there would be 'no compromise', not only on the creation of a federal Prime Minister by the Constitutional Conference, but also on the establishment of the office of Deputy Prime Minister. Since it was almost certain that the Prime Minister would be drawn from the Northern People's Congress (probably being Abubakar Tafawa Balewa, that party's Deputy Leader), Mbadiwe, as Leader of the N.C.N.C. Federal Parliamentary Party, envisaged the position of Deputy for himself. The Deputy, as described by the N.C.N.C. Constitutional Committee, would almost be a second Prime Minister, since 'The Federal Prime Minister shall exercise his powers with the consent of his deputy.'[29] This was strongly criticized by Dr Azikiwe:

The National President holds the view that it is indefensible that the powers of the Prime Minister should be exercised by the consent of his deputy. A solution to the present political situation is to have an understanding in the form of a Coalition Agreement.[30]

The stage was thus being set at the caucus on 15 April for a future clash between the N.C.N.C. National President and his chief lieutenant on a matter of some importance.

This unofficial meeting was the most significant but not the only manifestation of the turmoil in the party in that week in April 1957. Tension was greatly heightened by a curious incident on the 16th. As Dr Azikiwe's car entered the grounds of Government House, the Governor-General's residence, where the Premiers' meeting was to be held, a stone was thrown at it by a man, later determined in the courts to be insane. In the heightened imagination of the N.C.N.C. National President this became another assassination attempt, and was seen in a context with the activities of some of his lieutenants. Some of those who had caucused on the 15th formed a 'Peace Committee', which wrote to Zik on the eve of the N.E.C. meeting that 'it is absolutely necessary that our deliberations be free from bitterness, envy, hate and enmity'.[31] Referring somewhat mysteriously to 'that dispute', the Peace Committee asked that it be settled before the meeting, or that it be kept out of all deliberations; Adegoke Adelabu had been charged with responsibility in this regard.*

On the morning of Thursday, the 18th, when the National Executive Committee meeting at the Lagos City College in Yaba was opened by an apology from Dr Azikiwe for the shortness of the notice given for the meeting and an announcement that the first item on the agenda was an 'Exchange of views between party leaders, parliamentarians and the National President', everyone must have known that 'the dispute' was out in the open.[32] When Dr Mbadiwe began to speak on behalf of the Federal Parliamentary Party he first sympathized with the National President on his recent 'escape from assassination' and then went on to launch a heavy attack on him. The five matters he raised amply illustrated the declining trust between Nnamdi Azikiwe and those who should have been his closest collaborators. Why, Mbadiwe asked, despite a pledge to the contrary by the N.E.C., had certain Ministers been dropped in a re-shuffle after the recent Eastern election? Why had the Ikpeazu Report not been published, so that the name of the late Mbonu Ojike might be cleared? In the light of recent statements in the Eastern House of Assembly, could the party be sure that Azikiwe was sincere in his expressed desire to hand over control of the African Continental

---

* This Committee appears to be the first manifestation of what was later known as the 'Elders' Peace Committee', of which Alhaji Soule and H. O. Davies were prominent members. See pp. 420–1.

Bank to the regional government? In the light of the 'gossip and suspicions' which were 'rampant in the Party', with allegations current that some people were plotting to overthrow the National President, could there be clarification of the position of the Zikist National Vanguard, which had become prominent during the Eastern election, and which some feared was 'Zik's own Regiment', his private army?[33] How did one explain the growing 'inaccessibility' of the National President?

For the morning session, however, the dispute remained suppressed. Dr Azikiwe thanked the assembly for their congratulations on his escape from 'the assassin's bullet', although he was 'not, however, happy about some office bearers of the Party who could not visit him after the incident'.[34] Ignoring Mbadiwe's question about the cabinet shuffle, he stated that the Ikpeazu Report had not been published because it was adverse to Ojike, and the members of the commission had been divided in their opinion, the African Continental Bank was to be handed over to the Eastern Government, he knew nothing about the 'formation and running' of the Vanguard and did not believe in 'the gossip and rumours always afloat in party circles'. Lastly, Dr Azikiwe declared that 'although he might have been guilty of seeming inaccessible, it was not intentional, rather it was to conserve energy for further service to the people'.[35]

Although the critics of Azikiwe can hardly have been satisfied with his answer, the N.E.C. then turned its attention to a report by M. I. Okpara on the Premiers' Conference, and to the proposals which the party was to make at the Constitutional Conference. It was agreed that there should be a second chamber of the federal legislature, that independence should be granted in 1959, and that henceforth there should be no expatriate members of the Federal Council of Ministers. From the point of view of those who had caucused on 15 April, other proposals were less satisfactory; as we have already seen, the franchise in the North was to be different from that in the other regions, contrary to what Adelabu, Mbadiwe and their associates wanted, and it was now suggested that no change should be made in the list of subjects under federal jurisdiction. The proposals put before the N.E.C. made no mention of other matters regarded by the caucus as of great importance.* While the caucus had insisted that the police and the judiciary

---

* The full list of proposals put before the N.E.C. was as follows: (1) a bi-cameral federal legislature; (2) a Federal Prime Minister, with a Deputy; (3) expatriates no longer to be members of the Federal Council of Ministers, and the number of Ministers to be increased; (4) universal adult suffrage in the South, but votes for men only in the North; (5) 'The creation of States agreed upon generally as conducive to Nigerian unity'; (6) no change in the list of subjects under federal jurisdiction; (7) revenue allocation between regions and center to be fixed by a special commission; (8) independence in 1959; and (9) the boundary of Lagos Federal Territory to be

must be brought under federal control, the contrary was now suggested, and in keeping with what had been decided at the Premiers' meeting, there was no reference in the N.E.C. proposals to the Mid-West State. Of special moment to Adegoke Adelabu was the lack of mention of any policy to be adopted regarding the granting of self-government to the Western Region.

Nevertheless, there was no attempt at this meeting to dispute the proposals and the National Executive Committee endorsed them for reference to the Special Convention. Doubtless, Adelabu and the others believed that more effective pressure could be brought behind the scenes than openly at such a large meeting of party leaders as that at the City College, or the much larger assembly which gathered on the following morning (Friday 19 April) at the Glover Memorial Hall in central Lagos for the Convention.

The opening session of the Convention was devoted to an address by the N.C.N.C. National President. It was a speech of great importance, for in it Dr Azikiwe openly faced his critics, discussed the ills of the party, and made his own suggestions for their remedies. From the beginning he took an heroic if sombre stance which could not easily be challenged before such a gathering. 'We meet under abnormal conditions', he said, 'because there is widespread rumour that there is a rift among your leadership and an attempt has been made on the life of your National President.'[36] He confessed himself puzzled at what had occurred: 'I do not know what was the motive for this second attempt on my life. I am at a quandary to appreciate why people would conspire to take away human life in order to gratify their desires. If the motive is political, then I see no reason why I should not be told bluntly that since I have outlived my usefulness to the country I should step down.' Declaring that his life was threatened by a group of 'Brutuses and Cassiuses', he concluded the first part of his speech with what amounted to a resignation from his leadership of the party:

God knows I bear no grudge and have no hatred for any person and I harbour no ill-will against any man or woman. But I know that I am staying too long as National President of this great Party, and I am bound to hurt feelings and create unnecessary complications in the relationship of those who guide and control the destiny of the N.C.N.C. I must go and I must give way before these brave soldiers become frustrated and disillusioned. If that should happen and they are discomforted, you will have to lose not only my services but also their great contributions to the success of this great Party. These preliminary remarks are intended as an indication that I do not wish to stand for re-election when the time comes for the Party to elect its officers for the forthcoming year.

extended to a twenty mile radius. ('Constitutional Conference Committee: Proposals. . .', p. 3.)

368

Dr Azikiwe then went on to try to diagnose the cause of the party's sickness. During the twelve years of existence of the party, a period of adaptation and learning, 'an imperceptible conflict has developed between party loyalty and parliamentary leadership.' This was especially true of the federal legislators, for 'the peculiar nature of our federal system of government. . . makes it possible for the majority party to have absolute control of its Ministers in the Executive Councils of the Regions, whilst the position is reversed in the Federal Council of Ministers'. Azikiwe thus drew the attention of his listeners once more to the problems which had plunged the party into crisis in 1952–3 and seemed about to do so again.* Ever since the Macpherson Constitution came into effect in 1951, giving the party some access to power, the N.C.N.C. had faced two very difficult problems. First, how was central control to be exerted over powerful local 'barons' (like Adelabu), who had to be wooed into throwing their support behind the N.C.N.C.? Second, was the party to retain any 'national' meaning, or was it to become merely a vehicle for winning power in the regions, giving its members but not the national party access to sources of patronage and disbursable wealth? It was extremely important to have such resources at the party's disposal, in order to retain the loyalty of local leaders who felt no 'ideological' commitment to the N.C.N.C., but it was also essential in terms of the N.C.N.C.'s own commitment to Nigerian independence for it to play a national role. This is what made the place of the Federal Parliamentary Party so important, for while it could claim to represent the most important interest of the N.C.N.C. in terms of its history as a nationalist party with Nigeria-wide interests, it was subject to no real control by the party as such. Dr Mbadiwe, Kola Balogun and the other federal Ministers could regard themselves as the 'real' N.C.N.C., while paying little heed to Nnamdi Azikiwe, far off in Enugu.

Zik was not in charge in Lagos. If it was not his fault that he had not gone to the center in January 1952, he had made no effort to do so in the federal election of 1954, when he could have been easily elected from an eastern constituency. Nevertheless he tried in his address to explain why he had gone to the East in 1953 and became its Premier in 1954. In a wounded fashion he declared that

Since the Lyttelton Constitution became the organic law of this country I have been subjected to insulting remarks by various critics who thought that it was a

---

* Sklar, *Nigerian Political Parties*, p. 203, summarizes these as 'the inconsistency of a unitary party within a federal state'. It might be asserted that the unitary nature of the N.C.N.C. was always more a matter of theory than practice. Both the N.C.N.C. and the Nigerian constitution tended rather to reflect the heterogeneous nature of Nigeria itself.

pleasure for me to serve as Premier and opined that I detested the idea of serving in the centre for fear that I would not be at the top of the ladder there. I want to take this opportunity to puncture this myth and to say that in spite of the personal inconvenience entailed, I have always been ready to serve the cause of Nigerian freedom either at the federal or regional level in any capacity it pleases my party to ordain.

Still, Azikiwe did not choose to attack Mbadiwe and Balogun openly, contenting himself with commenting on the 'general lack of efficient machinery in our party organisation', and with recommending that N.C.N.C. parliamentarians be brought under control by forbidding them to hold party office or to be members of government corporations. (In what was perhaps an oblique move against Balogun, Secretary of the party since 1951, he also suggested that no person should hold national party office for more than two terms, unless two-thirds of the delegates at a Convention voted otherwise.) Dr Azikiwe turned to the forthcoming Constitutional Conference only briefly, asking for a clear mandate on what had been the failure at the Premiers' Conference to decide whether to press for independence or regional autonomy as the first item on the agenda in London. When the National President sat down he was followed by a debate on his Address in which Adelabu, Mbadiwe and the others kept the basic issues under cover. The only decision of note was to set up a Special Committee to make recommendations for the re-organization of the party; H. O. Davies was to be its chairman, and G. B. Akinyede (secretary of the caucus meeting on 15 April) and Adebayo Asaya were also members.

After a long break, the Convention met again at 3.45 p.m. with Adegoke Adelabu, First National Vice-President of the party, in the chair. Azikiwe had sent a note promising to be present by 5.30 p.m., but in fact he did not come at all. The reason for his absence is not clear; probably he hoped to avoid committing himself during the election of officers, which was scheduled for that afternoon. Whether because of his absence or for some other reason, there was no effective discussion of the N.E.C. proposals for party policy at the Constitutional Conference. Dr Okpara gave his report on the meeting of the Premiers and the proposals were endorsed without change. Thus Dr Azikiwe did not get the clear mandate for which he had asked on an issue which was to prove to be one of the most contentious of the Conference.

After a rather dull beginning, however, the afternoon session was to end in high drama. Kola Balogun had foreseen that the election might present an opportunity for trouble and in announcing the Convention he had ruled that only delegates from fully paid-up branches with letters of authority from their branch chairman and secretary would be admitted and allowed to

370

vote.[37] In all, 102 branches were represented; 64 of these were from the Western Region, a disproportion probably related to ease of access to Lagos, although it may also have been related to Balogun's strict control of entry to the hall. In addition to branch delegates, a crowd of National Officers, ordinary members of the N.E.C., and N.C.N.C. legislators was in attendance.

In the election of officers the three highest were unopposed. Despite his categorical statement of the morning Nnamdi Azikiwe had been prevailed on to stand again as National President, and at this juncture no one was prepared to challenge him openly. Similarly, no one was prepared to contest against Adegoke Adelabu for the office of First National Vice-President, and K. O. Mbadiwe was elected to fill the vacant place of Mbonu Ojike as Second Vice-President. For the office of National Secretary there were three nominations. Kola Balogun sought another year as the director of the party's organization, but two other men, perhaps having caught an inference from what the National President had said in his Address, now sought to dispossess Balogun. Adeniran Ogunsanya was a lawyer from Ikorodu and as one of Azikiwe's strongest supporters had been re-elected President-General of the Zikist National Vanguard at its first convention in January. He was known as one of the party's young militants. The candidature of the other, G. B. Akinyede, who had attended the unofficial caucus with Balogun, demonstrated that it had not yet solidified into a working group with agreed aims.

What happened next is best described in the words of the report of the Convention:

Messrs Akinyede and Ogunsanya were voted for and their votes recorded: while Chief Kolawole Balogun was being voted for, disorder crept into the election business because Hon. Benson came in and tried to stop the Chairman, Hon. A. Adelabu from continuing with the meeting with the election business, his reason of argument being that it was not proper to carry on the meeting in the absence of the National President. The confusion that ensued was so greatly embarrassing and disappointing that the convention was forced to adjourn at about 7 p.m.[38]*

---

* Fred Anyiam gives a rather more colorful description of the incident in his *Men and Matters in Nigerian Politics*, p. 47, but, presumably writing from memory, he describes Mbadiwe as being in the chair, and makes him the central figure (and chief villain), not Balogun. 'Dr. Azikiwe absented himself from the afternoon session and Dr. Mbadiwe thought that his hour of victory had come. He made himself the chairman, being the leader of the Parliamentary Party and the self-appointed successor to the leadership of the party. He rushed to the election of the National President and on his way to getting himself installed his immediate second, the Honourable T. O. S. Benson appeared and walked to the dais and demanded that no more election of officers should proceed since the National President had refused to attend.

The division among the N.C.N.C. leaders was now completely in the open and when the Convention met again at 9.00 p.m., with the intention of completing the election of a National Secretary, Azikiwe was forced to intervene. He did not come to the session in person but wrote a note to Adegoke Adelabu, who was again in the chair, advising postponement 'until passions died down'. After some debate this was accepted. If Zik's authority was sufficient to postpone, it did not provide a basis for a fresh start.

The Convention prolonged its adjournment throughout the next day, and did not meet again until 12.30 p.m. on Sunday, 21 April. In the meantime, Adelabu and some other delegates left for home. The election was never completed, Kola Balogun remaining National Secretary by default. After hearing Zik remind them that 'We must sink our differences in the interest of this great Party if we are loyal, sincere and want political freedom', the remaining delegates agreed that officers should be elected at the Annual Convention, to be held at Aba in the East after the Constitutional Conference. However, a committee of seven under J. M. Udochi from the Mid-West was set up 'to investigate the grave allegations in the Presidential Address against party leaders and make recommendations for internal security'.[39] The Convention also passed a motion calling on the Secretary of State to take measures to protect the lives of Azikiwe and other delegates to the London Conference.

A spate of unrelated items concluded the session.* The Convention finally

Dr. Mbadiwe insisted that the meeting was in order. Thereupon Mr. Benson pounced on him and shouted in annoyance, "Since this jagajaga man entered the NCNC, there has been chaos, intrigue, attempted assassination and bad faith in the party." Pandemonium ensued and in an attempt to protect his brother Dr. Mbadiwe, Mr. Green Mbadiwe received a dirty slap from one of those present and he fell head-long. Mr. Benson seized the National Secretary's book while Chief Kola Balogun ran for his dear life leaving his cap behind. Thus Mr. Benson saved the party from the political opportunist who wanted to get to the top by fair or foul means.'

* One of them was a matter close to Adelabu's heart, a re-affirmation of the party's will to press for the inquiry into the affairs of the Government of the West. A committee of three was set up to consider a request by Dr Obi's Dynamic Party for affiliation with the N.C.N.C. It was announced that a number of those who had left the party in previous years, including Jaja Wachuku (see pp. 253 and 254), had been re-admitted. On a motion from the floor, Mokwugo Okoye and Osita Agwuna, the radicals who had been expelled at the Ibadan Convention in 1955 (see pp. 260-2) were among those allowed back. The letter which they had written early in April 1957 to Azikiwe seeking re-admission, however, can hardly be described as a humble one: 'it is our candid opinion that our expulsion from the NCNC has neither improved the fortunes of the Party nor helped towards the achievement of its major objective – a Socialist Commonwealth – and with our record of service and our youth we have no reason to believe that our cause is a lost one'. They set a time limit for the N.C.N.C. to agree to take them back again, and to make their position even more

adjourned at about 4.00 p.m. Its main purpose of ratifying the N.E.C. policy proposals for the Constitutional Conference had been achieved, but on the eve of that Conference the differences among the N.C.N.C. leaders had finally come into the open and had been prevented from exploding only because of the need for a façade of unity in London. The Aba Convention was still to come.

The party prepared its memoranda and held further discussions on tactics. Individual delegates began to make personal plans. Adegoke Adelabu, for instance, was concerned with his personal finances. Never very secure, often extremely precarious, they had been a source of distraction from his political interests which he had hoped would resolve them. As we noted in Chapter 11, the loss of his income as a Federal Minister, the largest regular income he ever had, was a serious blow. In the latter part of 1956, having failed to secure public office as Premier of the West, he turned once again to private business in order to recoup his fortunes, working, as usual, with the Younan family. According to records in his personal papers, between 20 November and 17 December 1956, he bought assorted cloth worth £1758 from Anthony Younan, paying off £1000 in five installments during the week of 10–17 December. Part of this cloth he had made up by a tailor into identical costumes with caps which he sold to his party followers at £10. 0. 0d. each, raising some £900 in this way between 18 December 1956 and 12 February 1957. It is tempting to see this venture as a speculation made under pressure; from his surviving bank records we know that he had a balance of £1030 at the end of August 1956, and the refusal of the Western Region Government to pay his salary as Opposition leader deprived him of his regular income. The £1000 paid to Anthony Younan may therefore have represented his last working capital, and the venture an attempt to exploit one of his few remaining assets, the loyalty of his followers, who at Ikire alone bought £100 worth of blue plush costumes. As the surviving records stand, in mid-February 1957 Adelabu had still to make over £800 in order to cover his expenses on this speculation. It is quite possible that in the end he lost money, typical of the pattern of his business experience.

The payment of his arrears of salary in January would have removed the immediate pressures upon him, but by the time he and J. E. Otobo flew to London on 7 May he must already have been making elaborate plans for new business ventures. As we have noted, he would arrive in Britain two weeks before the other Western delegates coming by sea, and he used this time to make commercial contacts.

clear added, 'We ask for nothing and promise nothing more than the right to work together with you in the service of our common cause.' (Agwuna and Okoye to Azikiwe, 5 April 1957, A.P.)

Once in London, from his room in the Washington Hotel in the select area of Mayfair, he wrote to the Board of Trade and the Japanese Embassy to ask for lists of exports which might be sold on the Nigerian market through his 'Anglo-Nigerian Trading Company', for which he had stationery printed giving his hotel as its address. He apparently also dabbled with the idea of entering the timber business, for we know that on 20 May he was taken by his cousin, Tunde Alaka, still in London working for his law degree, to see the director of a firm which sold sawmill equipment. He also met and became friends with a London taxi-driver whom he interested in the Trading Company.

A list of nine items which Adelabu compiled at this time, a very cryptic one to be sure, shows some of the ways in which he hoped to make money. Renewed sales of *Africa in Ebullition* were to raise £1000, he hoped to make £25,000 out of 'libel cases', and £5000 from a 'federal contract'. He seems to have calculated the receipt of £2000 from the sale of 'Adelabu cloth', a textile printed with his picture which was to become a matter of controversy after his death, and £5000 from his trading company. Two other items are 'Muslim Bank', and 'Akuko Press', each of £5000. Almost certainly these represent potential business interests of N. B. Soule, who founded a Muslim Bank in Lagos in mid-1958, and who early in 1957 had plans to finance a new press which would possibly take over the *Southern Nigeria Defender*. It is a measure both of Adelabu's eternal optimism and of his lack of business acumen that he felt able to calculate such income from businesses which did not yet exist. Nevertheless, he seemed to believe that an income of £50,000 awaited him.

Adelabu's other activities in London are not known to us. He seems to have written few letters during this period and did not record his impressions of the capital of the British Commonwealth and Empire. He was photographed feeding the pigeons in Trafalgar Square with K. O. S. Are, another conference delegate, and two anonymous young ladies, but the extent to which he availed himself of the other pleasures of the metropolis is not ascertainable. His eldest son, on behalf of his wives, felt compelled to write requesting him 'not to fight with anybody' and not to drink 'too much beer'.[40] In any case, he was in London officially as the leader of the delegation of the Western N.C.N.C., and on 21 May the Constitutional Conference was due to open.

Sanya Onabamiro, as zealous as Secretary to the N.C.N.C. Delegation as he had been as Election Secretary in the West just over a year before, had done his best to brief his colleagues well. Knowing Britain personally as he did, he took care to warn them of the wiles of the imperialist when met on his home ground:

Great care should be taken in answering clever questions put by innocent looking English 'friends' and no indiscreet information should be given at Cocktail Parties or Dinner Parties or during 'friendly chats' with English men or English *women*.[41]

Onabamiro also provided his delegation with notes on their chief adversaries, pointing out that

We should expect...to find Mr Awolowo the most fanatical advocate of regionalism at the Conference...Mr Awolowo is the one single person in the Action Group Delegation whom we shall need to watch carefully every minute of the Conference.[42]

Of Chief Awolowo's second in command it was noted that

Chief Akintola is regarded by those who claim to know him intimately as the popular 'Whipping Boy' of the Action Group Leadership. He is a mere vocal megaphone of his Party Leader's views without necessarily sharing those views himself. It is thought that Chief Akintola is not really a bad man himself when one gets to know him.[43]

On 21 May the N.C.N.C. delegates travelling by boat arrived. Having settled themselves in their hotels the party delegation caucused. On Thursday the 23rd, at 11.00 a.m., the whole galaxy of Nigerian and Cameroonian politicians and British colonial administrators, politicians and civil servants, fifty-five delegates and forty-four advisers, met together amid the gold and scarlet splendor of the Long Gallery of Lancaster House for the Opening Ceremony of the Conference. Alan Lennox-Boyd spoke in a manner befitting a Conservative Colonial Secretary, reminding the audience of Britain's imperial past:

We meet on the eve of Empire Day. It is a time when in these small islands, and throughout vast territories, we not only rejoice in the past but take up gladly the challenge of the future. The past is here for all the world to see, in the rule of law that prevails throughout Nigeria, in the justice, in the devotion of the public service, in the freedom of speech – some fruits of which we shall no doubt be hearing during the course of the next few weeks – in the protection of minorities, in the material prosperity, and in the sense of unity, which should enable Nigeria to grow into a great and respected nation.[44]

'As for the future', he went on, 'we shall all at this Conference have our contributions to make. Any suggestions which I may put forward by way of proposal or counter-proposal – and I know you will remember this should disagreements arise – will have one object in view, the prosperity, the good government, and the unity of Nigeria.'[45]

The Opening Ceremony was not a place for disagreements. The Sardauna of Sokoto contented himself with thanking the British Government 'whose enlightened and humane policy has made it possible for Colonial peoples to realise the goal of their political ambitions'. Chief Awolowo claimed that 'To many of us Britain is a second home', reminded the audience that in the agitation against British rule Nigerians had 'not shed a drop of British blood', and promised that in the future they would proceed 'by peaceful, orderly and democratic self-rule'.[46] Dr Azikiwe contrasted this conference with the last, in 1953, when 'mutual distrust and suspicion' led to a 'make-shift Constitution'. Now there were grounds for optimism.[47] Similarly suit-able speeches from Dr Endeley, Leader of Government Business in the Southern Cameroons, and Sir James Robertson, Governor-General of Nigeria and head of the Federation's official delegation, brought the Ceremony to a close.

The first Plenary Session of the Conference met after luncheon in a dif-ferent atmosphere. It was already clear that the measure of agreement reached at the Premiers' meeting in Lagos in the middle of April had sur-vived the move to the cooler climes of London only in an attenuated form. The three Premiers and Dr Endeley were still agreed on the demand for independence in 1959, but their other limited agreements, especially that on the procedure for the creation of new states, had evaporated. In his auto-biography Chief Awolowo blamed this on the N.C.N.C., which he claimed had angered the Northern People's Congress by submitting 'a welter of memoranda' on the creation of new states in the interval since the Premiers' meeting, 'the contents of which were diametrically opposed to the principles agreed to' in Lagos.[48] As a result, Awolowo said, the Sardauna announced that he would support only the agreement on an independence date, but nothing more.

The N.C.N.C. Delegation did in fact deliberately submit many memo-randa to the Conference. One related to the creation of new states in general, another to the specific case of the Mid-West State, while others came from organizations linked to the party – the Mid-West State Movement, the Cen-tral Yoruba State Movement and the Lagos and Colony State Movement.* Dr Onabamiro explained this tactic in one of his circulars to N.C.N.C. delegates:

I am informed that the Action Group Delegation is likely to employ the tech-

---

* The Lagos and Colony State Movement had been founded on 20 June 1955, with the object of creating a separate state made up of Lagos Federal Territory and the Colony Province of the Western Region. In 1956 its President-General was T. O. S. Benson, its Secretary-General was Prince Ade Ibikunle-Akitoye, scion of one of the royal houses of Lagos, and among its legal advisers were Adeniran Ogunsanya and H. O. Davies.

nique of inundating the Conference with a plethora of memoranda for the purpose of capturing the initiative of the Conference by leading discussions on issues which they have arranged to suit their own strategy. It is recalled that they tried this technique at the 1953 London Conference not without some success. We should be on our guard against a repeat practice of this technique, possibly by anticipating the issues to be raised and submitting counter-memoranda in advance for each session or refusing out-right to be committed to a discussion on a memorandum submitted by the Action Group if it does not particularly suit us to do so.[49]

As we have seen, the N.C.N.C. advocated the creation of at least fourteen small new states with increased central power over them. Nor was the Action Group's support of the creation of three new states in fact much more compatible with the N.P.C.'s blanket refusal to support any such proposals. Thus, the 'agreement' reached in Lagos was a temporary truce, broken once the Conference actually started. Indeed, as we will see later, the whole dispute was not so much over the exact number of new units to be created as over the fundamental character of the Nigerian political system as it was to develop from this point onward.

In this sharpened atmosphere, the Conference turned toward its business. A Steering Committee was set up to consider the daily agenda and procedure and to issue press releases, the only ones which would be permitted. Each major party had two members on the Steering Committee, Adelabu and Mbadiwe representing the N.C.N.C.* The Plenary Session adjourned, the Committee convened and a dispute immediately arose over the order of business for the Conference as proposed by the N.C.N.C.: first, the date for Nigerian independence, then the question of the units of the federation, then the creation of the Mid-West State if agreement could not be reached on new states in general, after this the distribution of power within the federation, then 'federal self-government in the 2-year transitional period', followed only then by 'state self-government in the 2-year transitional period', and then thirteen detailed problems associated with the last three items.[50] As we have already seen, the Action Group and Northern People's Congress in fact wanted internal self-government for the Regions to come first on the agenda, arguing that this was an item left over from the 1953–4 conference. At the meeting of the Steering Committee, Chiefs Awolowo and Williams for the Action Group joined with Abubakar Tafawa Balewa and Muhammadu Ribadu for the N.P.C. to out-argue Adegoke Adelabu and Nnamdi

* The official federal delegation also had two members on the Committee, and N.E.P.U., U.N.I.P., the United Middle Belt Congress, the Kamerun National Congress, the Kamerun National Democratic Party, and the Kamerun Peoples Party had one each. The Colonial Office also had two representatives, and provided the Secretary and the Press Officer.

Azikiwe, who himself attended in place of Mbadiwe, and Aminu Kano, the N.E.P.U. leader. As the minutes of the meeting recorded:

After considerable discussion, it was agreed that the items covering self-government for the Regions and independence for the Federation should be taken first and second. While accepting the majority view, Dr Azikiwe and Malam Aminu Kano asked that it should be recorded in the minutes of the committee that they did so with reservations.[51]

When this capitulation was reported back to the next Plenary Session on the 24th, however, the N.C.N.C. delegates rebelled. Raymond Njoku, who had succeeded Azikiwe as President of the Ibo State Union and was now federal Minister of Transport, questioned the authority of the Steering Committee to determine absolutely the order of the agenda, claiming the Conference had given the Committee no such power. Nigerians, he pointed out, were anxious to hear the views of the British Government on independence. K. O. Mbadiwe echoed these views; he asked that the rules of procedure be clarified to state whether such disputes would be decided by voting or in some other way. Ibrahim Imam, leader of the Bornu Youth Movement, a northern opposition party, supported them.

Alan Lennox-Boyd answered. The Committee was concerned with procedure, not policy, and it was customary for conferences to appoint such bodies in order to save time in preparing the agenda. Moreover,

On the question of Conference procedure, he did not think it would be wise to propose over-rigid rules; in his experience, decisions by agreement could normally be reached either because all concerned held identical views, or because some interests were ready to accommodate themselves to the majority view.[52]

The views of the Colonial Secretary ultimately prevailed, and, looking back over the Conference, one observer thought this had been the critical moment in its development.*

In assessing the parts played by the various delegations in the Conference Room what appear uppermost in my mind are the imperialist interests of the Secretary of State for the Colonies. From the very beginning the NCNC insisted that rules of procedure should be laid down. The Secretary of State flatly refused. The Action Group supported the Secretary of State. All other delegations kept quiet and the Secretary of State had his way. This victory of the Secretary of State assured the subsequent overwhelming victory of the U.K. delegation through the

---

* The observer was Chike Obi, who in the document quoted here was reporting as Secretary-General of the Dynamic Party, but who attended the Conference as an adviser to the N.C.N.C., which had accepted the affiliation of his party. Towards the end of the Conference Obi took over as Secretary of the N.C.N.C. Delegation from Sanyo Onabamiro, who had to leave London unexpectedly for family reasons.

Conference; for it made Lennox-Boyd a dictator to the Conference...The man treated us like children, thanks to the Action Group which not only failed to support the NCNC proposal for rules of procedure but in fact opposed that proposal and supported the Secretary of State, who, like the NCNC, knew all the time the true significance of the absence of a set of rules of procedure.[53]

It is impossible to say how far the Colonial Secretary consciously set himself to oppose the views of the N.C.N.C., but it is certain that his own views on the future constitutional development of Nigeria were far more in accord with those of the Action Group, and especially of the Northern People's Congress, than they were with the ideas of Dr Azikiwe and his party. As we shall see, Lennox-Boyd's control of the conference proceedings was constantly apparent, and the N.C.N.C. had no cause to feel that this control ever operated to its benefit.

Defeated in their attempt to keep control of the procedure in the full Conference, rather than in the Steering Committee, the N.C.N.C. delegates had also to go along with their leader's reluctant acceptance of the placing of regional self-government first on the agenda. As Chike Obi put it, 'the gallant NCNC–NEPU defenders of Nigerian Unity had to choose either to walk out and bring the Conference to an end on its second day or to tolerate an agenda' in which independence for Nigeria in 1959 was subordinated to the question of regional self-government.[54] In fact, they did try to make a fight of it at the third Plenary Session on Monday 27 May, when the Colonial Secretary urged that self-government should be discussed in the context of the present regions, without ruling out the possibility of future changes. Chief Awolowo, the Sardauna and Dr Endeley agreed, but Azikiwe and the representatives of two minor parties held out for discussion of new states first. Adelabu and Dennis Osadebay insisted that their support for Western self-government was conditional upon the prior creation of a Mid-West State. The Action Group leaders countered that the motion for a Mid-West State passed in the Western House of Assembly in July 1955 had not been an official one although tabled by an Action Group Member, while the Motion in December of that year calling for the granting of regional autonomy was a government motion, which the Opposition had supported. Mbadiwe suggested a compromise. Why not discuss the Mid-West issue separately from the other states, and give the Action Group the chance to declare its stand? Alan Lennox-Boyd again spoke, emphasizing the difficulties involved in the new states issue while assuring delegates of his open mind on the subject. When the Sardauna stressed the importance of the undertaking on regional autonomy made by the British Government in 1953, and Lennox-Boyd re-affirmed the intention to observe that undertaking, resistance began to crumble. The U.M.B.C. and N.E.P.U. delegations announced

379

that they wanted further time to circulate memoranda on new states anyway, and it was finally agreed to meet the next day to consider a memorandum on the constitutions of self-governing regions presented by Lennox-Boyd as Chairman. The next six Plenary Sessions, lasting until 4 June, in fact discussed the changes necessary to allow the East and West to become self-governing immediately, and the North in 1959.

In all this Adegoke Adelabu took an active part, speaking always in favor of the increase of the powers of the central government relative to those of the regions. Thus, in the Plenary Session held on 28 May, he spoke in favor of giving the Governor-General the power to act quickly and decisively to intervene when there was a conflict between the center and the regions. At the sixth and seventh Plenary Sessions, on 30 and 31 May, the vexed question of the judiciary was discussed. The Action Group and N.P.C. wished to retain the regional framework established in 1954. The N.C.N.C. was prepared to have both federal and regional (or 'state') judiciaries, but wanted to subordinate the latter to the former.[55] If anything, Adelabu was prepared to go further than this. No doubt remembering his own experience of courts in the Western Region, he asked that the whole judiciary be brought under federal control before self-government was granted to the regions.

Adelabu faced his biggest challenge at the eighth Plenary Session of the Conference on Monday, 3 June when the actual requests by the regional governments for internal autonomy for their areas were discussed. It was clear that the request of the Action Group Government would be granted. The best the Western N.C.N.C. and its leader could hope for was the acceptance of such pre-conditions as the creation of the Mid-West State. As the N.C.N.C. Delegation had stated in a memorandum presented to the Conference on its second day, the N.C.N.C. Members of the Western House of Assembly had supported the motion in December 1955 calling for internal self-government for the region on the understanding that the creation of the Mid-West State would come first. Therefore,

If the two motions on the Mid-West and on self-government are taken together, they represent two dependent clauses of a contractual relationship between the Government and the Opposition in the Western House of Assembly. Immediately the obligation contained in either of the two motions is abrogated or falls short of fulfilment, the obligation contained in the other *ipso facto* loses its binding force. Therefore it is not only irrelevant but immaterial to point at the legislative sanction obtained for self-government in 1955 as the N.C.N.C. Opposition are under no obligation to respect it if the Government Party fails to fulfill the pledge it gave by being a party to the passage of the Mid-West Motion.[56]

In his speech in the debate on the Address in the Western House of Assembly on 26 March Adelabu had already referred to this stand on the part of the N.C.N.C., though he had not then used the 'contractual' argument. On that occasion he had also referred to certain constitutional 'safeguards' as pre-conditions for Western autonomy. He now argued that the N.C.N.C. demand for constitutional guarantees should be respected since the party had won the last federal election in the region and was accordingly its spokesman in the federal Parliament and Council of Ministers. They were fearful of the use to which the Action Group Government might put its new powers, which was why they wanted the Mid-West State to be created before anything else was done. 'Moreover', as the minutes reported Adelabu's speech, 'the Western Region Government had, by its actions and tendencies, instilled fears in the minds of the Opposition. They had shown a lack of respect for the conventions normally observed in democratic countries: for example, certain Action Group Ministers had remained members of private money-making concerns after assuming office. There was also the case of the Alafin of Oyo who had been banished by the Western Region Government.'[57] The latter case could have been prevented had there been a non-partisan Council of Chiefs whose function would be to approve the appointment and deposition of chiefs by the Western Government, which would be represented on the Council, as would the Opposition, the judiciary and the chiefs themselves. This 'safeguard' should be written into the constitution, and Adelabu listed eight more, including the principle that no person should be subject to legal penalties unless personally found guilty (a reference to the new Riot Damages Bill and its principle of collective punishment), and the need for re-drawing constituencies on a population basis. Echoes of the struggle for Ibadan were also present, for he asked that no local council not democratically elected should have a life of more than six months.*

Chief Awolowo responded. He promised to be brief. Only the British Government, not the Western Government, could create a Mid-West State and it should be dealt with along with the other proposed new states at the appropriate place on the agenda. The question of the Alafin of Oyo 'had been raised before in the appropriate forum' in Nigeria and his Government had dealt with it fully. He did not feel that he was called upon to reopen the issue or to defend before the Conference the action taken by the Western Region Government.[58] On the subject of safeguards Chief Awolowo was equally firm.

As regards constitutional safeguards, Mr Adelabu's suggestions amounted in fact to the legal draftsmen in the United Kingdom giving the Western Region a series of model laws on such matters as for example, local councils, the franchise and so forth. He thought this would be a very dangerous and unusual thing to

---

* By this time the Ibadan Provisional District Council had been in power for fourteen months.

do...The Constitutional safeguards demanded by Mr. Adelabu seemed to him an attempt to make the Government of the Western Region the creature of the Opposition.[59]

Everything now depended on the position taken by the Colonial Secretary, but his first words held little hope for Adelabu. He did not think a detailed consideration of the internal affairs of each region would be 'to the advantage of the Conference as a whole'. Then came the deluge.

He suggested that certain of the points made by Mr Adelabu were of a kind made by Oppositions all over the world. Other points were already covered by existing agenda items (for example, the structure of the Federal Government including franchise and electoral law, and provision for the guarantee of fundamental rights), and there would be opportunity for full discussion at the appropriate time.[60]

The offer of regional self-government had been made in 1953 in respect of the regions then existing and the 'duly elected and constituted' government of the West now asked for it; 'accordingly Her Majesty's Government were bound to honour their pledge', which need not prejudice the question of new states, to be discussed in due course. 'It seemed to him', he concluded, 'that, now that the question [of regional self-government] had been fully ventilated, this subject, as a separate item on the agenda, should be regarded as closed.'[61]

With the Western N.C.N.C. case rapidly foundering, Mbadiwe tried to salvage something by proposing that Adelabu's list of safeguards be circulated for private discussion with the Secretary of State, insisting that 'The points should not be completely ignored.' This provoked a further strong statement from Chief Awolowo, who

was not prepared to discuss in this way the internal administration of the Western Region...He could not...accept a situation in which the Opposition, having refused to discuss these matters with him, should come to this Conference to condemn his Government's behaviour. He was still prepared to discuss these matters with the Opposition through the usual channels and would be ready to do so outside the Conference before returning to Nigeria. He had always followed, in this as in other respects, the conventions obtaining in the United Kingdom, to the full extent possible.[62]

At this point, the Sardauna of Sokoto intervened, urging delegates to 'goodwill and co-operation'. Thirty-two million Nigerians were waiting for their independence, and 'it was most unfortunate that personalities and local politics should be brought into the discussions'. The appeal had the desired effect. Dr Azikiwe concluded the debate. The discussion had been useful and 'he particularly welcomed Chief Awolowo's willingness to have further discussions with the Leader of the Opposition in the Western House of Assembly'. 'On this understanding, and given that a number of the matters which had been raised could be pursued further under the relevant items of the agenda, he agreed that this subject, as a separate item for discussion, could be regarded as closed.'[63]

Thus, Adelabu had fought his first major battle at the Constitutional Conference and lost. Internal self-government for the West (and for the East) would now go into effect without any necessary preconditions; the Mid-West State was still to be discussed, and the only possible constitutional guarantees were those which might be written incidentally into the federal constitution. His own party's President had agreed to this, trusting to the good faith of the Action Group leader, which Adelabu could never do. In the name of principle, 'personalities and local politics' had been eschewed, but for Adelabu this was what politics was about. To him the Constitutional Conference was another round in his battle with Awolowo for political power in the Western Region. Defeated in the election a year before, the campaign for a Commission of Inquiry a failure, he now received another set-back. All his hopes were thus rapidly coming to depend on the Central Yoruba State.

The Conference now turned to the issue of the creation of new states. The Plenary Sessions of 4 and 5 June were taken up with the statements of the major parties on this question. These positions we have already seen. The Action Group, somewhat shaken by the N.P.C.'s repudiation of the Premiers' agreement according to Chief Awolowo's account, had been persuaded by him to remain firm in demanding the creation of the C.O.R., Mid-West and Middle Belt States.[64] The N.P.C. was adamant in opposing the creation of new states either at that time or in the future, declaring that 'It is clear from the fantastic demands now being made for the creation of more States in Nigeria that the real idea behind the move is indirectly to introduce a unitary form of government which all political parties have now agreed cannot work under the present circumstances.'[65] This shaft was aimed, of course, at the N.C.N.C.'s advocacy of many states and a strengthened central government holding the residual legislative powers given by the 1954 constitution to the regions.* In its memorandum on the subject the N.C.N.C. pointed out that

Nigeria as a nation or state is a British creation. It is not by any means pre-existing or co-existent individual states coming together to form a Federal union as in the case of the U.S.A. or Australia. For 60 years Britain ruled Nigeria like one unit. Five years ago the present three Regions were created. They were not

* Awolowo, *Awo*, p. 190, also describes the N.C.N.C. proposals as 'a backdoor reversion to a unitary system'.

based on language, religion, ethnic grouping, cultural affinity or any of the well known federal factors. Their creation was based so far as can be ascertained solely on administrative convenience. It is therefore futile to quote precedents of federations which are of voluntary union of pre-existing states instead of facing the reality of a unitary state deciding to break up into component units primarily for administrative convenience and only secondarily to give recognition to diversities.[66]

The memorandum went on to distinguish four evils of the division into three regions: the 'absurdity' of the great size of the North, with three-quarters of the land area and perhaps three-fifths of the population; the 'emphasis, magnification and encouragement of the cankerworm of tribalism'; the use of regional governments to persecute political opponents; and the 'dangerous rivalry' between the federal and regional governments, 'because the units are so few and each Region is too large'.[67] As a remedy the memorandum recommended that new states be set up on the basis of the former provinces which, however, could voluntarily group together. A States Boundary Commission should thus investigate the possibility of setting up a Rivers, Middle Belt, Ogoja, Calabar, Owerri-Rivers and Central Yoruba State and report by June 1958; the Mid-West State did not need investigation, and should be set up immediately.[68]

The Conference met in Plenary Session on Thursday, 6 June, to consider a statement by the Colonial Secretary on the subject of new states. The Secretary began by assuring delegates that 'I have read all the memoranda about new States – every one of them and every word of them.'[69] Many of them, he went on, evoked the principle of self-determination; but what of Cyprus, where 'chaos and bloodshed' would result if this principle were adhered to, he asked? 'How easy life would be' (and this phrase was repeated twice in the same paragraph), 'if the only guiding star we had to follow was the principle of self-determination.'[70] Lennox-Boyd then in effect virtually discounted the memoranda:

I have tried to be dispassionate in my judgements and tried to understand how I would feel if I thought my people were in danger of being forgotten or downtrodden by some majority Government. But I have also tried to remember that most of the memoranda were written by politicians and, being a politician myself, remember that sometimes one takes a slightly different view if the people one approves of are in power than if the people one disapproves of are in power.[71]

Having briefly summarized the position of the major political parties on the issue he then put the point of view of his own Government:

The principal United Kingdom interest is not in either preserving the existing Regions for the sake of doing so or breaking them up, but in developing as quickly as possible and on the firmest basis a system of good government, including adequate safeguards for minorities, which will enable Nigeria to progress steadily as a self-governing and independent nation.[72]

He stressed the difficulty and expense of restructuring the administration at this stage and suggested that minorities could be protected without creating new states for them.

He then discussed the critical question of Nigeria's colonial administrative history. 'The N.C.N.C. have also advanced the argument of principle', he wrote, 'that one State should not be so big as to dominate the rest. It may be that if we were starting from scratch and had a blank map of Nigeria we might achieve a better balance between the Regions. But the North has been the North for a long time – a historical fact with which all of us (including the North) must learn to live.' With these words he set the seal on the shape which Lord Lugard had given to Nigeria, and initiated the period of 'Northern domination' which was to last beyond the lifetime of Adegoke Adelabu and beyond independence, with which the South never did 'learn to live', and which culminated in the army coups of January and July 1966. It is difficult to know whether the Secretary of State intended the frivolous comparison he then advanced to be taken seriously as the foundation of his views. 'The Scots and the Welsh', he went on, 'might well argue that the English can always swamp them, and the possibility of this is actually greater in our unitary form of government than it is in Nigeria. I have not noticed, incidentally, that Lord Perth [Minister of State in the Colonial Office, and Lennox-Boyd's deputy], as a resident Scotsman, or the Governor-General, or the Governor of the West, are notably suppressed personalities, while all of us at Westminster are accustomed to fiery Welshmen playing a very large part in our affairs.'[73] Thus, whether seriously believed or not, Lennox-Boyd patly dismissed the most important issue in the constitutional and political evolution of an independent Nigeria.

A 'Minorities Commission', he went on, could be set up to investigate the feasibility of the Middle Belt, C.O.R. and Mid-West States if 'the establishment of the Commission would commit none of us to anything other than an enquiry into the facts and then consideration of those facts [but] the United Kingdom would be committed to nothing beyond this. I see innumerable dangers in any moves towards what might result in the fragmentation of Nigeria and I should want to be sure that the case for any new State was very sound, that support for it was broad-based, and that any alternative solution was impracticable, before I could agree that any new Government should be set up.'[74]

Although this lengthy statement by the Secretary of State was more upsetting to the N.C.N.C. Delegation than to the others, there were parts of it to which almost all the Nigerian delegations might object, and although Alan Lennox-Boyd met the Premiers in private conclave both before and after luncheon on that Thursday, it proved impossible to come to an agreement on his proposals. The Conference finally adjourned that afternoon for the Whitsuntide recess without progress.

The next Plenary Session was held rather more than a week later, on Friday 14 June. In the interval, the British Government had hoped the Nigerian leaders might come to an agreement among themselves, but this had not happened. The Sardauna of Sokoto, Abubakar Tafawa Balewa and Dr Azikiwe jointly urged that no mention be made of specific areas in the terms of reference for the proposed Minorities Commission. Their motives were of course different. The N.P.C. leaders disliked the prospect of an investigation in the area which might truncate the North by the creation of a Middle Belt State, while the N.C.N.C. wanted more than three new states to be considered. Nevertheless, they joined temporarily against Chief Awolowo, who took the view that if no limits were placed on the claims to be heard, then proceedings would be indefinitely prolonged and independence thus delayed beyond 1959. The Colonial Secretary expressed disappointment at the failure of the Premiers to agree. This issue was the 'first major point of difficulty' which the Conference had encountered, and the lack of agreement 'was bound to have some effect on the United Kingdom Government's attitude to other matters still to be considered by the Conference. . .It was a cause of concern to him that the proclaimed unity between the major parties did not, in fact, appear to exist.'[75]

The threat was plain, since 'other matters still to be considered' included the date of independence for the Federation. Lennox-Boyd argued that it would be impossible administratively to set up more than one new State from each region and it would therefore be futile for the Commission to consider more. It fell to Adegoke Adelabu to answer this, and his interest was direct, since if the Commission were to consider only one new state to be created out of the Western Region, it would obviously be the Mid-West, and his Central Yoruba State would go by the board. He therefore urged as a compromise that the six demands actually presented at the Conference should be considered by the Commission.* This would cover his own interests without giving the Commission 'a blank cheque to entertain additional demands'.[76]

The Secretary of State, rather than responding to this argument, tried to put pressure on the delegates by pointing out that the Conference was progressing more slowly than had been anticipated, with nineteen more items still on the agenda. Would the Conference, he asked, in the last resort

---

* These six were for the Mid-West, Central Yoruba, Lagos and Colony, C.O.R. Rivers, and Middle Belt States.

accept a ruling on this matter from the chair, that is, from himself? Nnamdi Azikiwe dug in his heels; after all, two out of the three major parties were agreed and there was no deadlock requiring such a ruling. Nor was the Sardauna disposed to agree with Lennox-Boyd, who thereupon adjourned for luncheon.

The Session did not begin again until 4.30, and the interval was spent in negotiations between Lennox-Boyd and the various delegations. Chief Awolowo, one of the major participants, later described these as 'protracted and nerve-wracking', with the Secretary of State submitting 'about three' different drafts of the terms of reference for the Commission in all.[77] In the end the N.C.N.C. scored a point but lost the match. Thus, the point was won that the Commission's terms of reference were not to contain any specific mention of proposed new states, but new states were on the other hand to be regarded as a 'last resort', and each must be proved to be economically and administratively viable. To create even one state, they were warned, would be 'an administrative problem of the first order', while 'the creation of more than one such state in any Region cannot now be contemplated'.[78] Thus the attempt by the N.C.N.C. to alter the fundamental shape of the federation had failed, and though he never admitted it publicly and perhaps not even to himself, so had Adelabu's proposal for a Central Yoruba State. This was his second defeat at the Conference; his campaign for constitutional 'safeguards' as a precondition for Western internal self-government had similarly come to naught, since with the decision on the Minorities Commission regional autonomy was now to go forward. From this point onward he seems to have lost interest in the Conference; his own direct personal concerns were not again to be touched, and he does not seem to have spoken at any of the nine subsequent Plenary Sessions.

By this time, too, his followers in Nigeria were becoming alarmed. On 10 June the *Daily Service* had reported that Adelabu and Awolowo had shared the same official car in London, and on the 13th had published a photograph of them ariving together at an Action Group London Branch dance. (See Plate 3.) However much this may have appealed to Colonial Office devotees of the Westminster parliamentary system, it greatly upset friends of the Leader of the Opposition. On 19 June Fasasi Adeshina, the Lagos contractor who was Adelabu's old friend and had been at the 15 April caucus meeting, wrote to him of the 'propaganda' of the *Daily Service*. The N.C.N.C. was 'not happy' while the Action Group was 'dancing in the streets every now and then...telling us that Adelabu have surrendered to Awolowo so that the matter of states does not come out...'.[79] Adeshina appealed to Adelabu, as 'the pillar that we depend on', to 'please try your possible best for us because if you do a piece of thing we here or Daily

Times must publish it'. In conclusion he adjured him to 'Send your photograph to us at home and explain to us your relationship between you and Awolowo.'

In London, out of his own milieu, Adelabu was being outmaneuvered by his enemies. He was unable to command personal publicity in the Constitutional Conference situation, nor was it conducive to his style of oratory or sense of political drama. The rather terse and impersonal press releases by the Steering Committee, of which he was a member but over which he had no control, could not convey to his followers at home his efforts on behalf of constitutional safeguards and the Central Yoruba State, yet he apparently felt constrained not to make his own pronouncements nor did he make any real attempt to keep people in Lagos and Ibadan informed by letter.* Not that there was any mutiny in his absence; but there was disquiet, a feeling that the Action Group was winning this next round of the battle which had been transferred to London.

Nevertheless, before the Conference ended there remained the decision as to the date of Nigeria's independence. All three major parties were still agreed on 1959, as they had been at the beginning of the Conference. On 17 June Alan Lennox-Boyd made his position clear at that day's Plenary Session in a statement on federal independence. He could not go to his colleagues in the British Cabinet, he said, and ask them for a 'blank Cheque' in favor of Nigerian independence; he must know how that check would be filled. Regional self-government had only just been agreed on for the East and West, and the largest region did not even want it yet, so it was essential to see how the federation would 'take the strain' of this new development. The Minorities Commission had also only just been accepted, and if it should recommend the creation of new states the whole structure of the federation might have to be reviewed. While he recognized that the independence of Ghana the previous March had spurred on the Nigerian political parties to emulate that example, it must be remembered that Ghana was a much smaller and more homogeneous country. In this respect, he felt that 'the Conference's recent discussion about the creation of new States had led to expressions of fear that went beyond normal political differences'.[80] Faced with this, an unofficial meeting of all Nigerian delegations was held under the chairmanship of the Sardauna of Sokoto in an attempt to cement their agreement further. An understanding was reached on almost all major features of the structure of the federal government, on interim arrangements

---

* He did write to Alhaji N. B. Soule, but he was away in Dahomey, attending to his business interests in Porto Novo. Adelabu had apparently also written to Adeshina asking for money; in his letter of 19 June Adeshina made excuses for being unable to oblige.

between 1957 and independence, and on the franchise: only the N.C.N.C. demand for a Deputy Prime Minister for the Federation was not generally adopted.*

This agreement smoothed the discussion during the next three days on such potentially contentious matters as the division of powers between the center and the regions and control of the police. As a result, on Friday 21 June, Lennox-Boyd made another statement on independence. Again he stressed the need to 'take the strain' of regional self-government, and to see what the Minorities Commission reported. He also seized on something which had emerged from the discussions of the past few days, an agreement among the Nigerian delegates that the Federal House of Representatives elected in 1954 should be allowed to run its full course. Since legally this might mean no dissolution before 12 January 1960, the Colonial Secretary interpreted this to mean that a federal election was to be expected in the dry season of 1959–60, that is in the last months of 1959 or the first of 1960, when weather conditions would be at their most favorable for the huge administrative task of organizing the election. 'If all goes well at that point', he promised, 'and the people are broadly united, as you assure me they are now, about the next step, the United Kingdom Government would be able to feel with a good conscience that its power of trusteeship was drawing to a close.'[81] A further conference might then be held, to consider the last steps to be taken by Nigeria to independence and membership of the Commonwealth, which Britain would sponsor.

This was scarcely likely to satisfy the Nigerian delegates, and in discussing the statement they urged the Secretary of State to be more specific. On Sunday 23 June, therefore (the Conference was now working without a break in order to meet its deadline), he made his final statement on the matter.

I understand that it is proposed that some time about January 1960 the new Nigerian Parliament will debate a resolution asking Her Majesty's Government to agree to full self-government within the Commonwealth by a date in 1960 which will have been mentioned in the resolution. In any case the constitutional machinery would take time and you would no doubt bear this very much in mind in coming to a conclusion as to what date you should ask for. It might therefore be (as many of you have urged) a good thing for there to be some informal consultation with us as to what sort of date was realistic. On receipt of your resolution Her Majesty's Government will consider it with sympathy and will then be prepared to fix a date when they would accede to the request. We could not at this stage give any undertaking that the date would be the same date as asked for in

---

* It is probable that Dr Azikiwe did not press this very hard. As we have seen, he had never been very happy about the idea, and by mid-1957 he can have had little desire to further K. O. Mbadiwe's ambitions.

the resolution, though we would do our utmost to meet the resolution in a reasonable and practicable manner. Delegates I hope know Her Majesty's Government well enough to be sure that they would not invent reasons for artificially extending the date. Her Majesty's Government would of course be very much guided in their choice of a date by the way everything was going, by how the two Regions now about to enjoy Regional self-government had taken the strain of this great step forward, and by how the country as a whole had faced up to the problems of minorities, on which a Commission would already have reported.[82]

This did not appeal to the Nigerian listeners at all, and when the Session adjourned the three Premiers and Dr Endeley met to prepare their own statement, which was made at the Plenary Session on the following day by the Sardauna of Sokoto. The leaders expressed their disappointment at the failure of Her Majesty's Government to name a specific date in 1960. The original proposal 'by the people of Nigeria' had been independence in 1959, 'and we have given consideration to a date in 1960 only because we appreciate that the solution to the various problems that must be disposed of before independence will take longer time than we had thought. Having gone thus far on the path of reason and realism, we had thought that the Secretary of State would accede to our united wishes.' The signatories therefore took note of what the Secretary of State had said, but reserved the right to pursue the matter further, 'with a view to impressing upon Her Majesty's Government the necessity for granting independence to the Federation of Nigeria not later than 2nd April, 1960'.[83]

Whatever reservations the Nigerian delegates might have, they were forced to accept what they could get. On the following day, Tuesday, 25 June 1957, after considering the draft report of the Conference and approving the terms of reference of the Minorities Commission, they heard Alan Lennox-Boyd, in his closing statement, praise their good humor, and Obafemi Awolowo commend the Secretary of State's 'geniality and patience' and his 'ingenuity in bringing out compromise proposals acceptable to all the Delegations'.[84] It can have given Adegoke Adelabu little real pleasure, though perhaps some sardonic amusement, to hear his old adversary single out Sir John Rankine, the Governor of the West, 'whom they looked on as their friend' for special praise. With further suitable rhetorical flourishes from Dr Azikiwe, the Sardauna, Dr Endeley and Sir James Robertson, the Conference finally adjourned, with the understanding that it would be resumed again the following year, when the Minorities Commission had had time to report and such questions as the allocation of revenue had been considered by the experts.

It was in varying moods that the Nigerian delegations left London to return home. By and large, the Northern People's Congress and the Action

Group could be well pleased with their efforts, despite their disappointment over the date of independence. The N.P.C. had beaten off the attempt to create a Middle Belt State, at least to the extent of having it referred to the Minorities Commission, and might reasonably infer from various statements by the Secretary of State that he did not intend to see the Northern Region reduced in size. The Action Group had not succeeded in getting new states created immediately, but felt that they still had a chance through the Minorities Commission. Moreover, they had seen Adegoke Adelabu completely thwarted in his attempt to impose conditions on the granting of internal self-government in the West. Finally, the N.P.C. and Action Group together had defeated the whole N.C.N.C. attempt to change the shape of the federation in a radical fashion which would shift the balance of power to the center.

The mood of the N.C.N.C. was much gloomier. In a statement made on his departure from London, on 11 July, Nnamdi Azikiwe described the Conference as 'a painful disappointment', though 'not a total failure'.[85] It had secured a larger measure of internal self-government for two regions, and for the federation as a whole, but it had failed to secure independence in 1959. There were two reasons for this, 'the immaturity of the Nigerian delegations', and 'the clever diplomacy of the Colonial Secretary'. Alan Lennox-Boyd and 'his galaxy of experts spared no effort to play on the vanity of the Nigerian delegations, whose gullibility in swallowing the soothing opium of flattery administered by experts in this brand of "White Magic" beats the imagination'.[86] As a result, the Nigerians had agreed to put independence second on the agenda, and then had accepted 1960 as the year when it would be granted. In this last matter, in particular, they had played into Lennox-Boyd's hands:

The spate of claims and counter-claims for separate states, the volley of allegations of oppression fired at a certain Regional Government, the exaggerated fears expressed by representatives of minorities against certain majority groups, and an apparent general feeling of insecurity, should the British depart from Nigeria, placed the Colonial Secretary at a vantage point. As a clever politician, he wasted no time in making capital out of these imponderables; hence he made it clear that he was not prepared to give a blank cheque for Nigerian independence.[87]*

Another observer, whose impressions of the Conference we have already quoted, gave a more detailed account of the tactics of the Colonial Secretary, with which – though hostile – we can hardly fail to agree.

Lennox-Boyd used his powers very well indeed. He supported the majority when

---

* The reference to 'the volley of allegations of oppression fired at a certain Regional Government' is obviously an indirect hit at Adelabu's campaign against the Action Group in the West.

the opinion of the majority tallied with his preconceived ideas. When this happened he ruled that the opinion of the majority should prevail. He supported the minority and ipso facto opposed the majority when it suited him. When this happened he argued that the British Government had responsibilities to the minority and that it would be difficult for him to convince his colleagues in the Cabinet.[88]

There is also much truth in Chike Obi's final verdict on the Conference:

The Nigerian Delegation to the Conference lost because it accepted battle with Lennox-Boyd on Lennox-Boyd's own ground and conditions. Lennox-Boyd like a clever general drew the line of battle and baited the Nigerian delegation into accepting battle on his own grounds.[89]

On 22 July Dr Azikiwe held a shipboard meeting on the way home with some of the other N.C.N.C. leaders to discuss future policy in the light of what had happened at the Conference. They discussed the same two major mistakes as Azikiwe had mentioned in his statement, but also felt that 'From nationalistic point of view, the conference was a partial success.'[90] 'In spotlighting these major mistakes', they felt, 'the treacherous role of the Action Group should be adequately stated.' The N.P.C. should also be 'constructively criticised', though, 'In dealing with the role of the N.P.C., tribute should be paid to its leader for his acts of statesmanship on a number of occasions.'[91] Thus the stage was being set for the coming-together of the N.C.N.C. and N.P.C. at the end of 1959 to form the coalition federal government which was to take Nigeria into independence.[92]

Another matter of great importance was discussed in the context of the N.C.N.C.'s experiences in London. During that time, with memories of the African Continental Bank crisis still fresh in their minds, the N.C.N.C. delegates had tried to preserve a nationalist posture; for example, they boycotted cocktail parties given by the *Daily Times* and the Bank of British West Africa. Now, the whole question of 'Attitude to Europeans' was discussed by the six men on board the M.V. *Apapa*. Their decision was that

Experience has shown that, in a country of our own level of political and economic evolution, open and emotional animosity towards expatriates is not only a most expensive luxury but a great tactical error. Agreed that a policy of evident fraternisation should now be pursued – with the National Leader giving the lead. We should not only be friendly but should appear to be so. This policy is to be applied officially and/or unofficially.[93]

Under pressure, then, the N.C.N.C. was changing, but Adegoke Adelabu was not. On the day that the meeting of the six was held, he returned to a tumultuous welcome in Ibadan. On his way back from Britain he had visited Northern Nigeria and made the Muslim pilgrimage to Mecca. All the speeches and negotiations in London had to him been merely another round in the battle with the Action Group. As he had done consistently since May 1956, when thwarted on one plane he planned to attack on another. Already he had begun to make plans for a 'New States Movement Front', which would seek to abolish the three regions and create new states, making this a condition for independence and campaigning in the federal election of 1959 on this platform.[94] He was nothing if not resilient.

CHAPTER 14

FINAL BATTLES

I am an egoist. I am not ashamed of it. These gramophone recordings praising me are all in the plan for political power. They are played in thousands of houses and my name is constantly in the subconscious memory of those who hear them.

Adegoke Adelabu, November 1957

Can we as a democratic organisation approve of the persistent acts of irresponsibility perpetrated by the little Caesars in our midst? How long shall we remain supine and see all our labours put to naught by small minded politicians whose chief goal is to advertise their little selves at the expense of a great organisation...?

Nnamdi Azikiwe, October 1957

Adelabu had flown from London on 27 June to the Northern Nigerian city of Kano, Nigeria's second international airport, and from there to Kaduna, the regional capital. While in Kaduna he stayed in the house of the Sardauna of Sokoto, who had also returned from London. On 2 July in an interview by telephone, the *Southern Nigeria Defender* asked him to comment on the Constitutional Conference, but had to be satisfied with reporting that 'In his present religious mood he appealed to all to reserve their comments until the full report was published.' He also promised to make a statement later.[1] On the 3rd he flew from Kano to Jedda, in Saudi Arabia, joining the stream of Nigerian Muslims who were making the Muslim pilgrimage to Mecca which in that year included Dauda Adegbenro, Western Region Minister of Land and one of the few prominent Muslims in the Action Group.*

It seems that his decision to make the hajj was a belated one, made while he was in London. He had not referred to such intentions in the message he had published earlier in the year on the occasion of the Muslim festival of Id el Fitr, even though he had specifically mentioned 'those preparing to undertake the pilgrimage to Mecca' nor had he discussed the idea with his intimates, who were greatly surprised when he sent for N. B. Soule to join him in the North for the trip to Mecca.[2]

---

* Returning to Nigeria on the same plane, they were carefully posed together for a photograph. (See Plate 5.)

There were probably several closely related motives for the trip, apart from the desire of any Muslim to visit the holy places and earn the title of Alhaji. He was aware of his reputation for riotous behavior, and continually shocking the respectable and the law-abiding; certainly his pilgrimage was an attempt to improve his public image. His behavior and public utterances were obviously more restrained after his return. As one of his co-religionists put it, 'Adelabu was an egoist and until he went on pilgrimage to Mecca, he could be intemperate in his actions.'[3]

Apparently the experience did have some genuine emotional impact on Adelabu. While it is a disappointment that he left no account of his trip to the Muslim holy places (his only recorded public comment being on 'the burning heat of the Saudi Arabian desert' made in a newspaper interview on his return), to his close friends he did relate a strange experience which he claimed to have had in Mecca. One day while out for a walk he lost his way, being completely unable to find his way back to where he was staying. His long-dead parents suddenly appeared to him in a vision. He greeted them in English and in Yoruba, but although they recognized him they could understand neither tongue. A small boy appeared, and translated his greetings from Yoruba into Arabic for them, whereupon they pointed out the way back to his lodgings. Taking it, he met those who had missed him and come to look for him.

According to his own account it was the Sardauna of Sokoto who suggested that he make the hajj. 'He convinced me that those who want to be great must move near God and after performing the pilgrimage, I am convinced more than ever.'[4] Moreover, the new Alhaji claimed that it was the Sardauna who had paid for his pilgrimage. Thus it seems very likely that a second motive was that of trying to move closer to the Northern leaders, and one of the best ways of doing this would undoubtedly have been to convince them of his sincerity as a Muslim. As we have seen, it is said that his drinking while a Federal Minister had given great offense to Abubakar Tafawa Balewa and the other N.P.C. Ministers. Now, perhaps, he sought to rehabilitate himself. He must also have been impressed, as the other southerners were, by the strength of purpose and discipline which the N.P.C. delegation had shown during the London Conference. In Chapter 6 we saw how in 'The Turning Point', written in 1952, he treated the North as politically subordinate to the East and West. By 1957 the N.P.C. and its region were beginning to make their mark on the Nigerian political scene; as we have already noted, some of the N.C.N.C. leaders were becoming aware of this development and Adelabu was probably among them.

His third motive may also have been related to his plans for his political future, and especially for winning support in the Western Region. At least

one out of every three Yorubas was a Muslim, and the proportion was if anything growing; moreover, the Muslims were most heavily concentrated in
that part of the Region which was foreseen as the Central Yoruba State. If
Islam could be made a political force in the West, with himself as its leader,
it might prove irresistible.

For some time, the Muslims of Lagos and the West had been restive, and
animosity among many of them had begun to focus on the Action Group
and its predominantly Christian leadership. The situation had some similarity to the Muslim disputes in Ibadan in 1953. The complaints of discrimination in education, which for many years were directed against the
British administration, were now being directed against the Action Group
Regional Government. The treatment of the ex-Alafin of Oyo, the most
prominent Muslim Yoruba traditional ruler, also upset his co-religionists.
This was a very confusing period for Muslim organizations. In May 1956
the *West African Pilot* reported that the Muslim Central Council in Lagos
had ordered all Muslims to resign from organizations which opposed the
return of the Alafin. In February 1957 the United Muslim Party, founded
in 1953 but hitherto confined to Lagos and the Colony area, decided to
extend its activities to include the whole Region. Plans were made for
establishing an organizational machine, launching a Muslim newspaper and
touring the Region on a 'Goodwill Mission'.[5] These meetings were attended
by such prominent Muslim figures as Alhaji A. R. Smith of Ilesha, President-
General of the Muslim Congress of Nigeria, and Alhaji El-Amin El-Kudaise
of Ijebu-Ode, also of the Congress; also associated with this move were
certain prominent Ibadan Muslims, among them Alhaji Amusa Inakoju and
Mustapha Alli (the Maiyegun Society leader). None of these, of course, was
a political ally of Adegoke Adelabu, but he was certainly privy to what was
going on and had an ally in M. R. B. Ottun, the original founder of the
U.M.P.

Over the next few months, however, the only achievement of the revitalized U.M.P. was to submit a memorandum to the Constitutional Conference,
which attempted to show in detail how 'The Muslims of the Western Region
have had a lot of experiences as to drive them to utmost desperation.'[6] On
27 July, however, two weeks after Adelabu returned from Mecca, Alhaji
Smith of the Muslim Congress joined with Y. P. O. Shodeinde, a prominent
Lagos Muslim, and Alhaji Inakoju in founding the National Muslim
League, a new political party of which Smith became President-General.
This move considerably alarmed the Action Group. On 12 October, in a
speech given to a party conference in Ibadan, Chief Awolowo declared that
'It is in the interest of all Nigerians that this new party should be nipped in
the bud.'[7] A few days later, the United Muslim Party surfaced again to

announce that it would press for the creation of a 'Muslim State', which earned for it a declaration of 'relentless war' by Chief Awolowo, speaking at the Annual Conference of the Egbe Omo Oduduwa at Oshogbo on 7 November. As for the League, the Action Group managed to win Alhaji Inakoju over to its side and by early December he had formed his United Muslim Council to rival the League. At its first conference on 12 January 1958, when the Council elected officers, it was revealed as an Action Group satellite; one of its Vice-Presidents was Inakoju, while its Treasurer was S. O. Gbadamosi, Federal Treasurer of the Action Group, and its Publicity Secretary, L. K. Jakande, was a prominent journalist on that party's newspapers. On 30 January the National Muslim League announced that it was changing its name to National Emancipation League, and that it would henceforward be open to people of all creeds.

Faced with the possibility of an attack upon it in the name of Islam, the Action Group had skillfully used a combination of threats, diplomacy and promises (such as providing funds for Arabic teaching in Muslim schools) to curb the new menace. Adelabu had lost a bitter and public battle over Islam to the Action Group in the 1953–4 election campaign. Unlike 1953, the groups involved in 1957–8 were largely outside of Ibadan and totally beyond his control. This time he made no call to action in his religion's name. In the Ibadan local elections expected in early 1958 such confusion, compounded by similar splits and confusion in the N.C.N.C. itself, would have been self-defeating. We must see, then, how Adelabu in fact began to mount his new campaign for power in Ibadan and beyond on his return to Nigeria.

He returned to Lagos by air on 14 July 1957, and travelled up to Ibadan on the 18th. Riding into the city on a white horse, clad in the full regalia of an alhaji, he was met by huge crowds all the way to Oke Oluokun, with three hundred hunters firing salvoes of welcome. Only two things marred his day of triumph. There was an affray in Isale-Ijebu, involving the Action Group Organizing Secretary for Ibadan, a sign that politics were still as bitter as ever. More irritating for Adelabu personally, when he arrived at the Central Mosque to pray he found that the Chief Imam, Muili Ayinde, refused to come out for him and indeed that the doors of the mosque were locked. His prayers, therefore, were brief, but not the feasting at the Taj Mahal which followed. The hero Penkelemesi had returned to his followers after an absence of more than ten weeks. Who cared what rich men, religious dignitaries or the Action Group thought? As the *Defender* put it in its editorial on the following day, he was not the first Ibadan alhaji, nor the first politician back from London, but 'There is something in the personality of the NCNC Opposition Leader in the Western House of Assembly that magnetises.'

397

On Saturday 20 July, the Lion of the West reported to the people on the Constitutional Conference at a great meeting at the Ibadan Race Course. The Conference had not gone well for the N.C.N.C. in general or Adelabu in particular, and it was not an easy task to put a favorable interpretation on events.[8] The N.C.N.C., he said, 'within the limits of human capabilities' had achieved its objects 'more than any other party delegation'. With regard to the allocation of functions between the center and the regions, 'we were able to keep the...exclusive list intact in all essentials and thereby gave a technical knockout to regional functions at the expense of the central government'. In general, the Conference had achieved a number of successes – adult male suffrage throughout the federation, a purely African Cabinet for the federation, and the decision to have a federal Prime Minister.

Despite his own rhetoric, however, Adegoke Adelabu knew that not even a 'technical knockout' had been won, and that to speak scornfully as he did of 'the thin shell and the inconsequential formula of regional home rule' did not really argue away the fact that the impending self-government for the West would consolidate the grip of the Action Group over it still further. Somehow in the clamor of his own words and in the security of a meeting in his own compound he allowed himself to make a bad mistake for the sake of his own personal prestige. At the London Conference he had not managed to get his 'safeguards' written into the constitution of the West before it became self-governing, nor had he pressed there for the Commission of Inquiry into the conduct of the Action Group Government for which he had campaigned so vigorously in the first few months of the year at home. Nevertheless, he now revived the issue. Although this was certainly not intended by the Colonial Office, he stated that the Minorities Commission which had been decided on in London was in fact to be such a Commission of Inquiry. He had already hinted at this in an interview given to the *Sunday Times* on his return to Nigeria, and in a speech at Glover Hall in Lagos on 17 July. Now, on 27 July at Oke Oluokun, he claimed the credit for its appointment, stating categorically that 'the commission is not a state boundary commission but a real commission of Inquiry. The terms of reference have been deliberately drawn so wide as to embrace anything and everything under the sun which in the opinion of the minorities might reasonably lead them to enter a state of fear whether those fears are well or ill-founded.'[9] According to some of the examples he now gave, 'minorities' could be followers of the ex-Alafin, or Mabolaje supporters, or even taxpayers who felt they had been victimized. Admittedly, the terms of reference of the Commission spoke of 'minorities' without qualification, but it was incredible of Adelabu to suggest that the Colonial Secretary had agreed to include anything other than ethnic and religious minorities in the Commission's terms of reference. At this point Adelabu was apparently betrayed into thinking he could force the Secretary's hand on a verbal ambiguity. It was not a very impressive demonstration of what he might have learned in London.

The Action Group was quick to take him up on these statements. Already on 20 July, speaking at a rally in Oyo, Chief S. L. Akintola had wagered Adelabu £100 that he could not show where in the report of the Conference the issue of the ex-Alafin was raised, or a Commission of Inquiry mentioned. On 4 August, A. M. A. Akinloye in turn wagered £1000 on the latter point. The Lion of the West made no reply.

Until the membership of the Minorities Commission was announced, and the date of its arrival in Nigeria, there was, in fact, little more that could be done. The Leader of the N.C.N.C. Opposition in the West turned to the state of the party and his own relations with its leader, Dr Azikiwe. The first matter was becoming of growing concern to all those actively associated with the N.C.N.C. We have already seen that in April the hard-working Adebayo Asaya had resigned as from 31 July, filled with disgust at his treatment by the party. While welcoming Adelabu back to Ibadan on 18 July, the *Defender* had spoken of the special need for discipline in the Western Working Committee and the curbing of 'irresponsible utterances' by 'certain party officials'. On 12 July a letter reached Adelabu's hands, written by the new Association of N.C.N.C. Constituency Secretaries, complaining of the lot of that ill-used body of professional party workers. Their request was for permanent appointments, vehicles and encouragement from the politicians, and they plaintively remarked that 'we feel that the Party has been very very ungrateful to us Secretaries who has [*sic*] sacrificed time, money and even life itself to make the NCNC what it is today in the Region'.[10] On 24 July Dr Azikiwe returned to Lagos, and on the following day, after a meeting of party leaders at K. O. Mbadiwe's house in Ikoyi, it was announced by Kola Balogun, as National Secretary of the N.C.N.C., that the Annual Convention of the party would be held in Jos in the last week of October. Everyone knew that the Lagos Special Convention in April had only postponed the crisis till the next convention. Now that the attention of disturbed party members was focused upon the end of October, the flood of comments upon the state of the party and suggestions for the remedying of its ills began to pour in, and Adelabu, as one of the most senior men in the party, received his share of these.

Tribalism, inadequate organization and the poor example of their leaders were the main concerns of the N.C.N.C. faithful in these weeks. For Adelabu, however, the issues were narrowing in effect to the question of the relations between himself and Nnamdi Azikiwe. We have in previous chapters traced in detail the significant events in this relationship – Adelabu's

399

resignation from his federal ministry, the dissolution of the Ibadan District Council, the N.C.N.C. President's apparently lukewarm attitude towards his lieutenant's campaigns against the Action Group in the West and his failure to give him any real support at the Constitutional Conference. With their return from London, the trend continued. Early in August the *Defender* published an article entitled 'Re-Assessing the London Conference Results' by Adeoye Adisa, a young Ibadan lawyer who was now rapidly emerging as one of Adelabu's most able lieutenants. Even if Adelabu had not actually inspired the piece, he must have approved of its contents, and it is significant, therefore, to find it remarking that Dr Azikiwe 'owes it to this great nation to get away completely from the rut of regional politics and concentrate on a more glorious task – the task of re-organising the only nationalist party in Nigeria on a sounder and more efficient basis'.[11] Another straw in the wind can be seen on 8 August, when the Eastern and Western Regions became internally self-governing. Dr Azikiwe and Chief Akintola exchanged messages of congratulation, and E. O. Fakayode published a message of congratulation to the Western Region Government. Adelabu and his followers remained studiously silent.

Matters came to a head in September. On Monday 2 September, the Federal House of Representatives met for the first time since the London Conference, and Abubakar Tafawa Balewa, now Prime Minister of the Federation, announced that the Action Group had joined the N.P.C. and the N.C.N.C. in a coalition or 'national' Government which had been sworn in the previous day.[12] This possibility had apparently first been raised 'behind the scenes' in London, and now it was publicly proclaimed by Dr Azikiwe to be a 'very wise decision to form a National Government in which all major political parties are represented'.[13] It was not readily apparent to some N.C.N.C. leaders that such a Government was necessary to carry out the final negotiations.* Thus, even before the announcement was made, T. O. S. Benson, deeply disquieted by news of the negotiations, wrote to Mbadiwe from his sickbed in Ikorodu pointing out that 'There is no Emergency at

* We are not certain which N.C.N.C. leaders were involved in this very important decision to invite the Action Group to join the Government. There was no meeting of the National Executive Committee to discuss it, nor does it appear that all the Officers of the party were consulted. Adelabu certainly was not. Apparently, the matter was raised in London by Azikiwe during discussions with the N.P.C. leaders and finally settled in Lagos by discussions between Abubakar Tafawa Balewa, K. O. Mbadiwe and other N.P.C. and N.C.N.C. Federal Ministers. We may have here another example of the conflict between the party as such and its legislators, more especially the Federal Parliamentary party. In this case, what would seem clearly to be an important matter of party policy was decided by a few federal legislators with the support of the National President.

present to warrant a National Government.'[14] Benson also pointed out that such a maneuver would destroy the N.C.N.C.'s claim to moral superiority over the Action Group, on the grounds that the former was part of the Federal Government, whereas its rival was only in control of a Region. On an entirely different level, Benson also pointed out that if the new portfolio of Lagos Affairs went to the Action Group, as was rumored, that party would have an undue advantage in subsequent local elections there. After the news broke D. K. Olumofin chose to make a more public protest; on 14 September the *Defender* published an 'Open Letter' from him to Abubakar, in which he commented that

It seems to me that we deceive ourselves and not the Colonial Secretary or the world, by forming a National Government which presents a semblance of unity that is artificial to the extreme.

The strongest reaction of all, however, came from two men in concert – Aminu Kano, President-General of the Northern Elements Progressive Union, and Adegoke Adelabu, First National Vice-President of the N.C.N.C. The N.E.P.U. Annual Conference for 1957 convened in Ibadan from 26 September to 2 October. This gave the two men the chance to get together. The opening session in the Odeon Cinema was attended by Adelabu, E. O. Fakayode, R. O. A. Akinjide and other N.C.N.C. notables, while Mbadiwe and U. O. Ndem, his Parliamentary Secretary, looked in on their way from the East to Lagos. Adelabu spoke of the solidarity of the N.C.N.C.–N.E.P.U. Alliance and Aminu Kano acidly remarked that 'The big leaders of Nigeria have called us to unite but have not told us what to do. They have not presented us with a concrete plan. We therefore suggest that some of the decisions of the London talks have either to be reversed or their implementation postponed until independence.'[15] In the following days the two demonstrated their closeness by riding in procession through the city on white horses. Their followers also took up the theme; at a party one speaker had described the two as similar personalities 'small in stature but with mighty heart and energy for work'.[16]

On 2 October the N.E.P.U. delegates were given a send-off dance at the Paradise Hotel. Ten days later, on 12 October, Aminu Kano and Adegoke Adelabu in a long manifesto in the *Daily Times* entitled 'The Dividing Ideological Line' published what was in fact a major attack on Nnamdi Azikiwe, K. O. Mbadiwe, Kola Balogun and the other leaders of the N.C.N.C. Federal Parliamentary Party who had agreed to the formation of a National Government.* Although the ideas and the actual wording seem

* The choice of newspaper was probably governed by the fact that, of those with national circulation, the *Daily Service* was Action Group, and therefore unthinkable,

401

more Adelabu's than Aminu Kano's, the two identified themselves as the 'standard bearers of the leftist wing of the NCNC–NEPU Alliance' and declared their obligation to those of their 'school of thought' to show how with a National Government 'the real and genuine dividing line in Nigerian politics has become blurred, confused and obscure. . .'.[17] It had never been discussed at any formal meeting of the Constitutional Conference or of its sub-committees and it was 'not the mandate either jointly or severally of the NCNC–NEPU Alliance'. It might be acceptable as 'a useful, though un-happy and risky insurance' of mutual agreement upon a date for indepen-dence but there was little hope of this.

As an unholy alliance of the reactionary forces of regionalism, it is a sinister con-spiracy against the genuine freedom and liberty of the Nigerian masses. By forcing the three major political parties, with directly opposite fundamental poli-tical beliefs, into a marriage of convenience and by lumping together what was hitherto Government and Opposition into an amorphous whole, the National Government has introduced an element of confusion into our orderly political development. It must be denounced as the handiwork of those who have vested interests in the present Regional Government set-up.[18]

Despite the obvious intensity of their feelings, Aminu Kano and Adegoke Adelabu were making no serious distortions in restating the fundamental issue underlying the development of the modern Nigerian political system. Was the balance of power in the federation to be tipped toward the regions or the center? This is what they meant when they went on to contrast the 'genuine Federalist School of thought' of the N.C.N.C.–N.E.P.U. Alliance with N.P.C.–A.G. Regionalism. Although the issue had been raised at the Constitutional Conference, they felt it had not been finally resolved. Now it was in danger of being forgotten or ignored in the name of a spurious unity.* In a sense the authors of the manifesto were themselves preoccupied with regional power, since they viewed politics as a struggle in which the major clashes came at the regional level. It must be remembered that these two and

and the *West African Pilot* would be most unlikely to publish such a direct attack on the N.C.N.C. leader. The *Daily Times* was expatriate-owned, being linked to the British *Daily Mirror* group, and claimed to be politically neutral. No doubt it also welcomed a 'scoop' such as this.

* Adelabu's chief opponent, Obafemi Awolowo, also opposed the formation of a National Government, on the different grounds that it would impede the Action Group's attempts to carry the struggle into the Northern Region and create a Middle Belt State. The Federal Executive Council of the Action Group took the decision to join the National Government while Awolowo was out of Nigeria, and he accepted this in the name of collective responsibility; this process of decision-making provides an interesting comparison with that in the N.C.N.C. (See Sklar, *Nigerian Political Parties*, p. 279.)

their followers were of all Nigerian politicians the most involved in direct political struggle; they knew from daily experience what it was like to be in opposition in the North and West, to be faced by other political parties and the many and varied uses to which the power of governments could be put. This could scarcely be appreciated by the Eastern leaders of the N.C.N.C., secure in their own control of a regional government, or the Federal Parliamentary Party, secure in its long-standing co-operation with the N.P.C. In another sense, then, Adelabu and Aminu were the most nationally minded of Nigerian political leaders. All too aware of the problems of virtually-autonomous regional power-structures, they wished the effective governmental powers to be vested in the center; thus their basic concern with regional power was to end it.

The demands of the manifesto, typically for Adelabu, were seven in number. First, following the next election, which would produce 'Nigeria's first sovereign Parliament duly elected on modern democratic direct adult suffrage', there must be a declaration of independence, 'with or without the consent of the United Kingdom Government'. To ensure democratic elections there must be universal suffrage (with votes for women as well as men in the North), and an independent Electoral Commission. Third, the center must be strengthened at the expense of the regions, with the police, judiciary, a united civil service, and education solely under the control of the central government, which would also have all residual legislative powers. There should be 'socialist economic planning', with nationalization of rail, ocean and air transport, mines, large-scale manufacturing, central banking, marketing boards, utilities and housing.* There should be an 'exhaustive enumeration' of fundamental human rights in the constitution, and speedy access to the courts when these were infringed. The sixth demand was for the creation of 'at least ten states as a lasting foundation for unity', and the last for 'the ultimate expansion of the Federation into a West African States Union embracing the whole of West Africa south of the Sahara'.[19]

Following this list of demands the manifesto made its clarion call:

Resurgent Progressive Federalism is at death grips with decadent Reactionary Regionalism. The dividing ideological line is clear, definite and distinct. There can be no compromise between the NPC–AG Alliance and the NCNC–NEPU Alliance. The present Balewa National Government is an NPC–Action Group

---

* Rail and air transport and electricity were already in effect nationalized, being run by public corporations, and a Central Bank had already been mooted. Bringing the marketing boards under central control would have destroyed the chief economic agency by which the regional power structures were financed. Public control of ocean transport and nationalization of large-scale factories would have hit hard at the big expatriate economic interests like Elder Dempster and the United Africa Company.

show with the NCNC Federal Parliamentary Party an unwilling partner under duress being coerced to serve the vested interests of one man at the top.[20]

Having thus relieved Dr Mbadiwe and the other N.C.N.C. federal parliamentarians of responsibility by placing the blame squarely on Nnamdi Azikiwe, Aminu and Adelabu concluded by listing the groups from whom they expected special support. In particular they referred to 'the masses', who 'do not want a regionalised Police Force to be used as an instrument of domestic tyranny by parties in control of Regional Governments', and the intellectuals 'as represented by the Student National Front', which had been formed at the University College at Ibadan before the London Conference to fight against regionalism. The manifesto ended on a note of hope:

The NCNC–NEPU Alliance, with the support of the new State Movementers, the masses and the intellectual elite, is destined under its new, radical, virile and militant leadership to take control of Nigeria's Ship of State in 1960.[21]

By making the most direct possible attack on the N.C.N.C. National President short of actually naming him, and by referring to new leadership, Aminu Kano and Adegoke Adelabu had openly challenged the ascendancy of Nnamdi Azikiwe, as well as the policies of his party. For the time being, the only reaction came from the Action Group, which strongly denied that it was in alliance with the N.P.C. Indeed, on 16 October Dr Azikiwe went on leave on the grounds of ill-health. But everyone knew that his answer must come at the N.C.N.C. Annual Convention.

Why Adelabu chose to break with his leader at this point is not certain but one plausible reason was his commitment to political struggle. To him the formation of the National Government was a sign that a deal had been made by the three major parties in order to be able to bargain more effectively with the Colonial Office. There was nothing wrong in this if the principles for which the N.C.N.C. stood were not being abandoned. However, precisely this must have occurred, he felt, because there was an unbridgeable gulf, a 'dividing ideological line', between the Action Group and the N.C.N.C. which the latter could cross only by giving up its principles.

Mixed up with this, undoubtedly, were his own ambition and his sense of personal pique at Dr Azikiwe. His faith in his own abilities could always be renewed by viewing his defeats in Ibadan, Lagos and London as the consequences of his subordinate position. This view was made more persuasive than it should have been by his continuing ability to control elections in Ibadan. He may even have partly believed that some concatenation of circumstances, perhaps of his own creation, would lead the Minorities Commission to propose his Central Yoruba State, and perhaps even to topple the government of Chief Awolowo. If this was so, he probably lost little thought over the contradiction between his goals of a Central Yoruba State under no serious control by others and a central government which would have greatly increased powers over such states. Such self-deception was made possible by his own ability to turn from one issue to another without his energies flagging, a dynamism which in turn attracted support not only in the West but from all over the country, especially from young people, who increasingly identified with him. Any prominent man in Nigeria attracts letters which judiciously combine admiration with requests for help. Reading those from this period, one is struck by the number in which the writer, while seeking money or some sort of patronage, was also genuinely moved by Adelabu.*

On the other hand, he did not break completely with the N.C.N.C. at this time. After all, he was Leader of the Opposition in the Western House of Assembly and there was little to be gained by denying himself that position and its salary. Furthermore, the months were slowly rolling by since the announcement in late May 1957 that local government elections would be held in April 1958. The Action Group was already contemplating a division of the city and its rural districts prior to that election, and it probably seemed unwise to add to the number of battles to be fought or the uncertainty in the minds of the electorate which would have to be educated away from the N.C.N.C. and toward another alignment in those few remaining months. As we have seen previously, on 12 October Awolowo had given full warning that he would oppose vigorously a redrawing of the lines of battle on religious grounds and it probably seemed prudent not to take the party battles to the point of irrevocable split and subsequent reorganization.

As he waited for the Annual Convention and Zik's inevitable reaction to his attack on the national front, Adelabu again gave notice that he would pursue the question of the Commission of Inquiry in another fierce debate in the Western House of Assembly which began on 1 October. The Lion of the West was still carrying on the fight against the Action Group, even

---

* A fascinating letter of this period came from a northerner, a student at the Kaduna Medical Auxiliary School and 'the only Cow Fulani boy educated in my land Nguru District'. The writer had seen Adelabu outside 'your friend's House "Sardauna"...I purposily go there and had a good look at you. Before the following day you flew to Mecca.' He had been impressed by what he saw, having also heard Adelabu give a public lecture, and now offered him a novel kind of help: 'I admire you and read your face I knew that you are not, NOT!! Deceiving Nigeria in order to ride on Buick! No! Arrange with a simple honest man and come to me, I will send you One Thing that can Protect you against Any Metal Made Weapons! Just Dash I Repeat Medicine for Knive – Arrow – Cutlass – dane or every Metal Guns it will BREAK before the Person using it will come with in a reach or even when he intended to do befor HAND!!' (M. Jaji to Adelabu, 1 August 1957, A.P.)

if other N.C.N.C. leaders were not, and he provoked the usual strong reaction from his old enemies, both in the House of Assembly before it adjourned *sine die* on 3 October, and in the Action Group press. However, his main concern was with the forthcoming tour of the Minorities Commission, with its mandate 'to enquire into the fears of Minorities and the means of allaying them'. On 12 October, while on a campaign visit to Abeokuta, he told a meeting that 'at the London talks, I was able to convince the Colonial Secretary and the Conference delegates of the need for investigating the Western Government'. The inquiry, he said, would begin 'on or about' 23 November, and he alleged that the Action Group was destroying incriminating documents in the Ministries at Agodi.[22] Either by deliberate misrepresentation or because he was convinced that they were the same, he was still identifying the Minorities Commission with the Commission of Inquiry he had sought for nearly a year.

On 7 October the Secretary of the Western N.C.N.C. Parliamentary Party J. E. Otobo, had sent a letter to the Secretary of the Minorities Commission, a seconded administrative officer who was in Lagos making preliminary arrangements, to confirm that the Western N.C.N.C. would be giving evidence. On 14 October, the same day he inaugurated the campaign for the Ibadan local government elections with a meeting at Oje market, apparently not trusting Otobo's efficiency, Adelabu also sent two telegrams and a letter to confirm the same thing and to inform the Commission that the N.C.N.C. would call at least ten witnesses from each Division, well over 200 in all. He also informed the Secretary that Dingle Foot, his defense lawyer of earlier days, might appear on behalf of the Western N.C.N.C., since barristers were to be allowed to represent those giving evidence to the Commission.[23]

At the same time Adelabu cabled the London firm of solicitors, Rexworthy, Bonser and Wadkin, to inquire as to Foot's availability and his fees. On 16 October they replied that Foot would be available at a basic fee of £2928 and further 'refreshers' of £66. 3. od. for each day of the hearings on which he appeared after the first; the solicitors also asked for £100 advance to cover their own costs. The word immediately went out that money was necessary. Professor Sklar, who attended a meeting of the Mabolaje at Adelabu's compound on 19 October, has reported that the Central Executive Committee was 'counting out a pile of money' for Foot's fees when Adelabu introduced him to them, and on 23 October, a Wednesday, Adelabu cabled £300 on account.[24] Thus when Adelabu left Ibadan at the end of the week for the N.C.N.C. Annual Convention, a considerable financial campaign still had to be undertaken.

On 28, 29 and 30 October the Annual Convention of the party met at

Aba in the Eastern Region, not at Jos as originally planned.* Long awaited, it produced moments of high drama and a decisive shift in the balance of power in the N.C.N.C. Adegoke Adelabu was entitled to attend both as an Officer of the party and as a parliamentarian. On Monday, 28 October 1957, he and 350 other delegates assembled in the Rex Cinema to hear the Presidential Address by Azikiwe, who appeared at the Convention with a bodyguard of members of the Zikist National Vanguard, dressed in red and blue shirts.†

Azikiwe was still officially on sick-leave, and he began his speech with a rather plaintive reference to his health, alluding almost in the first sentence to going 'the way of our ancestors'.[25] 'I am speaking to you today', he said, 'not as one who enjoys good health, but because it is a point of duty for me to be here.' Looking back over the period since the last Convention in April, he expressed his 'utter disappointment at the way NCNC affairs have been mishandled'. 'A false impression has gained ground that the National President is a softie and all one has to do is to threaten him with a show of force and he will hold his peace. The result is that members think that they can be a law unto themselves.' Without mentioning names, he referred to cases of indiscipline in the Eastern and Western N.C.N.C. and then demanded,

Compatriots, can we as a responsible Party condone these deliberate assaults on democracy? Can we as a democratic organisation approve of the persistent acts of irresponsibility perpetrated by the little Caesars in our midst? How long shall we remain supine and see all our labours put to naught by small minded politicians whose chief goal is to advertise their little selves at the expense of a great organisation whose very existence means so much to millions of our people?

For his part, the National President continued, 'I am convinced that a drastic control of the NCNC, even in a totalitarian manner, has become necessary. The situation in our rank and file is to be likened to the Great Plague in London which required a Great Fire to purify it.' 'Believe me, compatriots', he declared, 'I will be equal to the job if you will give the green signal.'

Having given this plain warning to his opponents, Dr Azikiwe turned to the question of the National Government.

For years now, your great Party has shouted the slogans of 'One Nigeria' and 'A strong Centre' throughout the country. When now an opportunity was offered

* The reasons for the change of venue are not clear; possibly Azikiwe felt more sure of support in his own region.
† The most valuable account of the Aba Convention is in Sklar, *Nigerian Political Parties*, pp. 195–203. Sklar had the great good fortune to be present at the plenary sessions of this Convention, and has kindly supplied further details in private correspondence with the authors.

to your leaders and their followers to translate into positive action what they had theorised and vociferated about all these months, it is with deep regret that I noticed how some of our colleagues developed cold feet and vituperated the National Government instead of giving it their wholehearted support.

'Mine has been the misfortune', he lamented, 'to lead an undisciplined army and so it was no surprise for me to receive impertinent telegrams from enraged NCNCers threatening me with hell-fire and brimstone if I supported the formation of a National Government.' Nevertheless, it had his support – 'because it will reduce party bickerings, it will settle party squabbles, it will minimise mutual suspicions and jealousies, and it will provide our Federal Ministers with an atmosphere that would be more conducive to the common good'.

One wonders what passed through Adelabu's mind when he heard this virtual repudiation of all his past struggles against the Action Group and confirmation of the fears he and Aminu Kano had expressed in their manifesto. It was directly to that document that the National President now turned.

In this connection may I disclose that I was very much ashamed when the National Vice-President of our great Party and the leader of the NEPU, which is in alliance with the NCNC, reviled the National Government. Apart from the fact that neither of the two assailants of the National Government had the courtesy to notify the Party of their intentions, it is the height of tactlessness, since six of the Federal Ministers are NCNCers.

Whilst I will readily concede to others a right to their opinions, I must assert that identification of the National Government as 'an unholy alliance' is to say the least a most irresponsible statement to make in public.

What the National President was in fact requesting was wide powers to discipline dissidents within the party. He reviewed the constitution of the N.C.N.C. to support his contention that the President had no real powers, other than the last word on the interpretation of the Constitution itself. 'I have come to the conclusion', he declared, 'that the NCNC Constitution must now be revised to vest the National President with power befitting a great political party of the stature and reputation of the NCNC.' He was giving notice, therefore, of a motion which would give him discretionary powers to initiate action against any individual for breaches of party discipline, to dissolve any party organ, and to disaffiliate any branches or member unions that went against the party. Such powers, if they existed, were all too likely to be invoked against Adegoke Adelabu, and as if to confirm this Azikiwe returned at the end of his speech to the issue of the National Government.

Left to me alone, I would even suggest that, after the next Federal elections, nationalists of Nigeria should declare a political truce and proclaim a moratorium on political parties for at least five years. Then they should run a National Government so that the new independent country may pass through its teething troubles with the least difficulty.

Nevertheless, Adelabu was not provoked into speaking in the debate on the Presidential Address which followed. Both Kola Balogun and K. O. Mbadiwe spoke, the former rather non-committally, the latter more strongly against the motion which their leader was proposing. Mbadiwe took as his theme a contrast between the 'philosophical' Gandhi and the 'administrative' Nehru, pointing out that the Indian Party had needed both – 'We want a team to lead the party and not one man.'[26] Jaja Wachuku, the turbulent lawyer who had only just been re-admitted to the party, also opposed Azikiwe's motion, on the grounds that it should have been proposed by someone else, since its rejection would amount to a vote of no confidence in the National President. In the end there was no vote, and the motion and Address were referred to the National Executive Committee.

In these circumstances, Azikiwe dropped his motion, but he had another weapon. On the third day of the Convention a motion was proposed and seconded by two men from Adelabu's own Western N.C.N.C., Babatunji Olowofoyeku, the lawyer from Ilesha, and Adeniran Ogunsanya, the Ikeja lawyer who had stood against Balogun for the office of Secretary in April. The motion was a simple one: until the attainment of independence, the National President was to be given the power to run the party through a 'cabinet' system, choosing his own National Officers rather than having them elected by the Annual Convention. The cabinet system had in fact been used between 1948 and 1951, when the procedure was changed at the Kano Convention. Now it was resisted vehemently by those who would be most affected if it were adopted again – the present Officers, who might hope for re-election but doubted that they would be chosen by Azikiwe if it were left to him. Kola Balogun challenged it as being incompatible with democratic principles; it was a good principle for running a government, but not a party. It was communistic, he suggested, provoking uproar from the floor and intervention from the chair by Azikiwe.[27] Mbadiwe proposed an amendment to the motion, that the present system of election of Officers be retained until the committee set up under Chief H. O. Davies to report on reorganization of the party had done so. The cabinet system, he maintained amid constant heckling, had failed before; it was undemocratic because it prevented opposition within the party. Adegoke Adelabu seconded the amendment. Like Balogun, he distinguished between governments and parties; and like Mbadiwe he called the cabinet system undemocratic for parties. Personally he declared his complete confidence in the National President, but the 'ideologists' of the N.C.N.C. assembled together were greater than any one man. All interests in the party, he said, must be respected and given a chance of representation, as the elective system gave an opportunity for a balancing of interests. He ended his speech with an insistence on the importance of ideology – he followed Zik because of the ideology of the party, which must not be allowed to die.

The debate which followed was a fierce one, marked in particular by a bitter clash between Dr Azikiwe and Kola Balogun, with the National President accusing the latter of trying to pack the Convention by the accrediting of delegates who would be favorable to himself. When it came to voting on the motion and amendment, however, indications were quite to the contrary: the amendment proposed by Mbadiwe and Adelabu lost overwhelmingly on a voice vote, and the original motion was similarly carried. At this point, Adegoke Adelabu walked out of the Convention hall.

The following day, 31 October, Dr Azikiwe announced his choice of Officers. All three new names were men unequivocally loyal to himself, even if less well-known than those they replaced. Kola Balogun was replaced as National Secretary by F. S. McEwen, Principal of the Lagos City College, General Manager of the *West African Pilot* and active in Lagos politics. K. O. Mbadiwe lost his position as Second National Vice-President to Raymond Njoku, the dapper Federal Minister of Transport and former President of the Ibo State Union. Adelabu ceded his place as First National Vice-President to J. O. Fadahunsi, an 'elder statesman' of the Western N.C.N.C. with whom he had never been very friendly. Chief Festus Okotie-Eboh, the National Treasurer, and the other officers kept their positions. Thus the balance of power in the party had shifted decisively in favor of Nnamdi Azikiwe. In the next few days the newspapers of the Zik Group pushed the lesson home. In Ibadan the *Defender*, which on a previous occasion had demanded that Adelabu resign his chairmanship of the Ibadan Council, in its editorial 'A Wise Decision' on 1 November declared that 'The need to put the right men in the right places in the party is a long felt one.' In an editorial the next day entitled 'Universal Brotherhood', the *Defender* announced that 'we strongly support condemnation of certain party leaders who would not work with duly elected officers because of petty group jealousies', and pointed out that 'the NCNC cannot exist as a party under the leadership of conceited tin-gods'. In following days, however, it had to change its tune somewhat. Faced with considerable gloating in the Action Group press over the N.C.N.C.'s troubles, it had to insist that recent events did not represent the 'degrading' or 'demoting' of Mbadiwe, Balogun and Adelabu; after all, the last was still Leader of the N.C.N.C. Opposition in the Western legislature, Chairman of the Western Working Committee and a member of the National Executive Committee.*

Adelabu himself took no part in all this press commentary, and made no other moves.† He was deeply involved in a number of local and regional matters which awaited his attention upon his return to Ibadan. There was the difficult matter of financing Dingle Foot's appearance for the inquiry and he was increasingly preoccupied with the approaching elections, in particular with the question once again of tax, and with a plan by the Action Group and administrative officers to divide the city of Ibadan from its surrounding rural areas.

On 4 November, Foot's solicitors wrote that they had been unable to obtain any documents relevant to the Commission from the Colonial Office, on the grounds that these were confidential, and no 'satisfactory or useful information' from the Western Nigeria Office in London, so Adelabu was asked to send his proposed basic memorandum to Foot. The same letter contained the welcome news that Foot's fees would be reduced to a basic fee of £2378. 17. 6d. and 'refreshers' of £55. 2. 6d. for each day after the first week.‡ However, Adelabu was now asked for £2150 in advance; Foot's air passage could then be booked. Given his conflict with the party, Adelabu could not afford to fail and he again appealed to his followers for funds. On the 7th he cabled a further £500. On the 12th Rexworthy, Bonser and Wadkin again wrote. They had arranged to see the Secretary of the Commission in London the following day, but there was to be a further expense; Dingle Foot wanted his solicitor to come to Nigeria to handle the documents for the case. Air passage and a fee of fifty guineas a day for seven days would come to £617. 10. 0d. The balance to be paid was now £2296. 7. 6d.

On 13 November the solicitors wrote once more. T. O. Kellock, Foot's Junior Counsel, would fly out on 26 November, and Foot a few days later. If this was satisfactory, the balance was to be paid by the 20th. In answer Adelabu sent a further £200, but he was having difficulty in raising the necessary funds; various individuals and groups were being tapped, even down to the small societies affiliated to the Mabolaje.§ Rexworthy, Bonser

---

* All three had been re-elected to the N.E.C. at the Aba Convention.

† On 4 November the *Nigerian Tribune* did report an interview with him at which he was claimed to have remarked that the Convention had given Azikiwe 'a rope with which to hang himself'; but such a report in a hostile newspaper must be treated with care.

‡ It should be pointed out that this included travel, accommodation and other expenses for Foot and his Junior Counsel, and also the latter's fee. The letters and cables from Rexworthy, Bonser and Wadkin are in the Adelabu Papers.

§ Thus on 9 November, for instance, the Ababi Olorun Kosi Party of Oke Oluokun contributed eleven guineas to the fund.

and Wadkin began to put on the pressure. A cable came on 18 November saying that if Foot were to leave London on the 22nd, as was now planned, the balance of his fee must be sent by return. Another on the 19th warned that he would not leave London unless the balance was paid by the 21st. A third cable on the 21st announced that the air passage had been cancelled pending the arrival of the balance. On that day, in fact, Adelabu issued a press release announcing that Dingle Foot had been briefed by the Western N.C.N.C. to appear before the Minorities Commission. The money was raised somehow, and Foot was in Ibadan to appear before the Commission when it moved from Lagos to Ibadan and began its hearings there on 29 November.

Meanwhile, Adelabu's party colleagues were left to carry on the battle that Adelabu and Aminu Kano had opened with their manifesto. Mbadiwe's first reaction after the Convention was to embark on a two-day fast in Lagos 'to invoke God's guidance in solving the problems of Nigeria'.[28] It was Kola Balogun who most actively took up the struggle. On 12 November he wrote to Azikiwe, accusing him of packing the Convention with improperly accredited delegates. Its decisions were therefore null and void. At a press conference announcing this he commented that 'Nigeria is too big to be run by one man no matter how gifted.'[29] On the 13th Adewale Fashanu, the President of the Zikist National Vanguard (which was said to have supplied the disputed delegates), sent a telegram to the N.C.N.C. National President pressing for further action against Balogun, and another to the former National Secretary, challenging him to contest his Oshun constituency again, so that the Z.N.V. could campaign against him. On 15 November Azikiwe instructed F. S. McEwen, Balogun's successor in office, to summon him to defend himself against charges of indiscipline. The National Officers of the N.C.N.C., Azikiwe and the men he had recently appointed, were acting now as a central Working Committee of the party, such a body being provided for in the revised party constitution of 1955 and empowered to make decisions between full meetings of the National Executive Committee. On 15 December this body suspended Balogun from membership of the N.C.N.C., pending disciplinary action by the N.E.C. Balogun fought back; in a letter dated 18 December he denied the right of the C.W.C. to suspend him without a hearing, which in fact he had not had. Moreover, he carefully refused to recognize McEwen as his successor, addressing his letter to Chief Gogo Abbey as Administrative Secretary, not to the 'General Manager of the West African Pilot'.[30]

Throughout this time, Adelabu took no action which would commit him openly to further opposition to Azikiwe. His stance in this regard was of great concern to his supporters, many of whom wrote to him. Yet Adelabu took no perceptible notice of letters urging him to continue an active national role. Throughout November he was preoccupied with the approaching Minorities Commission and the problem of financing his part in it, and the approaching local government elections. On 29 May 1957, the Electoral Commissioner had announced that such elections would take place in April 1958 and on 14 October Adelabu had formally launched the Grand Alliance campaign in Ibadan. From an interview in November, it seems that Adelabu was once again in his best, humorous election form. A *Daily Times* reporter told how he had visited Adelabu at the Taj Mahal for lunch.

As we sat outside his house, three young girls and two young men were passing by and he stopped them. He said, 'You are all well dressed. When are you getting married and will the third girl be my wife?' There was much laughter.

Later, I asked him: 'Why did you do that?' and he answered: 'I want power. The next election is approaching and this is one way of winning the hearts of the young men and women that I am young in heart.'[31]

Rumors had circulated in Ibadan in May 1957 while Adelabu was in London that the division of the Ibadan District Council into one urban and several rural councils was being considered, and in Adelabu's absence L. A. Lawal sought confirmation from the Minister of Local Government of the rumor warning that small rural councils would face difficult financial problems.[32] The Grand Alliance made this even more explicit a few days later, warning that 'The Creation of new small councils...meant that taxes and rates would be tripled if not quadrupled.'[33] Some British officials were of the belief that both urban and rural areas would be better served by Councils specially designed for their purposes, while the Action Group believed that the N.C.N.C. was sure to carry most of the rural vote, but could be defeated in the urban wards. By dividing Ibadan District and sacrificing the rural areas to the N.C.N.C., the Action Group could hope to win a city council election. A. M. A. Akinloye took a special interest in this project, according to the *Defender*.[34]

Government's initial idea had been that sub-committees of the existing council or 'area' committees might meet some rural needs, but on 8 November the Ibadan Provisional Council instructed its Secretary to seek the status of City for Ibadan.[35] A meeting was accordingly held on 16 October by Minister of Local Government Alhaji Adegbenro, D. A. Murphy, his Permanent Secretary, the Local Government Adviser for Ibadan Division E. W. Pratt and another British official. The Minister 'explained that he wished to discuss reorganisation of the present Ibadan District Council with the idea of breaking it down into smaller units as had been proposed by Mr. Schofield', who had formerly been a District Officer in charge of tax collection in

Ibadan.[36] Schofield's proposal was in exact contradiction to that made in 1953 by B. J. Cooper, the Council's first Administrative Secretary, who had recommended the continuation of the single, all-purpose council created after the Hayley Committee, earning the comment that his report showed 'some lack of foresight'. At that time Awolowo, as Minister of Local Government, had accepted Cooper's report 'without reservation' and cautioned that Ibadan District was 'one of the most conservative areas in Yorubaland'. He was 'personally satisfied with the progress of Ibadan on all fronts', he had said, and in 'due course, say three years hence, the Ibadan elites will see the necessity for the creation of an Urban District Council for Ibadan, and a number of Rural District Councils'.[37]

Three years and more had now passed and Awolowo was pursuing as Premier what he had originally foreseen as Minister of Local Government. On 5 November Adegbenro invited five officials, six members each of the Action Group and the N.C.N.C., and Ronald Wraith, a British political scientist then teaching a course in public administration at the University College of Ibadan, for further discussion. Adelabu was one of those invited for the N.C.N.C., and promptly refused. 'The present proposed meeting is not based on any political reality or statutory grounds', he wrote, 'and therefore is unacceptable.'[38] Throughout this week, as we have seen, Adelabu was trying desperately to collect Foot's fee, and when the meeting was finally held on 12 November the N.C.N.C. was not represented. Akinloye and J. A. Akinlotan attended for the Action Group and Akinloye stated that while he favored separate Councils, a connecting Divisional Council should also be established 'to prevent separation of town and Districts'.[39] D. A. Murphy pointed out to Akinloye that he had been a member of the Hayley Committee that had approved the existing Council structure and that if a change were to be made an equally thorough investigation would have to be made again. He did not see how this could be done prior to the April elections. This Akinloye sharply contested. In 1953, they had not been as familiar with modern local government as they were now. The proposed changes could in fact be instituted by a British officer in a few weeks, and he urged the Minister to put the appropriate machinery into motion as quickly as possible. The Minister held out some hope that this could in fact occur. 'If this were the case it would be within Government's competence to postpone the elections in Ibadan District until reorganisation had been completed.'

A version of these minutes was then prepared and sent to the Council which at its meeting on 25 November accepted the rural-urban-divisional council plan urged by Akinloye. A further meeting was called by Adegbenro on 3 December and was attended by Olubadan Akinyele and five other senior chiefs, the Rev. Alayande and S. A. Akinfenwa for the Provisional

Council and Akinlotan and Akinloye for the Action Group. Adegbenro announced that although he had invited the seven Ibadan members of the House of Assembly and two additional N.C.N.C. representatives, he had learned that morning that they would not be present. Akinloye's plan was accepted, although his further proposal to make the Divisional Council the rating authority was rejected, and this decision was announced in the papers. E. W. Pratt was instructed to make necessary arrangements.

Thus, while Adelabu was hoping to regain control of the Ibadan Council as the basis of his enlarged Yoruba Central State, the Action Group Government, for a variety of long-standing and opportunistic reasons, was threatening him with the same kind of boundary revision which he was hoping to use to dismember the Western Region and the Action Group. The Government now had the advantage of having the administrative officers under their orders, and it is clear that Government felt that Olubadan Akinyele and the senior chiefs, who included such former Adelabu supporters as Kobiowu, Akinwale Mato and Solagbade, could carry the urban election for the Action Group.

The reason for Adelabu's absence at the meeting of 3 December was that, as so frequently in the past, he was already occupied elsewhere when Government announced a meeting or an ultimatum. Government's action in this instance seems particularly pointed in that F. R. A. Williams, Minister of Justice, was similarly engaged. On 29 November the Minorities Commission had opened its hearings in Ibadan. Presided over by Sir Henry Willink, Master of Magdelene College, Cambridge, it also included the Director of the London Institute of Race Relations, a former official of the Indian Civil Service, and a former Deputy Governor of the Gold Coast. Facing them was a constellation of legal talent, including Dingle Foot and T. N. Kellock, appearing for the N.C.N.C. Opposition and the Central Yoruba State Movement, Webber Egbe for the Mid-West State Movement, and Rotimi Williams for the Western Region Government. At the very beginning of the hearings Foot raised two crucial matters. First of all, could the Western N.C.N.C. be described as a 'minority'? After an adjournment of fifteen minutes, the Commission decided affirmatively but within 'certain limitations'; the London Conference had really intended minorities to be ethnic or religious in this context, not political.* Foot would be allowed to try to

* The Commission later summed up its views on this point as follows: 'We thought that the Conference and the Secretary of State had meant us to be concerned with minorities of a permanent nature, ethnic or religious, not with a purely political minority, such as an Opposition. We were therefore not prepared to listen to a political opposition speaking on its own behalf as a political minority. But we were ready to hear an Opposition on the general political situation because their views and

show that the Western Government had taken excessive powers, but not to cite individual cases. The second matter related to procedure. Did the Commission have powers to subpoena witnesses and to protect them from criminal and civil actions which might result from what they said? No ruling on this point was given that day.

The following morning Dingle Foot pressed for an answer, suggesting that the matter be referred to the Colonial Secretary. Rotimi Williams formally protested on behalf of the Action Group Government (which cabled its objections to the Colonial Office) against what was felt to be developing into a full-scale judicial inquiry into the whole range of its recent activities, in other words, exactly what Adelabu had hoped for and promised! The terms of reference of the Commission were now called into question, therefore, and its activities virtually paralyzed.* On Monday, 2 December, the Commission heard only comparatively unimportant evidence and Dingle Foot flew to London to see the Colonial Secretary. On the 3rd, while the Ibadan council re-organization meeting was being held, Adelabu issued a press release in which he tried to show that the Government, not himself, was questioning the authority of the Commission, and what the consequences of this action must be. Thus, 'If the Western Region Government wants the scope of the present Commission of Inquiry re-opened *ipso facto* Regional self-government for the Western Region must be re-opened.'[40]

On 3 December the Commission and Adelabu with it moved north to Oyo for hearings there on the 4th. The Commission had already thwarted

their evidence might throw light on the fears of minorities.' (*Report of the Commission*, p. 5.)

* The terms of reference were as follows:

1 To ascertain the facts about the fears of minorities in any part of Nigeria and to propose means of allaying those fears whether well or ill founded.

2 To advise what safeguards should be included for this purpose in the Constitution of Nigeria.

3 If, but only if, no other solution seems to the Commission to meet the case, then as a last resort to make detailed recommendations for the creation of one or more new States, and in that case:

(*a*) to specify the precise area to be included in such State or States;

(*b*) to recommend the Governmental and administrative structure most appropriate for it;

(*c*) to assess whether any State recommended would be viable from an economic and administrative point of view and what the effect of its creation would be on the Region or Regions from which it would be created and on the Federation.

4 To report its findings and recommendations to the Secretary of State for the Colonies. (*Nigeria: Report of the Commission appointed to enquire into the fears of Minorities and the means of allaying them*, Cmd. 505, London: H.M.S.O., 1958, p. iii.)

Adelabu's hope of having the ex-Alafin give evidence there, on the grounds that he was banned from Oyo Division, although it had indicated its willingness to consider an application for him to be heard in Lagos when it returned there later in the month.[41] In the event, the hearing was adjourned three hours early because the N.C.N.C.-Oyo Parapo Alliance refused to give evidence until the Colonial Secretary gave his ruling, and there was no sitting the following day, and one for only forty minutes on 6 December.

The really decisive events were taking place in London. Matters were made more difficult by the fact that on the foggy winter night of 3 December the Colonial Secretary had slipped and broken a bone in his left shoulder. On the 5th, however, it was announced that he would consider Dingle Foot's submission. Prognostications were not very hopeful all the same; on 7 December the *Daily Times* reported that Foot had seen officials at the Colonial Office, but 'It is considered most unlikely, however, that the Colonial Office will support Mr. Foot.'

Tempers deteriorated. When the Commission opened its hearings in Benin on 9 December, the normally jovial Rotimi Williams walked out with the Action Group team on the grounds that the Western Region Government had the right to be heard first on the subject of the Mid-West State, but that the Commission had secretly promised priority to one of the Opposition lawyers. On the 12th, after an appeal to the Action Group Government by the Governor of the Western Region, it agreed to take part once again, but it was not until 14 December that the air was really cleared. On that day the Secretary of State announced his decision: witnesses before the Commission would not be given judicial privilege.

This was a serious defeat for Adelabu. Without the power to subpoena further witnesses, or to protect those coming forward voluntarily from possible reprisals for what they might say, there was no chance of the Commission being turned into something approaching a full-scale investigation of the conduct of the Action Group Government. He now had to continue the fight at a severe disadvantage since the refusal of the N.C.N.C. to co-operate with the Commission in Ibadan and Oyo meant that its evidence had not been fully presented, while the Commission was due to move on to the East on 3 January, and then to the North. Nevertheless, confident that he would be heard, Adelabu announced from Lagos on 24 December that further, unscheduled, hearings would be held in Ibadan at a date to be announced.

The Commission, however, at its second session in Lagos adopted a tougher attitude after the Secretary of State's ruling. Dingle Foot, back from London, appeared for the United Muslim Party and the Lagos and Colony State Movement, both of which were seeking the creation of that new region, but on 28 December the Commission ruled that the people of Lagos and Colony Province did not constitute a minority, and that the position of Lagos, as federal territory, had already been decided in London. On Monday 30 December, the Commission in ruling on a fourteen-point submission by Foot stated that they would only hear evidence relating to fears of minorities and not to the complaints of the N.C.N.C. Opposition in the West; they would not deal with such individual matters as the case of the ex-Alafin, the dissolution of the Ibadan District Council, or allegations of bias in the award of government scholarships, and, contrary to Adelabu's expectation, there would be no more hearings in Ibadan. The case of the Western N.C.N.C. must be presented in Lagos by 1.30 p.m. on 2 January 1958.

That Thursday morning, Foot, Adelabu and the others did the best they could, knowing that whatever they said would not turn the Minorities Commission into a Commission of Inquiry into the affairs of the Western Government and that Lennox-Boyd and the Commission would not be moved even by expensive British legal supplications. The Lion of the West, the ex-Alafin and P. A. Afolabi gave evidence, attempting to make as general an attack on the Western Region Government as possible. Dingle Foot argued that various pieces of Governmental legislation on such matters as local government, riots, and native courts, taken together seemed to increase ministerial powers and created fears in the minds of minorities, of whatever kind. Thus, the creation of a few new states was not the only answer to the problem; it would be better to make each province a separate unit of the federation. In his evidence Adelabu continued this theme, in effect challenging the Commission to consider new states immediately rather than as a last resort. It was Britain's responsibility to solve the minorities problem, he said, because Britain created it. The present constitutional structure was a mistake; what was needed (he now reiterated his whole case) to allay the fears of minorities of all sorts was a federation made up of the present provinces as states, with a strong central government. Somewhat illogically, he also asked for a Central Yoruba State made up of Ibadan, Oyo and Ondo Provinces. Although the London Conference had allayed certain minority fears, it had failed to provide constitutional safeguards for federal control of the police, constitutional protection for the position of traditional rulers, and elections based on a uniform, federally-controlled system.

Adelabu and Foot thus scored only an irrelevant success when the Commission agreed to tolerate evidence for these few hours which went far beyond the scope of ethnic minority fears. There could be no hope that when the Commission reported (in July 1958) it would speak to N.C.N.C. fears.*

* Thus, its final comment on the question of the Central Yoruba State and the Ondo Central State was that although in those areas 'there is an element of local and

With that great capacity of his to shift his attention from one level of politics to another, and under the pressure of events, in these last months Adelabu turned to the question of his own political power. It seems probable that the course his career would follow remained unclear to him, but whatever path he next took, two things would remain basic: his relations with the N.C.N.C. and his control over Ibadan.

In the first weeks of January 1958, the Ibadan election campaign began in earnest and once again the question of taxes was an issue. The Provisional Council had faced the problem of inadequate revenue in its first weeks in office in 1956 when a special sub-committee was appointed to consider property rating. Delay was initially incurred since many of the relevant files had been taken by Commissioner Nicholson to England for the preparation of his report and they had not yet been returned.[42] By October 1956 when the Finance and Tax Committee dealt with the problem, the tax season was just opening and they determined that it would be 'politically inexpedient' to introduce property rating at that time.[43] Furthermore, since the law under which such a plan might eventually be enforced applied to all of the Western Region, 'it was considered advisable to see it applied to other places before applying it to Ibadan'.

In 1957, the Provisional Council experienced considerable difficulty in collecting tax and even greater difficulty in finding funds to meet its expanding services. Under pressure from the Government, and since time was insufficient to introduce a property rating system before the Council would be in serious financial straits, for the 1957–8 season the Council increased the general income tax by seven shillings and six pence, the water rate from six shillings to twelve and bicycle licenses from ten to fifteen shillings. Such increases occurred elsewhere in the Region under a new income tax law and the new local government law, which forced local governments to collect more revenue for education and general purposes.[44] Protest, as the elections neared, increased throughout the Region. Petitions complaining of arbitrary and discriminatory tax increases were systematically gathered in every ward in Ibadan and forwarded to the Governor.[45] A list compiled by Adelabu's clerk giving the name, ward, occupation and 1956–7 and 1957–8 tax assessments of thirty-nine taxpayers, of whom twenty-eight were farmers, showed that their total tax had increased from £60. 14. 4d. to £249. 7. 0d. Unrest over such increases was widespread in the Region. In Okitipupa Division rioting required sending fifteen lorry-loads of Nigeria Police from Ibadan on 13 January and the placing of the Division under virtual martial

sectional feelings, this is really political opposition on party lines, and for the Opposition to ask for a separate state would make nonsense of parliamentary democracy'. (*Report of the Commission*, p. 28.)

law under the Peace Preservation Ordinance. Two days later, Adegoke Adelabu took advantage of this situation to issue a press release calling for a meeting of the House of Assembly to discuss the situation in Okitipupa, and citing previous cases of similar disturbances in Ijebu, Ibarapa, Egbado, Oyo, Ogbomosho, Oshogbo and Remo Divisions. It was no coincidence, he asserted, that tax trouble nearly always came in areas controlled by the Action Group, whereas where the N.C.N.C. controlled the local council 'Tax collection has been more relatively smooth and peaceful.'[46] Not that the N.C.N.C. was opposed to higher taxes as such – 'We believe that higher tax collection is the inescapable price of better Social Services and amenities and general progress.' It was the methods used in collection which were the cause of the trouble.

At this point, Adelabu virtually disappeared from sight for an entire month. On 20 January, the *Defender* announced that he had gone on 'sick leave' as of the 18th. There was a £50,000 libel suit by the Amalgamated Press hanging over his head as a result of his allegation that in printing the electors' lists in 1956 the Press had falsified them, and the hearings had just been adjourned till 31 March. Possibly he was feeling the strain and drinking again. We do not even know where he spent these weeks. His 'illness', following his preoccupation with the Willinck Commission and the election campaign in Ibadan, led him to miss a number of important meetings in Lagos and the Region.

As we have seen, in the first weeks of November after the Aba Convention, it was Kola Balogun who bore the main burden of resistance to Dr Azikiwe and his new Central Working Committee. By mid-November, another force was at work, the Elders' Peace Committee, composed in the main of senior members of the Lagos Democratic Party which we have already seen as an active force at the time of the N.C.N.C. Special Convention in April. While the Elders' Peace Committee in theory was seeking to mediate between the National President and Balogun, its preference was certainly for the former National Secretary, and it is hardly surprising that Dr Azikiwe refused its mediation. On 17 December this provoked the Elders into a public statement in which they described Balogun's suspension from the party by the C.W.C. as 'unreasonable'. Since their mediation had been refused 'they had to conclude that those who decided to suspend Chief Balogun were not motivated by the best interests of the party'.[47] A terse reply was given by F. U. Anyiam, the Acting National Publicity Secretary of the party. The Elders had no constitutional existence in the N.C.N.C., and it was 'pure waste of time treating with a body that is not existing'.[48]

Matters might finally have been brought to a head by another Special Convention of the N.C.N.C., which was summoned to meet on 30 January in Enugu. On 29 January, the National Executive Committee of the N.C.N.C., at its pre-Convention meeting, agreed only to censure K. O. Mbadiwe, who had said that he would apologize to the Convention. The suspension of Balogun was ratified indefinitely, but his case could not be decided finally, as he failed to appear in Enugu, though he gave no reasons. Moreover, Nnamdi Azikiwe himself did not attend. His mother had died three days before. Adelabu also failed to surface from his sick leave begun on the 18th. Thus, the Convention failed to bring the clash between Dr Azikiwe and his dissident lieutenants to a final head. (It was to come in June when they produced their 'Zik Must Go' letter.) The maneuvering continued. The day after the Convention in Enugu the opposition to the National President in Lagos and the West gathered at a meeting at Alhaji Soule's house called by the Elders' Peace Committee. It was attended by thirty-nine delegates, including all the Ibadan legislators, led in Adelabu's absence by L. Ade Bello. The national party crisis, it seemed, was to be critically linked to Ibadan.

In Ibadan, the implementation of the Action Group's plan for a pre-election dismembering of the Ibadan District Council area was running aground. E. W. Pratt had found it necessary to consider the implications of the proposals in more detail than had been originally foreseen. In particular, he had found it impossible to persuade the rural areas of the value of the scheme or to determine by any relatively objective standard how boundary lines in the rural areas would be drawn which would at once provide for administrative efficiency and population balance while taking into account the ties among clusters of villages traditionally bound together through the urban lineages. He therefore urged that a Boundary Committee be appointed.

By the middle of January, it was widely believed that Government had chosen 24 March, and not a day in April, as Ibadan polling date and yet no boundary committee had been appointed. By this time a combination of events had perhaps led the Action Group to decide that they could win a single Ibadan election without the trouble of forming new Councils, some of which they might not control. That the local N.C.N.C. feared the loss of the Districts was made clear when Majekodunmi Oduyoye, Oshilaja's son and N.C.N.C. Principal Organizing Secretary for Ibadan, announced that 'There is no doubt that the motive behind the split is to make it easy to capture Ibadan from the NCNC.'[49] Regionally and nationally the N.C.N.C. was in a state of confusion and Adelabu was well aware that he would not be able to rely on either the chiefs, particularly the Olubadan, or other prestigious N.C.N.C. leaders, especially Azikiwe, as he had in 1954.

Still a further reason for not pursuing the original plan was that Adelabu and the N.C.N.C. were once again protesting tax collection and the Action

421

Group Provisional Council was faced in February with the possibility of a considerably worse collection than that which had been used to justify Adelabu's dismissal from the Council in 1956. To delay the election until this possibility became a fact would have placed Government in an extremely embarrassing position. Rather than postponing the elections, Government seems to have decided to slow down the re-organization program and to use Adelabu's difficulties to their advantage.

During his absence, further petitions alleging tax discrimination were gathered in Ibadan by lawyers Adisa and Akinjide.[50] On 27 January, they led an N.C.N.C. delegation to complain to the Minister of Local Government about the manner in which taxes had been assessed. The Council was already in serious trouble. At the Finance and Rating Committee meeting of 22 January, the Council Secretary and the Local Government Adviser had warned that only eleven per cent of the goal of £550,000 had been collected, and that only 13,410 of the estimated 120,000 taxpayers had actually paid. The Local Government Adviser reported that he had discovered that many members of the Assessment Committees had not even paid their own rates and should progress in these regards not be made quickly, 'he would have no alternative but to bring to the notice of the Minister this bad situation which would, he was sure, cast a slur on the Olubadan of Ibadan and Council if the Minister should declare publicly the Council [to be] in default'. Under this threat, the Council initiated a vigorous collection program. Raiding was renewed, and fearing trouble, on 1 February the authorities placed 300 Nigeria Police on stand-by, with reinforcements brought in from Abeokuta. However, there was no trouble, even when apprentices demonstrated on 14 February against a decision not to exempt them from taxes.

Against this background, the planning begun at N. B. Soule's house in January continued. On Saturday 8 February, Kola Balogun met with some of the Elders at his home in Oshun Division to plan a new organization, the Egbe Yoruba Parapo, and on the 10th, it was announced in Oshogbo that the Egbe would be launched in Ibadan on 15 February. The inauguration was held at the Ibadan Race Course and was attended by Balogun, H. O. Davies and Alhaji Soule who mentioned donating £500 to the new cause. The principal speaker was the Lion of the West, Alhaji Adegoke Adelabu, emerging after weeks of absence as the Egbe's General Secretary.* The main aim of the Egbe Yoruba Parapo, he declared, was to further the solidarity of the Yoruba people in the same way that the Ibo State Union served its people. Seeming half to admit that such 'tribal' organizations had dangerous poten-

* The other officers of the Egbe were President: Alhaji Soule; Vice-Presidents: Chief H. O. Davies, A. O. Joaquim and Chief J. A. Oshibogun; Treasurer: P. A. Afolabi; Legal Adviser: Kola Balogun; Auditor: G. B. Akinyede.

tialities, he affirmed that the Egbe was prepared to dissolve itself if the Ibo State Union did the same. For the moment, however, it would remain in existence as an ally of the N.C.N.C., and the Ibos must not attempt to interfere with it. Indeed, he went further than this in affirming Yoruba group feeling, declaring that 'The careerists within the camp of the followership of the NCNC, who have debased themselves into tools in the hands of those who stand to gain by lack of solidarity among the Yoruba leaders of the NCNC, who are traitors to the Yoruba Nation, must realise that their days are numbered.'[51]

What was Adelabu trying to do at this point? The formation of the Egbe Yoruba Parapo seems at first sight dangerously close to the sort of 'tribalism', the pandering to a sense of cultural exclusiveness, which had for years bedevilled the N.C.N.C. and Nigerian politics in general. So it was interpreted by those who disapproved of what Adelabu was doing. On the same day as the Ibadan Race Course meeting, T. O. S. Benson, J. O. Fadahunsi and two other Yoruba N.C.N.C. leaders issued a statement warning their followers against the Egbe. Five days later Adeniran Ogunsanya challenged Adelabu to name those he had described as 'careerists'. 'It is a thing for regret', he said, 'that a man of the calibre of Alhaji Adelabu who has been the party's National Vice-President for two years and is still the Chairman of the NCNC Western Working Committee should now demote himself to be General Secretary of a tribal clique within the NCNC.'[52] On 22 February a meeting of the Zikist National Vanguard at N.C.N.C. National Headquarters in Lagos was addressed by Fred Anyiam, who as well as being acting National Publicity Secretary was also President of the Lagos branch of the Vanguard. Although he placed the major blame on Mbadiwe for the activities of the Elders' Peace Committee and the Egbe Yoruba Parapo, he was also reported as saying that Adelabu was the enemy of the N.C.N.C. and had threatened to beat up Zik if he came to Ibadan!

Such interpretations of Adelabu's actions and words were not unreasonable in the circumstances. He was indeed attempting to organize support among the Yoruba people – or such of them as followed the N.C.N.C. – by appealing to their sense of cultural identity, just as he might have appealed to Islam had the Action Group not so skillfully undermined such an effort. He had to have a firm basis for his political ambitions, and although Ibadan was the foundation of his strength it was not enough to satisfy all those ambitions.* He had hoped – and perhaps still hoped – to become Premier

* An interesting illustration of Adelabu's view of Ibadan and its relations with the rest of Yorubaland is in a letter written to members of a new Planning Committee he set up just after his return from Mecca: 'This is the top level thinking organ of the N.C.N.C. in Ibadan and therefore the Central Planning Body for the N.C.N.C. in

of the West, or at least of the Yoruba West if the Mid-West State came into being. Alternatively, he had hoped to rule in a new Central Yoruba State. By February 1958 his political future in these respects was very uncertain, but whatever happened he had to have as large a following in the Yoruba West as possible. Previously he had sought to acquire this within the general framework of the N.C.N.C. Now, though he was still not prepared to break completely with that party, he wished to build up his own organization within it, an ally of the N.C.N.C. rather than a constituent part, something he could use as his own personal machine on a regional basis, a sort of Mabolaje writ large. Thus he was applying to political party organization the view that it should be a free association of culturally distinct groups.* Correspondingly, R. O. A. Akinjide had organized forty-one Ibadan villages to protest on the Parapo inaugural day against the disintegration of the Ibadan District Council area.

Throughout February, E. W. Pratt had continued his investigations of the re-organization proposal and late that month he felt compelled to do what Akinloye had hoped would not be necessary when he conducted a public hearing at Mapo Hall in order to give opposing interests the opportunity to state their positions. By this time, however, the N.C.N.C. felt so certain of their position that they walked out of the meeting in protest. The Action Group had suffered a further embarrassment when thirty-one members of the Assessment Committees appointed by the Council were arrested for failure to pay their taxes before the deadline.[53] However, if things were not going well for the Action Group, the Ibadan N.C.N.C. leaders had a less than certain course to plot between the alternatives of appearing as law-abiding citizens and protesting tax assessments, between successfully contesting the election and disagreement with the parent party, and indeed among the personal disputes within the party caused by Adelabu's far-flung and often conflicting interests with their resultant sporadic leadership of his local party, and the increasing self-assertion within the party of its other leaders. The triggering incident which brought such a dispute into the open was perhaps a disturbing incident of arson against the house of a tax assessment committee member in which ten Mabolaje members were called

the Yoruba West.' (Adelabu and S. L. A. Elliott to Ibadan N.C.N.C. legislators and others, 31 July 1957, A.P.)

* He was apparently not without support in the ranks of the Ibo State Union, a body which was itself in some dispute with Azikiwe (see Sklar, *Nigerian Political Parties*, pp. 205–7). On 21 February the Administrative Secretary of the Port Harcourt branch of the Ibo State Union sent a telegram to Adelabu congratulating him on the formation of the Egbe Yoruba Parapo. Characteristically, he then sent copies to Benson, Ogunsanya and some of his other critics with the message 'See what tolerance can do?'

for questioning by the police. Whatever the immediate cause, on 26 February, E. A. Fakayode, L. Ade Bello, R. O. A. Akinjide, S. L. Lana and four others protested to Adelabu his nomination of Adebayo Adeyinka, S. L. Elliott and Isau Lawal to the Executive Committee of the Ibadan N.C.N.C.[54] So serious was this dispute that the eight dissenters stated they were willing to put their case before the urban and rural units of the party. We do not know what became of this dispute, but the chronology of events suggests that the response of Adelabu and the party to the taxation program of the Action Group Provisional Council, which had been led by two of the dissenters, was very much at issue.

On Sunday 2 March, Adelabu had the opportunity to clarify his views on a variety of national and local issues to his comrades in the N.C.N.C. when he presided over a meeting of the Western Working Committee in the Itoro Hall at Ijebu-Ode. Certainly he seemed to make some effort to mollify his recent critics. He described Nnamdi Azikiwe as the 'human symbol of our party solidarity and Nigerian unity', and said that 'Dr. Zik's twenty-five-year service to the nation has laid down a tradition which will channel our various efforts to one goal.' Yet in his references to 'our various efforts' which had to be channeled to one goal, to 'permissible' disagreement, and to the need for 'dexterity in the evolution of suitable formulae to harmonise different viewpoints and interests', he was in an oblique way restating the justification he had already given for the existence of the Egbe Yoruba Parapo; the Yorubas in the N.C.N.C. must have their own organization, just as the Ibos had.*

At a mass meeting later in the day he was, in fact, rather more explicit. Speaking before a gathering which included K. O. Mbadiwe, Festus Okotie-Eboh, F. S. McEwen, T. O. S. Benson, F. U. Anyiam, J. O. Fadahunsi and Adeniran Ogunsanya, he denied that the Yorubas were planning to break away from the N.C.N.C. On the other hand, he again justified the Egbe Yoruba Parapo as a cultural organization and counterpart of the Ibo State Union. One at least of those who heard him felt him to be unrepentant: when Ogunsanya spoke he attacked the Egbe and demanded its dissolution, and was booed for his pains by a section of the crowd, which included a large delegation from Ibadan.[55]

Adelabu also urged his listeners to pay their taxes and then seek political redress in the coming local government elections. He returned to this theme on 8 March at a rally in Itoku Square, in Abeokuta. Taxes must be paid, he said, 'even if it meant pawning their furniture and wearing apparels'.[56]

* The full text of this speech has not survived and this account is therefore based only on a report in the *Defender* for 4 March 1958. We do not feel we are reading too much into this admittedly incomplete account.

The solution to grievances was to vote against the Action Group in the local elections.* How serious this matter still remained is indicated by the fact that the Ibadan Council, which had on a previous occasion rejected property tax in the city as inappropriate until a similar system was instituted throughout the Region, on 3 March had passed a resolution urging that steps be taken to institute it as quickly as possible. This they had done in what were still thought to be the very last weeks of the Provisional Council's tenure in office. Under the urging of Adelabu and some but not all N.C.N.C. leaders, tax collection was proceeding peacefully in the Region and in Ibadan. In Okitipupa Division things were back to normal and it was possible to revoke the proclamation imposing stringent security measures. In Ibadan there was quiet if not success. By 31 March, only £292,984 of the £550,000 had been collected.[57]

Thus the image Adelabu was striving to present in these weeks was quite consistently one of respectability. On Tuesday 11 March, the Western House of Assembly met again for its Budget session. During the debates over the next few days Adelabu, as Leader of the Opposition, took an active part, keeping his temper even when his old adversary, Chief Rotimi Williams, once again taxed him with his part in the Akinbiyi slapping case. Indeed, according to two of his fellow Opposition members, when the N.C.N.C. Parliamentary Party met on 17 March he put great emphasis on the need for responsible behavior. In a memorandum which he circulated he wrote that 'The use of invectives must not be applied in debates in this honourable House. . .in all our criticisms we must show a sense of reasonable and responsible approach to Government measures and. . .the Opposition must remember at all times that it forms part of the machinery of the Western Region.'[58] When he spoke at the meeting he opened his remarks by saying that 'you cannot curse your opponent all the time, you cannot abuse your opponent all the time, let us have a meeting [of the House] this time that should be constructive'.[59] Not that his temperament was entirely suppressed. The very next day, when accused of repetition by Anthony Enahoro, another old opponent, he shot back the retort that 'in a very short while the Government front Bench will soon realise that the more they become sensitive the more will I continue to repeat until it hurts'.[60] Yet there is no doubt that the outward image was of a new Adelabu. It was left to other N.C.N.C. Members to speak of Government measures as 'oppressive, repressive, suppressive, unprogressive, undemocratic, chaotic, diabolic, barbaric, tribalistic, obnoxious, malicious, riotous, wolfish, selfish, childish, inhuman, untraditional and ungodly'.[61] This Adelabu was not the one of the

---

* Some Grand Alliance leaders had taken their cue from their leader; Obadara Atanda, for instance, the Maiyegun League elder, was reported to be urging farmers to pay their taxes. (S.N.D., 5 February 1958.)

battle for a Royal Commission of Inquiry. It was rather one who, at the end of what was to be his last speech in the House, on 20 March, assured the Government that

the time has gone when anybody may come to this House to make reckless accusations against the Government...But full information must be given at the appropriate time, so that, not only Government supporters, but also those of us who are the watchdogs of the public interest, as a virile Opposition, can tell the electorate at large that we are not going to allow anything as shocking as the newspapers would like to portray as happening, in the running of the Government of this Region.[62]

Whether this new 'Parliamentary' Adelabu would have proved to be a consistent characterization is now only a matter for speculation; this was not only his last speech, but his last appearance in the Western House of Assembly.

It was true that temperament and the Action Group's ability to control the timing of events had led him to an outburst in the *Defender* that very morning. The day before, on 19 March, Alhaji Adegbenro finally announced the dates of the local government elections in the House of Assembly: they were to be spread over a period of more than two months, from 8 April to 15 June, with different parts of the region polling at different times; Ibadan Division's councils were to be elected between 1 and 15 June. This provoked Adelabu to an immediate reply. In his statement to the *Defender*, published on the 20th, he pointed out that on the whole Action Group strongholds were scheduled to poll early and N.C.N.C. ones late – 'Ibadan in particular has been put last so that the results there which are certain to be an overwhelming defeat for the government party may not be in a position to influence voters in other constituencies.' Not only this, but the staggering of polling would permit 'any rich political party to attempt to transport masses of voters from a non-voting area on a particular day into a voting area for the purposes of impersonation'. Just as seriously, June elections postponed the time when Adelabu could assert his authority over his party by re-capturing the Council and its chairmanship. Although Pratt's activities had come to a halt, the Action Group was now willing to contest the election without the division of Ibadan District, since it had timed the election to suit itself. This meant a continuing period for Adelabu of the difficulties which it had appeared already were so serious that the Action Group was willing to oppose him without dividing the Council's jurisdiction. Insofar as these difficulties involved a dispute within the Grand Alliance as to whether to protest against taxes or pay them, perhaps Adelabu better than the Government itself knew the dangers involved in continuing to thwart established authority and in delaying the return of authority over Ibadan and the Grand Alliance to the weaver's son from Oke Oluokun.

CHAPTER 15

DEATH OF A HERO

> Death!...
> Thou hast rendered us powerless
> And we are bound to take things 'so-so'...
> > A Schoolboy Poet on Adelabu's death,
> > 1962

> ...his battle day is past. It is we who still toil and battle, who will worry
> where life's journey may yet lead us.
> > Anthony Enahoro, March 1958

> We do not...wish to continue to desecrate the memory of the late
> Adelabu by being unable to champion the cause of the people of Ibadan.
> > Two former N.C.N.C. legislators,
> > February, 1961

In the late afternoon of Tuesday, 25 March 1958, at a place called Ode
Remo, fifty-one miles north of Lagos on the road to Ibadan, Adegoke
Adelabu died amid the tearing of metal and the breaking of glass. The ash-
grey Peugeot saloon in which he was riding collided head-on with a light
yellow Austin with such force that the latter somersaulted and came to rest
upside down facing back the way it had come. Those who arrived first on
the scene found the Peugeot beginning to catch fire. Extinguishing it, they
discovered that only one of the Peugeot's four occupants was alive, the driver
having escaped with injuries. The corpse in the front passenger's seat was
not immediately recognized as that of the Lion of the West. The driver of the
other car was unharmed, his own two passengers, both British representatives
of the Royal Exchange Assurance Company, having been slightly injured.
The injured and the dead were taken to the nearest hospital, at Shagamu.

Adelabu had suffered multiple injuries and died immediately. Dr Abiodun
Adesanya of the Shagamu General Hospital, who performed the postmortem
on 26 March in the presence of Adelabu's old friend, J. M. Johnson, found
that

> ...there were abrasions all over the face, right leg and right forearm. There were
> abrasions like cogwheel marks over the chest, both sides and the left arm. There

was a compound fracture of the left forearm bone and a simple fracture of the left femur. The sternum was fractured...several ribs on both sides and the chest cavity [were] broken. The left lung was turned and there was a hemorrhage into the pleural cavity. The heart was ruptured both anteriorly and posteriorly. The liver was also ruptured and there was blood in the peritoneal cavity. There was no evidence of disease in the viscera.[1]

Before it was possible to publicize the doctor's finding that there were no other injuries, in particular no gunshot wounds, rumor spread among Adelabu's followers that he had in fact been murdered; that he had been waylaid and shot by agents of the Action Group.*

The driver of the car in which Adelabu died was his business partner of some years, Albert Younan. Adelabu had maintained close relations with this family of Lebanese merchants, including its head, Anthony Younan, who had died in December 1957. It was the belief of Adelabu's relatives and many of his associates that these relations contributed to his death. For some time the Younans had been selling cloth bearing Adelabu's name and picture, a commodity which had an assured sale in Ibadan, and, as Adelabu's business partner, Albert profited from this.[2] Two shipments of this cloth put on sale while Adelabu was still a minister sold well, and sales declined only after his death.† The relations between the Ibadan politician and the Lebanese merchant had been financially rewarding.

Many people also believed that a special cloth had been ordered by the Younans in readiness for the regional election of 1956, a cloth distinguished by a design showing Adelabu as Premier holding the keys to the Western House of Assembly.[3] According to this story, when Adelabu failed to become Premier, the Younans were placed in grave financial jeopardy, since they

* Steve Iweanya, editor of the *Southern Nigeria Defender* at the time, insisted in an interview with one of the authors that this was so, claiming to have seen the body of Adelabu, with bullet holes in the head and armpits. The car, he claimed, had been deliberately crashed to make it look like an accident, and Action Group doctors posted to all hospitals and mortuaries to which the body might have been taken! Such views are reflected in a play written by an author of the popular 'Onitsha Market literature' school, which Bernth Lindfors brought to our attention. It portrays Adelabu at the beginning of an election campaign addressing a meeting and praising the National Government (*sic*) and Azikiwe, and offering his life for the party. The crowd vows to kill twenty of his enemies if he should die and, ignoring his wife's pleas, Adelabu leaves for Lagos on 'National Duty'. Ijebu Action Groupers meanwhile have conspired with an Ijebu to produce hallucinations in the driver of Adelabu's car, who crashes on the way home. A riot follows in which twenty persons are killed, and then Adelabu is buried. (Ogali A. A. Ogali, *Adelabu* (*A Drama*), Onitsha: the author, n.d.)

† From a manuscript note in the Adelabu Papers, written while he was in London, it appears that Adelabu himself hoped for an income of £2000 from such textiles in the near future.

had secured a loan from the African Continental Bank to finance the speculation. Therefore, on 25 March 1958 Albert Younan took Adelabu to Lagos
to plead with the Bank for further credit for Younan, and when Adelabu
failed, Younan tried to commit suicide by crashing his car, succeeding only
in injuring himself badly and killing Adelabu and his two followers. All this
is denied by Younan, who maintains that there was no special cloth printed
for the 1956 election and therefore no financial loss, that he and Adelabu,
as frequently in the past, had gone together to Lagos on unrelated business,
that he had left Adelabu at the house of Festus Okotie-Eboh and called for
him there when he was ready to return to Ibadan.[4]

Nevertheless, Albert Younan was under some sort of stress at the time.
A letter dated 24 March 1958 and accepted by Younan as his, was tendered
by Mojid Agbaje, appearing as the lawyer for Adelabu's family at the
coroners' inquest held from 27–30 May. It read:

Dear Alhaji,
    Good morning. I am sorry that I am still a trouble to you. But I am in need to
[sic] your valuable help. I am still receiving telephone warnings every day that
I should comply by [sic] the contents of that letter I showed to you last time.
    Still nine days to go. I am too worried. I beg you by the name of Allah to help
me urgently. Please, please, give your definite reply. Thank you.[5]

During the inquest Younan's lawyer, S. O. Lambo, also intervened at one
point to state that if some matters were pursued 'certain grave revelations
which will not be pleasant to hear' might emerge.[6] An air of mystery therefore remains around the question of the business relations between the
Younan family and Adelabu and the link between them and his death. It is
clear that Adelabu lent his personality to help sell textiles, that Albert
Younan was experiencing business difficulties in March 1958, and that he
did appeal to Adelabu for help on the basis of their personal friendship.
Whether or not these facts were as closely interrelated as some would have
it we do not know.

When news of the accident reached Ibadan on Tuesday evening the city
passed into a state of shock. On Wednesday morning the *Defender* carried
a front-page picture of him headed 'Tragedy Strikes'. The *Daily Times*
carried a banner headline 'Adelabu Is Dead', and the *Daily Service* scooped
the rest with a picture of the two cars covering half the front page and the
claim to describe 'How It Happened'. Over the next few days the *Defender*
made a special feature of short tributes from a wide range of his peers – Dr
Ikejiani, Chief Okotie-Eboh, members of the United Muslim Party, H. O.
Davies, the Oba of Lagos, J. M. Johnson, Dr S. O. Biobaku (Secretary to the
Western Region Government and his schoolmate at Government College),

Fred Anyiam, R. A. Fani-Kayode of the Action Group, D. K. Olumofin and many more. Interestingly, such tributes did not come from Mojid Agbaje, E. O. Fakayode or his other N.C.N.C. associates in Ibadan, but Akinpelu Obisesan, who had heard of Adelabu's death at 10.30 p.m. on the night of the 25th, noted in his diary on 26 March that it came 'to the great dismay of his enemies & friends alike' and paid tribute by comparing him to Nnamdi Azikiwe.

The House of Assembly was in session on the morning of the 26th and after the Speaker read a letter of sympathy from the Deputy-Governor, the prearranged business for the day was adjourned and Anthony Enahoro, as Leader of the House, proposed an extraordinary adjournment for the rest of the day as a tribute to the dead Leader of the Opposition. Perhaps mindful of their previous battles, Enahoro's tribute to his old opponent was a rather guarded one:

We did not agree with him or his methods, and he, too, did not agree with us or our policies. Nevertheless, he was a tireless and doughty fighter who stood firmly by the things he cherished, and it may be that when the history of these times comes to be written, that is the one attribute of Alhaji Adelabu which will be remembered better than any other.[7]

Yet it was on a gracious note that the Leader of the House concluded:

Yes, Sir, Alhadji Adelabu had an eventful innings, but his task is now over and his battle-day is past. It is we who still toil and battle, who will worry where life's journey may yet lead us. His own journey is ended, and he ended it, Mr. Speaker, as he lived – as he might well have chosen to die if the Angel of Death had given him a choice: spectacularly.

Not for him lingering in painful illness, nor the obscurity of retirement in old age. He has gone like a meteor which, having blazed a trail in the skies, disappears while yet in its glory. And so he died while the House is in session on Private Members' Day – his own day – and we are all here to do him the honour which is his due.[8]

Enahoro's motion for adjournment was seconded briefly by J. O. Fadahunsi, then Dennis Osadebay and J. E. Otobo spoke for the Opposition, the former weeping as he did so, both of them also bearing witness to their Leader's recent change of heart and desire for a 'reasonable and responsible' attitude in the House. It was left to Chief Awolowo to have the last word about the man who had so keenly desired to take his place as Premier of the Region. In the circumstances it was a generous tribute:

Alhaji Adegoke Adelabu was, in his lifetime, and ever since he entered into politics, a fighter first and last, with all the characteristics of a fighter. He was fearless, formidable, forthright, often caustic, and uncompromising. Consequently,

431

to some of us, it appeared that he had no use for social and diplomatic niceties, as we know and practice them today. For the same reason, he found it difficult to draw a line between political differences and personal relations.

But as he was uncompromising in his opposition to his political opponents, so he was in every cause that he believed in and espoused, and in particular, in the cause of Nigerian freedom.

Alhaji Adegoke Adelabu has been cut off, when his political fortunes were just approaching their zenith, and our great country is on the threshold of independence, for which he had fought in the front line of battle with other Nigerian nationalists.

In his death, the NCNC, both as the Opposition in this House and as a Nigerian political Party, has lost a very able, indomitable and extremely resourceful leader, and Nigeria a most colourful, versatile and undoubted nationalist.[9]

At 10.55 the House adjourned for the day, having agreed to send a delegation of six Members from the Government benches, six from the Opposition and the Speaker and Clerk of the House as its representatives at the funeral to be held that afternoon.

A huge gathering, estimated at more than 75,000 people, many of them weeping, had assembled by the time the body reached Ibadan from Shagamu in an N.C.N.C. party van at midday. The crowd was so dense that it took three hours for the funeral procession of over fifty vehicles to move from the city outskirts at Molete via Oja'ba and Oranyan in the center of the city to Oke Oluokun, where Adelabu was to be buried in the compound surrounding the Taj Mahal. At his house the crowd was so thickly pressed that the body, wrapped in white cloth, had to be passed over their heads from the van to the house. (The coffin, which K. O. Mbadiwe had presented on behalf of the N.C.N.C., must have been delivered earlier.) Waiting for the corpse when it arrived at about 3.30 p.m. were Dr Mbadiwe, who had come to give the funeral oration, and the dignitaries of the Grand Alliance, the House of Assembly and the N.C.N.C. One N.C.N.C. leader conspicuous by his absence was Party President Dr Nnamdi Azikiwe, who sent a message from Enugu in which he remarked of Penkelemesi – 'as we fondly nicknamed him' – that 'He was a man of conviction and did not disguise his feelings on any particular issue; he was loyal and knew where to hold himself in dignified restraint.'[10] Some of Adelabu's devoted supporters might have been forgiven for doubting the sincerity of this in the light of the recent relations between Azikiwe and Adelabu. They certainly did not forgive Azikiwe for his failure to attend, and the delegation he sent to represent him from the Eastern N.C.N.C., headed by Dr Michael Okpara, in fact arrived after the body had been lowered into the grave. Significantly, the burial ceremony was highlighted by Mbadiwe's speech urging the people of

Ibadan to keep faith with the N.C.N.C. As we shall see, Adegoke Adelabu dead and buried was still a political force, and one which was not necessarily advantageous to the N.C.N.C. Indeed, another political party, the Northern People's Congress, made a point of adding its tribute a few days later. On 29 March Alhaji Muhammadu Ribadu, Federal Minister of Lagos Affairs, Mines and Power, and Inuwa Wada, Federal Minister of Works, visited the Taj Mahal on the orders of the Sardauna of Sokoto and Abubakar Tafawa Balewa to pay condolences and pray at the grave of a fellow Muslim.

The burial day of the Lion of the West was also the birthday of a wistfully hopeful movement, the 'Adelabu Resurrection Party', formed that morning 'to mark the great occasion when Hon Alhaji Adegoke Adelabu died' and 'to study and examine the philosophy of his life and foster it to the eternal glory of this country'.[11] Late that afternoon, however, a very different commemoration of the sorrowful occasion began. Obisesan recorded in his Diary for that day that over 6000 people paraded through the city, stoning Mapo Hall, the courts at Oke Are, and other public buildings. According to the *Daily Service*, three people were killed during the funeral in various parts of the city, and after the funeral a group led by Obadara Atanda, the Maiyegun League and Mabolaje leader, attacked the house of Alhaji Y. S. Ola Ishola, who, they claimed, fired on them in return.[12] Several other prominent Action Groupers had their houses damaged; market stalls were wrecked and beatings were also reported.

However, the violence which was to rock Ibadan Division for nearly a week in fact developed in the villages, not in the city itself, two days after the funeral. On Thursday, the city was relatively quiet, but there were reports of burnings and beatings from outlying communities. On Friday, the 28th, as reports of murders began to come in, patrols of police began circulating in rural areas. At least eighty persons were arrested, but at Arulogun the mob overwhelmed the police and forced them to dance and shout 'Ade! Ade!' While lawyers Agbaje, Adisa and Fakayode began virtually non-stop court appearances on behalf of arrested N.C.N.C. members, the police continued to transport hundreds of people to jail compounds and police barracks. By Sunday, the 30th, at least 300 were under arrest, 8 police had been injured by gunshots, and 12 other deaths were reported. Contingents of the Nigeria Police were being brought in from the Eastern Region and Lagos, and it was necessary to move arrested persons to jails in Ilesha and Abeokuta, since the Ibadan prison was already full.* At the army barracks, a company of Hausa troops not under orders was discovered fully

---

* Alan Milner, 'The Maintenance of Public Order in Nigeria', in *The Politics and Administration of Nigerian Government*, edited by L. Franklin Blitz (New York: Praeger, 1965), p. 199, states that 'over a thousand' police were called in from elsewhere.

dressed and equipped and standing at attention by its officers and the Secretary of the Ibadan Council, who made frequent visits to the soldiers to assure them that *if* their services were required, they would be *immediately* notified. Reportedly, the company voluntarily remained on ready status for three days, hoping for an invitation to join the fray. On 1 April, Government issued an Extraordinary Gazette, proclaiming an emergency in the Council areas of Ibadan, Oyo, Aiyedade and Iwo. It demanded that all arms be surrendered to police stations within twelve hours, and imposed a curfew from 7 p.m. to 6 a.m. until further notice. To be out after 7 p.m. required a written police permit or subjected the violator to a penalty of £50 or thirty days in jail. Public processions were banned.

For days reports of violent death poured in from the villages. Of eighteen riot deaths which we have traced, seven of the victims bore Christian names, three were tax clerks or assessors, and practically all were said to be members or supporters of the Action Group.* Villagers testified that N.C.N.C. leaders had urged them to avenge the death of Adelabu, which was attributed to the Action Group.[13] Having killed Bello Aiki, a Tax Assessment Committee member, the mob dispersed shouting 'Bello get up and assess me now' and 'Ade! Ade!! Ade!!!'[14] Justice R. A. Doherty concluded that the N.C.N.C. and the problem of tax assessment were at the center of the violence. During the course of this trial, Justice Doherty summed up the emerging pattern of violence, noting that the damage was exclusively upon the persons and property of Action Group members, that the background of the murders was 'political', and that the violence everywhere was marked by clashes between opposing party organizations.[15] This raised difficult problems for the courts, he noted, since the accused virtually all claimed innocence on the basis of alibis which were to be substantiated by other party members, thus making it difficult for the court to know whom to believe. At a trial in September 1959, Defense Counsel Mojid Agbaje admitted that it was common knowledge that N.C.N.C. members had attacked the Action Group, and Justice Samuel Quashie-Idun paid him 'full compliments' for his candor.[16]

The sheer magnitude of the violence created severe problems for the judiciary as well as for the police. Justice Adeyinka Morgan had 190 persons appear before him on 31 March 1958; 32 of these were charged with the murder of 5 persons; the remand of an earlier group of 68 persons brought before him on the previous Friday was extended to 8 April under the pressure of the court load.[17] By 2 April, 334 persons had been arrested.[18]† Upon arrest the accused were brought before witnesses in a 'line-up' or 'parade'

* Milner puts the number of deaths at sixteen (ibid., p. 199).
† Milner states that 826 were charged in all (ibid., p. 199); Sklar says 'more than 600', *Nigerian Political Parties*, p. 305.

for identification, but the police in some cases allegedly stated to witnesses that those in the parade were suspects and this procedural irregularity and contradictory identification evidence led to the dismissal of many suspects and witnesses.

The defense as well as the prosecution suffered under the stress. No defendant had chosen an Action Group counsel and under the sheer load upon them the N.C.N.C. lawyers frequently lost track of who was to defend whom; Justice Doherty threatened to remove briefs from Akinjide and Fakayode for failing to be in court while the accused whose lives they were supposed to be defending were on the witness stand.[19] Such errors led to frequent appeals against sentences by lower courts which were often upheld by higher ones. Richard Sklar estimated that 'more than 100' were charged with murder and that 64 of these were initially sentenced to death, but that 34 convictions had been reversed by 24 April 1959.[20] In that month appeals were also in process for another seventeen, but these later appeals were much less successful. The first execution finally took place on 24 May 1960. Seven more were hanged on the 25th; two executions were carried out on the 26th and four on the 27th. On 5 August four more were executed, bringing the total to eighteen. Thus some twenty-eight months of death and the fear of death, if not the memory of it, came to an end. In all, perhaps some thirty-nine lives were brought to an end as a result of the events of 25 March 1958 on the Lagos–Ibadan road.* Even then, this figure is undoubtedly a conservative one. The bodies of persons believed to have been killed were occasionally not found, and some instances of failure to report a murder were thought to have occurred through fear of still further retribution. Conflicting evidence and inconsistencies on the part of those supposed to identify rioters, on the other hand, undoubtedly gained release for some persons who bore equal responsibility for crimes with those who were punished. In the fury, the Adelabu Resurrection Party was never heard of again, and the traditional 'second burial' ceremony, held thirty days after the dead man's funeral, passed virtually unnoticed.

The realization, confirmed in the court trials, that the riots were not just the product of some blind anomie, was immediate and widespread.† The

---

* Our list of executions was originally officially compiled by the Northern People's Congress branch in Ibadan, and was supplied to us by two of its former Organizing Secretaries. The names of the accused noted as executed are correctly spelled, and also are to be found in newspapers and court records, and we believe the list to be accurate, though possibly incomplete. The list includes twenty-five names, with execution dates for eighteen; we are unsure of the fate of the remaining seven. Thus, the total number of dead includes Adelabu and his two travelling companions, eighteen murdered in the riots, and eighteen executed for murder.

† Peter Lloyd discusses this riot briefly in *Africa in Social Change* (Harmondsworth:

fact that the riots were so largely limited to rural areas suggests that the city had been consciously avoided, that someone had been aware that a protest could not be secretly planned in the city where the forces of protest, once unleashed, might become uncontrollable. It is interesting that the first public discussion of causes came from the *Southern Nigeria Defender*, voice of the N.C.N.C. On the first Saturday after the funeral, in a front-page lead article, it reported:

Rumour is very rife in Ibadan and environs that certain highly placed leaders of the community are busy instigating the relevant authorities to get NCNC leaders, Mogajis and staunch supporters into trouble as the planners of the present wave of lawlessness and disorder.[21]

It reported speculations that plans were being made to issue warrants for the arrest of N.C.N.C. leaders and 'the almost incontrovertible story' that this was an attempt to demoralize the N.C.N.C. as the local government elections approached. The *Defender* also quoted an N.C.N.C. leader's response to their question as to whether the party had planned a 'coup':

It is not in our context to climb to the top through foul means – we are mourning the late Adelabu – our leader in a spirit of real sorrow and nobody in this frame of mind will think of rioting or disorder as the right thing to embark upon.[22]

At stake, also, was something greater than party differences; as a *Tribune* editorial put it,

Only last August, Western Nigeria assumed self-governing status. That, in itself, is an evidence of the faith Britain has in the ability of the African to rule himself. That faith must not be shaken. . .[23]

This was a difficult position for the *Defender* to take because it was, at last, the Action Group's ability to govern which might be questioned, while the *Defender* recognized that it was necessary to identify as quickly as possible the causes and persons responsible for the riots in order to hasten their end.

Penguin Books, 1967), pp. 251–2. He mistakenly gives the year as 1957 and refers to Adelabu still again as a charismatic leader of 'the Ibadan people'. He asserts that Adelabu was looked to to restore the town 'to its former glory', a reward in the opinion of the present writers which most people would have set aside for a new water tap, a maternity clinic, a newly paved road or a job, in fact the issues with which Adelabu's Council dealt. Lloyd suggests that Ibadan's 'apparent exploitation' by other Yoruba groups led to the 'immediate response' of gangs of youths roaming the streets in the areas inhabited by strangers, overturning cars. As we have seen, strangers were not subjected to violence; indeed the Ijebu quarter of the city and the Division were the quietest. This interpretation is curiously mixed in that Lloyd sees violence as without obvious leadership or clear social aims, and as a form of aggression resulting from frustration. However, in the Ibadan case he admits that 'individuals sought to use this period of apparent license to settle old grievances'.

Concerned more with security than with politics, the police opened four temporary rural police stations and eventually succeeded in re-establishing order without the help of the army. On 15 April, the ban on public processions was extended by the Governor for another month, thus limiting the number of people that could legally congregate. These measures, however, could not prevent the murders and woundings, nor the very serious damage to property.

Following initial attacks on houses of prominent Action Groupers in Ibadan (as well as on the house of Chief Kobiowu who had become a supporter of Olubadan Akinyele), destruction broke out in village after village. Damage to property followed very clear patterns in method, targets and location. Houses were first stoned, their contents were then piled up and soaked with kerosene and ignited. Thatch roofs were burned and tin roofs were systematically hacked up with matchets. Money was stolen and foodstuffs were either destroyed or removed. In the property damage cases, the question of responsibility and guilt again arose. A massive attempt was made not only to determine who the guilty parties were, but also, in the cases of property damage, who had suffered specific losses in order that compensation could be paid. To this end, Justice Adeyinka Morgan, who had only been promoted to the High Court a few days earlier, was appointed Sole Commissioner on 17 April.

The Morgan Commission was to ascertain the amount of compensation to be paid to victims of the riots, rather than the total amount of damage done in the disaster. Under the Riot Damages Law, passed in March 1956, provision was made for compensation to be paid from public funds to those who had suffered property damage (but not to relatives of murder victims). This bill, according to the *Defender*, was passed during an 'era of unprecedented oppression, suppression, coercion and vindictiveness', and the N.C.N.C. members of the Western House of Assembly, including all Ibadan N.C.N.C. members, opposed it.[24] While the Minister of Local Government was later to claim that an overwhelming number of local councils had approved the bill in a survey taken by his Ministry before its passing, it was also true that an overwhelming number of councils were supporters of the Action Group Government. The Bill provided that an area stipulated by Government as a 'riot area' could be ordered to pay through a special levy 'a proportion' of compensation for damages suffered by individuals. The punitive aspect of the bill was stressed when Government announced that Ibadan's proportion of the compensation was to be 99.9 per cent, leaving a tiny percentage to be paid by the Government.

On 1 May 1958 Ibadan was officially declared a riot area under the law. As the *Nigerian Tribune* warned Ibadan residents, 'Thou, tighten your loins because YOU HAVE TO PAY FOR THE DAMAGES. . .'[25] The Action Group clearly intended to go beyond compensation, and this intention was probably reinforced by the N.C.N.C. victory in the Ibadan District Council election in June. As Minister of Local Government Adegbenro stated in explaining the Government's policy on a subsequent occasion, in addition to suppressing 'unconstitutional and violent action in support of political claims', punishing those responsible and compensating those who had 'suffered loss as a result of public disorder', it was also necessary to instill the idea 'in the minds of the public that respect for law and order will effectively prevent any disturbances of the peace in the future'. It was, he continued, 'the duty of all citizens in any community to ensure that the law and order is [sic] maintained and, therefore, if a breach of the peace does occur every citizen in the community is to some extent to blame, even if he himself was not directly involved or did his best to prevent it'. In further and conflicting terms he stated that 'the main cost of providing compensation shall fall on those persons who have been shown to have been chiefly responsible'; he hoped the 'lesson' of Ibadan would be 'well learnt' throughout the Region.[26] In practice this meant that compensation was to be collected from all persons, except those who had successfully filed damage claims, who had been liable to pay taxes in Ibadan in the 1957–8 tax year ending on 31 March.

Some 1023 claims were submitted.[27] Many of them were eventually disallowed, but a total of £54,747. 0. 0d. was accepted, of which only £10,705. 13. 11d. was in Ibadan town itself.* The actual amount of the rate levied to pay for the damage and the method of its collection were to be determined by the Ibadan District Council, and collected by 31 May 1960, at which time compensation payments would begin.

The N.C.N.C.-controlled Council, as ordered by the Minister of Local Government, met to discuss these questions on 8 February 1960, at which time it appointed a special *ad hoc* Committee to study the relevant documents. Sensing delay and disgruntlement over the collective guilt aspects of the Riot Damages Bill, Minister Adegbenro met with the Council on 16 February to explain the difference. The present ordinance, he said, unlike the earlier Collective Punishment Ordinance based on an English statute of 1888, exacted a levy for compensation to victims, rather than a fine which did not compensate victims. It was true, he admitted, that innocent people, including himself and other Ministers resident in Ibadan, would be required to pay, but in riotous assemblies where identification of individuals was

---

* A village chief claimed £700 worth of damage by fire to his 'super-natural power room', and his son, an 'international native doctor' submitted a separate claim for £209. 15. 6d. for burned properties. (The chief claimed to have been shot at three times, but his powers had protected him from harm.) N.T., 11 August 1958.

impossible the principle of 'collective responsibility' could not be ignored. Not entirely satisfied, the *ad hoc* Committee recommended a 3s. 6d. *per capita* levy in the city and £1. 11. 0d. for the villages, but it also urged that the Government approve a four-year loan to the Council as the compensation fund, rather than levy an immediate tax, that the Government increase its proportion to ten per cent, that all villages be subjected to the tax just as all wards of the town were, regardless of whether any damage had occurred in them, and, finally, that the deadline for payment of the tax be extended to 31 July 1960. Government refused to budge on any of these points, in spite of the pleas of a delegation to the Premier including Bishop Akinyele, Olubadan Akinyele, the Chief Imam and others on 26 April. In the meantime, the Council had prepared forms and established taxation procedures, and N.C.N.C. Councillors, stirred by the heckling and prodding of their Action Group colleagues, made speeches in the Council in favour of payment.[28] A. M. F. Agbaje, the new Chairman of the Council, made a tour of rural areas urging compliance, and Adeoye Adisa, who had once opposed the Riot Damages Bill so bitterly, promised a two-man touring delegation to rural villages.[29] All of this came at a time, however, when the N.C.N.C.'s Western Planning Committee in a release by R. A. Fani-Kayode was calling for abrogation of the law as creating hardships intolerable to civilized people.[30] Mojid Agbaje and his lieutenant Majekodunmi Oduyoye publicly disassociated themselves from their party's stand and accused Fani-Kayode (who had crossed from the Action Group to the N.C.N.C. at the end of 1959) of being a 'new comer' to the party, 'tactless' and engaging in deceit and causing havoc in the local N.C.N.C.[31] In November 1960 nearly £30,000 of the levy was still outstanding.

The death of Adelabu was thus the beginning of a series of events inextricably woven into the political conflicts of the time. It is clear, as Sklar has pointed out, that ethnicity (in the form of intra-Yoruba rivalries) was not a factor in the bloody rioting which followed that event. In fact, the most peaceful rural area was that along the Akanran road through the Obisesan family farms to Ijebu Ode. Party affiliation was the dominant theme. The attackers were largely supporters of the N.C.N.C. and the objects of their hostility were those supporting or responsible for the tax and educational policies of the Action Group. Given this structuring of the violence, it is possible to consider the hypothesis that the riots were in some sense planned. As we have already seen, the *Defender* was immediately concerned to dispel the belief in any N.C.N.C. responsibility for the riots, an attempt which court evidence strongly refuted. The real question is not whether the N.C.N.C. was involved as the N.C.N.C., but at what level this involvement took place. At no time were the names of any Ibadan N.C.N.C. leaders specifically mentioned. The present authors have been told by one investigating authority, however, that for some considerable time the Western Region Government was of the belief that demonstrations had been planned to protest the increase in taxes during the 1957–8 season, and that these demonstrations were to include the destruction of property by matchetting and fire. Government also believed that top N.C.N.C. leaders were involved in this planning, which was sufficiently developed at the time of Adelabu's death to be virtually self-executing at the local level. Government had hoped, we were informed, to bring a conspiracy charge against N.C.N.C. leaders, a plan which was eventually discarded. It would have been necessary to charge conspiracy for preparation of an anti-tax demonstration, which had not occurred, and the prosecution of a conspiracy charge would certainly have involved the N.C.N.C. leaders who were laboring in the courts to defend the N.C.N.C. village rank and file, thus opening the Government to the charge of conspiring against the accused, a charge which would have seemed the more plausible since the evidence, according to our source, was inadequate.

Perhaps, however, even the successful prosecution of a conspiracy charge would have been wide of the mark. It might have warned political agitators of the limits beyond which Government would not tolerate opposition, but it would have missed what may have been the basic underlying forces behind the violence. We have seen in Chapter 1 that mass civic violence had long been a part of the Ibadan political system. When the city was composed of parts (the major military chieftaincy houses) each more powerful than the force the city council itself could command, the punishment for crimes of a political nature, where the accused enjoyed the protection of his own compound and kin, often required the declaration by some authority that the property and person of the accused and his kin could be destroyed by the general public. Always involved were a perceived wrong, accompanied by public outrage, inadequate official enforcement agencies, an authoritative signal that destructive activities could be undertaken with a sense of public approval, followed by organized, publicly executed, verbally articulated acts of punishment against wrong-doers. The characteristics of this pattern appear to have occurred repeatedly in the Ibadan riots of 1958. The Action Group had done wrong, official government recourse was lacking, the N.C.N.C. had legitimized action by those with a sense of grievance, and justice was done.

In an earlier time, when Ibadan was a more cohesive community, more closely directing its own destiny, such violence as a form of community participation might have been absorbed. However, in 1958 the scale of Ibadan's political involvement had been enlarged beyond the horizons of many of its citizens, making of the community but a part of the regional political system. The regional authorities, rather than responding with appreciation to community action, had unleashed the police, the courts and financial retribution upon the defenders of justice, eventually granting restitution to those who had been previously identified as the wrong-doers. The morality of the issue was fought out by lawyers in courts where the judges wore wigs and spoke English, where it became clear that 'the truth' would be punished, and where the purchase of conflicting evidence could often gain one his release. Today, a visitor to the home of a person incontrovertibly responsible for one of the crimes committed during the 1958 riots, would be welcomed and entertained. The details of the killings and burnings would be described in the detail that only a witness or participant could master, but an admission of guilt as defined in the courts would be solemnly denied. Even if one's host were clearly lying about his participation, there would be a grain of truth in his profession of innocence. It is sometimes said that the only language some people will understand is the universal language of force. Probably the language of force has as many mutually unintelligible dialects as any language, a fact which should be taken into account by those who would speak the language or seek to understand such matters as guilt and innocence in terms of it.

During the months after his death in which tragedy struck at the foes and friends of Adelabu alike, his family also had to face their loss. Private grief was reinforced by financial uncertainty. Unlike his father, Adelabu had left no will, nor, for that matter, had he left a great inheritance. We have frequently had occasion to note the uncertainty of his finances; the last record of his bank balance to have survived showed him with a credit of £1070 at Barclays Bank on 30 July 1957, which accords reasonably well with an estimate of £2000 given by his cousin at a court hearing in April 1959. Yet at the same time Adelabu had been heavily in debt, owing 'an unknown amount' to certain commercial firms and the Bank of West Africa according to the same cousin. There was thus little if any money for his dependents, and yet when he died there were seventeen women who claimed to be his wives, at least nine of whom the family still regard as such by customary law since they had borne him children, and sixteen living children (with another still to be born) for whom to provide.

The only recourse seemed to be to the law, to fix responsibility for the death of the husband and father. The Coroner on 30 May 1958 found both drivers involved in the accident to have been negligent, but at the preliminary hearing in Ijebu Ode Magistrate's Court in July it was ruled that Albert Younan had no case to answer. The other driver was tried for dangerous driving in September, found guilty, and sentenced to pay a fine of £20 or serve two months in prison. It would have been pointless to sue the guilty driver for damages, for he had no money. The Adelabu family therefore filed a civil suit for £100,000 against the firms of Younan and Sons and the Royal Exchange Assurance Company, which had owned the other car and employed the other driver, while the family of one of those who had died with him claimed £10,000. In April 1959 the case was heard in the High Court of the Western Region before Mr Justice Quashie-Idun; his final ruling was that no case had been made against the insurance company, but that Younan and Sons must pay £6030 and £350 costs to Adelabu's children and £580, with £105 costs, to those of the other man.* In their turn, Adelabu's family was to pay the Royal Exchange Assurance Company £180 costs, and the other family £52. 10. od. Thus the Court had ruled that Albert Younan had driven negligently and the other driver had not.

However, this was only the beginning of the battle. An appeal by the defendants to the Federal Supreme Court secured a reversal of the damages award. A counter-appeal by the family to the Privy Council in Britain then remained a constitutional possibility, but at this stage the matter was settled out of court, by an agreement to pay the family a sum said to be about £3000. With that, the wives and children dispersed; today the family no longer lives in the Taj Mahal and its compound. Only the grave remains, and, at the end of 1964, one solitary former wife.

Adelabu's political legacy included the Egbe Yoruba Parapo and the record of his gradually worsening relations with Dr Azikiwe, which seemed at the time of his death to be verging on a final break with the N.C.N.C. There was also the apparently more substantial legacy of the N.C.N.C.–Mabolaje Grand Alliance, which he had founded and led to electoral victory in 1954 and 1956. The leaders of the N.C.N.C. knew that to retain the support of the majority of the Ibadan electorate they must preserve the Grand Alliance intact. There were thus two key questions after 25 March 1958. Could the Grand Alliance hold together without its dominant figure? Could the Mabolaje itself continue to exist now that its moving spirit was dead?

These two questions were inextricably intertwined.† In face of the need to defend N.C.N.C. supporters in the courts and to fight the local government

---

* Afusatu Adepate, aged twenty, was awarded £200, and Raufu Aderibigbe, aged sixteen £150.

† A detailed account of events up to the end of 1958 and an overall assessment of the Grand Alliance may be found in Sklar, *Nigerian Political Parties*, pp. 306–20, and a discussion over a somewhat longer time perspective in Mackintosh, *Nigerian Government*, pp. 346–9. The present author's differences with these commentators have in some cases already been made clear. Others should emerge in the course of the next few pages.

election, the Mabolaje and N.C.N.C. held together. By polling day on 21 June 1958, however, signs of stress were already beginning to appear.

On Friday 13 June, Nnamdi Azikiwe paid his delayed visit to the grave of Adelabu; he led the crowd in a version of the song 'John Brown's Body', publicly promised party scholarships to assure the education of the dead hero's children, and donated £100 to provide immediate assistance for them. Then he moved on to Lagos for a meeting of the N.C.N.C. National Executive Committee, where he was presented with the 'Zik Must Go' letter, in which thirty-one influential members of the party, including K. O. Mbadiwe and Kola Balogun, demanded his replacement, culminating the long process of growing dissatisfaction and intrigue discussed in previous chapters.* Adegoke Adelabu certainly had felt this dissatisfaction and engaged in the intrigue, and people very close to him are convinced that he would have signed the letter. Some of those who had been closest to him did sign – Alhaji N. B. Soule, Alhaji K. O. S. Are and Fasasi Adeshina. Another of the Ibadan legislators, L. S. Salami, also signed, as did P. A. Afolabi of Oyo and H. O. Davies. Probably Adegoke Adelabu would have followed suit had he been alive.

As it was, Mojid Agbaje, who was present at the meeting on 14 June, took the immediate opportunity to disavow the offending letter on behalf of the Grand Alliance. K. O. S. Are and L. S. Salami very soon withdrew their signatures, and it rapidly became apparent that the real contest was to be between two rival Ibo leaders, Azikiwe and Mbadiwe. The major part of the struggle was thus fought out in the East, and in these circumstances resulted in almost complete victory for Azikiwe. On the other hand, the Grand Alliance was not prompt to declare its collective loyalty, despite Agbaje's action; it was not until 17 July that it declared itself to be united in support of Dr Azikiwe.[32] The real problem at this time was less the question of the link between the Mabolaje and the N.C.N.C. than that of who was to inherit the mantle of Adegoke Adelabu and take control of the former organization. The two main contestants for this position were Adeoye Adisa, who had returned to Ibadan from his law studies in Britain at the end of 1956 and rapidly risen to prominence as one of the Alliance's lawyers, and Mojid Agbaje, also active in the last two years as a party lawyer. Both scored personal triumphs towards the end of June 1958. On the 26th Adisa was victorious in the bye-election for Adelabu's old seat in the House of Assembly, Ibadan South West, while on the 29th Agbaje was chosen as Chairman of the Western Working Committee, one of Adelabu's roles which had briefly passed to H. O. Davies. Each had thus secured part of the inheritance, but

* A detailed account of the meeting of 14 June and its aftermath may be found in Sklar, *Nigerian Political Parties*, pp. 219–30.

443

it was Adisa who made the most determined attempt to cultivate the Adelabu style. Since his return he had lived modestly in his family's compound at Oja'gbo, and was to be seen riding his bicycle along the narrow alleys, dressed in his academic robes and master's hood. In contrast, Agbaje, the son of a rich man who had sent him to study abroad, was already embarked on a conventionally successful career and was probably temperamentally unsuited to make an appeal to the masses. Within a few months after Adelabu's death, such temperamental differences and rival ambitions were dividing the organization and the leaders who had served, often uneasily, as his lieutenants. The conflict was no longer the familiar one between the educated N.C.N.C. leaders and the Mabolaje personified by Adelabu, for now the Mabolaje itself began to fall apart as different elements within it aligned with Adisa or Agbaje. Without the will of Penkelemesi to impose unity upon it this coalition of individuals and groups had no common identity to hold it together.

By mid-July a reclustering of allegiances around Adisa and Agbaje was complete, each also enlisting the support of another lawyer, R. O. A. Akinjide and E. O. Fakayode respectively. Among the Mabolaje stalwarts, Agbaje had the support of Alfa Elesinmeta and Mogaji Akere, while Adisa was backed by Mogaji Ebo-Elobi, Madam Hunmoani Apampa, the redoubtable Women's Wing leader, and the Alliance Youth. At this point Adisa was hailed by his supporters as Leader of the Grand Alliance, and on 20 July the Alliance Youth formed the Adelabu National Front. As Adisa knew, the dead hero's name was of great importance in the struggle, and he used the Taj Mahal as a meeting place for his faction and benefited from the fact that Madam Apampa lived next to the house and could act as virtual custodian of the grave. On 9 August the Agbaje faction elected Mogaji Akere as Leader. In December the two groups squared off against each other when the Agbaje faction expelled Adisa from the Grand Alliance. This resulted in the sending of a 'Peace Committee' by N.C.N.C. National Headquarters, under the chairmanship of Aminu Kano, the N.E.P.U. leader, to mediate in the quarrel. The Committee did not uphold the expulsion of Adisa, and for a time there was an uneasy peace. In July 1959, the conflict broke out again at another level, when the N.C.N.C. Working Committee met in Benin, with Adisa, Agbaje and T. O. S. Benson vying for the office of Chairman. The result was that no generally acceptable election was held, the Committee had to be dissolved, and its work was undertaken by the National Executive Committee.

In October 1959 the nomination of candidates for the approaching federal election again resulted in national intervention in local disputes. The national leadership of the N.C.N.C. was forced to choose between rival lists of Grand Alliance candidates presented by the Adisa and Agbaje groups, and in the event the choice was mishandled. T. O. S. Benson, the leading figure on the special committee set up by the national party to recommend candidates for the eight new Ibadan federal constituencies, favored Adisa. He seems to have won over a majority of his colleagues, but their recommendation was publicly overridden by Dr Azikiwe, for whom Agbaje represented the dependable core of N.C.N.C. support in Ibadan. Adisa and his supporters thereupon severed their alliance with the N.C.N.C., asserted themselves as the true and independent 'Hand' Mabolaje, rather than as formerly the true spokesmen of the Grand Alliance, contested seven of the eight seats (not Ibarapa), and won six, against both the Action Group and Agbaje's N.C.N.C. candidates.* Adisa and Akinjide were now working with K. O. S. Are. They were able to use Adelabu's name to good advantage, to maintain effective contacts with the old Mabolaje ward organizations, and to find a source of funds in the Northern People's Congress, anxious at this time to find allies in the south. Apparently using Alhaji Are as a channel, the N.P.C. provided £28,000 and fourteen vehicles for the election campaign.[33] In return, the Mabolaje declared its public support for the N.P.C. after the election, helping to raise its strength in the new Federal House of Representatives to 148 members out of 312.

From this point onward, Ibadan politics became more and more kaleidoscopic. Realizing its mistake, the N.C.N.C. shifted its support in the Western Region election of August 1960 from Agbaje to Adisa. Again both put up slates. The result was a further decline over the elections in which Adelabu had led the campaign, the Action Group taking five of the fourteen Ibadan Division seats and Adisa's recreated N.C.N.C.–Mabolaje Grand Alliance the other nine. Agbaje and all his candidates were defeated.† By December, however, the Grand Alliance had undergone an important realignment, allying itself with the N.P.C. instead of the N.C.N.C. and setting up branches in other parts of the West, such as Abeokuta and Ondo. In that month a meeting attended by two N.P.C. Federal Ministers elected Alhaji Are as President-General of the Western Region N.P.C.–Mabolaje Grand Alliance. In February 1961, however, Are and Adisa expelled each other from the Alliance, further weakening the party just as the triennial local government elections once more approached. Adisa's group went back to

* The Action Group won the seventh as a result of the split in the former Grand Alliance vote. The Hand was the electoral symbol used by the Mabolaje.
† In honor of the Maiyegun League, Adisa selected Obadara Atanda's son as a candidate, a poor, young inexperienced man with little formal education, and set him against Agbaje, the wealthy, suave lawyer, certain that the electorate would 'punish' Agbaje by ignoring his expensive campaign and electing a man who differed from him so greatly.

the N.C.N.C., although Adisa allowed R. O. A. Akinjide to assume its leadership. After an intense campaign the N.C.N.C. announced a boycott on the eve of the election on the ground that its candidates had been prevented from campaigning freely, a view for which there was considerable justification. Equally significant was the fact that the Action Group was extremely well-prepared, relying on the support of Olubadan Akinyele, his senior chiefs and many of Adelabu's former mogajis, and on the superb organization provided by a senior government official who was an Ibadan son and A. M. A. Akinloye. The Action Group thus captured all forty-six Council seats, and Akinloye became its Chairman.

Here the story may end. The party against which Adelabu had fought for his entire political life had learned the lessons of Ibadan politics Adelabu had previously mastered, and through the Regional Government it was willing to apply increasing pressure to convince the people of Ibadan that unless they changed their party allegiance they could expect no amenities for their city to be provided by the government. Developments in Ibadan would have been influenced more and more by its inclusion within the wider political system even had Adelabu lived. This wider system was increasingly that of the Federation as a whole. The intrusion of the Northern People's Congress into Western Region politics has already been noted, while in May 1962 the declaration of an Emergency in the West by the N.P.C.–N.C.N.C. coalition government irrevocably determined the direction of Nigerian politics.[34]

Throughout all this, beginning indeed as soon as he died, it was the fate of the political legacy of the Lion of the West to be reduced to a name which could be invoked without the fear that he would reappear. Those unsung yeomen of Nigerian politics, the organizing secretaries, still occasionally assured their masters that 'we have fulfilled our promises through several oath takings at the grave side of the Late Alhaji Adelabu not to betray the party', but the party of Adelabu, only a few years after his death, was gone.[35] His unique presence had held together the disparate set of elements of the N.C.N.C.–Mabolaje Grand Alliance without ever making a viable machine or even an inheritable organization of them. There was now no one with sufficiently ruthless determination to override the personal rivalries of the N.C.N.C. lawyers, to hold together the conglomeration of Maiyegun League leaders, dance groups, welfare societies and market women which he had temporarily aligned. With the man gone, the name became increasingly irrelevant and sacred. Thus, two Mabolaje Members of the House of Assembly could even justify their leaving the party in the name of the fallen leader.

If we continue to follow it we shall be destroying the objectives which motivated the late Alhaji Adelabu to propagate the ideals of the NCNC in Ibadan. We do not also wish to continue to desecrate the memory of the late Adelabu by being unable to champion the cause of the people of Ibadan.[36]

It is ironic that the self-styled critic, artist and Spiritualistic Nationalist should become a source of political legitimacy which could be used to justify the sort of opportunistic shift of allegiance which formed part of the political stock-in-trade in pre-coup Nigeria. Yet, as a political leader thrown up during a period of rapid political and institutional change, it is not surprising that his life should be of greater significance as an illustration of certain processes at work than as the history of a man successfully involved in the crystallization of definite political forms. In the terms of the title of this book, borrowed from Adelabu's own invocation to Nigerian nationalists, both his country and he himself paid the 'Price of Liberty'. From May 1962 onward the Nigerian political system gradually shook itself almost to pieces in a series of crises, culminating in two military coups, cruel massacres, and a long and bitter civil war. During the process of decolonization which was the subject of this book, viewed through the experience of one man, Nigeria paid the price of liberty in three ways. First, it gave birth to a political elite whose members were, for the most part, more concerned with power and its rewards than national unity or the welfare of the masses. Second, the parties which the elite controlled were not suitable instruments for promoting unity or for doing anything with the majority of citizens other than to attempt their manipulation for the benefit of the elite. Third, the institutional structure which emerged from the unequal bargaining between the Colonial Office and the Nigerian leaders was unable to impose any control on the intra-elite conflict which increased after mid-1962, and if anything served to exacerbate it. It is hoped that all three of these aspects of decolonization have been amply illustrated in this study.

The fate of many of those who were involved in this story reveals the basic uncertainties of independent Nigeria. The chiefs of Ibadan, long stripped of real power, resigned themselves to whatever honors they could still attain. Sir Isaac Akinyele, the Olubadan, died in May 1965, to be succeeded for a short time by Chief Kobiowu and on his death by Chief Aminu. That other outmoded group, the British officials, also contented themselves in many cases with retirement and honors. Such was the case with Sir James Robertson and Sir John Rankine. Others found new careers – D. A. Murphy with the Government of Guinea, John Hayley with the United Nations, T. M. Shankland, now Sir Thomas, as provost of a Scottish town. Some of the Nigerian politicians and officials also turned to less perilous pursuits. Thus Kola Balogun became an ambassador, Rotimi Williams and V. O. Esan returned to the law, Osita Agwuna became a chief in his home area, and Bello Abasi, D. T. Akinbiyi, E. A. Adeyemo and J. M. Johnson concentrated on their business enterprises. J. L. Ogunsola, the ex-Alafin, Alfa Elesinmeta, N. B. Soule, and Akinpelu Obisesan died peacefully. The Sardauna of Sokoto, Abubakar Tafawa Balewa, S. L. Akintola, and Festus Okotie-Eboh died violently at the hands of army officers in January 1966. The largest group have pursued their political careers and so far survived. J. O. Fadahunsi became Governor of the West, and found it a more contentious position than he expected. Such was the experience of Nnamdi Azikiwe, who attempted to become father of all his people, first as Governor-General, then as President of Nigeria. Dennis Osadebay became Premier of the new Mid-Western Region. K. O. Mbadiwe, T. O. S. Benson, A. M. A. Akinloye, and Chief Omo-Osagie became Federal Ministers; S. D. Onabamiro, Mojid Agbaje, Adeoye Adisa, R. O. A. Akinjide, L. Ade Bello and D. K. Olumofin all managed to become regional Ministers by judicious changes of party allegiance. The military take-over in January 1966 drove them all from office and some into house arrest or prison. Dr Mbadiwe was touring the United States seeking support for secessionist Biafra as this book was being finished. Only Obafemi Awolowo and Anthony Enahoro were in positions of power. Sentenced to ten and fifteen years in prison respectively in 1963, labeled as conspirators who wished to seize power by force, the second military coup of July 1966 resulted in their release and membership in the new military government of General Gowon.

The most recent change of fortune for Awolowo and Enahoro would not have pleased Adegoke Adelabu, though he might have appreciated its irony. Irony, indeed, is a quality which must dominate any final verdict upon his complex character. Certainly he paid a heavy personal price for his participation in gaining his country's liberty. Possessed of great natural intelligence, colonial Nigeria never gave him the education or the career opportunities which might have satisfied his ambitions and allowed a positive use of his intelligence. Instead he failed in business management for others, private enterprises of his own, and government service. Fully involved in politics by the beginning of 1952, he spent six years contributing – if sometimes unwillingly – to the self-seeking, manipulation and wheeling and dealing which marked Nigeria's political decolonization. Personal frustration was more often his lot than triumph, and much of what he was forced by circumstances to do was scarcely admirable.

Yet, in the end, it would be a brave biographer who attempted some moralizing judgement upon him. Rather it might be better to apply to him his own comments upon Salami Agbaje.

Would he have survived the turbulent vicissitudes of Ibadan political life if he had been less hardy, tough and ruthless? I think not. He may not be a paragon for our children to copy but there he is, a creature of his parentage, upbringing, environment and age. Where we may withhold our love we are at liberty to bestow our admiration if we are truthful and realistic. Too complex for summary judgement today he will become a simplified understandable personality with the passage of time.

No doubt were he alive now he would be planning his political comeback, possibly with the restoration of civil government in Nigeria he might at last have become Premier of the West. Such speculation is idle. He is dead, and he has no other memorials than this book, with all its limitations, and his children, to whom it is dedicated.

A NOTE ON BIBLIOGRAPHY AND SOURCES

In the end we decided not to attempt to compile an exhaustive bibliography. It may be that this was a result of our own exhaustion, but there are other justifications. We have given full publication details where citations have been made, and we want people to read our book and find these for themselves, not merely to treat a few pages of it as a useful booklist. Obviously, therefore, there are many items which we have found useful which are not directly cited; fortunately, several extensive bibliographies are to be found in the works of authors with more stamina than ourselves. Although it was published in 1963, Richard L. Sklar's *Nigerian Political Parties* is still the best bibliographical source for the period of decolonization. (It is also the indispensable foundation for any study of Nigerian politics before 1960.) References for all aspects of Yoruba life, including more recent items, may be found in Eva Krapf-Askari's *Yoruba Towns and Cities* (Oxford: Clarendon Press, 1969). Among publications in recent years attention should be drawn again to a work cited by us, *The City of Ibadan*, edited by Lloyd, Mabogunje and Awe. Lastly, mention may be made of a recent work which might be compared with our treatment of changes in local government and traditional authority, drawing its data from Northern Nigeria, C. S. Whitaker's *The Politics of Tradition* (Princeton: Princeton University Press, 1970).

To secondary sources we of course added the conventional primary ones, in our case newspapers, legislative debates, government publications and such pamphlet literature as existed. In an enterprise like ours interviews with those who had participated in the events described were also of great importance as sources of information, but even more for an understanding of the motives and perceptions of actors. In this respect we must confess some inadequacies. Interviews were possible with some Ibadan figures and with such of the British administrators as could be traced in retirement or in new careers. However, we made the decision to reserve some of our key interviews – with Kola Balogun and Dr Mbadiwe, for example – until after we had mastered the other material. The reason for this decision was simple, namely that we felt we could have much more productive interviews when we knew exactly what questions arose from our piecing together of events. As it happened, such a stage was not reached until long after both authors had left Nigeria. One made a return trip in April 1966, but the situation of uncertainty after the first coup and during the first military government made it difficult to find people (the answer to inquiries about one ex-minister was 'He is hiding outside the city, but his mother might tell you where if you can find her in the market'). There were other complications, and the result is an absence of total interview coverage; the most notable figure not talked to is undoubtedly Dr Nnamdi Azikiwe.

A much better situation prevailed in terms of personal and other unpublished documents; indeed one of the reasons for the length of time which this book has taken to write has been the profusion of these at our disposal. For some incidents we have had three or more accounts to balance against one another, a rare treat for students of Africa. Special mention should again be made of the Obisesan Diaries and Papers, an incredibly rich source which we only skimmed; Chief Obisesan himself deserves a full-length biography, based on a proper study of his records. Our great good fortune in gaining access to the archives of the Ibadan District Council and Ministry of Local Government of the West should also be stressed once more.

Undoubtedly, however, Adegoke Adelabu's own papers are the foundation of our study, and we were immensely blessed in getting free access to them. Pen-kelemesi was not a systematic man, despite his administrative experience, which encouraged him more to keep lists of what to do and in what order than actually to do them. Fortunately, he did keep many of his incoming letters and copies of some of those he sent. His papers when first examined were undoubtedly in more than usual disarray; our first lengthy task was to identify all items, even to the point of tracing which loose sheets of papers came after other loose sheets. When this was done a rare treasure stood revealed, dividable into four main categories of unequal bulk. First, there were many items concerning Adelabu's personal affairs. These, we feel, have enabled us to see the formation of the personality of a central figure in the post-war Nigerian political elite in much closer perspective than has been possible before, which is a major justification for this study. Second, the papers contained a very large number of internal documents of the N.C.N.C.; if our work is taken together with Sklar's, we can now say that this party is one of the most extensively documented in all the literature on African political parties. A third major category of documents are those related to the local politics and administration of Ibadan, by no means all of which could be used here, but which one of the authors hopes to employ in a future study. The fourth 'category' is, more precisely, only one file (incidentally, one of only two properly organized files in the whole collection): this contains the papers of the 1957 London Constitutional Conference, not officially to be available until 1987. These made it vividly possible to understand how such a crucial nodal point in the dialectic of decolonization really worked.

There were hundreds of other items, including, for example, a rich array of requests for non-political help from individuals and organizations, but the above were the main delights. Thanks to them we were able to come so close to Adelabu that keeping ourselves at a constant distance of objectivity became a recurrent problem. We have tried to do this, even at times at the expense of seeming censorious, and we hope that it will be judged by our readers that we have made adequate use of the superb sources available to us.

ENDNOTES

Note: Certain references are abbreviated throughout. Thus A.P. stands for Adelabu Papers; S.N.D. for *Southern Nigeria Defender*; N.T. for *Nigerian Tribune*; D.S. for *Daily Service*; W.A.P. for *West African Pilot*; and D.T. for *Daily Times*. 'PADID' and 'Ibaprof' references are to local government files kept in Ibadan.

CHAPTER I   *(pages 1–15)*

1 See also Akin Mabogunje, 'The Morphology of Ibadan' in P. C. Lloyd, A. L. Mabogunje and B. Awe (eds.), *The City of Ibadan* (Cambridge: University Press, 1967), and Joel Splansky, 'The Concentric Zone Theory of City Structures as applied in an African City: Ibadan, Nigeria', *Yearbook of the Association of Pacific Coast Geography*, vol. 25, 1966.

2 The myths of origin of the Yoruba may be found in Michael Crowder, *A Short History of Nigeria* (New York: Praeger, revised edition, 1966), pp. 53–4 and p. 341 notes 1–4, and O. Johnson (ed.), Samuel Johnson, *The History of the Yorubas* (Lagos: C.M.S. (Nigeria) Bookshops, 1921), Chapters I and II. This latter volume is still the standard reference work for pre-colonial Yoruba history.

3 I. A. Akinjogbin, 'The Prelude to the Yoruba Civil Wars of the Nineteenth Century', *Odu* (University of Ife Journal of African Studies), vol. I, no. 2, January 1965. See also Robert S. Smith's *Kingdoms of the Yoruba* (London: Methuen, 1969).

4 J. F. Ade Ajayi and Robert S. Smith, *Yoruba Warfare in the Nineteenth Century* (Cambridge: University Press, 1964), pp. 9–12.

5 Bolanle Awe, 'Ibadan: Its Early Beginnings', in Lloyd, Mabogunje and Awe, *The City of Ibadan*.

6 Based on interviews with members of the Oluokun and Adelabu families carried out by Emmanuel Oluyemi Latunji in July 1967.

7 Johnson, *History*, p. 324.

8 Gideon Sjoberg, *The Preindustrial City* (Glencoe: The Free Press, 1960), passim, but especially pp. 96 and 250–1.

9 For this war see Johnson, *History*, Chapter XVIII, and Ade Ajayi and Smith, *Yoruba Warfare in the Nineteenth Century*, especially Part II.

10 A. G. Hopkins, 'Economic Imperialism in West Africa: Lagos, 1880–92', *The Economic History Review*, vol. XXI, no. 3, 1968.

11 An outline discussion of the period 1893–1963 may be found in George Jenkins, 'Government and Politics in Ibadan', in Lloyd, Mabogunje and Awe, *The City of Ibadan*.

12 See Akin Mabogunje, 'The Ijebu', and C. Okonjo, 'The Western Ibo', in Lloyd *et al.*, *The City of Ibadan*.

13 Lugard's career, and his contribution to the ideas of 'indirect rule' are very fully

452

discussed in Margery Perham's *Lugard: The Years of Adventure, 1858–1898.* (London: Collins, 1956), and *Lugard, The Years of Authority, 1898–1945* (London: Collins, 1960).

14 Obisesan to the Secretary, Negro Literary Society, Lagos, 16 March 1920, draft letter, Obisesan Correspondence. The Society later changed its name to the Young African League.

15 Obisesan Diary, 4 and 18 March, and 1 July 1920. For Blyden see Hollis R. Lynch, *Edward Wilmot Blyden: Pan-Negro Patriot* (London: Oxford University Press, 1967); for Garvey, Edmund David Cronon, *Black Moses* (Madison: University of Wisconsin Press, 1955).

16 Obisesan Diary, 17 June 1921.

17 Ibid., 25 April and 21 July 1922.

18 Ibid., 13 August and 23 September 1922 and 8 April 1923; Evidence of the Butcher Commission, vol. I, p. 14, National Archives.

19 District Officer Oshogbo to Resident Oyo Province, circular, 3 May 1935, PADID 127, vol. II.

20 Resident to A. D. O. 27 August 1935, PADID 127, vol. II.

21 Obisesan Diary, 18 July 1945.

22 Declaration of Native Law and Custom (regarding chieftaincy promotion) of 1946.

23 Annual Report, 1948, PADID 2518.

24 Obafemi Awolowo, *Awo: the Autobiography of Chief Obafemi Awolowo* (London: Cambridge University Press, 1960), pp. 118–20.

25 Obisesan Diary, 24 March 1947.

26 Extracts from the famous despatch by Arthur Creech Jones, Secretary of State for the Colonies, are conveniently reprinted in A. H. M. Kirk-Greene (ed.), *The Principles of Native Administration in Nigeria* (London: Oxford University Press, 1965), pp. 238–45.

27 See Coleman, *Background to Nationalism*, Chapter 14.

CHAPTER 2

1 Adelabu's 'Diary', 18 November 1936, A.P. Since Adelabu was only four or five years old when she died, most of what he knew of her must have been told to him by relatives after her death.

2 'Diary', 18 November 1936.

3 Adelabu to 'EHLR re plight', 1938 (only date), A.P.

4 Adelabu to Senior District Officer, November 1950 (no exact date), A.P.

5 *Africa in Ebullition* (Ibadan: the author, n.d. but 1952), pp. 109–10.

6 Ibid., p. 110.

7 Powell to E. F. G. Haig, 22 August 1938, A.P.

8 Interview with Dr A. S. Agbaje, May 1963.

9 Adelabu to Haig, 1938 (only date), A.P.

10 Adelabu to D. D. Jones, General Manager, U.A.C., Lagos, 27 December 1952, A.P.

11 Powell to Haig, 22 August 1938, A.P. After his advice, Adelabu did not see Powell for at least two years.

12 E. H. L. Richardson to Haig, 19 August 1938 and Adelabu to Haig, 1938, A.P. It will be remembered that in his will his father later asked why Adelabu 'calumniated' him. His cousin, who grew up with him, is unable to account for three sisters.

13 For an interesting discussion of Nnamdi Azikiwe's formative influences see K. A. B. Jones-Quartey, *A Life of Azikiwe* (Baltimore: Penguin Books, 1965), pp. 24–30.

14 Adelabu to D. T. Akinbiyi, 6 June 1936, letter in Chief Akinbiyi's possession.

15 'Diary', 18 November 1936, A.P.

16 *Ebullition*, p. 8.

17 Letters to University Correspondence College, Burlington House, Cambridge, 21 May 1939, and to the Director of Studies of Wolsey Hall, Oxford, n.d., but 1939, both A.P.

18 Adclabu to D. D. Jones, 27 December 1950. His work was no doubt aided by the fact that he had already prepared such a report during his first vacation at Yaba, which had helped him to get the job with U.A.C.

19 Richardson to Captain Haig, 1 August 1938, A.P.

20 Adelabu to Jones, 27 December 1950, A.P.

21 Second page of a copy of a letter, apparently to Richardson, n.d., A.P.

22 Manager of U.A.C. to J.A.S. Adelabu, 5 October 1937, A.P.

23 'Diary', 22 June 1943.

24 H. L. Ward Price, *Dark Subjects* (London: Jarrolds, 1939), p. 235.

25 *Annual Report*, Ibadan, 1938. The fall in prices continued: in May 1938 Akinpelu Obisesan noted a price of £8. 9. od. per ton. (Obisesan Diary, 17 May 1938.)

26 Memorandum to Richardson, 'My Future', 11 November 1937, A.P.

27 Adelabu to U.A.C. District Manager Ibadan, 19 February 1938; Manager U.A.C. to Adelabu, 28 February 1938, copy and original in A.P.

28 Adelabu to R. M. Williams, General Manager U.A.C., Lagos, 19 July 1938, A.P.

29 Richardson to Captain Haig, 19 August 1938, A.P.

30 Adelabu to Haig, 1938.

31 Obisesan Diary, 30 August 1938.

32 Obisesan Diary, 28 February 1939. William Nowell chaired a paliamentary commission which inquired into price fixing, the methods of the middlemen and a hold-up in sales; see *Report of the Commission on the Marketing of West African Cocoa* (Cmd. 5845, 1938).

33 Adelabu to the Ibadan Native Authority Council, 6 January 1944, A.P. This description of his tasks was substantiated in an interview with Captain W. J. W. Cheesman, who succeeded Haig as Registrar of Co-operative Societies, in 1965.

34 Obisesan Diary, 8 April 1943. For the quota system see Coleman, *Background to Nationalism*, pp. 81–2.

35 Obisesan Diary, 7 and 27 February 1939.

36 'Diary', 22 June 1943.

37 Obisesan Diary, 30 June, 1 July and 3 November 1941.

38 Adelabu to Ibadan Native Authority, 6 January 1944; 'Agreement re grant of farm-land between Mr. Samuel Bamigbade of Bale's Compound Apomu and Joseph Adegoke Sanusi Adelabu', 31 March 1940; Adelabu to Igbobi College Ibadan, 1 September 1944; 'Agreement between J. A. S. Adelabu and Warri Adegoke of Ile Agbele, Bere, Ibadan', 3 February 1945, all in A.P.

39 Adelabu to Native Authority, Ibadan Native Administration, 6 January 1944, A.P.

40 Adelabu to Jones, 27 December 1950, A.P.

41 Adelabu to District Manager, U.A.C., 30 April 1946, A.P.

42 J. T. Alexander, Labour and Staff Manager, Lagos Area U.A.C., to Adelabu, 9 and 17 May 1946, A.P.

43 Material in this paragraph is derived from an incomplete letter in the Adelabu Papers dated 28 March 1947 and almost certainly directed to a Mr Kay (initials unknown) of MacIver's Store, Ibadan, and from an interview with Albert Younan in April 1966.

44 Adelabu to Secretary, Institute of Social Science, University College of Ibadan, 17 November 1949, A.P.

CHAPTER 3

1 Resident P. V. Main to Secretary of the Western Provinces, 1 August 1947, PADID 2453, vol. 1.

2 Obisesan Diaries 10 and 21 April, 12 May and 17 November 1948.

3 Ibid., 10 September 1949.

4 Petitions of 8, 10 and 18 August and 8 September 1949, PADID 2453, vol. 1.

5 Annual Report, 1948, PADID 2518.

6 Agbaje Inquiry Evidence, vol. 11, pp. 323–4.

7 Latorera to I.P.A. Secretary, 29 September 1938, I.P.A. Papers.

8 F. P. Laosun to Secretary, Western Provinces, 8 July 1949, Maiyegun Society Records.

9 S.N.D., 20 August and 22 September 1949.

10 Fred U. Anyiam, *Men and Matters in Nigerian Politics, 1934–58* (Lagos: the author, n.d.), p. 37. Anyiam's memory apparently was faulty, for he speaks there of the Maiyegun Society, not of the League.

11 S.N.D., 5 December 1949.

12 Adelabu to the Senior District Officer, Ibadan, November 1950, A.P. This is a carbon copy without an exact date. The original was allegedly destroyed by the Chief Commissioner of the Western Province: see p. 73.

13 Ibid.

14 Obisesan Diary, 8 and 9 August 1933 and 21 February 1936.

15 Adelabu to Senior District Officer, Ibadan, November 1950, A.P.

16 Ibid.

17 Petition from the Junior Chiefs and Mogajis to the Olubadan-in-Council, 27 December 1949, reprinted in H. L. M. Butcher, *Report of the Commission of Inquiry into The Allegations of Misconduct Made Against Chief Salami Agbaje, the Otun Balogun of Ibadan, and allegations of inefficiency and Maladministration on the Part of the Ibadan and District Native Authority* (Lagos: Government Printer, 1951), pp. 16–21 (hereafter Butcher Report).

18 Obisesan Diary, 1 February 1950.

19 Ibid., 19 January 1950.

20 Ibid., 1 March 1950.

21 Ibid., 2 March 1950.

22 Adelabu to the Senior Resident, November 1950.

23 George Jenkins, 'An Informal Political Economy' in *Boston University Papers on Africa: Transition in African Politics*, Jeffrey Butler and A. A. Castagno (eds), (New York: Praeger, 1967).

24 Obisesan Diary, 23 February 1950.

25 Ibid., 22 June 1950; Handing Over Notes of Millikan to Phillips, PADID 931, vol. 11c.

26 Obisesan Diary, 21 June 1950.

27 Butcher Report, p. 23.
28 Agbaje Inquiry Evidence, vol. II, p. 326.
29 'Ibadan at the Cross-road: Plain Talk on Current Affairs', S.N.D. 29 and 30 August 1950; 'Ibadan Nobility – Old and New', S.N.D., 25 September 1950; 'Democracy and Free Speech', S.N.D., 21 September 1950.
30 Adelabu to the Senior Resident, November 1950.
31 Ibid.
32 Ibid.
33 S.N.D., 25 September 1950.
34 Ibid.
35 'Ibadan at the Cross-road: Plain Talk on Current Affairs', S.N.D., 29 August 1950.
36 S.N.D., 25 September 1950.
37 Adelabu to C. M. Booth, 30 September 1950, A.P.
38 Apparently he never received a reply; on 14 December he wrote to Booth again, commenting rather angrily that 'Mr Richardson has no doubt over-indulged me but you will agree, Sir, that it is no solution of the problem for you merely to ignore my appeal.' (Adelabu to Booth, 14 December 1950, A.P.)
39 Adelabu to Obisesan, November 1950 (only date), A.P.
40 Adelabu to General Manager, B.A.T.C., 14 December 1950, A.P.
41 Adelabu to A.D.O., 1 January 1951, A.P.
42 Ibid.
43 Adelabu to D. D. Jones, General Manager U.A.C., 27 December 1950, A.P.
44 Labour/Staff Manager, U.A.C. to Adelabu, 13 January 1951, A.P.
45 Divisional Council Minutes, 10 January 1951.

CHAPTER 4

1 Agbaje Inquiry Evidence, vol. II, p. 222 (hereafter A.I.E.).
2 See, for example, *ibid*., pp. 44, 59, 60, 78, 95 and 104–10.
3 Butcher Report, p. 49.
4 S.N.D., 8 February 1951.
5 'Resoluton of the Ibadan Progressive Union (Youth Group) on the Native Settlers' Resolution on the Ibadan and District Native Authority (Alienation of Land to Strangers) Rules 1949', printed, n.d., in author's possession.
6 S. Odulana and others, mimeographed invitation of 14 February 1951, Bello Abasi's Papers.
7 Obisesan Diary, 2 March 1951.
8 Butcher Report, pp. 54–7.
9 Adelabu to 'Dear Chief' (Saka Adebisi?), 8 March 1951, A.P.
10 See a statement by the Ogbomosho Parapo, 30 March 1951, PADID 2910/2.
11 Petition, 9 April 1951, PADID 2910/2.
12 Fred Anyiam to Governor Macpherson, 4 April 1951, PADID 2910/2.
13 Petition, PADID 2910/2.
14 Adelabu to Hayley, 14 April 1951, PADID 2930/2.
15 The Master Plan is in PADID 2930/2. All subsequent quotations are from it unless otherwise noted.
16 Adelabu to Hayley, as from The Secretariat, Egbe Omo Ibile Ibadan, the Taj Mahal, P.O. Box 188, Oke Oluokun, Ibadan, 23 April 1951, Ibaprof 1, 2930/2.
17 From a minute by Hayley on Adelabu's letter of 23 April.

18 The invitation is quoted in Awolowo, *Awo*, pp. 213–14: see Sklar, *Nigerian Political Parties*, pp. 101–12, and Post, *The Nigerian Federal Election of 1959* (London: Oxford University Press, 1963), pp. 31–6.

19 D.S., 21 March 1951. The release also appeared in the *Daily Times* of the same date.

20 Quotations here are from the *Southern Nigerian Defender*, 15 May 1951, which printed this speech under the title 'Onward Into the Battle'.

21 For relations between the Egbe Omo Oduduwa and the Action Group in 1950–1, see Awolowo, *Awo*, pp. 217–21, Sklar, *Nigerian Political Parties*, pp. 101–7, and Post, *Federal Election 1959*, pp. 32–5.

22 N.T., 23 May 1951.

23 Chief Obisesan took the chair, and Adelabu also spoke on 'The Dawn of a New Era'; no text of this speech has survived.

24 Bello Abasi and others to Hayley, 30 May 1951, Ibaprof 1, 2930/2.

25 Interview with John Hayley in New York, August 1965.

26 Obisesan Diary, 16 June 1951.

27 Abasi to Adelabu, 17 June 1951, A.P.

28 S.N.D., 22 June 1951.

29 District Officer, Ikeja, to Adelabu, 27 June 1951 and Adelabu to Town Clerk, Port Harcourt, July (only date) 1951, A.P.

30 N.T., 3 July 1951. The *Defender* of the same day changed the wording somewhat to give the release a more pro-N.C.N.C. slant.

31 Obisesan Diary, 25 June 1951. Present were E. A. Sanda, T. L. Oyesina, J. A. Ayorinde, S. O. Lanlehin, J. L. Ogunsola, Akinpelu Obisesan, Adegoke Adelabu, and A. M. A. Akinloye.

32 Obisesan Diary, 9 July 1951; S.N.D., 11 July 1951.

33 Obisesan Diary, 12 July 1951.

34 *Annual Report*, 1951, PADID 2931.

35 S.N.D., 28 July 1951.

36 Minutes of the Second Meeting of the Greater Ibadan Unity Grand Alliance Working Committee, 21 July 1951, typescript, A.P.

37 Obisesan Diary, 27 July 1951.

CHAPTER 5

1 See his article 'A Stab in the Back', S.N.D., 13 December 1951.

2 Quotations from a typescript, emphasis in the original. A. P. Sklar, *Nigerian Political Parties*, p. 294, refers to an I.P.P.–E.O.I. Bulletin No. 6. We have seen only two

3 N.T., 25 September 1951.

4 N.T., 13 October 1951.

5 *Ebullition*, p. 15.

6 Ibid., pp. 15–16.

7 S.N.D., 1 December 1951.

8 'Adelabu's Inordinate Love of Self' and 'Adelabu: the Apostle of Hate and Confusion', N.T., 20 and 21 December 1951.

9 See the report in the *West African Pilot*, 31 August 1951.

10 In *Ebullition*, p. 16, he says that he also spoke at a meeting in Isalegangan Square. This was not reported in the *Pilot*.

11 See *Ebullition*, p. 16, for a summary of this speech.

12 S.N.D., 13, 14 and 15 December 1951.

13 Bolaji B... to Adelabu, 19 December 1951, A.P.
14 S.N.D., 7 January 1952.
15 *Ebullition*, p. 21.
16 *Ebullition*, p. 20.
17 Voting figures taken from the *Western House of Assembly Debates Official Report: First Session, 7th, 8th, 10th and 18th January, 1952*, p. 16.
18 *Ebullition*, p. 22.
19 *Debates Official Reports*, p. 30.
20 Ibid., p. 31.
21 S.N.D., 17 January 1952.
22 Alhaji Babatunde Jose, 'My Friend, Adelabu', D.T., 27 March 1958.
23 N.T., 1 February 1952.

CHAPTER 6

1 *Africa in Ebullition*, pp. 10–11.
2 S.N.D., 30 August 1950.
3 This and the next four quotations are from the *Nigerian Tribune*, 26 and 30 January 1951.
4 Alaka to Adelabu, n.d. other than 'Wednesday', A.P.
5 Adelabu to Alaka, 24 October 1952, A.P.
6 Adelabu to General Manager, U.A.C., 27 December 1950, A.P.
7 'The Turning Point', manuscript draft, n.d. but late 1952, A.P., p. 21.
8 'The Case for a Militant Nigerian Nationalism', typescript, p. 3 (unnumbered), A.P.
9 Ibid., p. 4 (unnumbered).
10 Ibid., p. 5 (unnumbered).
11 *Ebullition*, p. 112.
12 Ibid., pp. 112–13.
13 Ibid., p. 29.
14 Ibid., pp. 34–5.
15 Ibid., p. 36.
16 Ibid., pp. 108–9.
17 Ibid., pp. 87–96, passim.
18 Ibid., p. 91.
19 Ibid., p. 96.
20 'Turning Point', p. 3.
21 Ibid., p. 19.
22 Ibid., p. 22.
23 Ibid., p. 23.
24 'Ibadan Has Turned Over a New Leaf', p. 3.
25 *Ebullition*, p. 27.
26 Ibid., p. 28.
27 Ibid., pp. 79–80.
28 Ibid., pp. 81–2.
29 'Turning Point', p. 5.
30 *Ebullition*, pp. 70–4, passim.
31 'Turning Point', reverse of p. 3. (This manuscript is written on one side of each sheet, with occasional interpolations on the reverse.)
32 'Case', p. 2 (unnumbered).

33 'Turning Point', p. 38.
34 Ibid., p. 37.
35 *Ebullition*, p. 78.
36 Ibid., p. 82.
37 Ibid., p. 23.
38 'Case', pp. 1–2 (unnumbered).
39 'New Leaf', pp. 1–2.
40 *Ebullition*, p. 97.
41 'Turning Point', p. 32. The first sentence in this quotation is an almost exact repetition of one on p. 23 of *Ebullition*.
42 *Ebullition*, pp. 100–2.
43 Ibid., p. 80.
44 'Turning Point', reverse of p. 5.
45 *Ebullition*, pp. 22–3.
46 'Turning Point', p. 27.
47 Ibid., p. 18, emphasis in the original.
48 Ibid., p. 23.
49 *Ebullition*, pp. 19-20.
50 Ibid., pp. 37–46, passim.
51 'Turning Point', p. 40.
52 Ibid., reverse of p. 40.
53 Ibid., p. 41.
54 Loc. cit.
55 Ibid., p. 44.
56 Ibid., p. 34.
57 Ibid., p. 45.

CHAPTER 7

1 'Turning Point', p. 11.
2 S.N.D., 26 April 1952.
3 See a letter from J. O. Bolumole, S.N.D., 10 November 1952.
4 'Turning Point', p. 11.
5 Ibid., p. 12.
6 S.N.D., editorial, 19 May 1952.
7 Ibid., 10 June 1952.
8 Ibid., 12 September 1952.
9 *Western House of Assembly Debates Official Report: First Session, 18th to 27th February, 1952*, p. 162.
10 Ibid., p. 262.
11 Tika-Tore Press to Adelabu, 15 February 1952, A.P.
12 *Ebullition*, p. 25.
13 Manuscript notes, n.d., A.P.
14 Rational Bookshop to Adelabu, 25 May 1952, A.P.
15 Zukogi to Adelabu, 19 May 1952, A.P.
16 S.N.D., 15 March 1952.
17 *Debates Official Report: First Session. Part I, 14th to 21st July, 1952*, p. 79.
18 Ibid., p. 166.
19 Ibid., *Part II, 22nd to 30th July, 1952*, p. 326.

20 Ibid., p. 381.
21 'Turning Point', p. 7.
22 Ibid., p. 8.
23 *Western House of Assembly Debates Official Report: Second Session Part II, 30th Jan.; 2nd to 5th Feb.; 4th to 6th May, 1953,* pp. 470–1.
24 Ibid., p. 472.
25 Ibid., p. 473.

CHAPTER 8

1 Undated note, A.P.
2 Junior Chiefs and Mogajis through Y. S. Ola Ishola to Council, 7 April 1942, INA 'Rebate'.
3 Schofield Report on Taxation in Ibadan, Ibaprof 1, 149/2.
4 Butcher Report, p. 56.
5 Mogbonjubola, Busari Keremi, Mustafa Motosho and Bale Onilu. Their signatures appear on a petition of 4 February 1952 to the Native Authority, the District Officer, the Resident, and the Lieutenant Governor, File 179. For another report of the meeting see S.N.D., 10 February 1953.
6 Memorandum of the Brooke Commission, 8 September 1950, Ibaprof 1, 1109 vol. IV.
7 Resident Ibadan Province to Executive, Ibadan, Telegram, 2 June 1952; District Officer Hayley to the President [the Olubadan], Judicial Court of Appeal, 14 June 1952, Ibaprof 1, 1109 vol. IV.
8 Ibaprof 1, 1109 vol. IV.
9 The Junior Chiefs and Mogajis to the Olubadan and Senior Chiefs, 6 March 1953, Ibaprof 1, 1109 vol. IV. This letter was apparently also sent to the President-General of the Egbe Omo Ibile.
10 Junior Chiefs and Recognised Mogajis to the Resident, the Lieutenant Governor and the Minister of Local Government, 27 March 1953, Ibaprof 1, 1109 vol. IV.
11 Minutes of the Inaugural Meeting of the Ibadan Tax Payers Association, A. P. Sklar's statement that the I.T.P.A. was founded in 1952 is wrong.
12 Constitution of the Ibadan Tax Payers Association, typescript copy, n.d., A.P.
13 Letter from Ibadan Tax Payers Association Secretary, 22 April 1953, A.P.
14 Ibadan Tax Payers Association to Senior District Officer, the Senior Resident, and the Ibadan Native Authority, 3 May 1953, PADID 2642/S.1., A.P.
15 Council Minutes, 4 May 1953.
16 See, for example, Sklar, *Nigerian Political Parties*, pp. 296–7.
17 The first meeting of the 'Local Government Inquiry Committee' was held on 14 April 1953 under Chief Akinyele's chairmanship. Other members included Dr Agbaje, H. A. Apampa, T. O. Oyesina, H. V. Olunloyo, S. Lana, Chief Aminu and District Officer Cooper. At this meeting the proposed rural–urban division was considered. (See Minutes of this meeting in PADID 2642/S.1.)
18 'Ibadan Tax Payers Battle for Democracy', typescript n.d., but mid-May 1953, A.P.
19 Lt. Governor's note on 1953 Annual Report, Ibaprof 1, 2634 vol. I.
20 The Minutes of this meeting and the receipt of a printing bill for £16. 5. od. for the membership cards are in the Adelabu Papers.
21 S.N.D., 16 and 17 July 1953.
22 Petition from the Ibadan Native Authority Assemblymen, c/o H. V. A. Olunloyo, n.d., but *ca.* 1 August 1953, Ibaprof 1, 1109 vol. IV.

23 Council Minutes, 10 August 1953.
24 M. A. Aboderin to the District Officer, 12 August 1953, Ibaprof 1, 1109 vol. IV.
25 'The Victory of Truth', unpublished typescript, n.d., but *ca.* July 1953, A.P.
26 S.N.D., 13 June 1953.
27 'Religion and Politics in Ibadan', typescript, n.d., but probably late June 1953, A.P.
28 Maiyegun Society to Olubadan and Chiefs, 19 July 1948, and Olubadan and Council to Chief Imam, 30 September 1948, PADID 2583.
29 Acting Resident to Senior District Officer, 13 October 1951, PADID 1093.
30 S.N.D., 23 August 1953.
31 Adelabu to Senior Resident, 4 September 1953, A.P.
32 Mustapha Alli to Resident, 1 October 1953, PADID 1093.
33 Adelabu, on behalf of the Central Working Committee of the Tax Payers Association, to the Resident, 10 September 1953, PADID 2583.
34 S.N.D., 11 September 1953. While the author of this article is not given, it seems to be Adelabu's work.
35 N.T., 28 September 1953; Council Minutes, 26 September 1953.
36 N.T., 19 September 1953.
37 S.N.D., 9 October 1953; Council Minutes, 8 October 1953.
38 See an undated carbon copy of a letter in October from Acting Permanent Secretary, Ministry of Local Government, to Resident, Ibaprof 1, 1109 vol. IV.
39 'The Struggle', S.N.D., 7 November 1953.
40 J. T. Ogungbade and others to N.C.N.C. leaders, 30 January 1953, A.P.
41 A valuable (though rare) source on Action Group organization in the period 1953–5 is *Action*, the party's internal news-sheet.
42 See articles by S. T. Oredein and O. Agungbiade Bamishe in *Action*, vol. I, no. 1, December 1953, and vol. I, no. 2, January 1954.
43 N.T., 20 November 1953.
44 Obisesan Diary, 13 February 1954.
45 This was printed in the *Defender* on 28 December as 'Election Communique Number One'.
46 Notes of the meeting of 18 March 1953 are in Ibaprof 1, 1359/S.25.
47 See letter of 25 March 1953 to District Officer i.c. Lands, Ibaprof 1, 1359/S.25.
48 Council Minutes, 21 September 1953.
49 Senior District Officer to Ibadan District Native Authority, 25 September 1953, Ibaprof 1, 1359/S.25.
50 Senior Superintendent of Police to Assistant Superintendent of Police, Ibadan, 30 December 1953, Ibaprof 1, 1359/S.25.
51 E. W. J. Nicholson, *Report of the Commission of Enquiry into the Administration of the Ibadan District Council*, Ibadan: Western Region Government, 1956, pp. 75–7.
52 Interview with Olubadan Akinyele, July 1963.
53 Minutes of a Special Meeting on 5 March 1953, Ibaprof 1, 1109 vol. IV.
54 A Nigerian Correspondent, 'Mr Adelabu has the Answers', *West Africa*, 12 March, 1955, p. 221.
55 S.N.D., 7 January 1954.
56 D.S., 16 March 1954.
57 See the report in N.T., 18 March 1954.
58 S.N.D., 20 March 1954.
59 D.S., 20 March 1954.

CHAPTER 9

1 'Zik' to Adelabu, telegram, 21 March 1954, A.P.
2 S.N.D., 22 March 1954.
3 Fadahunsi to Adelabu, 27 March 1954, A.P.
4 S.N.D., 9 April 1954. The *Daily Service* of the same date reported a majority of 34 votes for Adelabu against Chief Aminu.
5 S.N.D., 9, 10, 12 and 13 April 1954.
6 Obisesan Diary, 8 April 1954.
7 Obisesan Diary, 9 April 1954.
8 Regina *v.* Ibadan Judicial Council, Suit no. 1/136/53 in re A. R. Salami Applicant.
9 Minute, Lewis to Resident, 9 April 1954, Ibaprof 1, 1109 vol. IV.
10 Ibadan Nadmin to Executive Ibadan, telegram, 17 April 154, Ibaprof 1, 1109 vol. IV.
11 Acting Permanent Secretary Murphy to Resident, 25 March 1954, Ibaprof 1, 1109 vol. IV.
12 Edah to Adelabu, 13 April 1954, A.P.
13 Adeyemo to Secretary, Ibadan District Council, 31 May 1954, PADID 2571.
14 Adeyemo to Minister of Local Government 24 June 1954, PADID 2571.
15 Resident to Permanent Secretary, Ministry of Local Government, 10 July 1954, PADID 2571.
16 N.T., 30 June 1954.
17 Adeyemo to District Officer, 6 July 1954, PADID 2571.
18 D.S., 8 June 1954.
19 S.N.D., 5 May 1954.
20 S.N.D., 15 June 1954.
21 Resident to Senior Superintendent of Police, Ibadan Province, 14 June 1954, Ibaprof 1, 26/S.4.
22 Olubadan to S.D.O., 17 June 1954, Ibaprof 1, 26/S.4.
23 Secretary I.T.P.A. to Egbe Mabolaje, Shaki, September 1953 (only date), A.P.
24 S.N.D., 14 January 1954.
25 'National Council of Nigeria and the Cameroons: Report of the Fifth Annual Convention held at Enugu, from January 6–10th, 1954', mimeographed, p. 6., A.P.
26 Ibid., p. 7.
27 S.N.D., 14 January 1954.
28 'Report of Fifth Annual Convention', p. 15.
29 Loc. cit.
30 Onabamiro to Adelabu, 8 April 1954, A.P.
31 Okoye to Adelabu, 13 April 1954, A.P.
32 Eze to Adelabu, 8 April 1954, A.P.
33 Eze to Adelabu, 23 April 1954, A.P.
34 A.A. Olateju Akanmole to Adelabu, 10 May 1954, A.P.
35 'National Council of Nigeria and the Cameroons: Report of the Principal Organising Secretary on the Reorganisation of the Party, Presented to the N.E.C. in Session at Ibadan, Sunday July 4, 1954', mimeographed, p. 1., A.P.
36 Ibid., p. 3.
37 S.N.D., 14 July 1954.
38 Ibid., 27 August 1954.
39 Ibid., 31 August 1954.
40 Ibid., 7 September 1954.

41 Ibid., 8 September 1954.
42 D.S., 15 October 1954. See also the evidence of Maja before the Lloyd Commission of Inquiry, reported in S.N.D., 20 October 1954.
43 Minutes of the meeting, Ibaprof 1, 26/S.4.
44 Secretary, Ibadan District Council, to Assistant Local Government Inspector, Ibadan Division, 4 September 1954, Ibaprof 1, 547, vol. 24.
45 Assistant Local Government Inspector to Local Government Inspector, 13 July 1954, Ibaprof 1, 26/S.4.
46 S.N.D., 18 September 1954.
47 Memorandum from the meeting in Ibaprof 1, 26/S.4.
48 Minutes of the Ibadan District Council Finance Committee, 30 September 1954.
49 Report by the Senior District Officer on the conduct of polling, 12 November 1954, PADID 3224/S.11.
50 S.N.D. editorial, 2 November 1954.
51 Minutes of 'NCNC Grand Alliance' meeting, 10 July 1954, ledger in A.P. (see note on p. 203).
52 Benson and McEwen to Adelabu, telegram, 6 November 1954, A.P.
53 Report by the Senior District Officer on the conduct of polling.
54 Loc. cit.
55 S.N.D., 18 November 1954.
56 Ibid., 29 November 1954.
57 Obisesan Diary, 26 November 1953.

CHAPTER 10

1 D.T., 10 January 1955.
2 D.T., 11 January 1955.
3 'Budget Scheme', n.d. but presumably early January 1955, A.P.
4 'The N.C.N.C. Western Region Planning Committee: Minutes of Meeting', mimeographed, 15 March 1955, p. 3, A.P.
5 Copy of agreement, A.P.
6 Adelabu to Acting Senior District Officer, 2 February 1955, A.P.
7 S.N.D., 7 February 1955.
8 Minutes of this meeting in Ibaprof 1, 1109 vol. IV.
9 Minutes of the meeting of the Kingmakers, 12 February 1955, Ibaprof 1, 1109 vol. IV.
10 From a Minute on 12 May 1955 by D. A. Murphy, on a speech given on 16 February 1955 by Adelabu, Ibaprof 1, 1109 vol. IV.
11 Text of a radio broadcast by D. A. Murphy, 13 February 1955, Ibaprof 1, 1109 vol. IV.
12 S.N.D., 14 February 1955.
13 Obisesan Diary, 9 and 12 February 1955.
14 Obisesan Diary, 18 February 1955.
15 Acting Permanent Secretary, Ministry of Justice and Local Government to Local Government Adviser, 28 February 1955. PADID 2263.
16 D.S., 4 March 1955; S.N.D., 4 March 1955.
17 *Debates in the Federal House of Representatives. First Session, 8th to 31st March and 1st to 7th April, 1955, Volume I, 8th to 23rd March, 1955*, p. 71.
18 Ibid., p. 93.

19 Ibid., pp. 94–5.
20 Ibid., p. 95.
21 S.N.D., 19 March 1955.
22 Adelabu, J. M. Johnson, A. Adeyinka and L. A. Lawal to N.C.N.C. Federal Ministers, 23 March 1955, A.P.
23 *Debates in the Federal House, Volume II, 24th to 31st March and 1st to 7th April, 1955*, p. 725.
24 Ibid., p. 735.
25 S.N.D., 15 December 1954.
26 Obisesan Diary, 24 and 29 December 1954 and 19 January 1955.
27 S.N.D., 31 March 1955.
28 *Debates in the Federal House*, pp. 1008–11.
29 *Debates in the Federal House*, pp. 1025–6.
30 D.S., 19 April 1955.
31 S.N.D., 23 April 1955.
32 D.S., 21 April 1955.
33 Murphy to Permanent Secretary, Ministry of Local Government, 26 October 1954, Ibaprof 1, 2634 vol. 1.
34 Acting Senior District Officer to Resident, 5 February 1955, PADID 547, vol. 24.
35 S.N.D., 23 March 1955. Curiously, little was made of this dereliction by the N.C.N.C.
36 Council Minutes, 5 March 1955.
37 Nicholson Report, p. 59.
38 'Democracy on Trial', n.d. but April 1955, typescript, A.P.
39 Mokwugo Okoye, 'Statement at Trial for Conspiracy NCNC National Executive', mimeographed, 2 August 1954, p. 5, A.P.
40 Ibid., p. 5.
41 Loc. cit.
42 Agwuna, 'Report of the Principal Organising Secretary...', p. 6.
43 Okoye, 'Statement...', p. 4.
44 Agwuna to Balogun, 4 February 1955, A.P.
45 See Sklar, *Nigerian Political Parties*, pp. 150–1, n. 13, for a long quotation from this document.
46 S.N.D., 7 May 1955.
47 D.T., 7 May 1955.
48 S.N.D., 10 May 1955.
49 See D.T., 6 May and W.A.P., 7 May 1955.
50 Okoye to Adelabu, 25 April 1957, A.P.
51 W.A.P., 9 May 1955.
52 Mbadiwe to McEwen, 16 May 1955, A.P.
53 Adelabu to McEwen, 11 May 1955, A.P.
54 McEwen to Adelabu, 12 May 1955, A.P.
55 Mbadiwe to McEwen, 16 May 1955, A.P.
56 'National Council of Nigeria and the Cameroons, Meeting of Interim Working Committee held at Ibadan on 22 May 1955', mimeographed, A.P.
57 S.N.D., 2 June 1955.
58 Permanent Secretary, Ministry of Justice and Local Government, to Adelabu, 3 June 1955, A.P.
59 Adelabu to the Ministry of Local Government, June (only date) 1955, A.P.
60 S.N.D., 2 June 1955.

61 Olubadan Akinyele and eight other chiefs to the Minister of Local Government, 7 June 1955, Ibaprof 1, 1109 vol. IV.
62 'The N.C.N.C. Western Region Conference: Minutes of Meeting', mimeographed, A.P.
63 Asaya to the Western Working Committee, 26 July 1955, A.P.
64 D.S., 20 July 1955.
65 D.S., 6 and 10 August 1955.
66 Police *v* Adegoke Adelabu and Eight Others, MI/623c/55, Magistrates' Court Library, Onireke, Ibadan.
67 Nicholson Report, p. 130.
68 Ibid., p. 131.
69 Mbadiwe to Adelabu, 9 September 1955, A.P. It should be pointed out that in addition to sources cited, this discussion is based on documentary and oral sources which it was agreed should remain confidential.
70 Mbadiwe to Adelabu, 9 September 1955.
71 Adelabu to Mbadiwe, 9 September 1955, A.P.
72 D.T., 13 September 1955.
73 Nicholson Report, p. 131.
74 Ibid., p. 53.
75 Ibid., p. 99.
76 Ibid., p. 100.
77 Ibid., p. 101.
78 Ibid., p. 100.
79 Loc. cit.
80 Typescript in the Adelabu Papers, p. 3. This was presumably intended to be part of an official handout, possibly by the Government Information Service, but it does not seem to have seen the light of day.
81 Minutes of the Inaugural Meeting of the Ibadan District Council Chieftaincy Committee, 9 November 1955.
82 Adegoke Adelabu and L. Ade Bello *v.* Inspector-General of Police, High Court of Justice, 22 November 1955, *Western Region of Nigeria Law Reports, 1955–56*, pp. 6–12.
83 Obisesan Diary, 3 November 1955.
84 Mbadiwe to Adelabu, 14 December 1955, A.P.

CHAPTER II

1 *Nicholson Report*, p. 130.
2 Ibid., p. 128.
3 Ibid., p. 129.
4 Loc. cit.
5 Ibid., p. 129.
6 Ibid., p. 137.
7 Governor-General to Adelabu, 17 January 1956, A.P.
8 Adelabu to Governor-General, first draft, n.d., A.P.
9 Adelabu to Governor-General, second draft, n.d., A.P.
10 'Resolutions', 18 January 1956, typescript, A.P. This document was signed by 61 people, including Adelabu and S. L. A. Elliott, with 42 actual signatures and 19 thumb-prints.

11 D.T., 21 January 1956.

12 D.T., 26 January 1956.

13 Adelabu to Governor-General, 24 January 1956, A.P.

14 Governor-General to Adelabu, 25 January 1956, A.P.

15 D.T., 26 January 1956.

16 Azikiwe to Adelabu, 28 January 1956, A.P.

17 S.N.D., 30 January 1956.

18 Ibid.

19 S.N.D., 24 February 1956.

20 Secret Memorandum by Minister of Justice and Local Government, 27 February 1956, PADID 2642/S.1.

21 Local Government Inspector Murphy to Permanent Secretary, Ministry of Justice and Local Government, 24 February 1956, PADID 2642/S.1.

22 S.N.D., 2 March 1956.

23 Obisesan Diary, 16 March 1956.

24 S.N.D., 12 March 1956.

25 Ibid., 14 March 1956.

26 Ibid., 21 March 1956.

27 Ibid., 17 March 1956.

28 C. J. Mabey to Adelabu, 23 August 1956; J. Blackwell to Adelabu, 23 August 1956; G. B. A. Coker to Adelabu, 20 August 1956; T. O. S. Benson to Adelabu, 2 August 1957; A.P.

29 Provincial Adviser to Permanent Secretary, Ministry of Local Government, 7 March 1956, Ibaprof 1, 1359/S.25.

30 N.T., 15 March 1956.

31 This list, in his own handwriting, is in part of a notepad found among his papers. It is undated, but the last definite date in the list is 4 October 1955, and other material in the notepad seems to date from late October.

32 Adegoke Adelabu, 'Grand Election Conspiracy in the West', mimeographed, p. 1, A.P. This is undated, but from the internal evidence was written sometime between 26 October and 1 November; part of the manuscript draft for it is in the notepad referred to in note 31.

33 Ibid., p. 5.

34 Discussions of the franchise and registration can be found in the official *Report on the Holding of the 1956 Parliamentary Election to the Western House of Assembly, Nigeria,* Ibadan: Government Printer, 1957, pp. 1–6; Philip Whitaker, 'The Western Region of Nigeria, May 1956' in W. J. M. Mackenzie and Kenneth E. Robinson (eds.), *Five Elections in Africa* (Oxford: Clarendon Press, 1960), pp. 43–53; and P. C. Lloyd and K. W. J. Post, 'Where Should One Vote?', *Journal of African Administration,* vol. 11, no. 2, April 1960.

35 Onabamiro to Balogun, 16 August 1955, 'Memorandum on the Question of the nomination of Candidates for the General Election of 1956, to the Western House of Assembly', A.P.

36 Onabamiro to Adelabu, 10 October 1955, A.P.

37 Onabamiro to Adelabu, 9 November 1955, A.P.

38 Balogun to Adelabu, 8 October 1955, A.P.

39 Onabamiro to Adelabu, 17 November 1955, A.P.

40 For a discussion of these constituencies, see Whitaker, 'The Western Region of Nigeria', pp. 55 and 88–9.

41 S. D. Onabamiro, Nomination Application Form, 11 November 1955, A.P.

42 See the 'Report of Arbitration into Ibadan NCNC Affairs by a Committee of the NCNC, 26 April 1956', mimeographed, mentioned in Sklar, *Nigerian Political Parties*, p. 301.

43 Partial manuscript draft, n.d., A.P.

44 Chairman, Secretary, Treasurer and 1st and 2nd Vice-Chairmen, Oshogbo District N.C.N.C. to Adelabu, 11 February 1956, A.P.

45 'Report of the Commission of Enquiry into the Cause of NCNC Failure in the General Election in the Western Region', mimeographed, n.d., p. 16, A.P.

46 'Minutes of the Western Working Committee which was held at the District Council School Room, Mokola, University College Road, Ibadan on Saturday the 21st day of January 1956', mimeographed, A.P.

47 Adebayo Asaya, Circular letter NC/WR/1w/50, 30 April 1956, mimeographed, A.P.

48 For an account of the campaign, see Whitaker, pp. 59–66.

49 See, for example, the cartoon from the *Daily Service*, reproduced in Whitaker, facing p. 67.

50 'Report of the Commission of Enquiry...', Appendix D (pages in the appendices were unnumbered).

51 Ibid., Appendix E.

52 An account of the meeting is in Ibaprof 1, File 26/S.4, vol. 1.

53 Ibid.

54 Acting Senior Superintendent of Police, Ibadan and Oyo Provinces, circular, n.d., but received 10 May 1956, PADID 3360.

55 For summaries of these manifestoes see Whitaker, 'The Western Region of Nigeria', pp. 58–9.

56 The text of this speech was serialized in the *Southern Nigeria Defender*, 22–4 May 1956, from which all quotations are taken.

57 Onabamiro to candidates, 18 May 1956, A.P. Emphasis in the original.

58 Inspector-General of Police Complainant *v*. Adegoke Adelabu in re Chief D. T. Akinbiyi. Federal Supreme Court, 29 May 1956, *Western Region of Nigeria Law Reports*.

59 Inspector-General of Police Respondent *v*. Adegoke Adelabu and L. Ade Bello in re L. Ade Bello Apellant. Federal Supreme Court, 29 May 1956, Criminal Appeal: Ibadan Appeal no. 1/42. CA/55. *Western Region of Nigeria Law Reports*.

60 S.N.D., 31 May and 1 June 1956.

CHAPTER 12

1 'Submissions on the 1956 Regional Parliamentary Elections by the NCNC Western Parliamentary Party to the Governor, Western Region, Sir John Rankine, K.C.M.G., K.C.V.O.', typescript, A.P.

2 Enahoro, circular letter no. MHA.46, 12 June 1956, A.P.

3 S.N.D., 18 June 1956.

4 *Western Region of Nigeria House of Assembly Debates Official Report, Omnibus Issue No. 5, 2nd, 3rd, 4th, 5th and 6th July 1956*, col. 151.

5 Ibid., col. 158.

6 Acting Deputy Governor of the Western Region to Secretary, N.C.N.C. Parliamentary Committee, 26 July 1956, A.P.

7 Lennox-Boyd to Brockway, 30 July 1956, A.P.

8 Deputy Governor to Adelabu, 8 October 1956, A.P.
9 Deputy Governor to Adelabu, 19 October 1956, A.P.
10 Afolabi to Brockway, 10 August 1956, A.P.
11 See the *Report on Banking and Finance in Eastern Nigeria*, Eastern House of Assembly Sessional Paper no. 4 of 1956, Enugu: Government Printer, n.d., pp. 3–10; also the statement by Chief Awolowo in the Western House of Assembly on 21 December 1956 in *Western Region of Nigeria House of Assembly Debates Official Report, Omnibus Issue No. 6, 19th, 21st, and 22nd December, 1956*.
12 On this point, see the letter from Azikiwe to A. K. Blankson quoted on pp. 12–13 of the *Report on Banking and Finance in Eastern Nigeria*.
13 *The Economic Development of Nigeria* (Lagos: Federal Government Printer, 1954), p. 98.
14 For a full account of the Onitsha dispute and the Ikpeazu Inquiry see Sklar, *Nigerian Political Parties*, pp. 151–62. It must be remembered that Dr Azikiwe was himself a native of Onitsha.
15 Despatch no. WAF 39/3/55, 1 December 1951.
16 See the *Proceedings of the Tribunal Appointed to inquire into Allegations of Improper Conduct by the Premier of the Eastern Region of Nigeria in Connection with the Affairs of the African Continental Bank Limited and Other Relevant Matters* (Lagos: Federal Government Printers, 1957), p. 195.
17 See Sklar, *Nigerian Political Parties*, pp. 172–3, for a speech by Azikiwe in which he cited this and other examples of apparent double standards on the part of the British Government.
18 D.T., 17 June 1956.
19 'National Council of Nigeria and the Cameroons: Minutes of N.E.C. Meeting held at Onitsha on Thursday, 26 July 1956', mimeographed, p. 2, A.P.
20 'National Council of Nigeria and the Cameroons: Minutes of Special Convention held at Onitsha on Friday, 27 July 1956', mimeographed, p. 1, A.P.
21 D.T., 28 July 1956.
22 For the full text, see the D.T., 20 August 1956.
23 S.N.D., 24 and 25 August 1956.
24 Ibid., 28 August 1956.
25 'National Council of Nigeria and the Cameroons (Western Region): Minutes of the NCNC Parliamentary Party Meeting held on Friday, 14th September 1956 at the Party's Headquarters Mokola, Ibadan', mimeographed, p. 2, A.P.
26 S.N.D., 24 September 1956.
27 Ibid., 27 September 1956; Obisesan Diary, 24 September 1956; Senior Divisional Adviser to Deputy Governor, 25 September 1956, CA.13/7/1A.
28 T. A. Lamuye to Adelabu, 27 September 1956, A.P.
29 There is an undated statement of accounts for the Bureau made by Asaya to Adelabu in the Adelabu Papers, in which £12. 18. 0d. is given as expenditure.
30 Anonymous to Adelabu, n.d., A.P.
31 Azikiwe to Asaya, 26 October 1956, A.P.
32 Onabamiro, 'N.C.N.C., Western Region. Memorandum Prepared by the Secretary of the Western Working Committee for the Re-organisation of the Party in the Western Region', 23 October 1956, copy with manuscript notes, A.P.
33 Members of the W.W.C. for fifteen Divisions were appointed by Adelabu, 'subject to confirmation by Divisional Executives' on 23 October. (Adelabu, circular letter NC/WR/2/64, 23 October 1956, A.P.)

34 S.N.D., 16 November 1956.
35 Fadahunsi to Adelabu, 24 November 1956, NC/WR/298, A.P.
36 Council Minutes, 13 November 1956.
37 S.N.D., 24 November 1956; N.T., 10 December 1956.
38 S.N.D., 28 November 1956.
39 *Western Region of Nigeria House of Assembly Debates Official Report, Omnibus Issue No. 6, 19th, 21st and 22nd December, 1956*, cols. 23–4.
40 Ibid., col. 27.
41 Ibid., col. 28.
42 Ibid., col. 35.
43 Ibid., col. 42.
44 Loc. cit.
45 Ibid., col. 49.
46 Ibid., col. 50.
47 Ibid., col. 57.
48 Ibid., col. 63.
49 Ibid., col. 66.
50 Ibid., col. 69.
51 Ibid., col. 73.
52 Ibid., cols. 74–5.
53 Ibid., col. 78.
54 Ibid., cols. 80–1.
55 Ibid., cols. 82–3.
56 Ibid., cols. 89–90.
57 Ibid., col. 99.
58 Ibid., col. 109.
59 Ibid., col. 113.
60 Ibid., col. 116.
61 Ibid., col. 121.
62 Ibid., col. 128.
63 Adelabu to Governor, 24 December 1956, NC/WR/298, A.P.
64 S. O. Gbadamosi had given the figure as £53,700 during the debate. See *Debates Official Report*, col. 164.
65 Three different lists exist in the Adelabu Papers, only one is dated – 4 March 1957. There is no record in the statements of postage accounts in file NC/WR/298 of any material in fact being sent to any British publication, and if it was they ignored it.
66 Fadahunsi to Adelabu, 8 January 1957, NC/WR/298, A.P.
67 W.A.P., 15 January 1957.
68 Adelabu to Fadahunsi, 19 January 1957, NC/WR/298, A.P.
69 Adelabu to Governor, 26 February 1957, NC/WR/351/69, A.P.
70 Asaya to Adelabu, 28 February 1957, NC/WR/281/38, with separate statement of account, A.P.
71 Asaya to Benson, date uncertain but December 1956, NCN/WR/298/50, A.P.
72 Asaya to Adelabu, 28 February 1957, A.P.
73 'National Council of Nigeria and the Cameroons (Western Region), Minutes of the Joint Meeting of NCNC West', mimeographed, n.d., p. 2, A.P.
74 'Minutes', p. 4.
75 Deputy Governor to Adelabu, 4 March 1957, A.P.
76 Adelabu to Governor, 9 March 1957, A.P.

77 Asaya to Adelabu, 11 March 1957, with separate statement of account, A.P.
78 *Proceedings of the Tribunal*, p. 42. For one view of the findings of the Tribunal and the Eastern election see Sklar, *Nigerian Political Parties*, pp. 175–89; for another see J. H. Price, 'The Eastern Region of Nigeria, March 1957' in *Five Elections in Africa*, pp. 106–67.
79 W.A.P., 14 March 1957.
80 Deputy Governor to Adelabu, 13 March 1957, A.P.
81 Deputy Governor to Adelabu, 27 April 1957, A.P.

CHAPTER 13

1 *Western Region of Nigeria House of Assembly Debates Official Report, Omnibus Issue No. 7, 25th–29th March, 1st–4th April, 1957*, col. 28.
2 Ibid., col. 53.
3 Loc. cit.
4 Ibid., col. 55.
5 Ibid., col. 338.
6 Ibid., col. 342.
7 Ibid., cols. 342–3.
8 Ibid., col. 343.
9 Ibid., col. 595.
10 Adelabu to Awolowo, 11 April 1957, A.P.
11 'National Council of Nigeria and the Cameroons (Western Region) Regional Finance Committee, Minutes of Meeting 23/3/57', p. 1, mimeographed, A.P.
12 Adelabu to Mariere, 3 April 1957, A.P.
13 Thomas K. Boyo to Adelabu, 16 July 1956, A.P.
14 'National Council of Nigeria and the Cameroons (Western Region) 10% Subscriptions. February 1957 – Statement of Account', mimeographed, 4 March 1957, A.P.
15 Asaya to Adelabu, 1 August 1957, A.P.
16 Asaya to Adelabu, 4 March 1957, A.P.
17 Asaya to Azikiwe, 19 April 1957, A.P.
18 'National Council of Nigeria and the Cameroons (Western Region) Publication Committee Meeting', mimeographed, 22 March 1957, A.P.
19 An analysis of some of the problems of leadership may be found in Sklar, *Nigerian Political Parties*, pp. 143–51.
20 Ibid., p. 149.
21 Awolowo, *Awo*, p. 186.
22 Azikiwe to Adelabu, 9 April 1957, A.P.
23 'Second Thoughts on the Forthcoming Constitutional Conference on Reflection on Ghana Independence', mimeographed, 11 April 1957, A.P. Emphasis in the original.
24 Awolowo, *Awo*, pp. 187–8.
25 S. O. Ajai, Circular no. I.S.P./55/1, 31 August 1955, A.P.
26 Ajai to Adelabu, 12 August 1957, A.P.
27 'National Council of Nigeria and the Cameroons Constitutional Conference Committee: Proposals to be Placed before the National Executive Committee', mimeographed, p. 3, n.d., A.P.
28 'Extraordinary Meeting of NCNC Leaders', typescript, G. B. Akinyede, n.d., A.P.
29 '...Constitutional Conference Committee...', p. 2.

30 Ibid., Annexe I.
31 Peace Committee to Azikiwe, 18 April 1957, A.P.
32 'National Council of Nigeria and the Cameroons: NCNC National Executive Committee held at the Lagos City College, Yaba, Lagos, on 18th April, 1957, mimeographed, p. 1, A.P.
33 For the Zikist National Vanguard, see Sklar, *Nigerian Political Parties*, pp. 403–6.
34 'National Executive Committee...18th April, 1957', p. 2.
35 Ibid., p. 3.
36 'National President's Address 1957 NCNC Special Convention', mimeographed, p. 1, A.P. All direct quotations are from this source.
37 Balogun to all N.C.N.C. branches, N.E.C. members and parliamentarians, 4 April 1957, A.P.
38 N.C.N.C. Special Convention, April 1957, mimeographed minutes, p. 2, A.P.
39 Ibid., p. 3, A.P.
40 Aderibigbe Adelabu to his father, n.d., A.P.
41 Onabamiro to Members of the N.C.N.C. delegation, n.d., Ref. Sec. D/3, emphasis in the original, A.P.
42 Onabamiro to N.C.N.C. Delegates, 'Confidential Notes on Members of the Action Group Delegation to the Conference', 16 May 1957, A.P.
43 This comment is particularly interesting in view of the late Chief Akintola's role in the Action Group crisis of 1962. See John P. Mackintosh, 'The Action Group, The Crisis of 1962 and its Aftermath', in Mackintosh *et al.*, *Nigerian Government and Politics*, esp. pp. 441–50.
44 'Nigeria Constitutional Conference 1957: Record of Opening Ceremony held in the Long Gallery, Lancaster House on Tuesday 23rd May 1957 at 11 a.m.', mimeographed, Annex 1, p. 1, A.P.
45 Ibid., Annex 2, p. 1.
46 Ibid., Annex 3, p. 1.
47 Ibid., Annex 4, p. 1.
48 The account of the Conference from the Action Group point of view may be found in Awolowo, *Awo*, pp. 189–92, though only the new states issue is discussed. Another account is to be found in Ezera, *Constitutional Developments*, pp. 231–40. There is also the official *Report by the Nigeria Constitutional Conference held in London, May and June 1957*, Cmd. 207 (London: H.M.S.O., 1957); the Sardauna's account, *My Life*, pp. 203–8, is disappointingly unrevealing.
49 Onabamiro, 'Confidential Notes...', pp. 2–3.
50 'Nigeria Constitutional Conference Steering Committee: Minutes of a meeting held in the State Drawing Room, Lancaster House, London, S.W.1, on Thursday 23rd May, 1957, at 4 p.m.', mimeographed, p. 1, A.P.
51 Loc. cit.
52 'Nigeria Constitutional Conference: Minutes of the Second Plenary Meeting held in the State Drawing Room, Lancaster House, London, S.W.1, on Friday 24th May, 1957 at 10-30 a.m.', mimeographed, p. 6, A.P.
53 Chike Obi, 'Observations on the Nigerian Constitutional Conference', 31 July 1957, mimeographed, p. 1, A.P.
54 Ibid., p. 2.
55 'The Nigerian Constitutional Conference, London, 1957. Memorandum No. 12 (From the N.C.N.C. Delegation to the Conference (The Judiciary – Federal and State))', mimeographed, p. 1, A.P.

56 'Self-Government for Western Region: Memorandum by the NCNC Delegation', mimeographed, p. 1, A.P.
57 'Nigeria Constitutional Conference: Minutes of the Eighth Plenary Session held in the State Drawing Room, Lancaster House, London, S.W.1 on Monday 3rd June, 1957 at 10-30 a.m. and 3 p.m.', mimeographed, p. 4, A.P.
58 Ibid., p. 6.
59 Loc. cit.
60 Ibid., pp. 6–7.
61 Ibid., p. 7.
62 Loc. cit.
63 Loc. cit.
64 Awolowo, *Awo*, p. 189.
65 'Memorandum by Northern Peoples Congress Delegation: Creation of New States', mimeographed, 24 May 1957, p. 1, A.P.
66 'N.C.N.C. Delegation's Memorandum to the 1957 Constitution Conference: States as the Units of the Federation', mimeographed, 24 May 1957, p. 1, A.P.
67 Ibid., p. 1.
68 Ibid., p. 2.
69 Presumably, therefore, he had read two in which Adelabu had a special interest: 'A Memorandum Submitted by the Central Yoruba State Movement. Sponsored by the N.C.N.C. Delegation' (mimeographed, A.P.) and 'N.C.N.C.–Mabolaje Grand Alliance: Creation of Yoruba Central State', a submission dated 31 May 1957 and signed by all the Ibadan Grand Alliance legislators, A.P.
70 'Nigeria Constitutional Conference: Minutes of the Eleventh Plenary Session held in the State Drawing Room, Lancaster House, London, S.W.1 on Thursday 13th June, 1957 at 10-30 a.m.', mimeographed, p. 1, A.P.
71 Ibid., p. 2.
72 Ibid., p. 4.
73 Ibid., pp. 4–5.
74 Ibid., p. 6.
75 'Nigeria Constitutional Conference: Minutes of the Twelfth Plenary Session held in the State Drawing Room, Lancaster House, London, S.W.1, on Friday 14th June, 1957 at 10-30 a.m. and 4-40 p.m.', mimeographed, p. 2, A.P.
76 Ibid., p. 3.
77 *Awo*, p. 191.
78 News Release, Colonial Office Information Department, 14 June 1957, pp. 2–3, mimeographed, A.P. See also the official *Report by the Nigerian Constitutional Conference*, pp. 13–14.
79 Adeshina to Adelabu, 19 June 1957, A.P.
80 *Report by the Nigerian Constitutional Conference*, pp. 24–5.
81 Ibid., p. 25–6.
82 Ibid., p. 26.
83 Ibid., p. 27.
84 'Nigeria Constitutional Conference 1957: Minutes of the Twenty-First Plenary Session held in the State Drawing Room, Lancaster House, London, S.W.1 on Tuesday 25th June, 1957 at 2-45 p.m.', mimeographed, p. 5, A.P.
85 Nnamdi Azikiwe, *Zik: A Selection from the Speeches of Nnamdi Azikiwe* (London: Cambridge University Press, 1961), p. 135.
86 Ibid., p. 136.

87 Loc. cit.
88 Obi, 'Observations...', p. 1.
89 Ibid., p. 5.
90 'Draft Minutes of the Ad Hoc Committee Meeting of N.C.N.C. Ministers on board the M.V. *Apapa* – July 22, 1957', mimeographed, p. 2, A.P.
91 Ibid., pp. 2–3.
92 For a further discussion of this see K. W. J. Post, 'The National Council of Nigeria and the Cameroons, the Decision of December 1959', in Mackintosh *et al.*, *Nigerian Government and Politics*, pp. 405–26.
93 'Draft Minutes...', p. 4.
94 An undated pencilled note on the Front in Adelabu's handwriting was among his papers on the Constitutional Conference.

CHAPTER 14

1 S.N.D., 16 July 1957.
2 Ibid., 30 April 1957.
3 Alhaji Babatunde Jose, 'My Friend, Adelabu', D.T., 27 March 1958.
4 Ibid.
5 Manuscript minutes of a meeting of the Special Working Committee of the U.M.P. held in Ibadan on 24 February 1957, A.P.
6 *United Muslim Party Representations Addressed to the Right Honourable the Secretary of State for the Colonies on Nigerian Constitutional Conference Opening in London May 23rd, 1957* (Abeokuta: Nigerian Blessed Press, n.d.), p. 6.
7 D.S., 14 October 1957.
8 For the full text of the speech see S.N.D., 22 and 23 July 1957.
9 The text of this speech is in S.N.D., 29 and 30 July 1957.
10 Association of N.C.N.C. Constituency Secretaries to Secretary of Western Working Committee, 12 July 1957, A.P.
11 S.N.D., 2 August 1957.
12 See the correspondence between Abubakar and Rotimi Williams, D.T., 31 August 1957. Chief S. L. Akintola became the new Minister of Communications and Aviation and Ayo Rosiji Minister of Health. The Kamerun National Congress retained its single portfolio.
13 W.A.P., 4 October 1957; Azikiwe to Abubakar, telegram, 3 September 1957, copy in A.P.
14 Benson to Mbadiwe, 29 August 1957, A.P.
15 S.N.D., 28 September 1957.
16 Ibid., 2 October 1957.
17 All quotations used here are taken from the typewritten, signed copy in Adelabu's Papers. This passage is from p. 1.
18 'Dividing Ideological Line', p. 2.
19 The demands are listed on p. 3 of the original.
20 'Dividing Ideological Line', p. 3.
21 Ibid., p. 4.
22 S.N.D., 14 October 1957.
23 Otobo to Secretary, Minorities Commission, 7 October 1957, A.P.; Adelabu to Secretary, two telegrams and a letter, 14 October 1957, A.P.
24 Sklar, *Nigerian Political Parties*, p. 319.

25 All quotations from Azikiwe's address are taken from W.A.P., 29 and 30 October 1957.
26 D.T., 29 October 1957.
27 This account is entirely from Sklar, *Nigerian Political Parties*, pp. 196–203.
28 S.N.D., 7 November 1957.
29 D.T., 13 November 1957.
30 D.S., 19 November 1957.
31 Jose, 'My Friend Adelabu'.
32 Lawal to Minister of Local Government, 22 May 1957, PADID 3467 vol. I.
33 S.N.D., 1 June 1957.
34 Ibid., 2 July 1957.
35 Circular of 19 September 1957 from the Minister of Justice and Local Government; and Secretary, Ibadan Provisional District Council to Permanent Secretary, Ministry of Justice and Local Government, 11 October 1957, PADID 3467 vol. I.
36 Minutes of this meeting are in PADID 3467 vol. I.
37 Ibid.
38 Adelabu to Minister of Local Government, 7 November 1957, PADID 3467 vol. I.
39 Minutes of this meeting are in PADID 3467 vol. I.
40 D.T., 5 December 1957.
41 Secretary, Minorities Commission to Adelabu, 29 November 1957, A.P.
42 Secretary, I.P.D.C., to Senior Divisional Adviser, 28 March 1956, Ibaprof 1, 2634 vol. I.
43 Minutes of Finance Committee, 18 October 1956.
44 The income tax law is in Western Region Gazette no. 11 of 7 March 1957; the new Local Government Law is in the Supplement to the Western Region Gazette no. 16 of 11 April 1957.
45 In November, for example, petitions on the levying of taxes were collected from Wards North West 1, 2, 3, 4 and 5 and North 1, 2 and 3. Copies of these are in the Adelabu Papers.
46 The release was published in the *Defender*, 15 January, 1958.
47 D.T., 18 December 1957.
48 W.A.P., 20 December 1957.
49 S.N.D., 18 January 1958.
50 See the *Defender* for 20 and 24 January 1958 for fifteen of these. Lawyer Fakayode also co-operated in preparing these petitions.
51 S.N.D., 17 February 1958.
52 D.S., 21 February 1958.
53 N.T., 20 February 1958.
54 Fakayode *et al.*, to Adelabu, 26 February 1958, A.P.
55 D.T., 4 March 1958.
56 S.N.D., 10 March 1958.
57 Finance and Rates Committee Minutes, 23 April 1958.
58 J. Otobo in *Western Region of Nigeria House of Assembly Debates Official Report, Omnibus Issue No. 10, 11th–14th, 17th–21st, 24th–28th and 31st March, 1st and 2nd April, 1958*, cols. 471–2.
59 Dennis Osadebay, ibid., col. 470.
60 Ibid., col. 160.
61 V. I. Amadasun in a debate on the Communal Land Rights (Vesting in Trustees) Bill, 21 March, 1958, ibid., col. 310.

62 Debate on the Supplementary Appropriation Bill, 19 March, ibid., col. 197. Adelabu was present but did not speak on the 20th and was absent on the 21st.

CHAPTER 15

1 D.T., 28 May 1958.
2 These details and the following discussion are based on an interview with Albert Younan in April 1966.
3 For a version of this story see Sklar, *Nigerian Political Parties*, pp. 303–4.
4 This seems to have been confirmed by Chief Okotie-Eboh: see the *Daily Times*, 26 March 1958.
5 D.T., 31 May 1958.
6 D.T., 30 May 1958.
7 *Western Region of Nigeria House of Assembly Debates Official Report, Omnibus Issue No. 10, 11th–14th, 17th–21st, 24th–28th and 31st March, 1st and 2nd April, 1958*, cols. 466–7.
8 Ibid., cols. 467–8.
9 Ibid., cols. 472–3.
10 D.T., 27 March 1958.
11 S.N.D., 27 March 1958.
12 Ibid., 29 March 1958.
13 D.S., 2 June 1958.
14 N.T., 21 May and 31 October 1958.
15 N.T., 30 August 1958.
16 N.T., 17 September 1959.
17 S.N.D., 1 April 1958.
18 S.N.D., 3 April 1958.
19 N.T., 21 October 1958.
20 Sklar, *Nigerian Political Parties*, pp. 305–6, with references to the *Daily Service* of 13 May 1958 and the *Daily Times* of 24 April 1959.
21 S.N.D., 29 March 1958.
22 Loc. cit.
23 N.T., 31 March 1958.
24 S.N.D., editorial, 29 March 1957.
25 N.T., 3 May 1958.
26 Alhaji D. S. Adegbenro, 'Government Policy with Regard to Damages occasioned during a Riot', Foreword, *The Council* (a civil servants' magazine), no. 54, February 1960.
27 S.N.D., 4 June 1958.
28 Council Minutes, 4 May 1960.
29 N.T., 18 May 1960.
30 W.A.P., 19 May 1960.
31 N.T., 23 May 1960.
32 See the release in the *Daily Times*, 18 July 1958.
33 Interview with Alhaji K. O. S. Are, 1963.
34 A brief summary of events in Ibadan after May 1962 may be found in Mackintosh, *Nigerian Government and Politics*, pp. 355–7.

35 Ibadan Organising Secretaries to Secretary, Planning Committee, N.C.N.C. National Headquarters, 19 September 1961, File 33, 'Ibadan Elections', N.C.N.C. Western Region Office.
36 N.T., 1 February 1961.

INDEX

Aba Division, 253, 326, 372, 407

Ababi Olorun Kosi Party, 411

Abasi, Bello, 22, 25, 27, 67, 68, 77, 80, 94, 96, 97, 98, 105, 106, 109, 119, 142, 143, 162, 164, 165, 178, 179, 181, 182, 232, 331, 448

Abayomi, Sir Kofo, 232

Abbey, Chief Gogo, 293, 296, 412

Abdallah, Habib Raji, 138

Abell, A. F., 55

Abeokuta, 3, 28, 47, 406, 422, 425, 433, 445

Abeokuta, Alake of, 173, 230, 243, 326

Abeokuta-Ijebu-Colony State, 360

Abeokuta Province, 363

Abimbola, Iyalode, 171, 247

Aboderin, J. C., 20, 21, 96, 108

Aboderin, Moyo, 96, 99, 105, 106, 109, 110, 111, 178, 229, 266, 267, 337

Aboh Division, 308

Action Group,
    and the Amalgamated Press, 322, 329, 331, 333, 338, 406, 410
    Benin Conference 1952, 153, 155
    and the Benin-Delta Peoples Party, 362
    Benin Provincial Action Group, 91
    and British administration, 152
    Central Ministers, 156
    Christian/Muslim affiliation, 394, 396, 397, 423
    as a cohesive force, 181
    and the Ibadan Divisional Council, 220
    Federal Executive Council, 402
    and I.C.C., 143, 144
    and Ijebus, 114
    and I.P.P., 120
    Mid-Western Action Group, 91, 92, 94, 107
    N.P.C.–N.C.N.C. coalition, 400
    Opposition, 246, 251

Owo Conference 1951, 90, 95

Party, 90–3, 95, 96, 98, 107–13, 116, 117, 118, 129, 131, 132, 139, 141, 149, 151, 153, 156, 158, 176, 178, 179, 184, 186, 187, 191–5, 197, 198, 199, 209, 216, 217, 218, 220, 221, 222, 224, 228, 230, 232, 233, 234, 236, 237, 239–44, 249, 250, 257, 263, 264, 266, 268, 270, 271, 275, 278, 285, 288, 290, 292, 295, 297, 298, 300–5, 307–14, 316, 321, 322, 324, 326, 327, 329, 330, 331, 333, 334, 337, 340, 341, 345, 348, 350, 352, 353, 359, 360, 361, 375–80, 383, 387, 388, 391, 392, 393, 397, 399, 401, 403–6, 408, 411, 413, 414, 415, 417, 420, 421, 424, 426, 427, 429, 431, 433–40, 445, 446

party organization, 185, 229, 238

and the Provisional Council, 287, 288, 289, 322, 415, 422, 425, 426

Regional Conference, 1955, 361

Regional Government, 145, 148, 201, 211, 216, 229, 230, 239, 252–5, 258, 278, 280, 282, 289, 292, 294, 310, 318, 319, 323, 325, 328, 330, 342, 343, 349, 351, 353, 363, 365, 380, 381, 398, 415, 416, 417, 437

temporary alliance with N.C.N.C., 218, 219

U.N.I.P. Alliance, 243

Warri Conference 1953, 185

Adamawa, 244

Adebisi, Chief Saka, 72, 93, 99

Adebola, Haroun P., 117, 138, 145, 148

Adebowale, Chief, 364

Adedipe, B. A., 271

Adedoyin, Adeleke, 117, 118, 313

Adegbenro, Alhaji Dauda, 394, 413, 414, 415, 427, 438

Adeitan, Sinotu, 34, 35

Index

Index

Index

490

Index